World Anthropology

General Editor

SOL TAX

Patrons

CLAUDE LÉVI-STRAUSS
MARGARET MEAD
LAILA SHUKRY EL HAMAMSY
M. N. SRINIVAS

MOUTON PUBLISHERS · THE HAGUE · PARIS
DISTRIBUTED IN THE USA AND CANADA BY ALDINE, CHICAGO

Views of the Past

Views of the Past

Essays in Old World Prehistory and
Paleoanthropology

Editor

LESLIE G. FREEMAN

MOUTON PUBLISHERS · THE HAGUE · PARIS

DISTRIBUTED IN THE USA AND CANADA BY ALDINE, CHICAGO

913.031
V671

GN
771
.I57
1973

General Editor's Preface

The character of the human species was largely formed during the long Paleolithic, which becomes known to us only as prehistorians piece together the clues that they find in the record. As these accumulate, the imaginative speculations that once perforce dominated the sparser evidence give way to disciplined use of data, starting always with the time and the place of the newest discoveries. The exercise of the archeologist's imagination comes now in discovering new ways to uncover more and better evidence in particular sites and to find ways to make available to colleagues both the data and the methods. The present book shows off some of the newest paleoanthropology as it emerges in Europe, Asia, and Africa and its details are painstakingly communicated to the world's prehistorians.

Like most contemporary sciences, anthropology is a product of the European tradition. Some argue that it is a product of colonialism, with one small and self-interested part of the species dominating the study of the whole. If we are to understand the species, our science needs substantial input from scholars who represent a variety of the world's cultures. It was a deliberate purpose of the IXth International Congress of Anthropological and Ethnological Sciences to provide impetus in this direction. The *World Anthropology* volumes, therefore, offer a first glimpse of a human science in which members from all societies have played an active role. Each of the books is designed to be self-contained; each is an attempt to update its particular sector of scientific knowledge and is written by specialists from all parts of the world. Each volume should be read and reviewed individually as a separate volume on its own given subject. The set as a whole will indicate what changes are in store for anthropology as scholars from the developing countries join in studying the species of which we are all a part.

The IXth Congress was planned from the beginning not only to include as many of the scholars from every part of the world as possible, but also with a view toward the eventual publication of the papers in high-quality volumes. At previous Congresses scholars were invited to bring papers which were then read out loud. They were necessarily limited in length; many were only summarized; there was little time for discussion; and the sparse discussion could only be in one language. The IXth Congress was an experiment aimed at changing this. Papers were written with the intention of exchanging them before the Congress, particularly in extensive pre-Congress sessions; they were not intended to be read aloud at the Congress, that time being devoted to discussions — discussions which were simultaneously and professionally translated into five languages. The method for eliciting the papers was structured to make as representative a sample as was allowable when scholarly creativity — hence self-selection — was critically important. Scholars were asked both to propose papers of their own and to suggest topics for sessions of the Congress which they might edit into volumes. All were then informed of the suggestions and encouraged to rethink their own papers and the topics. The process, therefore, was a continuous one of feedback and exchange and it has continued to be so even after the Congress. The some two thousand papers comprising *World Anthropology* certainly then offer a substantial sample of world anthropology. It has been said that anthropology is at a turning point; if this is so, these volumes will be the historical direction markers.

As might have been foreseen in the first post-colonial generation, the large majority of the Congress papers (82 percent) are the work of scholars identified with the industrialized world which fathered our traditional discipline and the institution of the Congress itself: Eastern Europe (15 percent); Western Europe (16 percent); North America (47 percent); Japan, South Africa, Australia, and New Zealand (4 percent). Only 18 percent of the papers are from developing areas: Africa (4 percent); Asia-Oceania (9 percent); Latin America (5 percent). Aside from the substantial representation from the U.S.S.R. and the nations of Eastern Europe, a significant difference between this corpus of written material and that of other Congresses is the addition of the large proportion of contributions from Africa, Asia, and Latin America. "Only 18 percent" is two to four times as great a proportion as that of other Congresses; moreover, 18 percent of 2,000 papers is 360 papers, 10 times the number of "Third World" papers presented at previous Congresses. In fact, these 360 papers are more than the total of *all* papers published after the last International Congress of Anthropological and Ethnological Sciences which was held in the United States (Philadelphia, 1956).

The significance of the increase is not simply quantitative. The input of scholars from areas which have until recently been no more than subject matter for anthropology represents both feedback and also long-awaited theoretical contributions from the perspectives of very different cultural, social, and historical traditions. Many who attended the IXth Congress were convinced that anthropology would not be the same in the future. The fact that the next Congress (India, 1978) will be our first in the "Third World" may be symbolic of the change. Meanwhile, sober consideration of the present set of books will show how much, and just where and how, our discipline is being revolutionized.

The present book is one of perhaps a dozen in this series which treat what might be called the "middle" development of the species. Between the books describing the emergence of hominid forms — books on primatology and human evolution — and those sampling the incredible variety and complexity of the lives and problems of historic peoples, are these relatively few volumes which provide material to explore "human nature" in its generic and specific characteristics.

Chicago, Illinois   SOL TAX
June 20, 1978

Table of Contents

Introduction

LESLIE G. FREEMAN

THE PAPERS

All but one of the articles that make up this volume were prepared for the IXth ICAES. Most were volunteered papers, selected for incorporation in Session 312 on Behavioral Paleoanthropology (Monday, September 3, 1973), chaired by E. Aguirre and L. G. Freeman. The session title was deliberately inclusive, and, as is usual with volunteered papers, the contributions were diverse. Some of the contributions represented dimensions of traditional prehistory that are not central to behavioral paleoanthropology, and vice versa. But with its broad interdisciplinary perspective and its international base the study of the human past can encompass many approaches. All specialists can learn a great deal from colleagues with different viewpoints, and for the field to progress we must consciously and deliberately weigh each approach, incorporating what is good from each before rejecting the rest.

It is my own belief that modern prehistory will advance beyond its traditional limits only insofar as it truly proceeds to the most intensive possible analyses of residues of past behavioral adaptations in largely undisturbed human occupation sites, instead of stopping short of this

The panel of discussants for this session included, in addition to the volume editor, Dr. Fekri Hassan, of Southern Methodist University, Dr. Eduardo Ripoll-Perello, director of the Provincial Archeological Museum, Barcelona, and Dr. Luis Pericot-García, Professor Emeritus of Prehistory, University of Barcelona. Time allotted for discussion was unfortunately severely curtailed. Therefore, no transcript of discussions is included. Remarks from the floor by Professor Pavel Boriskovskij, directed to the paper by Singer and Wymer, have been appended to that article as a comment. Professor Boriskovskij's comment has been amplified by the addition of two bibliographic references in Russian, documenting work to which he alludes. The volume editor is responsible for the English transliteration of those sources and for the translation of the chapter by González Echegaray. The volume editor also thanks Gertrude Tax for her invaluable help in correcting proof.

goal, content with the reconstruction of conjectural temporal sequences of artifact development. Until the nature of past adaptations is understood in considerable detail, the developmental sequences we can construct remain insubstantial. The sketches of industrial evolution that we learned as students were useful mnemonic devices (though they told us nothing about the lifeways of the people who authored those industries), but the changes in the sequences that have become necessary over the last twenty years show how flimsy the structure really was. Nevertheless, to say that the construction of temporal sequences of industrial evolution should no longer be our only or our foremost aim is not to say that their construction should be entirely abandoned. They are convenient frameworks for ordering the data from intensive studies of single occupations, and without orderly frameworks mastering the piecemeal detail of diverse intensive investigations is an impossible task. However, one needs to recognize the chronological sequences as but one subsidiary part of the paleoanthropologist's goals — a part which is more useful as an aid to remembering material relevant to other goals than as an end in itself — while bearing in mind that sequences now accepted as up-to-date will undoubtedly prove to be further from the truth than most of us can imagine. (In defense of this observation, which is far from the majority opinion among prehistorians today, one might cite the extensive changes wrought in the Aurignacian-Perigordian and Iberomaurusian-Capsian developmental sequences since the 1950's or the fact that the stages proposed by Leakey or Breuil for the Lower Paleolithic have generally been abandoned.) Where the ability to date the events of the past with reference to some absolute timescale has been most limited, the detailed developmental sequences of industrial change are likely to prove highly unsatisfactory.

There is, naturally, much interest in the discovery of absolute chronometric techniques for the dating of events in those shadow zones. The first paper in this volume, by Turnbull, Taylor, and Hare, discusses one promising new technique developed as a spinoff of studies on the chemical nature of amino acids. The method may help order deposits containing fossil bone accumulated at almost any time during the Upper Cenozoic.

Even if all problems of absolute dating were resolved for the timespan encompassing the hominid career, the construction of sequences of industrial evolution would still pose problems. In the first place, immense areas of the Old World are almost virgin territory to prehistory. For vast periods of time the prehistoric record is pitifully fragmentary; for some areas the situation is far worse than for others. Usually, appropriate deposits where vestiges of past cultural behavior might be expected have been lost through erosion. Often, however, the gaps in knowledge are due as much to lack of exploration as to any other cause. In their paper on a survey conducted in northwest Iran, Singer and Wymer add more evidence of ephemeral Lower Paleolithic occupation in a region that is largely unknown. Although their discoveries are meager, they are at least suggestive of directions for further research, as Boriskovskij underlines in his comment.

In some cases, the available sample of materials for study is inadequate because major categories of relevant evidence have gone unrecognized. Of all classes of artifacts from Lower and Middle Paleolithic occupations, bone tools are the most frequently neglected, and sometimes they have been missed altogether. The preliminary report on the large and striking series of Mousterian worked bones from Cueva Morín makes the point that the preconceptions that retouched bone implements must conform to patterned overall forms have kept prehistorians from perceiving retouched edges, no matter how regular, on amorphous bone fragments. An examination of other faunal collections from Paleolithic occupations shows that the Morín case is by no means unique.

Even when there is some guarantee that the samples to be compared are reasonably representative of all artifacts from their respective horizons, other factors than the passage of time are likely to correlate with interassemblage differences. Most comparisons of artifact types rely almost exclusively on evaluations of gross morphology (including metrical attributes). It has, nevertheless, been acknowledged for some time that morphologically similar pieces may have served different technological functions, and that pieces with different forms may sometimes have been used in the same way. Certainly, studies of formal change through time are most likely to produce meaningful results when it can be shown that the artifacts in question were functionally equivalent. The closest approach to an understanding of the body motions involved in tool use, and thus of artifact function in a very basic sense, is derived from the study of microscopic wear traces on the working surfaces of the tools themselves. This approach is far from satisfactory because (1) few collected artifacts in most collections bear any noticeable wear traces, and (2) the few that do cannot normally be studied under ideal conditions. A partial remedy for the latter problem is suggested by Straus and Walker, who propose the production of transparent replicas that may be studied as exhaustively as desired without permanent alteration of the surface of the original specimen. The paper on occupation floor distributions used a quantitative technique for the definition of covariant constellations of artifact types and faunal remains that seem to be functionally distinct, and then uses the constellations thus defined 'u delineate activity-specific areas in single occupation horizons. Potentially, such techniques permit the definition of functionally equivalent areas in different occupations, which can then be compared to identify formal and stylistic contrasts between functionally similar toolkits. One aspect of the statistical techniques employed in the study is the evaluation of the contribution of random error to interassemblage difference. Not all collections that seem different, subjectively, are necessarily so, and the contribution of chance to apparent interassemblage difference must be evaluated if reasonable interpretations of past cultural behavior are to be made. In their report on excavations at La Riera, Clark and Richards employ another set of statistical techniques to compare collections of artifacts and fauna from several natural strata. Yet other tests, including a multivariate clustering technique, are used by Hassan to perfect the typology of the Sebilian, to assess relationships among Sebilian sites themselves, and to attempt to relate the distinctive Sebilian to other industrial complexes in the Nile valley.

Major obstacles to the assessment of relations between industrial complexes arise when the type-localities that have been used to define prehistoric cultural entities were either impoverished or inadequately studied. González Echegaray reviews the Neuville-Garrod scheme currently used to classify Upper Paleolithic stages in Palestine and finds it inadequate. Basing his conclusions on richer collections from the more extensive stratigraphic sequences in Palestine, he proposes a new set of stage definitions for the Levantine Upper Paleolithic period. A much larger region — the whole of north-central Eurasia — is the subject of an ambitious study by Shimkin, whose review of the most important Upper Paleolithic occurrences in this fascinating area searches out similarities between Siberian materials and those from occupations on the Russian plain. Shimkin calls special attention to the manifest cultural complexity shown by the archeological record and points out several important directions for future study.

The last three papers in the collection show different approaches to the study of past ecosystems and man's place in them. Fedele combines observations on the unique adaptive demands forced on cultural and biological systems by survival in the Alpine zone with documentation of man's presence in the Italian Alps during prehistoric times in making a preliminary step toward understanding cultural mastery of hostile environments. Saxon compares Mesolithic and early Neolithic occupations from both ends of the Mediterranean, postulating that increased specialization involving a few resources, coupled with a decline of those resources, may have led to the collapse of the economic base and the crash of populations of traditionally exploited species and, thus, in fact, have paved the way for the introduction of herd animals and the Mediterranean agricultural complex. Last, Luchterhand proposes that successful mid-Pleistocene hominid colonization of eastern Asia may have depended on the disruption of local environments, a disturbance that would produce a broader spectrum of exploitable resources than would more stable ecological systems. Hominid penetration of the area seems to be directly associated with the larger radiation of modern grazing ungulates. This may be due not to early man's reliance on those species but, rather, to the fact that an increase of both short- and long-term fluctuations in available water would have favored the establishment of both grazing animals and broad-spectrum hunting-gathering peoples.

We all recognize that political and linguistic boundaries are, all too often, effective barriers to the interchange of scientific information and ideas. In a rapidly growing field such as ours, a constant effort to bridge those barriers is essential, if only because we stand in danger of traveling up avenues others have learned to be blind alleys when we work in isolation. The diversity of viewpoints on the past illustrated by collections such as this one is to the great long-run advantage of our field. We are all most grateful to the IXth ICAES for having provided us with this forum.

Amino Acid Dating of Pleistocene Fossil Materials: Olduvai Gorge, Tanzania

P. E. HARE, H. F. TURNBULL and R. E. TAYLOR

One of the problems facing students of hominid evolution is the lack of any sufficiently precise and accurate means for directly determining the ages of fossil specimens dating from a large portion of the Middle and Upper Pleistocene (Isaac 1973). Bio-stratigraphic approaches and geo-chronological techniques such as potassium–argon do provide important temporal information, but what is needed is some means for accurately dating the fossil material itself rather than assessing its age indirectly through associated geological or paleontological contexts.

The feasibility of a biochemical approach to chronometrics grew out of studies in basic amino acid research beginning in the 1950's which showed that there were significant temporal variations in the amino acid make-up of fossiliferous materials (Abelson 1954). Hare (1962) was the first to make detailed studies of these variations by analyzing a series of radiocarbon dated *Mytilus californianus* shells collected from coastal archeological sites in Southern and Baja California. These samples, which ranged in age from 400 to 34,000 radiocarbon years, varied considerably in their amino acid composition when compared with one another and with recent shells. What was most interesting, however, was that it appeared that the ratios of amino acid degradation products to their respective parental amino acid reactants varied linearly with respect to time for samples from similar postdepositional environments. This suggested the possibility that residual amino acid ratios in fossil material might be quantified and used as an indicator of the fossil's age.

In the years that followed these initial studies, several groups of investigators, using somewhat different approaches, have continued to study the implications of temporal alterations in the amino acid configuration of various types of fossil materials. These investigations have used both variations in amino acid ratios (i.e. the ratio of a particular amino acid degradation product to its parent amino acid) as well as racemization (and empimerization) processes for shell, bone, and teeth. The orientation of these studies has embraced basic geochemical and oceanographic studies (Hare and Abelson 1964, 1968; Hare and Mitterer 1967, 1969; Hare 1965, 1967, 1969, 1971; Kvenvolden *et al*. 1970; Bada *et al*. 1970; Wehmiller and Hare 1971; Bada 1972a; Bada and Schroeder 1972), as well as geochronometric/archeochronometric interests (Turekian and Bada 1972; Bada 1972b; Bada *et al*. 1973b; Bada and Protsch 1973; Bada *et al*. 1974a, 1974b; Hare *et al*. 1974). Since the reaction rates are of a chemical nature, they are temperature sensitive and amino acid analyses of terrestrial and oceanic materials have also been applied to geothermometric questions (Schroeder and Bada 1973; Bada *et al*. 1973a).

Although the initial studies by Abelson at the Carnegie Institution of Washington had included the analysis of fossil bone — as well as shells and teeth — it was tentatively concluded that because of its generally porous structure, bone would be a poor candidate on which to base a reliable amino acid dating method. Thus subsequent studies by the Carnegie group focused on mollusk shells and foraminifera (e.g. Hare and Mitterer 1969). The utilization of bone for amino acid geochronology was reinitiated by Bada and his collaborators at the Scripps Institution of Oceanography beginning in the early 1970's. They have provided the most extensive data on dates based on amino acid ratios utilizing the racemization reaction of aspartic acid and, to a lesser extent, isoleucine. They have attempted to eliminate the problem of evaluating average temperature conditions by using a calibration procedure in which the intrinsic rate of amino acid racemization for a particular site is determined by measuring the extent of racemization in a radiocarbon dated sample. After such a calibration step has been performed, other bone samples from that site and/or other localities in a presumably similar temperature environment are assigned dates using the calibrated racemization rate (cf. Bada and Protsch 1973).

It has been suggested, however, that even if a calibration procedure could accurately represent regional temperature regimes, the effective temperature history of specific samples at specific sites could certainly be impacted by variations in depositional contexts over time. Such considerations may be occasionally significant since, in the case of isoleucine for example, an error in temperature estimates of ±2°C would yield an age error of about ±50 percent (cf. Bada 1972b). Ignoring for a moment the problem of effective temperature constraints for specific samples, questions have also been raised and directed toward the problems inherent in utilizing racemization values in bone as the basis of a dating method in the absence of a careful examination of other geochemical parameters such as soil pH and eH (oxidation–reduction potential) and differential leaching depending on the degree of available moisture (Hare 1973). The porous structure of the vast majority of fossil bones makes this last parameter of particular significance. As the age of a given sample increases, the chances of contamination with non-*in situ* organics increases. Certain tests have been proposed to estimate the degree to which such modern contamination is present. However, if such is indicated, there is little that can be done to remove the contaminants and thus much less reliance can be placed on the calculated ages (Bada and Protsch 1973).

Previously published amino acid analysis of bone from Olduvai Gorge, Tanzania, suggested that the analyzed sample was contaminated to the point that only a minimum age could be calculated (Bada and Protsch 1973). Experiments conducted to determine the fossil structures least subject to contamination and leaching problems suggest that the enamel fraction of tooth structures appears to approximate a closed geochemical system. In order to compare the results obtained on bone samples from Olduvai Gorge, we have examined a series of fossil bovid teeth kindly supplied to us by the late L. S. B. Leakey from various stratigraphic zones dated by potassium–argon, fission track, paleomagnetic and biostratigraphic methods (Table 1). Amino acid analysis of the samples shows progressive changes that may be correlated with the stratigraphic position of the samples. The ratio of alloisoleucine to isoleucine (L-isoleucine/D-alloisoleucine) increased from 0.92 to 1.21 with increasing age of the deposits. Modern teeth have alloisoleucine to isoleucine ratios near 0. If we use the sample from the base of Bed I as the calibration sample and assume the age as 1.8×10^6 years, then the ages of the remaining samples can be calculated by equation (1).

$$t(\text{yrs}) = \frac{1}{1.8k} \, 1n \left(\frac{1 + \text{D/L}}{1 - 0.8 \, \text{D/L}} \right) \qquad (1)$$

where t is time in years, D/L is the D-alloisoleucine to L-isoleucine ratio, and k is the rate constant from the calibration sample ($1.3 \times 10^{-6}/\text{yr}^{-1}$).

Table 1. Amino acid ratios on samples of bovid teeth excavated from various time horizons at Olduvai Gorge, Tanzania

Stratigraphic horizon*	Estimated age ($\times 10^6$) yrs**	ALLO/ISO	Age ($\times 10^6$ yrs) calculated by equation 1
Bed III/IV	0.8 ± 0.2	$0.92 \, (\pm .01)$	0.84 ± 0.1
Upper Bed II	1.3 ± 0.1	1.00	0.98 ± 0.1
Lower Bed II	1.65 ± 0.05	$1.17 \, (\pm .06)$	1.5 ± 0.3
Top of Bed I	1.72 ± 0.02	1.09	1.2 ± 0.1
Base of Bed I	1.80 ± 0.03	1.21	calibration

* Based on information supplied by Dr. L. S. B. Leakey.
** Best estimates by Dr. Richard Hay without knowing locality data.

Examination of Table 1 suggests a good correlation between the age of the deposit and the calculated isoleucine racemization age. The age of each stratigraphic unit was provided by Professor Richard Hay, Department of Geology and Geophysics, University of California, Berkeley. However, since the provenience of each sample was supplied only with the designations listed in Table 1, the absence of specific-locality data prevents an evaluation of the degree to which the association between the sample and the designated stratigraphic unit is a direct one. This is especially important in the case of the sample from Bed I (1.8 m.y.), which was used to calibrate the racemization rate for the site. Possible contamination of the samples would lower the D/L ratios, making the samples appear younger than they really are. It is significant that none of the ages are older than the associated stratigraphic ages. Two of the samples have ages within the limits of experimental error while two others have ages somewhat too young.

Prior studies involving artificial heating of bone and teeth under simulated natural conditions have shown that the racemization rate of L-isoleucine in these materials is more than an order of magnitude slower than for mollusk shells. The data from Olduvai agree with these previous laboratory studies. This slower rate makes tooth enamel a useful sample material for amino acid dating of Early Pleistocene samples.

Amino acid dating may be a useful technique to apply in the direct dating of fossil teeth in the radiocarbon dating range and beyond. In contrast to the radiocarbon method, very small sample sizes are required (on the order of a few milligrams) because of the great sensitivity of amino acid analyzers. The potential drawback of the technique is due in part to the chemical nature of the reactions and the consequent effects of such environmental parameters as temperature, leaching, and pH. Many of these variables can be simulated in the laboratory and, as additional data become available, it should be possible to refine the application of amino acid reactions for the purpose of providing chronological controls to samples of interest to paleoanthropologists and archeologists.

REFERENCES

ABELSON, P. H.
  1954   Amino acids in fossils. *Science* 119:576.
BADA, J. L.
  1971   Kinetics of the nonbiological decomposition and racemization of amino acid in natural waters, in *Non-equilibrium systems in natural water chemistry*. Advances in Chemistry Series 106:309–331. Washington: American Chemical Society.
  1972a Kinetics of racemization of amino acids as a function of pH. *Journal of the American Chemical Society* 94:1371–1373.

1972b The dating of fossil bones using the racemization of isoleucine. *Earth and Planetary Science Letters* 15:223–231.

BADA, J. L., K. A. KVENVOLDEN, E. PETERSON
1973b Racemization of amino acids in bones. *Nature* 245:309–310.

BADA, J. L., B. P. LUYENDYK, J. B. MAYNARD
1970 Marine sediments: dating by the racemization of amino acids. *Science* 170:730–732.

BADA, J. L., R. PROTSCH
1973 Racemization reaction of aspartic acid and its use in dating fossil bones. *Proceedings of the National Academy of Sciences* 70:1131–1134.

BADA, J. L., R. PROTSCH, R. A. SCHROEDER
1973a The racemization reaction of isoleucine used as a paleotemperature indicator. *Nature* 241:394.

BADA, J. L., R. A. SCHROEDER
1972 Racemization of isoleucine in calcareous marine sediments: kinetics and mechanism. *Earth and Planetary Science Letters* 15:1–11.

BADA, J. L., R. A. SCHROEDER, G. F. CARTER
1974a New evidence for the antiquity of man in North America deduced from aspartic acid racemization. *Science* 184:791–793.

BADA, J. L., R. A. SCHROEDER, R. PROTSCH, R. BERGER
1974b Concordance of collagen-based radiocarbon and aspartic-acid racemization ages. *Proceedings of the National Academy of Science* 71:914–917.

HARE, P. E.
1962 "The amino acid composition of the organic matrix of some recent shells of some West Coast species of *Mytilus*." Unpublished doctoral dissertation. California Institute of Technology.
1965 Amino acid artifacts in organic geochemistry. *Carnegie Institution of Washington Yearbook* 64:232–235.
1967 Amino acid composition of the extrapallial fluid in molusks. *Carnegie Institution of Washington Yearbook* 65:364–365.
1969 "Geochemistry of proteins, peptides, and amino acids," in *Organic Geochemistry*. Edited by G. Eglington and M. T. J. Murphy, 134–145. New York: Springer-Verlag.
1971 Effects of hydrolysis on the racemization rates of amino acids. *Carnegie Institution of Washington Yearbook* 70:256–258.
1973 Amino acid dating — a history and an evaluation. *Museum Applied Center for Archaeology Newsletter* 10:4–7.

HARE, P. E., P. H. ABELSON
1964 Proteins in mollusk shells. *Carnegie Institution of Washington Yearbook* 63:267–270.
1968 Racemization of amino acids in fossil shells. *Carnegie Institution of Washington Yearbook* 66:526–528.

HARE, P. E., R. M. MITTERER
1967 Nonprotein amino acids in fossil shells. *Carnegie Institution of Washington Yearbook* 65:362–364.
1969 Laboratory simulation of amino acid diagenesis in fossils. *Carnegie Institution of Washington Yearbook* 67:205–208.

HARE, P. E., D. J. ORTNER, D. W. VONENDT, R. E. TAYLOR
1974 Amino acid dating of bone and teeth. *Geological Society of America Abstracts* 6:778.

ISAAC, G. LL.
1973 "Chronology and the tempo of cultural change," in *Calibration of hominoid evolution*. Edited by W. W. Bishop and J. A. Miller, 381–430. Edinburgh: Scottish Academic Press.

KVENVOLDEN, K. A., E. PETERSON, F. S. BROWN
1970 Racemization of amino acids in sediments from Saanich Inlet, British Columbia. *Science* 169:1079.

SCHROEDER, R. A., J. L. BADA
1973 Glacial-postglacial temperature differences deduced from aspartic acid racemization in fossil bones. *Science* 182:479.

TUREKIAN, K. K., J. L. BADA
1972 "The dating of fossil bones," in *Calibration of hominoid evolution*. Edited by W. W. Bishop and J. A. Miller, 171–185. Edinburgh: Scottish Academic Press.

WEHMILLER, J., P. E. HARE
1971 Racemization of amino acids in marine sediments. *Science* 173:907–911.

A Hand-Ax from Northwest Iran: The Question of Human Movement Between Africa and Asia in the Lower Paleolithic Period

RONALD SINGER and JOHN J. WYMER

Cameron (1936: 1) provides an excellent thumbnail sketch of the topographical setting of the country formerly known as Persia:

Iran, a plateau with numerous large depressions, is cradled between two mountain ranges sweeping majestically from the knotted heights of Armenia north of the Fertile Crescent. One wing, a lofty ridge known as the Elburz, advances eastward along the south of the Caspian, where it reaches its climax in the towering peak of the Demavend. Continuing eastward, it dwindles away in the steppes of Khurasan, where it meets the line of the Hindu Kush coming from the

Our 1970 expedition, consisting of ourselves, Dr. E. L. Boné, University of Louvain and University of Chicago, and a geologist, Dr. A. Iranpanah, University of Tehran, could not have been organized so smoothly without the kind cooperation of many colleagues and friends in Iran and the United States, to whom we are grateful. Dr. E. Firouz, Director of the Game and Fish Department of Iran, and his assistant, Dr. Fred Harrington, and Dr. Chamsddine, M. H. Mojidi, Vice-Chancellor for Research and Graduate Studies, and Dr. J. Jenab, Dean of the Faculty of Science, University of Tehran, kindly arranged for Dr. Iranpanah to accompany us. Mr. M. Taymans, the Belgian Ambassador to Iran, His Excellency Dr. M. Eghbal, president of the National Iranian Oil Company, and Dr. I. Stöcklin, Geological Survey of Iran, were extremely helpful and generously kind. We are also thankful to Dr. R. Braidwood, University of Chicago, Dr. H. E. Wright, University of Minnesota, Dr. E. Morris, Colorado State University, Dr. D. Lay, University of Chicago, now at the University of Michigan, and Mr. Grant Meyer, Peabody Museum, Yale University, for useful help and advice. Our thanks are also due Mr. Youtan Badaloff, interpreter and driver, and Ali-Akbar Baiat-Turk, driver.

The investigations were carried out with funds received from the USPHS grant GM 10113, the Wenner-Gren Foundation for Anthropological Research, Inc., and the Dr. Wallace and Clara Abbott Memorial Fund of the University of Chicago. Concepts developed in this paper resulted from investigations supported by NSF grants GS-1658 and GS-2907.

Without the skill and expert guidance of Dr. Iranpanah, based on his excellent knowledge of the geology of Iran, much time and effort would have been wasted. We are extremely grateful to him.

Dr. Philip Smith, University of Montreal, kindly provided useful comments on the manuscript.

opposite direction, from the Pamirs, the "roof of the world." The second wing, called the Zagros ranges, curves gently southeastward, then still more south. In numerous parallel folds it skirts the eastern edge of fertile Babylonia, forms a glittering and almost impassable barrier on the eastern shore of the Persian Gulf, and, after advancing over the desolate regions along the Indian Ocean, turns sharply northward through Baluchistan and Afghanistan to join other mountains spreading, like the Hindu Kush, fanlike from the Pamirs.

Recently, Smith (1971) gave a thorough overview of the Paleolithic of Iran. He mentions that:

The Iranian Plateau beyond the Zagros Mountains rises to elevations of 1,200–1,800 m., while the Zagros itself has peak elevations between ca. 2,000–4,000 m. Climatologically the Plateau is a part of the great Asiatic land mass and considerably different from the oceanic region of the Levant. This seems to have been true in Pleistocene times as well.

Lower Paleolithic industries are found over most of the African continent and much of India. In both areas are industries of simple flakes and cores, as well as industries with hand-axes. The typological similarities of the more developed hand-ax industries (compare the "twisted" ovate hand-axes of the Madras Acheulian and in Bed III at Olduvai Gorge) are more likely to be the result of cultural connection rather than independent evolution, and it is also possible that there was a connection between these continents from the time of the earliest human activity. These distributions of Lower Paleolithic industries are linked with the major problem of human evolution, for there must still be doubt as to whether the earliest hominids evolved in Africa and spread eastward or evolved independently in southeast Asia and perhaps spread westward, or both. Answers can only be speculative until reliably dated industries with associated hominid remains are found in Late Pliocene or Early Pleistocene deposits in southeast Asia, but the suggestion of human migration and contact between Africa and India is a strong one, particularly during the relatively advanced hunting communities of the Acheulian stage. If this is the case, Lower Paleolithic sites must exist in the immediate areas. The country of Iran presents an obvious corridor, a connecting link between the Far East and the Near East and beyond. The similarity between mammals and primates (including hominids) of Africa, Europe, and Asia from, at least, Miocene times onward is strongly suggestive of intercontinental migrations. From Plio-Pleistocene times, the likely land-link is Iran. In the historic period migratory movements and warriors' campaigns have frequently swept across its borders.

A few archeological expeditions have been conducted to search for this evidence. Mousterian and Baradostian industries of the Late Pleistocene have been found in western Iran and around the shores of the Caspian Sea (Coon 1951, McBurney 1964; Young and Smith 1966; Hole and Flannery 1967), but the only evidence of anything that could be earlier in these regions was reported by Braidwood (1960a, 1960b; Braidwood and Howe 1960) from near Kermanshah. Braidwood (1960b) refers to "flint hand-axes of standard Acheulian type, with associated flake tools, from surface hilltop scatters." One hand-ax is illustrated (1960a:695, Fig. 1), and this was on display at the National Archeological Museum in Tehran in 1970, labeled as coming from Tepe Gakieh, Kermanshah. The USAF Aeronautical Approach Chart (Map 428 A IV, 1:250,000) shows "Gakia" (as pointed out to us by Dr. Braidwood) as being 14 kilometers due east of Kermanshah at 34° 13' north latitude and 47° 13' east longitude. Dr. Elizabeth A. Morris, who discovered the hand-ax on the Braidwood expedition, states that *only one* hand-ax was found, but that numerous flakes and cores of similar material were found in the vicinity. These latter were assigned to several later occupations on the basis of their typology and the lack of the pronounced surface alteration evident on the hand-ax (personal communication). The upper surface of the hand-ax was darker and more patinated than the lower: it was found lying on one flat side. In the same area they found potsherds of various cultural affinities and recent artifacts probably originating in the nearby village. She states that it was their opinion at the time that the locality ("within 100 feet of the edge of the Kara Su River with its one or two lower terraces," at an elevation approximately 1,260 meters above sea level, and "on a surface with few, if any, cobbles"), which was near what became a travel route, had probably been occupied intermittently throughout the prehistoric and historic periods. (This hand-ax will be referred to again on page 21.)

Another expedition, by G. W. Hume, in 1967 (Hume 1969), discovered choppers, cores, and flakes on the high terrace of the Ladiz River in Baluchistan but no Acheulian artifacts. Apart from a mention of some Paleolithic artifacts on the alluvial terraces near Tehran (Rieben 1966), there is apparently nothing else to indicate the presence of man in the Early or Middle Pleistocene period.

In 1970 an expedition was organized by one of us (Ronald Singer). The main purpose of the expedition was to search for pre-Mousterian Lower Paleolithic sites that might assist us in solving the problems outlined earlier. It was hoped that chance exposures or surface indications might lead to the discovery of stratified sites, ideally with human, faunal, and floral remains. Several factors determined that in the limited time available a search should be made in northwest Iran, in the provinces of Azerbaijan, Kurdistan, and Kermanshah. The factors considered were

1.   The distribution of hand-axes in the neighboring countries — Armenia, Turkey, Iraq — and farther west, to the shores of the Mediterranean and the Red Sea.

2. The geographical barriers of the Syro-Arabian desert and within Iran.
3. The distribution in northwest Iraq of geological deposits of Early or Middle Pleistocene age.
4. The availability in Iran of suitable stone for making hand-axes.

These considerations are amplified below:

HAND-AX DISTRIBUTION

Acheulian hand-axes have been found, mainly on the surface, in very great numbers at sites in Egypt and Sudan, particularly along the Nile. They are numerous in Somaliland, so it is clear that northeast Africa was frequented by hunters in the Middle Pleisocene, although many of the hand-axes may belong to the Late Pleistocene, taking the division between the Mindel-Riss Interglacial and the Riss Glaciation as the boundary between Middle and Late. Hand-axes in the thirty meter terrace gravels of the Nile presumably relate to Middle Pleistocene occupation of the region. This makes a starting point for considering any possible diffusion of the Acheulian industry into (or from) southwest Asia.

Except in areas fringing the Mediterranean, finds of Acheulian hand-axes in southwest Asia are scanty, and, in most cases, there is no good evidence to show whether they are of Middle or Late Pleistocene age, or even earlier. Typology is not sufficient to date individual or small assemblages of hand-axes, but the Palestinian cave sites give a sequence of dated industries: a crude flake industry (sometimes described as Tayacian), an Acheulian industry and Jabrudian, succeeded by Levallois-Mousterian. The succession is thought to span the period represented in northwest Europe by the Last Interglacial and the first half of the Last Glaciation. Hand-axes commonly occur in the Acheulian and Jabrudian industries. Earlier Acheulian industries of Middle Pleistocene date, on the basis of associated fauna, occur in Jordan and Syria.

The main sites with hand-axes in the countries to the west of Iran are listed below, together with some pre-Mousterian flake or pebble tool industries.

Israel, Lebanon, and West Jordan

Paleolithic material is abundant in this region, around the eastern shores of the Mediterranean Sea. It is not certain whether much of it is Middle or Late Pleistocene, but those sites that have some claim to be considered earlier than the Mousterian industries of Israel are listed below, together with those dated more convincingly to the Middle Pleistocene period, or earlier. A useful account of some of the first sites discovered is given by Zumoffen (1897), and a more recent survey has been published by J. D. Clark (1966). The key to the local succession, at least during the Early–Late Pleistocene, is the site at Mount Carmel (Garrod and Bate 1937) and at Jabrud (Rust 1950) with evaluations by R. Neuville (1951), J. Waechter (1962), F. Clark Howell (1959), R. J. Braidwood and B. Howe (1960), K. P. Oakley (1964:149), and J. M. Coles and E. S. Higgs (1969).

Jisr Banāt Yaqūb.　A river terrace of the Jordan. Hand-axes associated with *Elephas trogontherii*, *Stegodon*, and rhinoceros, below later hand-ax levels and Levalloisian (Stekelis 1960).

'Ubeidiyeh.　A lacustrine site in the Jordan valley. Three phases of a "pebble-tool" industry have been recognized (called Israel Variant of the Oldowan) below a similar industry also containing crude hand-axes (Stekelis 1966).

Hazorea.　A lacustrine or spring site with a sealed industry containing hand-axes (Anati and Haas 1967; Avnimelech 1967).

Adlun.　A Jabrudian industry overlying pre-Aurignacian (that is a blade industry with some hand-axes), in a beach deposit at twelve meters above sea level. Hand-axes were also found in caves in this district associated with fauna and hearths (Zumoffen 1908).

Mount Carmel — Cave Et-Tabun.　Jabrudian overlies an industry of flakes with some Levallois technique, flake tools of mainly unspecialized forms, and cores, sometimes called Tabunian (Howell 1959). Above is Levalloiso-Mousterian (Garrod and Bate 1937). A few hand-axes come from the lower levels of Skhūl.

Oumm Qatafa.　A cave site in the Judean Desert with a Tabunian industry at the base and developed Acheulian industries above. In between is an industry comparable to the Tabunian but with hand-axes (Neuville 1931).

Ras Beyrouth.　A rolled hand-ax was found in the slope breccia at forty-five meters below the upper (seventy to one hundred meters) terrace, and an unweathered hand-ax comes from soil above (Fleisch 1946).

Rephaim Baq'a.　Many artifacts including hand-axes, mainly rolled, from gravels near Jerusalem (Stekelis 1947). Six hand-axes are figured by Macalister (1912).

Abou-Sif.　A few hand-axes were found on the basal level below a Mousterian industry in this cave, also in the Judean Desert (Neuville 1951).

Doukha.　A late Acheulian open site is recorded by Zumoffen (1908).

Akbyeh.　A workshop site is recorded by Zumoffen (1908).

Jafr-Ma'an.   Surface finds are recorded associated with possible ancient lake shores and deflated surfaces. Crude cores, hand-axes, and flakes have been compared to the Abbevillian and Clactonian of Europe (Zeuner 1957).

Ma'an, Khatt-esh-Shihib, Jerash, Shu'eib Bridge, Wadi-el-Harith, Petra, and other sites.   Several surface finds of hand-axes have been made in Jordan, mainly during an expedition in 1955 or by previous workers. These are summarized by Zeuner (1957).

Jafr-Ma'an Road, Qa el Mukheizin, Corral 3, Khareneh II, Aqaba, Irbid Road, and other sites.   Zeuner has also reported surface finds of flakes and cores unassociated with hand-axes and concluded many represent an "industry essentially Clactonian rather than Tayacian in character." Levalloisian and Levalloiso-Mousterian are also found richly scattered in the area, on the surface or stratified in Late Pleistocene alluvial deposits (Zeuner 1957).

Sherah.   Hand-axes and Levalloisian cores are recorded in the Wadi Gaza under two and one-half meters of loess, apart from some eoliths and rostro-carinates in southern Palestine (Moir 1930), which would not now be regarded as artifacts by most workers.

Syria

Jabrud.   Shelter I at Jabrud has produced numerous hand-axes in industries referred to as Acheulo-Jabrudian, Jung Acheuléen, and Jabrudian (Rust 1950).

Turkey

In southeastern Anatolia hand-axes have been recorded, and also some on the shores of the Bosphorus (Bostanci 1961).

Iraq

Barda Balka.   Pebble tools, flake tools, and "Upper Acheulian" hand-axes have been recorded from gravels tentatively equated with the Last Glaciation (Wright and Howe 1951).

Cham Bazar, near Jarmo, and Eski Kelik.   A few hand-axes have come from the first two sites in gravel of comparable age to that of Barda Balka. At Eski Kelik an isolated hand-ax was found on the right bank of the Greater Zab (Braidwood and Howe 1960).

Saudi Arabia, Yemen, South Arabia and Oman

Paleolithic artifacts are fairly widespread in parts of south Arabia and comprise cores, flakes, and "choppers." Levallois cores and flakes are included, and, in the absence of hand-axes or stratigraphical evidence, it is unlikely that any of the artifacts are earlier than Late Pleistocene. Comparisons have been made with the Late Soan Industries of Pakistan (Caton-Thompson 1953). Acheulian artifacts have been reported from Arabia (Bordes 1968). Field (1961) refers to Lower Paleolithic implements from Rub' al Khali. Payne (1963) describes two surface hand-axes and other flint implements from Habarut in southern Arabia.

Armenia

(Šatani-Dár. A rich surface site of obsidian and basalt hand-axes is recorded here near Mount Artin (Bogutlu) at an altitude of 1,640 metres (Mongait 1961; Kernd'l 1961, 1963; Klein 1966).
Azykh Cave (Azykhskaya peshchera in Azerbaidzhan, SSR). A cave at 1,400 meters with hand-axes (Klein 1966).
In the South Osetian (in Georgian SSR) group of sites (Klein 1966) are the following:
Laché-Balta. A deposit here in the Caucasus contains hand-axes and Levallois flakes (Kernd'l 1961, 1963; Klein 1966). Laché is also referred to as Lashe and Laše.
Kudáro I. The cave is located on the side of a limestone massif called Mt. Chasavali. At an altitude of 1,650 meters is an Acheulian industry stratified beneath Mousterian (Kernd'l 1961, 1963; Klein 1966).

Ukraine

Hand-ax sites are recorded here and in Turkmenia on the Caspian Sea (Mongait 1961).

GEOGRAPHICAL BARRIERS

There is no evidence to show that the existing deserts of Syria, Arabia, and central Iran were much different in the Pleistocene period. Minor changes caused by climatic fluctuations may have made temporary differences in favor of movement, but it seems unlikely that the environment altered significantly. It does not appear that at any time these deserts could have supported the herds of animals that Lower Paleolithic hunters may have depended upon for survival. The movement of such hunters would be bound by such factors; a difficult terrain would have been less of a barrier than an area devoid of game. It seems most probable that migration gradually took place by movement from one favorable area to another. If the great deserts really were as inhospitable during all stages of the Pleistocene as they are now, then Lower Paleolithic sites would not be expected to occur in them. The total lack of hand-axes, or any Lower Paleolithic types, in these deserts, from Jordan to Baluchistan, substantiates this hypothesis. However, these areas are vast and have received little attention from archeologists. The absence of material may just reflect this lack of investigation.

PLEISTOCENE DEPOSITS IN IRAN

The only available geological map of Iran (published in 1959 by the National Iranian Oil Company) is at a scale of 1:2,500,000, although there is a 1:250,000 map of the Zanjan area (published in 1969 by the Geological Survey of Iran, Ministry of Economy). Outcrops of Pleistocene rocks are uncolored with little or no description of their type. Other outcrops are more loosely described as Plio-Pleistocene. Rieben (1966) has subdivided some of the Pleistocene deposits into three formations:

A. Hezadarreh formation   Early Pleistocene
B. Kahrizak formation   Middle Pleistocene
C. Tehran formation   Late Pleistocene — Holocene

More detailed studies concerning the possible glaciation of some of the mountainous areas of Iran have been made (Wright 1961), and the only definite evidence of glaciation was found in the Zardeh Kuh range of Kurdistan. Smith (1971) summarizes available information on the Pleistocene background of Iran.

   Large areas of Pleistocene deposits are mapped in northwest Iran, although there is nothing to indicate what stage or stages of the Pleistocene may be represented by them. The central desert area is also mapped as being covered by superficial deposits dated as Pleistocene. Iranian geologists accept the tentative nature of this map and are engaged on more detailed surveys.

AVAILABILITY OF SUITABLE ROCKS FOR MAKING STONE TOOLS

The volcanic rocks that are so prevalent in west Iran are varied, but they include few tractable materials that give good, sharp edges. A green, welded tuff from the Eocene flakes with a clean, conchoidal fracture, but the resulting edge is soft. Some sandstones and quartzites are sufficiently fine grained to work and occur everywhere, although rather sporadically. Quartz is found, but there is very little good-quality siliceous stone except in parts of the Zagros and Elburz Mountains, corresponding markedly with the distribution of the Mousterian, Barodostian, and later stone industries of Iran. The outcrops and distribution of suitable rocks for toolmaking are virtually unknown except for the known chert outcrops around Kermanshah, and little help could be gained by considering this factor in advance.

The decision to investigate the northwest corner of Iran was prompted by the proximity of hand-axes in Armenia and the possibility that the stray finds in Iraq were a link with the richer Lower Paleolithic area nearer the Mediterranean. The Zagros Mountains offer a reasonable hunting habitat from Armenia to the Persian Gulf, as do the valleys of the Tigris and Euphrates, but only one hand-ax is recorded from the Kermanshah area, as previously noted. If northwest Iran was found to contain hand-ax sites or other evidence of Lower Paleolithic activity, it would make a good starting point from which a possible southern or eastern distribution might be traced. On the geological map large areas between Tehran and Tabriz are referred to the Plio-Pleistocene or Pleistocene period, so conditions seemed hopeful.

The outcome of the expedition has, unfortunately, done nothing to corroborate this speculation; in fact, the negative evidence strongly suggests there was apparently no Lower Paleolithic activity in northwest Iran, with some minor exceptions.

The result of intensive searching of chance exposures, dry river beds, and bare surfaces, from September 9–20, along a route Tehran-Tabriz-Lake Urmia-Kermanshah-Hamadan produced but one hand-ax and a few other artifacts that dubiously qualify as products of Lower Paleolithic industries. It is not necessary to record here details of the many places that were searched, but the opportunities for both preservation and discovery of stone artifacts in much of the area seemed good. Wide plains of sheet gravel covered most of the lowland areas. Marked as Pleistocene or Plio-Pleistocene on the map, they were certainly post-Miocene, frequently overlying volcanic rocks of that era. However, it was not clear why many could not be Pliocene, although the evidence of faulting had enabled the Geological Survey of Iran to date some of these gravels as Pleistocene with more confidence. Exposures were common in road cuttings, quarries, and natural cliffs. Bare surfaces of these sheet gravels were commonly seen and searched. Dry river beds offered further good opportunities for finding artifacts. The latter did produce a few simple, undiagnostic flakes of fine-grained sandstone, in fresh condition and presumably of Neolithic or more recent date. An illuminating natural section of fine silt was seen along the main road, forty kilometers north-west of Zanjan. The river had cut a vertical cliff four and a half meters high in silty deposits. There were marked laminations, lenses and seams of fine gravel, and point bars of coarse material, the latter indicating that the direction of flow was parallel to the present river. The deposits rested on the coarse gravelly bed across which the river now intermittently flows. A few narrow, vertical-sided lateral gorges had been cut through the silt and in one was a crudely flaked "chopper" of fine-grained volcanic rock and three possible flakes. They were not *in situ* but may have been derived from the coarser element within the silt. However, *in situ* within the body of the silt, three meters from the surface, were a few sherds, two of a thin-lipped bowl of red ware and another of a harder white ware with strip decoration. It is conclusive that this thick and extensive accumulation of silt had been not only deposited recently but mainly eroded away. In such a mountainous region of tectonic instability this is perhaps to be expected. If similar conditions had existed in the Pleistocene, it would have been conducive for the preservation of cultural and faunal material under stratified conditions, even if it was derived.

HAND-AX: FORTY-SIX KILOMETERS SOUTHEAST OF TABRIZ

A routine stop for searching was made at a point about one kilometer before the road from Mianeh reached Lake Gouri Djöll (37°53′N latitude and 46°42′E longitude). The altitude here is about 1,600 meters. A small river bed on the east side of the road did not produce any artifacts, although sherds were plentiful at the top of an isolated hill nearby. On the opposite side of the road, on the surface of a low terrace about 8 meters above the road, Dr. A. Iranpanah picked up a hand-ax (see Figure 1). It is a medium-sized subcordate tool, in a very worn, weathered condition. It is made of quartzitic buff-colored sandstone and a calcareous concretion adheres to part of the face not illustrated. It would be impossible to attribute this hand-ax to any particular stage of the Acheulian industries, but it is well made in spite of the poor quality stone used. Its presence on the surface in a highly weathered, almost unrecognizable state tentatively suggests that the gravels of this particular part predate it. An hour's searching by all four members of the team failed to produce further artifacts of any type. The whole following morning was spent in the vicinity of the lake. Not a single artifact was found. The hand-ax represents, perhaps, a casual loss by an Acheulian hunter.

Only three other artifacts found elsewhere during the expedition may qualify as Lower Paleolithic products: A small worn artifact resembling a crude hand-ax found by R. Singer and a worn blade-like outer flake found by E. Boné came from an area sixteen kilometers west of Zarrinabad in Azerbaijan, close to an area of travertine mapped by the Geological Survey of Iran about two kilometers south of a village called Hedgi or E-djee. The travertine was exposed in a small stream bed and is a nodular, semiconsolidated calcareous mud. No trace of fossils could be found within it, although Dr. Iranpanah identified some dark specks as wood remains.

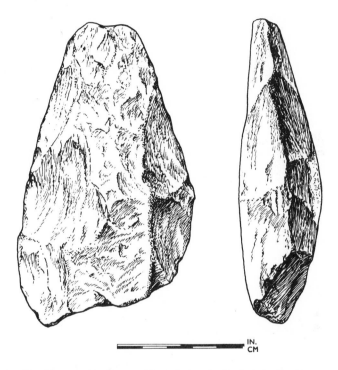

IN.
CM

Figure 1.   Hand-ax: weathered quartzitic sandstone, buff-colored, with calcareous concretion adhering to part of face not drawn. Recovered on surface of low terrace about eight meters above road twenty-nine miles southeast of Tabriz, Iran, September 13, 1970

The other artifact (see Figure 2) is a flake-blade of gray weathered quartzite with a plain striking platform. Calcareous concretions adhere in patches. It was found by J. Wymer, nine kilometers southeast of Zanjan beside the road to Qazvin, at a place where the road had been cut through the upper one to two meters of sheet gravel. The spoil from this cutting had been cast on the field to the side of the road and this flake was mixed with it.

These and all other materials collected were deposited with the Game and Fish Department, Tehran.

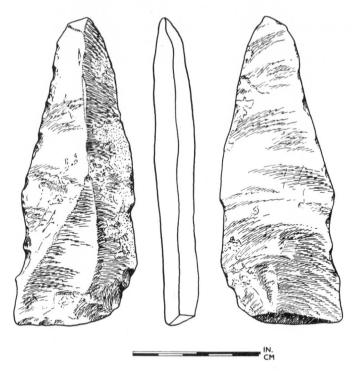

Figure 2.   Flake-blade with plain striking platform. Gray, weathered quartzite, with calcareous concretions adhering

CONCLUSION

The only hand-ax previously known from Iran is the one recorded by Braidwood in the Kermanshah area, and now in the National Museum in Tehran. The second hand-ax is the one recorded here. Until shown otherwise, it would seem that Acheulian activity in the Zagros area and in Azerbaijan was limited to hunting forays from a more favored area elsewhere. At present, the greater number of known hand-ax sites in the Caucasus–Black Sea area suggests that this may have been such an area, and a connection across Iraq and Turkey to the richer areas fringing the Mediterranean seaboard is inferred. The body of evidence at the moment, slender as it is, suggests that any possible connection between Pakistan, India, and Africa in the Early or Middle Pleistocene was along a southern route, skirting the Indian Ocean. The Arabian and Iranian deserts may have rendered such communication impossible, except during periods of low lea level, and the evidence sought may lie partly or completely to the south of the present coastline, submerged beneath the modern sea level.

Although no pebble tool or Oldowan type industry is known from Iran, intensive search along the eastern and southern boundaries of the country is certainly warranted. Smith (1971) aptly states:

A great deal of work must still be done before prehistorians will have a sound chronological and ecological framework in which to place their cultures, and the cooperation of natural scientists in the mapping of glacial and frozen ground features, study of inland lakes and the Caspian foreshore loesses, examination of extinct wadi systems, and construction of pollen sequences is a necessity for future Paleolithic work in Iran.

REFERENCES

ANATI, E., N. HAAS
   1967   The Hazorea Pleistocene site: a preliminary report. *Man* 2 (3):454–456.
AVNIMELECH, M. A.
   1967   A preliminary account of the geological situation of the prehistoric site near Hazorea. *Man* 2 (3):457–461.
BORDES, F.
   1968   *The old stone age.* London: Weidenfeld and Nicholson.
BOSTANCI, E. Y.
   1961   Research in South-East Anatolia: The Chellean and Acheulean industry of Dülük and Kartal. *Anatolia* 6:111–162.
BRAIDWOOD, R. J.
   1960a Seeking the world's first farmers in Persian Kurdistan: a full-scale investigation of prehistoric sites near Kermanshah. *Illustrated London News* 237:695–697.
   1960b Preliminary investigations concerning the origins of food-production in Iranian Kurdistan. *British Association for Advancement of Science* 17:214–218.
BRAIDWOOD, R. J., B. HOWE
   1960   Prehistoric investigations in Iraqi Kurdistan. *Oriental Institute Studies in Ancient Oriental Civilization* 31:1–184. Chicago: University of Chicago Press.
CAMERON, G. G.
   1936   *History of early Iran.* Chicago: University of Chicago Press.
CATON-THOMPSON, G.
   1953   Some Palaeoliths from South Arabia. *Proceedings of the Prehistoric Society* 19:189–218.
CLARK, J. D.
   1966   Acheulian occupation sites in the Middle East and Africa; a study of cultural variability. *American Anthropologist* 68 (2), pt. 2:202–229.
COLES, J. M., E. S. HIGGS
   1969   *The archaeology of early man.* London: Faber and Faber.
COON, C. S.
   1951   *Cave explorations in Iran, 1949.* (Museum monographs.) Philadelphia: The University Museum.
FIELD, H.
   1961   Palaeolithic implements from the Rub' al Khali. *Man* (9):22–23.

FLEISCH, H.
1946   Position de l'Acheuléen à Râs-Beyrouth (Liban). *Bulletin de la Société préhistorique de France*, 43:293–299.

GARROD, D. A. E., D. M. A. BATE
1937   *The stone age of Mount Carmel: excavations at Wady el Mughara*, vol. 1. Oxford: Oxford University Press.

HOLE, F., K. V. FLANNERY
1967   The prehistory of Southwestern Iran: a preliminary report. *Proceedings of the Prehistoric Society*, 33:147–206.

HOWELL, F. C.
1959   Upper Pleistocene stratigraphy and early man in the Levant. *Proceedings of the American Philosophical Society* 103:1–65.

HUME, G. W.
1969   "Palaeolithic Research in Iran." Unpublished Dissertation submitted to National Science Foundation.

KERND'L, A.
1961   Übersicht über den Forschungsstand der Ur-und Frühgeschichte in der Sowjetunion-1, *Berliner Jahrbuch für Vor- und Frühgeschichte* 1:171–190.
1963   Übersicht über den Forschungsstand der Ur- und Frühgeschichte in der Sowjetunion-2, *Berliner Jahrbuch für Vor- und Frühgeschichte* 3:112–179.

KLEIN, R. G.
1966   Chellean and Acheulean on the territory of the Soviet Union: a critical review of the evidence as presented in the literature. *American Anthropologist* 68 (2), pt. 2:1–45.

MACALISTER, R. A. S.
1912   Paleolithic implements from Palestine. *Palestine Exploration Quarterly* 43:82–84.

McBURNEY, C. B. M.
1964   Preliminary report on Stone Age reconnaissance in northeastern Iran. *Proceedings of the Prehistoric Society* 30:382–399.

MOIR, J. R.
1930   Flint implements of Lower Palaeolithic types from Palestine. *Journal of the Royal Anthropological Institute* 60:485.

MONGAIT, A. L.
1961   *Archaeology in the U.S.S.R.* Translated by M. W. Thompson. Harmondsworth: Penguin Books.

NEUVILLE, R.
1931   L'Acheuléen supérieur de la grotte d'Oumm Qatafa (Palestine). *L'Anthropologie* 41:13–51, 249–263.
1951   Le Paléolithique et le Mesolithique du desert du Judée. Memoir 24. Paris: Archives de l'Institut de Paléontologie Humaine.

OAKLEY, K. P.
1964   *Frameworks for dating fossil man.* London: Weidenfeld and Nicolson.

PAYNE, J. C.
1963   A surface collection of flints from Habarut in Southern Arabia. *Man* 240:185–187.

RIEBEN, E. H.
1966   Geological observations on alluvial deposits in Northern Iran. *Geological Survey of Iran* Report no. 9, pp. 1–41.

RUST, A.
1950   *Die Hohlenfunde von Jabrud (Syrien).* Neumünster: Karl Wachholtz.

SMITH, P. E. L.
1971   The Palaeolithic of Iran. Mélanges de Préhistoire, d'Archéo-civilisation et d'Ethnologie offerts à André Varagnac. Paris: École Pratique des Hautes Études — VIeme Section, Centre de Recherches Historiques.

STEKELIS, M.
1947   Rephaim-Baq'a: a Palaeolithic station in the vicinity of Jerusalem. *Journal of Palestine Oriental Society* 21:80–97.
1960   The Palaeolithic deposits of Jisr Banat Yaqub. *Bulletin of the Research Council of Israel* 9G:61–90.
1966   *Archaeological excavations at 'Ubeidiya, 1960–1963.* Jerusalem: Israel Academy of Sciences and Humanities.

WAECHTER, J. D'A.
1962   The Middle and Upper Palaeolithic sequence in south west Asia. *Advancement of Science* 18 (75):497–498.

WRIGHT, H. E. JR.
1961   Pleistocene glaciations in Kurdistan, *Eiszeitalter und Gegenwart* 12:131–164.

WRIGHT, H. E. JR., B. HOWE
1951   Preliminary report on soundings at Barda Balka. *Summer* 7:107–118.

YOUNG, T. C., P. E. L. SMITH
1966   Research in the prehistory of central western Iran. *Science* 153: 386–391.

ZEUNER, F. E.
1957   Stone Age exploration in Jordan, vol. 1. *Palestine Exploration Quarterly* (89th year): 17–58.

ZUMOFFEN, G.
1897   L'age de la pierre en Phénicie. *L'Anthropologie* 8:272–283, 426–438.
1908   L'age de la pierre en Phénicie. *Anthropos* 3:431–455.

COMMENT by *P. Boriskovskij*

The article by Singer and Wymer is extremely interesting and deals with discoveries of great importance. The illustrations that accompany the article are striking. In their review of other Acheulean occurrences in neighboring regions, the authors quite rightly cite discoveries in the Caucasus (Laché Balta, Šatani-Dar, and so on). However, other discoveries have been made in recent years in central Asia, especially in Kazakhstan, north of Tashkent. There, Alpisba'ev (1961) and Medo'ev (1964), prehistorians of the Kazakh SSR, have found numerous Acheulean bifaces and pics, together with great numbers of choppers and chopping tools. Additionally, there are the famous finds in Pakistan made by Graziosi. I am certain that the continued pursuit of such investigations in Iran will lead to many similar discoveries. We may certainly expect to find many further Acheulean bifaces in that region in the future.

ALPISBA'EV, KH.A.
1961   Otkritie pamyatnikov drevnevo i pozdnevo paleolita v Yuzhnom Kazakhstane. *Sov'etskaya Arkheologiya*, No. 1.

MEDO'EV, A. G.
1964   Kamennii vek Sari-Arika v svete noveishikh issledovanij. *Izvestia* of the Akademiya Nauk of the Kazakh SSR, social sciences series, V. 6, Alma-Ata. (volume editor).

Mousterian Worked Bone from Cueva Morín (Santander, Spain): A Preliminary Description

LESLIE G. FREEMAN

In two campaigns during the period 1968–1969, a rich sequence of Mousterian occupations totaling nine archeological horizons was discovered at the site of Cueva Morín (Santander, Spain). These campaigns were conducted under the joint direction of Father J. González Echegaray, vice director of the Provincial Prehistoric Museum in Santander, and the author. Results of the analysis of materials recovered during the 1968–1969 seasons are now published in some detail (González Echegaray *et al.* 1971, 1973). This paper presents some more recent observations, based on the study of materials recovered from one important Mousterian occupation during both field seasons, and the author's comments on comparable materials from the nearby site of El Pendo.

Level 17 is exposed over about twenty square meters. This area is not extensive in absolute terms, but the site as a whole is small, and the total surface excavated, some forty square meters, includes the greater part of the area of likely distribution of Paleolithic occupation vestiges remaining within the cave; this is known from stratigraphic exposures left by clandestine excavators and refreshed during our fieldwork. A large proportion of the area of the site is known to have been extensively disturbed by excavations in the early part of the century (Conde de la Vega del Sella 1921; Carballo 1923, especially Plate 1). Earlier workers destroyed a considerable part of Level 17 during their digs, but this is not the sole reason why more extensive traces of the occupation were not recovered by our work. Rather, the occupation horizon actually becomes sparser toward the eastern and southeastern part of the cave interior. Thus, our excavations allow us to define the actual boundaries of this occupation level to a considerably greater degree than one would suspect judging from their limited areal extent.

The lithic artifact inventory from this level is still under study. However, several hundred retouched stone tools have been classified, and it is clear that Upper Level 17 might be assigned to the Mousterian of Acheulean Tradition facies. It differs from its French counterpart in that the bifaces common in French collections are replaced at Morín, as elsewhere in Cantabria, by unifacial cleavers made on flakes ("cleaver-flakes" (see Figure 1). The Bordes-type cumulative percentage graph of the flake-tool collection recovered during 1968 is virtually indistinguishable from that of Level 4 at Pech de l'Azé (see Figure 2) (Bordes 1954). The assemblage is technically nonlaminar, non-Levallois, and non-faceted. An alternative classification as a special typical Mousterian variant is possible.

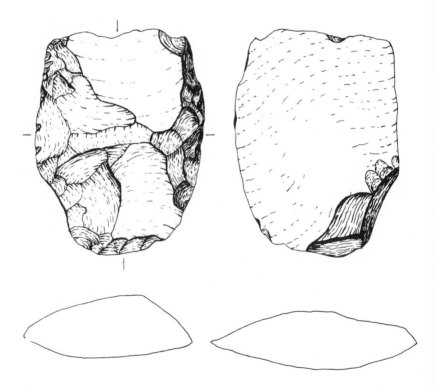

Figure 1. The cleaver-flake: characteristic tool of the Cantabrian Mousterian of Acheulean tradition (×0.6 of actual size)

It is not usual, in excavations of Paleolithic occupation horizons, that any appreciable quantity of industrial materials made of organic substances be brought to light. However, Upper Level 17 is an exception to this rule. In the 1968–1969 campaigns, 428 artificially worked fragments

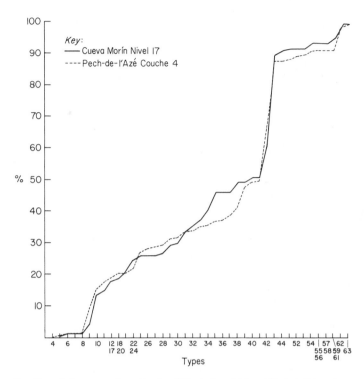

Figure 2.   Cumulative percentage graphs of Morín Level 17 and Pech de l'Aze 4 compared

of animal bone were recovered, and over 60 percent of these fragments appear to the author to be undeniable deliberately formed bone tools.[1]

Isolated pieces exhibiting deliberate, extensive, and continuous retouch have been reported from Middle and Lower Paleolithic contexts before, but such artifacts have never been found in great numbers. The quantity of apparent bone implements is not only absolutely large but also relatively large with respect both to the total number of bone fragments found and, equally important, to the total number of lithic implements recovered (only 416 shaped pieces). Large numbers of deliberately formed artifacts have, of course, been claimed for South African Australopithecine sites (Dart 1957 and elsewhere), for Choukoutien Locality I (Breuil 1932, 1938; Breuil and Barral 1955), for the

---

[1]   This statement is made after extensive examination of the literature on fortuitous "pseudo-tools" (see especially Pei 1938) and after consultation with Professor François Bordes at the University of Bordeaux. That the fragments are deliberate products of human activity is undeniable in the opinion of those who have seen the pieces, and I am not aware of any convincing evidence that such deliberately worked pieces can represent only the byproducts of other primary activities (such as butchering or grease extraction), although I have no doubt that much of the retouch on the other 40 percent of the pieces in question may be attributable to such processes.

Acheulean sites of Torralba and Ambrona (Howell 1966; Biberson and de Aguirre 1965; de Aguirre and Biberson 1967; Freeman and Butzer 1966) for the Middle Paleolithic localities of Castillo, la Quina, Grotte Neron, and other sites (Breuil 1950:97–99; Veyrier and Combier 1952), and most recently for Geula Cave (Dart 1967). However, with rare exceptions (Geula being one of them), the bone implements in question are minimally retouched and several categories of artifacts are identified, on statistical grounds, by the repetitive occurrence of similarly shaped fragments made on a variety of body parts or by repeated observations of similar treatment of the same body part from a given species. This is not the situation at Morín, where intentional manufacture of bone imple- ments can be recognized by the presence of deliberate retouch as clear and extensive as that on the most elaborately treated Middle Paleolithic stone tools. Strangely, the greater part of the bone tools to be described can be recognized *only* by the presence of the retouch they bear, and not by the shape of the bone fragment as a whole. Perhaps this fact has led former workers to pass over bone artifacts from other Mousterian occu- pations without giving them particular attention.

RAW MATERIALS

The following observations are based on pieces discovered during 1968, since the faunal identification was not complete for the 1969 collections at the time of writing.[2] This is only a preliminary diagnosis, and since it is based on small numbers of identifiable fragments, some of its details may not be completely trustworthy predictions of the state of the combined 1968–1969 collections. Publication of the Morín discoveries will not be completed for some time.

The worked bone in the 1968 collections was entirely from adult animals. By far the most abundant fragments are pieces of unidentifiable large long bone diaphyses. Assignment of these bits to given species or anatomical parts is simply not possible. Less than 20 percent of the fragments can be identified accurately. Of these, about 70 percent are pieces of bovid body parts. One of these is a bit of an upper tooth, but the rest are limb bones, with diaphysis fragments present to the near exclu- sion of epiphyses. All the longbones are represented. Bones of the feet (calcaneus, astragalus) are noted among the battered pieces.

Horse bones are rare, but limb bones (including metapodials) and dentition (apparently all the teeth are upper premolars and molars) of this species were recovered. Worked cervid bones are extremely rare and are primarily metapodials. No other species is represented in the worked

---

[2] Faunal identifications of Cueva Morín are being performed by Dr. Jesús Altuna, to whom the author is grateful for the information included here.

bone collection, but other species are very rare in the fauna from this level in any case.

The fauna from Upper Level 17, considered as a whole, is extremely poor in fragments other than those of limbs, feet, and teeth. Only about 1 percent of the bone assemblage consists of rib, scapula, pelvis, or vertebra fragments. Seventy percent of the limb bones are from lower limbs (metapodials, tibia, radius, ulna), the least meaty limb segments. These factors lead one to suspect that the faunal remains from this level do not simply represent food debris. Although it is still possible to think that the bones are primarily the remains of a marrow-extraction process or the preparation of bone grease (Leechman 1951), were this the case, there seems no reason why the upper limb bones, which also contain marrow and grease, should be absent. It seems most logical that the assemblage was deliberately selected from among the debris of meals and food processing and either retained at the site while garbage was disposed of elsewhere or else deliberately imported to Morín for some special purpose not directly related to primary food extraction. The single cervid antler from the 1968 collections is a cast specimen that must have been deliberately imported to the site for some such purpose. Although burned bone is present in the level, it seems unlikely that the mass of unburned osseous material was simply intended as fuel. In the first place, bone remains are intimately associated with numerous stone tools, and it seems improbable that a deliberately accumulated fuel supply would contain so much incombustible material. Secondly, burned fragments are rare and are not associated with hearths or other evidences of deliberate burning *in situ*. Lastly, if the bones were intended for imminent destruction, there is no reason why they should have been subjected to such extensive intentional retouch which, from the evidence at hand, seems to have been produced on the spot at Cueva Morín.

Bone Artifact Classification

While a number of bone implements apparently have direct analogues in the lithic flake-tool inventory, it would be inadvisable to attempt any major extension of the stone-tool terminology to embrace the bone pieces. The minimal categories recognized have been defined so as to keep them as free as possible of functional speculation.[3]

[3]   The designations "scraper-edged" and "skewer-like" are employed here without functional connotation. Until more is known of bone industries from Paleolithic contexts, it seems wise to ignore the functional load that some type-names bear. On the other hand, it is frequently stated that a "functional classification" of artifacts is a desideratum. Since any classification of material objects must be based on the physicochemical and associational attributes (including raw material, number and nature of flake-scars or striations, size, position, and so on) of the pieces classified, and since the functional significance of these

Table 1.   Categories of bone artifacts from Morín Upper Level 17

Categories	Totals
I. Flaked pieces	
A. Directly analogous to lithic flake-tools	
1. Lateral scraper-edged pieces	35
2. Terminal scraper-edged pieces	3
3. Notched pieces	47
4. Serrate pieces	36
5. Bec-like pieces	2
B. Directly analogous to lithic "bifacial" implements	
1. "Cleaver-flake-like" piece	1
C. With no true analogues in the lithic inventory	
1. Point-like pieces	3
2. Skewer-ended pieces	5
3. Para-becs, other pointed pieces	10
4. Chisel-ended pieces	16
5. Flaked teeth	8
6. Unclassifiable retouched pieces	132
II. Battered pieces	
A. Nicked pieces	16
B. Dented pieces	
1. Macrodented pieces	37
2. Nibbledented pieces	6
3. Anvildented pieces	4
III. Abraded pieces	
A. Smoothed pieces	1
B. Striated pieces	7
C. "Pushmarked" pieces	8
D. Sharp-edged pieces	2
E. Pockmarked (eroded) pieces	24
IV. Cut and engraved pieces	
A. Slice-marked pieces	14
B. Macaroni-marked pieces	11

In the classification presented in Table 1, four major categories of artifacts are recognized. These groups can be distinguished by the nature of the surface alteration of the basic bone raw material. The first division consists of all pieces with scars similar to those produced in stone during the flint-knapping process (roughly conchoidal flake-scars). Another category includes all battered pieces (pieces with nicks, dents, and

---

attributes is not directly evident, but must be based on a series of postclassificatory deductions derived in part from other considerations, the frequently mentioned but practically elusive "functional classification" can be recognized for the mythological beast that it is. It seems likely that no exhaustive and exclusively functional classification of Paleolithic implements will be possible until the invention of a "time machine" — in other words, never.

compression-marks of other sorts). A third group includes all so-called worn pieces (pieces with abrasions, striations, and eroded surfaces), and the last comprises pieces whose surfaces have been sliced or engraved by a sharp-edged implement.[4]

Flaked Pieces

Two-hundred and ninety-eight artifacts have been altered by apparently deliberate flake removals. Surfaces left by intentional flaking of reasonably fresh bone are quite easily distinguished from simple fractures (intentional or not) in fresh material and from accidental fractures (including "pseudo-conchoids") produced after an appreciable alteration of the organic bone structure. Deliberate flake-scars have some of the same characteristics that they possess in stone, including a marked negative concavity adjacent to the point of impact and, occasionally, small radial fissures or film — thin secondary (and often incompletely detached) flakes near the platform. Flakes produced after extensive alteration often follow a "splitting-plane" concentric with the long axis of the bone and parallel to its outer surface; sometimes these splitting planes are visible in section in bone and give it the appearance of weathered elephant tusk. The flake-terminus of a pseudo-conchoid in intensely weathered bone is frequently a vertical fracture at right angles to the flake axis, and a well-developed bulb is not frequently found. The pseudo-conchoid scar frequently has a very irregular (sometimes fibrous) surface and is sometimes of a strikingly different ("fresher") color than the patina borne by the weathered bone surface. Some of these characteristics occasionally occur in deliberate conchoidal flake scars, especially when a period of deliberate weathering is part of the artifact-manufacturing process, but when several are combined, the intentional nature of the retouch becomes very doubtful. A last, and certain, indication of the accidental nature of some "retouch" in moist weathered bone is given by the continued natural production of fresh similar scars while the bone dries or the generally fragile state of the find, which crumbles at the edges, producing fresh pseudo-conchoids and prismatic splinters if subjected to slight abrasion (such as that which accidentally occurs in bagging and storing the specimen).

No attempt to classify simple fractures has been made here. They are

---

[4]   Some pieces have been subjected to more than one kind of surface alteration, but in this preliminary classification no special provision is made for combined types. Each whole piece is classed with others according to the most extensive type of alteration it bears, as though that type were exclusively present. This practice has been followed for all combination-artifacts in the collection, although there is a substantial number of such pieces. Later publications will treat these pieces in more satisfactory and detailed fashion.

breaks at right angles to the plane of the bone surface (to the cylindrical surface of a longbone diaphysis, for example).[5]

Among the flaked pieces are 124 which are amazingly analogous to recognized lithic artifact types. These include scraper-edged pieces, notched pieces, serrate-edged or denticulate pieces, and bec-like pieces.

The "scraper-edged pieces" show continuous smooth, relatively straight or simple arcuate, concave or convex retouched edges. Retouch consists of regular diminutive[6] to normal expanding flake removals, usually produced on the bone inner table (interior surface of the compact bone) by percussion on the outer table (exterior surface). Thirty-five are laterally-retouched pieces, like stone sidescrapers (see Figures 3:2 and 4:1, 2), while three are terminally retouched pieces like stone endscrapers (one is a single-shouldered "endscraper" in bone).

Notched pieces are produced by drawing multiple diminutive to massive expanding flakes to produce a continuous simple deeply concave arcuate edge; the chord joining the terminal points of the concavity is usually quite short (see Figure 5:1, 3). Serrate pieces (see Figures 5:2 and 6) have retouched edges produced by the serial conjunction of more than two usually diminutive concavities to form a festoon. Projections between concavities may be sharp or blunted. The concavities are frequently produced by a single normal expanding flake removal.

Bec-like pieces have small single projections produced by convergent retouch, sometimes by convergent diminutive notches.

One flaked piece from this level is so similar to the cleaver flakes from some Cantabrian Mousterian occupations that it has been placed in a separate category (see Figure 7:1). The retouch on the trapezoidal segment of a large diaphysis is mostly concentrated at the transverse "distal," or "cleaver"-edge, and consists of massive to diminutive expanding and step-expanding flakes. The lateral margin and butt are formed by breaks. At several points on the outer table striations parallel and oblique to the long axis of the piece are barely discernible with the naked eye. These are apparently use-striations; they certainly were produced by abrasion rather than by slicing.

One-hundred and seventy-four flaked pieces have no apparent direct analogues among the lithic artifacts from the site. Some are vaguely reminiscent of specific stone-tool types, and a very small number look strikingly similar to given stone artifact types, but were produced by different techniques from those used in stone.

---

[5]   Such fractures are occasionally recognized as "bone burins," due apparently to a mistaken notion of the nature of burins in stone (Barandiarán 1967:302), but I have never seen a convincing bone burin from a Paleolithic site. (After recent discussions at Chicago, I believe that Barandiarán's diagnosis of bone burins now conforms to my own.)

[6]   Metrical characteristics are only described in this paper in relative terms. The pieces collected in 1969 have not yet been measured. More precision in metrical description will be provided in later publications.

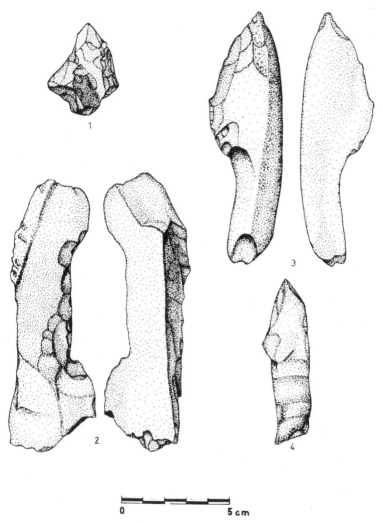

Figure 3. Point-like pieces (3, 4), concave lateral scraper-edged piece (2), and unclassifiable retouched piece (1)

Among these pieces are three that resemble stone "points." All three are roughly parallel-sided, flat-sectioned bone fragments with one extremity brought to a sharp point by flaking, cutting, and abrading (see Figure 3:3, 4). In all three cases, the parallel body of the piece has been flaked or abraded, thinning the base as though to form a stem for hafting.

The five skewer-ended pieces are long prismatic-sectioned sharply pointed awl-like artifacts (see Figure 8). The point may be bifacial, trihedral, or quadrilateral in section. The prismatic sectioned shaft and the point are produced by deliberate retouch, and the points are sometimes worn and polished. Ten other pieces (para-becs, and so on) are somewhat similar to stone "perforators." These include two elongated flat pointed objects, retouched on one surface, three pieces with broad or steep pointed projections like the stone artifacts called "becs," produced by irregular, sometimes alternate retouch, and five small sharply pointed splinters with scanty retouch or just marks of utilization; these last pieces may be fortuitous shapes that were chosen from a large mass of debris and used because of their suitable form.

The sixteen chisel-ended pieces (see Figure 9) are made on longbone fragments and have been retouched to form a straight or curved extremity produced in all cases but two by alternate or bifacial retouch. The pieces are arcuate in cross-section ("scoop-shaped"), and none is retouched

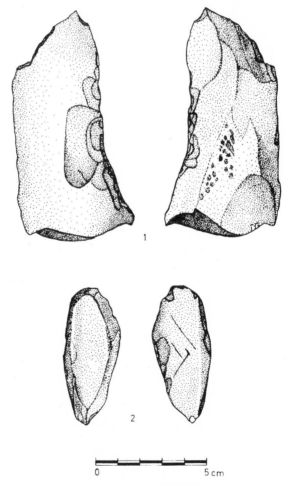

Figure 4.   Two scraper-edged pieces (one has bifacial retouch)

exclusively on the outer table; these factors and their greater overall size distinguish the chisel-ended pieces from endscraper-like pieces. Many of the chisel-ends occur in combination with other sorts of edges, especially notched and scraper-like ones.

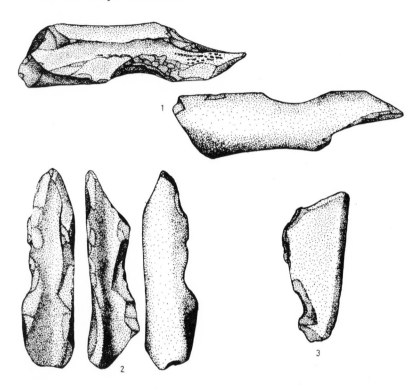

Figure 5.   Notched pieces (1, 3) and serrate piece with opposed notch (2)

Some years ago Pittard described regularly patterned marks indicating intentional breakage on bovid and equid teeth from the Mousterian levels of "les Rebieres" (Dordogne). He called attention to the presence of similar pieces at Spy and Ramioul (Pittard 1935a, 1935b, 1936). Patterns mentioned include the removal of roots from one or both sides of premolars and molars, cusp removal, splitting of a whole tooth, oblique fracture of a whole tooth, and (seldom) battering and flaking of the grinding surface. At Morín eight teeth show these patterns, especially root mutilation. Figure 10 shows bovid and equid molars from Level 17 with complete and unilateral root removal, as well as lateral flaking of the enamel on the tooth crown. There are, however, too few pieces of this sort at Morín to permit one to discern repetitive patterns of breakage or to decide if the breakage is intentional, or an accidental result of other operations on the skull and mandible. In teeth from other Cantabrian

Mousterian collections (Castillo, El Conde) similar breaks are found, and the high proportion of teeth to other body parts in some levels, even where bone preservation is exceptionally good, has previously inclined me to believe that teeth were deliberately selected for a specific use at some sites.

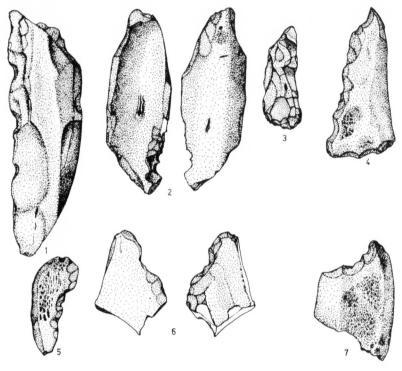

Figure 6.   Serrate pieces

One-hundred and thirty-six fragments have been called unclassifiable retouched pieces. Either they are so small in their entirety as to make a more specific assignment to another category impossible (see Figure 3:1), or the flake-scars they bear are irregularly distributed and do not conform to any recognizable pattern. Some of these pieces may simply be by-products of butchering practices or other deliberate manipulations of bone not related to tool-production.

Bone fragments that bear battering marks supposedly indicative of their use as hammers or anvils are a regularly recognized class of bone artifacts from Mousterian sites. Such pieces (and pointed splinters) are usually the only categories of bone artifacts mentioned from occupations of this age, and it is evidently felt by most scholars that the absence of other bone artifact types from such occupations is a normal and logical state of affairs. For example, Cheynier's discussion of the Mousterian collection at Pair-non-Pair mentions ". . . des Os-Enclumes nombreux; mais naturellement ni os ouvré ni ivoire" (1963:67). A rather impressive variety of battered pieces was recovered at Cueva Morín, but these totaled only sixty-three; they are only about half as abundant as the flaked pieces obviously analogous to lithic artifacts.

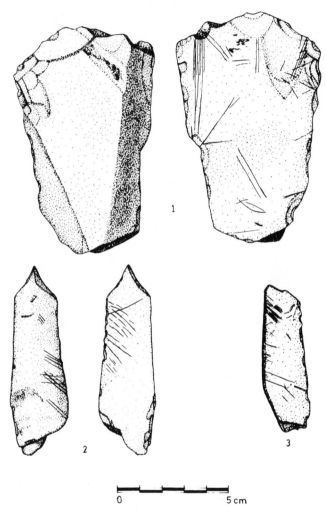

Figure 7. Cleaver-flake like piece (1) and two sharp-edged abraded pieces, all showing visible use-striations

Battered pieces from the Morín collection bear four distinct types of impact scars. Sixteen pieces show restricted clusters of short, sharp, generally parallel indentations with V-shaped cross sections, which are here called nicks. These always occur in patches, usually at one or both ends of an elongated bone fragment. Limited experimentation suggests that such pieces are bone hammers or compressors used in secondary retouch (this is also their traditional interpretation). The remaining pieces have marks I have called dents. Dents are regular or irregular, generally shallow depressions formed by compression of the bone tissue as much as by removal of material. The dent bottoms are either gently curved or flat. The thirty-seven macrodented pieces bear large irregular

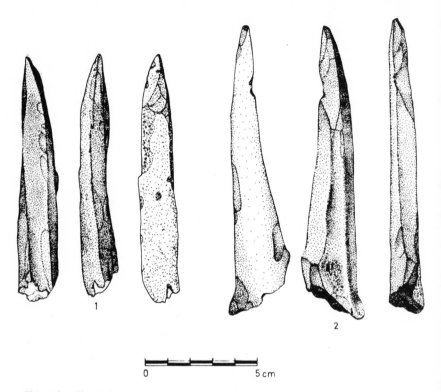

Figure 8. Skewer-ended pieces

dents, unevenly spaced over the bone surface. The six "nibbledented" pieces bear small, irregularly spaced shallow dents on the surface, sometimes near edges or pronounced convexities. Macrodents and nibbledents have been produced experimentally on bone fragments used as hammerstones in primary flaking and on bone pieces used as anvils or rests for bits of stone being flaked by bone or stone hammers. Anvildents, regularly shaped flat-bottomed depressions, usually triangular and sometimes curved in plan, and usually roughly equal in depth, generally occur in regularly spaced linear series (see Figure 11:1). The scars on an anvil-

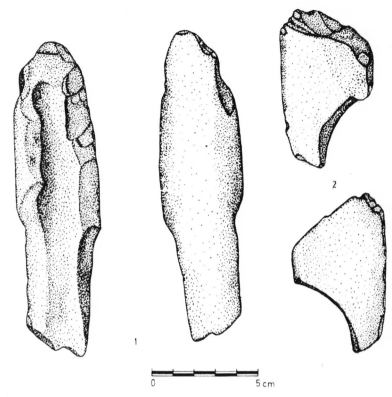

Figure 9.   Chisel-ended pieces

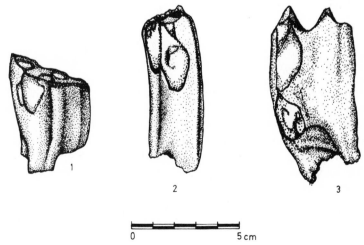

Figure 10. Flaked teeth

dented bone are so uniform that it is possible they were produced by repeatedly repositioning a single stone flake at intervals along the bone surface during secondary retouch by violent percussion. That mechanism is suggested by Semenov as responsible for the production of similar marks on mammoth foot-bones from Kiik-Koba and Kosh-Koba (1964:171, 175).

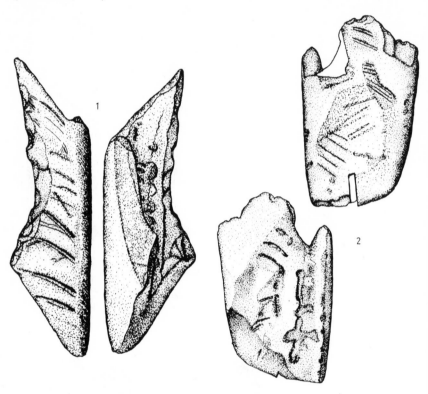

Figure 11.   Anvildented piece (1) and pushmarked piece with anvildents (2)

The collection includes forty-two fragments with surfaces altered by abrasion only. One artifact is called a smoothed piece. The cancellous tissue on this fragment seems to have been repeatedly rubbed against a hard surface. In the process the porous surface of the bone was crushed, filled, increased in density, and smoothed. Seven pieces bear dense parallel linear striations, clearly visible to the naked eye. Such marks could be the result of successive abrasions against a sharp projection or a rough granular surface. It is conceivable that if a sinew or other narrow fiber were sawed back and forth across a bone, similar scars would eventually result.

The abrasions on eight "pushmarked pieces" are the result of several recurrent applications of pressure from a hard, sharp object against a restricted bone surface. This action has produced deep scored grooves, which frequently terminate abruptly (nearly perpendicular to the long axis of the groove). Whether the bone was used as an active agent in the application of pressure or a stationary rest against which the pressure was applied cannot yet be determined. The grooves and pits produced during use of these pieces occur as frequently on the outer table as on the inner table of the bone (see Figure 11:2 and 12).

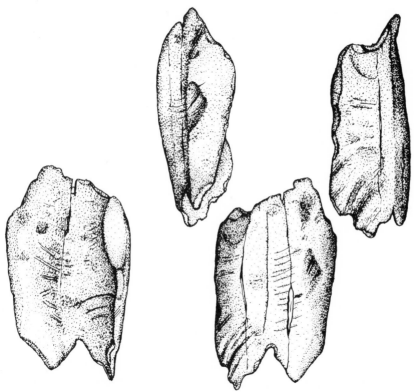

Figure 12.   Views of a pushmarked piece

Two pieces that present one or more sharp lateral margins bear parallel marks of abrasion. In one case (see Figure 7:2) these marks and small nicks depart from one sharp edge at an angle, a characteristic of use striations on stone "whittling knives," according to Semenov (1964:109). If the piece in question functioned as a knife, it could only have been used to cut quite soft materials. The second of these artifacts has use-nicks on its sharp edge and striations, but most of the striations depart from the blunt edge of the abrupt "back" opposed to the sharp margin (see Figure 7:3).

Twenty-four pieces are heavily worn over all surfaces. On some the worn surfaces appear to be formed by the continuous convergence of irregular pits or pockmarks. Many look eroded, as if by the action of acid. They are too severely altered to be extensively used hammer/anvils, but the mechanism responsible for their appearance has not been determined (see Figure 13).

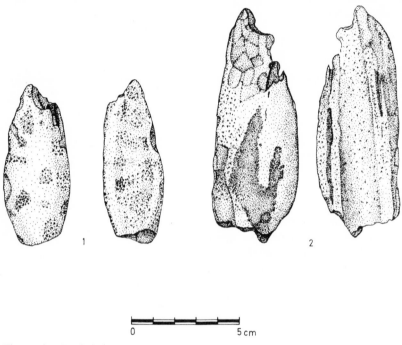

Figure 13.   Eroded pieces

Marks of cutting or engraving are found on twenty-one fragments. Fourteen of these show unevenly spaced and irregularly oriented marks of slicing by a sharp-edged hard object. Perhaps such pieces served as work surfaces atop which soft material such as skin was cut. Some of the slice-marks may simply be the result of butchering processes.

MOBILE ART

Whether or not Mousterian residents of France or Spain left enduring traces of primitive artistic endeavors on cave walls is a subject of cocktail-hour speculation among Old World prehistorians; treatment of the subject has not advanced beyond this stage due to the complete absence of recognizable evidence to substantiate claims on either side of the issue. Most authorities are willing to agree that Mousterian peoples did decorate *something* (their skins, tents, hides, and so on) with the rubbed nodules and sharpened pencils of mineral colorants discovered with some frequency in occupations of this age (Bordes 1952), but no artistic production of undoubted Mousterian origin has survived to be recognized as such.

According to a widely held theory, the origins of figurative art are to be sought in the:

... lines or incisions drawn on clay with several fingers or pronged palette-knives. These "macaroni" as they are called, to be found on many cave walls, which at first are merely a chaotic tangle of lines form the earliest "pictorial writing"; they probably also date from the Middle Aurignacian (Breuil and Berger-Kirchner 1961:21).

Good examples of "macaroni" from Spanish sites are figured for Hornos de la Peña and Altamira (Alcalde del Rio, Breuil, and Sierra, 1912:90, 196, Plate LVI) and for las Chimeneas in the Castillo complex (González Echegaray 1963:14). Such traces are also recognized in the French caves of Pech-Merle and Gargas (Leroi-Gourhan, 1965:Plates 304, 382; Nougier and Robert 1954).

Among the cut and engraved pieces recovered from Level 17 at Morín are eleven with surface markings strikingly coincident with the so-called macaroni. Most of the meanders are apparently due to natural causes but some of the lines are intentional. Often, deliberately engraved lines amplify or extend meanders which may have been naturally produced. The natural causes of these marks are not known. Some may be of superficial blood vessels like those known to occur on human remains (Wells 1963). The marks in question are meandering lines formed exclusively or in part by sets of two to four roughly parallel shallow, sometimes sharp-bottomed, incisions. They are not like natural traces formed by chemical etching, rodent gnawing, carnivore scratching, root or worm vermiculations, or any other unintentional natural process familiar to me or figured in the literature to the best of my knowledge (see especially Pei 1938:13–14, Plates 19, 20 for figures of such natural traces).

The meanders on five of the Morín fragments are haphazardly scattered over the (outer) bone surface. In one case they are arranged in widely spaced parallel sets. The most complex group of meanders is that on the bone fragment illustrated (see Plate 1). The extent to which this group may be formed by impressions of blood vessels has not yet been completely determined, and the piece is now under study. Some observers have attempted to see one or more zoomorphic figures in this jumble, but the fancied silhouettes are fortuitous. More of these pieces will be illustrated in detail in forthcoming publications. Although they are still enigmatic, the Morín engraved meanders constitute a potentially productive field of investigation for those concerned with the origins of artistic productions.[7]

Plate 1.   Macaroni-marked bone

SUMMARY

A combination of excellent conditions for bone preservation and the peculiar nature of the activities undertaken by the occupants of Morín Level 17 and the recovery, cleaning, and examination of all bone fragments (rather than just identifiable body parts) by the excavators during the 1968–1969 field season has permitted the identification of an elaborate Mousterian bone artifact industry. This industry is striking not only because it exhibits as much refinement and control of percussion retouch in the fabrication of bone tools as was exercised in stone nor solely because of the unprecedented variety of identifiable implement-types represented but also because of the great abundance of individual artifacts recovered. The total number of bone artifacts recognized is almost exactly as large as the total number of retouched stone artifacts

[7]   Professor Bordes has shown me pieces with analogous markings recovered from occupation levels at least as old as those at Cueva Morín in his excavations in southwest France. One of his pieces is probably of considerably greater antiquity. An enigmatic extensively worked Acheulian bone object recovered by Howell at Torralba in 1961 looks quite zoomorphic indeed, but the form of the piece may be related to the technological use to which it was put.

from the lithic assemblage in this level (about 450). If the bone pieces were omitted from the study of recovered artifacts, an impressive richness of detail concerning the technology of the Mousterian cave occupants would obviously be lost.

It is possible, even likely, that Morín Level 17 is an unusual occupation, and it may well be that Mousterian levels with abundant bone artifacts are in truth a great rarity. However, the number of Mousterian sites excavated in the past is so large that similar occupations have certainly been excavated in the past and the osseous artifact component simply overlooked.[8] In the future the prehistorian working with Middle Paleolithic occupations must obviously abandon the preconception that retouched bone implements can not exist in the levels he studies. The recognition of such pieces will be facilitated if the prehistorian also discards the idea that bone implements have to conform to patterned overall forms and concentrates on the search for retouched edges, no matter what the shape of the bone fragments on which such edges occur may be.

The identification of enigmatic "macaroni"-marked pieces in the Morín bone assemblage is of considerable potential interest for the student of Paleolithic art and expands the range of materials which must be taken into account in the search for the origins of esthetic expression. Even if these pieces only represent deliberate "doodled" amplifications and extensions of meander patterns produced largely by natural phenomena, they will add a new dimension to our appreciation of the accomplishments of Neanderthal men (the presumed authors of the Morín assemblage).

REFERENCES

ALCALDE DEL RIO, H., H. BREUIL, L. SIERRA
  1912   *Les cavernes de la région cantabrique (Espagne).* Monaco: S.A.S. le Prince Albert 1er de Monaco.
BARANDIARAN, I.
  1967   *El Paleomesolítico del Pirineo occidental.* Anejo de *Caesaraugusta*, III, Zaragoza.
BIBERSON, P., E. DE AGUIRRE
  1965   Experiences de taille d'outils préhistoriques dans des os d'éléphant. *Quaternaria* 7:165–183.
BORDES, F.
  1952   Sur l'usage probable de la peinture corporelle dans certaines tribus

---

[8]   In 1972 I was able to see the collections from international excavations in the cave of El Pendo, directed by the late Dr. J. Martínez Santa-Olalla from 1953 through 1957. Among the faunal remains from Level 16 at that site (a Denticulate Mousterian horizon) are 155 worked bones, including at least 45 flaked pieces and 2 with "macaroni" meanders. A detailed study of the Paleolithic collections from this most interesting site is now being prepared by González Echegaray.

moustériennes. *Bulletin de la Société Préhistorique Française* 1952:169–171.
1954   Les gisements du Pech-de-l'Azé (Dordogne). I — Le Moustérien de tradition Acheuléenne. *l'Anthropologie* 58:401–432.

BREUIL, H.
1932   Le feu et l'industrie de pierre et d'os dans le gisement du Sinanthropus à Chou-Kou-Tien. *l'Anthropologie* 42:1.
1938   The use of bone implements in the old Palaeolithic period. *Antiquity* 12:56–67.
1950   Collections préhistoriques de Rome, Monaco, Nice. *Bulletin de la Société préhistorique française* 67:97–99.

BREUIL, H., L. BARRAL
1955   Bois de cervidés et autres os travaillés sommairement au paléolithique ancien du vieux monde et au moustérien des grottes de Grimaldi et de l'Observatoire de Monaco. *Bulletin du Musée d'anthropologie préhistorique de Monaco*, Fasc. 2:4–26.

BREUIL, H., L. BERGER-KIRCHNER
1961   "Franco-Cantabrian rock art" in *The art of the stone age*. Edited by H. G. Bandi *et al*. 15–72. New York: Crown Publishers.

CARBALLO, J.
1923   *Excavaciones en la Cueva del Rey en Villanueva (Santander)*. Junta superior de excavaciones y antigüedades, Memoria 53.

CHEYNIER
1963   *La caverne de Pair-non-Pair*. Documents d'Aquitaine 3 (Bordeaux).

CONDE DE LA VEGA DEL SELLA
1921   *El Paleolítico de Cueva Morín (Santander) y notas para la climatología cuaternaria*. Comisión de investigaciones paleontológicas y prehistóricas, Memoria 29. Madrid.

DART, R.
1957   *The osteodontokeratic culture of Australopithecus prometheus*. Transvaal Museum, Memoir 10.
1967   Mousterian osteodontokeratic objects from Geula Cave (Haifa, Israel). *Quaternaria* 9:105–140.

DE AGUIRRE, E., P. BIBERSON
1967   Nota preliminar sobre el trabajo del hueso en el yacimiento achelense de Torralba del Moral. Madrid: *Noticiario Arqueológico Hispánico*.

FREEMAN, L. G., K. W. BUTZER
1966   The Acheulean station of Torralba, Spain. A progress report. *Quaternaria* 8:9–21.

GONZÁLEZ ECHEGARAY, J.
1963   *Cueva de las Chimeneas*. Excavaciones arqueológicas en España 21, Madrid.

GONZÁLEZ ECHEGARAY, J. *et al.*
1971   *Cueva Morín. Excavaciones 1966–1968*. Santander: Patronato de Cuevas Prehistóricas.
1973   *Cueva Morín. Excavaciones 1969*. Santander: Patronato de Cuevas Prehistóricas.

HOWELL, F. C.
1966   Observations on the earlier phases of the European Lower Paleolithic. *American Anthropologist* 68 (2):88–201.

LEECHMAN, D.
1951   Bone grease. *American Antiquity*, 16:355–356.

LEROI-GOURHAN, A.
1965   *Préhistoire de l'art occidental.* Paris: Lucien Mazenod.

NOUGIER, L. R., R. ROBERT
1954   *Pech-Merle de Cabrerets.* Toulouse: Edouard Privat.

PEI, W. C.
1938   Le rôle des animaux et des causes naturelles dans la cassure des os. *Palaeontologica Sinica*, n.s. D, 7.

PITTARD, E.
1935a Dents de *Bos* et d'*Equus* de la période moustérienne intentionellement brisées. *Société de Physique et Histoire Naturelle de Genéve.*

1935b Dents de *Bos* intentionellement fracturées (et sectionées) de la période moustérienne provenant de la station "les Rebières I" (Dordogne), *Bulletin de la Société Préhistorique Française* 32:554–558.

1936   Dents d'*Equus* intentionellement brisées (et sectionées) de la période moustérienne provenant de la station: les Rebières I (Dordogne). *Comptes rendus, XVI Congrés International d'Anthropologie* (1935):8.

SEMENOV, S. A.
1964   *Prehistoric technology.* New York: Barnes and Noble.

VEYRIER, M., J. COMBIER
1952   L'industrie osseuse moustérienne de la grotte Néron à Soyons (Ardeche). *l'Anthropologie* 56:383–385.

WELLS, C.
1963   Cortical grooves on the tibia. *Man* 137:112–114.

A Technique for Studying Microscopic Wear on Artifact Surfaces

LAWRENCE G. STRAUS and PHILIP WALKER

Microscopic traces of wear on prehistoric implements have been described at length by Semenov (1964) and, despite several criticisms by Bordes (1967), constitute one class of potential evidence in the delineation of the functional attributes of tools. This being simply a methodological outline, the important questions of sampling and representativeness are not treated, although they are recognized as crucial in the interpretation aspect of any program of artifact analysis. By the use of controlled analogy, parameters of motion, duration and angle of use, and inferences about the general range of raw material on which the artifacts were employed might be determinable from experiments. The regularity of the association of various types of wear (an unintentional by-product of artifact function) with intentional features of artifact morphology could provide strong evidence in support of hypotheses about artifact use at various levels of specificity. We propose a technique using transparent replicas of working edges (1) as an improved means of studying and recording the traces of experimentally produced wear and (2) as a method of discovering wear that is not visible by simple microscopic examination of prehistoric artifacts.

Semenov (1964) has suggested several techniques for staining and shadowing the surface of artifacts. This kind of preparation is necessary because of the lack of contrast shown by surfaces of translucent objects subjected to transmitted or reflected light. The transparent replica technique, which was developed by anatomists interested in the microtopography of teeth, overcomes many of the difficulties inherent in directly studying artifact surfaces (Dahlberg and Kinzey 1962; Scott and

We wish to thank Dr. William Hylander for suggesting the use of this technique. In addition, we would like to thank Dr. A. A. Dahlberg and Professor L. G. Freeman for their advice, encouragement, and aid.

Wyckoff 1949). This technique consists of the production of a resin (or collodion) replica of the surface of the artifact to be examined.

In order to obtain a transparent replica of an artifact (or part thereof), it is first necessary to make a rubber mold of the surface. The procedure outlined below is applicable to lithic artifacts — in our case, fine-grained European and Palestinian flint pieces with smooth surfaces. The steps involved are the following:

1. The artifact is cleaned in acetone or alcohol.
2. A rubber-base impression material is spread over the surface to be reproduced. We have found that rubber-base dental impression materials (for example, "Coe-flex") yield particularly good results. These materials are also quite convenient because they set quickly and can be removed from the artifact after only a few minutes.
3. After the rubber mold is removed from the artifact, it is surrounded by a plasticene dike about one-third of an inch high.
4. A viscous solution of polyvinyl alcohol and water is poured into the mold formed by the rubber impression and dike.
5. After it is dry and hard (one to two days later), the transparent polyvinyl alcohol surface replica is carefully removed from the rubber impression and mounted on a microscope slide.

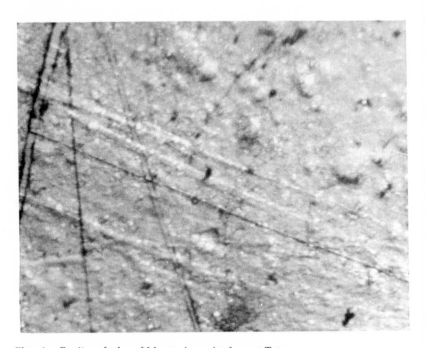

Plate 1.   Replica of edge of Mousterian point from et-Tatum

6. The surface can then be viewed and photographed microscopically, using various light intensities and angles, to provide the greatest clarity and contrast of any wear striations or use retouch present. We have found that for general purposes magnifications of from ×20 to ×100 are most useful (see Plates 1 and 2).

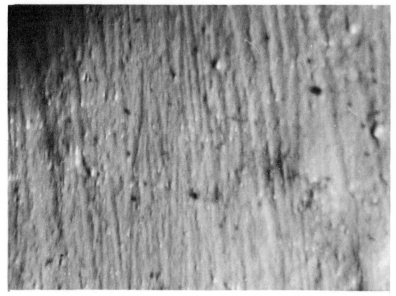

Plate 2. Replica of grinding striations on bit of a European Neolithic ground celt

Since the finished replica is somewhat flexible, it can be mounted on a flat microscope slide, which is particularly of value at higher magnifications, where depth of field is reduced. This same quality allows specific areas of the replica to be prepared for examination with the electron microscope. Scott and Wyckoff (1949) have taken electron micrographs of metallically shadowed replicas with high resolution at magnifications of ×10,000, although for archeological purposes, much lower magnifications would be of interest.

One of the subsidiary values of the technique is the fact that replicas can easily be made of museum specimens, which can then be used in comparative studies. This allows the application of electron microscopic and staining techniques, or other alterations, which would not otherwise be feasible. Using the technique one can clearly distinguish striations from natural or eroded microtopography on flint.

With good microscopic equipment the possibilities for locating subtle traces of wear on a replica are excellent. This technique consequently seems to be of significant value in helping to develop a less speculative science of prehistoric tool function.

REFERENCES

BORDES, F.
  1967   Considerations sur la typologie et les techniques dans le Paléolithique. *Quartär* 18:25–55.
DAHLBERG, A., W. KINZEY
  1962   Étude microscopique de l'abrasion et de l'attrition sur la surface des dents. *Bulletin du Groupement International pour la Recherche Scientifique en Stomatologie* 5:242–251.
SCOTT, D., R. WYCKOFF
  1949   Studies of tooth surface structure by optical and electron microscopy. *Journal of the American Dental Association* 39:275–282.
SEMENOV, S.
  1964   *Prehistoric technology.* Translated by M. W. Thompson. London: Cory, Adams and MacKay.

The Analysis of Some Occupation Floor Distributions from Earlier and Middle Paleolithic Sites in Spain

LESLIE G. FREEMAN

GENERAL CONSIDERATIONS

Historical Introduction

Anthropological archeology in the United States attempts the reconstruction of extinct sociocultural systems from their durable material remains. In the last twenty years the field has undergone intensive self-evaluation, partly manifest in efforts to establish archeological description and inference on a more objective and quantifiable basis.[1] The application of standard descriptive statistics (mean, mode, standard deviation) to artifact series and the use of quantitative tests (T test, analysis of variance, chi-square) to differentiate between series (as in artifact typology) are abundantly manifest in the literature. This paper is concerned with another and more strictly inferential thrust of the methodological "revolution" in archeology — the use of statistics in the discernment and explanation of occupation residue patterning at the supra-artifactual level.

This paper is not concerned with all attempts to discern and explain patterning in prehistoric residues but with only one subset of the group that searches for covariations of artifacts using multivariate techniques. Recent and stimulating growth in this field has involved the development and testing of two discrete explanatory models for patterning, but both now employ broadly analogous or identical multivariate analytical

---

[1] Although isolated earlier statistical applications are relatively numerous, the work of A. C. Spaulding (1960 and elsewhere) deserves especial mention as germinal. Much of the stimulus in the United States to the archeological use of standard techniques for statistical description and inference during the "modern" period can be traced directly to his work or to his students.

methods. A number of tests (cluster analysis, multiple regression, factor analysis) have been pressed into service with varying degrees of success. Some of these methods were first applied to archeological analyses at the University of Chicago in the 1960's by a group, including the author, working under the direction of L. R. Binford.

The two models proposed are: (1) that patterned occurrences of design ("stylistic") elements reflect the social organization and residence patterns of prehistoric groups and (2) that patterns in the frequency of occurrence of different artifact types reflect the performance of different activities by prehistoric social units. The two models are not *alternative* explanations of the same kinds of variation. Both may be equally correct in the most general sense, but their validation requires consideration of different aspects of the data. Nor were the models developed and applied completely independently.

Credit for pioneering the attempt to discern shifts in residence practices by the quantitative study of "stylistic" variables (ceramic rim sherd attributes) must go to James Deetz, who was engaged in such a study in the late 1950's (1960, 1965). However, his results were not generally known or easily available for the next few years. In 1961 Constance Cronin independently produced a study of painted pottery design elements, using the Robinson-Brainerd "coefficient of similarity" and concluding that there was a greater percentage of shared design elements between different pottery types at a single site than existed between samples of the same type of pottery from different sites (1962). W. A. Longacre next used a multiple regression analysis to relate spatial differentiation in the occurrence of pottery design elements at the Carter Ranch site to the presence of two "localized matrilineal groups" (1963, 1970). Longacre utilized some of the results of a previous study by Freeman and Brown (1964) in his work. James Hill used factor analysis in a study that combined a search for functional and stylistic aspects of data-patterning at the Broken K Pueblo (1965, 1970). Hill's work was the first of its kind to combine macrobotanical, faunal, and palynological evidence with the study of ceramics, lithic artifacts, and structural remnants from a single site. At about the same time Whallon sought to relate shifts in associations of ceramic design attributes on Owasco and Iroquois pottery to social structural change (1965, 1968).

An early example of multivariate quantitative testing designed to show that artifact frequency covariation may reflect the number and nature of different activities is that done by Freeman and Brown in 1962; simple and multiple regression analysis and chi-square tests were used to show that correlation in frequency of different pottery types at the Carter Ranch Pueblo could best be explained in functional terms (Freeman and Brown 1964; Brown and Freeman 1964). The next such test in sequence was my application of factor analysis to Cantabrian Mousterian artifact frequencies (1964, 1966), undertaken under Binford's direction. As far as I know, this was the first use of factor analysis on Paleolithic archeology.

L. R. Binford and S. R. Binford then undertook a similar test with Mousterian of Levallois facies artifact collections (1966). Their article has probably had as much impact on the thinking of English-speaking Paleolithic prehistorians as any other methodological paper published during the last fifteen years. More recently Binford (1972) has used results of a factor analysis of Acheulean assemblages in another major theoretical statement. The present paper is another attack on these problems. It differs from the Binfords' work in methodological detail; however, the differences are tactical, not strategic.

The two models just discussed are not independent, and their developmental histories are intertwined. Nonetheless, the distinction between them is more than arbitrary. It is no accident that studies of Paleolithic artifact assemblages have generally inclined to "functional" explanations of inter- and intra-assemblage difference, while social and residence structuring have mostly been sought in near-historic American Indian artifact series. The data available in the two cases are extremely different. In the first place, many of the Amerind sites studied have preserved vestiges of house rooms and ceremonial structures, whose characteristics may be expected to reflect residence patterns and social structure more than implements alone would. These are used as samples in analysis. From the universe of available variables, one set is usually chosen as especially appropriate for studies of internal structural differentiation within a society — ceramic "design" motifs. Although some of these may be more than decorative devices, most are very likely "stylistic" manifestations with little technological load. Functional differences between classes of aboriginal pottery are probably very restricted, as compared to the range of difference in function that may characterize distinct stone-tool types. As a result, studies that seek to explain attribute covariation as reflections of social structure or residence practices have chosen variables that are almost ideally relevant to the problem at hand: from a class of artifacts for which functional range is very limited, a set of extremely variable decorative attributes is chosen as variables for analysis. One final parameter usually characterizes such studies. Explanations of the variability isolated are sought in elaborate direct analogy with the ethnographically known cultural descendants of the prehistoric group whose remains are being examined. That is not inappropriate when direct historic links between the past case and that from the ethnographic present can be largely documented.

Paleolithic prehistory is another analytic universe. Direct evidence of residence patterns is rarely preserved and is fragmentary at best. Large permanent population aggregations such as those of the Pueblo Indians cannot be demonstrated. As a result, samples are generally whole occupation levels or spatial subdivisions of occupations made at the analyst's whim. The data available are lithic-artifact types (or classes of artifact attributes) and contextual information. Attribute clusters from artifacts or whole stone-tool types reflect a wide diversity of artifact functions. Stone is neither tractable nor plastic like clay. And deliberately decorated tools have not been documented before the latest Upper Paleolithic. The universe of variables available for study has far more potential "functional" (that is, technological) than "stylistic" significance. Since spatial patterning of artifact occurrences is only rarely associated with structural remnants, it cannot be assumed that the patterns observed offer more than a vague reflection of the existence of coresident units or corporate social groups. Generally speaking, the social units that serve directly to articulate a society with its environment are special-purpose task forces. It is such teams who are responsible for the accumulation of the Paleolithic occupation residues available for study. The teams need not equate with any kind of corporate social group. Last, direct ethnographic analogy must be avoided in interpretation as much as possible. No surviving group is the direct cultural heir of any Paleolithic society from the Old World. The ecosystems to which societies must adapt are constantly in flux, and the unending work of adaptation not only alters societies and people but also closes some potential avenues of future change as it opens up broad new adaptive vistas. In sum, the very nature of the available evidence makes the delineation of Paleolithic corporate groups and residence practices far more difficult than the recognition of the number and nature of tasks performed and the identification of the special-purpose teams responsible for task performance. That is not to say that attempts to delineate Paleolithic corporate groups should be abandoned — only to suggest that such attempts need to be vastly more sophisticated and elegant when applied to Paleolithic residues than in application to near-historic Amerind materials.

This study attempts to relate variability in artifact assemblages and context to the number and nature of discrete tasks performed by some prehistoric hunters in Spain. It uses data from two Paleolithic occurrences: Torralba (a multilevel Acheulean open-air site in Soria) and Cueva Morín (a multicomponent late Pleistocene cave site in Santander).

General Assumptions

The observational data available to a prehistorian are the durable residues of past human behavior and the contexts in which those residues

are found. When patterned occurrences of occupation residues are recovered from undisturbed contexts, patterned human behavior was
responsible for their production. Consistent patterning in several occupations is more likely to reflect culturally conditioned behavior than biological factors, and studies based on such consistent patterning may take for
granted its cultural foundations.[2]

Culture is the total configuration of patterned activities (which are not
simply referable to the biology of the actors) performed by a society,
including the materials used in or produced by those activities and the
social units responsible for activity performance. A social unit ("party,"
"task force," or "team") is any number of individuals (from one to n) who
contribute to activity performance. For this paper, all the listed designata
of social units are equivalent. An activity is purposeful behavior, whether
or not the performers can articulate their purpose. The common
terms "occupation," "pursuit," and "recreation" are all subsumed in "activity."

Patterned occurrences of occupation residues are a traditional subject
of archeological study, but a somewhat more precise definition is
intended than that used by most archeologists. One sort of "patterned
occurrence" of traditional concern was the "association," defined as a
spatial co-occurrence of items. Such co-occurrences were recognized and
defined subjectively. Often they were meaningful; but just as often they
were accidental and their interpretation was misleading. This paper is
concerned with discerning associations of two sorts: (1) significant patterns of covariation in the frequency of discrete classes of variables or
"linked frequency variations" and (2) significant tendencies for spatial
co-occurrence of discrete categories of variables or "spatial associations." Both linked frequency variations and spatial associations must
be objectively defined, using standard statistical techniques. Most of the
following discussion concerns material manifestations of these statistically determined associations. Groups of variables, each of which exhibits
similar patterns of linked frequency variations with respect to all other
variables, are called "clusters" or "constellations," while spatial co-
occurrences of limited sets of variables are called "clumps" ("spatial
configurations" or, at a later analytical stage, in this case specifically,
"activity-specific areas").

The rest of this paper documents the empirical search for clusters of
items from several Paleolithic occupations and the proof that such clusters tend to occur in discrete spatial clumps on the ground.

---

[2]   Although the line between culturally and biologically caused patterning may be hard to
define exactly in given cases, the problem is more important philosophically than practically
with the sorts of materials available for study, and the intervention of biological factors may
be considered either negligible or irrelevant for present purposes.

The Discernment of Clusters

As mentioned earlier, a number of multivariate techniques could be used to generate clusters of variables from prehistoric occupations and several have been so used with varying success. After some experimentation, the technique of factor analysis (Harman 1967) has proved to be the most convenient in practice and to yield the most satisfactory (elegant, intelligible, and replicable) results. (Actually, the words "factor analysis" are used here to indicate principal components analysis with rotation.) The technique has been criticized for reasons that are not always justifiable. It is true that factor analysis is not ideally suited to the analysis of prehistoric residues, but neither is any alternative test.

As input for factor analysis of the Torralba and Morín materials, matrices of product-moment correlation coefficients (Pearson's "r") calculated from the raw frequencies of a large number of variables from a smaller number of samples were used. Raw frequencies of zero were permitted, since they were observations of zero, not missed observations. This practice is open to serious objections. Pearson's "r" should be calculated only for samples from populations where the bivariate distribution of the variables in question is normal. Otherwise, standard assumptions about the distribution of values of the correlation coefficient may not be valid. Some of the variables sampled at Torralba and Morín have considerable positive skewness and/or kurtosis. Also, the correlation coefficient should be calculated from continuous values of variables, and raw frequencies are not continuous. However, these objections only have force when applied to the detailed interpretation of the correlation values, a task that is not attempted here. The values of "r" are regarded in this paper as so many measurements between pairs of points in n-dimensional space, without regard to whether or not specific distance measurements indicate significant relationship between the variables. Only one argument has been based on the significance of the value of "r," and that is the statement that no "significant" negative correlation coefficients occur in either matrix. In that case, I feel the conclusions are justified regardless of the exact values of the coefficients necessary for significance.

It should be noted that a variety of means have been proposed for the "standardization" of raw frequencies used in correlation analysis. No technique of standardization has yet proven its consistent and universal worth. One proposed technique, the calculation of "r" from relative frequencies of variables expressed as percentages of total sample contents, has several recognized disadvantages in the search for variable/variable as opposed to sample/sample correlations. This technique cannot help but produce spurious results as an artifact of the mathematics involved (see Miesch, Chao, and Cuttita 1966).

There were far fewer samples than variables from either site. It can be shown that such asymmetrical matrices have very severe drawbacks, and it could be urged that in this case multidimensional scaling or cluster analysis might better have been used. But there are equally valid objections to the other tests. Clustering techniques use as input some numerical measure of distance. In my opinion the most defensible distance measures are those derivable from Pearson's "r," but other measures are generally used.

These may be as simplistic as summed differences in the percentage representation of sets of characteristics of the observed variables (as the Robinson-Brainerd "coefficient of similarity") or quite complex, as are some measurements in vogue among biologists (Euclidean distance, Mahalanobis' d^2, and so on). There is no doubt that these indices measure something, but precisely what some of them express is difficult to define.[3] Since the indices are usually generated from attribute lists without controlling for correlation among the attributes compared, disproportionate weight may be given to causes for variation reflected in larger sets of attributes than other causes. Different procedural approaches to the assignment of a variable to a cluster produce contradictory results, and it has been said with justification that no single approach to cluster analysis has proved itself as a satisfactory archeological technique (Hodson 1970:317).

The best defense of factor analysis is that given by Sokal and Sneath: "factors which emerge in a simple structure solution have been shown to correspond to meaningful entities which reappear in related studies" (1963:195–196). In my experience, the variable clusters that are isolated by the factor model seldom coincide with those derived by currently used clustering procedures. While I am not happy with factor analysis for many reasons, and wish a more suitable test were available, I believe that all the suggested alternatives have even more serious drawbacks.

Factor analysis computations were done by the University of Chicago Computation Center, using the Harvard Data-Text Program. Factors with latent roots (eigenvalues) of 1.0 or higher were accepted as significant in the principal components solution. The significant factors were then subjected to rotation. It has been suggested that rotation is superfluous, since the principal components solution is mathematically unique. It is true that exactly the same variable clusters can be recognized in the principal components solution as are discoverable in the simple structure achieved by rotation. However, rotation is not a useless step. The resultant clusters are easier to pick from the factor solution after rotation than before. Rotation is an economical, timesaving procedure.

The generated factors are not, themselves, of interest. The relevant

---

[3] Euclidean distance and similar distance measures are, of course, themselves related to the product-moment correlation coefficient.

data for our purposes are the lists of variables associated with each factor. Rotated factor loadings express the extent to which variation in each variable is related to each of the underlying *tendencies* for variation (the factors). The factor loadings may be used to generate variable clusters, since some variables will be uniquely determined by one tendency for variation while others will be determined by other factors.

Lists of variables pertaining to each cluster are determined as follows. (1) By *arbitrary definition*, any variable exhibiting a loading of 0.800 or higher on any factor (and no loading as high as 0.500 on any other)[4] is said to be *uniquely determined* by that factor. (2) Any variable whose loading on one factor falls between 0.700 and 0.800, with no other loading as high as 0.500, is said to be *almost exclusively* determined by that factor. The list of variables uniquely or almost exclusively determined by a factor constitutes a cluster. Obviously, it is not really appropriate to call a lone uniquely determined variable a cluster. Less obvious, but equally true, is the observation that when only one variable is uniquely or almost exclusively determined by a factor, its "interpretation" in sociocultural terms is probably fruitless.

Conclusions based on the examination of lists of uniquely and almost exclusively monofactorial variables are more meaningful than conclusions based on other lists. As the value of the factor loadings for a variable drops, the factor model becomes less adequate as an explanation of the variance of that variable. It is certainly true that some variables must be partly determined by two or more factors, and that this may be reflected in considerably lower loadings than 0.800 on those factors. Therefore, middling loadings (above 0.500) on several factors might indicate that a variable was partly determined by more than one of the isolated tendencies for variation. However, middling factor loadings also may occur when there is poor fit between the factor model and variation in the variables in question. The inclusion of additional observations in such cases will sometimes result in the generation of a previously undemonstrated factor, uniquely determining those variables. For that reason, the partial determination of variation by two or more factors may be spurious. It would be irresponsible to rely heavily on such variables for cultural interpretation. It would, nonetheless, be equally irresponsible to ignore them altogether.

Two other arbitrary definitions are needed to cover such cases. *A variable with loadings on one or more factors higher than 0.500 is said to be partially determined by each of those factors, and mostly determined by*

---

[4]   This arbitrary definition reflects the empirical fact that a loading of 0.800 or more is a statement that at least 64 percent of the total variability in the variable is determined by the factor. Normally, with more than three or four factors, there are few cases where a variable has 64 percent of its variability determined by one factor and over 25 percent (loading of 0.500) determined by a second. The threshold values were adopted for their convenience in the case at hand. In other cases they might not be ideal, and could be altered as necessary.

the factor with the highest loading.[5] Partially determined variables are not included in the strict definition of clusters.

So far, rules for the recognition of variable clusters have been presented, but there has been no attempt at the abstract interpretation of clustering in sociocultural terms. As a matter of fact, no abstract definition (other than that the clusters show patterned covariation in frequency) can be presented. Interpretation can only be meaningful in concrete empirical application. A cluster in the abstract has no fixed sociocultural referent.

Discernment of Spatial Patterning, Especially Specialized Activity Loci

All prehistorians must have observed that recovered artifacts are often not homogeneously, uniformly distributed over the surface of the occupation levels they have excavated. Nonetheless, even after the impression of nonhomogeneous distributions has been verified statistically, it is often difficult to interpret this discovery. If there are only a few objects of the class in question, and the area excavated is large, one would not expect to find the objects all over the surface. Micro-movements and item realignments due to geological processes can produce nonrandom distributions, too. Thus some significant differences in spatial occurrence, as determined by standard tests, may be culturally meaningless.

On the other hand, certain sorts of variable clusters should tend to be found in different spatial positions within an occupation for reasons related to the structure and functioning of extinct sociocultural systems. Clusters that are the material embodiment of boundary-indicative mechanisms restricted to distinct identity-conscious social units (professional badges, other status-indicative devices, material symbols of distinct coextant ideological systems, for example) should be found in the restricted space utilized by any such units that were confined to distinct localities on the site. Clusters of implements used together for different restricted sets of related (technological) activities might often be found in different places as well (toilet utensils, butchering equipment, food storage vessels, for example). These observations are part of the common sense theoretical inventory of most archeologists. Once again, the causes of spatial patterning can only be determined in concrete empirical application.

[5] Statisticians who use the factor test often assume that any factor loading below 0.400 should be disregarded; to be useful for interpretive purposes, a factor should account for at least 16 percent of the variability in a variable under consideration. In the light of the reservations about the suitability of these data for factor analysis, I think it safer to raise the arbitrary cutoff in this case to 0.500. Acceptance of this value means that unless 25 percent of the variance in a variable is determined by a factor, it will not be considered determined by that factor at all.

Strangely, attempts to define differential spatial distributions of prehistoric residues quantitatively are rare in the professional literature. This is even stranger when one recalls that many archeologists have a strong interest in discovering such distributions. In fact, the study of prehistoric spatial distributions is still in its infancy.

Many workers are aware of a battery of tests suited to the study of spatial positioning. Sometimes, applications are less than satisfying because their limits are not understood. If one only needs to know whether a distribution of points in a given space is "random" or "clumped," the nearest-neighbor test is appropriate (Clark and Evans 1954). However, that test will not specify the number of clumps that can meaningfully be distinguished nor will it locate them in space or bound them, nor be used directly to compare the positions of clumps of different kinds. If the space in question can be divided into meaningful subunits (structural remnants, equal-area grid squares of ideal size and position[6]), the tendency for distributions of distinct data classes within the subunits to associate or segregate can be measured by the phi-coefficient = Kendall's partial rank correlation coefficient (Siegel 1956:223–229). A simple chi-square test will do essentially the same thing (in fact, the phi-coefficient and chi-square can be derived from each other). Probably these techniques have been used in classroom demonstrations and student projects literally hundreds of times. Very recently, Whallon has undertaken a series of explorations of the potential of these tests (1973a, 1973b, 1974). His work is sure to lead to a resurgence of interest in the techniques. I have the impression that the earlier lack of published uses of these tests was partly due to the feeling by their practitioners that they are pedestrian or that in specific application they have led to inconclusive results. One other reason for their neglect seems to reside in the fact that prehistorians often want to do something unnecessarily complicated. In this case, one suspects that most workers ideally want a statistical test that will draw "objective" limits around spatial distributions and, at the same time, compare the spatial positions of different kinds of things. But such a test is unnecessary for most of the questions the archeologist needs to answer.

In its simplest form, the spatial question that prehistorians most fre-

---

[6]   The problem with this technique is the practical difficulty in specifying just what grid size and position are ideal. A choice of any one set of parameters gives different results from those obtainable using other grid sizes, positions, and orientations. To circumvent this difficulty, Whallon has used a method called dimensional analysis of variance, successively doubling grid sizes to produce larger and larger grid units. Even so, it is impossible to examine intermediate grid sizes by this technique, and even, if that were possible, the recognition of functionally restricted toolkits depends in this system on discovering similarities between the distributions of pairs of different types. Exhaustive application of the test thus requires that the distribution of each type be laboriously compared with the distribution of every other type in all combinations. And, in the end, there seems to be no way to resolve ambiguities when they arise.

quently ask is: "Do these different things tend to occur in different places in an occupation?" A completely satisfactory answer to that question can usually be obtained using chi-square. There is tremendous concern on the part of Paleolithic prehistorians with the discernment of differential spatial distributions, especially activity-specific areas, in prehistoric occupations. Since the chi-square test is widely known, one would expect that the literature would abound in published demonstrations that activity-specific areas exist, yet it does not. The greatest cause of failure to isolate convincing activity areas on prehistoric occupation sites quantitatively seems not to be the theoretical weakness of the tests available, but the weakness of the models to be tested. Perhaps the greatest single weakness resides in a failure to recognize exactly which of the elements available for study are relevant to the discovery of specialized areas and their delineation in space.

A specification of the hidden assumptions involved in a search for areal specialization of function within prehistoric occupations may help to clarify these issues.

Assumption 1:   Prehistoric men performed markedly different activities in different places whenever space permitted.

Assumption 2:   The implements used together in a specific activity or its products and byproducts (or both) were usually abandoned together in a restricted area (whether abandonment was intentional or not).

Assumption 3:   Materials exclusively related to different activities were abandoned in different places.

Assumption 4:   The place of abandonment of materials related to an activity tends generally to coincide with the place of activity performance.

These four assumptions are neither equally probable nor equally necessary. The first three are absolutely essential; however, except in the broadest sense, they have never been proven valid. They are constructed of "common sense,"[7] but foundations of that material are notoriously liable to crumble. Nonetheless, we must at least proceed as though they might be true. The fourth assumption is not strictly necessary. Spatial differentiation by function in the most general sense could be demonstrated with the contents of garbage heaps quite well. However, there are ways in which specialized garbage dumps (in the sense of arbitrarily designated spatial depositories of wastes) can potentially be told from other areas of specialized activity performance. First of all, there are relatively unlimited ways of differentiating garbage dumps that will separate things used together and only one that consistently unites them. So, when things that covary in frequency in a sample of occupations, regard-

---

[7]   At least the first is. The basis of the other two is partly empirical, but quite subjective.

less of spatial position, are also found consistently to co-occur spatially in single occupations, it is less likely that the place of occurrence is a garbage heap and more likely that it is some other kind of specialized activity area. If, in addition, it can be shown that the spatial distribution of one of the classes of items in the covarying constellation places major constraints on the distributions of the other items, the areas are not simply arbitrarily designed garbage dumps. They are almost certainly the places of special activity performance. These considerations become an integral part of our framework if we hope to find the places where the different activities were actually undertaken.

These assumptions have important implications for research design. In the first place, not all kinds of sites and occupations will be equally fruitful sources of data for the recognition of functionally specific areas. Sites that have been subjected to severe postdepositional disturbance are obviously to be avoided, but some disturbance, provided that its extent is recognizable and that it is relatively slight, can be cautiously tolerated. Isolated short-term occupations will usually preserve evidence for areal specialization better than frequently reoccupied sites or single, continuous, long-term occupations. On the other hand, continuous long-term occupations may provide proof of a greater variety of distinct activities than ephemeral occupations (provided that the loci of specific activities have remained relatively constant throughout the period represented), simply because ephemeral occupations are often quite specialized.

If the area available for utilization is large, as is the case for most open-air sites and some very big caves and shelters, there is a better chance of distinguishing activity-specific areas than if usable space is restricted. A small cave site (Cueva Morín, for example) does not ordinarily provide ideal conditions for studies of areal differentiation.

It is obvious from the third assumption that not all functional items need be differentially distributed in space: only those exclusively related to a single set of activities would be expected to show clear spatial segregation. On the contrary, multipurpose items, used in more than one specific activity set, would cross the spatial boundaries defining the activity loci in question, and the more generalized an item, the more likely its distribution is to overlap all activity-specific areas. A failure to distinguish special purpose items from general purpose materials before searching for activity-specific loci is responsible for many past failures to demonstrate convincing spatial patterning of activity-performance.

In the absence of structural remnants most subjective "demonstrations" of spatial activity-segregation are inconclusive to a degree. On the other hand, in a search for objectivity it is possible to err in the other direction by adopting too mechanistic a conception of past human behavior. Prehistoric men are no more to be considered infallible automata than are modern men. A test that materials used in different tasks were abandoned in different places that does not allow the occasional loss of a toothpick in the bedroom or the use of a butcher-knife as a screwdriver is doomed to failure from the start. Even when butchering and stoneknapping are usually carried out in different areas, a butcher may very well sharpen his stone knife on the spot if it becomes too dull.

The phrase "specialized activities" has been used without definition up to this point. For this paper, there can be no overlap in the diagnostics of specialized activities. Conversely, any activities that produced distinctive diagnostic residues are specialized. The word "specialized" may mislead the incautious reader. I think most attempts to put intelligible labels on the activity-sets prehistorians study fall far wide of the truth by being over-specific (and that holds for my own labels as much as for those proposed by others). The only units produced by such analyses as the present one that have any objective reality are the independent clusters of covarying items and their spatial clumping. In passing from these units to inferences about their sociocultural meaning in the behavior systems that produced them, there is a tendency to assume that each represents a very limited number of different kinds of behavior; in fact, each may represent a large constellation of discrete but interrelated behavior patterns. We are inclined to infer that a cluster of implements reflects the activities of a craft as specialized as the modern butcher's when, in fact, it may reflect a kind of slicing that could be performed on vegetal materials as well as animal tissues and is as useful for ceremonial scarification as it is for food-processing. At present, there is no way out of this dilemma. The reader must, therefore, be aware that the functional designations the prehistorian uses are heuristic devices only and are usually at least partly in error. Nonetheless, such errors do not invalidate the existence of discovered variable clusters and distinctive spatial configurations.

With these preliminary remarks we may now begin the analysis of the cases at hand.

THE CASES

Torralba

Torralba, an open-air Acheulean site from the province of Soria, Spain, known as an archeological locality since 1909, was the subject of three seasons' intensive field investigation in 1961–1963 by F. Clark Howell and a team that included the author. Several short articles and a brief monograph about the new excavations have appeared, and a monograph of major length is soon to be submitted for publication (Butzer 1965; Howell, Butzer, and Aguirre 1963; Freeman 1975; Freeman and Butzer 1966).

Excavations at Torralba revealed ten major superimposed occupation surfaces and several smaller ones, most of them largely undisturbed, all of which yielded Earlier Acheulean artifacts, fauna, and botanical remains. On the basis of geology, pollen, and fauna, the sediments are dated to an early mid-Pleistocene glacial period. Festoons and pockets of frost-contorted ground and frost-patterned stone arrangements on prehistoric surfaces formed at several times during the period bracketed by human occupation of the site.

At the time it was utilized, Torralba was found along the edge of a valley bottom, containing marshes and ponds as well as a stream. The valley dissects the high, dry mountain and paramera systems that separate the southern from the northern submeseta. Game animals must always have been much more numerous in the valley than on the uplands and may have been seasonally exceptionally abundant during migrations of large herbivores.

No occupation level provided any evidence of structural remains (huts, tentrings, postholes, pits, trenches, and so on) although the excavation is relatively large (over 600 square meters in extent). Charcoal, though abundant, does not occur in the dense accumulations one would expect for deliberate fireplaces except in one level. Torralba cannot be called a "living site"; it is, rather, a series of "kill-sites" and "butchering areas." The site sediments may have been accumulated over the course of a relatively long period of time, but each occupation was probably very short lived.

Torralba hunters took several kinds of large herbivores. *Elephas antiquus, Equus caballus*, wild cattle, cervids including a primitive reindeer, and rhinoceros are represented. Carnivore remains and birds are rarely documented. There are no small animals. Apparently, the Acheulean hunters were rather opportunistic, taking any animal large enough to be spotted moving through the low valley-bottom vegetation (grasses, reeds). The most striking member of the faunal assemblage is certainly the huge extinct elephant, which is abundantly represented, but other animals outnumber it in every occupation. In several levels wild horses alone are as numerous as elephants. There is no denying that *Elephas antiquus* would have been by far the most abundant meat supply.

The maximum number of individual animals in any Torralba occupation is only fifteen. There is no significant difference in species representation from level to level: the same kinds of animals were being exploited in about the same proportions throughout the sequence. However, there are notable differences in the treatment of faunal remains in different levels. These are detailed in the forthcoming monograph.

The Torralba Variable Clusters

Raw data for the Torralba case are the frequencies of forty-seven variables in each of ten occupations (see Tables 1 and 2). These include both implements and faunal remains. All flake-tool frequencies are *counts of working edges* (except for unretouched flakes and utilized flakes, which, as is the case for the bifacial implements, are counts of whole artifacts).

The matrix of variable/variable intercorrelations is shown in Table 3. The fact that no negative correlation coefficients are nearly large enough to be identified as significant indicates that no variables can be said to replace each other in this occupation series. In other words, none of the variables increases in frequency at the expense of any other variable. Clearly, this strongly suggests that temporal change in popularity or stylistic difference between identity-conscious socio-cultural groups probably did not play a major role in causing the inter-assemblage variations at Torralba with which we are concerned.

Seven significant factors were generated by the factor analysis. Rotated factor loadings for the relationship of each variable to each of the seven underlying tendencies for variation are shown in Table 7. Table 5a lists

Table 1.   Torralba: identification of variables*

1. Endscrapers	26. Unworked equid teeth
2. Sidescrapers	27. Worked equid teeth
3. Perforator-borers	28. Equid skull
4. Burins, paraburins	29. Unworked equid limb including
5. Notches	metapodials
6. Abrupt retouched pieces	30. Worked equid limb including
7. Denticulates	metapodials
8. Retouched flakes	31. Equid scapulae
9. Utilized flakes	32. Equid feet excluding metapodials
10. Waste including biface trimming	33. Equid vertebrae
flakes	34. Equid pelvis
11. Bifaces	35. Bos teeth
12. Choppers, chopping tools, flaked	36. Bos skull
pebbles	37. Unworked bos limb including
13. Cores and "coreflakes"	metapodials
14. Elephant teeth	38. Worked bos limb including
15. Unworked elephant limbs	metapodials
16. Worked elephant limbs	39. Bos feet excluding metapodials
17. Unworked elephant ribs	40. Cervid (*Cervus*, *Dama*, large cervid
18. Worked elephant ribs	species) antler
19. Elephant skull	41. Cervid skull
20. Unworked elephant tusk	42. Cervid limb including metapodials
21. Worked elephant tusk	43. Cervid scapula
22. Elephant feet	44. Cervid feet excluding metapodials
23. Elephant scapulae	45. Cervid vertebrae
24. Elephant pelvis	46. Unworked indeterminate species
25. Elephant vertebrae	47. Worked indeterminate species

*Stone artifacts are *edges* except utilized flakes, waste, bifacial implements.

Table 2. Torralba: basic input (raw frequencies)

Variable number	Sample 1	Sample 2	Sample 3	Sample 4	Sample 5	Sample 6	Sample 7	Sample 8	Sample 9	Sample 10
1	7	1	2	2	0	0	0	0	3	2
2	23	0	8	17	5	3	1	3	13	5
3	2	2	4	8	4	0	3	4	8	4
4	2	0	2	1	2	0	2	0	1	1
5	5	5	6	10	0	0	1	2	8	3
6	3	1	0	0	2	2	0	0	0	4
7	12	7	5	23	5	2	8	6	7	6
8	7	3	3	9	5	3	4	4	10	7
9	10	5	7	9	10	6	4	0	10	26
10	13	2	14	11	10	10	4	0	13	58
11	5	2	2	10	0	0	2	0	8	3
12	3	1	3	1	1	1	0	0	2	2
13	7	2	0	6	2	2	1	1	5	3
14	16	0	5	8	4	2	4	0	10	5
15	11	0	4	3	1	0	0	1	16	1
16	31	2	5	21	3	4	0	0	7	2
17	13	0	6	6	3	0	2	0	15	2
18	16	1	6	11	2	4	1	7	12	2
19	4	0	2	10	4	2	1	2	12	2
20	17	0	2	9	2	1	5	2	16	0
21	13	0	4	5	2	1	0	0	2	6

22	0	18	1	0	1	3	11	4	0	11
23	0	5	0	0	0	0	2	1	0	8
24	2	5	0	1	1	1	1	1	0	9
25	6	22	2	3	1	6	11	2	1	33
26	13	18	0	2	2	17	7	4	5	21
27	9	5	1	0	1	2	14	5	1	11
28	2	4	2	1	1	3	2	3	0	5
29	9	1	1	0	0	2	3	1	0	6
30	9	6	0	7	1	2	10	5	1	8
31	3	2	2	0	1	2	4	2	0	7
32	4	6	0	1	0	1	6	4	0	7
33	4	2	1	0	0	2	3	2	0	11
34	0	0	0	1	2	6	5	6	4	4
35	0	1	0	1	2	2	8	1	1	0
36	3	1	0	2	0	0	9	0	0	5
37	3	1	2	2	1	0	2	0	0	4
38	3	2	0	0	2	1	3	0	0	5
39	8	1	1	0	0	3	2	1	0	1
40	2	5	0	5	0	1	3	5	1	15
41	4	1	0	1	0	1	2	2	0	2
42	1	1	0	0	2	1	7	0	1	2
43	2	1	0	1	1	1	2	1	1	4
44	0	0	1	1	2	10	4	3	0	2
45	0	0	7	0	0	2	1	2	0	3
46	42	31	7	10	25	26	66	21	10	85
47	24	25	3	11	9	10	60	26	4	64

Table 3.   Torralba: matrix of correlation coefficients

Variable number	Correlation coefficients									
	1	2	3	4	5	6	7	8	9	10
1	1.000	0.868	0.116	0.370	0.514	0.334	0.373	0.551	0.274	0.215
2	0.868	1.000	0.403	0.390	0.637	0.114	0.641	0.679	0.168	0.079
3	0.116	0.403	1.000	0.156	0.715	-0.443	0.563	0.641	0.187	0.096
4	0.370	0.390	0.156	1.000	0.037	0.069	0.150	0.323	0.136	0.120
5	0.514	0.637	0.715	0.037	1.000	-0.354	0.702	0.621	0.066	0.022
6	0.334	0.114	-0.443	0.069	-0.354	1.000	-0.210	0.165	0.725	0.694
7	0.373	0.641	0.563	0.150	0.702	-0.210	1.000	0.546	0.012	-0.069
8	0.551	0.679	0.641	0.323	0.621	0.165	0.546	1.000	0.495	0.396
9	0.274	0.168	0.187	0.136	0.066	0.725	0.012	0.495	1.000	0.974
10	0.215	0.079	0.096	0.120	0.022	0.694	-0.069	0.396	0.974	1.000
11	0.544	0.735	0.757	0.139	0.889	-0.205	0.799	0.856	0.194	0.120
12	0.774	0.614	0.058	0.425	0.426	0.364	0.011	0.419	0.412	0.423
13	0.766	0.855	0.359	0.166	0.576	0.290	0.659	0.838	0.306	0.183
14	0.926	0.961	0.324	0.423	0.536	0.279	0.444	0.705	0.304	0.211
15	0.698	0.675	0.444	0.378	0.511	-0.126	0.185	0.665	0.042	-0.020
16	0.859	0.945	0.224	0.362	0.571	0.171	0.719	0.559	0.082	-0.009
17	0.771	0.816	0.387	0.367	0.539	-0.003	0.248	0.707	0.087	0.026
18	0.815	0.922	0.498	0.255	0.680	-0.116	0.576	0.540	0.007	-0.088
19	0.314	0.640	0.803	0.102	0.676	-0.374	0.540	0.742	-0.037	-0.148
20	0.827	0.849	0.453	0.351	0.542	0.110	0.457	0.785	0.251	0.159
21	0.881	0.894	0.008	0.482	0.381	0.235	0.466	0.384	0.014	-0.048
22	0.637	0.811	0.670	0.225	0.726	-0.214	0.479	0.777	0.031	-0.073
23	0.928	0.888	0.218	0.341	0.498	0.131	0.363	0.589	0.059	-0.027
24	0.921	0.799	0.049	0.402	0.279	0.370	0.190	0.559	0.228	0.153

25	0.907	0.885	0.267	0.392	0.449	0.250	0.393	0.701	0.205	0.093
26	0.687	0.639	0.280	0.442	0.216	0.494	0.133	0.688	0.498	0.341
27	0.695	0.827	0.468	0.285	0.689	0.278	0.759	0.733	0.518	0.460
28	0.783	0.812	0.319	0.639	0.338	0.224	0.170	0.596	0.277	0.193
29	0.526	0.418	0.096	0.198	0.100	0.745	0.224	0.395	0.866	0.818
30	0.553	0.627	0.501	0.504	0.547	0.149	0.666	0.740	0.525	0.517
31	0.878	0.913	0.164	0.459	0.419	0.476	0.524	0.621	0.419	0.340
32	0.811	0.919	0.622	0.434	0.711	0.076	0.585	0.748	0.382	0.303
33	0.944	0.838	0.004	0.441	0.320	0.523	0.384	0.485	0.389	0.325
34	0.375	0.486	0.115	0.449	0.324	0.213	0.382	0.194	0.355	0.414
35	-0.260	0.077	0.337	-0.014	0.269	-0.205	0.545	0.252	-0.151	-0.251
36	0.407	0.695	0.426	0.262	0.562	-0.104	0.953	0.554	-0.048	-0.147
37	0.685	0.599	-0.022	0.331	0.161	0.552	0.427	0.547	0.509	0.495
38	0.727	0.748	0.096	-0.052	0.307	0.469	0.441	0.468	0.410	0.352
39	0.346	0.412	0.484	0.268	0.394	0.469	0.386	0.651	0.889	0.849
40	0.866	0.701	0.015	0.638	0.190	0.488	0.228	0.467	0.443	0.408
41	0.604	0.660	0.409	0.710	0.485	0.241	0.499	0.608	0.552	0.546
42	0.219	0.459	0.398	-0.104	0.490	0.253	0.748	0.604	0.473	0.422
43	0.842	0.875	0.008	0.537	0.288	0.371	0.501	0.529	0.180	0.125
44	-0.167	0.051	0.053	0.457	-0.224	0.232	0.062	0.104	0.134	0.038
45	0.546	0.600	-0.044	0.588	0.089	0.151	0.210	0.003	-0.077	-0.145
46	0.819	0.909	0.208	0.337	0.470	0.435	0.649	0.678	0.394	0.312
47	0.810	0.941	0.364	0.413	0.657	0.161	0.772	0.674	0.251	0.194

Table 3a

Variable number	Correlation coefficients									
	11	12	13	14	15	16	17	18	19	20
1	0.544	0.774	0.766	0.926	0.698	0.859	0.771	0.815	0.314	0.827
2	0.735	0.614	0.855	0.961	0.675	0.945	0.816	0.922	0.640	0.849
3	0.757	0.058	0.359	0.324	0.444	0.224	0.387	0.498	0.803	0.453
4	0.139	0.425	0.166	0.423	0.378	0.362	0.367	0.255	0.102	0.351
5	0.889	0.426	0.576	0.536	0.511	0.571	0.539	0.680	0.676	0.542
6	-0.205	0.364	0.290	0.279	-0.126	0.171	-0.003	-0.116	-0.374	0.110
7	0.799	0.011	0.659	0.444	0.185	0.719	0.248	0.576	0.540	0.457
8	0.856	0.419	0.838	0.705	0.665	0.559	0.707	0.540	0.742	0.785
9	0.194	0.412	0.306	0.304	0.042	0.082	0.087	0.007	-0.037	0.251
10	0.120	0.423	0.183	0.211	-0.020	-0.009	0.026	-0.088	-0.148	0.159
11	1.000	0.305	0.795	0.646	0.622	0.655	0.647	0.706	0.810	0.748
12	0.305	1.000	0.415	0.726	0.519	0.519	0.654	0.497	0.156	0.488
13	0.795	0.415	1.000	0.847	0.610	0.848	0.718	0.724	0.636	0.844
14	0.646	0.726	0.847	1.000	0.755	0.877	0.877	0.878	0.573	0.892
15	0.622	0.519	0.610	0.755	1.000	0.507	0.939	0.745	0.674	0.895
16	0.655	0.519	0.848	0.877	0.507	1.000	0.648	0.839	0.457	0.742
17	0.647	0.654	0.718	0.877	0.939	0.648	1.000	0.798	0.720	0.888
18	0.706	0.497	0.724	0.878	0.745	0.839	0.798	1.000	0.671	0.850
19	0.810	0.156	0.636	0.573	0.674	0.457	0.720	0.671	1.000	0.664
20	0.748	0.488	0.844	0.892	0.895	0.742	0.888	0.850	0.664	1.000
21	0.420	0.646	0.694	0.873	0.513	0.937	0.671	0.784	0.296	0.669
22	0.822	0.452	0.755	0.803	0.875	0.642	0.916	0.846	0.918	0.857
23	0.592	0.622	0.796	0.934	0.855	0.832	0.903	0.891	0.537	0.918
24	0.433	0.648	0.749	0.906	0.803	0.747	0.844	0.754	0.359	0.889

25	0.619	0.581	0.865	0.948	0.839	0.827	0.882	0.846	0.560	0.950
26	0.384	0.565	0.694	0.788	0.640	0.549	0.679	0.553	0.434	0.725
27	0.776	0.556	0.791	0.762	0.340	0.809	0.498	0.658	0.469	0.631
28	0.427	0.747	0.600	0.903	0.774	0.662	0.860	0.751	0.516	0.782
29	0.220	0.434	0.444	0.502	0.070	0.412	0.136	0.296	-0.081	0.398
30	0.738	0.381	0.620	0.585	0.428	0.589	0.434	0.492	0.368	0.656
31	0.542	0.691	0.817	0.923	0.473	0.912	0.651	0.732	0.350	0.729
32	0.782	0.651	0.750	0.910	0.715	0.790	0.786	0.894	0.657	0.857
33	0.414	0.700	0.738	0.890	0.509	0.868	0.619	0.720	0.168	0.741
34	0.242	0.585	0.193	0.408	-0.068	0.477	0.147	0.282	0.006	0.102
35	0.304	-0.267	0.222	-0.081	-0.281	0.162	-0.157	-0.074	0.367	-0.188
36	0.719	0.036	0.721	0.513	0.199	0.792	0.312	0.563	0.539	0.473
37	0.440	0.350	0.693	0.630	0.364	0.648	0.406	0.430	0.074	0.676
38	0.483	0.376	0.759	0.751	0.376	0.730	0.510	0.684	0.303	0.701
39	0.491	0.457	0.449	0.443	0.104	0.321	0.197	0.237	0.236	0.345
40	0.323	0.669	0.580	0.796	0.577	0.695	0.595	0.605	0.075	0.739
41	0.543	0.661	0.478	0.649	0.354	0.604	0.441	0.483	0.256	0.516
42	0.648	0.085	0.633	0.341	-0.075	0.487	0.100	0.250	0.386	0.271
43	0.470	0.564	0.778	0.866	0.510	0.913	0.661	0.692	0.300	0.732
44	-0.154	0.035	0.016	0.041	-0.269	0.071	-0.115	-0.171	0.060	-0.217
45	0.006	0.507	0.240	0.580	0.188	0.637	0.335	0.540	0.066	0.263
46	0.639	0.562	0.891	0.882	0.428	0.927	0.614	0.715	0.420	0.731
47	0.760	0.568	0.833	0.861	0.492	0.947	0.644	0.795	0.505	0.740

Table 3b

Variable number	Correlation coefficients									
	21	22	23	24	25	26	27	28	29	30
1	0.881	0.637	0.928	0.921	0.907	0.687	0.695	0.783	0.526	0.553
2	0.894	0.811	0.888	0.799	0.885	0.639	0.827	0.812	0.418	0.627
3	0.008	0.670	0.218	0.049	0.267	0.280	0.468	0.319	0.096	0.501
4	0.482	0.225	0.341	0.402	0.392	0.442	0.285	0.639	0.198	0.504
5	0.381	0.726	0.498	0.279	0.449	0.216	0.689	0.338	0.100	0.547
6	0.235	−0.214	0.131	0.370	0.250	0.494	0.278	0.224	0.745	0.149
7	0.466	0.479	0.363	0.190	0.393	0.133	0.759	0.170	0.224	0.666
8	0.384	0.777	0.589	0.559	0.701	0.688	0.733	0.596	0.395	0.740
9	0.014	0.031	0.059	0.228	0.205	0.498	0.518	0.277	0.866	0.525
10	−0.048	−0.073	−0.027	0.153	0.093	0.341	0.460	0.193	0.818	0.517
11	0.420	0.822	0.592	0.433	0.619	0.384	0.776	0.427	0.220	0.738
12	0.646	0.452	0.622	0.648	0.581	0.565	0.556	0.747	0.434	0.381
13	0.694	0.755	0.796	0.749	0.865	0.694	0.791	0.600	0.444	0.620
14	0.873	0.803	0.934	0.906	0.948	0.788	0.762	0.903	0.502	0.585
15	0.513	0.875	0.855	0.803	0.839	0.640	0.340	0.774	0.070	0.428
16	0.937	0.642	0.832	0.747	0.827	0.549	0.809	0.662	0.412	0.589
17	0.671	0.916	0.903	0.844	0.882	0.679	0.498	0.860	0.136	0.434
18	0.784	0.846	0.891	0.754	0.846	0.553	0.658	0.751	0.296	0.492
19	0.296	0.918	0.537	0.359	0.560	0.434	0.469	0.516	−0.081	0.368
20	0.669	0.857	0.918	0.889	0.950	0.725	0.631	0.782	0.398	0.656
21	1.000	0.549	0.848	0.809	0.812	0.558	0.655	0.758	0.357	0.438
22	0.549	1.000	0.808	0.664	0.803	0.614	0.558	0.735	0.069	0.448
23	0.848	0.808	1.000	0.953	0.974	0.707	0.560	0.827	0.295	0.446
24	0.809	0.664	0.953	1.000	0.962	0.777	0.502	0.838	0.437	0.449

25	0.812	0.803	0.974	0.962	1.000	0.818	0.610	0.847	0.406	0.523
26	0.558	0.614	0.707	0.777	0.818	1.000	0.481	0.828	0.535	0.360
27	0.655	0.558	0.560	0.502	0.610	0.481	1.000	0.538	0.663	0.821
28	0.758	0.735	0.827	0.838	0.847	0.828	0.538	1.000	0.394	0.447
29	0.357	0.069	0.295	0.437	0.406	0.535	0.663	0.394	1.000	0.598
30	0.438	0.448	0.446	0.449	0.523	0.360	0.821	0.447	0.598	1.000
31	0.901	0.562	0.783	0.796	0.824	0.705	0.860	0.782	0.666	0.649
32	0.714	0.815	0.796	0.720	0.812	0.661	0.844	0.825	0.544	0.747
33	0.900	0.465	0.828	0.878	0.847	0.691	0.732	0.754	0.691	0.589
34	0.514	0.079	0.152	0.140	0.133	0.067	0.694	0.372	0.479	0.549
35	-0.021	0.110	-0.214	-0.359	-0.141	-0.018	0.236	-0.170	-0.232	0.011
36	0.588	0.488	0.430	0.286	0.476	0.242	0.729	0.271	0.181	0.596
37	0.581	0.267	0.574	0.690	0.654	0.450	0.670	0.425	0.711	0.777
38	0.649	0.466	0.682	0.704	0.707	0.477	0.712	0.489	0.690	0.518
39	0.186	0.248	0.146	0.203	0.273	0.468	0.780	0.375	0.810	0.728
40	0.767	0.386	0.756	0.862	0.793	0.680	0.592	0.769	0.681	0.661
41	0.576	0.387	0.433	0.448	0.486	0.459	0.820	0.639	0.628	0.863
42	0.231	0.272	0.114	0.058	0.209	0.158	0.806	0.046	0.493	0.615
43	0.938	0.519	0.809	0.830	0.830	0.590	0.715	0.733	0.471	0.610
44	0.118	-0.076	-0.180	-0.143	-0.065	0.315	0.107	0.221	0.065	-0.065
45	0.794	0.240	0.498	0.471	0.461	0.436	0.361	0.665	0.253	0.114
46	0.849	0.577	0.744	0.735	0.796	0.628	0.903	0.667	0.632	0.689
47	0.852	0.650	0.745	0.667	0.756	0.490	0.930	0.653	0.499	0.777

Table 3c

Variable number	Correlation coefficients								
	31	32	33	34	35	36	37	38	39
1	0.878	0.811	0.944	0.375	-0.260	0.407	0.685	0.727	0.346
2	0.913	0.919	0.838	0.486	0.077	0.695	0.599	0.748	0.412
3	0.164	0.622	0.004	0.115	0.337	0.426	-0.022	0.096	0.484
4	0.459	0.434	0.441	0.449	-0.014	0.262	0.331	-0.052	0.268
5	0.419	0.711	0.320	0.324	0.269	0.562	0.161	0.307	0.394
6	0.476	0.076	0.523	0.213	-0.205	-0.104	0.552	0.469	0.469
7	0.524	0.585	0.384	0.382	0.545	0.953	0.427	0.441	0.386
8	0.621	0.748	0.485	0.194	0.252	0.554	0.547	0.468	0.651
9	0.419	0.382	0.389	0.355	-0.151	-0.048	0.509	0.410	0.889
10	0.340	0.303	0.325	0.414	-0.251	-0.147	0.495	0.352	0.849
11	0.542	0.782	0.414	0.242	0.304	0.719	0.440	0.483	0.491
12	0.691	0.651	0.700	0.585	-0.267	0.036	0.350	0.376	0.457
13	0.817	0.750	0.738	0.193	0.222	0.721	0.693	0.759	0.449
14	0.923	0.910	0.890	0.408	-0.081	0.513	0.630	0.751	0.443
15	0.473	0.715	0.509	-0.068	-0.281	0.199	0.364	0.376	0.104
16	0.912	0.790	0.868	0.477	0.162	0.792	0.648	0.730	0.321
17	0.651	0.786	0.619	0.147	-0.157	0.312	0.406	0.510	0.197
18	0.732	0.894	0.720	0.282	-0.074	0.563	0.430	0.684	0.237
19	0.350	0.657	0.168	0.006	0.367	0.539	0.074	0.303	0.236
20	0.729	0.857	0.741	0.102	-0.188	0.473	0.676	0.701	0.345
21	0.901	0.714	0.900	0.514	-0.021	0.588	0.581	0.649	0.186
22	0.562	0.815	0.465	0.079	0.110	0.488	0.267	0.466	0.248
23	0.783	0.796	0.828	0.152	-0.214	0.430	0.574	0.682	0.146
24	0.796	0.720	0.878	0.140	-0.359	0.286	0.690	0.704	0.203

25	0.824	0.812	0.847	0.133	-0.141	0.476	0.654	0.707	0.273
26	0.705	0.661	0.691	0.067	-0.018	0.242	0.450	0.477	0.468
27	0.860	0.844	0.732	0.694	0.236	0.729	0.670	0.712	0.780
28	0.782	0.825	0.754	0.372	-0.170	0.271	0.425	0.489	0.375
29	0.666	0.544	0.691	0.479	-0.232	0.181	0.711	0.690	0.810
30	0.649	0.747	0.589	0.549	0.011	0.596	0.777	0.518	0.728
31	1.000	0.827	0.947	0.612	0.031	0.613	0.743	0.786	0.568
32	0.827	1.000	0.761	0.509	-0.040	0.550	0.560	0.674	0.617
33	0.947	0.761	1.000	0.490	-0.223	0.454	0.793	0.792	0.441
34	0.612	0.509	0.490	1.000	0.103	0.379	0.351	0.323	0.606
35	0.031	-0.040	-0.223	0.103	1.000	0.617	-0.250	-0.213	0.132
36	0.613	0.550	0.454	0.379	0.617	1.000	0.458	0.449	0.308
37	0.743	0.560	0.793	0.351	-0.250	0.458	1.000	0.778	0.496
38	0.786	0.674	0.792	0.323	-0.213	0.449	0.778	1.000	0.440
39	0.568	0.617	0.441	0.606	0.132	0.308	0.496	0.440	1.000
40	0.824	0.713	0.924	0.427	-0.413	0.282	0.814	0.634	0.437
41	0.750	0.779	0.667	0.808	0.032	0.480	0.600	0.395	0.778
42	0.513	0.439	0.309	0.476	0.535	0.712	0.484	0.545	0.701
43	0.932	0.707	0.912	0.508	-0.021	0.640	0.787	0.724	0.315
44	0.201	-0.015	0.006	0.296	0.635	0.249	-0.175	-0.235	0.249
45	0.652	0.479	0.638	0.547	0.047	0.347	0.164	0.279	0.091
46	0.972	0.797	0.889	0.565	0.145	0.728	0.780	0.833	0.570
47	0.917	0.866	0.826	0.645	0.169	0.800	0.704	0.728	0.533

Table 3d

Variable number	40	41	42	43	Correlation coefficients 44	45	46	47
1	0.866	0.604	0.219	0.842	-0.167	0.546	0.819	0.810
2	0.701	0.660	0.459	0.875	0.051	0.600	0.909	0.941
3	0.015	0.409	0.398	0.008	0.053	-0.044	0.208	0.364
4	0.638	0.710	-0.104	0.537	0.457	0.588	0.337	0.413
5	0.190	0.485	0.490	0.288	-0.224	0.089	0.470	0.657
6	0.488	0.241	0.253	0.371	0.232	0.151	0.435	0.161
7	0.228	0.499	0.748	0.501	0.062	0.210	0.649	0.772
8	0.467	0.608	0.604	0.529	0.104	0.003	0.678	0.674
9	0.443	0.552	0.473	0.180	0.134	-0.077	0.394	0.251
10	0.408	0.546	0.422	0.125	0.038	-0.145	0.312	0.194
11	0.323	0.543	0.648	0.470	-0.154	0.006	0.639	0.760
12	0.669	0.661	0.085	0.564	0.035	0.507	0.562	0.568
13	0.580	0.478	0.633	0.778	0.016	0.240	0.891	0.833
14	0.796	0.649	0.341	0.866	0.041	0.580	0.882	0.861
15	0.577	0.354	-0.075	0.510	-0.269	0.188	0.428	0.492
16	0.695	0.604	0.487	0.913	0.071	0.637	0.927	0.947
17	0.595	0.441	0.100	0.661	-0.115	0.335	0.614	0.644
18	0.605	0.483	0.250	0.692	-0.171	0.540	0.715	0.795
19	0.075	0.256	0.386	0.300	0.060	0.066	0.420	0.505
20	0.739	0.516	0.271	0.732	-0.217	0.263	0.731	0.740
21	0.767	0.576	0.231	0.938	0.118	0.794	0.849	0.852
22	0.386	0.387	0.272	0.519	-0.076	0.240	0.577	0.650
23	0.756	0.433	0.114	0.809	-0.180	0.498	0.744	0.745
24	0.862	0.448	0.058	0.830	-0.143	0.471	0.735	0.667

	40	41	42	43	44	45	46	47
25	0.793	0.486	0.209	0.830	-0.065	0.461	0.796	0.756
26	0.680	0.459	0.158	0.590	0.315	0.436	0.628	0.490
27	0.592	0.820	0.806	0.715	0.107	0.361	0.903	0.930
28	0.769	0.639	0.046	0.733	0.221	0.665	0.667	0.653
29	0.681	0.628	0.493	0.471	0.065	0.253	0.632	0.499
30	0.661	0.863	0.615	0.610	-0.065	0.114	0.689	0.777
31	0.824	0.750	0.513	0.932	0.201	0.652	0.972	0.917
32	0.713	0.779	0.439	0.707	-0.015	0.479	0.797	0.866
33	0.924	0.667	0.309	0.912	0.006	0.638	0.889	0.826
34	0.427	0.808	0.476	0.508	0.296	0.547	0.565	0.645
35	-0.413	0.032	0.535	-0.021	0.635	0.047	0.145	0.169
36	0.282	0.480	0.712	0.640	0.249	0.347	0.728	0.800
37	0.814	0.600	0.484	0.787	-0.175	0.164	0.780	0.704
38	0.634	0.395	0.545	0.724	-0.235	0.279	0.833	0.728
39	0.437	0.778	0.701	0.315	0.249	0.091	0.570	0.533
40	1.000	0.723	0.113	0.830	-0.038	0.552	0.729	0.693
41	0.723	1.000	0.473	0.648	0.239	0.473	0.694	0.778
42	0.113	0.473	1.000	0.374	0.173	-0.055	0.664	0.636
43	0.830	0.648	0.374	1.000	0.134	0.640	0.918	0.883
44	-0.038	0.239	0.173	0.134	1.000	0.468	0.155	0.064
45	0.552	0.473	-0.055	0.640	0.468	1.000	0.519	0.527
46	0.729	0.694	0.664	0.918	0.155	0.519	1.000	0.945
47	0.693	0.778	0.636	0.883	0.064	0.527	0.945	1.000

Table 4.   Torralba: rotated factor loadings (orthogonal varimax, rotation by variable)

Variable number	Rotated factor loadings								Communality
	1	2	3	4	5	6	7	8	
1	-0.104	-0.182	0.148	-0.905	0.225	-0.162	0.051	-0.020	0.964
2	-0.335	-0.080	0.397	-0.813	0.207	0.050	0.046	0.093	0.994
3	-0.935	-0.133	0.226	0.039	-0.009	0.064	0.121	0.188	0.999
4	-0.045	-0.060	-0.022	-0.358	0.161	0.300	0.866	0.014	1.000
5	-0.711	0.015	0.413	-0.242	0.388	-0.186	-0.091	-0.078	0.934
6	0.523	-0.729	-0.046	-0.341	-0.081	0.182	-0.133	-0.134	0.999
7	-0.356	0.023	0.891	-0.188	0.054	-0.003	0.089	0.132	0.984
8	-0.611	-0.401	0.333	-0.437	-0.118	0.105	0.132	-0.348	1.000
9	-0.067	-0.990	-0.009	-0.085	0.029	0.035	0.033	-0.053	0.998
10	0.006	-0.977	-0.046	-0.002	0.132	-0.089	0.077	-0.105	0.998
11	-0.711	-0.115	0.551	-0.350	0.049	-0.145	0.029	-0.162	0.996
12	-0.120	-0.317	-0.189	-0.630	0.633	0.025	0.074	-0.199	0.993
13	-0.306	-0.225	0.514	-0.718	-0.134	0.055	-0.114	-0.201	0.998
14	-0.299	-0.206	0.185	-0.896	0.155	0.058	0.045	0.020	0.998
15	-0.577	0.066	-0.164	-0.721	-0.093	-0.192	0.196	-0.178	1.000
16	-0.109	-0.005	0.557	-0.791	0.184	0.053	0.045	0.086	0.993
17	-0.507	0.024	-0.051	-0.808	0.078	-0.038	0.068	-0.214	0.971
18	-0.469	0.072	0.243	-0.770	0.136	-0.124	-0.024	0.296	1.000
19	-0.849	0.115	0.249	-0.335	-0.105	0.162	-0.083	-0.061	0.955
20	-0.457	-0.160	0.169	-0.806	-0.168	-0.192	0.141	-0.042	0.999
21	0.060	0.066	0.314	-0.880	0.294	0.098	0.118	0.095	1.000
22	-0.746	0.074	0.134	-0.634	0.004	0.027	-0.040	-0.092	0.993

23	-0.264	0.040	0.092	-0.950	0.022	-0.116	0.029	-0.025	0.998
24	-0.086	-0.139	-0.020	-0.970	-0.065	-0.110	0.101	-0.071	1.000
25	-0.275	-0.106	0.135	-0.934	-0.107	-0.017	0.075	-0.049	0.996
26	-0.266	-0.401	-0.117	-0.736	-0.184	0.373	0.066	-0.036	0.966
27	-0.296	-0.459	0.620	-0.460	0.321	0.020	0.041	0.026	1.000
28	-0.328	-0.173	-0.140	-0.825	0.168	0.229	0.254	0.075	0.988
29	0.108	-0.862	0.182	-0.352	0.049	-0.056	0.038	0.268	0.992
30	-0.320	-0.475	0.524	-0.303	0.097	-0.239	0.486	-0.054	0.999
31	-0.038	-0.345	0.385	-0.803	0.233	0.145	0.088	0.055	0.999
32	-0.539	-0.295	0.254	-0.666	0.235	-0.046	0.154	0.183	1.000
33	0.098	-0.320	0.241	-0.873	0.173	-0.047	0.119	0.101	0.989
34	0.062	-0.335	0.367	-0.159	0.759	0.114	0.261	0.148	0.954
35	-0.225	0.171	0.596	0.278	0.002	0.662	-0.114	-0.151	0.987
36	-0.227	0.092	0.884	-0.319	-0.005	0.194	0.120	0.054	0.998
37	0.167	-0.484	0.440	-0.588	-0.148	-0.307	0.262	-0.090	0.994
38	-0.002	-0.396	0.388	-0.691	-0.047	-0.246	-0.271	0.195	0.958
39	-0.301	-0.860	0.285	-0.085	0.226	0.124	0.121	0.035	1.000
40	0.083	-0.374	0.057	-0.794	0.083	-0.143	0.419	0.084	0.991
41	-0.230	-0.483	0.319	-0.363	0.442	0.059	0.529	0.042	1.000
42	-0.208	-0.470	0.810	-0.022	0.081	0.102	-0.200	-0.098	0.987
43	0.096	-0.110	0.416	-0.846	0.114	0.065	0.236	-0.029	0.985
44	0.083	-0.108	0.097	0.058	0.064	0.957	0.207	0.045	0.997
45	0.160	0.131	0.052	-0.604	0.402	0.428	0.218	0.442	0.998
46	-0.069	-0.330	0.555	-0.736	0.145	0.103	0.010	-0.003	0.995
47	-0.224	-0.178	0.612	-0.661	0.290	-0.010	0.145	0.031	0.998
Sums CF Squares	6.555	6.721	6.981	18.262	2.424	2.480	2.222	.972	46.536

the uniquely determined variables for each factor and Table 5b the almost exclusively determined variables. Four of the variable groupings are true clusters, and there are three single variable isolates (which will not be interpreted further).

The interpretation of the factors is unimportant to the recognition of the clusters of variables associated with each. The clusters can be examined and discussed without reference to the nature of the underlying tendencies for variation that form them. It is not even my intent to present a thorough analysis of the clusters at this time; such an analysis is soon forthcoming in the final monograph on the site. Nonetheless, some interpretation is called for.

Table 5.

A.   Groupings of "uniquely" determined variables by factor

Factor 1
  Perforators/becs
  Elephant skull fragments
Factor 2
  Utilized flakes
  Unretouched flakes
  Unworked equid limb
  Bovid footbones
Factor 3
  Denticulates
  Bovid skull fragments
  Cervid limb fragments
Factor 4
  Endscrapers
  Sidescrapers
  Elephant teeth
  Unworked tusk
  Worked tusk
  Elephant scapulae
  Elephant pelvis
  Elephant vertebrae
  Equid skull fragments
  Equid scapulae
  Equid vertebrae
  Cervid scapulae
Factor 6
  cervid footbones
Factor 7
  Burins, paraburins

B. Groupings of "almost exclusively" determined variables by factor

Factor 1
  Notches
Factor 4
  Cervid antler
  Worked elephant rib
  Unworked equid teeth
Factor 5
  Equid pelvis

All evidence from the Torralba site suggests that it was the locus of a range of activities involving the killing of game animals, dressing out meat from the carcasses, some secondary stages in meat preparation, and, probably, limited consumption on the spot. The clusters seem to reflect these activities. Each of the four isolated clusters contains some lithic artifactual material and specific kinds of bone fragments. It is striking that both kinds of stone artifacts associated in the Factor 2 cluster are sharp-edged unretouched pieces: flakes with no visible evidence of deliberate retouch or utilization and flakes showing wear traces but no signs of intentional shaping. All three remaining clusters include only deliberately retouched shaped tools: perforators and becs for Factor 1, denticulates for Factor 3, and scraper-edged tools for Factor 4. Perhaps the kinds of bone fragments in the Factor 2 cluster are broken flaking implements, used in the production of the associated unretouched lithics, but they show no signs of such service; they may equally well be either implements used in, or residues of, an operation involving fine slicing by the sharp stone artifacts.

Associated with the scraper-edged implements in the Factor 4 cluster are three kinds of bone fragments: (1) There are broken bits of equid skull. (2) There are large, dense bones which carry little or no meat and which, from the butcher's viewpoint, project awkwardly from the carcass (elephant tusk fragments). (3) There are heavy, meat-bearing bones, which are generally bulky with respect to the meat on them, and which frequently present relatively extensive flat surfaces, from which the meat may be stripped quite conveniently. These are elephant scapula, pelvis, and vertebra (especially cervical vertebra) fragments, bits of equid scapulae and vertebrae, and deer scapulae. The scraper-edged pieces may be the tools used to strip flesh from these bone fragments, as necessary, in the early stages of heavy butchering. Bone residues might often have been abandoned in place as garbage, but some were apparently selected for bone-implement manufacture and used on the spot in the butchering process.

The Factor 1 and Factor 3 cluster at first look distinct, but on more intensive analysis they are seen to be similar. Both contain skull fragments of animals with massive heads and a complex cranial morphology. The skulls of both wild oxen and elephants have features that are necessary to sustain long, heavy horns or much heavier tusks. Extraction of the edible material from these creatures' heads requires some means of smashing the structure apart and some device for getting at edible fragments in nooks and crannies. The perforator-becs at Torralba would be suitable sharp-edged pointed probes for the latter process, and denticulates unite a series of small-pointed projections (and a series of hollow notches) in a working edge, which might have served a similar purpose. The Factor 1 cluster contains nothing like a battering tool, but the cervid limb bones (including the metapodials) in the Factor 3 cluster would serve the purpose well enough on the lighter parts of an aurochs cranium.

When variables that are almost exclusively determined by one factor are added to the clusters, they fit these interpretations quite well.[8] Another stone-tool type, notches, is added to the Factor 1 cluster. This makes parallels between the Factor 1 and Factor 3 clusters even more complete, since the first now has both perforators and notches, as individual and often rather large whole artifacts, while the second has a tool, the denticulate, that combines both these forms (usually on a somewhat smaller scale) on a single working edge. To the Factor 4 cluster may now be added cervid antler (meatless and awkward projections), unworked equid teeth, and worked elephant ribs, which seem quite at home with the rest of its bone contents. Equid pelvis fragments appear as the only associated variable for Factor 4.

It would be premature to press the analysis much further by adding material from Table 6 to the discussion, but a few suggestions seem worthwhile. Bifaces are partly associated with Factors 1 and 3, and both clusters have been characterized as related to butchering the skulls of the larger prey of the Torralba hunters. These tools certainly seem appropriate for the heavy battering associated with this process: the fact that

Table 6.   Groups of "partially determined" variables, by factor

---

Factor 1 and Factor 2
  Abrupt retouched pieces   (mostly *2*)
Factor 1 and Factor 3
  Bifaces   (mostly *1*)
Factor 1 and Factor 4
  Equid feet   (mostly *4*)
  Elephant ribs unworked   (mostly *4*)
  Elephant feet   (mostly *1*)
Factor 3
  Equid teeth worked
Factor 3 and Factor 4
  Cores (mostly *4*)
  Elephant limb worked   (mostly *4*)
  Indeterminate species, indeterminate bone unworked   (mostly *4*)
  Indeterminate species, indeterminate bone worked   (mostly *4*)
Factor 3 and Factor 6
  Bovid teeth   (mostly *6*)
Factor 4 and Factor 5
  Choppers, chopping tools
Factor 7
  Cervid skull

---

[8]   This narrative presentation is somewhat unfair. While the conclusions reached in this study are properly presented, the laboratory analysis really did not proceed in such gradual, logical, and compelling steps as my presentation does. Some conclusions about the nature of the clusters of uniquely determined variables were really only reached after an evaluation of the partially determined variable clusters. The present paper contains logical sequences of argument developed somewhat *a posteriori*.

bifaces are mostly related to the cluster containing elephant skull fragments is consonant with the suggested functional interpretation. Worked (in this case, flaked and battered) equid teeth are partially related to the Factor 3 cluster, and to be consistent they might be suspected as lighter-weight hammers. The items that are partially related to Factor 4 seem quite reasonable when added to the cluster; the fact that cores, choppers, and chopping tools are the added stone artifacts prompted a reexamination of these pieces and the discovery that a large proportion actually bears some scraper retouch, which had mistakenly been identified as heavy use (on the choppers) or platform regularization (on the cores) in my classification. Apparently, some chopper/chopping tools and (perhaps exhausted) cores were used for heavy-duty "scraping," in addition to their other functions. The interpretation is carried further in the monograph in preparation.

In summary, factor analysis of the Torralba materials resulted in the recognition of distinct clusters of variables, each of which is uniquely or almost exclusively determined by one of the seven significant tendencies for variation (or factors) isolated by the test. An examination of the matrix of bivariate correlations failed to reveal the significant negative correlation coefficients that would be produced were the temporal replacement of any variable by one or more others or the replacement of one or more variables popular in one sociocultural group or segment by variables popular in another responsible for the noted patterns of inter-assemblage variability. This coupled with the fact that items from each major cluster are found in virtually all the ten occupation horizons examined, and with other evidence, leads to a presumption with almost the strength of certainty that each cluster is a group of functionally related items, produced by or used in a distinct activity set. One can, of course, question the appropriateness of the test employed, but at least, in this case, all results would be consonant with the suggested interpretation.

Areal Specialization at Torralba

The data used in the factor analysis were the frequencies of variables from each of ten Torralba occupations, without regard to the spatial position of the variables within any occupation horizon. The results of that test are, therefore, independent of spatial considerations. The study of the Torralba Acheulean horizons may legitimately be carried a step further, using the factor analysis results to determine whether materials from different clusters have different spatial distributions within single occupations. If the variable clusters are activity-specific toolkits, they nonetheless might not occur in discrete and segregated spatial clumps, for reasons detailed above. However, if different clusters tend to be distributed in distinct areas, the argument that they are activity-specific toolkits will be strengthened.

There are occasional circumstances when the use of variables partially determined by a very few factors may yield useful results in the search for special activity areas. For the sake of simplicity and clarity, discussion will here be restricted to variables exclusively determined by just one factor. They should segregate best, as explained above. Two occupations have been chosen from those used in the factor test, Occupation 7 and Occupation 8. The former is the earlier, but both are late in the Torralba sequence. Figures 1 and 2 represent the excavated areas diagrammatically showing the distribution of items exclusively determined by each represented factor. These items are keyed to make the distribution more intelligible. Using a simple χ^2 test, it has been proved that the distribution of Factor 4 variables north of the L line is far denser than expectable, while other variables tend to be found to the south of that line, in Occupation 7. In Occupation 8, Factor 2 variables clump densely in the southernmost part of the excavation, south of the G line, while other exclusively determined variables are significantly differently distri-

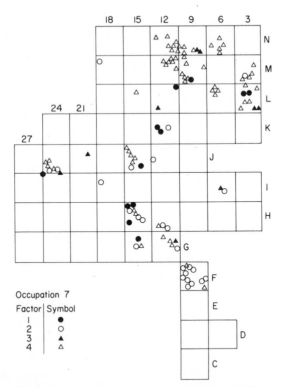

Figure 1.   The distribution of factor-specific items in Occupation 7 at Torralba. Distance between grid lines equals three meters

buted in space. Significant differences in spatial location of exclusively determined variables for two or more factors have been found in nine of the ten major occupations in the Torralba sequence. Simple as these words seem, they are all that is needed to prove that clumps of variables exclusively determined by different factors are found in different places in the Torralba occupations.

What are the alternatives to the conclusion that the factor-specific areas are activity-specific areas? If the conclusions had been determined subjectively, they might be strictly accidental and culturally meaningless, but a standard statistical test was used, and it can be shown that the probability that the differential distributions are due to chance is so small that this explanation can be ruled out. They could be due to changes in popularity of artifact types through time — if different factor-specific areas in one horizon could be shown to have accumulated at different times. This explanation can immediately be rejected, for two reasons. First, it seems unreasonable because the area distributions do not show any clear temporal trend. If Factor 4 items become popular later than Factor 2 materials, or vice versa, why are both kinds of items found on all

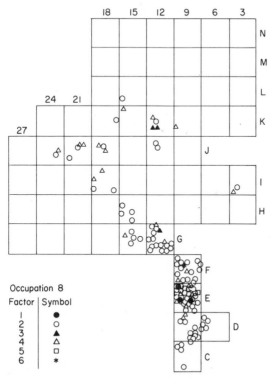

Figure 2. The distribution of factor-specific items in Occupation 8 at Torralba. Distance between grid lines equals three meters

92   LESLIE G. FREEMAN

the Torralba occupation floors, with no evidence for increase of one kind of material at the expense of others through time? One might suppose that these two groups might have been deposited during different seasons. (In fact, this argument really proposes a kind of functional explanation, rather than a strictly temporal one.) However, there is good evidence that the discrete spatial distributions were accumulated simultaneously, since the bones of a single individual were often found in clusters related to two or more different factors, recovered in different factor-specific areas. Second, the factor-specific clusters might be the stylistic boundary-indicators of different identity-conscious social groups or subgroups who occupied the site simultaneously. The argument that one social group used only denticulate tools and processed only bovid skulls, while another used only perforators and processed only elephant skull, and yet another used scraper-edged tools to process the limbs, vertebrae, and scapulae rejected by the other groups cannot be proved wrong but it seems so farfetched as to warrant no further consideration. The interpretation that spatial differentiation in the distribution of factor-specific materials in any Torralba occupation must reflect the existence of activity-specific areas, utilized by a single social group, and that those areas were utilized relatively synchronously, seems the most convincing.

Until now, only schematic diagrams of the Torralba occupations have been presented. Total distribution maps, showing all items recovered from the two levels discussed, have also been examined. The visual difference between the spatial distributions recognized objectively as distinctive is so marked as to provide an independent confirmation of the conclusions of this paper. In Occupation 7, the Factor 4 cluster is densest in the area of discovery of the nearly intact bones of a half elephant skeleton, interpreted as the locus of preliminary stages in the butchering of a single animal immediately adjacent to the kill spot. Materials from other clusters are densest in other areas, south of the elephant kill, where it is thought that secondary stages in the processing of many kills of a variety of animal species were simultaneously performed. The schematic map should be compared with the scale map of the northern part of this distribution published by Freeman and Butzer (1966). The dense distribution of Factor 2 materials, especially "waste" flakes, in Occupation 8 coincides with a rich lens-shaped heap of burned and decayed organic material (wood, bark, and so on), which may be the remains of a large smudge-fire, lit to smoke-dry meat or as an insect repellent.[9]

During the analysis of the Torralba materials, a number of discrete and

[9] In this Torralba occupation, the exact number of recovered wood fragments (mostly tiny splinters) is so great that it cannot be determined with precision. Since raw frequencies were used in the factor analysis, macrobotanical material could not be included in the test. In a previous factor analysis, using another measure of correlation, macrobotanical remains were almost exclusively determined by a factor that also determined waste flakes and utilized flakes. Probably wood fragments could be included in the Factor 2 cluster.

discontinuous area distributions of about 15 square meters and about 25 square meters in extent were noted. It is my subjective impression that areas of about this size (and perhaps some much larger) may reflect modal space requirements of consistent sorts at Torralba and other open-air sites.

No quantitative attempt to delineate the spatial boundaries of each activity-specific area in any occupation has been made in this paper. That is another problem, involving somewhat more difficulty than the one attacked here, and is treated in the final monograph on the Torralba site.[10] It is *not* an essential step for the present purpose, which only sought to demonstrate the presence of activity-specific areas. The technique used here proves that such areas exist, without incurring unnecessary complications.

Cueva Morín

Cueva Morín, a cave site in the Spanish province of Santander, was discovered in 1910. Like Torralba, Morín was extensively excavated in the early part of this century. Those investigations were the subject of two large monographs by the Conde de la Vega del Sella (1921) and Father Carballo (1923). In 1966 new research at the site was begun by the *Seminario de Prehistoria y Arqueología Sautuola*, directed by Father J. González Echegaray and Dr. M. A. García Guinea, and it was continued during 1968 and 1969 by an international team led by Father Echegaray and the author. Results of the new work are the subject of several articles and two monographic studies (González Echegaray *et al.* 1971, 1973; Freeman and González Echegaray 1970a, 1970b, 1972; Freeman 1968).

The site is noteworthy for its long Paleolithic stratigraphic sequence, including nine Mousterian levels and twelve Upper Paleolithic horizons, from Chatelperronian through Azilian. One earlier Aurignacian level yielded a semi-subterranean structure and an associated mortuary complex. In Mousterian Level 17 a dry stone wall divided the area occupied into two sectors with distinct artifactual and faunal contents. Artifacts from that level include the largest series of deliberately shaped bone tools ever reported from a Mousterian horizon. The entire Paleolithic occupation sequence can probably be assigned to the Weichsel Glaciation.

Located in a limestone "hum" in Karstic topography, the cave opens to the northwest some twenty-two meters above present active drainage.

[10] Procedures attempted to this end with encouraging preliminary results are based on distance measures and correlations between vectors in space or their end points. Once clumps are defined in preliminary fashion, discriminant functions will help define their boundaries.

The hum is seven kilometers from the south shore of the bay of Santander and only about two kilometers from the *ría* of Solía, and both these features provided access to marine and estuarine resources throughout the period of Paleolithic occupation. Although they were occasionally collected, mollusks do not seem to have constituted a faunal element of any dietary significance during the Mousterian occupations, to judge by their scarcity in the levels. The distance to the dissected uplands above 600 meters is relatively very short, but the alpine animals to be found above that limit were not consistently exploited by Mousterian hunters in the region.

In this paper discussion is restricted to three Morín occupations, whose artifactual contents have been assigned to a regional variant of the typical Mousterian facies. Levels 17 and 16 were accumulated under cold conditions, while Horizon 15 was deposited during a period of climatic amelioration (possibly at the beginning of Hengelo). The lapse of time between Occupations 16 and 15 could not have been great, judging from the striking similarities in their lithic artifact inventories. Level 17 seems to have been produced during intensive residence near the cave mouth. There is too little relevant information about Levels 16 and 15 to permit a similar affirmation. These two levels are known from small exposures. Visual indications of spatial differentiation are not striking in the distributions of materials in Levels 16 and 15, but the structural remnant (dry stone wall) forms a markedly distinctive visual referent for spatial patterning in Upper Level 17.

Each of the three levels contains remains of both forest-dwelling and open-country ungulate species, although the number of individuals represented is very small. Taken all together, the Morín Mousterian faunas indicate opportunistic exploitation of both the above habitats, with no greater concentration on any one species or habitat than any other. The bulk of meat taken would have come from the open-country ungulates (*Bos, Equus*), simply because they have larger individual body weights than the forest dwellers (*Cervus, Capreolus*). Bone remains from the two levels that concern us are highly fragmented and seem to include both food remains and bones used as raw materials for tool manufacture.

Morín Artifact Clusters

In many ways, the Morín Mousterian occupations are less than ideally suited to the sorts of investigations just illustrated with the Torralba materials. The excavation at Morín is much smaller. There are only nine Mousterian occupations. Of these, two cannot be used because of the small size of the artifact collection from each, and four more are only known from exposures of one or two square meters. The remaining three levels (17, 16, 15) are more extensively exposed, but their contents are different, which limits the points of comparison between them. (Only Level 17 contained substantial faunal remains.) Since pollen and mac-robotanical materials are not preserved in these levels, analysis must rest on comparisons of lithic artifact contents alone. Fortunately all three occupations may be assigned to one industrial facies — the typical Mous-terian — for that at least maximizes the comparability of the three artifact assemblages.

Fortunately, other evidence may be brought to bear on the study of the Morín occupations. For the last eleven years, I have collected evidence concerning Lower and Middle Paleolithic occupations in Spain. My doc-toral dissertation, presented in 1964, is based substantially on results of a factor analysis using frequencies of fifty-one stone-artifact types from fourteen Cantabrian Mousterian artifact collections. While all the theoretical objections raised against the use of factor analysis on the Torralba materials apply even more strongly to the Cantabrian data, where samples vary widely in size, it is interesting to note that substantial additions of new information gathered in 1966 and 1968 have been incorporated in two successive recalculations but have not altered the artifact clusters defined by the 1964 test. The fourteen collections examined come from sites on Spain's Cantabrian coast and the adjacent sector of the French Pyrenees (Abri Olha) and include the material from earlier excavations at Morín itself. Although ideally one would like to work only with recently excavated material, there is simply not enough of it; nonetheless, the available results, based on museum collections, seem to have considerable validity in attempts to discern activity-patterning at Cueva Morín.

Only the most summary statement of the factor analysis results is necessary here. A list of the artifact types used is given in Tables 7 and 8. Table 9 shows the matrix of variable/variable correlation coefficients. The correlation matrix, again, shows that there is not one single case of significant negative correlation between any pair of variables, a fact that has the same implications it did at Torralba. Fewer significant factors were generated from the Cantabrian Mousterian collections, due, no doubt, to the fact that no data were available except the stone artifact frequencies. (Only three factors had latent roots above 1.0 in the princi-pal components solution.) Rotated factor loadings for the significant factors are shown in Table 10.

Although there are three significant factors, one exclusively deter-mines *just* geologically crushed pieces, which were deliberately included as a check on results.[11] Variables uniquely determined by Factors 1 and 2

[11]   Since geological crushing should act in "random" fashion rather than selectively on the lithic assemblages in a level, test results would have been suspect had this variable clustered

are listed in Table 11. All told, thirty-one of the fifty-one variables used in the test are uniquely determined by single factors.

Variables uniquely determined by Factor 1 are almost all scraper-edged pieces. Six of the types associated with Factor 2 have sharp slicing edges, and four are heavy duty chopping-cleaving implements. Probably abrupt retouched sidescrapers in this classification are really not scrapers but should be considered a sort of atypical backed knife. All but one of the remaining types are the chisel-ended burins and the burinating becs. These lists look subjectively like coherent clusters of activity-specific implements, one set used for "scraping," the other for slicing, splitting, and rending tasks. Two variables are "almost exclusively" determined by Factor 2 — blades and bifaces. They fit the characterization of the Factor 2 cluster nicely.

The Morín Case: Discerning Activity-Specific Areas

If the clusters defined by the factor analysis of Morín Mousterian artifact types have distinct technological functions, there should be some Mousterian occupations within which the clusters have different spatial distributions. On the other hand, a failure to discern such differences, especially in an intensively occupied site with a restricted surface area, would not contradict the hypothesis that the two clusters are tool-constellations used for different technological purposes. By reason of their restricted extent, and the even smaller size of my exposures, I had no high expectations about proving the existence of activity-specific areas in the Morín Mousterian horizons. Rather surprisingly, differential spatial distribution of lithics from the two clusters was demonstrable in each of the three occupations tested.

Although results of the Morín analysis may only be stated in summary fashion, since the appearance of the final monographic treatment of the distributions is still some time away, the spatial segregation of materials from the two clusters is quite striking. In both Levels 15 and 16, Factor 1 materials are more abundantly represented near the present cave mouth, while the Factor 2 cluster is more densely distributed toward the interior. The distribution in Level 17 is complicated by the existence of an artificial wall, which divides the occupied area into two sectors. The densest distribution of bones and lithics in this level is found on the side of the wall toward the cave entrance. Within this rich area there seem to be internal distinctions in the occupation debris, and there are certainly significant differences across the dry wall. More of the Factor 1 cluster is on the side

with others. As expected, variation in geologically crushed pieces was isolated as idiosyncratic.

Table 7.   List of artifact types used in the Cantabrian Mousterian study

Type number	Type name
1	Levallois flakes (typical)
2	Levallois flakes (atypical)
3	Pseudo-Levallois points
4	Mousterian points
5	Limaces
6	Simple straight sidescrapers
7	Simple convex sidescrapers
8	Simple concave sidescrapers
9	Double straight-convex sidescrapers
10	Double straight-concave sidescrapers
11	Double biconvex sidescrapers
12	Convergent straight sidescrapers
13	Convergent convex sidescrapers
14	Canted sidescrapers
15	Transverse straight sidescrapers
16	Transverse convex sidescrapers
17	Transverse concave sidescrapers
18	Sidescrapers on ventral surface
19	Abrupt retouched sidescrapers
20	Thinned-back sidescrapers
21	Bifacially retouched sidescrapers
22	Alternately retouched sidescrapers
23	Typical endscrapers
24	Atypical endscrapers
25	Typical burins
26	Atypical burins
27	Typical perforators
28	Atypical perforators
29	Atypical backed knives
30	Natural backed knives
31	Raclettes
32	Truncated flakes
33	Notches
34	Denticulates
35	Alternate burinating becs
36	Pieces with ventral retouch
37	Pieces with coarse abrupt alternate (crushing) retouch
38	Pieces with fine abrupt alternate retouch
39	Pieces with bifacial retouch
40	Tayac points
41	Endnotched pieces
42	Choppers
43	Chopping-tools
44	Unclassifiable retouched pieces
45	Debris
46	Flakes
47	Blades
48	Bifaces
49	Cleaver-flakes
50	Other bifacial tools
51	Nuclei

Table 8.   Cantabrian Mousterian basic input (raw frequencies)

Variable number	1	2	3	4	5	6	Sample 7	8	9	10	11	12	13	14
1	65	21	0	2	0	1	7	13	1	10	0	0	0	2
2	95	53	5	11	0	0	3	0	3	11	1	9	12	9
3	12	1	0	0	0	1	0	2	1	3	0	4	0	2
4	14	15	1	0	3	0	0	5	0	1	0	0	0	0
5	16	24	3	0	0	1	0	3	0	0	0	0	0	3
6	80	127	10	1	5	0	2	5	0	2	6	2	3	8
7	380	580	39	3	12	8	23	39	11	10	13	6	6	11
8	29	38	3	0	2	0	2	0	0	0	0	0	4	3
9	41	36	4	1	0	2	2	0	0	0	0	0	0	0
10	2	8	1	0	0	0	1	0	0	0	1	1	1	1
11	63	78	4	2	0	1	1	7	0	0	1	0	0	0
12	30	36	4	0	2	0	0	0	0	1	1	1	1	0
13	73	69	6	2	4	1	2	3	0	0	0	0	0	0
14	52	136	7	1	11	0	1	9	0	2	0	0	0	1
15	27	60	2	0	0	0	0	1	1	1	0	0	1	0
16	127	407	20	2	6	1	8	20	1	6	3	1	0	6
17	2	12	0	0	3	0	0	0	0	0	0	1	2	0
18	46	105	4	0	0	3	3	3	1	3	3	1	1	4
19	7	4	0	0	0	0	0	2	0	0	0	0	0	1
20	19	97	7	1	1	0	0	4	0	0	0	0	0	3
21	40	137	4	0	2	5	2	3	0	1	0	0	0	1
22	40	84	4	1	2	1	3	6	0	3	2	1	2	2
23	13	41	1	0	4	1	2	5	0	0	2	2	12	4

Floor														
24	9	35	7	5	3	5	6	5	0	2	1	5	38	34
25	0	3	0	0	1	0	1	0	0	0	0	1	11	25
26	2	3	0	1	2	1	0	1	0	0	1	1	14	14
27	1	3	1	1	6	2	0	0	1	1	0	0	19	11
28	7	17	2	0	4	7	1	3	0	2	0	0	32	36
29	1	0	2	0	3	1	0	0	1	0	0	2	4	9
30	0	2	6	1	0	1	2	2	3	2	1	2	15	49
31	10	0	4	0	2	0	0	0	0	1	0	0	6	5
32	3	2	0	0	0	0	0	1	0	0	1	0	4	10
33	0	43	10	6	7	2	4	2	0	1	4	3	109	88
34	217	208	94	11	52	42	49	16	3	22	8	30	511	782
35	10	0	0	1	0	0	1	1	1	0	0	0	17	36
36	0	0	0	1	2	1	1	3	0	0	0	0	53	12
37	5	18	170	65	0	1	0	0	0	0	0	0	3	13
38	7	33	44	18	0	0	1	3	0	0	0	6	83	99
39	0	5	12	3	1	0	0	2	2	1	1	2	28	89
40	2	1	0	0	1	2	3	0	0	1	0	1	39	59
41	5	7	1	2	0	0	0	0	2	0	0	0	18	6
42	1	0	0	0	0	1	0	0	0	0	0	1	3	9
43	2	0	0	1	1	1	8	1	0	3	6	6	17	70
44	30	0	2	3	2	2	8	5	0	2	1	11	153	114
45	69	26	63	0	2	4	1	0	3	2	1	0	43	65
46	475	300	549	85	11	11	8	10	9	2	29	28	530	772
47	53	18	29	8	0	2	1	2	2	0	46	5	29	110
48	1	0	1	1	0	0	23	20	2	2	0	12	7	31
49	0	0	0	0	0	1	0	46	6	0	37	70	1	303
50	3	0	2	1	1	4	13	9	2	4	3	5	19	35
51	34	50	19	11	6	21	8	9	2	6	6	5	266	374

Table 9. Cantabrian Mousterian: matrix of bivariate correlation coefficients

Variable no.	1	2	3	4	5	6	7	8	9	10
1	1.000	0.933	0.884	0.821	0.705	0.683	0.707	0.739	0.863	0.373
2	0.933	1.000	0.807	0.865	0.829	0.828	0.836	0.879	0.950	0.571
3	0.884	0.807	1.000	0.577	0.454	0.426	0.444	0.488	0.649	0.117
4	0.821	0.865	0.577	1.000	0.950	0.942	0.951	0.944	0.946	0.761
5	0.705	0.829	0.454	0.950	1.000	0.991	0.991	0.982	0.945	0.896
6	0.683	0.828	0.426	0.942	0.991	1.000	0.998	0.990	0.945	0.916
7	0.707	0.836	0.444	0.951	0.991	0.998	1.000	0.989	0.953	0.904
8	0.739	0.879	0.488	0.944	0.982	0.990	0.989	1.000	0.968	0.871
9	0.863	0.950	0.649	0.946	0.945	0.945	0.953	0.968	1.000	0.756
10	0.373	0.571	0.117	0.761	0.896	0.916	0.904	0.871	0.756	1.000
11	0.780	0.888	0.532	0.969	0.985	0.987	0.993	0.989	0.978	0.851
12	0.769	0.894	0.535	0.958	0.978	0.986	0.988	0.991	0.982	0.852
13	0.850	0.941	0.626	0.965	0.957	0.959	0.965	0.977	0.997	0.775
14	0.531	0.691	0.245	0.895	0.960	0.974	0.970	0.942	0.855	0.954
15	0.583	0.747	0.310	0.902	0.973	0.987	0.985	0.964	0.891	0.948
16	0.480	0.651	0.193	0.858	0.946	0.960	0.956	0.923	0.825	0.971
17	0.278	0.494	0.015	0.741	0.818	0.858	0.846	0.822	0.675	0.907
18	0.572	0.734	0.299	0.894	0.972	0.985	0.982	0.960	0.884	0.958
19	0.941	0.930	0.789	0.912	0.845	0.815	0.831	0.849	0.919	0.553
20	0.375	0.564	0.088	0.799	0.910	0.924	0.916	0.877	0.756	0.975
21	0.461	0.638	0.177	0.845	0.939	0.954	0.950	0.917	0.816	0.970
22	0.602	0.752	0.324	0.916	0.978	0.989	0.988	0.966	0.896	0.946
23	0.423	0.614	0.139	0.813	0.895	0.915	0.905	0.895	0.765	0.923
24	0.596	0.760	0.410	0.722	0.754	0.771	0.764	0.821	0.757	0.642

25	0.496	0.933	0.844	0.798	0.785	0.792	0.863	0.825	0.984	0.960
26	0.782	0.975	0.978	0.953	0.952	0.943	0.921	0.597	0.942	0.819
27	0.863	0.876	0.936	0.944	0.946	0.921	0.874	0.411	0.787	0.633
28	0.679	0.910	0.923	0.875	0.873	0.863	0.857	0.608	0.916	0.791
29	0.452	0.862	0.753	0.720	0.709	0.722	0.764	0.884	0.927	0.901
30	0.390	0.861	0.747	0.689	0.680	0.701	0.767	0.899	0.946	0.942
31	0.730	0.761	0.789	0.778	0.792	0.785	0.740	0.621	0.756	0.608
32	0.449	0.903	0.812	0.753	0.739	0.739	0.808	0.794	0.972	0.940
33	0.811	0.907	0.959	0.926	0.934	0.925	0.873	0.501	0.871	0.703
34	0.615	0.927	0.897	0.843	0.843	0.852	0.864	0.760	0.968	0.879
35	0.531	0.913	0.837	0.789	0.785	0.806	0.836	0.819	0.958	0.929
36	0.973	0.773	0.886	0.925	0.929	0.908	0.806	0.119	0.587	0.410
37	-0.004	-0.125	-0.140	-0.130	-0.118	-0.157	-0.172	0.176	-0.056	-0.140
38	0.701	0.897	0.884	0.850	0.852	0.833	0.827	0.676	0.905	0.765
39	0.408	0.884	0.765	0.715	0.701	0.706	0.789	0.891	0.963	0.953
40	0.649	0.983	0.925	0.899	0.889	0.895	0.935	0.755	0.979	0.928
41	0.886	0.723	0.857	0.846	0.866	0.850	0.715	0.145	0.605	0.375
42	0.409	0.887	0.769	0.719	0.708	0.726	0.785	0.844	0.957	0.941
43	0.324	0.851	0.714	0.668	0.651	0.672	0.783	0.876	0.933	0.972
44	0.883	0.957	0.988	0.986	0.989	0.991	0.941	0.504	0.865	0.736
45	0.409	0.506	0.516	0.454	0.477	0.496	0.423	0.621	0.604	0.461
46	0.536	0.698	0.694	0.635	0.651	0.655	0.609	0.700	0.778	0.628
47	0.264	0.675	0.577	0.503	0.510	0.530	0.544	0.788	0.827	0.761
48	0.164	0.542	0.418	0.412	0.374	0.430	0.567	0.580	0.544	0.744
49	0.106	0.692	0.513	0.449	0.428	0.451	0.558	0.832	0.812	0.880
50	0.514	0.899	0.808	0.795	0.769	0.799	0.895	0.758	0.892	0.949
51	0.673	0.979	0.939	0.904	0.897	0.897	0.918	0.731	0.981	0.900

Table 9. (continued)

Variable no.	11	12	13	14	15	16	17	18	19	20
1	0.780	0.769	0.850	0.531	0.583	0.480	0.278	0.572	0.941	0.375
2	0.888	0.894	0.941	0.691	0.747	0.651	0.494	0.734	0.930	0.564
3	0.532	0.535	0.626	0.245	0.310	0.193	0.015	0.299	0.789	0.088
4	0.969	0.958	0.965	0.895	0.902	0.858	0.741	0.894	0.912	0.799
5	0.985	0.978	0.957	0.960	0.973	0.946	0.818	0.972	0.845	0.910
6	0.987	0.986	0.959	0.974	0.987	0.960	0.858	0.985	0.815	0.924
7	0.993	0.988	0.965	0.970	0.985	0.956	0.846	0.982	0.831	0.916
8	0.989	0.991	0.977	0.942	0.964	0.923	0.822	0.960	0.849	0.877
9	0.978	0.982	0.997	0.855	0.891	0.825	0.675	0.884	0.919	0.756
10	0.851	0.852	0.775	0.954	0.948	0.971	0.907	0.958	0.553	0.975
11	1.000	0.994	0.987	0.938	0.960	0.917	0.789	0.955	0.883	0.865
12	0.994	1.000	0.989	0.932	0.954	0.908	0.792	0.948	0.867	0.856
13	0.987	0.989	1.000	0.880	0.910	0.849	0.714	0.902	0.918	0.783
14	0.938	0.932	0.880	1.000	0.993	0.996	0.935	0.993	0.695	0.981
15	0.960	0.954	0.910	0.993	1.000	0.990	0.912	0.998	0.735	0.968
16	0.917	0.908	0.849	0.996	0.990	1.000	0.936	0.992	0.653	0.993
17	0.789	0.792	0.714	0.935	0.912	0.936	1.000	0.907	0.477	0.947
18	0.955	0.948	0.902	0.993	0.998	0.992	0.907	1.000	0.725	0.971
19	0.883	0.867	0.918	0.695	0.735	0.653	0.477	0.725	1.000	0.568
20	0.865	0.856	0.783	0.981	0.968	0.993	0.947	0.971	0.568	1.000
21	0.909	0.900	0.839	0.993	0.988	0.999	0.942	0.990	0.635	0.993
22	0.965	0.957	0.916	0.994	0.998	0.989	0.902	0.998	0.749	0.964
23	0.866	0.852	0.795	0.952	0.946	0.956	0.950	0.946	0.607	0.952
24	0.776	0.768	0.768	0.706	0.747	0.695	0.677	0.733	0.690	0.653

25	0.859	0.864	0.922	0.639	0.693	0.591	0.434	0.679	0.945	0.496
26	0.971	0.970	0.977	0.869	0.910	0.847	0.720	0.902	0.890	0.785
27	0.930	0.924	0.894	0.934	0.955	0.927	0.858	0.950	0.734	0.892
28	0.898	0.896	0.914	0.782	0.830	0.757	0.684	0.816	0.867	0.692
29	0.776	0.795	0.843	0.562	0.623	0.523	0.338	0.611	0.854	0.435
30	0.759	0.770	0.841	0.507	0.566	0.456	0.285	0.557	0.920	0.358
31	0.777	0.792	0.772	0.738	0.760	0.723	0.650	0.764	0.691	0.684
32	0.819	0.821	0.888	0.587	0.647	0.541	0.395	0.631	0.905	0.444
33	0.931	0.926	0.918	0.872	0.906	0.858	0.781	0.901	0.818	0.814
34	0.885	0.887	0.923	0.715	0.767	0.680	0.554	0.757	0.929	0.604
35	0.843	0.847	0.900	0.635	0.686	0.593	0.414	0.683	0.949	0.506
36	0.877	0.865	0.798	0.981	0.974	0.993	0.944	0.978	0.584	0.993
37	-0.130	-0.100	-0.131	-0.143	-0.125	-0.131	-0.074	-0.121	-0.149	-0.131
38	0.877	0.889	0.895	0.749	0.797	0.725	0.637	0.788	0.821	0.660
39	0.786	0.799	0.866	0.536	0.596	0.484	0.325	0.582	0.909	0.382
40	0.941	0.943	0.979	0.774	0.817	0.733	0.580	0.806	0.965	0.651
41	0.810	0.800	0.742	0.880	0.891	0.893	0.881	0.897	0.564	0.893
42	0.788	0.800	0.867	0.543	0.602	0.494	0.311	0.587	0.928	0.399
43	0.748	0.753	0.834	0.483	0.535	0.425	0.237	0.520	0.923	0.322
44	0.984	0.982	0.966	0.940	0.960	0.925	0.798	0.960	0.863	0.881
45	0.475	0.490	0.498	0.369	0.414	0.360	0.304	0.419	0.546	0.324
46	0.664	0.679	0.692	0.530	0.582	0.512	0.436	0.581	0.698	0.459
47	0.577	0.584	0.654	0.335	0.398	0.297	0.139	0.391	0.744	0.219
48	0.471	0.446	0.526	0.266	0.282	0.227	0.007	0.281	0.671	0.147
49	0.538	0.558	0.657	0.235	0.298	0.179	-0.023	0.283	0.754	0.074
50	0.848	0.834	0.894	0.654	0.685	0.607	0.415	0.676	0.960	0.518
51	0.942	0.945	0.975	0.783	0.830	0.747	0.611	0.819	0.948	0.668

Table 9. (continued)

Variable no.	21	22	23	24	25	26	27	28	29	30
1	0.461	0.602	0.423	0.596	0.960	0.819	0.633	0.791	0.901	0.942
2	0.638	0.752	0.614	0.760	0.984	0.942	0.787	0.916	0.927	0.946
3	0.177	0.324	0.139	0.410	0.825	0.597	0.411	0.608	0.884	0.899
4	0.845	0.916	0.813	0.722	0.863	0.921	0.874	0.857	0.764	0.767
5	0.939	0.978	0.895	0.754	0.792	0.943	0.921	0.863	0.722	0.701
6	0.954	0.989	0.915	0.771	0.785	0.952	0.946	0.873	0.709	0.680
7	0.950	0.988	0.905	0.764	0.798	0.953	0.944	0.875	0.720	0.689
8	0.917	0.966	0.895	0.821	0.844	0.978	0.936	0.923	0.753	0.747
9	0.816	0.896	0.765	0.757	0.933	0.975	0.876	0.910	0.862	0.861
10	0.970	0.946	0.923	0.642	0.496	0.782	0.863	0.679	0.452	0.390
11	0.909	0.965	0.866	0.776	0.859	0.971	0.930	0.898	0.776	0.759
12	0.900	0.957	0.852	0.768	0.864	0.970	0.924	0.896	0.795	0.770
13	0.839	0.916	0.795	0.768	0.922	0.977	0.894	0.914	0.843	0.841
14	0.993	0.994	0.952	0.706	0.639	0.869	0.934	0.782	0.562	0.507
15	0.988	0.998	0.946	0.747	0.693	0.910	0.955	0.830	0.623	0.566
16	0.999	0.989	0.956	0.695	0.591	0.847	0.927	0.757	0.523	0.456
17	0.942	0.902	0.950	0.677	0.434	0.720	0.858	0.684	0.338	0.285
18	0.990	0.998	0.946	0.733	0.679	0.902	0.950	0.816	0.611	0.557
19	0.635	0.749	0.607	0.690	0.945	0.890	0.734	0.867	0.854	0.920
20	0.993	0.964	0.952	0.653	0.496	0.785	0.892	0.692	0.435	0.358
21	1.000	0.985	0.956	0.687	0.577	0.838	0.925	0.749	0.510	0.443
22	0.985	1.000	0.945	0.745	0.703	0.911	0.950	0.828	0.626	0.577
23	0.956	0.945	1.000	0.823	0.567	0.823	0.895	0.799	0.429	0.421
24	0.687	0.745	0.823	1.000	0.750	0.845	0.775	0.927	0.576	0.630

25	0.577	0.703	0.567	0.750	1.000	0.910	0.732	0.899	0.916	0.957
26	0.838	0.911	0.823	0.845	0.910	1.000	0.926	0.961	0.826	0.818
27	0.925	0.950	0.895	0.775	0.732	0.926	1.000	0.874	0.707	0.594
28	0.749	0.828	0.799	0.927	0.899	0.961	0.874	1.000	0.780	0.812
29	0.510	0.626	0.429	0.576	0.916	0.826	0.707	0.780	1.000	0.908
30	0.443	0.577	0.421	0.630	0.957	0.818	0.594	0.812	0.908	1.000
31	0.717	0.761	0.679	0.606	0.670	0.779	0.793	0.735	0.750	0.693
32	0.528	0.656	0.536	0.759	0.984	0.886	0.681	0.891	0.864	0.944
33	0.852	0.906	0.897	0.925	0.830	0.965	0.914	0.964	0.717	0.741
34	0.668	0.772	0.694	0.849	0.953	0.946	0.800	0.959	0.869	0.928
35	0.580	0.698	0.553	0.683	0.954	0.894	0.704	0.867	0.890	0.975
36	0.995	0.971	0.950	0.661	0.520	0.805	0.915	0.715	0.457	0.379
37	-0.129	—	-0.108	-0.036	-0.098	-0.148	-0.124	-0.128	-0.016	-0.004
38	0.717	0.799	0.743	0.854	0.879	0.903	0.806	0.902	0.805	0.827
39	0.471	0.606	0.447	0.661	0.979	0.838	0.635	0.827	0.924	0.978
40	0.721	0.824	0.685	0.751	0.976	0.959	0.827	0.919	0.899	0.925
41	0.899	0.884	0.960	0.844	0.545	0.810	0.863	0.804	0.423	0.435
42	0.478	0.608	0.428	0.618	0.965	0.845	0.623	0.818	0.913	0.971
43	0.406	0.550	0.370	0.577	0.964	0.792	0.559	0.766	0.892	0.966
44	0.917	0.965	0.876	0.767	0.822	0.964	0.924	0.892	0.754	0.750
45	0.354	0.413	0.411	0.568	0.535	0.545	0.435	0.604	0.572	0.663
46	0.504	0.582	0.559	0.731	0.725	0.729	0.601	0.769	0.711	0.791
47	0.283	0.405	0.285	0.533	0.788	0.671	0.415	0.669	0.734	0.881
48	0.198	0.321	0.175	0.295	0.629	0.437	0.209	0.401	0.519	0.626
49	0.160	0.312	0.111	0.409	0.855	0.612	0.321	0.589	0.816	0.889
50	0.586	0.706	0.542	0.605	0.922	0.832	0.650	0.787	0.817	0.893
51	0.736	0.834	0.724	0.813	0.970	0.974	0.844	0.953	0.881	0.917

Table 9. (continued)

Variable no.	31	32	33	34	35	36	37	38	39	40
1	0.608	0.940	0.703	0.879	0.929	0.410	-0.140	0.765	0.953	0.928
2	0.756	0.972	0.871	0.968	0.958	0.587	-0.056	0.935	0.963	0.979
3	0.621	0.794	0.501	0.760	0.819	0.119	0.176	0.676	0.891	0.755
4	0.740	0.808	0.873	0.864	0.836	0.806	-0.172	0.827	0.789	0.935
5	0.785	0.739	0.925	0.852	0.806	0.908	-0.157	0.833	0.706	0.895
6	0.792	0.739	0.934	0.843	0.785	0.929	-0.118	0.852	0.701	0.889
7	0.778	0.753	0.926	0.843	0.789	0.925	-0.130	0.850	0.715	0.899
8	0.789	0.812	0.959	0.897	0.837	0.886	-0.140	0.884	0.765	0.925
9	0.761	0.903	0.907	0.927	0.913	0.773	-0.125	0.897	0.884	0.983
10	0.730	0.449	0.811	0.615	0.531	0.973	-0.004	0.701	0.408	0.649
11	0.777	0.819	0.931	0.885	0.843	0.877	-0.130	0.877	0.786	0.941
12	0.792	0.821	0.926	0.887	0.847	0.865	-0.100	0.889	0.799	0.943
13	0.772	0.888	0.918	0.923	0.900	0.798	-0.131	0.895	0.866	0.979
14	0.738	0.587	0.872	0.715	0.635	0.981	-0.143	0.749	0.536	0.774
15	0.760	0.647	0.906	0.767	0.686	0.974	-0.125	0.797	0.596	0.817
16	0.723	0.541	0.858	0.680	0.593	0.993	-0.131	0.725	0.484	0.733
17	0.650	0.395	0.781	0.554	0.414	0.944	-0.074	0.637	0.325	0.580
18	0.764	0.631	0.901	0.757	0.683	0.978	-0.121	0.788	0.582	0.806
19	0.691	0.905	0.818	0.929	0.949	0.584	-0.149	0.821	0.909	0.965
20	0.684	0.444	0.814	0.604	0.506	0.993	-0.131	0.660	0.382	0.651
21	0.717	0.528	0.852	0.668	0.580	0.995	-0.129	0.717	0.471	0.721
22	0.761	0.656	0.906	0.772	0.698	0.971	-0.130	0.799	0.606	0.824
23	0.679	0.536	0.897	0.694	0.553	0.950	-0.108	0.743	0.447	0.685
24	0.606	0.759	0.925	0.849	0.683	0.661	-0.036	0.854	0.661	0.751

25	0.976	0.979	0.879	−0.098	0.520	0.954	0.953	0.830	0.984	0.670
26	0.959	0.838	0.903	−0.148	0.805	0.894	0.946	0.965	0.886	0.779
27	0.827	0.635	0.806	−0.124	0.915	0.704	0.800	0.914	0.681	0.793
28	0.919	0.827	0.902	−0.128	0.715	0.867	0.959	0.964	0.891	0.735
29	0.899	0.924	0.805	0.016	0.457	0.890	0.869	0.717	0.864	0.750
30	0.925	0.978	0.827	−0.004	0.379	0.975	0.928	0.741	0.944	0.693
31	0.751	0.672	0.822	0.282	0.692	0.741	0.795	0.798	0.613	1.000
32	0.946	0.969	0.862	−0.105	0.475	0.932	0.935	0.812	1.000	0.613
33	0.885	0.747	0.910	−0.074	0.822	0.828	0.931	1.000	0.812	0.798
34	0.958	0.916	0.921	−0.050	0.618	0.959	1.000	0.931	0.935	0.795
35	0.957	0.941	0.837	−0.110	0.524	1.000	0.959	0.828	0.932	0.741
36	0.672	0.411	0.677	−0.126	1.000	0.524	0.618	0.822	0.475	0.692
37	−0.113	0.048	0.254	1.000	−0.126	−0.110	−0.050	−0.074	−0.105	0.282
38	0.897	0.871	1.000	0.254	0.677	0.837	0.921	0.910	0.862	0.822
39	0.940	1.000	0.871	0.048	0.411	0.941	0.916	0.747	0.969	0.672
40	1.000	0.940	0.897	−0.113	0.672	0.957	0.958	0.885	0.946	0.751
41	0.649	0.432	0.741	−0.074	0.891	0.571	0.712	0.910	0.522	0.689
42	0.940	0.965	0.795	−0.125	0.415	0.958	0.909	0.737	0.953	0.626
43	0.919	0.972	0.765	−0.112	0.340	0.933	0.873	0.676	0.951	0.566
44	0.918	0.746	0.857	−0.135	0.887	0.852	0.890	0.943	0.777	0.823
45	0.546	0.581	0.702	0.419	0.316	0.658	0.713	0.640	0.521	0.816
46	0.730	0.754	0.878	0.387	0.460	0.787	0.856	0.794	0.713	0.865
47	0.745	0.828	0.705	0.083	0.223	0.855	0.813	0.639	0.817	0.628
48	0.587	0.626	0.404	−0.208	0.159	0.591	0.502	0.324	0.621	0.195
49	0.764	0.897	0.607	−0.106	0.093	0.813	0.719	0.466	0.870	0.367
50	0.934	0.897	0.764	−0.181	0.537	0.904	0.857	0.729	0.898	0.603
51	0.993	0.932	0.928	−0.078	0.690	0.953	0.978	0.924	0.950	0.771

Table 9. (continued)

Variable no.	41	42	43	44	45	46	47	48	49	50	51
1	0.375	0.941	0.972	0.736	0.461	0.628	0.761	0.744	0.880	0.949	0.900
2	0.605	0.957	0.933	0.865	0.604	0.778	0.827	0.544	0.812	0.892	0.981
3	0.145	0.844	0.876	0.504	0.621	0.700	0.788	0.580	0.832	0.758	0.731
4	0.715	0.785	0.783	0.941	0.423	0.609	0.544	0.567	0.558	0.895	0.918
5	0.850	0.726	0.672	0.991	0.496	0.655	0.530	0.430	0.451	0.799	0.897
6	0.866	0.708	0.651	0.989	0.477	0.651	0.510	0.374	0.428	0.769	0.897
7	0.846	0.719	0.668	0.986	0.454	0.635	0.503	0.412	0.449	0.795	0.904
8	0.857	0.769	0.714	0.988	0.516	0.694	0.577	0.418	0.513	0.808	0.939
9	0.723	0.887	0.851	0.957	0.506	0.698	0.675	0.542	0.692	0.899	0.979
10	0.886	0.409	0.324	0.883	0.409	0.536	0.264	0.164	0.106	0.514	0.673
11	0.810	0.788	0.748	0.984	0.475	0.664	0.577	0.471	0.538	0.848	0.942
12	0.800	0.800	0.753	0.982	0.490	0.679	0.584	0.446	0.558	0.834	0.945
13	0.742	0.867	0.834	0.966	0.498	0.692	0.654	0.526	0.657	0.894	0.975
14	0.880	0.543	0.483	0.940	0.369	0.530	0.335	0.266	0.235	0.654	0.783
15	0.891	0.602	0.535	0.960	0.414	0.582	0.398	0.282	0.298	0.685	0.830
16	0.893	0.494	0.425	0.925	0.360	0.512	0.297	0.227	0.179	0.607	0.747
17	0.881	0.311	0.237	0.798	0.304	0.436	0.139	0.007	-0.023	0.415	0.611
18	0.897	0.587	0.520	0.960	0.419	0.581	0.391	0.281	0.283	0.676	0.819
19	0.564	0.928	0.923	0.863	0.546	0.698	0.744	0.671	0.754	0.960	0.948
20	0.893	0.399	0.322	0.881	0.324	0.459	0.219	0.147	0.074	0.518	0.668
21	0.899	0.478	0.406	0.917	0.354	0.504	0.283	0.198	0.160	0.586	0.736
22	0.884	0.608	0.550	0.965	0.413	0.582	0.405	0.321	0.312	0.706	0.834
23	0.960	0.428	0.370	0.876	0.411	0.559	0.285	0.175	0.111	0.542	0.724
24	0.844	0.618	0.577	0.767	0.568	0.731	0.533	0.295	0.409	0.605	0.813

	41	42	43	44	45	46	47	48	49	50	51
25	0.545	0.965	0.964	0.822	0.535	0.725	0.788	0.629	0.855	0.922	0.970
26	0.810	0.845	0.792	0.964	0.545	0.729	0.671	0.437	0.612	0.832	0.974
27	0.863	0.623	0.559	0.924	0.435	0.601	0.415	0.209	0.321	0.650	0.844
28	0.804	0.818	0.766	0.892	0.604	0.769	0.669	0.401	0.589	0.787	0.953
29	0.423	0.913	0.892	0.754	0.572	0.711	0.734	0.519	0.816	0.817	0.881
30	0.435	0.971	0.966	0.750	0.663	0.791	0.881	0.626	0.889	0.893	0.917
31	0.689	0.626	0.566	0.823	0.816	0.865	0.628	0.195	0.367	0.603	0.771
32	0.522	0.953	0.951	0.777	0.521	0.713	0.817	0.621	0.870	0.898	0.950
33	0.910	0.737	0.676	0.943	0.640	0.794	0.639	0.324	0.466	0.729	0.924
34	0.712	0.909	0.873	0.890	0.713	0.856	0.813	0.502	0.719	0.857	0.978
35	0.571	0.958	0.933	0.852	0.658	0.787	0.855	0.591	0.813	0.904	0.953
36	0.891	0.415	0.340	0.887	0.316	0.460	0.223	0.159	0.093	0.537	0.690
37	-0.074	-0.125	-0.112	-0.135	0.419	0.387	0.083	-0.208	-0.106	-0.181	-0.078
38	0.741	0.795	0.765	0.857	0.702	0.878	0.705	0.404	0.607	0.764	0.928
39	0.432	0.965	0.972	0.746	0.581	0.754	0.828	0.626	0.897	0.897	0.932
40	0.649	0.940	0.919	0.918	0.546	0.730	0.745	0.587	0.764	0.934	0.933
41	1.000	0.423	0.335	0.847	0.527	0.640	0.363	0.047	0.093	0.450	0.707
42	0.423	1.000	0.978	0.767	0.541	0.696	0.858	0.615	0.910	0.904	0.925
43	0.335	0.978	1.000	0.705	0.474	0.643	0.824	0.710	0.937	0.928	0.892
44	0.847	0.767	0.705	1.000	0.558	0.710	0.599	0.419	0.493	0.810	0.925
45	0.527	0.541	0.474	0.558	1.000	0.955	0.748	0.134	0.364	0.424	0.598
46	0.640	0.696	0.643	0.710	0.955	1.000	0.810	0.260	0.513	0.595	0.779
47	0.363	0.858	0.824	0.599	0.748	0.810	1.000	0.398	0.781	0.682	0.759
48	0.047	0.615	0.710	0.419	0.134	0.260	0.398	1.000	0.726	0.821	0.534
49	0.093	0.910	0.937	0.493	0.364	0.513	0.781	0.726	1.000	0.812	0.734
50	0.450	0.904	0.928	0.810	0.424	0.595	0.682	0.821	0.812	1.000	0.901
51	0.707	0.925	0.892	0.925	0.598	0.779	0.759	0.534	0.734	0.901	1.000

Table 10. Cantabrian Mousterian rotated factor loadings for rotation no. 1

Variable no.	Rotated factor loadings, orthogonal varimax				Communality
	1	2	3	4	
1	−0.285	−0.944	−0.008	0.001	0.973
2	−0.472	−0.843	0.124	0.183	0.983
3	0.011	−0.912	0.329	−0.007	0.940
4	−0.746	−0.631	−0.021	−0.039	0.957
5	−0.855	−0.497	0.045	0.049	0.983
6	−0.879	−0.465	0.063	0.068	0.997
7	−0.870	−0.489	0.038	0.037	0.999
8	−0.823	−0.542	0.047	0.146	0.995
9	−0.685	−0.717	0.040	0.059	0.989
10	−0.961	−0.121	0.156	0.002	0.962
11	−0.809	−0.582	0.035	0.047	0.997
12	−0.800	−0.586	0.067	0.048	0.990
13	−0.716	−0.690	0.035	0.059	0.994
14	−0.959	−0.275	0.020	0.015	0.997
15	−0.938	−0.336	0.044	0.059	0.997
16	−0.975	−0.216	0.031	0.020	0.998
17	−0.960	−0.010	0.056	0.132	0.943
18	−0.942	−0.322	0.053	0.048	0.996
19	−0.480	−0.841	0.026	0.053	0.942
20	−0.990	−0.105	0.030	0.022	0.993
21	−0.978	−0.196	0.033	0.030	0.996
22	−0.933	−0.354	0.037	0.038	0.999
23	−0.942	−0.156	0.038	0.242	0.972
24	−0.608	−0.436	0.079	0.568	0.888
25	−0.408	−0.890	0.040	0.161	0.987
26	−0.719	−0.646	0.044	0.225	0.988
27	−0.865	−0.379	0.068	0.154	0.921
28	−0.629	−0.636	0.058	0.408	0.971
29	−0.343	−0.848	0.209	0.004	0.881
30	−0.254	−0.930	0.185	0.140	0.985
31	−0.623	−0.443	0.573	0.068	0.918
32	−0.355	−0.887	0.013	0.234	0.968
33	−0.756	−0.511	0.136	0.380	0.994
34	−0.516	−0.772	0.173	0.320	0.994
35	−0.408	−0.865	0.122	0.171	0.959
36	−0.987	−0.131	0.026	0.018	0.992
37	0.130	0.102	0.893	−0.140	0.845
38	−0.592	−0.636	0.370	0.216	0.938
39	−0.289	−0.925	0.168	0.096	0.977
40	−0.571	−0.810	0.057	0.093	0.995
41	−0.874	−0.132	0.125	0.422	0.976
42	−0.293	−0.930	0.044	0.119	0.967
43	−0.220	−0.969	0.009	0.041	0.989
44	−0.821	−0.539	0.089	0.099	0.983
45	−0.237	−0.428	0.718	0.377	0.897
46	−0.371	−0.563	0.627	0.360	0.978
47	−0.096	−0.799	0.315	0.323	0.851
48	−0.079	−0.755	−0.229	−0.311	0.725
49	0.033	−0.971	−0.037	0.011	0.945
50	−0.434	−0.869	−0.065	−0.104	0.959
51	−0.589	−0.776	0.098	0.189	0.995
Sums of Squares	23.453	20.949	2.737	1.916	49.055

Table 11. Variables in Cantabrian Mousterian collections

Factor 1	Factor 2
Uniquely determined by a single factor	
Limaces	Typical Levallois flakes
Simple straight sidescrapers	Atypical Levallois flakes
Simple convex sidescrapers	Pseudo-levallois points
Double straight-concave sidescrapers	Abrupt retouched sidescrapers
Canted sidescrapers	Typical burins
Transverse straight sidescrapers	Atypical backed knives
Transverse convex sidescrapers	Natural backed knives
Transverse concave sidescrapers	Truncated flakes
Sidescrapers on ventral surface	Alternate burinating becs
Sidescrapers with dorsal thinning	Pieces with bifacial retouch
Bifacially retouched sidescrapers	Choppers
Alternate retouched sidescrapers	Chopping-tools
Typical endscrapers	Cleaver-flakes
Typical perforators	Discs, pics
Pieces with ventral retouch	
Endnotched pieces	
Almost exclusively determined by a single factor	
	Blades
	Bifaces

of the wall toward the cave mouth than would be expected by chance alone.[12]

As in the Torralba case, the examination of occupation distributions in Mousterian levels at Cueva Morín provides clear evidence that the positions of abandonment of materials related to different clusters isolated by factor analysis tend to be segregated. The most economical explanation of the tendency is that the clusters represent constellations of items produced by distinct activity-sets and that the position of abandonment of the items specific to an activity-set tends to coincide with the loci of activity-performance. When other categories of data (besides lithic artifacts) can be included in tests of the Morín distributions, it may be predicted that activity differentiation will become objectively easier and that an increase in the number of recognizably distinctive divisions of major activities will probably occur.

It is my subjective impression that bounded distributions sometimes do occur in the Morín levels and that they are generally much more restricted

---

[12] The chi-square tests are significant at the $a = <.05$ level of probability (Occupation 15) and the $<.01$ level (Occupation 16). For Level 17, the difference between the area toward the cave interior and a *part* of the accumulation on the entry side of the wall is significant at the $a = <.05$ level. Subareas on the entry side will be delineated precisely in a forthcoming publication.

than at Torralba. Certain small distributions (two and one-half to three square meters, ca. ten square meters) seem recurrent as spatial divisions in both Mousterian and Upper Paleolithic horizons. This impression has not yet been empirically validated.

After this study was completed, all the remaining Mousterian occupations at Morín (except Level 22) were examined to see whether differential spatial distributions would be discoverable in occupations known from such small (less than three square meters) areal exposures. In no case could significant tendencies for nonrandom distributions be proven from these small exposures, even though the quantities of recovered artifacts were relatively large in all cases and despite the fact that in Level 17 interior there seemed to be visual indications of area specialization.

CONCLUSIONS AND SPECULATIONS

By means of factor analysis distinct clusters of similarly varying artifactual (and contextual) items have been discerned in Paleolithic occupation residues. Under certain conditions, elements of different clusters can be shown to occur in different places in both cave and open-air occupations. The clusters seem to reflect real socio-cultural characteristics of the prehistoric groups that produced the residues. Cluster-specific areas are often found to have visually distinctive characteristics, independent of the variables used to discern the clusters or differentiate their spatial positions objectively. In the cases examined in this paper, the most economical explanation of these facts is that each cluster is the distinctive set of implements, products, and byproducts of a limited range of technological operations or activities. Spatial differentiation in cluster distribution probably reflects the existence of activity-specific areas within single occupations.

The recognition of variable clusters is a complex quantitative operation which must precede the search for spatial differentiation.[13] Once that is done, the demonstration of different spatial utilization seems to be a simpler, more straightforward, logical and practical task, which can be performed with elementary statistical procedures.

The number of discrete clusters that can be generated from Paleolithic data may be expected to depend not just on the number and nature of different activities undertaken during an occupation but also (and perhaps even more at this primitive stage of methodological develop-

---

[13] There is an exception to this generalization. J. A. Brown is currently attempting to delineate activity-specific areas directly from spatial distributions, with a technique involving analysis of residuals. The approach looks fruitful, but it is more difficult in practice than the technique I have outlined.

ment) on the number and kinds of different data classes available for study. One would expect that occupations accumulated during the year-round utilization of sites for a large range of activities (as is perhaps the case for Cueva Morín Level 17 and must also be true for some of the samples used in the Cantabrian Mousterian factors test) would generate more activity-specific clusters than ephemeral occupations that were accumulated during the performance of hunting, butchering, and meat-processing activities alone. Yet the reverse occurs with these data. In fact, the problem is more complex. The Acheulean butchering site produced more distinct clusters than the Mousterian case, partly because a wide range of faunal data could be used in factor generation at Torralba, while contextual information was unusable in the Mousterian study.

Activity-specific areas defined by cluster distributions are harder to discern in the cave occupations studied than at Torralba. That certainly reflects the fact that activity loci could be spaced farther apart in the open-air site than in the cave and probably that continued occupation of the restricted cave surface led to some blurring of activity-area boundaries. It also certainly reflects inadequacies in the data available for cluster generation. Spatial clumps of specific-artifact types are obviously present in some Morín horizons, but their precise significance cannot be determined without the evidence necessary to subdivide clusters produced by the factor analysis.

The size of bounded activity-specific spatial accumulations is a datum the importance of which is only briefly mentioned here. Spatial clumps in caves look subjectively smaller than those in open-air sites. That seems reasonable, considering the relative sizes of areas generally available in the two kinds of occurrences. But it may reflect something more than different restrictions on "spreading out." I suggest that the size of activity loci also reflects other factors, and that one important factor is the size of the human body and minimal individual spatial needs.[14] The two and one-half to three square meter accumulation subjectively noted in some cave occupations may be the space utilized by a single human agent. If that is so, the size of activity loci might reflect the number of team members engaged in task performance at a given locus (the number of personnel in a social unit). Obviously, this suggestion is subject to severe qualifications; other factors, such as the dimensions of manipulated materials, also condition locus size. Also, these comments refer only to areal spreads of activity-specific materials, not to the size of structural features such as hearths, postholes, or buildings.

---

[14]   I recognize that spatial "needs" are subject to cultural modification (Hall 1966). That is not terribly important here. A stationary individual can conveniently reach an area of two and one-half to three square meters, and this dimension is related only to stature and reach, which vary within a limited range among European populations of genus *Homo*, living or extinct. This area would, of course, be smaller for *Homo habilis* and the Australopithecines.

In some Torralba occupations several restricted distributions have been defined the contents of which are statistically indistinguishable. This is exactly what one would expect if several social units were simultaneously engaged in the more-or-less independent performance of the same set of activities. The occurrence of separate clumps of similar materials may potentially indicate the number of social units responsible for the accumulation of a body of occupation residues. If this information can be coupled with hypotheses about the number of personnel responsible for accumulations of given dimensions, we shall have another important line of reasoning to bring to bear on the estimation of the size of prehistoric social groups.

The last two paragraphs are extremely speculative; they are presented to suggest some of the directions future research might take. It is fair to say that no one can foresee the potential of such studies in all their possible ramifications. Attempts to discern functional and stylistic attributes of Paleolithic artifacts, to describe activity-specific variable clusters, and to define specialized activity loci are still in the most primitive developmental stage. That makes our era an especially exciting one for methodologically oriented prehistorians. Almost anyone with the time, intelligence, and interest can contribute fundamentally to the development of techniques that will produce a quantum change in our ability to reconstruct extinct sociocultural systems from their surviving residues.[15]

REFERENCES

BINFORD, L. R.
  1972 *An archeological perspective.* New York: Seminar.
BINFORD, L. R., S. BINFORD
  1966 A preliminary analysis of functional variability in the Mousterian of Levallois facies. *American Anthropologist,* n.s. 68(2): part 2.
BROWN, J., L. G. FREEMAN
  1964 A UNIVAC analysis of sherd frequencies from the Carter Ranch Pueblo, eastern Arizona. *American Antiquity* 30(2): part 1, 162–167.
BUTZER, K. W.
  1965 Acheulian occupation sites at Torralba and Ambrona: their geology. *Science* 150:1718–1722.
CARBALLO, J.
  1923 *Excavaciones en la Cueva del Rey, en Villanueva* (Santander). Junta Superior de Excavaciones y Antigüedades 53.
CLARK, P., F. EVANS
  1954 Distance to nearest neighbor as a measure of spatial relationships in populations. *Ecology* 35(4):445–453.

---

[15] Although a considerable body of work on spatial analysis in archaeology has been done since this paper was written (some of it by the author), it has not been possible to incorporate it here. None of it, however, would really change this paper.

CONDE DE LA VEGA DEL SELLA
1921   *El paleolítico de Cueva Morín (Santander) y notas para la climatología cuaternaria.* Comisión de Investigaciones Paleontológicas y Prehistóricas, Memoria 29.

CRONIN, C.
1962   "An analysis of pottery design elements, indicating possible relationships between three decorated types," in *Chapters in the Prehistory of eastern Arizona.* Edited by P. S. Martin *et al. Fieldiana Anthropology* 53:105–114.

DEETZ, J.
1960   *"An archaeological approach to kinship change in eighteenth-century Arikara culture."* Unpublished Ph.D. dissertation, Harvard University.
1965   *The dynamics of stylistic change in Arikara ceramics.* Illinois Studies in Anthropology 4.

FREEMAN, L. G.
1964   *"Mousterian developments in Cantabrian Spain."* Unpublished Ph.D. dissertation, University of Chicago.
1966   The nature of Mousterian facies in Cantabrian Spain. *American Anthropologist,* n.s. 68(2) part 2:230–237.
1968   Cueva Morín: a European Paleolithic site. *Current Anthropology* 9:541.
1975   "Acheulian sites and stratigraphy in Iberia and the Maghreb," in *After the Australopithecines.* Edited by Karl W. Butzer and Glynn Ll. Isaac, 661–743. World Anthropology. The Hague: Mouton.

FREEMAN, L. G., J. BROWN
1964   "Statistical analysis of Carter Ranch pottery," in *Chapters in the prehistory of eastern Arizona.* Volume two. Edited by P. S. Martin *et al. Fieldiana Anthropology* 55:126–154.

FREEMAN, L. G., K. W. BUTZER
1966   The Acheulean station of Torralba (Spain). A progress report. *Quaternaria* 8:9–21.

FREEMAN, L. G., J. GONZÁLEZ ECHEGARAY
1970a Aurignacian structural features and burials at Cueva Morín (Santander, Spain). *Nature* 226:722–726.
1970b Enterramientos auriñacienses en la cueva de Morín (Santander). *Boletín de la Real Sociedad Española de Historia Natural (Biol.)* 68:101–105.
1972   *La Sombra de un cazador de la Edad de Piedra.* Santander: Diputación Provincial.

GONZÁLEZ ECHEGARAY, J. *et al.*
1971   *Cueva Morín. Excavaciones 1966–1968.* Santander: Patronato de las Cuevas Prehistóricas.
1973   *Cueva Morin. Excavaciones 1969.* Santander: Patronato de las Cuevas Prehistóricas.

HALL, E.
1966   *The hidden dimension.* Garden City, N.Y.: Doubleday.

HARMAN, H.
1967   *Modern factor analysis.* Chicago: University of Chicago Press.

HILL, J.
1965   "Broken K: a prehistoric society in eastern Arizona." Unpublished Ph.D. dissertation, University of Chicago.
1970   *Broken K pueblo.* Tucson: University of Arizona Press.

HODSON, F.
1970   Cluster analysis and archaeology: some new developments and applications. *World Archaeology* 1(3):299–320.

HOWELL, F. C., K. W. BUTZER, E. AGUIRRE
1963   Noticia preliminar sobre el emplazamiento acheulense de Torralba (Soria). *Excavaciones arqueólogicas en España X.*

LONGACRE, W.
1963   *"Archaeology as anthropology: a case study."* Unpublished Ph.D. dissertation, University of Chicago.
1970   *Archaeology as anthropology. A case study.* University of Arizona Anthropological Papers, 17. Tucson: University of Arizona Press.

MIESCH, A., E. CHAO, F. CUTTITA
1966   Multivariate analysis of geochemical data on tektites. *The Journal of Geology* 5(2):673–691.

SIEGEL, S.
1956   *Nonparametric statistics for the behavioral sciences.* New York: McGraw-Hill.

SOKAL, R., P. SNEATH
1963   *Principles of numerical taxonomy.* San Francisco: W. H. Freeman.

SPAULDING, A. C.
1960   "Statistical description and comparison of artifact assemblages," in *The application of quantitative methods in archaeology.* Edited by R. F. Heizer and S. F. Cook, 60–92. Viking Fund Publications in Anthropology 28. Chicago: Quadrangle Books.

WHALLON, R.
1965   *"The Owasco period: a reanalysis."* Unpublished Ph.D. dissertation, University of Chicago.
1968   "Investigations of late prehistoric social organization in New York State," in *New perspectives in archeology.* Edited by S. R. Binford and L. R. Binford, 223–244. Chicago: Aldine.
1973a   "Spatial analysis of Palaeolithic occupation areas," in *The explanation of culture change.* Edited by C. Renfrew, 115–130. Pittsburgh: University of Pittsburgh Press.
1973b   Spatial analysis of occupation floors I: application of dimensional analysis of variance. *American Antiquity* 38:266–278.
1974   Spatial analysis of occupation floors II: application of nearest neighbor analysis. *American Antiquity* 39.

Late and Post-Pleistocene Industries and Fauna from the Cave Site of La Riera (Province of Asturias, Spain)

GEOFFREY A. CLARK and LINDA R. RICHARDS

INTRODUCTION

In the summer of 1969 the Comisión de Investigaciones Arqueológicas granted permission to conduct small-scale test excavations in four sites known to contain cultural deposits attributed to the Asturian of Cantabria (Conde de la Vega del Sella 1914, 1923, 1930). The Cantabrian

Many Spanish friends and colleagues contributed to the research upon which this report is based. Dr. Martín Almagro-Basch, Director Nacional de la Comisaría de Investigaciones Arqueológicas, kindly granted permission to undertake tests at La Riera. Personnel at the Museo Nacional de Ciencias Naturales (Madrid), Museo Arqueológico Nacional (Madrid), and the Museo Arqueológico Provincial (Oviedo) made collections attributed to the site available for study. Personnel at the latter institution were instrumental in relocating the site and in furnishing some of the equipment necessary for excavation. Thanks are also due Srta. María-Dolores Brandis García, Department of Anthropology, Universidad de Madrid, and Sr. Antonio Álvarez, of the Oviedo museum staff, who assisted Clark in the field. Clark's wife, Valerie, shared in the processing of the excavated material and is responsible for many of the illustrations. Lawrence G. Straus, Department of Anthropology, University of Chicago, and Dr. Edward Spicer, Department of Anthropology, University of Arizona, assisted in data collection. Dr. Jesús Altuna, Museo de San Telmo, San Sebastián, Guipúzcoa, identified the mammalian faunal remains; Dr. Benito Madariaga de la Campa, Instituto Oceanográfico de Madrid (Santander office), classified the marine fauna. Professor Josefa Menéndez-Amor, Laboratorio de Palinología, Museo Nacional de Ciencias Naturales (Madrid), conducted pollen analyses on sediment samples from La Riera which were, unfortunately, devoid of preserved pollen. Sediment samples from the conchero at the site were analyzed by Dr. Karl W. Butzer and Daniel C. Bowman, Paleoecology Laboratory, University of Chicago. Dr. Leslie G. Freeman, Department of Anthropology, University of Chicago, and Dr. Joaquin G. Echegaray, Vice Director, Museo Provincial de Arqueología y Prehistoria, Santander, checked and verified Clark's classification of lithic implements according to the de Sonneville-Bordes and Perrot (1954, 1955, 1956) typological format. National Science Foundation Graduate Fellowships awarded to Clark in 1968, 1969, 1970, and 1971 provided subsistence in the field and during the write-up period. A National Science Foundation Dissertation Aid Grant (No. GS-3169) provided funds for radiocarbon determinations. Travel abroad was paid for by Ford Foundation awards to Dr. Freeman and Dr. R. Braidwood.

Asturian occurs in caves situated along the coastal portions of the provinces of Asturias and Santander in northern Spain (see Figure 1). The
assemblage is characterized mainly by a crude industry in quartzite.
Asturian industrial remains are found in shell midden deposits called
"concheros." Recent radiocarbon determinations indicate a late Boreal
and early Atlantic date, between 7,000 and 9,000 B.P. (Butzer 1971:531).

The four sites tested in Asturias were Penicial (Conde de la Vega del
Sella 1914), Coberizas (Conde de la Vega del Sella 1923:49), La Riera,
and Balmori (Conde de la Vega del Sella 1923:45–49, 1930). This
report's objectives are to review and analyze prior investigation at the
cave site of La Riera, Posada de Llanes, Asturias, and to describe the
results of tests conducted there in 1969. A prior synthetic work summarizes data pertinent to the Cantabrian Asturian (Clark 1971a); a shorter
paper describes and interprets fauna associated with Asturian sites (Clark
1971b:1244–1257). This material will not be reviewed here.

La Riera is an important site because it has been a "touchstone" for
Cantabrian prehistorians for many years. The Late and Post-Pleistocene
sequence preserved there figures in every important attempt at synthesis
of the north Spanish Upper Paleolithic (Almagro-Basch 1947:408–417,
1960:200, 201, 208, 304, 311–314, 1963:245–285; Barandiarán 1967;
Jordá-Cerdá 1957; Obermaier 1924, 1925).

LOCATION AND SETTING

Cueva de La Riera:
Coordinates: 01°09′58″ west longitude (Madridmer.), 43°25′47″ north latitude.
Elevations: Between 50 and 60 meters above sea level; 4.94 meters above the
level of the nearest flowing water (Río Calabres).
Distance from Sea: 1.5 kilometers.

La Riera is a solution cavity formed in the southern face of a small,
east/west trending, limestone plateau called the Llera. Of Lower Car-
boniferous or Devonian age (Martínez-Álvarez 1965: map), the Llera is
bounded on the north by the Cantabrian Sea, where it ends abruptly in a
series of cliffs except where penetrated by inlets at the towns of Barro,
Niembro, and Celorio (Clark 1971a:78). The average elevation of the
Llera is about forty meters (maximum elevation 315 meters). It is
covered today with a deciduous forest, broken in many places by heather
(*Calluna vulgaris*, *Erica* spp.)/gorse (*Ulex* spp.) matorral.

The cave and rock shelter called La Riera is situated 100 meters east
and slightly south of the famous Upper Paleolithic site of Cueto de la
Mina, at the eastern end of the Posada Valley (Conde de la Vega del Sella
1916). Both cave and shelter face toward the west. La Riera was discovered by the Conde de la Vega del Sella in 1916; he excavated it in

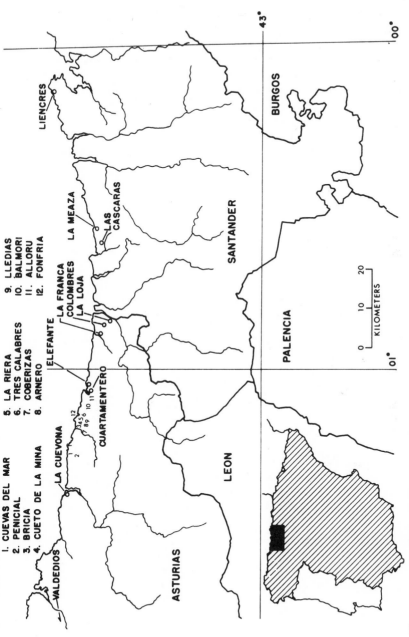

Figure 1. Late and Post-Pleistocene cave and open-air sites in the coastal portions of eastern Asturias and Santander

collaboration with Hugo Obermaier during the following year (Obermaier 1924:175, 346).

Originally the rock shelter was small and inconspicuous, measuring only eight meters across by five meters deep (see Figures 2 and 3). The cavern entrance was completely blocked by a massive deposit of conchero. A layer of soil had formed on top of the shell mound, so that the existence of the cave was not apparent to the casual observer; there were no surface indications of the important cultural deposits it contained. The Conde, however, found a small opening at the shelter base that communicated with the hidden cavern by means of a tortuous crawlway (Conde de la Vega del Sella 1930:6,7).

The cave itself consisted of a single irregular chamber, some twelve meters long, between six and ten meters wide, with a ceiling less than two

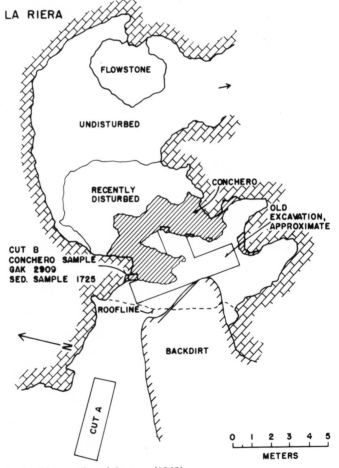

Figure 2.   La Riera: plan of the cave (1969)

LA RIERA

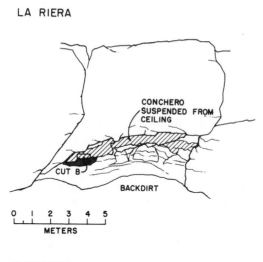

CONCHERO
SUSPENDED FROM
CEILING

CUT B

BACKDIRT

0   1   2   3   4   5
METERS

ELEVATION

Figure 3.   La Riera: elevation of the cave (1969)

meters high (see Figures 2 and 3). The interior was characterized by dripstone formations, now largely destroyed. The floor was covered entirely by a flowstone, which the Conde pierced with an iron bar to determine whether archeological levels were present. In doing so, he exposed the shell mass, noted earlier, which penetrated into the cave interior in the form of a wedge. It is important to bear in mind that the cultural deposits at the foot of the shelter and in the cave entrance and interior were sealed in by this stalagmitic crust, precluding any possible mixture from a disturbance subsequent to its formation. This unusual circumstance and the fact that the cave had been hidden from view for millennia insured a stratigraphic sequence free of mixture (Conde de la Vega del Sella 1930:9).

PRIOR INVESTIGATION

The 1917 excavations were conducted in two phases. (1) A trench of unspecified dimensions was excavated parallel to the long axis of the cave, transecting both the deposits in the shelter and those in the cave mouth. The objective was to create a passageway for backdirt, deposited to the right of the entrance, and to permit natural light to enter the cave to facilitate excavation. (2) A similar trench was excavated parallel to the long axis of the shelter, in order to tap the deposits there, and to verify the stratigraphic sequence revealed by the first sounding. The second trench, perpendicular to the first, formed either a "T" or a "+" with it (which is not made clear in the published report). The stratigraphic sequence summarized on the following pages occurs at the conjunction of the two tests. The approximate location of these old soundings is indicated in Figure 2.

At least four and possibly as many as six cultural deposits were recovered from the site. Bedrock was never reached at any point in the excavations. The oldest assemblage recorded *in situ* pertained to the Upper Solutrean (Jordá-Cerdá 1957:63). The stratigraphic sequence is presented in reverse order to that provided in the original text. Level thicknesses are crude approximations from original surfaces taken from the section provided by the Conde (Conde de la Vega del Sella 1930:8). Estimations in the shelter are from ground level; those in the cave are calculated from the top of the stalagmitic crust. Extensive summarization of, commentary on, and analysis of this material are thought justifiable on four grounds. (1) The original source is written in Spanish, is long out of print, and is not generally available to English-speaking prehistorians. (2) A systematic and exhaustive restudy of the collections has been impossible since 1941, when debitage and fauna from the site were discarded[1] and the finer retouched pieces divided among various museums.[2] (3) One of the authors (G. Clark) has had the opportunity to examine much of what remains of the original collections. (4) As a consequence of his own excavations there, he is familiar with the site itself.

Level K: ? — 157 cm. (shelter)
     ? — 91 cm. (cave)

The oldest deposit exposed in the excavation is a yellow cave clay of undetermined thickness. The sediment contains a few charcoal flakes near the top and some éboulis but is sterile with respect to industrial remains. It is not otherwise described (Conde de la Vega del Sella 1930:7–10).

Level J: 157 — 122/117 cm. (shelter)
   91 — 56/51 cm. (cave)

Level J is the oldest cultural level exposed in the excavation. The sedimentary

[1]   Conde de la Vega del Sella died on September 28, 1941. Until his death, extensive faunal and lithic collections were stored at his summer home in Nueva (Asturias). During the 1940's these unlabeled collections were broken up and dispersed among various museums, principally the Museo Arqueológico Provincial (Oviedo) and the Museo Nacional de Ciencias Naturales (Madrid). At some point after the death of the Count, débitage and pieces regarded as unsuitable for display were combined for efficiency in storage into large bushel basket containers. Some half-dozen of these bushel baskets are stored at the Museo Arqueológico Provincial (Oviedo). They contain thousands of quartzite artifacts, now utterly useless because there are no provenience data to link them with any single site or group of sites, much less to levels within sites.
[2]   Salvageable collections are housed in the Museo Arqueológico Provincial (Oviedo), the Museo Arqueológico Provincial (Barcelona) and the Museo Nacional de Ciencias Naturales (Madrid). The present marqués keeps a small collection in his house in Llanes (Asturias).

matrix, thirty-five to forty centimeters thick, is not described in detail. It consists of a sandy clay similar in texture to that of Level K, but of a darker gray or gray-brown color. Industrial remains, attributed to the Upper Solutrean by the Conde (1923:48, 1930:35), are localized near the cave entrance and at the foot of the shelter. They do not extend far into the cave itself; there, the cultural component of Level J is represented only by ash and charcoal flecks.

The industry in stone consists of a few nucleiform endscrapers.[3] Endscrapers made on thick flakes, sometimes approaching circular forms, are slightly more numerous; simple endscrapers made on laterally retouched blades also occur. One piece figured in the text as a nucleiform endscraper is almost certainly a discoidal flake core or a chopping tool. As is the case generally with Solutrean industries (de Sonneville-Bordes 1963:252), endscrapers are more numerous than burins. The latter category includes canted dihedral burins and burins on breaks; both are illustrated as occurring on retouched blades. Finely made single and double perforators occur on both flakes and blades. One piece is combined with a notch. No microlithic tools are recorded in the assemblage. Both flint and quartzite are utilized as raw material.

The characteristically Solutrean pieces include at least two unifacially retouched shouldered points in flint and what may be a fragment of a third. One magnificent laurel leaf with a concave base is figured, along with a fragment of a second. A broken willow leaf point from which a burin blow appears to have been struck is also represented.

Ground quartz and quartzite discs with edges showing wear are interpreted as polishing stones. Compressors, thought to have been used for pressure flaking, also occur (Conde de la Vega del Sella 1930:40).

The Level J bone industry is both plentiful and varied. The type most commonly represented is a Magdalenian-like beveled base, circular-sectioned antler point; four examples are figured in the text and several more are preserved in the Museo Arqueológico Provincial, Oviedo. The surface of the bevel is usually engraved with a series of parallel lines. The characteristic Solutrean curved antler point, with marked medial flattening, is also present. Two such pieces are illustrated; one is a textbook example. The foregoing were erroneously considered arrowheads by the Conde (1930:40). Larger, more massive, circular, and oval-sectioned pieces also occur. Characterized by basal engraving, they were thought to be spear points. Some finely made needles and awls complete the Level J inventory.

Jordá-Cerdá (1957:63), citing the shouldered and concave-based points and medially flattened pieces, places the Solutrean at La Riera in his Phase III (Upper Solutrean).

Fauna listed include *Equus caballus*, *Cervus elaphus*, *Capra ibex pyrenaica*, *Vulpes vulpes*, and *Canis lupus*. Mollusca exploited consist of *Patella vulgata sautuola*, *Littorina littorea*, and *Littorina obtussata*. Relative frequencies for the different species are not given.

Level I: 122/117 — about 115 cm. (shelter)
      56/51 — about 50 cm. (cave)

This level consists of a thin level of gray clay, somewhat lighter in color than that of Level J and apparently archeologically sterile.

[3] Lithic terminology and type descriptions in this paper conform to those developed for the Upper Paleolithic of western Europe by de Sonneville-Bordes and Perrot (1954, 1955, 1956).

Level H: about 115 — 108 cm. (shelter)
     about   50 —   40 cm. (cave)

    Level H consists of a black, organic clayey sediment similar to, although darker
than, that of Level J. The industrial component was identified as Late Magdalenian by the Conde (1930:31, 35). The level merges with Level F at the rear of the
cave (see Figure 4). The lithic industry was not separated from that of Level F
because no sedimentological distinction could be made between the two deposits.
For a discussion of the assemblage, see Level F.

LA RIERA

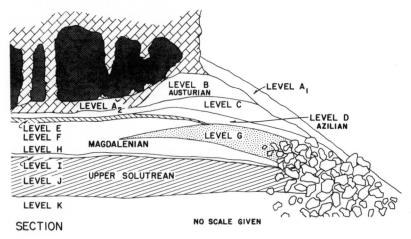

Figure 4.   La Riera: section through the 1917 excavations; no scale given (modified after
Conde de la Vega del Sella 1930:8–10)

Level G: 108 — 78 cm. (shelter)
      40 — 35 cm. (cave)

    The stratum designated Level G is interposed between Levels H and F in the
rock shelter and the mouth of the cave. It consists of a wedge of red clay, some
twenty to thirty centimeters thick (shelter), which contrasts sharply with the
darker sediments of the levels that occur above and below it.
    Level G contained an industry described as Acheulean by the Conde. Its
occurrence in the middle of a deposit of Magdalenian age is explained by postulating a landslide. The Acheulean pieces were believed to have been deposited
originally on the platform above the site. During the late Magdalenian, they fell
from the slope above the shelter and thus became incorporated in the Level H to F
depositional sequence (Conde de la Vega del Sella 1930:8–10, 45, 46; Obermaier
1924:175).
    The industry, exclusively in quartz and quartzite, consists of only six pieces. All
are retouched, however, and are figured in the Conde's text. Five of the pieces are
manufactured on cobbles. Only one piece appears to be bifacial. It is a quartzite
hand-axe, amygdaloid in plan and biconvex in section, flaked over both faces and
retouched secondarily on the margins. The butt of the piece is not worked,

however, presenting the exterior surface of the cobble. There are three unifacial pieces that, because of cutting edges transverse to the long axes of the pieces, might be called cleavers. Two are retouched over the whole of one surface; the other piece is retouched only around the circumference. All three exhibit secondary marginal retouch.

The four artifacts described above are designated "hachas" (axes, cleavers) by the Conde. A fifth piece appears to have been a discoidal core, split from a spherical quartzite cobble and worked unifacially on the ventral surface around three-quarters of the circumference using the unmodified (dorsal) surface as a striking platform. The margins show secondary retouch, suggesting classification as a chopper. The final piece is a concave-convex transverse sidescraper, made on a flake with a prepared striking platform. Retouch is irregular and is restricted to the margins of the ventral surface. These pieces are on display at the Museo Nacional de Ciencias Naturales in Madrid.

Two red deer mandibles (*Cervus elaphus*) constitute the only faunal remains reported from Level G.

In spite of the distinctive nature of the industry and of the sedimentary context in which it occurs, I am inclined to believe that the small collection belongs with the Magdalenian levels with which it is associated. Large quartzite implements of "archaic" appearance are a common component of Magdalenian levels, as is also the case with the Level B "cache" at Cueto de la Mina. The evidence suggests a "heavy duty" toolkit reserved for a specific activity or set of activities, involving chopping or cutting. It is not necessary to postulate an Achulean intrusion to account for the appearance of "archaic" tools in Upper Paleolithic assemblages.

Level F: 35 — 23 cm. (cave)

Level F consists of a black, organic sediment, identical with that of Level H. It occurs as a separate entity only in the mouth of the cave, where deposits of from seven to twelve centimeters thick are recorded. It is absent beneath the shelter overhang, and it grades imperceptibly into Level H farther back in the cave interior (see Figure 4). Like Level H, the industry is classified as Late Magdalenian (Conde de la Vega del Sella 1930:30, 31).

Because the Conde considered Levels H and F representative of a single period of deposition, he made no effort to distinguish the artifacts recovered from below the red clay wedge (Level G) from those taken from the sediments above it. The distinction may have been an important one, because the Conde himself later remarks that the deposits designated Level F contain harpoons, whereas the Level H sediments do not (1930:31, 32). Once again, the area showing densest occupation is restricted to the cave entrance. The lithic industry from the two levels was described as a single unit.

The most numerous tool category appears to be that of endscrapers; at least eleven are figured in the text, and several more examples are preserved in the Museo Arqueológico Provincial (Oviedo). Nucleiform pieces make up the most common type. They occur both on small flint bladelet cores and on large and massive quartzite flake cores. Carinate forms also occur. Endscrapers made on flakes are present in some frequency; often they are retouched around the entire circumference of the piece, except for the butt. Endscrapers on blades seem to be rare.

Burins are said to be present in "their various forms" (Conde de la Vega del Sella 1930:26), but only a straight dihedral burin manufactured on a blade is depicted. Other pieces called burins cannot be classified because no burin blows are indicated on the illustrations. There are a few subrectangular blade fragments showing continuous abrupt marginal retouch on one or more edges. One such piece resembles a giant raclette. Other blades are intentionally denticulated. One large blade is clearly backed; the edge opposite the backing is slightly retouched. Five blades showing only irregular-use flaking are also figured.

Although much is made of the large quartzite pieces, the industry in flint is hardly described at all. In addition to the massive nucleiform endscrapers, a huge atypical perforator (or bec) and a nondescript flake core in quartzite also are illustrated in the site report. No mention is made of a microlithic component, an element to be expected in a Late Magdalenian assemblage.

The industry in bone includes two uniserial harpoons, both recovered from Level F. The rest of the pieces cannot be fixed as to level, although it is stated that no harpoons were recovered from Level H. The most common pieces are quadrangular-sectioned points of cervid antler, usually engraved with parallel or hatched line motifs. One such piece has a beveled base. Smaller, more finely made oval or circular-sectioned beveled base points also occur, along with the needle and awl fragments common to all Upper Paleolithic industries.

Jordá-Cerdá (1957:64) classifies the Magdalenian levels from La Riera in his "Initial Upper Magdalenian," a phase that corresponds to Magdalenian V in the French sequence. The agreement is good with respect to all criteria except for that of microliths. As noted above, no microliths occur in either Levels H or F. The presence of bladelet cores, however, indicates that they were very likely manufactured and simply not recovered by the excavators.

Faunal remains consist of *Equus caballus*, *Bison priscus*, *Cervus elaphus*, *Capra ibex pyrenaica*, *Meles meles*, *Rupicapra rupicapra*, *Vulpes vulpes*, *Canis lupus*, and an unidentified long-legged wading fowl. Mollusca recovered consist of *Patella vulgata sautuola*, *Littorina littorea*, *Littorina obtussata*, *Trivia europaea*, *Pectunculus glycimeris* and *Turritella triplicata* (Conde de la Vega del Sella 1930:35). No frequency data were provided.

Level E: 78 — 76 cm. (shelter)
        23 — 21 cm. (cave)

A thin clay layer on top of Level F separates it from Level D (Azilian). Although present in the cave, the sediment does not extend much beyond the base of the rock shelter (see Figure 4). It is described only as being a limestone decalcification product, lighter in color than the organic sediments of Level F (Conde de la Vega del Sella 1930:8, 18, 25). No mention is made of faunal or cultural debris.

Level D: 76 — 69 cm. (shelter)

Level D is classified as Azilian by the Conde (1923:47, 1930:18–25). The sedimentary matrix is a red clay, in marked contrast with the darker sediments of Levels E and F (Conde de la Vega del Sella 1930:9). Again, lithic debris is concentrated at the foot of the rock shelter.

The industry includes an impressive array of small endscrapers made on diminutive flakes and blades. Flake endscrapers, retouched around three-quarters of their circumferences, are common. A few truly circular forms occur. Simple endscrapers on small blades are present in high frequency; two pieces figured approach "thumbnail" dimensions. Carinate and nucleiform endscrapers made on small bladelet cores are also represented. An unusual component is a set of four nosed or shouldered endscrapers. They are made on larger blades and flakes, at least two of which also show lateral retouch. A blade with a convex truncation and a Aurignacian-like blade with continuous scalar retouch on both edges are figured in the Conde's text.

Burins are said to be numerous. Like the endscraper series, they are diminutive, occurring on small blades (frequent) and flakes (rare). Straight and canted, simple, and multiple dihedral burins are most common. One blade figured in the site report shows an angle burin on a break at one end, combined with a burin struck off a convex truncation at the other.

In marked contrast to Level F, the microlithic component is abundantly represented. It consists in the main of simple backed bladelets, but truncated, backed and truncated bladelets, and microgravettes also occur. Some of the latter are large enough to qualify as true Gravette points. "Azilian points," however, are apparently absent. No good geometrics are noted or illustrated; none appear in the museum collections.

The industry in bone includes the characteristic flat Azilian harpoon with basal perforation; the illustrated example is of cervid antler. Also of note is a long, cylindrical piece that is engraved with a zigzag pattern, said to be characteristic of the Azilian of Cantabria (Conde de la Vega del Sella 1930:25). The rest of the pieces consist of various kinds of points. One is small and double, with a circular section; one is large, possibly double (one end is broken off) with an oval section; a third is quadrangular in section with a single point and shows a series of engraved, subparallel lines; a fourth is clearly an awl or punch, made from a rib bone, the proximal end of which is still preserved.

Ornaments include a perforated canine tooth and examples of *Littorina littorea* and *Trivia europaea* through which holes had been drilled for attachment or suspension. An ochre lump showing use facets also was recovered.

Faunal remains included *Equus caballus*, *Bos* species, *Cervus elaphus*, *Capreolus capreolus*, *Rupicapra rupicapra*, *Canis lupus*, *Vulpes vulpes*, and *Meles meles*. Salmon vertebrae (*Salmo* species) and the bones of the leopard (*Felis pardus*) are noteworthy, since they are not recorded from earlier levels in the site. Occurrence of leopard so late in time is regarded as unusual; the remains may not be correctly identified. Kurtén (1968:87, 88) asserts that the leopard became extinct in western Europe towards the end of the Würm IV stadial. Only two mollusca are listed: *Patella vulgata* (no size indicated) and *Littorina littorea*.

Level C: 69 — 39 cm. (shelter)
      21 — 15 cm. (cave)

Level C consists of a deposit of red clay, attaining a maximum thickness of twenty-five to thirty centimeters under the rock shelter, much thinner inside the cave (see Figure 4). Archeologically sterile, it is otherwise not described.

Level B: 39 — 20 cm. (shelter)
      15 — 10 cm. (cave)

Level B consists of a huge Asturian shell midden, extending across the entire width of the shelter mouth (eight meters) and penetrating into the cave interior to a point at least eight meters from the entrance (Figures 2, 3, and 4). As mentioned before, this deposit completely obstructed the cavern mouth prior to excavation. Maximum thickness (approximately thirty centimeters) was at the foot of the shelter. The deposit thins out rapidly inside the cave and under the shelter overhang.

Conchero remnants also exist on the shelter walls, attesting to a mound of even greater extent, now largely destroyed by erosion.

The matrix consists of brown silts and darker greasy organic sediments occasionally appearing as ephemeral layers within the deposit. The main constituents of the midden, however, are millions of loose shells and bone fragments, both in extraordinarily fine states of preservation. Those portions of the deposit situated inside the cave were indurated near the top by the flowstone formations capping the stratigraphic sequence.

The industry, exclusively in quartzite, is present in greater abundance and variety than at any Asturian station excavated so far. Also, a number of bone tools were recovered (Conde de la Vega del Sella 1930:11–18).

No terrestrial fauna are listed for Level B. The molluscan constituents, however, are presented in some detail. As is usually the case with Asturian concheros, *Patella vulgata* (of small and medium dimensions) and *Trochocochlea crassa* are present in great numbers; *Cardium edulis* is said to be abundant. A few examples each of *Mytilus edulis*, *Astralium rugosus*, and *Triton nodiferus* were also recovered from the deposit. Sea urchins (*Paracentrotus lividus* = "*Taxoneptes lividus*") are present in quantity, mostly in the form of spines. Crab claws identified as those of *Cancer pagurus* are also present (Conde de la Vega del Sella 1930:18).

Level A: 20 — 0 cm. (shelter)
    10 — 0 cm. (cave)

Level A consists of two kinds of sediments, both of which mark the end of the depositional sequence at the site.

Level A_1 is the designation used to refer to the modern soil cover formed atop the shell midden where the latter occurs beneath the rock shelter in the open air. Level A_1 is a dark brown to black soil with small limestone inclusions. It attains a maximum thickness of about twenty-five centimeters; it is archeologically sterile.

Level A_2 designates the stalagmitic crust formed on top of Levels B and C in the interior of the cave. It attains a maximum thickness of about ten centimeters; like Level A_1, it is archeologically sterile (Conde de la Vega del Sella 1930:9).

Except for the description and commentary presented above, which is concerned primarily with the characteristics of the industrial succession, the La Riera lithic data do not admit of detailed analysis. It would be unwise to attempt more sophisticated inquiry, given that the material is clearly selected and probably does not constitute a representative sample of any of the industrial complexes recorded. Nevertheless, it is probably safe to assert, from qualitative evidence alone, that the succession of gross industrial complexes is accurately described.

If this be accepted, it is then possible to discuss, at least in general terms, the faunal assemblages associated with the industrial remains present in the site. An analysis of this kind suffers from the absence of quantitative information. No bone counts are presented, nor is there any way to estimate the minimum number of individual animals taken in any given level. A second problem is that of potentially inaccurate identification: faunal collections were deliberately discarded subsequent to excavation and cannot be reexamined by competent specialists today.

Level J mammalian fauna include a mixture of open (*Equus caballus*, *Canis lupus*), woodland (*Cervus elaphus*), alpine (*Capra ibex pyrenaica*) and indifferent (*Vulpes vulpes*) forms, which, because no relative frequencies are given, provide little paleoecological information. A date toward the end of the Würm III stadial, or the beginning of the Würm III/IV interstadial[4] would be expected for Level J on the basis of the Upper Solutrean industry which it contains (González Echegaray 1966:1–12). If the gross generalizations about habitat given above are regarded as being at least approximately correct, the evidence suggests two hypotheses, which should be the subject of future testing: (1) the paleoclimate in coastal Asturias never became so markedly cold during the Würm as to preclude the existence of forest dwellers (for example, *Cervus elaphus*); and (2) a number of different biotopes were exploited during the Solutrean occupation at La Riera, in that animals that may probably be regarded as food sources (*Equus caballus*, *Cervus elaphus*, *Capra ibex*) were taken from at least three distinct environmental zones. It is beyond this paper's scope to attempt to discuss in detail the wealth of ecological data that can be derived from an ecologically oriented investigation of prehistoric faunal remains. Fortunately, such a detailed synthesis already exists. An article by Freeman (1973) evaluates mammalian faunas recovered from seventy-seven Paleolithic occupation levels in Cantabrian Spain. Much valuable information regarding contemporary habitats, food preferences, behavior, and hunting practices is summarized in the Freeman article and used to generate hypotheses about Pleistocene paleoecology. No attempt will be made to incorporate this material into the present study because the quality of the La Riera faunal data do not permit such inferences to be made.

Level J molluscan fauna attest to water temperatures slightly cooler than those of the present, as indicated by the apparent absence of thermophile species (*Trochocochlea crassa*, *Mytilus edulis*) found in the area today. The giant form of the limpet (*Patella vulgata sautuola*), locally extinct since the end of the Pleistocene, also suggests a somewhat cooler marine environment (Clark 1971a). Inferences that may be drawn from molluscan faunas are discussed at greater length elsewhere (Clark 1971b).

Level F fauna are also mixed, but a higher proportion of open-country dwellers may be represented. Horse (*Equus caballus*), wolf (*Canis lupus*), and bison (*Bison priscus*) (Kurtén 1968:185–186) all suggest open-steppe environments, whereas red deer (*Cervus elaphus*) and badger

---

[4] Würm subdivisions follow the commonly used system of Bordes (1968:222, 223), although the chronology is that developed for the Late Pleistocene of Cantabria (González Echegaray 1966:1–12).

(*Meles meles*) attest to forested lands. Alpine forms include pyrenean ibex (*Capra ibex pyrenaica*) and chamois (*Rupicapra rupicapra*). The red fox (*Vulpes vulpes*) is indifferent to rigorous environmental requirements. Again, quantitative data are absent and no estimation of relative frequency is provided. Level F may confidently be assigned to the Upper Magdalenian and is thought to be the temporal (and partly typological) equivalent of Magdalenian IV and /or V in France. This would suggest an early-to-middle Würm IV stadial date (González Echegaray 1966:1–12; Bordes 1968:222, 223) and somewhat wetter, colder climatic conditions relative to final Solutrean times (González Echegaray 1966:1–12). To the extent that the sparse faunal evidence can be considered to reflect a colder paleoclimate, it is possible to explain the apparent increase in species adapted to open country.

The molluscan faunal spectrum is more varied than that of Level J; however, the microenvironmental requirements of the species listed do not indicate any change in sea-water temperature or salinity when compared with the mollusks from the Solutrean level. Recent excavations at the site suggest that the winkle (*Littorina* spp.) and the limpet (*Patella vulgata sautuola*) probably predominated, but we cannot assert that this was the case on the textual data provided.

The Azilian occupation is represented by Level D. It may be distinguished from the Upper Magdalenian only by the appearance of the characteristic flattened harpoon; the lithic assemblages are closely similar in the Cantabrian zone. Nine species of mammals are recorded for Level D. Only horse (*Equus caballus*) and wolf (*Canis lupus*) may reasonably be claimed open-country-adapted species. Red deer (*Cervus elaphus*), roe deer (*Capreolus capreolus*), badger (*Meles meles*), leopard ("*Felis pardus*" = *Panthera pardus*), and the large bovid (*Bos* sp., *primigenius*?) are creatures adapted to open-deciduous forest and forest-margin biotopes. Of some note are salmon bones (*Salmo* spp.), not recorded from earlier levels in the site. Neither quantitative data nor subjective estimations of frequency (abundant, scarce, and so on) were included in the original publication. So far as the data permit conclusions to be drawn, an apparent reversal in the proportions of open- to forest-adapted species is suggested, perhaps in keeping with an early Holocene date. It can be suggested that forested biotopes became more widespread in the area subsequent to Würm IV times, but in the absence of palynological data and more adequately described faunal remains, this must remain only a speculation. Chamois (*Rupicapra rupicapra*), the single alpine species present, indicates only that the foothills of the Cantabrian Mountains continue to have been exploited, although probably not very intensively. Evidence from other sites summarized by Freeman (1973) suggests that chamois seldom constitute a major element in Cantabrian late Pleistocene cave faunas.

Only two species of marine shellfish are listed for Level D: limpets (*Patella vulgata*) and winkles (*Littorina littorea*). The absence of the subspecific designation "sautuola," indicating the large Pleistocene limpet, suggests that the modern form is present, in contrast to earlier levels, but this assertion cannot be demonstrated. *Littorina littorea* is the taxonomic designation used for both the substantially larger Pleistocene winkle and its modern counterpart.

The Asturian occupation in the site corresponds to Level B. Inexplicably, no terrestrial fauna are listed in the original publication (but, see below). The shellfish remains consist, for the most part, of limpets (*Patella* spp.) of modern dimensions and top-shells (*Trochocochlea crassa*),[5] the latter a comparatively thermophile species. Both species are said to be abundant (Conde de la Vega del Sella 1930:18). Cardial shells (*Cardium edulis*), also common, indicate nothing about sea-water temperature, but scarce thermophile mussels (*Mytilus edulis*), like top-shells present for the first time, suggest a warming trend. A single example of *Astralium rugosus* and some fragments attributed to *Triton nodiferus* also were recovered, along with great quantities of sea urchin spines and shells (*Paracentrotus lividus*)[6] and some crab claws (*Cancer pagurus*) (Conde de la Vega del Sella 1930:18). It may be inferred from the absence of cold and cool water indicators that, by Austurian times, the mean sea-water temperature had risen somewhat when compared with temperatures characteristic of the Late Pleistocene (Clark 1971b: 1245–1247). The Asturian deposits mark the end of cultural deposition in the cave.

RECENT EXCAVATIONS

La Riera was tested by Clark during July 1969. A large test pit, designated Cut A, was placed outside the cave entrance along the left side of the rockshelter (see Figure 2). The location of Cut A was determined by a desire to sample undisturbed deposits outside the cave mouth. It was speculated that occupation surfaces pertaining to the latter periods might occur there because the Asturian level, in particular, seemed to have consisted of a large trash heap. No mention of features was made in the published accounts, and by Asturian times it seems likely that the cave mouth was largely filled with cultural debris, precluding its use as a living space. Old photographs indicate that the backdirt from the Conde's excavations in the cave interior was heaped up to the right of the cave mouth, leaving the left side intact (Conde de la Vega del Sella 1930:6, 7).

The location of a second, smaller test, Cut B, was determined by the

---

[5] *Trochus lineatus* in the original text.
[6] *Taxoneptes lividus* in the original text.

presence of a broad band of conchero adhering to the cave ceiling (see Figures 2 and 3) and extending across the entrance. This conchero was assumed to be the same one referred to by the Conde (1923:45–48, 1930:11–14), an assumption later verified by recovery of the characteristic picks from these sediments.

In both cuts excavation was done according to natural levels; all sediments removed from the test pits were screened (one-eighth-inch mesh) by the crew during the course of excavation. Because-the work was conducted as part of a research program investigating the Cantabrian Asturian, there were three principal objectives. (1) Given the poor quality of faunal collections from the site, emphasis was placed upon obtaining large quantities of faunal remains, especially from the poorly known Asturian occupation (see Tables 1 and 2). (2) Although it appears that considerable numbers of lithics were recovered from the Asturian conchero, the description of this important corpus of material leaves much to be desired. No counts of artifact types or of débitage categories were presented; the inventory given in Tables 3 to 7 comprises all Asturian industrial remains from La Riera that can be located today. The almost total absence of débitage attests to selection in these collections. Thus, a second objective was to obtain a representative sample of the Asturian lithic industry. (3) Because of recent attempts to assign Lower or Middle Paleolithic dates to the Asturian (Jordá-Cerdá 1957:66, 67,

Table 1. La Riera — Fauna by cuts, levels: marine mollusks, echinoderms, terrestrial mollusks, osseous fishes, crustaceans

Species	Museum collections	A_1	A_2	A_3	A_4	Subtotal A	Conchero samples	B_1	Subtotal B	Total
Patella spp.	—	219	323	14		556	1,427	872	2,299	2,855
P. vulgata sautuola	—	3				3			—	3
Trochocochlea crassa	8	62	63	7		132	406	345	751	891
Littorina littorea	—	2				2			—	2
Cardium edule	8	1	2			3		4	4	15
Nassa reticulata	—					—	2	6	8	8
Halyotis tuberculata	2					—			—	2
Triton nodiferus	3					—			—	3
Mytilus edulis	2					—			—	2
Unidentified marine	—	24	56			80	52	20	72	152
Paracentrotus lividus	—		1			1	57	33	90	91
Helix nemoralis	4	2	2			4	76	31	107	115
Helix arbustorum	—	2	4	1		7	20	24	44	51
Unidentified terrestrial	—	1	1	1		3	2	6	8	11
Solea spp.	2					—		1	1	3
Teleostomi Indeterminate	—					—	17	45	62	62
Cancer pagurus	—					—		1	1	1
Total by level	29		316	452	23	—	791	2,059	1,388	3,447	4,267

Table 2.   La Riera — Mammalian fauna by cuts, levels

Species	Museum collec- tions	A₁	A₂	A₃	A₄	Sub- total A	Conchero samples	B₁	Sub- total B	Total
Cervus elaphus (W)	—	17	2	4	30	53	22	6	28	81
Capreolus capreolus (W)	—					—	3	1	4	4
Equus caballus (O)	—	1				1			—	1
Capra ibex pyren. (A)	—	2				2			—	2
Glis glis (I)	—					—	1		1	1
Rodentia indet. (I)	—		1			1		8	8	9
Aves indet. (I)	—					—		R	R	R
Unidentified bone	P	261	42	59	191	553	71	56	127	680
Total by level	P	281	45	63	221	610	97	71	168	778

Key: W = woodland; O = open country; A = alpine; I = indifferent; R = rare; P = present

1958:19–21, 1959:63–66; González 1965:35–39; Pericot-García 1964:48–50; Hernández-Pacheco *et al.* 1957:24), the recovery of charcoal for radiocarbon assay was also deemed important. All three of these objectives were attained.

CUT A

Cut A consisted of a trench four meters long by one meter wide. As Figure 2 indicates, the trench parallels the north wall of the rockshelter and extends beyond it in an easterly direction, descending the slope in

Table 3.   La Riera — Asturian industry: débitage (quartzite)

Types	Museum collec- tions	A₁	A₂	A₃	A₄	Sub- total A	Conchero samples	B₁	Sub- total B	Total
Cobbles, unmodified	—			1		1	1		1	2
Pebbles, unmodified	1	2	2	3		7			—	8
Split cobble segments	1		4	2	1	7	1		1	9
Nucleus, flakes	1	3	5	3		11	1		1	13
Nucleus, blades/ bladelets	—		1	1	1	3			—	3
Nucleus, mixed	1	2			2	4			—	5
Flakes, plain	7	55	48	44	35	182	2	6	8	197
Flakes, trimming	—	8	11	8	4	31	1		1	32
Flakes, core renewal	—	1				1			—	1
Flakes, platform renewal	—			1		1			—	1
Blades	6	10	7	1	5	23			—	29
Bladelets	—	8	5	7	7	27			—	27
Total by level	17	89	83	71	55	298	6	6	12	327

front of the site. Cut A was excavated as a step trench; the easternmost meter was dug in arbitrary ten centimeter levels to a depth of forty centimeters. When it became apparent that natural stratigraphic levels could be discerned, these were employed instead, each level being stripped off in succession throughout the rest of the excavation. The northeast corner of the trench served as the point of attachment for an arbitrary datum from which all depth measurements were taken. Because of the marked slope in front of the cave (22°), an arbitrary datum was essential for accurate vertical measurement. The Cut A section revealed the presence of four major strata (see Figure 5).

Table 4.   La Riera — Asturian industry: retouched and modified pieces (quartzite)

Types	Museum collections	A_1	A_2	A_3	A_4	Subtotal A	Conchero samples	B_1	Subtotal B	Total
Cobble hammerstones	3	1				1			—	4
Cobble, bitruncated	—		1			1			—	1
Pick, Asturian	50		2	1		3	1		1	54
Choppers, large	3					—			—	3
Choppers, small	2					—			—	2
Choppers, double	1					—			—	1
Chopping tools, small	1	1				1			—	2
Bifaces, partial	2					—			—	2
Endscraper, nucleiform	—		2	1		3			—	3
Hammerstone/ chopping tool	—			1		1			—	1
Denticulate, flake	—	3	2	2	1	8			—	8
Denticulate, blade/ bladelet	—	1				1			—	1
Denticulate, double	1					—			—	1
Notch, flake	—	3	2	1		6			—	6
Wedge, flake	—				1	1			—	1
Perforator, atypical	—				1	1			—	1
Sidescraper, lateral convex	1					—			—	1
Perforator/ denticulate	—	1				1			—	1
Total by level	64	9	9	7	3	28	1	—	1	93

Level 1

Level 1 consists of the uppermost part of the humic horizons of the present-day soil, an A(B)C woodland podsol. A_{00} (surface litter), A_0 (fermentation horizon), and A_1 (a brown, mull-humus) horizons are present with an abundant microfauna (interpretation mine, terms from

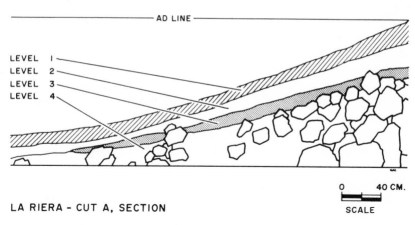

LA RIERA - CUT A, SECTION

Figure 5.   La Riera: Cut A — Section (1969)

Butzer 1971:79–85). In contrast to lower levels very few limestone fragments appear in Level 1. Texture is cohesive when damp but becomes crumbly after it has dried out. In the natural state lumps of soil frequently adhere to rootlets. Level 1 averages ten centimeters in thickness, but exceeds twenty centimeters in the eastern end of the trench. No metal fragments and only two potsherds appeared in the area exposed by Cut A, suggesting that occupation of the shelter had essentially ceased after Level 1 times. There are no indications of disturbance in the Level 1 section; this is surprising when it is noted that it is the surficial layer but perhaps is understandable given the appearance of the site prior to

Table 5.   La Riera — Asturian industry: débitage (flint)

Types	Museum collections	A_1	A_2	A_3	A_4	Sub-total A	Conchero samples	B_1	Sub-total B	Total
Nucleus, flakes	—		1	1	1	3			—	3
Nucleus, blades	—		1			1			—	1
Nucleus, bladelets	—			1	1	2			—	2
Nucleus, mixed	—	2			1	3	3	1	4	7
Flakes, plain	—	40	35	25	13	113	1		1	114
Flakes, trimming	—	6	6	6		18			—	18
Flakes, core renewal	—	1				1			—	1
Flakes, platform renewal	—	1				1			—	1
Blades	—	4	9		3	16			—	16
Bladelets	—	7	4	6	9	26			—	26
Burin spalls	—	1				1			—	1
Total by level	—	62	56	39	28	185	4	1	5	190

excavation. It can be conclusively demonstrated that Level 1 is distinct from the Conde's spoilheap, the edge of which is located some three to five meters southeast of Cut A.

The remains of terrestrial fauna in Level 1 were fairly abundant, although few bone fragments could be identified (see Table 2). The bones of red deer (*Cervus elaphus*) predominated, but the identifiable sample was so small as to preclude drawing any conclusions from it. Horse (*Equus caballus*) and ibex (*Capra ibex*) were also identified. Faunal material of marine origin was confined solely to shell fragments. These were small and their state of decay advanced, making species identification difficult. However, shellfish remains are predominantly those of modern limpets (*Patella* spp.) and topshells (*Trochocochlea crassa*), indicating a Post-Pleistocene time range.

The state of shell preservation in Level 1 is important if it is asserted that the Level 1 soil is intact. The shells occur as fragments, very fragile and flaky, as a consequence of extensive decalcification brought about by

Table 6.   La Riera — Asturian industry: retouched and modified pieces (flint)

Types	Museum collections	A_1	A_2	A_3	A_4	Sub-total A	Conchero samples	B_1	Sub-total B	Total
Endscraper, flake	—		1			1			—	1
Endscraper, nucleiform	—	1	2	3		6			—	6
Perforator, atypical	—	1	1			2			—	2
Burin, straight dihedral	—				1	1			—	1
Burin, angle on a break	—				1	1			—	1
Burin, multiple dihedral	—	2			1	3			—	3
Burin, nucleiform	—				1	1			—	1
Truncated piece, oblique concave	—	1			1	2			—	2
Truncated piece, oblique convex	—	1				1			—	1
Bitruncated piece	—				1	1			—	1
Denticulate, flake	—	3	1	1	1	6			—	6
Sidescraper, simple lateral straight	—	1		1		2			—	2
Sidescraper, simple lateral convex	—				1	1			—	1
Bladelet, backed	—		1		1	2			—	2
Bladelet, partially backed	—	3				3			—	3
Bladelet, truncated	—				1	1			—	1
Continuously retouched piece	—				1	1			—	1
Notch/denticulate	—	1				1			—	1
Total by level	—	14	6	5	11	36	—	—	—	36

prolonged exposure to the elements. Decay was no doubt accelerated by the acidic conditions that characterize the humic horizons in which they are found. The condition of the shells in Level 1 (and in Cut A in general) stands in marked contrast to those present in the Conde's spoilheap, only a few meters distant. The latter, removed from sediments in the cave interior, and exposed to the elements for only fifty years, are without exception complete specimens, as durable as the day they were collected

Table 7.   La Riera — Asturian industry: miscellaneous

Types	Museum collections	A₁	A₂	A₃	A₄	Sub-total A	Conchero samples	B₁	Sub-total B	Total
Quartz										
Pebbles, unmodified	—					—	1		1	1
Crystals, unmodified	—	24	5	3		32			—	32
Flakes	—	16	4	6	4	30		2	2	32
Bladelets	—	2				2			—	2
Endscraper, thick shd.	—		1			1			—	1
Notch, flake	—		1			1			—	1
Wedge, flake	—	1				1			—	1
Denticulate, flake	—	1				1			—	1
Burin, straight dihedral	—			1		1			—	1
Chunks, ground	—	1				1			—	1
Sandstone										
Chunks	—		2			2			—	2
Nucleus, flake	—		2			2			—	2
Limestone										
Stalagmites, fragments	—	3				3			—	3
Flakes	—		5	3	1	9			—	9
Blades	—		1			1			—	1
Bone										
Points, oval section	—	1	1			2			—	2
Punches/awls/ perforators	—	1				1			—	1
Sharpened splinters/ needle fragments	3					—			—	3
Bone with cutting marks	—	17	2	7	11	37		1	1	38
Other										
Potsherds, hand turned	—	2	2			4			—	4
Facetted ochre nodules	—	1			2	3			—	3
Total by level	3	70	26	19	19	134	1	3	4	141

and distinguishable from contemporary examples only by fading. The stratigraphy indicates that, in spite of shallow depth, there are no signs of disturbance in Level 1. That the Level 1 sediments are unmixed is borne out by the shells they contain, which can be readily distinguished from those in the nearby spoilheap, the nearest and potentially most dangerous source of contamination.

The Level 1 lithic inventory is summarized in Tables 3 to 7. As is evident from the tables, stone artifactual materials were not particularly numerous and retouched pieces were extremely scarce. Perhaps most noteworthy is the evidence for bladelets, both in flint and quartzite, along with the mixed flake/bladelet cores from which they were detached. The presence of tiny trimming flakes (Clark 1971a:266, 267) indicates that secondary retouching, as well as the production of flakes and blades, was an activity conducted at La Riera during the Level 1 occupation. Although Level 1 cannot be assigned to any given industrial complex on the basis of qualitative evidence alone, the proportions of artifacts in the retouched and débitage categories are similar to those from Levels 2 and 3, which are assigned to the Asturian on other grounds. It is suggested that Level 1 may be a portion of the Asturian conchero found in the cave, modified by the chemical action of humus formation but not altered in content since Asturian times. Stratification above Asturian levels in Cut A indicates a Post-Pleistocene date for the Level 1 occupation, less than or equal to 8,900 years B.P.

Level 2

Level 2 consists of a crumbly, dark-brown organic soil, a continuation of the A_1 humic horizon first seen in Level 1. It can be distinguished from the lower part of Level 1 on the basis of color (darker), texture (more plastic when moist), and inclusions. Small fragments of limestone derived from spalling off the shelter walls are much more prevalent. Level 2 averages fifteen centimeters in thickness at the east end of the trench, but pinches out to less than ten centimeters at the west end (see Figure 5).

Level 2 differs in no significant respects from Level 1 in the type of fauna found; the same two species of shellfish (*Patella* spp., and *Trochocochlea crassa*) predominate, although frequencies are undoubtedly inflated due to the poor state of preservation. Identifiable mammalian faunal remains are confined to those of the red deer (*Cervus elaphus*), the predominant form throughout the La Riera sequence.

The Level 2 lithic industry can be attributed with certainty to the Asturian; two classical examples of the characteristic unifacial pick were recovered from the Level 2 soil horizon. These conform in all important particulars to the type definitions presented by the Conde de la Vega del

Sella (1923:14) and Clark (1971a:268, 269); they are depicted in Figure 6. The picks are only significant, however, in their limited roles as index fossils; the type is well- (indeed, over-) represented in the museum collections (see Figure 7 and Table 4). The Level 2 lithic inventory is significant because it provides, for the first time, a fairly detailed picture of an Asturian industry as a whole. What is immediately evident is the comparative importance of quartzite as a raw material in this flint-poor region; just under 60 percent of the Level 2 lithics are of fine- to medium-grained quartzite. Most commonly found are the unretouched flakes mentioned in the older literature (Conde de la Vega del Sella 1923, 1930) but never saved; these account for 71 percent of the Level 2 quartzite débitage total. A variety of nuclei are present; flake cores predominate. A surprising element consists of some dozen quartzite blades and bladelets; no mention of a blade technology appears in the classical literature. Nuclei from which blades and bladelets were detached were also recovered. Retouched quartzite implements are scarce. About the only forms that occur with any regularity other than the much-noted picks are flake notches, denticulates, and nucleiform endscrapers (de Sonneville-Bordes and Perrot 1956:552). More extensive excavations could be expected to produce good series of these tools; that they are common elements at many Asturian sites is suggested by the detailed reevaluation of the Asturian lithic industry as a whole (Clark 1971a:307–309).

The flint industry is all the more noteworthy because flint artifacts are never mentioned in connection with Asturian industries in the classical literature (Conde de la Vega del Sella 1914, 1923, 1930; Jordá-Cerdá 1959). As usual, débitage predominates, comprising 90 percent of the Level 2 flint inventory. Lamellar elements are again present, along with the cores from which they were detached. Retouched flint artifacts are too few to permit extensive comment (see Table 6). Unique items include a fragment of an oval-sectioned bone point; similar objects were recovered from Level 1, from the Asturian conchero at La Riera (Conde de la Vega del Sella 1923:24, 25), and from the Asturian deposits at the ill-fated site of La Franca (Conde de la Vega del Sella 1923:24, 25). Two hand-turned potsherds were also found. Ceramics evidently occur sporadically and in extremely low density in levels attributed to the Asturian at Bricia (now in collections at the Museo Arqueológico Provincial, Oviedo) and at the badly disturbed cave site of Lledías (Uría-Ríu 1941, 1944), as well as at La Riera. The possibilities of disturbance prior to excavation, mixing of level designations in poorly provenienced museum collections, and intentional counterfeiting (in the case of Lledías) cannot be ruled out.

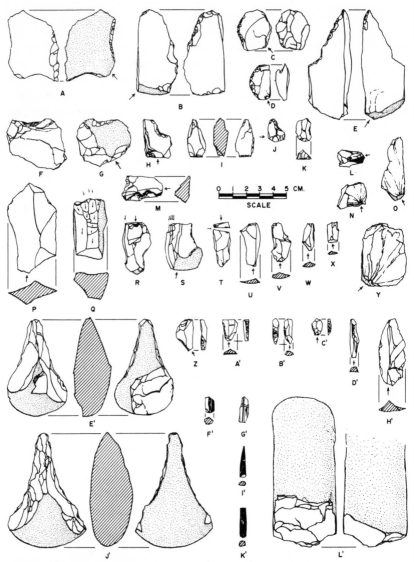

Figure 6. La Riera — Cut A, Levels 1 (Asturian?) and 2 (Asturian):
Level 1: A, B — denticulated flakes; C — atypical transverse sidescraper or denticulate; E
— perforator/denticulate; G — notch; I — wedge (see also Clark 1971a:275); K —
microendscraper; L — crystal showing battering; M — platform renewal flake; R — straight
dihedral burin; S — multiple dihedral burin; Z — piece with oblique concave truncation; A',
B' — backed bladelets, partial; D' — *hojita del borde de nucleo*; F' — beveled crystal; G' —
incised bone; I' — bone point tip; L' — chopping tool on elongated pebble. A–C, E, G, I, L'
are quartzite; K, M, R, S, Z, A', B', D' are flint; L and F' are quartz; G' and I' are bone
Level 2: D — convex lateral sidescraper; F, H — notches; J — thick, shouldered microendscraper; N, O, Y — flakes; P — blade; Q — nucleiform burin in a bladelet core; T —
angle burin on a break; U–X — small blades, bladelets; C' — backed bladelet, partial; E', J'
— unifacial Asturian picks (tip of J' heavily worn from use); H' — blade showing edge wear

Level 3

Level 3 is also attributed to the Asturian. The Level 2/3 contact is characterized by a distinct color change; Level 3 is browner, more clayey, and finer in texture than Level 2. It may represent the transition from an A_1 to a B horizon. Some roots and soil organisms penetrate to Level 3 depths but not to the extent that they are present in the overlying levels. Shell declines dramatically in frequency, as is indicated by Table 1. The quantity of éboulis, on the other hand, increases strikingly *vis-à-vis* more recent levels. The size of limestone fragments also increases noticeably. Level 3 averages about thirteen centimeters in thickness.

The Level 3 faunal collection is distinguished from that of Level 2 only by its sparseness; the familiar limpet/topshell combination is in evidence as before, supporting the assignment of the level to the Asturian. Red deer (*Cervus elaphus*) continue to represent the principal ungulate exploited.

Industrial remains in Level 3 closely parallel those in Level 2, both in kind and in the proportion of artifacts present. A typical pick was recovered, suggesting assignment to the Asturian. The comparatively high frequencies in the débitage categories mirror those in Level 2. Among the retouched pieces flake denticulates and notches and nucleiform endscrapers again predominate. A blade technology is unmistakably present; it is manifest not only in the blades and bladelets themselves but in unmistakable bladelet cores. Sparseness of industrial remains precludes any additional comment about type frequencies. At first impressions, at least, Levels 2 and 3 seem to be closely similar.

Level 4

The Level 3/4 contact is very irregular (see Figure 5), but Level 4 is markedly different in texture and color from the Level 1 to 3 sequence that overlies it. Level 4 averages about fifty centimeters in thickness over the area exposed in Cut A. Whereas the later levels appear to be various subdivisions within the A and B horizons of a soil, the Level 4 matrix consists of a fine, dense yellow clay. Level 4 appears to represent the partially disintegrated (C_1) and intact (C_2) parent material upon which the weathering ((B)) and humic (A) horizons have developed. Bedrock was not reached in the excavation. It is inferred that the D horizon (bedrock) is the same Devonian limestone in which La Riera has formed. Angular limestone chunks are present in the clay and are much larger

from use; K' — fragment of bone awl or point. F, H, P, U, V, E', J', H' are quartzite; D, Q, T, W, X, C' are flint; J is quartz; N, O, Y are limestone; K' is bone

than in any of the subsequent levels, with dimensions not uncommonly surpassing 25 by 50 centimeters. Further excavation revealed a layer of larger, impenetrable limestone blocks, apparently the remains of an overhanging shelter that in antiquity extended far out in front of the

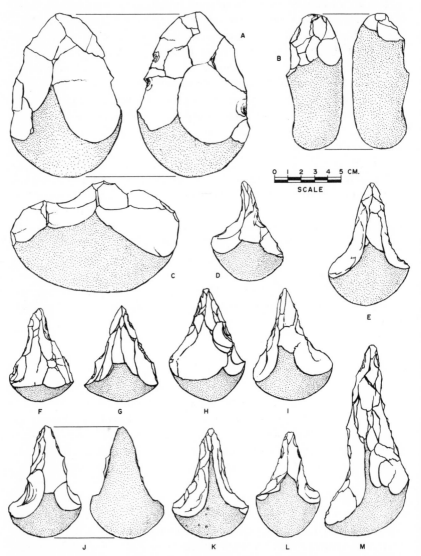

Figure 7. La Riera — Asturian artifacts from Spanish museums: A — partial biface reminiscent of Acheulean pieces; B — chopping tool on elongated pebble; C — large chopper; D–M — Asturian picks. All pieces are made on quartzite cobbles. Museo Arqueológico Provincial (Oviedo): A, E, H–L; Museo Arqueológico Nacional (Madrid): F; Museo Nacional de Ciencias Naturales (Madrid): B–D, G, M

present entrance to the cave. If these deposits may be correlated with those that contained Vega del Sella's so-called Acheulean intrusion (Conde de la Vega del Sella 1930:8–10, 45, 46), then it can be inferred, if we accept his stratigraphy for the cave entrance at face value, that the

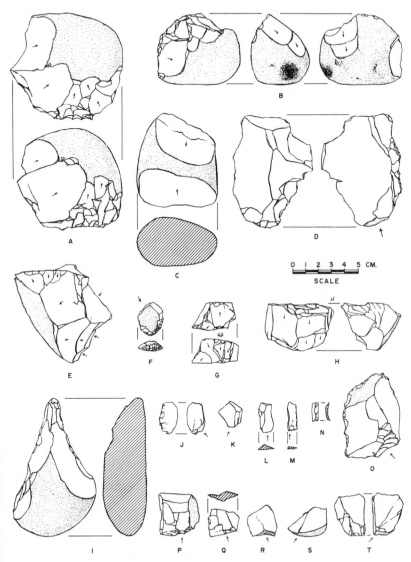

Figure 8. La Riera — Cut A, Level 3 (Asturian): A — nucleiform endscraper; B — chopping tool/hammerstone; C — bitruncated cobble; D — double inverse denticulate; E — flake core; F — simple endscraper on a flake; G — bladelet core; H — mixed core; I — unifacial Asturian pick; J, K, P–T primary and secondary flakes; L–N bladelets; O — atypical denticulate, A–E, H, I–K, M, O–T are quartzite; F, G, L, N are flint

collapse took place during the Magdalenian occupation (see Figure 4). The survey team was not equipped to penetrate this massive deposit of rockfall, and consequently the excavation of Cut A ended when the dense layer of rock was encountered. It may be the case that more cultural levels underlie Level 4, but a full-scale excavation would be required to determine whether or not this is the case.

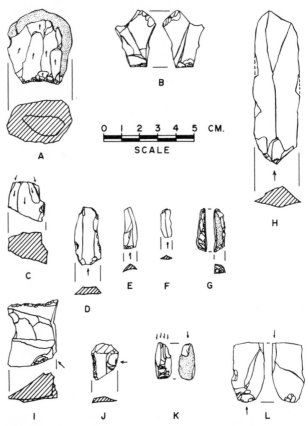

Figure 9.   La Riera — Cut A, Level 4 (unknown): A — nucleiform endscraper made on a bladelet core; B — double wedge (see also Clark 1971a:275); C — mixed core; D — small blade showing use; E, F — bladelets; G — atypical backed and truncated bladelet; H — blade; I — denticulate; J — truncated piece; K — multiple dihedral burin; L — straight dihedral burin. B, H, I are quartzite; A, C–G, J–L are flint

Level 4 fauna exhibited the trends already evident in Level 3. As Table 1 indicates, shellfish remains were nonexistent, due, no doubt, to factors of preservation[7] rather than nonexploitation. Only the bones of red deer

[7]   Shellfish were systematically exploited throughout the Late Pleistocene in coastal Cantabria. The Upper Paleolithic levels at La Riera, Cueto de la Mina, and Balmori consist in the main of shell (Conde de la Vega del Sella 1916, 1923, 1930; Clark 1971a, 1971b).

(*Cervus elaphus*) were recovered from Level 4, but these were more prevalent here than in any other level. Again, a woodland environment is postulated on the scant evidence available.

Level 4 lithics cannot be attributed on qualitative grounds to any industry; diagnostic pieces that would permit such an assignation to be made do not occur. Level 4 lithics are generally similar to the worked stone inventories from Levels 1 to 3. Modified quartzite pieces are so scarce as to preclude any comment; retouched flint shows the preeminence of nucleiform endscrapers noted above.

CUT B

The area designated Cut B lies along the north wall of the cave, under the overhang. Cut B sampled the Asturian conchero, which extends across the cave mouth in a broad band (see Figures 2 and 3). At the point sampled the conchero is suspended about 125 centimeters above the present floor, and is approximately 40 centimeters thick. The deposit consists of a bone and shell breccia, of variable induration, shot through with lenses and pockets of brown silty sediments and ephemeral travertine layers. No consistent stratigraphy is discernible; a single "level" (B_1) was defined. Geological deposition in the cave was terminated by a thick (approximately twenty-five centimeters) flowstone cap, which covered the Asturian midden.

Industry, as in all Asturian concheros, was negligible. However, one characteristic unifacial pick was recovered from the area sampled by Cut B, confirming its assignment (on faunal grounds) to the Asturian.

Other points along the conchero were sampled for shell content prior to the period of excavation, in March and June 1969 (see Figure 2 and Tables 1 and 2).

A radiocarbon determination (GaK 2909) obtained on charcoal (37.7 grams) taken from a pocket in the Cut B exposure was 8,909± 309 B.P., corrected for the new half-life (Kigoshi 1970, personal communication). This determination is taken to date the Asturian occupation at the site. It tallies almost exactly with a charcoal determination (GaK 2906; 35.1 grams) from the Asturian conchero at the type site, Cueva del Penicial (8,909±185 B.P.) (Kigoshi 1970, personal communication).

Sediments from the conchero at La Riera (Sample Number 1725) were analyzed as part of a series from Asturian sites by Karl W. Butzer and Daniel C. Bowman (1971:615–622), of the University of Chicago Paleoecology Laboratory. Their findings point to the high carbonate content (70–75 percent) generally characteristic of conchero deposits; pH's in the 7.6–8.2 range are thought to be the result of excessive free lime. The noncarbonate residue noted above ("brown silty sediments") may be more accurately described as a "clayey silt" with a high (30–37.5 percent) clay component. There is no positive evidence of eolian deposition in the Asturian conchero; frosting of quartz grains (which is common in the La Riera conchero) is attributed to chemical attack in a highly alkaline carbonate environment (Butzer and Bowman 1971:618). There is no indication of sedimentary processes different from those which have characterized Cantabria since the end of the Pleistocene. There is no evidence in the sedimentological analysis of the Asturian series for either a climate cooler than that of today or for marked variation in the abundance of precipitation. These findings lend stature to the assertion that the Asturian is a Post-Pleistocene phenomenon.

ANALYSIS

To summarize the results of the test excavations, it has been tentatively concluded that the following industrial complexes are represented at La Riera:

Cut A	Cut B
Level 1: unknown, possibly Asturian	Level 1: Asturian
Level 2: Asturian	
Level 3: Asturian	
Level 4: unknown	

Problems with assigning "cultural" affiliations arise from small sample size. Rather than depend exclusively upon archeological "index fossils" (for example, Asturian picks), a rigorous statistical method was adopted to attempt to assess differences and similarities among the various levels.

The Kolmogorov–Smirnov Test

The statistical test selected for level comparisons is called the Kolmogorov–Smirnov two-sample test (Siegel 1956:127–136). The test is used to determine whether or not two independent samples have been drawn from populations with identical or similar underlying distributions. It is a nonparametric or distribution free test; a normal distribution is not assumed to underlie the populations from which the samples are drawn. The rationale for using the Kolmogorov–Smirnov two-sample test with such data as these is given by Goodman (1954).

There are two different forms of the Kolmogorov–Smirnov two-sample test — a one-tailed test and a two-tailed test. The one-tailed test is used to determine ". . . whether or not the values of the population from which one of the samples was drawn are stochastically larger than the values of the population from which the other sample was drawn . . ." (Siegel 1956:127). The one-tailed test predicts directionality of difference. The two-tailed test indicates only whether or not there *are* differences in the distributions from which the two samples are drawn. In this paper we are concerned only with the latter case; hence, the two-tailed test is appropriate. Statistically speaking, when two independent samples have been drawn from the same population, they should show only random deviations from the population distribution and the cumulative distributions of both samples should be fairly close to each other. If at some point in the cumulative distributions there is a large amount of difference, then there is reason to suspect that the samples may have been drawn from two different populations. In this test, the null hypothesis (H_0) is a hypothesis of no difference; it specifies that the samples were drawn from the same population. The alternative hypothesis (H_1) is simply that the samples were drawn from different populations. In the Kolmogorov–Smirnov test, if the deviation between the cumulative distributions of the two samples is large enough, it is evidence for rejecting H_0.

In order to apply the Kolmogorov–Smirnov two-sample test, the numerical frequencies of the observations in the two samples to be compared are entered in a table. The numerical frequencies of the observations are then converted to relative frequencies and the relative frequencies are cumulated separately for each sample. Sample sizes, which need not be equal, are designated n_1 and n_2. A constraint on the valid application of the test is that the sample size must exceed forty in both cases. Sn_1 (X) is the observed cumulative step function of one of the samples, and Sn_2 (X) is the observed cumulative step function of the other sample. The maximum absolute difference between the two cumulative distributions is then determined according to the formula:

$$D = \text{maximum} | Sn_1(X) - Sn_2(X) |.$$

Stated more simply, one determines at what point the two cumulative distributions differ by the largest amount; this is D.

The level of significance (a) for the Kolmogorov–Smirnov test as applied in this report has been set arbitrarily at 0.001. This means that the probability of Type I error (rejecting H_0 when in fact it is true) is less than or equal to 0.001. A result leading to erroneous rejection of H_0 occurs only once in a thousand times due to chance alone. With some qualifications (for example, an increase in the probability of a Type 2 error), the level of significance expresses the amount of confidence that can be placed in the decision to accept or reject H_0.

When D has been determined, a table of critical values of D (Siegel 1956:279) is consulted in order to determine a value (Cr) for samples of sizes n_1 and n_2, at specified a levels. The formula used to determine Cr at the 0.001 level of significance is

$$1.95 \sqrt{\frac{n_1 + n_2.}{n_1 n_2}}$$

If the observed D is greater than or equal to Cr, H_0 may be rejected at the chosen level of significance, and it is concluded that H_1 applies: the two samples were drawn from different populations. If D is less than Cr, H_0 cannot be rejected.

The following example serves to illustrate the method. Two of the three levels classified as Asturian on the basis of the occurrence of the characteristic pick (A_2 and A_3) are compared according to the overall characteristics of their lithic industries. Table 8 indicates raw counts by type, relative frequencies, cumulative frequencies, and differences by type across the two samples. In Table 8:

$$D = 0.062. \ Cr = 1.95 \sqrt{\frac{111 + 141}{(111)(141)}} = 1.95(.1269) = 0.247.$$

$D(0.062)$ is less than Cr (0.247); H_0 cannot be rejected. It is concluded, if a probability of Type 1 error = 0.001 is acceptable, that the lithic assemblages from A_2 and A_3 have in fact been drawn from populations with identical or closely similar underlying distributions.

Lithic and faunal data were analyzed. Minimal sample size, greater than forty, precluded comparison of the following stratigraphic units with each other or with any other units:

Cut A
Level 3 (fauna)
Level 4 (fauna)

Cut B
Conchero sample (=CS) (lithics)
Level 1 (lithics)

Faunal material was present in sufficient quantity for valid comparison in the units listed below:

A_1 CS (Conchero sample)   A (all levels)
A_2 B_1 B (all levels)

For paired levels, six nonreflexive comparisons are possible, plus the comparison of the Cut A sequence with Cut B. The results of the pairwise comparisons are summarized below, specified as equivalent (=) or not equivalent (≠) in the statistical sense defined above.

Levels Compared	D	Cr	n_1	n_2
$A_1 = A_2$	0.051	0.143	316	451
$A_1 = CS$	0.031	0.118	316	1983
$A_1 = B_1$	0.036	0.122	316	1302
$A_2 = CS$	0.069	0.102	451	1983
$A_2 = B_1$	0.078	0.106	451	1302
$CS = B_1$	0.065	0.068	1983	1302
$A = B$	0.072	0.077	791	3447

From this, it can be concluded that the 1969 excavations sampled a faunistically homogeneous series of levels. In no case was it possible to reject the null hypothesis in the pairwise comparisons presented above. It may be asserted on both faunal and industrial grounds that these levels pertain to Asturian occupations. Whether Levels A_3 and A_4 belong to the same faunal universe could not be ascertained; sample sizes were too small to permit analysis.

Table 8.   La Riera: Kolmogorov-Smirnov two-sample test – an example comparing A_2/A_3 lithics

Type	Cut A, Level 2			Cut A, Level 3			
	Count	Percent	Cum. percent	Count	Percent	Cum. percent	Difference
Nuclei, flint	2	0.014	0.014	2	0.018	0.018	0.004
Nuclei, quartzite	6	0.042	0.056	4	0.036	0.054	0.002
Flakes, flint	35	0.248	0.304	25	0.227	0.281	0.023
Flakes, quartzite	48	0.340	0.644	44	0.400	0.681	0.037
Trimming flakes, flint	6	0.042	0.686	6	0.054	0.735	0.049
Trimming flakes, qte.	11	0.078	0.764	8	0.072	0.807	0.043
Blades, flint	9	0.064	0.828	—	—	0.807	0.021
Blades, quartzite	7	0.050	0.878	1	0.009	0.816	0.062*
Bladelets, flint	4	0.028	0.906	6	0.054	0.870	0.036
Bladelets, quartzite	5	0.035	0.941	7	0.063	0.933	0.008
Burins	2	0.014	0.955	—	—	0.933	0.022
Denticulates, flint	1	0.007	0.962	1	0.009	0.942	0.020
Denticulates, quartzite	2	0.014	0.976	2	0.018	0.960	0.016
Backed bladelets	1	0.007	0.983	—	—	0.960	0.023
Endscrapers	—	—	0.983	4	0.036	0.996	0.013
Notches	2	0.014	0.997	1	0.009	1.005	0.008
Total	111 (n_1)	0.997	0.997	141 (n_2)	1.005	1.005	

* $D = 0.062$

Artifacts were scarcer than faunal material. Retouched pieces and unworked manufacturing debris were placed together to increase sample size. In no case did the number of retouched pieces by themselves exceed forty. Only major types were compared (see also Table 8). Sufficient quantities of worked stone were recovered only from Cut A. All four levels produced lithic counts greater than forty when débitage and retouched pieces were combined. Six nonreflexive pairwise comparisons are possible. Results are given below.

Levels Compared	D	Cr	n_1	n_2
$A_1=A_2$	0.080	0.224	164	141
$A_1=A_3$	0.083	0.240	164	111
$A_1=A_4$	0.088	0.256	164	90
$A_2=A_3$	0.062	0.247	141	111
$A_2=A_4$	0.157	0.220	141	90
$A_3=A_4$	0.165	0.277	111	90

The homogeneity evident in the faunal analysis appears to be confirmed by the analysis of the lithic data. Levels A_1, A_2, A_3, and A_4 are alike with respect to artifactual content; they may be regarded as samples drawn from a single population, at least insofar as variation is accurately measured by the type categories used in this study. The Cut A sequence is assignable to the Asturian. No evidence for the Pleistocene occupations so clearly present in the cave interior was forthcoming from the 1969 excavations.

REFERENCES

ALMAGRO-BASCH, MARTÍN
  1947 "España Prehistórica," in *Historia de España*, Volume 1, Edited by Ramón Menéndez-Pidal, 408–417. Madrid: Publicaciones de Espasa-Calpé.
  1960 *Manual de Historia Universal.* Volume 1 (Prehistoria), 311–317. Madrid: Publicaciones de Espasa-Calpé.
  1963 "El Paleolítico Español." *Historia de España* (third edition). Edited by Ramón Menéndez-Pidal. Madrid: Publicaciones de Espasa-Calpé.
BARANDIARÁN, IGNACIO
  1967 *El Paleomesolítico del Pirineo Occidental.* Zaragoza: Anejo de Caesaraugusta.
BORDES, FRANÇOIS
  1961 Typologie du Paléolithique Ancien et Moyen. *Publications de l'Institut de Préhistoire de l'Université de Bordeaux.* Memoire No. 1, Bordeaux: Imprimeries Delmas.
  1968 *The old Stone Age.* New York: McGraw-Hill.
BUTZER, KARL
  1971 *Environment and archeology: an ecological approach to prehistory* (second edition, revised). Chicago: Aldine–Atherton.
BUTZER, KARL, DANIEL C. BOWMAN
  1971 "Some sediments from Asturian archeological levels from sites in Cantabrian Spain," in *The Asturian of Cantabria: A re-evaluation.* Unpublished Ph.D. Dissertation, University of Chicago.
CLARK, GEOFFREY
  1971a *The Asturian of Cantabria: A re-evaluation.* Unpublished Ph.D. Dissertation. University of Chicago.

1971b The Asturian of Cantabria: subsistence base and the evidence for Post-Pleistocene climatic shifts. *American Anthropologist*, 73 (5):1244–1257.

CONDE DE LA VEGA DEL SELLA
1914   La Cueva del Penicial (Asturias). *Comisión de Investigaciones Paleontológicas y Prehistóricas*, Memoria Núm. 4, Madrid: Museo Nacional de Ciencias Naturales.
1916   El Paleolítico de Cueto de la Mina. *Comisión de Investigaciones Paleontológicas y Prehistóricas*, Memoria Núm. 13, Madrid: Museo Nacional de Ciencias Naturales.
1923   El Asturiense; Nueva Industria Pre-Neolítica. *Comisión de Investigaciones Paleontológicas y Prehistóricas*, Memoria Núm. 32 (Serie Prehistórica Núm. 27). Madrid; Museo Nacional de Ciencias Naturales.
1930   Las Cuevas de La Riera y Balmori. *Comisión de Investigaciones Paleontológicas y Prehistóricas*, Memoria Núm. 38 (Serie Prehistórica Núm. 29). Madrid: Museo Nacional de Ciencias Naturales.

DE SONNEVILLE-BORDES, DENISE
1963   Upper paleolithic cultures in Western Europe. *Science* 142 (3590):347–355.

DE SONNEVILLE-BORDES, DENISE, JEAN PERROT
1954   Lexique Typologique du Paléolithique Superieur. *Bulletin de la Société Préhistorique Française*, 51:327–334.
1955   Lexique Typologique du Paléolithique Superieur. *Bulletin de la Société Préhistorique Française*, 52:76–78.
1956   Lexique Typologique du Paléolithique Superieur. *Bulletin de la Société Préhistorique Française*, 53:547–559.

FREEMAN, LESLIE G.
1973   The significance of mammalian faunas from Paleolithic occupations in Cantabrian Spain. *American Antiquity* 38 (1):3–44.

GONZÁLEZ ECHEGARAY, JOAQUÍN
1966   Sobre la cronología de la glaciación Wurmiense en la Costa Cantábrica. *Ampurias* (28):1–12.

GONZÁLEZ, JOSÉ MANUEL
1965   Localización de un pico asturiense en Luarca (Asturias). *Valdedíos*, 35–39. Oviedo.

GOODMAN, L. A.
1954   Kolmogorov–Smirnov tests for psychological research. *Psychological Bulletin* 51:160–168.

HERNÁNDEZ-PACHECO, F., N. LLOPIS-LLADÓ, F. JORDÁ-CERDÁ, J. A. MARTÍNEZ
1957   *Livret-Guide de l'Excursion N_2 — Le Quaternaire de la Region Cantabrique*. Inqua: Vième Congrès International; Oviedo: Diputación Provincial de Asturias.

JORDÁ-CERDÁ, FRANCISCO
1957   *Prehistoria de la Region Cantábrica*. Oviedo: Diputación Provincial de Asturias, Servicio de Investigaciones Arqueológicas.
1958   *Avance al Estudio de la Cueva de La Lloseta (Ardines, Ribadesella, Asturias)*. Oviedo: Diputación Provincial de Asturias, Servicio de Investigaciones Arqueológicas.
1959   *Revision de la Cronología del Asturiense*. V° Congreso Nacional de Arqueología (1957). Zaragoza: Seminario de Arqueología, Universidad de Zaragoza.

152   GEOFFREY A. CLARK, LINDA R. RICHARDS

KURTÉN, BJÖRN
1968   *Pleistocene mammals of Europe.* Chicago: Aldine.
MARTÍNEZ-ÁLVAREZ, J. A.
1965   *Rasgos Geológicos de la Zona Oriental de Asturias.* Instituto de Estudios Asturianos, Oviedo: Excma. Diputación Provincial de Asturias.
OBERMAIER, HUGO
1924   *Fossil man in Spain.* Hispanic Society of America, New Haven; Conn.: Yale University Press.
1925   *El Hombre Fósil.* Comisión de Investigaciones Paleontológicas y Prehistóricas, Memoria Núm. 9 (second edition). Madrid: Museo Nacional de Ciencias Naturales.
PERICOT-GARCÍA, LUIS
1964   Medio Siglo de Prehistoria Hispánica. Barcelona: Publicaciones de la Universidad de Barcelona.
SIEGEL, SIDNEY
1956   *Non-parametric statistics for the behavioral sciences.* New York: McGraw-Hill.
URÍA-RÍU, JUAN
1941   La Caverna de Lledías (Llanes, Asturias). *Archivo Español de Arqueología*, Memoria, Núm. 42. Madrid.
1944   La Caverna Prehistórica de "El Cuetú" Lledías (Asturias) y sus Pinturas Rupestres. Ministerio de Educación Nacional, *Comisaría General de Excavaciones Arqueológicas* — Informes y Memorias Núm. 6. Madrid.

The Sebilian of the Nile Valley: Some New Concepts

FEKRI A. HASSAN

In 1920, the Sebilian was first discovered in the Kom Ombo Plain by Edmond Vignard, who described the industry in a series of articles published betwen 1923 and 1955 (Vignard 1923, 1928, 1934a, 1934b, 1935, 1955a, 1955b). Until the recent work in the Nile Valley during the sixties, the Sebilian was regarded as the major Upper Paleolithic industry in the area. The presence of "Mousterian" discoidal cores and Levallois cores, the predominance of flakes, and the low frequency of the so called "Upper Paleolithic tools" in the Sebilian led to the belief that the Nile Valley was a culturally stagnant area during the Late Paleolithic.

This belief cannot be substantiated any longer as a result of the discovery of many industries rich in blades, burins, backed bladelets, and other typically Upper Paleolithic and Late Paleolithic tools during the 1960's (Wendorf and Said 1967; Smith 1967; Wendorf, Said, and Schild 1970). Recent studies have also provided new data on the Sebilian that necessitate a reexamination of the Sebilian concept as a whole and its place in Egyptian prehistory. The present study is an attempt to achieve this goal and to investigate, in addition, some of the ecological and cultural dimensions of the Sebilian.

The Sebilian as envisioned by Vignard (1928, 1934b, 1955b) consists of three evolutionary stages associated stratigraphically with three flood benches. According to Vignard, the Lower Sebilian is characterized by the predominance of diorite as raw material, "Mousterian" discoidal cores, Levallois cores, a large number of basally truncated flakes with and

Needless to say this study could not have been possible without the excellent analysis of the Sebilian sites from Nubia by Dr. A. E. Marks and Dr. Fred Wendorf. I am also especially indebted to Dr. Wendorf and Dr. Marks, who provided valuable suggestions and criticisms throughout the stages of this work, and who were a source of continuous support and encouragement.

without oblique lateral truncation, a predominance of flakes, and extreme rarity or absence of microburins. The Upper Sebilian, in contrast, is characterized by exclusive utilization of chert, a predominance of opposed platform cores, a low frequency of Levallois flakes, an abundance of microburins, a low frequency of basally truncated and double truncated flakes, and a relatively high blade index.

The Middle Sebilian is regarded as an intermediate stage in the development of the Lower Sebilian into the Upper Sebilian, showing an increase in blades, microlith geometrics, microburins, and a decrease in the frequency of Levallois flakes, basally truncated flakes, and double truncated flakes from the former to the latter. In the Middle Sebilian, the raw material utilized is chert and the proportion of opposed platform cores is pronounced. Although Vignard's subdivisions are widely disseminated in the literature, the validity of the subdivision has been questioned by Huzayyin (1941:262), Caton-Thompson (1946:108), and McBurney (1960:144–145).

Smith (1966) has affirmed the reality of Vignard's Lower Sebilian. The study, now under way, of a number of Sebilian sites from Kom Ombo by Smith promises some modifications, particularly in the delineation of the Upper Sebilian (Smith 1966:37; Butzer and Hansen 1968:165). It is interesting to note here that sixteen newly discovered sites in Nubia and Upper Egypt were found to be more similar to Vignard's Sebilian I (Lower Sebilian) than to any other stage. Although in some sites the frequency of microburins is high, the overall tool and core typology supports neither the line of development suggested by Vignard nor any other line of evolutionary change of considerable magnitude.

Although the so called "Upper Sebilian" could be in part phyletically related to the "Lower Sebilian," the differences between the two outweigh the similarities. The link between the "Middle Sebilian" and the "Upper Sebilian" is also weak, considering that the "Upper Sebilian" elements are rare to absent and that the possibility that sites are mixed cannot be excluded. In fact, without a preconceived evolutionary framework, the Upper Sebilian can be regarded as a separate industry.

Although a final decision must await the completion of the studies by Smith, the term Sebilian will be used throughout this work to mean essentially Vignard's Sebilian I (Lower Sebilian). To extend this term to an industry rich in microlith geometrics, blades, stylized endscrapers, and opposed platform cores, but poor in basally and double truncated pieces, would be confusing.

The data utilized in the present work come mainly from the detailed studies by Marks (1968) and Wendorf (1968a) on Sebilian sites from Nubia, and those by Hassan (i.p.) and Hassan and Wendorf (i.p.) on sites from Upper Egypt. The locations of these sites are shown in Figure 1. The codes for the sites are as follows:

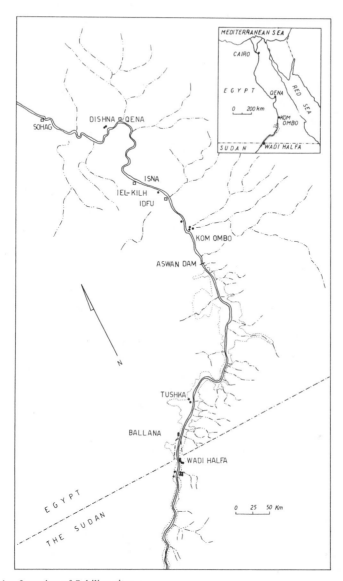

Figure 1.   Location of Sebilian sites

Second Cataract Region: 1042, 2010A, 2010B, 83, 2013, 1024A,
    1024C, 81, 2005 (Marks 1968),
Tushka, Egyptian Nubia: 8886 (Wendorf 1968a),
Ballana, Egyptian Nubia: 8899A, 8899B, 8898 (Wendorf 1968a),
Dishna, Upper Egypt: E61M1A, E61M1B (Hassan i.p.), and
El-Kilh, Upper Egypt: E71P3 (Hassan and Wendorf i.p.).

CHRONOLOGY OF THE SEBILIAN

The Sebilian was regarded by Vignard (1934b:174) as an Upper Paleolithic industry contemporaneous with the Aurignacian and Magdalenian in Europe. Caton-Thompson (1946:117), partially in agreement with Vignard, considered the Sebilian as being contemporaneous with the "Cave Mousterian and Chatelperronian." Recent reassessment of the Pleistocene geology of the Nile Valley and the application of the radiocarbon technique, on the other hand, indicate that the Sebilian dates between ca. 13,000 B.C. and ca. 9,000 B.C. (Smith 1967:146–147; Wendorf 1968b:1048; Wendorf and Schild i.p.).

In Nubia two radiocarbon dates, 9,050 ± 120 B.C. (WSU–144) and 8,975 ± 140 B.C. (WSU–188), are available in association with site 1024A (Marks 1968:468). Site 1024C, in a similar stratigraphic position to 1024A, is probably contemporaneous with it. Both sites are therefore partially contemporaneous with the Post-Sahaba recession of Wendorf and Schild (i.p.). Other sites from the Second Cataract region in Nubia are most probably contemporaneous with the Sahaba Aggradation (Marks 1968:469), which dates between ca. 12,000 B.C. and 10,000 B.C. (Wendorf and Schild i.p.). The sites from the Ballana area are believed also to be contemporaneous with the Sahaba Aggradation (Wendorf, personal communication). The site at Tushka, in a similar stratigraphic position to the Ballana sites (Wendorf 1968a:947), is probably also contemporaneous with the Sahaba Aggradation.

In the Kom Ombo Plain three dates, 12,000 + 1,190, — 1,400 B.C.; 10,690 ± 320 B.C.; and 11,240 ± 340 B.C. were obtained on shells associated with *in situ* artifacts comparable with Vignard's Sebilian I and II (Smith 1967:147). Two other dates, 11,610 ± 120 B.C. and 11,120 ± 160 B.C., are probably indicative of the age of an assemblage described as Sebilian II from an *in situ* occurrence near Gebel Silsila (Smith 1967:147). Butzer and Hansen (1968:163–164), on the other hand, associate Sebilian I and II with Channel A of the Gebel Silsila Formation (ca. 15,000–12,500 B.C.) and Sebilian III with Channel B of the same formation (ca. 12,000–10,000 B.C.). Since the exact location of Sebilian I in the sediments of Channel A is unknown, the oldest Sebilian sites at Kom Ombo may date at ca. 14,000–13,000 B.C. or at most at ca. 15,000 B.C.

At El-Kilh and Dishna, the sites are dated by the help of a burnt silt layer which serves as a chronostratigraphic marker (Wendorf, Said, and Schild 1970). This layer, dated at 10,550 ± 230 B.C., is located stratigraphically in the upper part of the Sahaba Formation. At El-Kilh the site is located directly below this layer, whereas at Dishna the sites are located directly above it.

In sum, the Sebilian is firmly dated by radiocarbon dating between ca.

12,000 B.C. and 9,000 B.C. The lower range of the Sebilian on the basis of stratigraphic evidence may, however, be dated at ca. 13,000 B.C. or at most ca. 15,000 B.C.

THE LITHIC ARTIFACTS OF THE SEBILIAN

Raw Materials

The kinds of raw materials utilized for the manufacture of Sebilian tools, though limited by the locally available materials, indicate a specific pattern of selectivity. In Nubia, for example, most of the Sebilian artifacts are made on ferruginous sandstone. Little or no use is made of the riverine flint pebbles which are widely utilized in most of the Upper and Late Paleolithic in the area (Wendorf 1968b:1048). Sebilian sites in Nubia also contain artifacts made on dacite and meta-quartzite, but the frequency of these materials is generally low (see Table 1). Two sites (2010A, 1042), however, have a high content of dacite and meta-quartzite. In Nubia, the ferruginous sandstone is available from the inselbergs of the Nubia Sandstone bordering the Nile (Marks 1968:474). The dacite and meta-quartzite, on the other hand, are available from the limited outcrops of the basement complex or from old Nile gravels (Wendorf 1968a:815).

In the Kom Ombo Plain, where ferruginous sandstone is available from the Nubia Sandstone exposures and cobbles of igneous and metamorphic rocks are common in old wadi beds, the artifacts of Sebilian I are made from diorite, porphyritic igneous rocks, quartz, and sandstone (Vignard 1928:200). Sebilian II and Sebilian III, on the other hand, are characterized by the utilization of flint and chalcedony, most probably derived from the old Nile gravels found in abandoned channels.

At El-Kilh and Dishna in Upper Egypt, the material used consists predominantly of chert, which is locally present as bands and concretions in the Lower Eocene limestones (Thebes Formation). It should be noted, however, that the nearest limestone outcrops to El-Kilh are some tens of kilometers northward.

Relative Frequency of Major Artifact Categories

In most of the Sebilian sites, débitage flakes, tools, and debris are the most frequent constituents. Primary flakes and cores are usually far less frequent (see Figure 2). In a few sites (1042, 2010A, 2010B) the frequency of debris is anomalously low. This is mainly a result of deflation (Marks 1968:471), which reduces the numbers of the small chips — the

Table 1. Raw materials utilized at Sebilian sites

	Ferruginous sandstone	Dacite	Meta-quartzite	Diorite	Nilotic flint	Egyptian chert
Second Cataract						
Khor Musa area						
2010A	50.6	40.5	8.9	—	—	—
1042	77.1	11.6	11.3	—	—	—
2010B	81.3	12.1	6.6	—	—	—
1024C	84.8	6.6	8.6	—	—	—
1024A	92.8	4.3	2.9	—	—	—
Jebel es-Sahaba area						
83	97.7	2.3	—	—	—	—
81	94.4	4.7	0.9	—	—	—
2005	94.6	3.4	2.0	—	—	—
2013	96.5	2.2	1.3	—	—	—
Ballana						
8898	100.0	—	—	—	—	—
8899B	98.4	1.5	—	—	0.1	—
8899A	97.5	2.5	—	—	—	—
Tushka						
8866-A	100.0	—	—	—	—	—
Kom Ombo						
Sebilian I	common	—	—	predom-inant	present	—
Sebilian II	present	—	—	present	common	—
El-Kilh						
E71P3	—	—	—	—	5.5	95.5
Dishna						
E61M1A and B	—	—	—	—	—	100.0

major component of the debris. Marks (1968:471) has observed also that these sites show anomalous density of artifacts. Excluding these sites, the ratio of debris to cores is between 3:1 to 31:1. The average is 11:1 for all sites (see Table 2). The ratio of blanks to cores is between 5:1 and 28:1 with an average of 17:1.[1] The ratio of primary flakes to cores is between 1:1 and 5:1 with an average of 2:1, a low ratio, considering the limited use of primary flakes as retouched tools. According to Marks (1968:473), this may indicate that the cores were prepared somewhere outside the site area.

---

[1] The term blanks is used here to denote both unretouched and retouched Levallois and non-Levallois flakes and blades. The blank-to-core ratio is therefore a measure of the productivity of the core technique used, given a wide margin of error.

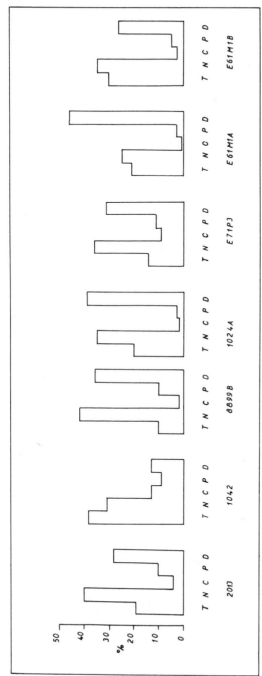

Figure 2.   Histograms showing frequency of lithic artifact categories in Sebilian sites (*T*: tools, *N*: non-Levallois débitage, *C*: cores, *P*: primary flakes, and *D*: debris [chips and chunks])

Table 2.   Ratio of various flaking products to cores

	Second Cataract							Ballana	Kilh	Dishna	
	1042	2010A	2010B	83	2013	1024A	1024C	8899B	E71P3	E61M1A	E61M1B
Blanks: cores	5 : 1	8 : 1	13 : 1	19 : 1	15 : 1	28 : 1	18 : 1	26 : 1	6 : 1	30 : 1	22 : 1
Primary flakes: cores	1 : 1	1 : 1	1 : 1	4 : 1	3 : 1	2 : 1	1 : 1	5 : 1	1 : 1	3 : 1	2 : 1
Debris: cores	1 : 1	2 : 1	2 : 1	5 : 1	7 : 1	20 : 1	17 : 1	18 : 1	3 : 1	31 : 1	9 : 1

Table 3.   Major core types in Sebilian sites

Cores	Kom Ombo	Second Cataract									Tushka	Ballana			Dishna		Kilh
		1042	2010A	2010B	2005	83	81	2013	1024A	1024C	8886	8899A	8899B	8898	E61M1A	E61M1B	E71P3
Discoidal	+	49	38	13	23	21	6	15	10	20	9	1	5	4	1	1	16
Levallois	+	14	5	2	11	13	2	4	7	5	3	1	2	1	1	4	54
Single platform		3													1	1	2
Opposed, double platform	+	10		2					1								6
Crossed, double platform						1			1								
Marginal						8		3									1
Unpatterned and others		23	25	10	46	16	6	15	4	25			3		3		6
Total		99	68	27	83	59	14	37	23	50	12	2	10	5	6	6	85

Cores

Discoidal cores are the most frequent, followed by Levallois-flake cores
(see Table 3). Opposed platform cores, single platform cores, and 90°
(crossed) cores (*à plans croisés*) are extremely infrequent.

The discoidal cores are usually flat, ranging in size from 35 to 100
millimeters, with an irregular, oval outline. In Nubia, the discoidal cores
are made on sandstone tablets (*plaquettes*) and occasionally on small
cobbles (Marks 1968). The discoidal cores in the Sebilian sites are similar
to those from Nubia, except for the raw material used. They are also
similar to those reported by Vignard (1923). The discoidal cores from
El-Kilh, on the other hand, are smaller, ranging in size from 20 to 40
millimeters. These cores are made on small cobbles, resembling those
designated as "discoidal cores, Type II" by Marks (1968:490).

Levallois flake cores are generally unstylized. Some of these cores
appear as if they were "a compromise between a true Levallois core and a
flat 'Mousterian' discoidal core" (Marks 1968:488). These cores are
predominant at El-Kilh.

Single platform cores are recorded in one site only in Nubia, but are
present in all the three sites in Upper Egypt. Opposed platform cores are
more frequent in Nubia than single platform cores. Both, however, are
rare. In Kom Ombo, according to Vignard (1923), this core type appears
first in Sebilian II.

In addition to the above standard types, a high percentage of the cores
are unpatterned. Bifacially flaked *plaquette* fragments, so called "marginal cores," are present in three Nubian sites (Marks 1968).

Débitage

The flaking products (*débitage*) in all Sebilian sites consist mainly of
non-Levallois flakes and debris. Blades and Levallois flakes are not
abundant (see Table 4). The average indices for these two components
are 5.2 and 11.5, respectively. It is interesting to note that the relative
frequency of Levallois cores, 21.4 percent, is higher than that of Levallois
flakes. This may be related to the lower productivity of the Levallois
technique.

Faceting platforms in preparation for the detachment of flakes was
common (see Table 4). In general, the faceting index for the Nubian
assemblages is higher than that of the assemblages from Upper Egypt.
This is probably related to the better quality of the raw material used in
the latter.

Table 4. Technological indices of Sebilian sites

Index	Second Cataract									Ballana		Tushka Kilh		Dishna	
	1041	2010A	83	2013	2010B	2005	81	1024A	1024C	8898	8899B	8886	E71P3	E61M1A	E61M1B
IL	13.8	10.9	14.3	10.9	13.6	22.2	11.1	15.1	9.8	3.8	6.9	2.2	7.1	15.1	16.3
IF	77.6	75.3	70.7	75.7	78.4	61.4	63.9	63.1	56.8	73.2	71.6	85.0	47.4	54.8	45.3
IFs	45.9	46.1	46.2	48.6	52.8	37.9	42.7	35.0	31.9	51.1	55.0	66.2	22.4	39.8	24.6
Ib	4.7	7.1	3.7	4.2	2.3	2.9	7.9	5.1	4.1	5.0	3.7	5.1	3.6	11.5	6.5

Key: IL: Levallois index; IF: faceting index; IFs: restricted faceting index; and Ib: blade index (for definitions see Marks 1968:467)

Tools

The Sebilian is characterized by the abundance of truncations and the paucity of other tool types. Notches and denticulates are common minor constituents. Backed macrolithic flakes and microburins, a diagnostic débitage product generally grouped with tools, are also common minor elements. Endscrapers and burins, also rare, are present in 50 percent of the sites. Sidescrapers and perforators are still more scarce, being present in only 30 percent of the sites (see Table 5).

Most of the tools, with the exception of truncations, are generally unstylized. Notches and denticulates are produced by retouched and unretouched notching; burins by blows parallel to the axis struck from both snapped and truncated platforms; and endscrapers by poor retouch. The perforators were formed by alternated retouch.

Microburins are particularly common in sites 1024A, 1024C, 8898, and 8899B. The first two sites date at ca. 9,000 B.C. and belong thus to the later part of the Sebilian. Microburins are not, however, absent completely from older sites. Sites 8898 and 8899B, for example, belong to the Sahaba Formation, and probably date at least at 11,000 B.C. Microburins are absent in Sebilian I at Ezbet el-Sebil. In Sebilian II, microburins amount to 1.9 and 3.0 percent at Burg el-Makkazin and Ezbet el-Sebil, respectively (Vignard 1955b).

Truncations in all Sebilian sites are manufactured on flakes. Truncated blades are rare. The flakes are generally between 30 and 50 millimeters in size (see Figure 3), except at El-Kilh where the flakes average 23.8

Table 5. Relative frequency of major typological elements (in percent)

	LEV	N and D	ES	SS	BK	T	PERF	BU	GEOM	MICBU	Total
E7 1P3	22.4	5.2	2.6	—	9.5	60.3	—	—	—	—	100.0
E6 1M1	32.6	15.2	—	—	—	50.0	—	2.2	—	—	100.0
E6 1M1A	29.1	17.7	2.5	—	2.5	40.5	1.3	5.1	1.3	—	100.0
88 86	3.6	3.6	—	—	4.3	86.2	—	—	—	2.2	99.9
10 42	24.9	5.2	—	0.7	6.6	61.9	—	0.4	—	0.4	100.1
20 10A	15.2	2.8	1.4	1.4	4.7	71.6	—	0.5	—	2.4	100.0
83	25.3	7.7	0.6	—	6.9	57.0	0.6	0.4	—	1.5	100.0
20 10B	16.8	5.4	2.0	1.0	3.0	66.5	0.5	0.5	—	4.9	100.6
20 05	32.3	7.0	3.5	0.7	2.1	51.4	—	—	—	2.8	99.8
81	16.0	2.1	—	1.1	3.2	74.5	—	—	—	3.2	100.1
20 13	24.2	7.0	0.5	—	3.7	62.3	—	—	—	2.3	100.0
10 24A	16.7	5.0	0.3	—	4.2	58.8	—	—	—	15.0	100.0
10 24C	18.0	2.9	—	—	1.5	64.6	—	0.5	—	12.6	100.1
88 98	24.5	1.5	—	—	5.1	45.4	—	—	—	23.5	100.0
88 99B	37.1	2.5	—	—	0.8	43.9	—	1.7	—	13.9	99.9

Key: LEV: Levallois elements; N and D: notches and denticulates; ES: endscrapers; SS: sidescrapers; BK: simple backing; T: truncations; PERF: perforators; BU: burins; GEOM: geometrics; and MICBU: microburins.

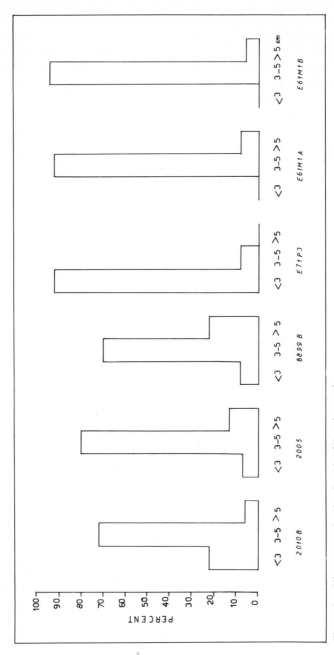

Figure 3.   Histograms showing length of Sebilian tools

millimeters. The truncations are generally formed by steep retouch (80–85 degrees), with squamous, medium- to coarse-sized scars. Oblique truncations are predominantly located on the left side (Marks 1968:477–479) both in Nubia and Upper Egypt. This could be a result of a consistent manufactural habit. Since the retouch is predominantly produced by a force directed from the ventral side, this habit may have consisted of holding the blank in the left hand with the bulbar side toward the workman, assuming right-handedness.

On the basis of shape, the truncated flakes belong to three major classes (see Figure 4). The modal type in the first class consists of a

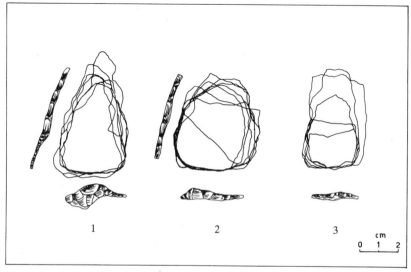

Figure 4.   Modal types of the shape of Sebilian truncated flakes (E61M1A, E61M1B) include type 1 (triangular flake); type 2 (broad flake); and type 3 (elongated flake)

triangular flake with basal truncation and/or left-sided, oblique truncation. The angle between the truncations is about 65 degrees; the basal truncation is straight, and the length/width ratio of the piece is ca. 1.4:1. The modal type in the second class consists of a broad flake with a basal truncation with or without backing. The piece usually has a length/width ratio of ca. 1.1:1. The third class is typified by an elongate flake (length/ width ratio of ca. 1.8:1) usually with a basal truncation only. Typologically, truncated and backed pieces can be broadly classified into three major subclasses: (1) basal truncations, (2) oblique (distal and lateral) truncations plus simple backing, and (3) double truncations plus basal truncations and backing.

The relative frequency of these categories (see Figure 5) reveals an overall similarity, although the range of variation is about 30–40 percent. Three subclusters, in fact, may be identified: the first includes 2005, 83,

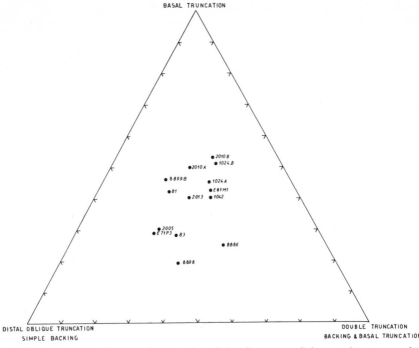

Figure 5.   Ternary diagram showing the relative frequency of three major groups of truncated pieces

E71P3, and 8898; the second includes 2010A, 2010B, 2013, 81, 1042, 1024A, 8899B, and E61M1; and the third consists of 8886 only. Although these subclusters may represent stylistic differences, random variability cannot be excluded on account of the small numbers of the truncated pieces in individual assemblages. The average content of truncated pieces is about 120, with a range between 23 and 266 pieces. This allows for about ±8.5 percent as an average confidence interval at a confidence level of 0.05.

INTERSITE FUNCTIONAL VARIABILITY

The Sebilian sites display a uniform predominance of truncated pieces and an extremely low frequency of other tool classes (see Table 5). The frequency of the major subclasses of truncations is, in addition, quite similar (see Figure 5). Moreover, the frequency of other tool classes shows considerable homogeneity (see Figure 6). Notches and denticulated pieces are the predominant minor constituents in most of the assemblages. Only in three samples — 2005, 2010B, and 2010A — is the frequency of notches and denticulates closely matched by that of

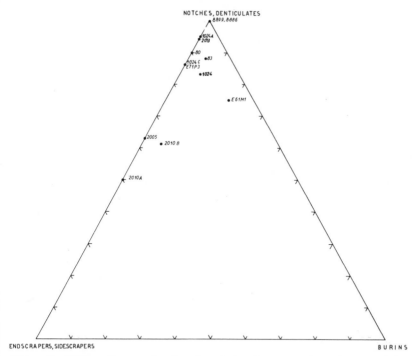

Figure 6. Ternary diagram showing the relative frequency of notches/denticulates, endscrapers/sidescrapers, and burins

endscrapers and sidescrapers. Although it is conceivable that these sites represent areas where a different activity was carried out, any statement on functional variability, on account of the exceedingly small numbers of the tools involved, cannot be strongly emphasized.

The overall similarity in the proportions of the lithic categories, the size of the sites (which will be discussed in the following pages), and in the frequency of various tool categories indicates that similar activities were probably carried out in most of the sites. There is no compelling reason to suspect that there is any significant functional variability between the sites.

THE TAXONOMY OF THE SEBILIAN

Comparison between the major tool categories using an "average link clustering" technique (Parks 1970) shows that the Sebilian sites belong to one major cluster (see Figure 7). Site E61M1A is the least similar to other sites. This is particularly emphasized when the factor measurements are unweighted (see Figure 7A), but when the factor measurements are weighted according to percent of total variance accounted for by each

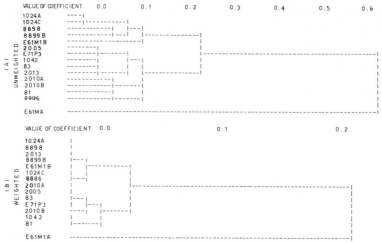

Figure 7. Q-mode dendrograms showing coefficient of similarity between Sebilian sites

factor, E61M1A falls with the other sites at a high level of similarity. Table 5 shows that E61M1A is close to 83. It differs from most other sites in its relative richness in denticulates and notches and the presence of many of the minor constituents. The clustering technique used calculates the similarity coefficient using the simple distance function

$$D_{1,2} \left[\sum_{i=1}^{M} (X_{i1} - X_{i2}) \frac{2}{M} \right]^{\frac{1}{2}}.$$

Each sample is compared with all other samples across all variables to produce a Q-mode similarity matrix. Figure 7 is a copy of the dendrogram plotted by the line printer as part of the output. The data used are those listed in Table 5.

THE SEBILIAN TOOLKIT

Truncated pieces represent the most common specialized and stylized tools in the Sebilian "kit." The rest of the tools, sparse and poorly made, constitute a cluster not unlike that described by Binford and Binford (1966) as an unidentified toolkit, consisting of endscrapers, sidescrapers, burins, and perforators. Standard point types are only represented by unretouched and retouched Levallois points in small numbers. Large cutting tools are absent. Unretouched flakes are twice as abundant as tools, and were probably utilized.

This combination of notches, denticulates, perforators, sidescrapers, and unretouched flakes constitute a kit oriented mainly toward cutting, shredding, and other light duties, probably, involved in food preparation and the manufacture of wooden tools. The predominant truncations, on the other hand, pose a problem. Vignard (1923) viewed these tools as "points." However, the distal end of the truncated flakes is not usually sharp. If these tools were used as "points" they were probably hafted on spears used at a close distance.

The high frequency of distal breakage (about 50 percent of all flakes are broken distally), in contrast with the low frequency of lateral and basal breakage (both account for 7.5 percent), indicates that the pieces were subjected during their use to a force diagonal or perpendicular to the distal segment of the flake. This could happen if the pieces were used for stabbing or chiseling with the distal edge. Some pieces also show pseudo-burin breaks, which are common to used projectile points as a result of hitting an impenetrable surface, for example, bone or rock, at a high force. Other pieces show in addition to the distal break a diagonal basio-lateral break, which could have resulted from breaking the edge against a hard surface, inducing a shock wave from a haft.

Truncated pieces could have been used for splitting, using the unmodified edge, either hafted or unhafted. The exact manner of hafting is difficult to reconstruct because of the peculiarity of the diagonal truncation. The predominance of truncated pieces in Sebilian sites, where several activities were apparently carried out, suggests that these tools could have been multifunctional.

THE SEBILIAN: SOME ECOLOGICAL AND CULTURAL ASPECTS

Sebilian sites vary in size from 60 square meters to 400 square meters, with the exception of one site which covers 5,000 square meters (Marks 1968:471). Sites larger than 60–70 square meters, however, show a progressive decrease in the density of artifacts per square meter as the area of the site increases. The large sites show also a low frequency of debris, which consists mainly of small, light chips. It seems thus that the increase in the area of those sites is mainly a result of deflation, which leads to spreading the artifacts on a large area leading to a decrease in the density of artifacts.

Chips and other small debris would also suffer from selective removal because of their lighter weight. This suggests that the sites, regardless of the size of their present area, may have had an original area of about 60–70 square meters. Cook (1972) has estimated that minimum space requirements for a single person are on the order of four square meters. The total area of the sites thus may have been occupied by two or three families. It is interesting to note here that the scatter pattern of artifacts in one of the Nubian sites (Marks 1968: Figure 31) shows two major clusters, each of which can be covered by a circle, 2.5 meters in radius and 20 square meters in area.

The Sebilian sites must have been loci for some stone-working activity judging by the presence of cores, debris, and primary flakes, but it cannot be stated that these sites were primarily workshops because of the high density of tools, the low frequency of core-trimming flakes, and primary flakes. The sites do not seem, either, to represent transient specialized kill sites.

The presence of bone fragments in several sites, some systematically broken (Butzer and Hansen 1968:164), on the other hand, may indicate that processing of animal food was carried out at these sites. The presence of hearths and fire pits (Vignard 1923:5–13; Butzer and Hansen 1968:163; Marks 1968:512) seems to confirm this conclusion. It is not unlikely, thus, that the Sebilian sites were multiactivity sites serving as stations for stone-working, food-processing, shelter, and other domestic activities, that is, home-base campsites.

The subsistence pattern of the groups that dwelt in these sites can be inferred from the faunal remains which have been described by Gaillard (1934), Gautier (1968), and Churcher (1972). These remains consist mainly of *Bos primigenius* (wild cattle), *Alcelaphus buselaphus* (bubal hartebeest), *Equus asinus africanus* (Nubian wild ass), *Gazella dorcas* (Dorcas gazelle), and *Gazella rufifrons* (red-fronted gazelle). Although catfish remains (*Clarias anguilaris*) were identified in Middle Sebilian sites (Gaillard 1934; Churcher 1972), they are absent in Sebilian I. They are also absent in all the Nubian sites and the other sites from Upper Egypt, though they are common in many other Upper and Late Paleolithic sites in these areas (Greenwood 1968). The major subsistence activity therefore seems to have consisted of hunting large terrestrial mammals (Wendorf 1968b:1048).

The mammals hunted belong to two main biomes, the wooded, well-watered savanna of the flood plain, which supported herds of wild cattle, and the savanna grasslands surrounding the flood plain, which was preferred by the herds of hartebeest, Dorcas gazelle, and the Nubian wild ass (Churcher 1972:125). The Sebilian sites, at the edge of the flood plain, are centrally located between these two biomes. During the dry season, the hartebeest, gazelle, and Nubian wild ass herds would approach the river and become accessible to the hunters. During the rainy season, as these herds retreat to the wadis outside the flood plain, forays into that area or even relocation of the home-base campsites could have been necessitated. If the latter situation was the case, the Sebilian sites probably represent thus seasonal home-base campsites. The small size of the sites probably also indicates that the sites were not year-round settlements.

The Sebilian sites are encountered along a stretch of about 600 kilometers from the Second Cataract to the neighborhood of Qena (see Figure 1). The overall similarity in the typological and technological aspects of the collections found at these sites indicates a considerable amount of contact between the inhabitants of those sites. Although these peoples were sympatric with others who possessed very different toolkits and technological skills, namely, those with Esnan, Menchian, Qadan, and probably Sebekian, Ballanan, and Silsilian technology (Wendorf 1968b; Smith 1967; Wendorf, Said, and Schild 1970; Wendorf and Schild i.p.) the exchange of technological knowledge and tool designs must have been minimal. The Sebilian differs significantly in its basic manufactural techniques and toolkit from any of these industries. The Sebilian does not also show temporal variability similar to that of the Halfan or the Gemaian/Qadan (Wendorf 1968b).

The absence of good control on the date of each site and the small size of the samples, in fact, makes it difficult to detect any systematic variability. The variability in the numbers of microburins could be either functional or developmental. Two of the sites rich in microburins are dated by radiocarbon at ca. 9,000 B.C. Two other sites, similarly rich in microburins, are not dated chronometrically and their position in the Sahaba Formation indicates that they are older. The two young sites also show a higher ratio of ferruginous sandstone than other sites from the same area. Does this reflect a progressive use of that material? One may be in fact tempted to think that the raw material utilized during the early phases of the Sebilian consisted of ferruginous sandstone and igneous/metamorphic rocks (for example, 2010A and Sebilian I at Kom Ombo), followed by a progressive adoption of the ferruginous sandstone. The utilization of chert as in site E61M1A and other sites north of the sandstone belt could be a later development.

The dating of this site and El-Kilh site indicates an age of ca. 11,000–10,000 B.C. One may even speculate further that this temporal variability in the kind of raw material utilized indicates that the Sebilian was originally developed in an area where igneous/metamorphic rocks are abundant. Since the distribution of the Sebilian sites indicates that the industry was probably confined to northern Sudan and southern Egypt (see Figure 1), this may indicate that the Sebilian spread into the Nile Valley from the southeastern rim of the Sahara, where igneous/metamorphic exposures are numerous. This area with savanna vegetation could have supported large terrestrial animals, namely the hartebeest. As these hunters moved northward and as they became more adapted to the riverine environment they started to make use of its raw materials, namely, the Nilotic flint gravels and the chert slabs in the Eocene limestone formations. This is only *speculative* and does not explain the similarity between some of the aspects of the basic technology of the Sebilian and other older industries in the Nile Valley.

One site which either indicates temporal variability or regional differentiation is the El-Kilh site. The tools in this site are significantly smaller than those in other Sebilian sites and a high proportion of the cores consist of a peculiar Levallois core type, a compromise between the standard Levallois core and the discoidal core. This site, however, does not resemble the predominantly microlithic "Sebilian III." In all other aspects, as we have noted above, it closely resembles other Sebilian sites from Nubia. The Sebilian sites at Dishna show a relatively high frequency of single and double platform cores, a lower faceting index, a higher content of notches, denticulates, and retouched pieces, but are otherwise very similar to the Nubian sites. It should be also noted that the sample size from these sites is low, and that the raw material used is chert.

THE ORIGINS OF THE SEBILIAN

The Sebilian cannot be affiliated with any industry in the Nile Valley or elsewhere because of its unique richness in truncated flakes, its predominantly flake débitage, its discoidal and Levallois cores, and its poverty in tool types, with the exception of truncations. Vignard (1923) maintained that the Sebilian developed out of indigenous Mousterian. Caton-Thompson (1946), on the other hand, regarded the Sebilian as a derivative of the "Levalloisian." Both authors developed their ideas on the assumption, now refuted, that the Sebilian dates back to the early part of the Upper Paleolithic and on the basis of the presence of "Mousterian" discoidal and Levallois cores not unlike those found in the Egyptian Middle Paleolithic. The recent dating of the Sebilian at ca. 13,000 B.C. to ca. 9,000 B.C. means that there is a time gap of at least 15,000 years between the end of the Middle Paleolithic and the beginning of the Sebilian. The specialized character of the Sebilian also does not indicate that the Sebilian is a late "Middle Paleolithic survival."

The Khormusan, an industry dating between ca. 21,000 and 17,000 B.C. and believed to be a continuation of the "Levalloisian tradition" (Wendorf 1968b:1046), does not qualify as a direct "progenitor" (Marks 1968:525). This conclusion is reached on the basis of extremely low index of truncations, and the high index of burins, denticulates, and scrapers. The Khormusan shares with the Sebilian, however, the predominance of flake débitage, the presence of Levallois flakes (the index is higher in the Khormusan), a high index of faceting, and the presence of Levallois and discoidal cores.

Another industry, the Gemaian, associated with the lower part of the Sahaba Formation (Shiner 1968:538), is similar both to the Sebilian and the Khormusan in its richness in flake débitage, but it differs from both by its higher microlithic content, low Levallois index, and the presence of leaf-shaped points. This industry is too close in time to the Sebilian to have contributed to its development. It is also considerably different both typologically and technologically.

These three industries — the Khormusan, the Gemaian, and Sebilian — however, are quite distinct from a group of industries spanning the period between ca. 18,000 B.C. and 12,000 B.C. characterized by opposed platform cores mainly on small pebbles, backed bladelets, a high blade index, and microlith geometrics in various proportions. These industries include the Halfan, the Idfuan, the Fakhurian, the Ballanan, the Sebekian, Complex "D," the Silsilian and Complex "E." These industries have some affinities to the Ibero-Maurosian (Wendorf 1965; Smith 1967; Wendorf 1968b; Wendorf, Said, and Schild 1970; Wendorf and Schild i.p.).

It should be, however, stressed that these sites show great typological and technological variability and are not related except in a most general way. By comparison, however, the Sebilian is closer to the Khormusan than to any of these industries. But, although the Khormusan shares some basic technological aspects with the Sebilian there is no direct link between the two. The Khormusan, in fact, shows an evolutionary trend in a direction widely divergent from the Sebilian (Marks 1968:387). The few similarities between the Sebilian and the Khormusan — an industry recalling some elements of the Levalloisian tradition — suggest, however, that the Sebilian could be at least in part a product of an industry of the same tradition as the Khormusan.

To date no firm connection between the Sebilian and any extra-Nilotic group is established, although the double truncations of the Sebilian recall the *petits tranchets* of the Tshitolian of West Africa and the Central African Republic (Marks 1968:525–531). The *petits tranchets* are, however, stylistically different, consisting generally of two parallel distal and basal truncations instead of the basal and lateral, oblique truncation of the double truncated pieces of the Sebilian. The Tshitolian is also characterized by biconical cores, cone-bottom discoidal cores, lanceolate bifaces, leaf-shaped points, core-axes, hand-axes, choppers, picks, core choppers — all absent in the Sebilian. The faceting index of Tshitolian flakes is also much lower than that of the Sebilian (an excellent review of the Tshitolian may be found in Clark [1963]). The Tshitolian cannot be much older than the Sebilian, since the earlier Tshitolian is dated at ca. 12,000 B.C.

Therefore, if the similarity between the Sebilian and the Tshitolian is not a matter of convergence, an alternative suggested by Marks (1968:528), both industries may have been influenced by an older industry that is yet to be unearthed in the area west of the Nile between the Second Cataract and the West African forest, along the southeastern rim of the Sahara. This area, with savanna vegetation during the Late Pleistocene, could have supported a relatively high biomass of herbivores, providing an area favorable for hunting.

It should be noted that connections between the western fringe of the Nile Valley in Nubia and northern Sudan and West Africa are suggested by the presence of assemblages related to the Sangoan/Lupemban or Lupemban at Khor Abu Anga and near the Second Cataract in northern Sudan (Marks 1968:530). The Tshitolian, however, shows strong affiliation to the Lupemban and seems to be part of a long-standing West African tradition — the Sangoan/Lupemban/Tshitolian tradition. The Sebilian could only have been slightly influenced by this tradition because of the basic differences involved. More work in the southeastern fringe of the Sahara and on the eastern fringe of the Nile in northern Sudan in the future may throw more light on the problem of the origin of the Sebilian.

The clues available so far only suggest that the Sebilian is not derived from the northern part of the lower Nile basin, that it has no close relationship to industries known in the Nile Valley, in the Levant, or in Northwest Africa, that it resembles the Tshitolian in the predominance of truncated pieces but is stylistically different, and that it shares a few technological traits with the Middle Paleolithic and Khormusan in the Nile Valley. Partially the problem in attempting to interpret the origin of the Sebilian stems from the fact that the Sebilian is typologically highly specialized, therefore, close affinities with older more generalized industries are hard to establish. Also, the Sebilian could be of mixed indigenous and extra-Nilotic origin, which would pose a serious problem in attempting to derive it from a single industry.

REFERENCES

BINFORD, L. R., S. R. BINFORD
  1966   A preliminary analysis of functional variability in the Mousterian of
         Levallois facies. *American Anthropologist* 68(2):238–295.
BUTZER, K., C. L. HANSEN
  1968   *Desert and river in Nubia.* Madison: University of Wisconsin Press.
CATON-THOMPSON, G.
  1946   The Levalloisian industries of Egypt. *Proceedings of the Prehistoric
         Society* 12:57–120.
CHURCHER, C. S.
  1972   *Late Pleistocene vertebrate from archaeological sites in the plain of Kom
         Ombo.* Royal Ontario Museum Contribution 82.
CLARK, J. D.
  1963   *Prehistoric cultures of northeast Angola and their significance in tropical
         Africa.* Lisbon: Subsidies para a Historia, Arqueologia e Ethnografia
         des Povos da Lunda. Museu do Dundo.

COOK, S. F.
1972 *Prehistoric demography.* (Module 16.) Reading, Mass: Addison-Wesley.

GAILLARD, A.
1934 *Contribution à l'étude de la faune préhistorique de l'Égypte.* Lyon: Archive Musée d'Histoire Naturelle, Volume 14, Mémoire 3.

GAUTIER, A.
1968 "Mammalian remains of the northern Sudan and Southern Egypt," in *The prehistory of Nubia.* Edited by F. Wendorf. Dallas: Southern Methodist University Press.

GREENWOOD, P. H.
1968 "Fish remains," in *The prehistory of Nubia.* Edited by F. Wendorf. Dallas: Southern Methodist University Press.

HASSAN, F. A.
i.p. Note on Sebilian sites from Dishna. *Chronique d'Égypte.*

HASSAN, F. A., F. WENDORF
i.p. *A Sebilian assemblage from El-Kilh, Idfu.*

HUZAYYIN, S.
1941 *The place of Egypt in prehistory.* Cairo: Mémoir de l'Institut d'Egypte, v. 43.

MARKS, A. E.
1968 "The Sebilian industry of the Second Cataract," in *The prehistory of Nubia.* Edited by F. Wendorf. Dallas: Southern Methodist University Press.

McBURNEY, C. B. M.
1960 *The Stone Age of northern Africa.* Harmondsworth, Middlesex: Pelican Books.

PARKS, J. M.
1970 *Fortran IV program for Q-mode cluster analysis on distance function with printed dendrogram.* Computer Contribution 46, State Geological Survey. Lawrence: The University of Kansas.

SHINER, J. L.
1968 "The Khartoum Variant Industry," in *The prehistory of Nubia.* Edited by F. Wendorf. Dallas: Southern Methodist University Press.

SMITH, P. E. L.
1966 New prehistoric investigation at Kom Ombo (Upper Egypt). *Zephyrus* 27:31–45.
1967 New investigations in the late Pleistocene archaeology of the Kom Ombo Plain (Upper Egypt). *Quaternaria* 9:141–152.

VIGNARD, E.
1923 Une nouvelle industrie lithique: le Sébilien. *Bull. Institut Français d'Archéologie Orientale* 21:1–76.
1928 Une nouvelle industrie lithique: le Sébilien. *Bull. Société Préhistorique Française* 25:200–220.
1934a Les microburins Tardenoisiens du Sébilien. *Congrès Préhistorique de France*, Tenth Session, 66–106.
1934b Le Paléolithique en Égypte. *Mémoirs de l'Institut Français d'Archéologie Orientale* 66:165–175.
1935 Le microburin est-il Sébilien? *Bull. Société Préhistorique Française* 44:298–313.
1955a Un kjoekkenmödding sur la rive droite du Wadi-Shaït dans le nord de Kom-Ombo (Haute-Égypte). *Bull. Société Préhistorique Française* 52:703–708.

1955b   Les stations et industries Sébiliennes du Burg el Makkazin, Région de Kom-Ombo (Haute-Égypte). *Bull. Société Préhistorique Française* 52:437–452.

WENDORF, F., *editor*
1965   *Contributions to the prehistory of Nubia.* Dallas: Fort Burgwin Research Center and Southern Methodist University Press.
1968a   "Late Paleolithic sites in Egyptian Nubia," in *The prehistory of Nubia.* Edited by F. Wendorf. Dallas: Southern Methodist University Press.
1968b   "Summary of Nubian prehistory," in *The prehistory of Nubia.* Edited by F. Wendorf. Dallas: Southern Methodist University Press.

WENDORF, F., R. SAID
1967   Paleolithic remains in the Nile Valley. *Nature* 215:244–247.

WENDORF, F., R. SAID, R. SCHILD
1970   Egyptian prehistory: some new concepts. *Science* 169:1161–1171.

WENDORF, F., R. SCHILD
i.p.   Late Paleolithic stratigraphy in the lower Nile Valley of Egypt (tentative title).

Notes Toward a Systematization of the Upper Paleolithic in Palestine

J. GONZÁLEZ ECHEGARAY

The importance of the Upper Paleolithic industrial sequence in the Levant is well established. The sequence is possibly crucial for an understanding of the prehistory of the Old World in its entirety. This study is of special interest due to the fact that, despite the efforts of eminent prehistorians, a satisfactory, precise, and coherent scheme of the development of Paleolithic industrial complexes in Palestine has yet to be developed. The situation is aggravated by the fact that there is not even uniformity in basic terminological usage. Naturally, in a paper such as this, I do not pretend to resolve a problem of such magnitude; rather, I present an overview of the present situation and indicate what I suppose may prove to be some fruitful directions that might contribute to the definition and refinement of a basic systematic framework as research progresses in the region.

There have been two fundamental attempts at systematization of the Palestinian sequence in the not-too-distant past. These are the syntheses presented by Neuville (1951) and Garrod (1957, 1962). Actually, Neuville had already sketched his scheme in the *Revue Biblique* some years earlier (Neuville 1934). It is based on his own excavations in the Desert of Judea, realized at the sites of Erq el-Ahmar, Et-Tabban, Umm Naqus, and El-Khiam, as well as in the cave of Jebel Qafzeh in Galilee, and takes account also of the stratigraphic sequence of the Mugharet el-Wad in Mt. Carmel, excavated by Dorothy **Garrod**. According to Neuville, the Upper Paleolithic may be divided into six **stages**, which are called simply, Phase I through Phase VI.

Phase I is characterized by the persistence of relatively large proportions of "Levalloiso-Mousterian" artifact types. There are also abundant elements typical of Upper Paleolithic industries: backed knives, simple endscrapers on blades, burins, especially those made on flakes, and the famous Emireh points, with retouch on the basal part of the ventral surface. To this phase correspond Level B at Et-Tabban, Level E at Jebel Qafzeh, and Level F at Mugharet el-Wad.

In the second phase appear pieces "intermediate between Chatelperron and Gravette points." The retouch on these pieces is not always abrupt; it is sometimes semiabrupt or even flat. Horizons assignable to this phase are Level F at Erq el-Ahmar and Level D at Jebel Qafzeh.

The third phase is characterized by the presence of Font-Yves points and would correspond to Level D at Erq el-Ahmar and possibly to Level C at Jebel Qafzeh and to Level D at Mugharet el-Wad.

The next phase has abundant keeled and nosed endscrapers. Font-Yves points are present but scarce. Backed knives are very rare. Level B at Erq el-Ahmar and Level D at Mugharet el-Wad are characteristic.

In the fifth phase, keeled and nucleiform endscrapers abound, as do angle burins (especially the "oblique burin on a notch") and polyhedral burins. Some microliths appear. Level C at Mugharet el-Wad and Level E at El-Khiam (1933 excavations) are attributed to this phase.

Finally, in the sixth phase, microliths become numerous, and there are abundant endscrapers on blades, normal dihedral burins, and nucleiform endscrapers. This phase appears in Level D at El-Khiam (1933 excavations) and corresponds to Level C at El-Kebarah.

Garrod was relatively uncritical of Neuville's scheme and, with the exception of some small but original modifications, adopted it almost in its entirety. She did, however, attempt to fit Rust's results (1950) at Yabrud to the developmental scheme and, at the same time, proposed new stage designations.

Thus, Neuville's Phase I became the Emiran, represented principally by Level F at Mugharet el-Wad and Level 7 at Yabrud II, as well as sites like El-Emireh (Turville-Petre and Keith 1927; Garrod, 1955), the Abu Halka shelter in Lebanon (Haller 1942–1943) and others. The Emiran is defined as an industry with a "flake and core element which is identical with that of the Upper Levalloiso-Mousterian, associated with blades and blade-cores and curved knife-blades with blunted back which resemble those of the Chatelperronian" (Garrod 1962).

Neuville's second phase is practically eliminated in Garrod's scheme. It "has been found only in a very few sites, where it is poorly represented, and its separate existence is not absolutely certain" (Garrod 1962).

For the third and fourth phases of Neuville, Garrod created a separate period, which she called the Antelian, a name proposed earlier by Menghin and derived from that of the cave of Antelias in Lebanon, where the industry in question was first recognized. Artifact assemblages of the period have quite an Aurignacian allure. Garrod divides the Antelian into two stages: a lower and an upper. The Lower Antelian would be equivalent to Neuville's Phase III, the Upper, to his Phase IV. In the

Lower Antelian, Levalloisian elements that disappear in the subsequent stage still survive. The Aurignacian character of the Upper Antelian is more marked. In general, the Antelian is characterized by keeled and nosed endscrapers, prismatic burins, and blades with marginal retouch. Font-Yves points are numerous in the Lower Antelian. Levels 2–5 of Yabrud II should correspond *en bloc* to this stage; Level 1 at the same site should be Upper Antelian.

Neuville's Phase V becomes the Atlitian, a name Garrod used for this industry from the time it was first discovered at the Mugharet el-Wad (Garrod and Bate 1937). Its principal characteristics are the presence of nucleiform endscrapers and prismatic burins.

Phase VI receives the name Kebaran, by which it was already designated when it was identified at the site of Kebarah (Turville-Petre 1932). Garrod had reservations about the recognition of the Kebaran as the terminal stage of the Upper Paleolithic, recognizing the possibility that it would eventually prove to be a Mesolithic industry.

Neuville's system has admittedly had considerable utility and its merit as a pioneering attempt must obviously be acknowledged. However, it has a major weakness, residing in the fact that it was based primarily on a sequence of poor and generally unrepresentative assemblages found at Erq el-Ahmar in the Desert of Judea. Neuville complemented this primary sequence with first-hand observations made during his excavations of other sites in the same region, but, with one exception, those sites were even poorer in Upper Paleolithic stratigraphy than Erq el-Ahmar. The exception, El-Khiam, is a rich site, but it was inadequately excavated for reasons beyond Neuville's control.[1] Neuville knew the materials from Mugharet el-Wad well, but he only utilized the stratigraphy of that site as a reference point for his scheme rather than as its basis. As a result, the stratigraphic sequences of the most important Paleolithic localities in the Levant can be reconciled with the Neuville framework only with considerable difficulty.

It seems logical that the process to be followed in establishing a classification of the Palestinian Paleolithic should, in principle, have been the contrary one: such a classification should be founded on the ample stratigraphic successions from the principal sites in the region and only afterward should an attempt to fit poorer, less complete sequences to the general scheme be made. Naturally, this procedure is also subject to errors, but it is certainly a preferable alternative, given that conclusions derived from the study of large numbers of artifacts from a relatively complete sequence are always sounder than those obtained from scant collections or sequences in which lacunae abound.

[1] He fell ill during the excavations, which were completed by his foreman, Ibrahim Shabriyeh, who, although highly competent and experienced in fieldwork, naturally lacked the requisite scientific preparation for the direction of such a complicated operation.

The most complete sequences excavated to date in the zone in question come from the Mugharet el-Wad, Ksar Akil, Yabrud, and El-Khiam. The Paleolithic stratigraphy at Mugharet el-Wad was the following, from base to top: Level G = Upper Levalloiso-Mousterian; Level F = Upper Levalloiso-Mousterian at base, "Lower Aurignacian" at surface; E = Middle Aurignacian; D_1 and D_2 = Middle Aurignacian; C = Atlitian (Garrod and Bate 1937). This stratigraphy links with that of the neighboring cave of Mugharet et-Tabun, where Level B coincides with Level G of Mugharet el-Wad: that is to say, both yielded an Upper Levalloiso-Mousterian. From Level B, strata at Tabun, in descending order, were Level C = Lower Levalloiso-Mousterian, Level D = Lower Levalloiso-Mousterian, Level E (with four subdivisions) = Upper Acheulean (Micoquian), Level F = Upper Acheulean, and Level G = "Tayacian" (Garrod and Bate 1937). One may conclude that the two caves together provide one of the world's most complete Upper Pleistocene stratigraphic sequences.

Another site that seems to present a complete Upper Paleolithic stratigraphy is Ksar Akil in Lebanon (Ewing 1947), but, unhappily, its materials have not been adequately studied and published; as yet they are not sufficiently secure for utilization. New excavations by Tixier should restore Ksar Akil to a position of importance.

The third site is Shelter II at Yabrud, in the Syrian Antilebanon. Its Paleolithic stratigraphy was described by A. Rust, the excavator, in the following terms (from base to top): Levels 10–8 = Upper Mousterian, Level 7 = Early Aurignacian; Level 6 = primitive Aurignacian; Levels 5–4 = Middle Aurignacian; Level 3 = recent Aurignacian; Level 2 = recent Aurignacian (Atlitian?); and Level 1 = Final Aurignacian (Micro-Aurignacian). As was the case for the two Mount Carmel sites, this important series is completed with the stratigraphy in nearby Shelter I, as follows (from top to bottom): Levels 2–4 (whose most recent portion is broadly contemporary with Level 10 in Shelter II) = Mousterian; Level 5 = Micromousterian; Levels 6–11 = Mousterian; Level 12 = Final Acheulean; Level 13 = Preaurignacian; Level 14 = Yabrudian; Level 15 = Preaurignacian; Level 16 = Yabrudian; Level 17 = Acheulean; Level 18 = Micoquian; Level 19 = Acheulean?; Levels 20–22 = Yabrudian; Level 23 = Acheulean; and Levels 24–25 = Yabrudian (Rust 1950; Solecki and Solecki 1966, Solecki 1970). This most important stratigraphy and that from the El-Wad/Et-Tabun occurrences comprise the most complete sequences in the region.

The fourth key site for the study of the regional Upper Paleolithic is the terrace of El-Khiam in the Desert of Judea, according to the excavations realized there by the author in 1962. The number of retouched pieces found in the excavation of Upper Paleolithic strata amounts to 8,367 (from a total of 51,125 pieces of all kinds), an indication of the great value of the assemblages for the quantitative definition of the different stages represented in the site. At El-Khiam, the levels that concern us are (from bottom to top): Levels 12, 11_d and 11_c = Primitive Aurignacian; Levels 11_b and 11_a = Middle Aurignacian; Level 10 = Recent Aurignacian; Level 9 = Atlitian; and Levels 8–6 = Kebaran (González Echegaray 1964). Attention is called to the clarity of the stratigraphic succession: despite the fact that El-Khiam is a sloping terrace, the levels were completely distinguishable in color and texture, and the differences were easily followed during excavation. In fact, later laboratory analyses of sediment samples from El-Khiam also show these obvious differences (Pérez Mateos 1966). Other well-stratified Paleolithic sites with levels on an 18 percent slope, comparable to the situation discovered at El-Khiam in 1962, are not infrequent.[2]

In fact, the six-stage system of development of Upper Paleolithic industries envisioned by Neuville does not seem consonant with the information provided by the complex stratigraphic successions just reviewed. Suffice it to say that his supposed Phase II is not represented in any of the more important sites, its only point of reference being the Erq el-Ahmar shelter, Levels F and E, with seventy-six and forty-seven pieces, respectively. It is also claimed to be represented at Jebel Qafzeh and Ksar Akil, sites that have not yet been adequately studied. Phase III, characterized by Font-Yves points, also lacks foundation since such points appear in several clearly distinct stages of the Upper Paleolithic in the Near East and are found in practically all levels at Yabrud and El-Khiam. In Level E at Qafzeh, with Emireh points, considered as representative of Phase I, thirty-five Font-Yves points were found, according to Stekelis (1956). Phase IV is defined on the basis of the presence of high proportions of keeled and nosed endscrapers. But in Level B of Erq el-Ahmar, the type-level according to Neuville, such pieces do not amount to more than 37.6 percent of all endscrapers, a proportion noticeably lower than that found in most Paleolithic levels at El-Khiam, where the index of these types (IGAr) reaches 84.6, 60.4, 47.8, 56.4, and 47.8.[3] As a result, it is evident that this criterion is not simply insufficient to diagnose the supposed fourth phase; it is self-contradictory, since there are more endscrapers of these kinds in earlier levels and fewer in precisely the horizons where they should, theoretically, be most abundant.

The crisis in which Neuville's theory finds itself is clearly evidenced by

[2]   The presence of microliths in the Upper Paleolithic levels has aroused some doubts about a possible contamination of levels, due to the gradient. The doubts are illfounded. Today it is well known that microliths occur throughout the European Upper Paleolithic, from the Dufour bladelets of the Aurignacian 0 to backed bladelets and microburins in the Gravettian and triangles in Magdalenian levels.

[3]   The exceptions to this observation are Level 12, with only sixty-two tools, where IGAr is only 27.3, and Level 9 (Atlitian) where it is 26.2.

the results of the excavations at Yabrud and the most recent work at El-Khiam, data that were, of course, not available to Neuville in 1951.[4] Even Garrod, in her most recent treatment of the question, still did not have the El-Khiam results, although she did incorporate Rust's work on Yabrud and was obviously aware of the difficulties inherent in reconciling Rust's results with Neuville's stages. In fact, in her attempt to maintain the general outlines of Neuville's system, she found it necessary to resort to a series of dangerous transpositions. Rust had tried to establish a reasonable equivalence between strata at Yabrud II and Mugharet el-Wad. According to Rust, Level 7 at Yabrud (Early Aurignacian) should be equated with Level F at El-Wad; Yabrud Level 6 would be without equivalent in the Carmel stratigraphy; Level 5 would correspond to Level E; Level 4 would correlate with El-Wad D_2; Level 3 with D_1, and Level 2 would be comparable to El-Wad Level C.

Garrod clearly saw that these correlations could not be reconciled with Neuville's scheme, since in each Yabrud level from 5 to 2 there were Font-Yves points. On the other hand, Level 2 itself is very rich in keeled scrapers, a condition that obliged her to place it more closely in relation to Neuville's Phase IV. As a result, the ample stratigraphy of Yabrud II had necessarily to be compressed by Garrod in the following way: Level 7 at Yabrud = Level F at El-Wad, Level 6 = without equivalent at El-Wad, Levels 5–2 at Yabrud = Level E at El-Wad, and Yabrud Level 1 = El-Wad Levels D_2 and D_1. "Je suis convaincue" — she says — "que la succession de l'abri II est moins complète qu'il ne le croit" (Garrod 1957).

Given the renewed excavations of El-Khiam, it is no longer possible, in my opinion, to continue to maintain the old Neuville-Garrod system. Above all, it is essential that terms that have direct referents in the European Paleolithic industrial sequence be abandoned. Such terms — particularly the terms Chatelperronian and Aurignacian, the latter employed first by Garrod and Bate (1937), later by Rust (1950) and myself (González Echegaray 1964) — do an injustice to the individualistic nature of industrial complexes in the Near East. In this respect we agree completely with the observations of F. Hours (1966). Neuville's work, from this viewpoint, was praiseworthy in avoiding misleading terminological usage. Garrod, as we have seen, proposed a new nomenclature that, for the moment, seems viable and that I have adopted on one occasion (González Echegaray 1963). For the Preaurignacian stage — to which I shall return presently — she proposes the name Amudian (Garrod and Kirkbride 1961). The equivalent of the European Chatelperronian is called the Emiran (Garrod 1955). What we might correlate with the typical Aurignacian is designated the Antelian (Garrod 1957). The ter-

[4] A note in Neuville's text says: "Je corrigeais les dernières épreuves de ce travaille lorsque me parvint le tres important ouvrage d'Alfred Rust . . ." (1951:260).

minal phase of the Upper Paleolithic, already very specialized, would be the Atlitian (Garrod and Bate 1937). Finally, in my opinion, as an early Mesolithic industry, we have the Kebaran (Turville-Petre 1932). I have utilized these designations in an attempt to formulate a new classification of the different stages of Paleolithic development in the Levant. However, it is necessary to forget, in major part, the content and stratigraphic correlations of the industries described by Garrod under these names, since her system was crippled by its excessive faithfulness to the classification proposed by Neuville.

AMUDIAN

This industry was first identified in Yabrud Shelter II by Rust, who called it "Preaurignacian" (Rust 1950). It has been studied by Bordes (1955, 1960). Garrod identified it later in Levels E_b and E_a at Mugharet et-Tabun, intercalated with the Acheuleo-Yabrudian (Garrod 1956), an observation later confirmed by Jelinek (Jelinek *et al.* 1973). Garrod also identified it in Mugharet ez-Zuttiyeh, and discovered an intact level at the Zumoffen Shelter on the Lebanese coast (Garrod and Kirkbride 1961). It is evident that ample series of the so-called Levalloiso-Mousterian were found above the Amudian (itself atop the Yabrudian) in Yabrud and Et-Tabun, as well as on the Lebanese coast, if, as seems undeniable, the site of Ras el-Kelb is the chronological continuation of Zumoffen (Garrod and Henri-Martin 1961). The dating of the Levalloiso-Mousterian in the Levant is problematical. While Bordes (1960) assigns it to the Würm II/III interstadial, and the subsequent Würm III stadial, which would make it contemporaneous with the earliest European Upper Paleolithic, Garrod thought it older — the equivalent of Würm I/II — an opinion that seems to agree better with the few radiocarbon dates from the region, for example, the date of 55,000 B.P. for Ras el-Kelb. Zeuner maintained that Abri Zumoffen corresponds to the "storm beach" of the 6 meter terrace, which would equate with the Würm I/II interstadial (1961). Recently, W. Farrand has asserted that the Amudian level at Tabun (E) corresponds to that interstadial, so that the Yabrud "Preaurignacian" would be placed at the beginning of the following stadial during which the Levalloiso-Mousterian developed also (1972). The date for the Amudian that would agree best with present evidence would therefore be the Würm I/II interstadial, with isolated and ephemeral survivals into the subsequent stadial. This is a very early date, which can still not be said to be completely secure. Date notwithstanding, the Amudian is an industry of undoubted Upper Paleolithic type, albeit primitive, and has great similarities to the later "Aurignacian." Bordes showed that there is less difference between the Amudian of Yabrud I and Level 7 (Aurignacian) of Yabrud II than between the latter and Level 6, also classified as Aurignacian. The industry is characterized by an abundance of blades, keeled and nosed endscrapers, and a significant number of burins (especially angle-burins and burins on retouched truncation) as well as different kinds of blades with continuous "nibbled" retouch along the edges. It is clear that the Amudian is older than any other yet-known Upper Paleolithic industry in Europe. Possibly, as has been suggested, the Amudian marks the arrival in the Levant of the first waves of Aurignacian industries, which later were absorbed by the local Levalloiso–Mousterians; such waves would naturally arrive in the Levant before they were felt in Europe (Aurignacian 0) during the Würm II/III interstadial.

EMIRAN

Following the Levalloiso-Mousterian, in which there can be noted certain survivals of Upper Paleolithic forms, the Emiran complex appears. Emiran industries include backed knives, abundant angle burins, and Emireh points, whose identification and exact classification seem, in my opinion, to require revision. As is known, the latter are triangular points, (Levallois points according to Bordes) the bases of which have been retouched on the ventral as well as the dorsal surfaces. During the Emiran, there is a persistence of such "Mousterian" types as sidescrapers. Sites with Emiran horizons include Mugharet el-Wad, where the industry was not sufficiently well stratigraphically differentiated from the Levalloiso-Mousterian found in contact with it in Level F. It also appears, probably well stratified, in Ksar Akil and Abu Halka. According to Neuville's description (1951), collections from Level E at Jebel Qafzeh and Level B at Et-Tabban, both with Emireh points, belong here. The eponymous site of Mugharet el-Emireh (Garrod 1955) pertains to this phase, as, perhaps, does the cave of Amud in Galilee, as Watanabe would have it (1968, 1970). Level 7 at Yabrud II has also been compared with El-Wad Level F (Rust 1950), but Bordes (1955) notes its closer typological relationship to Level 15 at Yabrud I (that is to say, the Amudian). In any case, there is at least one atypical Chatelperron in this level, and it could chronologically have accumulated during the time when the Emiran period was developing in the Levant, as a case of independent and convergent cultural development.

The Emiran was regarded skeptically by Stekelis, who denied that the Emireh point is a valid "guide fossil" (1956). Recently, Bar-Yosef and Vandermeersch, who consider that all "Emiran" occupations are disturbed, have removed the phase from the industrial sequence in Palestine (1972). Nevertheless, such criticisms must be received cautiously, since the geological proofs offered are quite debatable. For the moment, it seems prudent to continue using the term Emiran for an early phase of the Upper Paleolithic which frequently has Chatelperron points (as Garrod did). Besides, the phase seems well represented outside Palestine in Lebanon (Levels XXV to XXI at Ksar Akil, Levels IVe and IVf at Abu Halka and Levels VII to V at Antelias (Hours, Copeland and Aurenche 1973). Any subdivision within the Emiran would be premature. The Emiran should correspond to the end of the Würm II/III interstadial, immediately following the Levalloiso-Mousterian. The case would parallel that of the European Chatelperronian. The fauna at Emireh, including rhinoceros and hippopotamus, seems congruent with such an interpretation. In the stratigraphy of Qafzeh, Level E, which has been called Emiran, also indicates dry conditions.

In continuation, we have the major stage of the Upper Paleolithic of the Near East, quite similar to the European Aurignacian, which, I believe, should be called the Antelian. This corresponds to what is now called Levantine Aurignacian B, since A is a phase restricted to Lebanon (Levels 7 and 9 at Ksar Akil). Doubtless, this represents the second wave of Aurignacian elements to reach the Levant, perhaps from some center in Russia or Anatolia (as Bordes suggested). This wave arrives when its presence has already been noted in western Europe, where it coexists with the Perigordian without mixture. In Lebanon, Syria, and Palestine the Aurignacian complex partly fuses with traditional elements already present in the region — that is, with the Emiran — and, in any case, pursues an autonomous evolutionary course with respect to its more or less distant relatives, the distinct European Aurignacian facies. In the Antelian, in my judgment, three successive stages may conveniently be recognized. These may be called Antelian I, II, and III.

ANTELIAN

In the Antelian I we still have an industry with a strong flake element. Types of "Mousterian" affinities, sidescrapers and denticulates, for example, are abundant, but with them are found numerous endscrapers of clearly Aurignacian type, such as keeled and nosed forms. As for burins, the most frequent type is the dihedral burin, while burins on retouched truncation are far scarcer. Backed elements are rare or nonexistent; but Font-Yves points are found as well as the first Dufour bladelets. As can be seen, almost all these attributes are characteristically Aurignacian. The bone industry includes punches with unworked bases and some handsome specimens with circular cross-section. To this phase may be assigned Level 6 at Yabrud II, El-Wad E, and the complex of Levels 12–11$_d$ and 11$_c$ at El-Khiam. Possibly the site of El-Quseir (Perrot 1955) belongs in the very earliest stages of this phase.

To amplify these observations, some characteristic indices of Level VI at Yabrud II are compared with Level 11_c at El-Khiam, the collection which best represents the complex.

Indexes	Level 6, Yabrud II	Level 11_c, El-Khiam
IG	44.7	34.6
IB	21.5	22.4
IGA	12.1	21
IBd	12.1	15.8
IBt	6.5	5.1
75 (denticulates)	12.1	6.7

For Level E at El-Wad and Level E at Kebarah the endscraper indexes are 58.3 and 51.8 and the burin indexes 21.6 and 5.4 respectively.

The Antelian II is distinguished by a distinct diminution of the Aurignacian endscrapers, especially the nosed forms, with respect to the anterior phase. Font-Yves points also tend to decrease in abundance, at least at El-Wad and El-Khiam. From indices of 7.4 at El-Wad and 14.2 at Kebarah, the level drops to 1.0 at El-Wad and 0.9 at Kebarah. At El-Khiam from 0.7 in Level 11_c it drops to 0.6 in Level 11_b and 0.1 in Level 11_a. In this site, there is an increase of backed pieces and Dufour bladelets. In general, the blade industry is better represented than it was earlier, and "Mousterian" types are less frequent. The bone industry includes oval-sectioned biconical sagaies. Key sites for the Antelian II are Level D_2 at El-Wad, the Level 4–5 complex at Yabrud II, and Levels 11_b and 11_a at El-Khiam. The greater part of the Paleolithic strata at Erq el-Ahmar probably belong to this phase.

It seems that the Antelian II marks the local evolution of an anterior stage with somewhat more typically "Aurignacian" character. The increment of "Perigordian" elements is a noteworthy factor separating Antelian evolution somewhat from the European Aurignacian.

As an illustration, some indices from Level 4 at Yabrud II are compared with those from Level 11_a at El-Khiam. When these figures are contrasted with those for the Antelian I, significant differences may be noted.

Indexes	Level 4, Yabrud II	Level 11_a, El-Khiam
IG	36.1	14.8
IB	25.6	16.2
IGA	7.3	8.3
IBd	13.4	10.1
IBt	4.5	5.0
75 (denticulates)	4.2	3.9

The following phase of industrial development, the Antelian III, sees a rapid disappearance of "Mousterian" elements. For example, sidescrapers decrease. From 4.8 in Level D_2 at El-Wad and 5.2 in Level D_2 at Kebarah, we now find 3.7 at El-Wad and 2.7 at Kebarah. From 2.3 in

Level 11$_b$ at El-Khiam and 1.1 in Level 11$_a$, the index drops to 1.0 in Level 10. The blade industry augments appreciably, and bladelets gradually acquire more importance within that category. Burins on retouched truncation become abundant and are sometimes very handsome. There are also many kinds of combined endscraper-burin. Backed elements seem to diminish, even though they still persist in El-Wad. Typical occurrences would be El-Wad Level D$_1$, Level 3 at Yabrud II, and El-Khiam 10.

In turn, at El-Wad and Kebarah the endscraper index augments greatly, although that does not happen at Yabrud. Once more, we present for comparison some critical indices from the Yabrud and El-Khiam collections, noting that they should be contrasted with those presented earlier. (It must, of course, be remembered that each site has its own peculiarities.)

Indexes	Level 3, Yabrud II	Level 10, El-Khiam
IG	26.9	21.4
IB	30.8	22.9
IGA	8.2	10.2
IBd	20.7	9.7
IBt	5.8	12
75 (denticulates)	7.8	2.4

The Antelian should correspond in general terms with the Würm III. At Qafzeh, levels later than E show an abrupt change to colder climatic conditions. Within the cold stage, there was a period of intense humidity, related to a resumption of the process of karstification. This can be seen in caves with "chimneys," where deposits were deformed by dissolution and collapse of underlying levels. But, in general, conditions were rather dry, as it seems is indicated by the stratigraphy at Qafzeh.

ATLITIAN

Finally, within the Upper Paleolithic, we come to the Atlitian, the characteristics of which separate it somewhat from the Antelian proper, although in a general way the Atlitian still belongs to the "Aurignacian" tradition. In some ways the Atlitian foreshadows developments to come in the rich regional Mesolithic. There are already some microliths, which tend to geometric forms. At times, the keeled endscraper categories diminish notably. In all cases, endscrapers on blades and small circular flakes and, especially, nucleiform endscrapers have increased.

Typical occupations are Level C at Mugharet el-Wad and Level 9 at El-Khiam. Possibly Level 2 at Yabrud II belongs here, as well as the site of Ain el-Quedeirat (Buzy 1929). Level 9 at El-Khiam, which I consider

Atlitian, has been classified by Bar-Yosef as Kebaran Geometric A (1970, 1975). I cannot accept his interpretation, either as concerns the lithics (only 19 percent of the tools are microliths) or as concerns the sedimentology, because neither body of evidence shows any fundamental difference from the preceding level, which all agree is clearly Upper Paleolithic. Attribution of Atlitian development to Würm interstadial III/IV is probably not far wrong, but there is no direct proof of this age at present. The lack of exact data about the latest phases of Würm (Pluvial C) in Palestine does not permit many concrete conclusions, but in any case it seems certain that at that time a process of desiccation set in that continues, despite minor fluctuations, until the present day.

KEBARAN

With the description of the Atlitian, discussion of Upper Paleolithic industries in the Levant has finished; in my opinion, the following Kebaran industry is earliest Mesolithic (González Echegaray 1966). This opinion is based on two considerations: geology and industrial characteristics. In the first place, the Kebaran develops during a postpluvial climatic period with characteristics such as those of present regional climate, as is especially clear at El- Khiam (Pérez Mateos 1966). In the second place, the industry is clearly "Mesolithic": there is a preponderance of microlithic elements, including geometric forms (triangles, trapezes, segments of circles, and such like), as may be demonstrated at either El-Khiam, where such tools make up 40 percent of retouched pieces, or at Kebarah itself. The distinction established by Bar-Yosef (1970), between an earlier simple Kebaran and a later Geometric Kebaran is certainly a fundamental one. Paradoxical though it may appear, the period during which the Kebaran evolves should coincide chronologically with the closing phases of the Pleistocene in Europe. In the El-Khiam terrace, three successive developmental phases attributable to the Kebaran were identified. Each was successively more "Mesolithic"-looking than its predecessor. In its last moments, the Kebaran at El-Khiam was already contemporary with the Natufian.

Schematically, this would be my interpretation of the Upper Paleolithic in Palestine:

Periods	Yabrud II	El-Khiam	El-Wad	Kebarah	Other sites
Atlitian	2	9	C	—	Ain el-Qedeirat
Antelian III	3	10	D_1	D_1	
Antelian II	5–4	11_b–11_a	D_2	D_2	Erq el-Ahmar
Antelian I	6	12–11_d–11_c	E	E	El-Quseir
Emiran	7	—	F	—	El-Emireh, Et-Tabban

REFERENCES

BAR-YOSEF, O.
1970 "The Epipalaeolithic cultures of Palestine." Unpublished Ph.D. dissertation, Hebrew University, Jerusalem.
1975 "The Epipalaeolithic in Palestine and Sinai," in *Problems in Prehistory: North Africa and the Levant.* Edited by F. Wendorf and A. E. Marks. Dallas: Southern Methodist University Press.

BAR-YOSEF, O., B. VANDERMEERSCH
1972 "The stratigraphical and cultural problems of the passage from the Middle to Upper Paleolithic in Palestinian caves," in *The origin of Homo Sapiens.* Proceedings, Paris Symposium, 221-225. Paris: UNESCO.

BORDES, F.
1955 Le Paléolithique inferieur et moyen à Jabrud (Syrie) et la question du Pre-Aurignacien, *L'Anthropologie* 59:486–507.
1960 Le Pré-Aurignacien de Yabroud (Syrie), et son incidence sur la chronologie du Quaternaire en Moyen Orient. *The Bulletin of the Research Council of Israel* 9G (2–3):91–103.

BUZY, D.
1929 Une station magdalénienne dans le Negueb (Ain el Qedeirat). *Revue Biblique* 38:364–381.

EWING, J. F.
1947 Preliminary note on the Excavations at the Palaeolithic Site of Ksar Akil. *Antiquity* 21:186–197.

FARRAND, W. R.
1972 "Geological correlation of prehistoric sites in the Levant," in *The origin of Homo Sapiens.* Proceedings, Paris Symposium, 227–235. Paris: UNESCO.

GARROD, D. A. E.
1955 The Mugharet el- Emireh in Lower Galilee: type station of the Emiran industry. *Journal of the Royal Anthropological Institute* 85:1–22.
1956 Acheuléo-Jabroudien et "Pré-Aurignacien" de la Grotte du Taboun (Mont Carmel); étude stratigraphique et chronológique. *Quaternaria* 3:39–59.
1957 Notes sur le Paleolithique Supérieur du Moyen Orient, *Bulletín de la Société Préhistorique Française* 54:439–446.
1962 An outline of Pleistocene prehistory in Palestine-Lebanon-Syria. *Quaternaria* 6:541–546.

GARROD, D. A. E., D. M. A. BATE
1937 *The Stone Age of Mount Carmel,* volume 1. Oxford: Oxford University Press.

GARROD, D. A. E., G. HENRI-MARTIN
1961 Rapport préliminaire sur la fouille d'une grotte au Ras el Kelb. *Bulletin du Musée de Beyrouth* 16:61–67.

GARROD, D. A. E., D. KIRKBRIDE
1961 Excavation of the Abri Zumoffen, a Paleolithic rock-shelter near Adlun, South Lebanon, 1958. *Bulletin du Musée de Beyrouth* 16:7–45.

GONZÁLEZ ECHEGARAY, J.
1963   Nouvelles fouilles á "El Khiam," *Revue Biblique* 70:94–119.
1964   *Excavaciones en la terraza de "El Khiam" (Jordania), I. Estudio del Yacimiento y los niveles paleoliticos.* Madrid: Biblioteca Praehistórica Hispana.
1966   *Excavaciones en la terraza de "El Khiam" (Jordania) II, Los niveles meso-neoliticos, estudio de la fauna, flora y análisis de las tierras del yacimiento.* Madrid: Biblioteca Praehistórica Hispana.

HALLER, J.
1942–1943   L'Abri de Abou Halka (Tripoli), *Bulletin du Musée de Beyrouth* 6:1–20.

HOURS, F.
1966   Bibliographie, *Mélanges de l'Université Saint-Joseph* 42:291–292.

HOURS, F., L. COPELAND, O. AURENCHE
1973   Les industries paléolithiques du Proche-Orient. Essai de corrélation. *L'Anthropologie* 77:229–280, 437–496.

JELINEK, A. J., W. R. FARRAND, G. HAAS, et al.
1973   New excavations at the Tabun cave, Mount Carmel, Israel, 1967–1972: a preliminary report. *Paléorient* 1:151–183.

NEUVILLE, R.
1934   Le Préhistorique de Palestine, *Revue Biblique* 43:237–259.
1951   *Le Paléolithique et le Mesolithique du Desert de Judée.* Paris: Archives de l'Institut de Paléontologie Humaine. Memoir. 24.

PÉREZ MATEOS, J.
1966   "Estudio mineralógico y morfoscópico de unas muestras de tierras procedentes del yacimiento de El Khiam (Jordania)," in *Excavaciones de la Terraza de "El Khiam' (Jordania), II, Los Niveles mesoneoliticos. Estudio de la Fauna, Flora y Análisis de las tierras del yacimiento.* J. González Echegaray. Madrid: Biblioteca Praehistórica Hispana.

PERROT, J.
1955   Le Paléolithique supérieur d'El Quseir et de Masar an Na'aj (Palestine). *Bulletin de la Société Préhistorique française* 52:493–506.
1968   La préhistoire palestinienne. *Supplément, Dictionnaire de la Bible.* Volume 8:286–446.

RUST, A.
1950   *Die Höhlenfunde von Jabrud (Syrien),* Neumünster: Offa-Bücher.

SOLECKI, R.
1970   "A sketch of the Columbia University archaeological investigations at Yabrud (Syria)," in *Frühe Menschheit und Umwelt.* I (Fundamenta A, 2), 199–211.

SOLECKI, R., ROSE SOLECKI
1966   New data from Yabroud, Syria. Preliminary report of the Columbia University Archaeological investigations, *Annales Archéologiques Syriennes* 16(2):121–153.

STEKELIS, M.
1956   Nouvelles fouilles dans la grotte de Kebara. *Congresso Internacional de Ciencias Prehistóricas y Protohistóricas, Actas de la IV sesión, Madrid 1954,* 385–389. Zaragoza.

TURVILLE-PETRE, F.
1932   Excavations in the Mugharet el-Kebarah, *Journal of Royal Anthropological Institute* 62:270–279.

TURVILLE-PETRE, F., A. KEITH
   1927   *Researches in prehistoric Galilee 1925–1926, and a report on the Galilee skull.* London.
WATANABE, H.
   1968   "Flake production in a transitional industry from the Amud Cave, Israel, A statistical approach to Paleolithic Techno-typology," in *La Préhistoire, Problemes et Tendences,* pp. 499–509.
   1970   "A Palaeolithic industry from the Amud Cave" in *The Amud man and his cave site.* Edited by H. Suzuki and F. Takai, 77–114. Tokyo.
ZEUNER, F. E.
   1961   The shore line chronology of the Paleolithic of Abri Zumoffen, Adlun caves, Lebanon. *Bulletin du Musée de Beyrouth* 16:49–60.

The Upper Paleolithic in North-Central Eurasia: Evidence and Problems

EDITH M. SHIMKIN

This paper was written with a two-fold purpose in mind. The first was to examine selected sites on the Russian plain, in north Russia, the Urals, and western and central Siberia, for specific similarities and differences in various features such as dwelling remains, burials, art, and so on within the overall Upper Paleolithic culture of the area. The treatment of these similarities and differences among sites has necessarily been selective, depending on available information and the immense span of both time and area encompassed. The majority of the sources used were Russian-language sources published within recent years, with additional reference to general background studies in English such as those of Coles and Higgs (1969) and Butzer (1964).

As indicated, the emphasis has been on features such as dwelling

The author wishes to express her appreciation to Professor Ralph T. Fisher, Jr., Director, Russian and East European Languages, for provision of typing and Xeroxing costs. Thanks are also due to Professor Clark E. Cunningham, Chairman, Department of Anthropology, for providing office space. Professor Eugene Giles, Department of Anthropology, kindly reviewed the materials pertaining to possible domestication of the wolf in the Ukraine. Mr. James A. Bier, cartographer, Department of Geography, prepared the map (Figure 1) and gave other technical assistance. Mr. Ben Parker, Department of Anthropology, Photo-laboratory, made the photographs of the illustrative material (Figures 2, 3, and 4). Mrs. B. A. Gudauskus, stenographic services, typed the manuscript, tables, and site list. The author also wishes to thank Professor D. B. Shimkin, Department of Anthropology, for many helpful suggestions and criticisms, assistance in the evaluation of source materials, and joint preparation of data for the map and site list. All of the above are at the University of Illinois at Urbana.

The initial research involved in the preparation for the paper was begun during the academic year 1970–1971, at the Center for Advanced Study in the Behavioral Sciences, Stanford, California. The help of Dr. O. Meredith Wilson, director, and the generous provision of office space and other facilities of the Center are gratefully acknowledged. Also the author wishes to express appreciation to Dr. Henry Field, Miami, Florida, who made available the Soviet radiocarbon date lists subsequently published in translation in *Radiocarbon* (1968, 1970, 1972).

remains and hearths, burials (although the data on Upper Paleolithic burials are generally scanty), faunal remains and estimates of viable group size, bone tools and weapons, and art, rather than on stone typologies. This last cultural feature is treated briefly in a section written by Demitri B. Shimkin. However, definitive qualitative and quantitative evaluations of the relationships between stone typologies require the judgments, based upon examination and classification of the actual tools, of experts in the field. Radiocarbon datings, mostly obtained in Soviet laboratories, which are available for some sites, are given in the site list, Appendix 1.

The second purpose is to determine, on the basis of the data presented in this paper, the particular problems that require solution, insofar as existing and new information permits, and to define further the relationships between the Upper Paleolithic of European Russia and Siberia. Hence, both the data in this paper and the tentative conclusions at the end should be regarded as furnishing a basis for further discussion and interpretations, taking into account always the continuing and extensive investigations of the many Soviet scientists involved with these complex problems.

NOMENCLATURE: GLACIAL AND INTERGLACIAL PERIODS

Soviet nomenclature for glacial and interglacial periods in both European Russia and Siberia differs somewhat from that generally in use in western Europe and the United States. For the area of the Russian plain, the Riss-Würm (or Eem) Interglacial is called the *Mikulino*; for Siberia, it is termed the *Kazantsev*.[1] The following, final (Upper Pleistocene) glacial epoch in the Old World, generally called the Würm, is often referred to as the *Valday* (with stadials), in European Russia. However, some Soviet scientists, simultaneously or alternatively, use the western term. Additionally, the first phase of the Valday is sometimes called the *Kalinin* Glaciation with oscillations, and the final glacial phase, the *Ostashkov*, which was preceded by an intervening interglacial called the *Mologo-Sheksnya*, or *Bryansk interval*, is tentatively equated with the Paudorf (ca. 30–25,000 B.P.). Warm intervals, occurring within the early Valday (or Kalinin) are referred to either as "warm periods" or by the western terms — Ammersfort and Brørup.

For Siberia, the first Upper Pleistocene glaciation is called the *Zyryanka* and its final phase, the *Sartan*. The interglacial period preceding the onset of the Sartan is referred to as the *Karginsk*. However, Cherdyntsev *et al.* (1969) have proposed the term *Karginsk Interglacial*

[1] With a few minor exceptions, the transliteration system used throughout this paper is that of the U.S. Board on Geographic Names.

Complex for a somewhat longer period, beginning about 45,000 B.P. with alternating cold and warm phases (including the "Karginsk proper") and ending at about 25,000 B.P. with the onset of the Sartan. The proposed term was based on the authors' conclusions after reviewing radiocarbon datings primarily for the area of central Siberia obtained by the laboratory of the Geological Institute of the USSR Academy of Sciences. The terms Bølling and Allerød for the warm periods of the terminal Pleistocene are also commonly used by Soviet scientists.

RADIOCARBON DATING

In addition to the radiocarbon datings of archeological samples obtained for some (but not all) of the Upper Paleolithic sites in the Soviet Union (cited in Appendix I), a great many geological samples pertaining to the Upper Pleistocene have been obtained and published by Soviet laboratories.[2] These date descriptions, as well as those still available only in Russian-language publications (mainly *Geokhimiya* and the Bulletin of the Commission for the Study of the Quaternary Period, *BKIChP*), contain details of the stratigraphy of the particular location where the sample was obtained, presumed geologic age, relevant palynological analyses, and evaluation of the result in conjunction with other datings. A new laboratory of the Siberian Branch of the USSR Academy of Sciences at Novosibirsk (SOAN) is now obtaining extensive datings for the river systems of western Siberia, especially for the upper and middle reaches of the Ob' and Irtysh systems, so far little studied by other Soviet laboratories.

CRITICAL FEATURES OF THE PALEOGEOGRAPHY

While the map of north-central Eurasia during the Upper Paleolithic (see Figure 1) is necessarily generalized and encompasses, of course, an immense area, it is believed that it reflects the major features of the paleogeography of the region at about 20,000 B.P.[3]

As indicated, the Fenno-Scandian and Ural ice caps were not joined. In Siberia, in addition to the Taymyr ice cap, there was mountain glaciation

---

[2] A number of these have been published in the United States, particularly Cherdyntsev *et al.* (1968 — Geological Institute, USSR Academy of Sciences, GIN); Vinogradov *et al.* (1966, 1968 — Vernadsky Institute, Mo); Arslanov (1968 — Khlopin Institute, Le); Arslanov, Gromova, and Rudneyev (1968 — All Union Geological Institute, LC); and Punning, Liiva, and Ilves (1968 — Turtu Laboratory, TA).

[3] Sources used in compiling the map are listed separately at the end of the References; for technical reasons it was not possible to include on the map the entire western portion of the USSR.

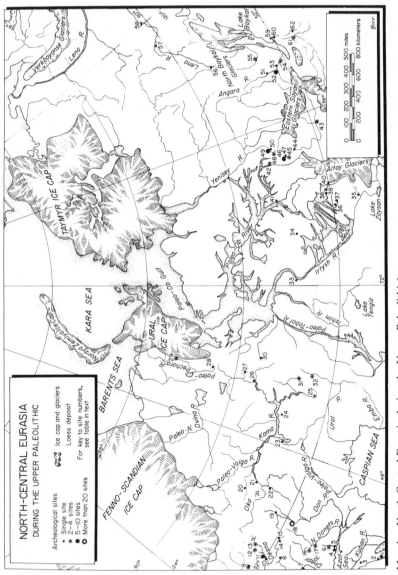

Map 1.   North-Central Eurasia during the Upper Paleolithic.[a]

in the Altay, Sayan, Baykal, and Verkholensk systems. While the Fenno-Scandian ice cap was very thick, with a maximum depth in its central portion of 2.5 to 3 kilometers (Grichuk *et al.* 1966:5), the Ural ice cap probably did not exceed 300 meters in height and the edge of the Taymyr ice cap is believed not to have exceeded some 50 meters in height.

Meltwaters from the ice caps (as well as the mountain glaciations of Siberia) formed glacial lakes and flooded the river systems. The Volga and Kama systems and the Caspian basin received meltwaters from the Fenno-Scandian ice cap. The corresponding late Valday transgression of the Caspian is called the Late Khvalinsk, which was not particularly extensive, with a rise in level of about two meters (Kvasov 1966:179). To what extent previous glaciations coincided with transgressions in the Caspian-lower Volga region or whether the periods of greatest flooding were connected with interglacials and the retreat and melting of the ice

Key to Map 1:
1. Akhshtyr Group
2. Vorontsov Cave
3. Il'skaya Camp
4. Muralovka
5. Mar'yeva Gora
6. Amvrosiyevka Group
7. Dneprovo-Kamenka
8. Gontsy Settlement[b]
9. Grensk Group
10. Mezin Settlement
11. Pushkari Settlement Group
12. Yeliseyevichi Settlement Group
13. Timonovka Settlement Group
14. Avdeyevo Settlement
15. Kursk I
16. Sharukanskaya Group
17. Min'yevskaya Group
18. Kostenki-Borshevo Settlement Group
19. Gagarino Settlement
20. Sungir'
21. Karacharovo
22. Podsosenka Verkhnyaya
23. Undory Site
24. Deukovskaya
25. Kapova Cave
26. Talitskiy
27. Bliznetsova Cave
28. Bear Cave (Medvezh'ya Peshchera)
29. Byzovaya Settlement Group
30. Bear Rock Cave (Medved' Kamen' Grot)
31. Yuryuzan Cave Group
32. Smelovskaya Cave Group
33. Chernoozer'ye
34. Vol'chya Griva
35. Bukhtarma Cave (Malyy Grot)
36. Tuekta
37. Ust'-Kanskaya Cave
38. Biyisk
39. Srostki Camp
40. Ust'-Kuyum
41. Tomsk Camp
42. Achinsk
43. Angachi Camp Group
44. Buzonovo I
45. Bateni (Tashtyk) Camp Group
46. Kokorevo Camp Group
47. Ulazy
48. Biryusa Camp Group
49. Afontova Gora Settlement Group
50. Pereselencheskiy Punkt Settlement (?)
51. Krasnyy Yar
52. Mal'ta Settlement Group
53. Buret' Settlement
54. Irkutsk Camp (?) Group
55. Makarovo Camp Group
56. Chastinskaya
57. Nyuya
58. At-Daban
59. Sannyy Mys
60. Oshurkovo
61. Nyangi Camp (?) Group
62. Dureny

[a] Compiled by D. B. Shimkin and E. M. Shimkin, University of Illinois, Urbana (see Bibliography for map sources); cartography by James A. Bier, Department of Geography. University of Illinois, Urbana.
[b] Settlement refers to a site with permanent or semipermanent dwellings.

cap still seems unresolved (Lyubin 1970:21). Hence, just when and for how long there existed the extensive barrier to human movement from European Russia into Siberia postulated by Bader (Lyubin 1970:21) cannot be determined. Likewise, while the water barriers in Siberia, shown on the map, are believed to have existed during the last glacial phase, exact details of their extent and duration are lacking.

Transgressions and regressions in the Black and Azov seas seem fairly well established in relation to glacials and interglacials. The second regression, called the Late Karangat, occurred at the beginning of the Valday, when the level of the Black Sea was 122 meters below its present level. The Novo-Euxine regression occurred during the Ostashkov (Lyubin 1970:21; Velichko, Ivanova, and Muramov 1969:Table 1; Kvasov 1966:178, Figure 1).

Meltwaters from the Ural and Taymyr ice caps, combined with isostatic depression of the west Siberian plain, formed the extensive Paleo-Ob' Gulf and flooded areas of the Paleo-Tobol, Ishim, Irytsh, and Ob' river systems. The southern Irtysh system also received meltwaters from the Altay mountain glaciation. While there was flooding of the lower Yenisey and Lena, their middle and southward reaches (as well as the course of the Angara) approximated those of today. Generally, the dissection or downcutting (*vrezaniye*) of the Russian river systems occurred during periods of glaciation, including the earlier ones of the Middle Pleistocene.

There are, of course, earlier horizons of loess deposited during previous glaciations. In European Russia, loess depositions (shown on the map in hatching) extend north to the basins of the Oka and Kama, south to the Ukraine, and west into areas of central Europe not shown on the map. In Siberia, as indicated, loess areas occur along the upper reaches of the Paleo-Tobol, Irtysh, and Yenisey rivers. The Afontova Gora sites on the upper Yenisey are located in one of these loess areas.[4] There are also loess deposits farther east along the Lena River. These richer soils and associated higher bioproductivity appear to have been significant general determinants of the locations of Upper Paleolithic sites.

In the European portion of the USSR, according to the periodization proposed by Velichko, Ivanova, and Muramov (1969: Table 1), Loess I pertains to the Kalinin (early Valday); Bryansk fossil soil to the Bryansk Interval during the Mologo-Sheksnya; and Loess II and III, separated by a layer of gley or subaqueous soil formation (*ogleveniye*), to the Ostashkov. Above Loess III at the end of the final glaciation is a horizon of late glacial soil, with contemporary soil pertaining, of course, to the succeeding Holocene.

Connected with glacial episodes are the processes related to freezing

---

[4]   For convenience, the Yenisey system south of Krasnoyarsk is referred to as the "upper Yenisey," although it is more properly considered the middle Yenisey by Soviet geographers.

and thawing of the soil — solifluction, cryoturbation, ice-wedge casts, and so on. Fossil soils, peat, plant remains, and wood are sampled to determine their relationship to interglacial or interstadial periods. For example, a sample of plant remains with inclusions of wood fragments from the Terrace of the Yenisey, dated at 32,500 ± 700 by the Geological Institute, came from a sandy layer overlying Zyryanka glacial deposits. These plant remains were associated by Kind and Troitskiy, who collected the sample, with the Karginsk Interglacial; the fact that the layer from which the sample was obtained was disturbed by frost processes indicated to the collectors that it was related to the beginning of the Sartan cooling (GIN–99) (Cherdyntsev *et al.* 1968:434).

Likewise, a number of datings of fossil soils, with disturbances by solifluction and ice-wedge casts (related to the onset of the Ostashkov), from Vladimir Oblast' are near and relevant to the site at Sungir' (Cherdyntsev *et al.* 1968:421–422, 429). Archeologically, however, the study of the site itself has been greatly complicated by the presence of these phenomena because of the disturbance of the cultural horizon.

Another specialized subject of great complexity is the study of the formation of river terraces. Since the majority of Upper Paleolithic sites, both in European Russia and Siberia, as well as those in the Urals, are located on river terraces or ravines opening on to the contemporary floodplains, the interpretation of data bearing on their formation is of great importance to the archeologist. In the section on dwellings (see pages 201–227), the situation of each site discussed is briefly sketched, but for detailed information on the relationship of sites to terrace formation, the reader must turn to the writings of experts in the field; some of these materials are listed in the bibliography.

PALEOCLIMATE, VEGETATION, AND FAUNA

The climatic oscillations of the Upper Pleistocene, as with earlier glacial and interglacial periods, are reflected in what is generally referred to as the periglacial environment. The actual climatic changes involved in these oscillations are only gradually being analyzed in sufficient detail for reliable results. Attempts of this sort have included those of Grichuk (1969) for the central Don region of European Russia and of Sher (1971) for northeastern Siberia.

For the Russian plain, especially its southern portion, data on vegetation during the last phases of the Valday (approximately from 35,000 to 10,000 B.P.) are less full than for the Mousterian period because of the lack of vegetal remains in existing deposits. In the Kostenki region on the Don, however, a series of pollen-analysis diagrams provide sufficient information (although with some omissions) to reconstruct the types of vegetation and from them a model of the climatic oscillations occurring during the Bryansk Interval and the onset of the much colder period of the final Ostashkov Glaciation (Grichuk 1969:58–59).

Very briefly summarized, Grichuk's reconstruction of the climatic changes at Kostenki XVII is as follows:

During the existence of the lower cultural horizon at Kostenki XVII, just prior to, or at the beginning of the Bryansk interval, climatic conditions were more severe than in that portion of the Don at present. Mean July temperatures were approximately 4° and January ones 6° below the present ones (15°C versus 19.8°C; −18°C versus −9.8°C), with a frost-free period of only some three months, and a snow-cover lying for nearly one and a half months longer than at present. (At present, the frost-free period for this region of the Don lasts 138 days; the snow-cover lay [sic] for 150 to 180 days compared with 100 days, while its depth reached 50 centimeters as opposed to 30 centimeters under contemporary conditions.)

In the warm period of the climatic optimum of the Bryansk Interval, climatic conditions changed appreciably: summer temperatures approximated today's with winter temperatures almost 5°C higher, the frost-free period lasted about six months of the year, and the mean duration of the snow-cover was 2.5 months (1969:64–65, Figure 18).

With time the climate worsened, but Grichuk (1969:64) believes that at the time the upper cultural horizon of Kostenki XVII was occupied, the climate was still milder than at present. At the time of the accumulation of the upper horizons of loams correlated with Kostenki I–1, the climate became very severe, with mean January temperatures 8 to 9°C below present temperatures and a corresponding increase in the duration of the snow-cover. At the time Kostenki XIX was occupied, data indicate even more severe conditions, but they are too incomplete to construct a detailed model (Grichuk 1969:65).

On the basis of extensive literature on the study of the region's vegetation, Grichuk has constructed a map (1969: Figure 19) showing the vegetation zones of eastern Europe during the maximum of the final (Ostashkov) glacial advance. This map shows tentative distributions of a general periglacial vegetation, in which the following seven associations are distinguished: (1) a thin birch and larch forest with tundra and steppe groupings adjacent to the ice cap, (2) mountain tundra and Alpine meadows, (3) forest-steppe with birch, pine, and evidently larch forests, (4) steppe with boreal vegetative groupings; (5) forest-steppe with deciduous admixtures; (6) spruce and fir piedmont forests; and (7) mixed forests of the southern upland regions. Of these associations, the most important for man were those of the forest-steppe and steppe.

For a detailed discussion of the periglacial environment as well as the plant associations for Siberia, the reader may consult the relevant passages on Sher's work (1971), to be found in the section on *Faunal remains, hunting specialization and methods, and population estimates* (see pages 235–254). Also, in the same section, data on the environment and faunal associations at Bear Cave in the Urals, as presented by Guslitser and Kanivets (1965), are reviewed. Finally for a discussion of the fauna connected with the Upper Paleolithic sites on the Russian plain as well as in the Urals see the section on *faunal remains* (see pages 237–241).

DWELLINGS

One feature of the Upper Paleolithic mammoth subsistence tradition to which Soviet scientists have devoted increasing attention since the late 1920's has been the excavation and study of permanent or semipermanent dwellings. The site at Gagarino in Voronezh Oblast', discovered by Zamyatnin in 1927, was the first studied in the USSR. Since then, a total of about thirty dwelling remnants have been reported on.

Rogachev (1970b:434) believes that the invention of permanent winter dwellings was necessitated by the combination of a deteriorating winter climate and the absence of caves on the eastern European plain. Pidoplichko (1969:5), on the other hand, emphasizes that mammoth hunting as a subsistence base made possible the existence of permanent or semipermanent settlements, leading logically to the construction of permanent dwellings.

Modifications of cave dwellings dating to Mousterian times are known in the Soviet Union — for example, at Kiik-Koba (hearths) and Chokurcha (mammoth bone collection placed in front of the entrance), both in the Crimea, as well as elsewhere in Europe. Traces of hearths and stone walls were observed by Gorodtsov at Il'skaya *stoyanka* [campsite], an open-air Mousterian site in the North Caucasus.

The first genuine house remains of mammoth bone, however, appear to be at Molodova I on the middle Dnestr, with some indications of possible dwelling remains also at nearby Molodova V, Horizon 11. These remains at Molodova I are in Horizon 4, considered to be late Mousterian. A sample of charcoal from one of the hearths in the dwelling was dated to >44,000 B.P. (GrN–3659; Vogel and Waterbolk 1967:119), while charcoal from Horizon 11 at Molodova V was dated by the same laboratory at >40,000 B.P. (GrN–4017; Vogel and Waterbolk 1967:119). Hence, it appears that dwelling construction of this type was already a feature of Late Mousterian culture on the Russian plain.

General Features

Boriskovskiy (1958:3–19) in his discussion of the study of these dwellings, points out some of their characteristics and problems connected with excavation. Previously many such dwelling remains have gone unrecognized, either because of incorrect excavation methods, destruction, or displacement of the remains as a result of natural processes such as solifluction (as is the case at Sungir') or because of destruction by modern road or building construction, especially since many Upper Paleolithic sites on the Russian plain are located on river banks favorable for human occupation to this day. In addition, Rogachev points out that the excavator must possess a specialized knowledge of Quaternary deposits.

Basically, a "checkerboard square" system of excavation must be followed: each square meter must be excavated and studied before one proceeds to the next. An attempt must be made to delineate the ancient soil surface (*pol* or *pod*) on which the inhabitants lived, as well as to identify the foundation boundaries. Hearths, storage pits, and other intentionally dug depressions, such as occasional graves, extend downward, below the living surface. The ancient living surface is often indicated by its coloration by ashes, charcoal, and especially red ocher. The inventory of flint, bone tools, and their fragments, bone and ivory ornaments and statuettes, small animal bones, bits of charcoal and ocher form the first layer covering the living surface. On top of these remains lie the large bones, skulls, tusks, and reindeer horns that formed the framework and covered the roof. Sometimes bones or tusks were dug vertically into the periphery of the dwelling to form part of the framework and are found in their original position; the same applies when stone slabs were used as construction material. The outline of these two layers of materials theoretically delineates the structure boundaries. In cases where the dwelling floor was dug into the earth below the ancient exterior surface, the remains of the earthen foundation wall thus formed can often be recognized.

However, many difficulties arise. At many sites, particularly in the Ukraine and on the Don, rodent activity may disturb the cultural layer and make the identification of intentionally constructed pits difficult. Soil processes and water action, ice wedge casts, and so on have similar effects. The delimitation of exact boundaries is by no means agreed upon (Klein 1969a: Figure 34). Yefimenko (1958) and Grigor'yev (1967) assign different boundaries to the "long house" at Kostenki I Horizon 1, leading to quite different possible interpretations of the relationship of the peripheral habitation pits to the main structure. The entrance to a dwelling is often tentatively identified by an accumulation of cultural debris and sometimes an open-air hearth just outside the structure, but often an entrance cannot be definitely recognized, although the dwelling orientation may give a clue to the position of an entranceway. Hides covering the dwelling and wooden poles probably used for construction of the framework do not survive; hence, much of the interpretation concerning the exact use of these materials is highly speculative. In some cases, interior hearths appear to be mere patches of ash and charcoal while others are elaborately constructed with draught trenches or lined with stone slabs. Such stone-lined hearths occur at many open-air sites, especially late sites in Siberia; the presence of such a feature, therefore, does not in itself indicate a dwelling.

DWELLING TYPES. Dwellings fall into two major categories. The first is a small round or oval structure with a diameter of four to six meters, with a single hearth, usually in the center. Sometimes these small dwellings were on the surface, sometimes constructed in a shallow excavation.

The second type is the so-called long house, an oval structure of considerably larger dimensions with several hearths, often along the long axis of the dwelling. There are individual variations, however. The dwelling at Pushkari I is believed, from the placement of the three hearths, to have consisted of three round dwellings joined together. Those at Avdeyevo and Kostenki I Horizon 1 had deep and large pits attached. These were believed to be for habitation (as opposed to storage) purposes. In contrast, two of the dwellings at the Siberian site at Mal'ta appear to have been rectangular, dug into the river terrace with the long side opening to the river. The only analogous remains on the Russian plain are at Timonovka, where the remains of six dwellings were rectangular (eleven and a half to twelve by three to three and a half meters) and dug in to 3 to 3.5 meters, each with one hearth either in the center or end of the building (Boriskovskiy 1958:11).

European Russia

SITE 1. The dwelling remains at Molodova I Horizon 4 (also discussed by Klein 1969b:263) contain two rings of mammoth bone; the outer dimensions are ten by seven meters, and the inner ones are estimated to be eight by five meters. There is no information on probable entranceways, internal divisions, or special internal or external features. Eleven patches of ash and charcoal were identified, but no central hearth. The inventory included a large number of flints and broken bones. Large bones used as building material for the framework and as anchors for a roof of skins included twelve skulls, thirty-four flat bones from scapulae and pelvises, more than fifty long bones, fourteen tusks, and five lower jaws. Molodova I, on the Dnestr, has not only the oldest dwelling remnants in the territory of the Soviet Union, but apparently the most westerly. The remains listed in Table 1 are arranged in geographical order, generally running from southwest to northeast.

SITE 2. Mezhirich (Site 2), Dobranichevka (Site 3), Mezin (Site 4), and Gontsy (Site 5) are Upper Paleolithic sites in the Ukraine (all located to the east of Molodova I), which are discussed in great detail by Pidoplichko (1969). In addition to his analysis of these four sites, he devotes a chapter to the material at Kiyevo-Kirillovskoye site, based on the notes and drawings of an earlier excavator, V. V. Khyvoyko, and museum collections, since the site itself, located in Kiev, is now covered by modern buildings. On the basis of this information, Pidoplichko believes that the site contained four round structures built of mammoth bone, each with a central hearth, as well as exterior hearths.

Mezhirich is believed to have been a multidwelling settlement, although only one dwelling has been studied in detail. The site was first excavated in 1966 under Pidoplichko's direction. It lies on a promontory in the area between the Ros' and Rosava rivers in the midst of a stratum of loessal loam with layers of fine-grained sand. This stratum shows less evidence of rodent activity than the overlying loessal loam and contemporary soil which contains extensive rodent burrows. The cultural horizon is at a depth of approximately two and one-third meters from the contemporary surface. Palynological analysis at the site and neighboring ravines showed pine, oak (depth, about four meters), linden, cherry (depth, about one and a half meters), grasses and spores of fern and sphagnum mosses. The faunal complex is of the forest-steppe type with mammoth predominating.

The excavation of the dwelling itself showed that an estimated 385 bones, including large fragments, were used in its construction. The foundation was made of twenty-five skulls, of which twenty-three were dug into the ground to a depth of forty centimeters, with the frontal bones facing inward; pelvic and long bones and earth filled in the interstices between the skulls. The remaining two skulls, dug in only to a depth of twenty centimeters, constituted part of the facade arch. A special outer facing (*obkladka*) of lower jaws and earth strengthened the foundation. The framework above the foundation consisted of twelve skulls of young and half-grown mammoths, plus scapulae, long bones, pelvic bones, and vertebrae. Thirty-five mammoth tusks and other bones found on top of the cultural layer were probably used to anchor a roof made of skins.

The facade arch was evidently made partly of tusks and partly of poles and wattle and probably was screened with skins. An outer wall of mammoth bones apparently served to protect the entrance.

The central hearth was surrounded by mammoth bones dug into the earth, perhaps serving as some sort of spit or other cooking device. Other special internal features were evidence of a "workshop" north of the hearth and a "storeroom" along one wall. Small bits of red and yellow ocher were found inside the dwelling. The inventory included over 300 flint tools and about 4,300 unretouched pieces. The painted mammoth skulls and line drawing on a piece of mammoth ivory from this site will be discussed in the section on art. Stylized statuettes of women made from mammoth ivory, bone, and antler artifacts, pieces of worked amber (found locally and along the Dnepr), a shark's tooth, and shells were also found.

The two exterior hearths may have served as dumps for "kitchen debris," since they contained a significant quantity of flint, bones, ocher, amber, and other objects; they also served as open fireplaces outside the dwelling. The excavator believes the dwelling was abandoned peacefully, probably because of a scarcity of game. (Color photographs [Pidoplichko 1969, Figure 62, opposite p. 138] show the reconstructed framework in the Paleontological Museum of the Ukrainian Academy of Sciences in Kiev.)

SITE 3.   Dobranichevka, which was excavated by Shovkoplyas and Pidoplichko in 1952–1953, is situated to the east of the Supoy River on the Tashanka, a streamlet that flows into the Supoy. The Supoy, in turn, is an eastern tributary of the Dnepr, and its western bank forms part of an ancient loess terrace above the floodplain of the Dnepr. At the time the site was occupied it overlooked the floodplain of the Supoy, which was wooded and an ideal feeding spot for mammoth; this probably explains the site choice, in spite of its northern exposure.

The cultural remains lie in loess at a depth of one and a half to two meters below the present surface and sixteen to seventeen meters above the low floodplain of the Supoy. There is evidence of rodent activity to a depth of about three meters from the surface of the contemporary soil. Most of the rodent bones found at the site belong to a period later than its occupation, although the rodent species found all existed at the time the site was occupied. Mammoth predominated among the faunal remains.

The dwelling itself is round and rather small, compared with those at Mezin (Site 4) and Mezhirich, with an inner area of not more than twelve square meters. Although Pidoplichko (1969) refers to the dwelling as a surface one, its inner floor was actually about twenty centimeters below the outside surface; hence, it is classified here as semisubterranean. As with Mezhirich, the bone foundation was made of ten mammoth skulls and other mammoth bones and earth. The small earthen wall formed by the excavation surrounded the bone foundation. The framework was made up of smaller bones, and, according to Pidoplichko's theories about the dwelling's construction, wooden poles were inserted into openings of the bones in the foundation, thus preserving them better than if they had

Table 1. Remains of Upper Paleolithic dwellings: North-central Eurasia

Site	Form	Surface or semi-subterranean	Entranceways a. Orientation b. Type	Walls and framework: Types	Probable roof structure	Internal divisions	Hearths	Interior pits	Red ocher	Special internal features	Peripheral and/or external features
EUROPEAN USSR											
1. Molodova I Horizon 4 (Late Mousterian), Dnestr River W. Ukraine >44,000 (GrN-3659)	Oval (10×7m)	surface	...	mammoth tusks, skulls and bones	...	...	multiple (11)	...	+	...	...
2. Mezhirich, between Ros' and Rosava Rivers, Cherkassk Obl.	Round (5.5–6m. diam.)	surface	a: S; b: facade arch	mammoth bones and earth; frame of bones and poles(?)	skins; mammoth skulls and tusks	...	single (ca. 50cm diam.)	...	+	+[a]	+ (2 open hearth patches; protective wall); rodent activity
3. Dobranichevka, Tashanka and Supoy Rivers, Dnepr valley, Kiev Obl.	round (ca. 4m. diam.)	semisubterranean (ca. 20 cm. below surface)	a: S(?); b: ...	mammoth skulls and long bones	skins; mammoth tusks	...	single	—	+	...	+ (open hearth; storage pit and wall); rodent activity
4. Mezin, W. bank, Desna River, Chernigov Obl.	round (5.5m. diam.)	semisubterranean (ca. 50 cm. below surface)	a: SE; b: facade arch	mammoth skulls and bones; frame of bones and	skins; mammoth tusks and reindeer antlers	+[a]	multiple (3)	—	+	+ (religious corner)[a]	+ (hearth; storage pits; wall on NE)

5. Gontsy, Uday River, Poltava Obl.	round (ca. 5m. diam.)	surface	a: S; b: facade arch	mammoth skulls; mammoth scapulae and tusks	...	single (70–80 cm. diam.)	−	+	−	+ (open hearth; storage pits)
6. Pushkari I, W. bank, Desna River Chernigov Obl.	compound-oval (12×4m.)	semisubterranean (depth 30 cm.)	...	low earthen wall; mammoth bones and tusks	+ (3 connected dwellings)	multiple (3)[a]	+ (post holes around each hearth)	...	+[a]	...
7. Yeliseyevichi, Sudost' River Desna valley, Bryansk Obl. 33,000±400 (GIN-80)	round (ca. 8m. diam.)	surface	a: ...; b: passageway	mammoth bones	...	single (?)	+	+	...	attached "religious" structure; passageway to river[a]
8. Avdeyevo, Ragozna River br. of Seym, Kursk Obl.	compound-oval (40×15–19m.)	semisubterranean (40–60 cm. below surface)	a: ...; b: corridor type	low earthen wall; mammoth bones and poles	see last column	multiple	+	+	+ (upright long bones indicate "workshops")	attached 2-chambered dugout (zemlyanka) 3.5×2m. with corridor entrance; outer wall of mammoth bone

Table 1. (*continued*)

Site	Form	Surface or semi-subterranean	Entranceways a. Orientation b. Type	Walls and framework: Types	Probable roof structure	Internal divisions	Hearths	Interior pits	Red ocher	Special internal features	Peripheral and/or external features
Kostenki sites Don River Voronezh Obl.:											
9. Kostenki I, Horizon 1, 14,020±60 (GIN-86)	compound-oval (35×15-16m.)	surface	...	mammoth bones	skins; possibly several roofs	+ (habitation dugouts connected to main house by a step)	multiple (11 along long axis; also cooking hearths)	storage pits on floor of long house; post holes; work areas	+	+	12 storage pits; 4 habitation dugouts; remains of adjoining structure
10. Kostenki IV (Aleksandrov-skaya) Horizon 1, W. dwelling.	round (ca. 6m. diam.)	semisub-terranean (max. depth 50 cm.)	a: SW(?) b:[a]	stone slabs; mammoth bones and tusks	skins (?); 2 lion crania[a]	—	multiple[a]	storage pits	+	+	—
11. Kostenki IV, Horizon 1, E. dwelling.	round (6-6.5m. diam.)	semisub-terranean depth, 30-40 cm.)	a: SW(?) b: ...	stone slabs; mammoth bones and tusks; earthen bank on S.	skins(?)	—	multiple (6)[a]	storage pits	+	—	—
12. Kostenki IV, Horizon 2 S. dwelling.	oval (34×5.5m.)	semisub-terranean (av. depth, 20-30 cm.; max. 40 cm.)	a: NE b: step	earthen walls; bones and stones	gabled(?)	+ (2 earthen ridges)	multiple (10)[a]	storage pits (48); post holes (4)	+	+	—

Site	Shape/size	Construction	Orientation	Walls	Roof	Hearth	Pits/postholes			Notes
13. Kostenki IV, Horizon 2, N. dwelling.	oval (23×5.5m.)	semisubterranean (depth, 20–35 cm.)	a: N(?) b: ...	bones and stones	gabled(?)	multiple (9 midline; cooking)[a]	23 (storage and post-holes)[a]	+	...	...
14. Kostenki II, Complex I.	oval (8×6.5m.)	semisubterranean (depth not given)	a: NE(?) b: ...	mammoth bones and tusks	...	single	+[a]	+	—	+ (possible outer fence to NE; pit with burial; bones and hearth patches in Complex II)
15. Kostenki VIII, (Tel'manskaya), Horizon 1.	round (5.2–5.6m. diam.)	semisubterranean (depth, 50–70cm.)	a: W[a] b: ...	earthen wall: mammoth bone	skins and bone supported by earthen wall(?); lion cranium	SW (near entrance)	+ (7[a])	+	+[a]	...
16. Gagarino, E. bank Don River Voronezh Obl.	round (4.5–5.5m. diam.)	semisubterranean (depth, 25–50cm.)	a: NE b: entrance corridor(?)	earthen wall; stone slabs and mammoth bones	skins and bones(?)	single	1 storage	+	...	+ (peripheral storage pit)

NORTH RUSSIA, URALS AND W. SIBERIA[a]

UPPER YENISEY AND ANGARA REGIONS

Site	Shape/size	Construction	Orientation	Walls	Roof	Hearth	Pits/postholes			Notes
17. Afontova Gora II, lower horizon W bank, upper Yenisey River, Krasnoyarsk Kray 20,900±300 (GIN-117)	oval (ca. 10×5–6m.)	semisubterranean (depth, 150–175 cm.)[a]	a: NE(?) b:[a]	earthen walls (slanted to 45°); mammoth bones	...	multiple (?) ... with stones	+[a]	...	+[a]	...

Table 1. (continued)

Site	Form	Surface or sub-subterranean	Entrance-ways a. Orientation b. Type	Walls and framework: Types	Probable roof structure	Internal divisions	Hearths	Interior pits	Red ocher	Special internal features	Peripheral and/or external features
18. Buret' (dwelling No. 2), E bank, Angara River, Irkutsk Obl.	oval (ca. 5-6× 4m.)	semi-subterranean	a: W(?) b: corridor type	earthen walls; stone slabs; bones; inner embankment for poles	probably cupola type	...	multiple (?)	...	...	...	corridor entrance
Mal'ta, W bank, Belaya River, br. of Angara, Irkutsk Obl.											
19. Dwelling A (1956 excavation).	rectangular (ca. 14×6m.)	semi-subterranean (depth ca. 55 cm. at back; 10 cm. at front)	a: NE(?) b:[a]	earthen walls; limestone slabs; mammoth and rhinoceros bones; tusks	mammoth hide(?) supported by poles; held down by antlers	[a]	multiple (3); one lined with stone slabs	+ (storage dug into walls; bone sockets for poles)	+	+ ("male" and "female" sections)[a]	no outside storage pits at Mal'ta sites; debris on terrace slope
20. Third dwelling (1957 excavations).	rectangular (9×3 to 4m?[a])	semi-subterranean	a: NE(?) b:[a]	earthen wall, poles	skins with slabs and antlers	...	surface (20–25 cm. above floor)	+ (1 storage dug into wall)	+	...	...

21. Fourth dwelling (1957 excavation).	oval(?)[a]	surface	a: NE(?) b:[a]	stone slabs; mammoth and rhinoceros skulls	thin slabs; reindeer antlers; poles and skins	...	—[a]	...	+[a]	+[a]
22. Fifth dwelling (1957 excavation).	round (ca. 4.5m. diam.)	surface	a: ... b: ...	bones stone slabs; reindeer antlers	skins(?)	...	surface (lined with stone slabs)	...	+("male" and "female" sections)[a]	+[a]
23. First and Second dwellings (1957 excavation).	round	semi-subterranean(?)	a: ... b: ...	...	...	...	surface	+[a]	...	...

Sources: 1. Molodova I: Klein 1969b:263; Rogachev 1970a:67, Figure 1. 2. Mezhirich: Pidoplichko 1969:111–114. 3. Dobranichevka: Pidoplichko 1969:62–76. 4. Mezin: Pidoplichko 1969:77–110. 5. Gontsy: Pidoplichko 1969:45–61. 6. Pushkari I: Boriskovskiy 1958:8–10; Yefimenko 1953:451–452. 7. Yeliseyevichi: Beregovaya 1960:63. 8. Avdeyevo: Yefimenko 1953:436–437: 9–15. Kostenki sites: Beregovaya 1960:45–48: Pidoplichko 1969:75; Rogachev 1970:67–75, Figures 2–4; Klein 1969a (pages and figures as follows: 9. 116–121, Figures 34 and 35; 10. 180–186, Figures 62 and 63; 11. 180–186, Figures 62 and 63; 12. 170–175, Figures 58 and 59; 13. 174–175, Figures 58 and 60; 14. 146, 150–151, Figures 52 and 53; 15. 141, 143, Figure 50). 16. Gagarino: Yefimenko 1953:439–441, Figure 151. 17. Afontova Gora II: Yefimenko 1953:573–577, Figures 276–279; Cherdyntsev *et al.,* 1968:435. 18. Buret': Boriskovskiy 1958:8, Figure 2; Yefimenko 1953:482–483. 19. Mal'ta: Dwelling A. Gerasimov 1964:9–14, Figures 2–5. 20. Third dwelling: Gerasimov 1964:20–27, Figures 14 and 15. 21. Fourth dwelling: Gerasimov 1964:24–27, Figures 17 and 19. 22. Fifth dwelling: Gerasimov 1964:28–29, Figures 19 and 21. 23. First and second dwellings. Gerasimov 1964:17–20.

Key: +   Present.
    —   Absent.
    ...   No information.
    ?   Tentative interpretation.
    [a]   See text.

been driven into the earth. The dwelling roof was probably made of skins held down by mammoth tusks.

Evidence on an entranceway was not clear, but it was probably oriented toward the south. The area inside the dwelling contained a hearth near the entry. Flint, and bone tools and fragments occurred both inside the dwelling and in the large ash accumulation, probably also a summer fireplace, just outside the dwelling by the supposed entrance. The fact that the exterior hearth was not in constant use is shown by the presence of "kitchen debris" untouched by fire. A large storage pit was located northeast of the dwelling. The diameter at the upper edge was 2 meters, and at the bottom, 1.7 meters, and its depth was 1.2 meters. It contained remains of mammoth, bison, musk-ox, reindeer, bear, wolf, wolverine, and arctic fox, evidently intended for future use of one sort or another; some bones showed traces of working. A bone punch, flint fragments and tools, a flake of mountain crystal, and ashes and coals were also found in the pit. Within the dwelling were pieces of amber, tools, and ocher.

In 1967 when excavations at the site were continued by Shovkoplyas, two more dwellings very similar to the one just described were discovered. One of the dwellings had a small interior hearth, which had been dug into the earth. A large exterior storage pit and a flint "workshop" were also found.

SITE 4.   The remains of the dwelling at Mezin were discovered by Pidoplichko and Shovkoplyas in 1954 and excavated the following year. The site, which has been known since the 1900's, lies on the slopes of a ravine on the western bank of the Desna, north of its confluence with the Dnepr at Kiev. The geology of the site is interpreted by Pidoplichko as follows:

The cultural horizon is at the base of a loessal layer deposited upon older boulder clay and covered by a series of primary and redeposited sediments — loess, loam and sand — which reached to a depth of some 5 meters prior to erosion (1969:77–81).

Although the bones of contemporary rodent species were found among the faunal remains, there is no mention of rodent burrows. Mammoth, reindeer, horse, and musk-ox predominate among large food animals; also common are wolf, arctic fox, and collared lemming (*Dicrostonyx*).

Remains of five dwellings are believed present at the site; the dwelling described is in Excavation II. It was dug into the ground slightly; the low earthen wall thus formed and a circle of mammoth skulls made up the foundation of the house. The framework, as with other dwellings of the same type, was probably of poles and bones. The roof of skins was probably held down by reindeer antlers found on top of the bone accumulation. The position in which a wolf skull was found indicates that it also probably was placed on the roof.

The facade arch at the entranceway (facing south) was apparently constructed from two upended mammoth skulls with tusks inserted into the alveolar openings; the ends of the tusks in turn were joined by a piece of mammoth ivory to form an unbroken archway (Pidoplichko 1969:90, Figure 29). There may possibly have been a skin-covered passageway leading from the facade arch.

Special internal features are the apparent division of the dwelling into eastern and western portions. The "religious corner" (Pidoplichko 1969:97–98) was in the western portion (Quadrant 24 and part of 25). The objects found included mammoth bones painted with ocher and an anthropomorphic figurine. One of the mammoth skulls found in the eastern half of the dwelling (Quadrant 33) also was partially painted with red ocher.

The Mezin dwelling lacked a permanent central hearth (although three interior ash accumulations were identified) and interior storage pits. The inventory included retouched and unretouched flints, bone articles, amber, shells, and ocher (Pidoplichko 1969: Figures 27 and 37).

External features include storage pits filled with bone, to the east and northeast of the dwelling, hearths, and a protective wall made of bone. Some of the pits, containing flints and debris, were believed to have existed prior to the construction of the dwelling. The largest hearth (Quadrants 18 and 19), containing flints, shells, amber, charred bone and ash, bone artifacts, may indicate that a temporary dwelling of branches, skins, and grasses existed there first, while the inhabitants collected bones for the more permanent structure.

SITE 5. The cultural horizon at Gontsy site, which is located on the south bank of the Uday River, a branch of the Dnepr, is at a depth of 2.2 meters from the contemporary surface of the first terrace above the floodplain. It lies within a band of varved loam, some 6 meters thick, underlain by layered sand. At the time of its existence it was in an area of gallery vegetation suitable for mammoth. Remains of this animal predominate among the faunal collection, followed by reindeer, hare, and arctic fox. Horse and musk-ox were not found.

Since Gontsy has been known since the 1870's, with excavations carried on at intervals through the 1930's, Pidoplichko's description of the dwelling (evidently discovered in 1935) is drawn from the literature and examination of osteological materials in various museums. It is not clear how much of the site itself is still in existence at the present time. The dwelling, apparently similar to the one at Mezhirich (Site 2), seems not to have possessed any unique features. The inventory within the dwelling included flints, a hammer made of reindeer horn, needles of mammoth ivory and bone, and a piece of mammoth tusk with traces of working. A pierced fragment of the lower jaw of a bear with attached canine tooth and a single wolf canine tooth were possibly amulets. The outside storage pits contained the usual flint chips and fragments of tools, tusks, ocher, and bone. Much of the mammoth bone was from very young specimens.

SITE 6.   Puskhari I, on the elevated western bank of the Desna in the northern Ukraine, contains the remnants of several semisubterranean dwellings. The one dwelling that has been studied is a compound oval of much larger dimensions than those previously described at Mezhirich, Dobranichevka, Mezin, and Gontsy. It was possibly made up of three round dwellings joined together, in view of the three hearths along the long axis and the pits surrounding the hearths, which could have served as post holes. Mammoth tusks, their thick ends inserted into the ground, evidently were part of the outer framework. The house, if constructed in this manner, would have had three cupola-like roofs, forming gables. Judging from the drawing of the possible outward appearance, Boriskovskiy (1958:9, Figure 3) who excavated the dwelling, believed there was a single entrance. Hence, the dwelling at Pushkari I in its mode of construction appears to be transitional to the "long houses" found at Avdeyevo and the Kostenki sites.

The faunal complex at the site was of the tundra-steppe type, including mammoth, horse, reindeer, wolf, arctic fox, and two species of lemming. Bones from an estimated sixty-five mammoths were used in dwelling construction. The inventory included bone fragments, tools, flint chips, and so on; ornaments and religious objects are not mentioned.

SITE 7.   Yeliseyevichi, as well as Timonovka, Yudinovo, and Suponevo, which also are discussed in the following pages, is located in Bryansk Oblast', north of the Ukrainian sites already discussed, but still in the basin of the Desna. The Sudost' River on which Yeliseyevichi and Yudinovo lie is a western branch of the Desna; Timonovka and Suponevo are on the western bank of the Desna itself.

The dwelling at Yeliseyevichi is round and somewhat larger than those at Mezhirich, Mezin, Dobranichevka, and Gontsy. It was constructed of mammoth bone and does not appear to have any special internal features. An oval pit filled with cultural debris was found in the middle of the dwelling; whether this was also the location of the hearth is not clear. Two peripheral features are especially interesting. A second round cup-shaped structure made of mammoth scapulae, with a lower diameter of 0.85 meters and an upper of 1.6 meters, was attached to the dwelling; it may have served a religious purpose. The other feature is a passageway (6 by 1.5 meters) constructed of mammoth bone, leading from the river to the campsite. The 1970 discovery of hearths, one containing decayed, charred mammoth bones, and a large storage pit on the edge of the site indicated an entire settlement (Grekhova 1971:47).

The inventory at Yeliseyevichi includes flint and bone tools (including needles), female statuettes of ivory, and other art objects. One of the scapulae in the attached structure bears fifteen vertical incised strokes; small pits around the inside circumference contained slabs of mammoth ivory with geometric ornamentation.

The ^{14}C date for Yeliseyevichi shown in Table 1 is for wood from the base of the hearth [*sic*] at a depth of 2.3 meters in a stratum of loessal loam. If the site is analogous to Pavlov, as stated in the date description, the date appears too old (that is, the sample was probably not contemporaneous with the site). Three dates for Pavlov — 26,000 ± 350 (GIN–104), 24,800 ± 150 (GRO–1325), and 26,400 ± 230 (GRO–1242) — all for charcoal, are in good concordance, and it is not likely that Yeliseyevichi is older than the more westerly site in Czechoslovakia (Cherdyntsev *et al.* 1968:426, 430).

The atypical dwelling remains at Timonovka have already been described. Ruins of two mammoth-bone dwellings were discovered in 1947 at Yudinovo. The larger structure is oval and about twenty meters long; the smaller is round and about five meters in diameter. Both have single hearths and are delimited by walls of mammoth bone. The inventories are reportedly similar to those at Yeliseyevichi. Shells of *Nassa reticulata* found there are believed to be the farthest northern finds of this Black Sea mollusk.

Suponevo contains ruins of two types of dwellings: (1) permanent semisubterranean dwellings with excavated hearths and mammoth bone construction and (2) temporary dwellings without hearths and bone accumulations. Mammoth predominated among the faunal remains. The flint inventory is similar to that at Timonovka; a large collection of bone and horn artifacts and ornaments was also found.

SITE 8. Avdeyevo is somewhat east of the Yeliseyevichi group on the Ragozna River near its confluence with the Seym, an eastern branch of the Desna, and to the west of the Kostenki sites on the Don, though in about the same latitude. It is located in a portion of the central Russian upland that was never glaciated, lying between the Don and Dnepr tongues of the maximum (Dnepr) glaciation.

The fauna belong to the steppe-tundra type: mammoth, rhinoceros, horse, reindeer, musk-ox, saiga antelope, brown bear, wolf, fox, steppe marmot, and birds. The cultural horizon lies about 1.1 to 1.6 meters from the surface of the river terrace under chernozem and brown loam in a layer of greenish sand evidently of alluvial origin. The northeastern portion of the site has been destroyed by a new course of the Ragozna River.

The site and the dwelling (excavated by Rogachev in 1949) have much in common with Kostenki I Horizon 1. The dwelling surface of the large oval structure contains multiple hearths, evidently randomly distributed, and small pits. The attached *zemlyanka* (one of several at the site) was filled with bones evidently used for the roof; a musk-ox skull found in a position indicating that it had been placed on the roof recalls the one found in a similar position at Kostenki I. The *zemlyanka* evidently had a corridor type of entrance. Unfortunately, the literature does not contain a plan of this dwelling and dugout so a clear and complete description is not possible.

The inventory at Avdeyevo, both flint and bone, recalls Kostenki I. Of particular interest is a massive mattock of mammoth ivory. There were also many ornaments and statuettes of humans and animals.

The Kostenki Sites

SITES 9–15.   This famous group of sites, located in the Don basin near the city of Voronezh, lies to the east of those in the Desna basin. The sites are spread along the slopes of ravines above the contemporary floodplain on the west bank of the Don. At least some of the sites must have been occupied for a long period of time during the Upper Paleolithic, judging from the stratigraphy, ^{14}C dates, and other evidence. Unfortunately, except for Kostenki I, radiocarbon dates are not available for the sites where there are dwelling remnants. An attempt at correlating other dated sites in the group with those discussed below is included in the section on the general problems of dating.

The Kostenki group has been known for many years; among Soviet scientists who have studied various sites are Yefimenko, Zamyatnin, Abramova, Rogachev, Boriskovskiy, and Lazukov. An English-language study appeared in 1969 (Klein 1969b). It should be borne in mind: (1) many of the sites have been disturbed not only by erosion and rodent activity but also by earlier excavations and the digging and building activities of the present-day inhabitants, and (2) the sites show great variability in flint assemblages, art objects, and other characteristics, so that they can by no means be regarded as belonging to a single *culture*.

In addition to the dwelling remains tabulated in Table 1, a number of sites contain cultural remains centered around hearth remnants with bones and red ocher present, indicating possible ancient structures but without sufficient data to permit tabulation. Kostenki VIII (Tel'manskaya), Horizons 2 and 3 (discussed below under Kostenki VIII, Horizon 1); Kostenki I Horizons 3 and 5; Kostenki XI (Anosovka II) Horizons 1 and 2; Kostenki XV (Gorodtsovskaya) where in 1952 Rogachev found the remains of a round dwelling and a burial; Kostenki III, Kostenki XVII

(Spitsynskaya), Horizon 2 and Kostenki XIV (Markina Gora I) Horizon 2 have hearth remnants and red ocher, but no structural remnants. Borshevo II Horizons 3 and 1 have bone collections that may have been parts of dwellings. Kostenki XVIII appears to have had remnants of what may have been either a small habitation pit or possibly a grave with cremated remains. Bone collections at Kostenki XVI (Ulyanka) include one hearth and ten pits in one portion of the cultural horizon; the second bone collection is associated with seven pits. The cultural inventory at Point A in the upper horizon of Kostenki XI lies within a collection of mammoth bones, suggesting the presence of a dwelling. No remnants of either structures or hearths have been reported for Streletskaya I, Kostenki VI (Streletskaya II), Kostenki XII (Volkovskaya) Horizon 3, Kostenki XI (Anosovka II) Horizon 5, or Borshevo I and II.

SITE 9. Kostenki I Horizon 1 (as well as Horizons 2 and 3) occurs in gray-brown loessal loam; Horizon 1 lies at a depth of 1.1 to 1.4 meters from the surface. As already mentioned, there has been disagreement as to the peripheral outlines of the *long house*. These difficulties are a result of the disturbances caused by earlier excavation procedures and rodent activity. Yefimenko's suggestion that the entire area of the house was covered with a mammoth hide roof seems unrealistic; possibly lighter hides were used, or there were several gabled roofs, as suggested for Pushkari I.

Some of the hearths within the long house had draft-trenches to provide air to the fire. One of the two adjoining deep habitation pits also had a hearth. This pit was filled with mammoth tusks, which presumably weighted the roof. As at Avdeyevo, the position of a complete musk-ox skull indicated that it had been placed on the roof. The figure-eight shape of the pit suggested that it had been two-chambered; a step led from each chamber into the main structure.

Other adjoining and peripheral features of the main structure include remains of a semisubterranean dwelling containing a central hearth and pits on the southwest. The dimensions were possibly eight by six and a half meters and the depth was about 60 centimeters. In the 1950's, Rogachev found fragments of a nearby structure containing seven pits; four were believed to be habitation pits and the remaining three storage pits.

Kostenki I Horizon 1 has a large flint and bone inventory (see Klein 1969a:123–124, Table 23) and many marl and ivory anthropomorphic and animal figurines. Faunal remains from this horizon include mammoth, horse, musk-ox and red deer, fox and arctic fox, reindeer (rare), rodents, and hare. If the date of 14,020 ± 60 (GIN–86; see appendix 1–58a on page 294) for charred bone "from the upper stratum, second dwelling," is relevant, then the dwelling pertains to a relatively late period.

SITES 10–13.   Although both Horizons 1 and 2 at Kostenki IV have been disturbed by erosion and rodent activity, there are clear remnants of four dwellings — round in the upper level and oval in the lower level. All four dwellings, however, have multiple hearths and storage pits, some of which may be post holes.

A specific feature of the dwellings in both levels is the presence of sandstone slabs, presumably used for construction. Adjoining or peripheral dwelling remnants, pits, or hearth patches have not been reported. Two lion crania were found on top of the accumulation in the western dwelling, in Horizon 1, suggesting that they had been placed on the roof. The hearths in the northern oval dwelling of the second horizon are arranged in three groups, indicating the possibility that the house was of the three-gabled type, similar to Pushkari I.

Faunal remains for both horizons include mammoth, horse, reindeer, cave lion, wolf, fox and arctic fox, and many hare and rodent bones. The artifact assemblage at Kostenki IV Horizon 2 differs markedly from that at Kostenki I Horizon 1, leading Klein (1969a:175) to conclude that the sites are not related in spite of some superficial similarities in the dwellings. Likewise, the flints from Kostenki IV Horizon 1 are "unique among Kostenki-Borshevo assemblages" (Klein 1969a:193). Kostenki IV Horizon 1 also contained many ivory and marl objects.

SITE 14.   Kostenki II Complex I contains dwelling remains reported to be semisubterranean, although the depth beneath the ancient surface is not given (Beregovaya 1960:52). No storage pits were found on the living level, but underlying sandy sediments may have caused their disappearance (Klein 1969a:150). In addition, reconstruction was made difficult by "early, relatively unsystematic excavations and pits dug by local farmers" (Klein 1969a:146). Mammoth bones on the northeastern edge of the dwelling may have formed an outer protective fence (as in the Ukrainian sites); possibly the entrance also was located in this area.

Bones and hearths in Complex II (approximately fifty meters to the northeast) did not show indications of a dwelling and may have been areas of outdoor activity. The description of the round accumulation of bones (mostly mammoth) and two depressed ashy spots in Complex III may indicate the ruins of another dwelling.

The flint inventory at Kostenki II varies within the three complexes. It also differs from those of Kostenki I and VIII, but it is said to resemble that of Kostenki XI (Anosovka II) to the south across Anosov Ravine. The most interesting special feature of Kostenki II is the adjacent burial, described in the section devoted to that subject (see pages 227–232).

SITE 15.   The dwelling at Kostenki VIII (Tel'manskaya) Horizon 1, discovered in 1937, lies at a depth of about two meters from the surface.

Although the dwelling is round, the hearth is not centered, but located in the southwestern portion, near the presumed western entrance. Two of the interior storage pits were partially overlain by the hearth and may antedate it. One pit contained charred wood, an unusual find for these sites. Faunal remains (including also mammoth, reindeer, bison, hare, and arctic fox) were notable for the large number of wolf paws found in anatomical order, recalling similar finds at Mezin in the Ukraine. A lion cranium had probably been placed over the entrance. Again, the flint inventory at Kostenki VIII Horizon 1 differs markedly from those at the other Kostenki sites (with the exception of Kostenki V, located to the north on another ravine) demonstrating the great variability found among the Kostenki sites as a group.

SITE 16. Gagarino, which lies on the upper reaches of the Don north of the Kostenki sites, is unique in its location on the northern slope of a ravine on the *eastern* bank of the river. The Don narrows considerably at this point, with only a small floodplain, and the fact that the north bank location overlooks the valley may explain Gagarino's situation. The cultural horizon lies under chernozem in loessal loam at a depth of about one meter; this depth, however, is not indicative of the age of the site in view of the diluvial deposits occurring in the area, especially along the ravine slopes.

Faunal remains are predominantly mammoth and arctic fox, with rhinoceros, reindeer, bison, and rodents also present. Limestone slabs found around the dwelling remains were probably part of the foundation. The inventory of flint and bone artifacts recalls Kostenki I Horizon 1, with which Zamyatnin believes Gagarino to be contemporaneous (Beregovaya 1960:59). Gagarino is famous for its female figurines, discussed in the section on art (see pages 269–284).

North Russia, the Urals, and Western Siberia

Known Upper Paleolithic sites, especially open-air sites, are much sparser in these areas than in the more southern portions of the eastern European plain. Because of their more northerly position, natural processes are particularly destructive of sites in north Russia and the Urals, and this is notable in the case of Sungir', discussed in the following pages. Insufficient exploration has also been a factor, but since the end of World War II the northern Urals have been the object of exploration and study by both geologists and archeologists for the purpose of illuminating their geologic history and paleoclimate, with particular reference to human occupation and migration into Siberia. In the case of the western Siberian lowland, known Paleolithic sites are very few. The explanation for this

blank on the archeological map of the USSR revolves (1) around the
possible sparsity of settlement during the Upper Paleolithic because of
the extensive flooding of the river systems, particularly the Paleo-Ob' and
(2) around poor preservation of sites because of natural conditions existing since the early Holocene in the western Siberian lowland, combined,
perhaps, with insufficient exploration to date.

NORTH RUSSIA.   The Sungir' campsite is some 250 kilometers north, and
slightly east, of Gagarino. It is located on a small stream called the Sungir'
near the city of Vladimir. The Sungir' flows into the Klyaz'ma, a western
branch of the Oka, which in turn joins the upper reaches of the Volga at
the city of Gor'kiy.

Since 1956 when Bader first investigated the site, the site has been the
object of much study and discussion as to its exact geologic age. The
conclusion of Tseytlin and Ivanova that it pertains to the beginning of the
Ostashkov, the final phase of the last glaciation on the Russian plain,
seems the most reasonable (Bader 1967:149). Two samples of wood
charcoal from the cultural horizon (depth not given) obtained by N. V.
Kind during Bader's 1967 excavations gave dates of 21,800 ± 1000
(GIN–326a, Cherdyntsev *et al.* 1969:184) and 22,500 ± 600
(GIN–326b; Cherdyntsev *et al.* 1969:184), which accord with this
estimate.[5]

The cultural horizon, at a depth of about four meters in fossil soil, has
been greatly disturbed:

The soil and lower strata of loam overlapping it, including the entire cultural
horizon, were subject to the action of solifluction processes. Also, the natural
position of objects and bones, destroyed hearths and other habitation details had
been disturbed by solifluction. . . . In spite of the above-mentioned destruction,
the campsite contains fauna, charcoal, ochre patches and rich [and] interesting
material of stone and bone artifacts (Bader 1965a:59).

The discovery of graves in 1964 and 1969 lends credence to the existence
of dwellings at the site. In the area excavated in 1969 Bader (1970:41)
mentions "several hearth pits, collections of large mammoth bones and
prepared stone tools around them," although, as in the case of the 1964
excavations when the adult burial was discovered, the outlines of a dwelling could not be discerned. In his report on the 1970 excavations, Bader
(1971a:33) speaks of continued investigation of the cultural inventory in
Excavation III, definitely regarded as a dwelling ruined by solifluction.
The contents of one of the "hearth pits" discovered in 1969 are detailed
as follows: bits of ocher and charcoal, two pieces of a large mammoth

[5]   Previously obtained dates of 16,200 ± 400 (soil) and 14,600 ± 600 (bone) (GIN–14 and
GIN–15; Cherdyntsev *et al.* 1968:422) are believed too young (Cherdyntsev *et al.*
1969:184).

tusk, a segment of a large reindeer horn, tail vertebrae of an arctic fox, a "unique" mammoth ivory tool formed like a "a narrow and very long small spade or trowel," and a stone spall with a worked end (Bader 1969:41).

THE URALS. Data on sites in the basin of the Volga and the basins of the river network in the southern and middle Urals do not indicate evidence of dwelling remains, except for Talitskiy site (*stoyanka Talitskogo*; this site is sometimes referred to as *Ostrovskaya stoyanka*) in the central Urals, on the lower reaches of the Chusovaya, east of its confluence with the Kama near Molotov. Here six hearths in pairs indicate the former existence of separate dwellings. At Ogurdinovo, a very late Paleolithic or possibly early Mesolithic site on the Kama, there are remains of a possible temporary dwelling; Deukovskaya, also on the Kama, contains an oval pit filled with charcoal and the bones of a young mammoth. Cave sites in the basin of the Ufa River to the south (mostly excavated by Bibikov in the late 1930's) appear to be temporary hunting camps, containing charcoal, ash, and tools in addition to rich faunal remains, although a round hearth, about one meter in diameter was found at Buranovskaya *peshchera* [cave]. Farther south, in the basin of the Ural River, Medved'-Kamen' Grot [Bear Rock Cave] contains traces of a hearth.

The sites to the north, in the Pechora basin, are of extraordinary interest. The problems connected with the study of this region are stated by Guslitser and Kanivets as follows:

In spite of significant efforts undertaken during the last decades for the study of the Quaternary deposits of the European northeast, many very important questions of the history of the Anthropocene of this territory remain unclear or controversial.

This is explainable first of all by the fact that as a basis [for understanding] the stratigraphic structures, methods have been followed which, in their application to the relatively short Quaternary period, can have only a secondary role. Data from the widely employed analysis of spores and pollen, diatoms, wood, buried peat bogs, mollusc shells, foraminifera, sponge spicules, etc., as a rule, permit clarification of the paleogeographic conditions for deposition but do not give direct evidence for the age of deposits, since plant species and numerous groups of animals have practically not changed since the Pliocene.

A reliable stratigraphic *schema* can be established only on the basis of the determination of the absolute age of deposits; the study of mammalian remains — the most changeable groups of animals, the evolution of which proceeded relatively rapidly during the course of the Quaternary period, as well as studies of the material culture of Paleolithic man (1965:86).

The passage quoted above is the authors' preliminary statement in their report on Bear Cave (*Medvezh'ya peshchera*) and the open-air site at Byzovaya, both in the Pechora basin. At Bear Cave, in a horizon of brown gravelly loam in the forward portion of the cave, there is evidence of Paleolithic cultural activity in addition to rich and varied Upper Pleistocene faunal remains. Many fragments of broken reindeer horns, showing no evidence of having been worked as tools, were distributed in separate heaps. This led Guslitser and Kanivets to the conclusion that the horns were used for holding down the roofs of dwellings under the cave vaults. Although a relatively large number of charcoal bits were noticed on the southwest edge of the excavation, there were no indications of especially constructed hearths. Two portions of musk-ox skulls with attached horns were found in the central portion of the excavated area (Guslitser and Kanivets 1965:94).

Byzovaya is the most northerly Paleolithic site discovered to date in European Russia. It is north of the 65th parallel, 175 kilometers south of the Arctic Circle on the right bank of the Pechora at the mouth of a small ravine. The fauna include reindeer, mammoth of a late type, and bones believed to belong to a polar bear. The 422 bones collected by Timofeyev in 1961–1962 were mostly mammoth. A worked flint was found in association with the faunal remains, but no traces of structures or hearths were noted. Other tools found around the site made from local flint were thought to show Upper Paleolithic traits. Mammoth bones from the site dated to 18,320 ± 280 (TA–121; Punning, Liiva, and Ilves (1968:379) would indicate a fairly late age.

WEST SIBERIA. Although west Siberian Upper Paleolithic sites are mainly located on the upper reaches of the Irtysh and Ob', not far from the Altay, two sites on the Siberian plain have been briefly reported in the recent literature.

Chernoozer'ye II (near the village of the same name and located not far from Omsk on the middle Irtysh) has several cultural horizons, the lowest of which is Upper Paleolithic. Remains of open-air campfires, one large hearth, two small pits, a flint workshop, stone and bone artifacts, and bones, but no dwelling remains, are reported. The fauna lack mammoth and rhinoceros; this horizon is believed to be late Paleolithic contemporaneous with Krasnyy Yar on the Angara (Gening 1969:198–199; Gening et al. 1970:187–188; Viktorov et al. 1971:197).

The other site is called Volch'ya Griva [Wolf Mane]; it is located in Kargatsk Rayon, west of Novosibirsk, Novosibirsk Oblast'. Mammoth bone was dated by the laboratory of the Siberian Branch of the USSR Academy of Sciences at Novosibirsk[6] at 14,200 ± 150 (SOAN–78; Firsov, Panychev, and Orlova 1972:196). The brief date description employs only the term "Paleolithic campsite"; no estimated geological or archeological age is given.

[6]   This laboratory began operation in August 1969; the half-life used is 5,568 years. A brief discussion of laboratory methods is given in the introduction to the list (Firsov et al. 1970:190).

Farther up the Irtysh (that is, to the south), the caves at Bukhtarma and Malyy Grot [Little Grotto] have indications of human modification; limestone slabs in front of the cave at Bukhtarma and the remains of a hearth in the center of Malyy Grot. These sites are believed to be late, similar to those at Kokorevo on the upper Yenisey. Other upper Irtysh sites contain no evidences of dwellings or cave modifications.

The middle and upper reaches of the Charysh River in the Altay foothills form the southern basin of the Ob' system. Among the many caves in the region, the one at Ust'-Kanskaya shows evidence of human occupation, with a stone and bone inventory and many faunal remains. There are no remains of campfires or hearths. The dry cave with its opening to the south overlooking the valley at an elevation of 1,050 meters was probably used only in warm weather. On the basis of the faunal remains, Rudenko (1961:213) believes human occupancy dated to a relatively warm period preceding the final Altay glaciation. Mammoth is absent, presumably because the mountain terrain was unfavorable, but woolly rhinoceros, horse, wild ass, gazelle and argali sheep, and spiral-horned antelope (*Spiroceros*), as well as cave hyena, fox, wolf, brown bear, badger, ermine, and rodents, are included in the faunal list. Rhinoceros, cave hyena, and spiral-horned antelope are, of course, now extinct; the horse and wild ass survive in parts of Mongolia and Tibet.

Sites along the Ob' appear to have been open-air camps without especially constructed hearths or traces of dwellings. Tomsk is the remnant of an open-air hunting camp containing remains of a young mammoth. Achinsk on the Chulym, a branch of the Ob', also contained mammoth bones in addition to charcoal and flints.

Central Siberia

SITE 17. Afontova Gora II has been known since 1884. The geographical feature from which it takes its name (Afontova mountain) is actually an outlier of the low mountains that surround the river valley in the Krasnoyarsk region. Today the Yenisey River at this point has a floodplain terrace averaging nine to twelve meters above normal water level, which forms the shoreline during the spring rise. Another terrace is at fifteen to eighteen meters above normal water level; it is not always discernible since it is masked with loess deposits. Afontova Gora II lies in these loess deposits, located on the western bank of the river at the foot of heights along the preexisting river bank. (Cultural remains at other points nearby are labeled Afontova Gora I, III, and IV.)

Afontova Gora II has two (or possibly three) cultural horizons; the dwelling remains are in the lower one, at a depth of about twelve meters. As noted in Table 1 (see p. 209), the dwelling at Afontova Gora II was unusually deep, a true *zemlyanka*. Dwelling remains at the other Afontova Gora sites, and apparently also at Pereselencheskiy Punkt nearby, are of the same type.

The faunal remains are notably diverse. They include species associated in later fauna with distinct environments (from tundra to dry steppe to mountain), and include reindeer (which is predominant), mammoth, hare, arctic fox, horse, antelope, mountain sheep, goat, wolf, bear, lion, rodents, and birds. (Mammoth and arctic fox are absent in the upper horizon.) Charcoal from the lower horizon was from willow and larch. The inventory included stone and bone tools, ornaments of soapstone, pierced fox teeth, and mammoth ivory beads. The lower cultural horizon also contained remains of a human hand and fragments of a child's skull, which G. F. Debets (1946) thought showed Mongoloid characteristics. The dwelling may have been occupied over a long period of time, but only at intervals in the warm season, as evidenced from the northward-facing location, shed reindeer horns, and waterbird bones.

SITE 18.   Buret', located on the eastern bank on the Angara not far from the mouth of the Angara, is usually regarded as a sister site to Mal'ta (Sites 19–23). Of the remains of four fairly well-preserved dwellings, the one designated Dwelling Number two is described in detail in the literature. As with Mal'ta, limestone slabs as well as bones from large animals were used for the framework; an inner low embankment was probably constructed as a base for a pole framework. The bones used for construction, in addition to mammoth and reindeer, included rhinoceros skulls, indicating, as at Mal'ta, a greater abundance of these animals than at sites in European Russia. A short corridor-like entrance faced the river, recalling the same feature at Gagarino on the Don.

The tool inventory at Buret' is very similar to that at Mal'ta; the unusual statuettes and nephrite disk are dealt with under the appropriate section.

Although Mal'ta (Sites 19–23) has been studied and written about since the 1920's, at the time Gerasimov, the original excavator, published his report on the 1956–1957 excavations,[7] there still appeared to be much disagreement about the site's geological age and its place in the archeological history of Siberia. The 1956–1957 excavations were carried on in conjunction with the survey of the Angara valley deposits as part of the preliminary work on the construction of the Bratsk reservoir. Whether, as a result of the reservoir construction, the site is still sufficiently preserved for study *in situ* is not clear, and a survey of recent literature does not indicate further work at Mal'ta. On the other hand, the

[7] Translated into English (with illustrations) from *Sovetskaya etnografiya*, No. 3, 1958:28–52, in *The archaeology and geomorphology of northern Asia: selected works.* Edited by Henry N. Michael. Toronto: University of Toronto Press, 1964.

description of the only available radiocarbon date gives the impression that the bones used for the sample were collected on the spot (GIN–97; Cherdyntsev *et al.* 1968:436). The date itself — 14,750 ± 120 — appears inconclusive, even though it was taken from "the lower cultural stratum," in view of the belief that Mal'ta belongs to the oldest group of Siberian Paleolithic sites. Except for the remnants of a site belonging to the much younger Baday culture on the southeastern periphery, Gerasimov believes that the basic Paleolithic cultural layer at Mal'ta (the area of the dwelling excavations) represents a single cultural horizon; he notes that unlike sites in European Russia there is almost no disturbance of the cultural horizon by rodent burrows (Gerasimov 1964:3–5).

Faunal remains collected before Gerasimov's 1956–1957 excavation had been placed in the Irkutsk Museum, and a portion of the collection was evidently lost. Gerasimov, however, reports that he found reindeer predominant (150 pairs of antlers); bones in anatomical position indicated that the flesh was eaten. Mammoth (eight specimens) were mostly young, and there were fourteen specimens of rhinoceros, thought to be of a different variety from the typical woolly rhinoceros. Large rhinoceros bones were used in constructing the framework of the dwelling. The number of predator bones at the site was small — fourteen arctic fox, four wolverine, and one each of lion and wolf. The lack of gnawing marks on bones at the site led Gerasimov to the conclusion that the domesticated dog was not present.

SITE 19. Dwelling A, the largest discovered at Mal'ta, is atypical in its rectangular outlines. Rhinoceros, as well as mammoth bones, were used in constructing the framework. Another atypical feature is the presence of storage pits dug into the earthen wall supporting the framework rather than into the living floor. Gerasimov believed that the long side of the dwelling facing the river was open, with a mammoth hide roof, in imitation of a rock shelter. If so, the framework must have been very strongly constructed to support the weight of a single hide roof of the necessary dimensions. The distribution of the artifact inventory with "hunting implements and representations of birds" near the right hearth, and "knives, scrapers, needles, awls, ornaments and female statuettes" near the left hearth, suggests "male" and "female" sections in the dwelling (Gerasimov 1964:17). No external storage pits or hearth patches are mentioned; kitchen debris was probably thrown down the terrace slope.

SITE 20. The "third" dwelling, excavated during the 1957 fieldwork, is also rectangular; since half of it had been destroyed by construction of an eighteenth-century sod house, the dimensions could only be tentatively determined, probably nine by three to four meters. The construction was believed similar to that of Dwelling A (Site 19); presumably the entrance also faced the river. An unusual feature is the construction of the single hearth, which had been raised above the living level. There was one storage pit, "a hiding place," dug into the rear wall, containing a statuette of a swan (Gerasimov 1964:24, Figure 16).

SITE 21. The "fourth dwelling," higher up the slope but believed to pertain to the same cultural horizon, had also been disturbed by the sod house; its remnants consisted of an "arcuate wall, constructed of [large] stone slabs, rhinoceros and mammoth skulls and their long bones . . ." (Gerasimov 1964:24, Figures 17a and b). The house was, therefore, presumably oval with the wide entrance facing the river. The house, evidently, did not have a specially constructed hearth, but it did have a fireplace at the entrance. One unusual interior find was a bull shoulder blade, which evidently had been a shelf; on top of it was a reindeer dorsal vertebra containing a female statuette. Another unusual find was a rhinoceros skull, which may have served both as a seat and a storage place.

SITE 22. The "fifth dwelling" was a small round structure with a clearly defined sunken central hearth lined with stone slabs. The walls had, evidently, been constructed of limestone slabs with a connecting framework of reindeer antlers. There was no discernible entranceway. As in Dwelling A, the distribution of artifacts on either side of the earth suggested "male" and "female" sections.

SITE 23. The "first" and "second" dwellings consisted only of remnants of depressed round areas with central hearths as a result of the destruction caused by roadwork. Bones of a young mammoth in a slab-lined pit or hollow were found in one dwelling. These two structures may have been tent-like summer dwellings (Gerasimov 1964:18) as bird and fish bones, absent in the other dwellings, were found in them.

Summary and Conclusions

A review of the foregoing materials reveals that the basic underlying feature of Upper Paleolithic dwellings in the territory of the Soviet Union is the use of large bones, mostly of mammoth, in the construction of foundations and lower walls of both permanent and semipermanent structures. Semisubterranean dwellings share the added feature, in most cases, of earthen embankments and lower walls, sometimes strengthened with stone slabs. Individual details of particular dwellings — size, shape, presence or absence of permanent hearths, storage pits, type and location of entrance, peripheral features, and so on — may vary greatly not only from site to site but within a site. Although the facade arch does appear to be unique for the Ukraine (Mezhirich, Mezin, Gontsy), examination of the data does not reveal one particular "western" (that is, European Russian) house type as opposed to an "eastern" (that is, Siberian) style. Instead, analogues occur between widely separated sites. Yeliseyevichi on the Desna and Buret' on the Angara both have corridor-like entrances. The only analogues to the two rectangular dwellings among those excavated at Mal'ta in the Angara regions are the remains of rectangular dwellings at Timonovka, like Yeliseyevichi in the basin of the Desna. The deeply excavated oval dwelling at Afontova Gora II in central Siberia recalls the peripheral habitation dugouts of the compound-oval dwelling at Kostenki I–1 on the Don. Hence, it appears that there is one basic pattern for dwellings unifying the whole of north-central Eurasia.

BURIALS

Although a number of authentic Mousterian burials are known for western Europe (Binford 1968:141), there appears to be only two reported for the present-day territory of the Soviet Union: burial of an adult male at Kiik-Koba in the Crimea and the child burial at Teshik-Tash in Uzbekistan.[8] Both are quite clearly intentional burials, associated with human cave habitations, and the human remains are of Neanderthal type in both cases. Although the site at Teshik-Tash should probably be regarded as pertaining to the Middle East from an archeological viewpoint, the burial has some features analogous to Upper Paleolithic burials on the Russian plain and in Siberia: (1) the apparent use of limestone slabs to surround and cover the body at Teshik-Tash suggests an affinity with the child's burial chamber found at Mal'ta (Sites 6 and 2), the pairs of goat horns delimiting the grave area recall the mammoth scapulae and tusks found at three of the Kostenki burials.

Likewise, Upper Paleolithic burials on the Russian plain and in Siberia appear to be far fewer than those known for western and central Europe and more recently discovered (Binford 1968:141). Table 2 charts the known Upper Paleolithic burials for the Soviet Union, even though in the case of the Kostenki sites information is far from complete.[9] Most important are the burials at Sungir' and Mal'ta not only for their obvious similarities but for the indications on clothing, ivory-working technology, and social organization at the Sungir' site.

[8] For a description of the Kiik-Koba burial, see Yefimenko 1953:194, 249, Figure 9; for Teshik-Tash, see Movius' review article (1953) of Okladnikov's report.
[9] See footnote to Table 2 concerning discrepancies in estimated ages for remains at the Kostenki sites. As noted, those given in Klein 1969a:236–237, Table A–4, are the ones listed.

Table 2. Upper Paleolithic burials: European, USSR and Siberia

Site	Remains						Grave pit					Grave inventory			Comments
	Sex	Age[a]	Position; orientation	Decoration	Orientation (long axis)	Shape	Dimensions; depth	Red ocher	Ash; charcoal; earth	Covering	Tools/weapons (stone and bone)	Ornaments[b] (not related to decoration of remains)	Special features	
EUROPEAN USSR														
1. Kostenki XV (Gorodtsovskaya)	male (?)	5–6[c]	sitting and contracted; head on knees (see comments)	pierced arctic fox teeth at head and knees	N–S	oval	1.24 × 0.8m.; 0.43m.	+; also yellow pigment	...	Mammoth scapulae; horse bones; possibly earth	flints; bone needle and polisher; bone knife	...	...	Skull and lower jaw separated from rest of skeleton; original position and orientation of head undetermined; grave pertains to cultural horizon, and dwelling remains; discovered 1952
2. Kostenki XVIII	male (?)	9–11[c]	contracted; on left side; head to SW; face to NW	—	N–S(?)	oval(?)	...; 1m. below surface	—	—	3 layers of mammoth long bones and portions of scapulae ca. 0.35m. thick	—	—	—	Grave disturbed; dimensions and exact depth of grave pit not known; no grave inventory, but alongside settlement discovered 1953

Site	Sex	Age	Position	Orientation	Grave shape	Dimensions	Ocher	Fill	Associated features			Skull/other	Remarks
3. Kostenki II (Zamyat-minskaya), Complex 1	male	30+	sitting position facing SE	SE–NW	oval	4×1.5m.	+ (small quantity)	+ (believed filled with earth to shoulder-level)	mammoth skulls and long bones forming burial chamber presumably roofed with perishable material	—	—	—	Grave to S.E. of associated house remains; Cro-Magnon type according to G. F. Debets; discovered 1953
4. Kostenki XIV (Markina Gora), below Horizon 3	male	20–25°	con-tracted (bound?) on left side; head to W	E–W	oval; trough-like bottom	0.99× 0.39m.; 0.30–0.48m.	bones and skull powdered with red ocher	+ (filling bottom of grave)	—	earth(?)	—	—	flints and bones in grave thought accidental; body may have been bound; skeleton showed "Negroid" traits according to G. F. Debets
5. Sungir[c]: A. Burial 1, Excavation 2	male	55–65	extended; head to NE; arms bent and crossed over torso; head raised	SW–NE	oval; trough-like shape	2.05 × 0.70m.; depth, 60–65 cm.; 8–9 cm. higher beneath head	+ (ivory beads and bracelets; clothed)[d]	+ (above covering and be-neath re-mains)	+ (ash, charcoal filling bottom)	red ocher patch SW–NE; rectangu-lar stone; female skull	+ (flint knife be-tween knees)	+?[d]	female skull (Euro-peoid) and stone slab on top of grave	evidence of Arctic-style clothing from dis-tribution of beads and config-uration of ocher; estimated height 5' 11"; weight, 156 lb; Cro-Magnon type (Debets 1967: 160–164); probably associa-ted with dwelling discovered 1964

Table 2. (*continued*)

Site	Sex	Age[a]	Remains		Orientation (long axis)	Grave pit					Grave inventory			Comments
			Position; orientation	Decoration		Shape	Dimensions; depth	Red ocher	Ash; charcoal; earth	Covering	Tools/weapons (stone and bone)	Ornaments[b] (not related to decoration of remains)	Special features	
B. Burial 2	male (2)	12–13; 7–9	extended; older child; head to NNE; younger: head to SW	ivory beads and pierced fox teeth; ivory pins; breast ornaments; clothed[d]	SW–NNE	oval(?)	length 3m.; depth 80 cm.	+ (as above)	...	...	+ (bone needle and other artifacts; ivory spears)[d]	?		evidence of clothing; probably associated with dwelling; discovered 1969
SIBERIA 6. Mal'ta	male	3–4	extended; arms extended along body; head raised	ivory coronet, necklace, bracelet	SW–NE	oval	1.15 × 0.68m.; depth, 60+cm.	+ (skull and skeleton colored red)	earthen fill	stone slabs forming burial chamber	+ (flints dagger)	bird statuette		associated with dwelling; skeletal remains too poorly preserved for anatomical study; discovered 1929

Sources: 1. Kostenki XV: Bader 1967: 144; Beregovaya 1960:56–57; Klein 1969a:94–96, 236–237. 2. Kostenki XVIII: Bader 1967:145; Beregovaya 1960:46; Klein 1969a:164, 236. 3. Kostenki II: Bader 1967:145; Beregovaya 1960:52; Klein 1969a:150–151, 236–237. 4. Kostenki XIV: Bader 1967:145; Beregovaya 1960:51; Klein 1969a:90, 91, Figure 23, 236–237. 5. A. Sungir': Bader 1967:151–159; B. Bader 1970:41–43. 6. Mal'ta: Bader 1967:145–146; Yefimenko 1953:479, Figures 238–239.

Key: +   Present.
    —   Absent.
    . . .   No information.
    ?   Tentative interpretation.
[a] Estimated.
[b] Not related to decoration.
[c] Note discrepancies in estimated ages for Kostenki burials between data given in Beregovaya 1960 and Bader 1967 and Klein 1969a:236–237 and Klein 1969a:236–237, Table A–4. The estimated ages given in Klein (1969a:236–237, Table A–4) are used since data are based on physical anthropological studies.
[d] See text.

All the burials tabulated have certain common elements: all are obviously deliberate interments; all the adults are male and the children presumably so; in all cases the complete corpse had been interred in an oval grave; all but one (Number 2) are definitely related to human habitations and contain red ocher. Orientation of the grave pit and position and orientation of the remains, and the presence or absence of decoration and a grave inventory vary. Three of the Kostenki burials (Numbers 1–3) had mammoth bone coverings (plus horse bones at Kostenki IV). In two of the Kostenki burials the deceased had evidently been placed in a sitting position; that of the adult at Kostenki II Complex I may have projected above the surface and been surrounded with a structure of mammoth bone roofed with some perishable material like wood.

THE SUNGIR' BURIALS SITES 5A AND 5B.   The adult burial at Sungir' is believed by Bader and others (Bader 1967:151) to pertain definitely to the cultural horizon of Excavation II. The Pleistocene age of the burial is also confirmed by the presence of an ice-wedge cast cutting through the grave and extending some ninety centimeters into the underlying fossil soil, loam, sand, and clay. There is disagreement between Bader and Gromov as to whether the grave was contemporaneous with the existence of permafrost (Bader 1967:158). The grave was first identified as a patch of red ocher on top of which were a stone slab and a female skull minus the lower jaw. It had probably been placed deliberately on the ocher patch as a marker and had previously been stripped of flesh, since there were no tooth marks of predators on it. Also, there were no teeth or post-cranial bones found.

Upon excavation, the grave was found to have a layer of ash and charcoal on the very bottom, in Gromov's opinion showing that it had been excavated by means of fire to melt permafrost. A flint scraper-like implement found under the left part of the pelvis was probably an accidental association. On top of the ash and charcoal was a thick layer of red ocher, covering part of the walls of the grave. The body had been laid in an extended position with the head slightly higher than the feet and the arms crossed over the pelvic area. A flint knife had been placed between the knees.

The skeleton, covered with rows of mammoth ivory beads, was that of an adult male between fifty-five and sixty-five years old. Debets, who gives no opinion as to the probable cause of death, classifies the skeleton as Cro-Magnon "in the broad sense of the term" (1967:160–164); the man's height and weight are estimated to have been about 161 centimeters and 55 kilograms.

Another layer of red ocher covered the skeleton. Above it were rows of larger ivory beads, which had possibly decorated some sort of shroud, and an additional layer of ocher. A pierced stone ornament found on the breast was thought to pertain to the rows of larger beads decorating the "shroud." The beads found in the burial totaled more than 3,500.

The position of the rows of beads on the skeleton and the configuration of the ocher covering it indicate that the body had been clothed. Three strands of beads surrounded the skull as though originally sewn onto a close-fitting cap; twenty pierced arctic fox teeth found in the region of the occiput were probably also part of the headgear. Seven unbroken transverse rows of beads lay across the upper torso and arms and reached to the waist, indicating that they had either been sewn directly (or on leather strips) to a pullover type of garment, similar to a parka. Strings of beads and very thin ivory bracelets encircled the upper arms and wrists. There were also bands of beads under the knees and at the ankles and feet; those under the knees were attached to bunches of bone pendants. Vertical rows of beads were distributed along the legs from the heels to the thighs, suggesting pants with attached footgear. The configuration of the ocher indicated folds, as though it had been poured over leather or fur.

The double child burial (Number 5B) at Sungir' has not been so fully reported.[10] Both children were interred in an extended position and thickly covered with red ocher and thousands of ivory beads. In addition, bracelets, rings, and breast ornaments adorned both skeletons. A horse figurine found was similar to another one found earlier at the site. Under the chins of both skeletons were long bone pins. Although the skeletons are reported to have been "well preserved" (Bader 1970:42), there is no anatomical information other than the presumed ages and sex, nor any indication that death was from other than natural causes. Rows of beads and pierced arctic fox teeth around the skulls suggested the same sort of cap as that worn by the adult; the long bone pins were presumably for fastening the upper garment, perhaps some sort of cloak. There is no information on the arrangement of beads on the torsos and legs.

In contrast to the adult burial, the double child burial contained an inventory of flint tools (not described in detail) and artifacts of horn, bone, and ivory, including a thin needle and two "batons"; of the sixteen "spears, darts and daggers" of ivory, two were remarkable for their length: 1.66 and 2.42 meters (Bader 1970:42–43).

From a technological standpoint, the length of these spears indicates knowledge of how to straighten ivory. The thousands of ivory beads found in the two burials also have not only technical but social implications. S. A. Semenov found that the beads had been drilled by means of a simple drill held between the palms; he estimated that the entire production time per bead, beginning with the cutting of the blank, would have taken thirty to sixty minutes. Taking an average production time of

---

[10] Bader's (1970) report is somewhat unclear: he speaks of "a second grave" containing "three burials," but describes only the double child burial found in 1969 (designated as 5B in Table 2).

forty-five minutes per bead, the 3,500 beads in the adult burial would have required 2,625 man-hours of labor (Bader 1967:156). Many of the beads had a surface luster indicating long usage; even so, the numbers of beads found in both burials would constitute an immense hoard representing the end-products of specialized work done over a long period of time.

There are also implications of social organization in the elaborateness of the burials themselves. The significance of child burials during the Upper Paleolithic in western Europe, such as the burial at Grimaldi, and those in the Soviet Union, including the one at Mal'ta (Number 6) cannot be explained beyond the obvious fact that the children were for some reason considered important enough to receive special mortuary treatment. The adult burial at Sungir' is notable for (1) the advanced age of the deceased, (2) the amount of ocher, (3) the immensely valuable decoration of the clothing and shroud indicating some sort of ritual dress, and (4) the very specific marking of the grave. Together, these factors tempt the use of the adjective "princely."

Indications of the type of clothing in which Sungir' man was buried have possible analogies to and contrasts with evidence from Upper Paleolithic art found in European Russia and Siberia. Bracelets are indicated on the arms of statuettes from Kostenki I, Avdeyevo, and Mal'ta and were probably a widespread item of personal decoration. Three statuettes from Kostenki I have bindings crossing the upper part of the breast. Bader finds an analogy in the three rows of beads across the breast of Sungir' man (Bader 1967:156); on the other hand, he does not take into account a possible sex differentiation in dress and ornaments since the Kostenki statuettes represent women. The distribution of beads and arctic fox teeth on the skulls of the Sungir' burials may have analogies with the shell headdresses of the child burial at Grimaldi (see Coles and Higgs 1969: Plate VI, opposite p. 225). Most interesting from the standpoint of the entire body covering is a comparison of Sungir' man's clothing with a statuette from Buret' (presumably also of a woman). This statuette appears to be clothed in a one-piece garment with attached hood and footgear; punctate markings may indicate the texture of fur.

MAL'TA. SITE 6.   The burial of the very young child discovered at Mal'ta in 1929 has many similarities to the Sungir' burials, but it is distinctive in that the stone slabs found in the grave indicate a burial chamber, analogous both to the Teshik-Tash burial, as previously mentioned, as well as to a number of western European burials (Grimaldi, Barma Grande, Combe-Capelle) (Bader 1967:143). The body, which was too poorly preserved for study, had been decorated with an ivory necklace and bracelet and what appeared to be an ivory coronet. The grave also contained a bird statuette, flints, and an ivory dagger — objects of adult usage — as in the case of the child burial at Sungir'. The descriptions of the grave do not mention indications of clothing and evidently ivory beads were not found.

Two general observations result from this summary. (1) The Mousterian child burial at Teshik-Tash appears to have analogies to that at Mal'ta and some in western Europe in the use of stone slabs to form a burial chamber, indicating as in the housing remains at Molodova I, cultural continuities in time and space between the Middle and Upper Paleolithic. (2) As with the evidence on dwellings, an overall unitary pattern, although variable in details, emerges for both European Russia and Siberia, with an underlying complex social organization functionally related to the requirements of a mammoth economy.

FAUNAL REMAINS, HUNTING SPECIALIZATION AND METHODS, AND POPULATION ESTIMATES

In reviewing the evidence on faunal remains, the large inferential component must be borne in mind. Faunal remains at Upper Paleolithic sites in the USSR have not been uniformly reported and analyzed. For some sites known for long periods of time (such as Kiyevo-Kirillovskoye site and Gontsy), osteological materials are scattered throughout various museums. In the case of Mal'ta, faunal materials placed in the Irkutsk Museum were never thoroughly studied, and a portion of them was subsequently lost (Gerasimov 1964:3).

The percentage of a given species in the faunal list of a particular site does not necessarily reflect its relative abundance or scarcity in the surrounding area. Faunal lists from sites in the same region may vary greatly in the percentages of a particular species; sometimes a species is entirely absent although it is known to have lived in the area. While mammoth does appear predominant, followed by reindeer, and yielding first place to the latter animal during the terminal Paleolithic as at Molodova V (see p. 236), faunal lists for Ukrainian sites, as analyzed by Pidoplichko (1969), exhibit considerable difference in the presence or absence of both large food animals and predators. For instance, for Dobranichevka neither horse nor rhinoceros is reported, for Mezhirich no rhinoceros and only one horse; for Mezin three rhinoceros and sixty-three horses are reported (Pidoplichko 1969:82). Likewise, among predators there is considerable variation in the numbers of wolf and arctic fox at various sites. Certain animals, such as musk-ox and wolverine, are represented throughout by only one or two individuals. Rhinoceros is also little represented in faunal lists for European Russia although the use of rhinoceros bone in the dwellings at Mal'ta and Buret' may indicate a greater abundance in central Siberia or, perhaps, more successful hunting. The specialized conditions (that is, the periglacial environment) responsible for the abundant faunal resources available to Upper Paleolithic man are discussed in the final portion of this section.

A discussion of faunal remains at the sites under consideration can be approached from three different viewpoints: (1) the timespan approach from the Mousterian to the terminal Paleolithic; (2) the area approach based on remains in sites in the Russian plain; north European Russia, the Urals and West Siberia; and Central Siberia, and (3) the discussion of the three or four most important animals by species.

Timespan at Molodova V

The timespan approach is exemplified by Ivanova's table on Molodova V in which she correlates data on fauna, mollusks, vegetation, stratigraphy, and ^{14}C dates (Ivanova 1966: Figure 20) with the cultural horizons of the site. It should be noted that there is a long period between Mousterian Horizon 11 and Upper Paleolithic Horizon 10, approximately 40–30,000 B.P., when the site was either unoccupied or only occasionally used; also only occasional cultural finds are reported for the period separating Horizons 7 and 6, about 23,000–17,000 B.P. Ivanova, however, includes a cautionary note against putting too much weight on faunal composition as an indicator of climatic conditions:

It is necessary to note that the mammalian faunal composition does not play a major role for these conclusions, *i.e.*, a colder climate than at present for the suite of loess formations. Such forms as the mammoth (early form) and reindeer are also known from Riss/Würm deposits. Hence, here the percentage composition of forms and the appearance of such cold-tolerant forms as the arctic fox (*Vulpes* [*Alopex*] *lagopus* L.) and the collared lemming (*Dicrostonyx torquatus* Pall.) are significant.

Furthermore, land mollusks living in the Dnestr area at present, such as large snails, are absent in cold periods, and

. . . are encountered only in Riss-Würm soil, and further only in the uppermost portion of the loess cross-section. At the time of the formation of the loess layer such boreal forms as *Vallonia tenuilabris* Al. Br., *Columella columella* Mart, not occurring in the Dnestr region at the present time, were widely distributed. Certain species of mollusks encountered in isolated horizons indicate a dry climate (Ivanova 1966).

From the standpoint of the primacy of large food animals, however, mammoth, reindeer, and horse are predominant for Upper Paleolithic Horizons 10 through 3, with mammoth absent in the terminal Paleolithic Horizon 2 and Mesolithic Horizons 1 and 1a.

Mammoth is "very abundant" in Mousterian Horizons 12, 12a and 11 (correlated with ^{14}C dates of approx. 45–40,000 B.P.) with reindeer *absent* and horse present only in Horizon 11. As mentioned earlier, mammoth is "present" in Upper Paleolithic horizons to about 14,000 B.P. The correlating ^{14}C date is 13,370 ± 540 — GIN–9, campfire charcoal (Cherdyntsev *et al.* 1968:421). However, for Horizons 10 through 1 and 1a, reindeer becomes the "very abundant" species, with horse also "very abundant" for Horizons 10–7, approximately 30–23,000 B.P., and "present" in Horizons 6 through 1a (approximately 16,500 B.P.).

Woolly rhinoceros is present or occurs as a single example only in some of the Mousterian and Upper Paleolithic horizons, though, surprisingly, it is identified as "present" in Mesolithic Horizon 1. Deer, moose, *Bos* species, and *Bison priscus* are either present or represented by single individuals throughout Upper Paleolithic Horizons 10–2, and all except *Bos* species are shown for the Mesolithic horizons. Species of deer and *Bison priscus* are reported for the Mousterian, with *Bos* species and moose absent. Musk-ox is not listed at all. Wolf, arctic fox, fox, and hare are not included in the list for the Mousterian period, but they are either present or represented by single individuals during the Upper Paleolithic. Arctic fox is absent in the Mesolithic horizons, placed by Ivanova in the terminal Upper Pleistocene. Somewhat contradictory in view of Ivanova's statement, quoted above, is the evidence for the collared lemming, listed as present in Mousterian Horizon 11, correlated by Ivanova with a warm period ["Brørup"] of the early Upper Pleistocene, and completely absent in all the upper horizons. Lion (*Panthera spelaea*) is listed only for Mousterian Horizon 11, though in other sites on the Russian plain it occurs during the Upper Paleolithic. Brown bear (*Ursus arctos*), likewise, is listed only for Mousterian Horizon 11, though it is also known for the Upper Paleolithic. Cave bear is completely absent. In general, however, this analysis by Ivanova confirms the general shift to the primacy of reindeer and horse over mammoth from the Mousterian period through the late Upper Paleolithic.

Faunal Remains by Areas

The preceding discussion of the faunal list for Molodova V indicates the general faunal composition for the Russian plain, at other sites in the Ukraine and along the Don. Musk-ox, as previously mentioned, occurs in the Ukraine and along the Don, though never in large numbers. Saiga antelope is present in the Don River sites, although not in the Ukraine. For the Kostenki sites, Klein (1969a: Table 9) shows mammoth, rhinoceros, horse, wild bovids (*Bos* and bison), red deer, reindeer, Arctic fox, wolf, and hare occurring in all levels of the second terrace and in the first terrace. Giant deer and saiga antelope occur in some but not all levels, whereas moose is present only in the first terrace. As in the Ukraine, brown bear had evidently replaced the cave bear. Kowalski (1967:359) states that the cave bear ". . . coexisted in Europe with the brown bear (*Ursus arctos*), but these two species were seldom found together." Cave lion occurs only in the upper humic bed of the second terrace and in the first terrace at the Kostenki sites. Klein (1969a:66) suggests that ". . . indicative of cold conditions is the absence or near absence anywhere in the deposits [at the Kostenki sites] of bones of wild boar (*Sus scrofa*)"; on the other hand, since the boar is associated with deciduous forest, the absence of sufficient deciduous trees may have been the key factor.

There are variations in faunal remains at individual Kostenki sites, indicating specialized hunting preferences. Kostenki XIV (Markina Gora), second cultural layer, is notable for the large number of horse bones, some in anatomical order. Slivers of horse bone from Layer 3, possibly synchronous with the burial (see Table 2, p. 228) have been dated to 14,300 ± 460 (GIN–79; Cherdyntsev *et al.* 1968:431). Kostenki I Horizon 1 contains mammoth and abundant horse but only one piece of reindeer antler; the second horizon also contains mammoth and horse; the third horizon contains mostly mammoth, but also horse and many arctic fox bones. Many fragments of deer antler are reported from the cultural level at Kostenki X (Anosovka I); hare predominates in the faunal remains at Kostenki IV. As previously mentioned, Kostenki VIII (Tel'manskaya) Horizon 1, in addition to a preponderance of mammoth and other large animals, contained large numbers of wolf bones including paws in anatomical order on the dwelling floor. Mammoth is absent in the upper cultural horizon of Borshevo II, although present in the two lower ones, but remains of horse, wild cattle, moose, and reindeer, as well as wolf, fox (but not arctic fox), hare and cave hyena occur in the upper horizon. This upper horizon is believed by Boriskovskiy to be transitional to the Mesolithic, which is apparently confirmed by the absence of mammoth and arctic fox and a date of 12,300 ± 100 (GIN–88) (Cherdyntsev *et al.* 1968:432) for humified alluvium underlying the lower cultural stratum. However, the reported presence of cave hyena again illustrates the contradictory nature of so much of the evidence on Soviet Upper Paleolithic sites.

For sites in north Russia, the Urals, and western Siberia, the composition of faunal remains at Byzovaya and Krutaya Gora in the far north and the variety of species in the Urals are of special interest. For Sungir', there is a preponderance of reindeer, but with many remains also of mammoth, horse, and arctic fox. Reindeer, followed by horse and fox, were believed to be the primary food animals. Gromov suggests "episodic" fire drives for a small type of mammoth. Other animals reported are arctic hare, collared lemming, wolf, brown bear, wolverine, cave lion, and birds.

Byzovaya, in the Pechora basin, contained reindeer, a late type of mammoth, musk-ox, wolf, arctic fox, and bones tentatively identified as those of polar bear. Krutaya Gora, an open-air site one and a half degrees south of the Arctic Circle and near Byzovaya, has two cultural layers, the lower regarded as exhibiting "Mousterian traits" and the upper, Paleolithic ones. The mammalian fauna of the Mousterian level have not been determined. Although a detailed faunal list for the upper layer is not available, analysis of both "tools and faunal data" led to the conclusion that this level is Upper Paleolithic (Guslitser, Kanivets, and Loseva 1970:163).

At Bear Cave, also in the Pechora basin, the analysis of osteological materials in the horizon of brown pebbly loam with Paleolithic cultural remains showed a preponderance of reindeer bones (2,271) followed by varying hare (*Lepus timidus*) (2,304), arctic fox (585), wolf (144), cave bear (414), horse (217), musk-ox (109), and mammoth (73). There were also large numbers of bird bones, including over 3,000 from the ptarmigan (*Lagopus* sp.). The list includes large numbers of vole bones, as well as bones of other rodents, squirrels, and various weasels.

In addition to mammoth, large animal remains included those of rhinoceros, *Bos* and *Bison* sp., moose, saiga antelope, and deer.

In the two upper horizons, mammoth diminishes and is then absent. There is, likewise, a diminution of large animals such as rhinoceros, *Bos* and *Bison*, musk-ox, horse, moose, saiga antelope, deer (absent entirely in the upper level), and reindeer, as well as wolf, arctic fox, and hare. Cave bear bones also diminish in numbers, with brown bear absent in the Upper Paleolithic horizon and then appearing in small numbers in the upper horizons. Bear Cave and another cave on a tributary of the upper Pechora are believed to be the northernmost finds of cave bear and cave lion remains.

Some of the bones in the faunal list were associated with human activity, including the reindeer antlers and musk-ox skull mentioned in the section on dwellings (see pages 201–227); other bones had obviously been brought into the cave by predators.

Although the fauna of the brown loam horizon generally represent what is referred to as the Upper Pleistocene "mammoth complex" (Guslitser and Kanivets 1965:89–91), some species usual for the complex, such as the Ob' lemming, large jerboa, and reddish suslik, were absent. Likewise, the land mollusk (*Vallonia tenuilabris*) associated with loess formations was not found, in contrast to the situation at Molodova V. Spore and pollen analyses indicated special ecological conditions — a warmer and wetter microclimate — at the cave mouth and in the ravine. The area surrounding the cave was, however, probably one of open areas with tree clumps or sparse forestation, a cold forest-steppe, especially in view of the absence of dwarf birch pollen. Also, bits of pine charcoal were found in the cave. The presence of saiga antelope and the steppe pika (*Ochotona*) were also indicators. At present, the pika occurs only as far north as the southern Urals and eastern Kazakhstan, while the saiga antelope does not live farther north than the fifty-second parallel. Likewise, the horse is a steppe and forest-steppe form; *Bison*, *Bos* sp. and skunk live in both steppe and forested areas. Marten and hazel grouse, also appearing in the faunal list, are forest dwellers. Guslitser and Kanivets (1965:92) also are of the opinion that the presence of horse, saiga antelope, wolf, and arctic fox indicates only a lighter winter snowfall during the period of the formation of the brown loam horizon.

In the more northern Pechora region, Pleistocene deposits in three of twenty-seven previously unknown caves on the middle course of the Ilych River (approx. lat. 62°30′N long. 58°00′E) contained "bones of mammoth, woolly rhinoceros, wild cattle, musk-ox, horses, cave bear and other mammals" (Guslitser and Kanivets 1965:98).

The Talitskiy site at the mouth of the Chusovaya contained mammoth, rhinoceros, reindeer, horse, hare, wolf, arctic fox, and lemmings (Beregovaya 1960:69). Other Urals sites, including numerous caves in the basins of the Kama, Ural, Chusovaya, and Ufa rivers, contained bones of reindeer, rhinoceros, horse, deer, moose, bison and *Bos* sp., saiga antelope, arctic fox, hare, rodents, and birds. Cave bear is sometimes mentioned, sometimes only "bear," presumably *Ursus arctos*. Mammoth is not uniformly reported; whether its absence is accidental for a particular site or explainable by ecological conditions or unfavorable terrain is not clear. Cave lion and hyena are also reported. In the basin of the Taliga, horse, reindeer, rhinoceros, *Bos*, deer, fox, hare, rodents, and birds, but no mammoth, are listed for Medved'-Kamen' Grot.

Except for Ust'-Kanskaya in the upper Ob' system, data on western Siberian sites are meager. Chernoozer'ye contained tentatively identified remains of moose, wild cattle, horse, fox, and hare, with mammoth and rhinoceros evidently absent. Mammoth bone found at Volch'ya Griva was dated to approximately 14,000 B.P. (see Table 3 page 243 and section on dwellings pages 201–227). Ust'-Kanskaya, as already pointed out, was notable for its mixture of mountain and dry-steppe or semidesert forms (yak, wild ass, horse, gazelle, spiral-horned antelope) with an absence of mammoth attributed to the altitude and local terrain.

The diversity of faunal remains at Afontova Gora II, on the upper Yenisey in central Siberia has already been discussed in the section on dwellings (see pages 201–227). Reindeer is predominant, with mammoth and arctic fox absent in the upper horizon. At Mal'ta and Buret', the two major Angara sites, reindeer, likewise, was predominant, although mammoth and rhinoceros were also important among large animals. Bird and fish bones were found at these central Siberian sites in contrast to their scarcity or absence in European Russian sites. Brief reports on recently discovered sites in the Angara region do not discuss faunal remains, except for mention of a rhinoceros long bone in association with artifacts at a site on the Ida River (Medvedev 1971:184, 1972:253). "Mammoth fauna" are reported in the valley of the Lena at recently discovered Makarovo III (Aksenov 1972:254).

Important Individual Species

MAMMOTH.   Table 3 summarizes radiocarbon datings for mammoth tissue and bone. Only two bone datings, open to question since results for bone are often too young, are available for the European USSR. When compared with the datings of soft parts from the Taymyr Peninsula and the Yakut ASSR, with the exception of the date for sinew from the Mamontova River (Number 11), both bone datings listed are relatively recent, as is the one for bone from western Siberia. The timespan within these datings is very long — some 30,000 years. The Siberian samples (as well as sample of rhinoceros) were from carcasses found in frozen ground, where the animals had died of natural causes, often from entrapment and suffocation, as in the case of the Berezovka mammoth. The number of frozen carcasses reported from Siberia, especially along the Lena, is very large, and at one time the Siberian trade in fossil ivory was of commercial importance. Examination of a number of the carcasses showed the animals to be in prime condition, indicating an abundance of food. Tolmachoff (1933) gives detailed information on the earlier history of frozen mammoth discoveries in Siberia.

The facts cited earlier may possibly have a bearing on differential causes of extinction in Siberia and European Russia. In European Russia, with its much larger human population, man may have played a part in extinction by destroying or greatly reducing the mammoth breeding stock. This theory is borne out by the large number of young and half-grown remains found in the Ukranian sites taken in conjunction with the late breeding age of elephant species, as pointed out by Krantz (1970:168–169). In the case of the mammoth, hunting practices may have been wasteful for unavoidable reasons. Also, human activities along migration routes and at watering places may have had a disturbing effect on the life cycles of animals.This effect would would probably have operated where Upper Paleolithic sites were located along river banks, precisely because of the abundance of animals in such areas. On the other hand, man and mammoth coexisted on the Russian plain for many thousands of years, as shown on Ivanova's analysis of the Molodova V horizons. Her table shows mammoth absent at the very end of the Upper

Paleolithic, correlated with radiocarbon dates in the 11,000 to 10,000 B.P. range; the youngest date for mammoth bone (Krantz 1970: Table 3) is 11,000 B.P. for Kostenki 2, second terrace. Mammoth, as well as other Upper Pleistocene species, survived the climatic oscillations of the last glacial period. Extinction in European Russia at the end of the Pleistocene may, therefore, have resulted from the complex interaction of

Table 3.   Radiocarbon datings of mammoth tissue and bone woolly rhinoceros tissue in European Russia and Siberia

Species	Location	Age (B.P.)	Lab. No. and Reference	Comments
MAMMOTH				
1. Blood and fat[a]	Berezovka R., Yakut ASSR., Siberia (lat. 67°30′N long. 155°30′E)	>39,000	T-299; Nydal 1961:180	See date description
2. Fat[a]	Sanga-Yuryakh (R.) Yakut ASSR., (mouth: approx lat. 72°10′N, long. 144°30′E)	>39,000	T-170; Nydal 1961:179	See date description
3. Fat[a]	Lena R. delta, Yakut ASSR., (lat. 72°00′N, long. 129°00′E)	>33,000	T-171; Nydal 1961:179	See date description; also No. 6 (Y-633)
4. Skin[a]	Gyda R., Gydanskiy Penin., Krasno-yarsk Kray, Sib. (approx. lat. 72°00′N, long. 78°00′E)	33,500±1000	T-298; Nydal 1961:180	Incorrectly given as Yakut ASSR in date description
5. Skin[a]	Mokhovaya R., delta of Yenisey, Krasno-yarsk Kray (approx. lat. 72°00′N, long. 84°00′E)	>32,500	T-169; Nydal 1961:179	Incorrectly given as Yakut ASSR in date description
6. Skin[a]	Lena R. delta, Yakut ASSR (same location as No.3)	>30,000	Y-633; Stuiver et al. 1960:53	Part of same sample as No. 3 (T-171)
7. Hair	Chekurovka settle-ment, Lena R. delta, Yakut ASSR (lat. 71°00′N, long. 127°40′E)	26,000±1600	Mo-215; Vinogradov et al. 1966:320	Discovered 1960
8. Tissue	Pyasina R., Taymyr Penin., C. Siberia (Pyasina: lat. 73°50′N, long. 87°10′E)	25,100±550;	LE-612; Dolukhanov, Romanova, and Semyontsov 1970:149	Discovered 1964

Table 3. (*continued*)

Species	Location	Age (B.P.)	Lab. No. and Reference	Comments
I. MAMMOTH				
9. Bone[b]	Byzovaya, Komi ASSR, N. Russia (lat.65°08'N, long.57°30'E)	18,320±280	TA–121; Punning *et al.* 1968:379	Collected 1964 by V. I. Kanivets
10. Bone[b]	Volch'ya Griva, Novosibirsk Obl., W. Siberia (approx. lat. 55°10'N, long. 80°15'E)	14,200±150	SOAN–78; Firsov, Panychev, and Orlova 1972:196	
11. Sinew[a]	Manontova R., Taymyr Penin. (approx. lat. 75°45'N, long. 99°00'E)	11,450±250	T–297; Nydal 1961: 179–180	Discovered 1948: "geologic conditions indicate . . . warm postglacial time"
12. Bone[b]	Kostenki II, Don R., Russia (lat. 51°24'N, long. 39°01'E)	11,000±200	GIN–93; Cherdyntsev *et al.* 1968:431	From 2nd terrace; possible assoc. with burial; see Table 2
II. WOOLY RHINOCEROS				
1. Skin[a]	Nochnoy brook, El'gi R., Yakut ASSR (approx. lat. 64°00'N, long. 138°00'E)	>38,000	T–172; Nydal 1961:179	Discovered 1948; only pretreatment with HCL

[a] See also text.
[b] All bone datings open to question; see Protsch and Berger 1973:235–239.

environmental and human factors; in Siberia, especially in the north central and northeastern areas, changes in natural conditions at the beginning of the Holocene may alone have brought about the mammoth's extinction.

REINDEER. In contrast to the mammoth, the reindeer was a successful survivor of the Pleistocene. The species extant in the USSR is *Rangifer tarandus,* which exists both in the wild state and as a domesticate of considerable economic importance. The southern boundary of distribution of the wild reindeer has moved north in historic times, in both Europian and Asiatic Russia, although as late as the beginning of the Christian era reindeer was still a winter migrant into the Ukraine (Pidoplichko 1969:29). During the Upper Paleolithic this was also believed to be the case, since the bones of young reindeer have not been found to date in Ukrainian sites (Pidoplichko 1969:68). The reindeer of Upper Paleolithic times was also widely distributed throughout Europe: in Ireland, England, France, and as far south as northern Spain. As previously noted, reindeer became predominant at Molodova V toward the end of the Upper Paleolithic; Pidoplichko reports it in the faunal lists for Dobranichivka, Mezhirich, Gontsy, and Mezin (eighty-three individuals) but not for Kiyevo-Kirillovskoye site, although it existed in the area at the time the site was occupied. Klein (1969a:67, Table 9) reports reindeer present in all terraces at the Kostenki-Borshevo sites. Sites in the Desna basin also contain reindeer remains; likewise, reindeer was found at Sungir' and the Urals sites, including a preponderance at Bear Cave. It is not clear whether reindeer was found in the western Siberian sites, and it is absent at Ust'-Kanskaya. Reindeer is predominant at Afontova Gora 2 and Mal'ta; it is also present in the other Angara sites.

HORSE.   Like the reindeer, the horse survived the Pleistocene, though now it is present in the Soviet Union mainly as a domesticate. It is a grass-eating herd animal, and in both the domestic and the wild state it is widely adapted to most landscapes and climates except for heavy forests and equatorial regions. The horse of the Upper Paleolithic is *Equus caballus,* and the Przewalski horse, now a nearly extinct semidesert inhabitant of Central Asia, is believed to be closely similar. The time of its extinction in Europe is in question; Kowalski (1967:359) believes that the wild horses reported in the Ukrainian steppes as late as the mid-nineteenth century were probably feral. Representations of horses in Upper Paleolithic art, mainly in French and Spanish cave paintings, vary widely, and it is impossible to tell whether they are all realistic representations. The black painted horse at Niaux, however, is anatomically very close to the Przewalski horse, with its short legs, heavy body, massive neck and head, and upright mane (Ucko and Rosenfeld 1967:82). The red painted horse at Kapova Cave in the Urals appears to have the same proportions and distinctive upright mane (Bader 1965c,Plate III).

OTHER LARGE HOOFED SPECIES.   In addition to reindeer and horse, bison, wild cattle, and various species of deer appear in faunal lists, varying in importance from site to site. Wild cattle (aurochs) became extinct in historic times. The giant deer *(Megaloceros)* also is extinct; moose, red deer, and roe deer have survived in various areas of Eurasia. The saiga is now confined to desert and semidesert areas of Asiatic Russia. The Pleistocene steppe bison *(Bison priscus)* is extinct; the European forest bison *(Bison bonasus),* which may be related, is a protected species. The musk-ox, always rare in the Upper Paleolithic and perhaps only a winter migrant into the Ukraine, has survived in the New World but not in Eurasia.

WOLF, FOX, ARCTIC FOX, HARE. Remains of wolf appear in most faunal lists. It would obviously have been important for its pelt; it was also probably eaten. The large numbers of wolf remains at Mezin and the characteristics of a one-year-old skull led Pidoplichko (1969:99–101, Table 103) to the conclusion that the wolf was in the process of domestication. In view of Professor Eugene Giles, who kindly reviewed the evidence presented by Pidoplichko, the points of contrast presented in the Table on page 103 of Pidoplichko are not taxonomically definitive in distinguishing the skulls of dogs and wolves. The anatomical variations of the "dog" from the Mezin site fall within those normal for the European Russian wolf; furthermore the argument deals with a single specimen.

Fox *(Vulpes)*, arctic fox *(Alopex lagopus)*, and hare, doubtless, also provided both pelts and meat. In addition, hare bones were used widely for small bone tools.

Hunting Methods

The methods employed for hunting mammoth and other large herd animals have been the object of much speculation. It is evident from remains found in the Caucasus and Crimea that the drive, wherein herds of animals were stampeded over cliffs or canyon walls, was practised in Mousterian times. For hunting mammoth during Upper Paleolithic times, Kowalski (1967:355) suggests the use of stampedes and pitfalls; Vereshchagin, the drive over ravine walls. This method would appear plausible in view of the location of many Upper Paleolithic sites, especially the Kostenki group, along riverbanks with ravines leading to floodplain watering places. The fire drive was another possible method. Vereshchagin also emphasizes the technological advance represented by the improvement of the flint or bone-tipped spear, as well as invention of the missile dart and flint axe (1967:373, 375–376). A noted previously, the long ivory spears found at Sungir' show that methods of straightening ivory had been discovered. The spear and dart would have made possible the hunting of solitary and, especially, young mammoth. Spears believed used for mammoth hunting found at Mezhirich had a maximum length of 37.0 centimeters, a width of 1.9 centimeters, and thickness of 1.7 centimeters, larger than the bison spears at Amvrosiyevka (Pidoplichko 1969:138). Other large herd animals such as bison were hunted by similar means or, perhaps, by the combined use of the drive and the spear, as evidenced by the bison kill at Amvrosiyevka in south Russia. A photograph of a bison shoulder blade from an unnamed "camp"on the Yenisey shows an embedded dart head of reindeer horn (Vereshchagin 1967: Figure 9). In the case of mammoth, it has been suggested that animals that had died from natural causes were also utilized.

Much has been made of the alleged wastefulness of the Upper Paleolithic hunter; this viewpoint, however, is disputed by Klein by analogy with the known full utilization of kills among primitive peoples today (1969a:223). Estimates advanced by various writers as to the degree of food utilization from kills will be discussed in the section on food supplies and population (see pages 247–248). The many raw materials provided from animal sources, in addition to meat, should always also be borne in mind — bone for fuel; bone, horn, and ivory for building materials, artifacts, and weapons, needles and fastenings for clothing, ornaments, and artistic/religious objects; hides, pelts, and sinew for house coverings, straps and ropes, thread, clothing; and so on. In fact, aside from flint and other stone and wood, animal resources provided all nonedible raw materials needed for survival.

Population Estimates

GENERAL STATEMENT.   Only very tentative estimates of population, based upon the size, number of settlements, and hypothetical food supplies, can be made for north-central Eurasia during the Upper Paleolithic. Certain generalizations, however, are stated below:

1.   The population of the Ukraine, Don, and Desna basins in European Russia was relatively dense, judging from the sheer number of Upper Paleolithic sites known for the area. Likewise, the complex social organization indicated by dwellings, elaborate burials, cultural inventories, and so on would require as a prerequisite moderately sized social units; this prerequisite would also apply for sites in central Siberia.

2.   Although man had successfully penetrated far to the north in European Russia (Krutaya Gora and Byzovaya) and many hunting camps (mostly caves) with rich faunal remains are known in the Urals, population numbers decreased to the north and east into western Siberia.

3.   Although human movement from European Russia into western Siberia may be assumed, the routes and time intervals remain unclear, especially in view of the water barriers of the Paleo-Tobol', Irtysh, and Ob' systems existing during the final glacial period. It is also possible that there was human movement into central Siberia from the south — the Altay region, Minusinsk basin, and Mongolian upland. Likewise, there may have been population movement from east to west during the final stages of the Sartan Glaciation.

4.   In central Siberia, in the upper Yenisey and Angara regions, there was fairly dense settlement (Afontova Gora sites, Mal'ta, and Buret' groups), with population numbers thinning out as man penetrated north

along the Lena. Generally, Upper Paleolithic sites in Siberia pertain to a later time horizon, although with some temporal overlap, judging from the radiocarbon dates for the Kostenki sites compared with those for Afontova Gora II and Mal'ta and the long Kokorevo series (see Appendix I).

5. Total population numbers may be assumed to have fluctuated considerably over time and from area to area. This would depend on climatic oscillations with resulting environmental changes, diminishing numbers of large game animals, seasonal scarcities of game especially in late winter and spring, epidemics, and so on. Group size also varied from settlement to settlement, subject to the conditions mentioned above, based on indications from the sites themselves. These possible variations are discussed in detail (see pages 249–251).

6. Sex ratios are impossible to determine. Nor can the widely assumed practice of infanticide, particularly female infanticide, be proven or disproven.

FOOD SUPPLIES.   Although there is evidence that on occasion many more herd animals were killed than could be consumed and that in some cases a kill of a full-grown mammoth could not be completely utilized because of the sheer size and weight of the beast, data from modern hunting societies show that very complete use is made of killed animals. The Nganasany of the Taymyr Peninsula as late as the 1930's utilized wild reindeer meat and fat for food; hides for clothing, blankets, straps, tent coverings, and storage containers; sinew for thread; hair for clothing decoration; horn (and mammoth ivory) for elements of domesticated reindeer harness; and bone for hide scrapers, and so on (Popov:1948).

Meat supplies were probably frozen for storage over the winter in pits (as indicated in the section on dwellings, see pages 201–227), thus assuring some continuity of food supply. If meat, fish, and possible vegetable products such as roots were cooked, this practice would have increased the utilization of food and served as a health measure. The prevalence of hearths in dwellings, temporary camps, and cave shelters with special construction features such as stone slab linings and the number of small hearths found in the "long house" at Kostenki I indicate the likelihood that cooking was practised routinely.

Presumably, meat from kills of large herbivores furnished the bulk of the diet. Wolves, foxes, and bears were probably also eaten, in addition to small game — hares, marmots, and so on. Although bird and fish bones have not been found to any extent in European Russian sites, waterfowl, eggs, and fish probably supplemented the diet during the spring and summer. Egg shells were found at Mezin (Pidoplichko:1969:85). The absence of their remains in European sites may possibly indicate that known sites, especially those with dwellings, were primarily for cold-weather occupancy. At Afontova Gora II, it will be recalled, the dwelling contained waterfowl bones and shed reindeer horns, indicating possible warm-weather occupancy. Roots, berries, and other plant foods probably also were gathered in the spring and summer.

DWELLING AND SITE OCCUPATION LENGTH.   Efforts to estimate length of occupancy of individual dwellings and sites from calculated food resources are highly tentative. Given an average family size of five to seven persons, the number of babies and young children would reduce daily caloric demands by as much as 40 percent.The adult male and female requirements would vary depending on activity. Outdoor hunting during cold weather would require a very large caloric intake — minimally 3,000 calories per day — whereas this requirement would be reduced during days of rest or relatively sedentary activity. Food requirements also vary in proportion to body size; the data from the few adult burials known for the Russian plain (see Table 2, pages 228–231) indicate that Cro-Magnon man was relatively tall. Sungir' man was estimated to have been about 5'11" tall but weighed only about 156 pounds. Only a very large number of skeletal measurements, however, could give sufficient data for reliable estimates of average adult height and weight, and there do not appear to be any female skeletal remains (other than the skull at Sungir'). In regard to family composition, even though *average* life expectancy was not beyond twenty to thirty years, there were probably some surviving adults no longer able to hunt, but capable of performing essential tasks such as tool and weapon making, bone and ivory work, preparation of skins and clothing, and so on. Note that in Table 2, one burial (Number 4) was that of a male estimated to be twenty to twenty-five years old, whereas two others (Numbers 3 and 5A) are of males over fifty years. Such people would have needed a smaller daily caloric intake than that of the young hunter, but to estimate their percentage of an average family or hunting group would be sheer guesswork.

Estimates of game animal weights also vary. Note, for instance. that Klein (1969a:222, Table 38) and Pidoplichko (1969:152) give different average body weights for mammoth, Klein using 4,540 kilograms, Pidoplichko, 2,500 kilograms. In the latter case, allowance was made for the large numbers of young and half-grown specimens killed; this more conservative estimate is probably more reliable. Killed weight minus bones is reduced, accordingly, to an average of 1,000 kilograms. For other important large game animals, wild cattle are calculated by Klein from "their nearest living relatives" at an average live weight over twice that given by Pidoplichko. Average body weights for reindeer given by the two authors are about the same, although Pidoplichko calculates a higher dressed weight — 100 kilograms versus 89. Wolves, an important component of aunal remains both in the Ukraine and on the Don, are given an average weight of 50 kilograms by Klein and only 25 kilograms by Pidoplichko. However, modern-day wolves vary greatly in size and weight, and it may be that their Upper Pleistocene relative on the Russian plain was larger than the living species. The modern Przewalski horse weighs 200 to 300 kilograms (Geptner, Nasimovich, and Vannikov 1961:723), but as with the case of the wolf the Upper Pleistocene ancestor may have been much larger, as indicated by both Pidoplichko and Klein, with an average weight of 400 to 450 kilograms. The caloric value of a kilogram of game varies seasonally; in the fall it may run as high as 5,000 calories from a fat animal and drop to perhaps 2,000 calories in the spring.

Other factors are the extent to which edible food from large animals was utilized, how much game may have been consumed at the time of a kill, and the amount of bones left behind on the spot. Another factor is the extent to which small game, fish, waterfowl, eggs, and vegetables may have supplemented large game supplies during the late spring, summer, and fall.

The resulting estimates of length of occupancy vary: Klein, assuming a group of fifty people requiring 114,000 calories (some 2,200 calories per person) for four of the Kostenki sites, estimates a four-year occupancy for Kostenki II, five and one-half months for Kostenki VIII (Tel'manskaya) (Horizon 1), between seven and eight months for Kostenki IV–2, and only forty-three days for Borshevo II–1 (Klein 1969a:222, Table 38). Pidoplichko, on the other hand, using an average of 800 to 1,000 gram daily requirement, estimates occupancy length for Dobranichevka, Mezin, Gontsy, and Kiyevo-Kirillovskoye at between seven and nine years and twenty years for the Mezhirich dwelling (Pidoplichko 1969:154). If his calculations are correct, his thesis of a semisettled population in the Ukraine during the Upper Paleolithic is borne out.

HEARTH AND DWELLING NUMBERS AND SETTLEMENT SIZE. The assumption of one family per hearth is probably reasonable; a conservative estimate of average family size is five persons, based on the 1926–1927 census figures for the Nganasany of the Taymyr Peninsula. Referring to the dwellings charted in Table 1, most of the round dwellings contain only one hearth, with oval and compound oval ones containing up to ten or eleven; thus, five to fifty people could have lived in a single dwelling. Note that the dwelling at Molodova I had eleven hearths, indicating the possibility of a dense population for the southern Ukraine in Mousterian times.

The settlement at Mezin is reported to have contained five dwellings; the one excavated has three hearths; assuming the other four dwellings contained one hearth each, seven families could have occupied the site. A conservative estimate of site population would, therefore, be thirty-five people; Pidoplichko quotes Bibikov as estimating a population of around fifty. In any event, a site population somewhere between these figures would represent a viable economic unit. Klein, likewise, estimates group size for the Kostenki sites at fifty persons. The large dwellings at Kostenki I and Kostenki IV (Table 1, Numbers 9, 12 and 13, see pages 208–209), as already pointed out, could have accommodated forty-five to fifty people; the dwelling at Avdeyevo (Table 1, Number 8, see page 207) is also a large compound oval, and the large rectangular dwellings at Mal'ta also could have held several families.

Around 500 Upper Paleolithic campsites are known for the Ukraine, most thickly clustered along the Dnestr and its tributaries. Many are multistratum, as with the Molodova group. The basin of the Don contains some thirty known sites, including twenty-one in the Kostenki group, many of which again are multistratum. Toward the north and east in the Desna, Sozh, Oka, Volga, Kama, and Chusovaya basins site numbers decrease. Since not all sites were occupied continuously, there is no way of estimating population numbers at a particular time, around 25,000 B.P., for example, without complete and reliable radiocarbon datings for the majority of the sites in the European USSR. So far this coverage does not exist, and its accomplishment would be a monumental task.

VIABLE GROUP SIZE.   For comparative purposes, data on the Nganasany, a migratory wild-reindeer hunting group living in the Taymyr Peninsula, may be relevant. In the 1930's all the Nganasany lived north of 70° north latitude in a very severe continental climate but with sparse winter snowfall. The Taymyr Peninsula was, of course, subject to glaciation during the Upper Pleistocene; the Nganasany were historical migrants, already acquainted with the use of iron, from south Siberia.

In the 1930's the Nganasany's total population was reported to be 699, occupying a total area of 132,574 square kilometers (Popov 1948:12). The population density, therefore, was 0.41 per 100 square kilometers, about the same as that for the Caribou Eskimo (Kroeber 1939:134). Fall migrations closely followed those of the reindeer south to the edge of the forest-tundra zone where the Nganasany winter. In the spring the reindeer were followed and hunted as far north as the Byrranga Plateau.

By the mid-nineteenth century the Nganasany had obtained firearms and had begun to herd domesticated reindeer for pulling their sleds, thus greatly increasing their mobility. Dogs were used for herding. Before they obtained firearms and introduced reindeer herding, their weapons were the bow and spear and movement was entirely on foot, with some use of man-drawn sleds. Formerly, also, the dugout (*zemlyanka*) was the winter dwelling; later, a tent, made of reindeer hides and poles, which could be loaded onto sleds for transport, came into year-round use. Clothing has continued to be made almost entirely of reindeer pelts, sewn with reindeer sinew. As late as the 1930's the mainstay of the diet was reindeer meat, supplemented by fish, and wild fowl, especially wild geese taken during the moulting season. Plant food was eaten during the early spring, frequently a time of starvation.

Traditionally, mass killings took place during the spring and fall at spots where the migrating reindeer crossed rivers or lakes. Also, at defined spots considered common property, reindeer were trapped with the aid of nets and blinds. Hunters with weapons (originally bows and later firearms) were stationed around the area to drive off beasts of prey; anyone not observing the regulations or interfering with the hunt was penalized by being required to donate his own domestic reindeer. Formerly, also, hunters were required to share their kills with their neighbors.

Before the Russian Revolution, there was a patrilineal clan structure, with the Avam section divided into five clans and the Vadeyev into six. Each clan was an exogamous unit, rather than territorial or economic. A Nganasany settlement as a rule consisted of families belonging to different clans. The social composition of these settlements sometimes consisted of households attached to the family of a wealthy man holding large numbers of domesticated reindeer.

According to the 1926–1927 Soviet census, the 5 Avam clans totaled 574 persons and 118 families, the number of families in the 5 clans varying from 14 to 39, and the number of persons per clan, 175 to 76. The Vadeyev, split into 6 clans, were less numerous, totaling only 224 persons and 41 families; the smallest clan consisted of only 11 persons all belonging to one family, while the largest contained 73 persons belonging to 15 families. For both groups, family size averaged 5 persons (Dolgikh 1952: Table 2). Six migration groups were formed from families belonging to different clans. From 2 or 3 to as many as 39 families from a particular clan could be found in each migration group; the groups themselves totaled from 13 to 42 families.[11] The termini of migrations to winter settlements were much closer together geographically than those for spring and summer, which fanned out to the north.

Conclusions

This examination of faunal resources, hunting methods, and population distributions is clearly of a preliminary nature, since only the most general features of the settlement of the immense area of north-central Eurasia, over the great timespan involved, can be indicated. Data on such areas as

[11] Note that Dolgikh's figure for total population according to the 1926–1927 census is 798 for Avam and Vadeyev. Popov gives only 699 persons for the Avam, Vadeyev, and Taymyr National Soviets during the 1930's, but he also reports eight migration groups.

western Siberia and the upland areas of the Irtysh and Yenisey are still inadequate; work underway at present by the radiocarbon laboratory of the Siberian Branch of the Academy of Sciences at Novosibirsk (laboratory designation SOAN) will in time make possible a more complete understanding of the paleogeography and paleoclimate of these areas.

Recent discoveries in northeastern Siberia, however, show that Upper Paleolithic man could survive in an environment even more challenging than that of north-central Eurasia. Mochanov (1972:251) reports the discovery of a Paleolithic campsite with mammoth bones and artifacts, on the Berelekh River, a branch of the Indigirka, at approximately 72° north latitude; it is probably the most northerly Paleolithic site in the world. Another site, on a brook flowing into the Kolyma at approximately 63° north latitude, contained flint implements. Both sites, as well as one discovered on the western shore of the Sea of Okhotsk, belong to the Dyuktay culture (see Semyontsov *et al.* 1972:357 for the Dyuktay Cave, Yakut ASSR, subseries; LE–784, Upper Paleolithic layer: 13,070 ± 90).

These sites, as well as those of north-central Eurasia under discussion in this paper, existed within a periglacial environment, the basic characteristics of which are described by Butzer (1964:105–119). Sher's study of natural conditions in the lower Kolyma region in northeast Siberia during the Upper Pleistocene using these concepts, probably has validity as well for north-central Siberia and even parts of the Urals and European Russia (Sher 1971:107–111).

During the Upper Pleistocene horses and bison dominated in the Kolyma area studied by Sher; mammoth and reindeer were represented, but musk-ox and rhinoceros were rare. The small mammals were similar to those in the contemporary fauna, although the hares, differing from today's varying hare, were close to those found at the Kostenki sites. Large predators included brown bear, wolf, and "cave cat."

Turning to the fossil flora, Sher notes that

> . . . in its assemblage of families, genera and species, determined from buried pollen, [the flora] scarcely differed from the contemporary. However, when we turn to vegetative associations, it must be noted that among them were [associations] absent at present in the lower reaches of the Kolyma or distributed locally (Sher 1971:108).

These associations included grasses (Gramineae), goosefoot (*lebeda*; Chenopodiaceae), and Artemisia, as well as those of green mosses, club mosses (*plauny*; Lycopodiaceae), Selaginella, Artemesia, and Carex. Along with these associations, spectra of contemporary type containing a large component of birch sections (*Nanae*) and other tundra bushes, plus sedges, grasses, and mosses, are also encountered. Other spectra show woody birch, willow, and alder (Sher 1971:108).

Under modern conditions Upper Pleistocene fauna, especially hoofed animals, could not live in the lower Kolyma (except in particular localities) because of the bushy vegetation, microrelief and viscous, water-saturated summer ground. Throughout north Eurasia, however, these same fauna — comprising a mixture of animals of open areas such as mammoth, horses, and bison; arctic forms such as the lemming, musk-ox, and arctic fox; and steppe forms such as the saiga antelope — subsisted on the periglacial vegetation, combining cold-adapted and xerophytic elements with sparse or absent arboreal vegetation. But, as Sher points out, many more concrete details are needed for an understanding of the present ecology of Upper Pleistocene fauna (1971:109). Presently favorable areas in extreme northeastern Siberia have meadow- , rock- , and tundra-steppe associations with a dominance of xerophytic and arctic-alpine species, indicating relict origin. Under the influence of intensified continentality, steppe, and tundra-steppe associations would have been widely distributed on southern slopes, with river valleys also favorable for steppe associations. Continental variants of tundra associations, including "forest-tundras," would have occurred on lowlands, while sheltered areas would have permitted the growth of thermophilic, although cold-resistant, vegetation. Soils in flat watersheds and depressions would have dried up much more completely than at present. The resulting postulated landscape would have had abundant short-grass pastures in valleys, light winter snow-cover, and a hard summer soil surface, capable of supporting large herds of grazers. Contemporary dry mountain areas of central Asia with light winter snow-cover are analogous.

Sher also deals with the complex problem of the depth of the active soil layer in summertime during the Pleistocene, accepting the simultaneous phenomenon of thick layers of permafrost. At present a relatively thin active layer (0.3 to 0.5 meters) under bush-sedge and sedge-moss associations with a tussocky microrelief is usually water-saturated in summer. During the Pleistocene intensive drying of the upper ground in the spring because of the light snow-cover and other factors, including the effects of dry-adapted vegetation, would have resulted in a hard surface. Sher concludes that during the Pleistocene the active layer probably was 0.6 to 1.0 meters thick in summer. Processes of soil instabilities (solifluction, cryoturbations, and so on) proceeded intensively in specific areas such as the northern slopes and during spring and autumn temperature shifts. Indirect evidence on the stability of the ground during the Pleistocene is provided by the relative narrowness of the hoof of the Late Pleistocene horse of the lower Kolyma compared with its contemporary European forms. Vegetation found in the stomachs of fossil animal remains or associations *in situ* confirm the nature of the vegetative associations. There are remains of saiga antelope, along with small horses and small short-horned bison, in the Aleshkin Suite pertaining to the end of the Sartan (ultimate) Glaciation, about 15,000 to 10,000 B.P., indicating extensive dry, hard expanses, thin snow-cover, a cold dry climate with about 300 millimeters of annual precipitation, and xerophytic vegetation by analogy with the conditions under which the saiga lives today. Evidently, the climate shifts during the Siberian interglacials, even allowing for the northward advance of forests, were not so drastic as to bring about extinction of the Upper Pleistocene fauna; on the other hand, the climatic alterations that ushered in the Holocene were sufficient to cause the extinction of many of the Pleistocene grazers without the agency of man.

Hence, Sher's data reveal in detail the combination of climatic factors, microrelief, and plant associations making possible the high bioproductivity of the periglacial environment (see also Butzer's discussion (1964:138). While Sher's study relates specifically to northeastern Siberia, its relevance to all of north-central Eurasia is evident.

STONE AND BONE ARTIFACTS

*Stone Typologies**

In 1951 S. N. Zamyatnin undertook a general classification of Upper Paleolithic cultures, using tool types as major, but not exclusive, criteria. He differentiated three major provinces: the European Periglacial, the Chinese-Siberian, and the Mediterranean-African. The last category included the Crimea and the Caucasus. North-central Eurasia between the mouth of the Oka River (44° east longitude) and the Altay foothills (82° east longitude) could not be classified for lack of data (Zamyatnin 1951:127–137).

Zamyatnin's regionalization has been both strengthened and modified by subsequent studies. Mousterian antecedents have been found for a division between central Europe, the Russian plain, and the Crimea, on the one hand, and the Caucasus and central Asia on the other. The Caucasus, however, exercised influences upon the Crimea, the Kostenki sites, and the Volga (Lyubin 1970:34). Farther to the east, Siberian-Mongolian and east Asiatic provinces have been distinguished for this same period (Lyubin 1970:35; Klein 1969b).

For the Upper Paleolithic, Grigor'yev (1970) has sought to identify the most important regional traditions and interregional influences in north-central Eurasia (see Appendix 1 for site list). The resulting pattern is much more complex than the one postulated by Zamyatnin. A central question raised by several archeologists but unresolved to Grigor'yev's satisfaction is the degree of continuity between Mousterian antecedents and Upper Paleolithic traditions in a number of regions.

---

*   This section was written by Demitri B. Shimkin. — *Editor*

A number of salient points in Grigor'yev's analysis may be summarized; the discussion below excludes the distinctive Transcaucasian traditions.

The longest regional sequence on the Russian plain is that for the Molodova culture, which may have had a Mousterian genesis, and which dates back to beyond 30,000 B.P. in its earliest Upper Paleolithic stage (Babin I, Lower Stratum). The second stage (typified by Molodova V, Stratum X) continues to ca. 28,000 B.P.; the third (typified by Molodova V, Stratum VII) lasted to ca. 23,000 B.P.; and the fourth (with Molodova V, Stratum I, as representative) ends about 10,000 B.P. Other sites in the western and central Ukraine, such as Lipa, some 200 kilometers north of Molodova, were also characterized by long local sequences, with only limited effects from interregional loans (Grigor'yev 1970).

In the Kostenki sites on the Don River the picture is very different. Instead of the gradual differentiation of long-lasting traditions, as to the west, both initial heterogeneity and temporal discontinuities are evident. In the Lower Stratum (Horizon 5) of Kostenki I is a seemingly archaic culture (*Streletskaya kul'tura*) perhaps derived from the North Caucasian Mousterian (Il'skaya; see Gorodtsov 1941; Yefimenko 1958). It includes:

. . . elongated sidescrapers (*skreblo*) with convex cutting edges, bifacially retouched; points and sidescraper knives, also bifacial, with two elongated, often convergent, edges. A large part of the inventory consists of endscrapers — almost all on flakes of shortened proportions, with retouched longitudinal sides and, often, retouched ventral surfaces. In form they are most often triangular, with straight or convex longitudinal edges and often sharpened at the butt. A few endscrapers are from thick pieces of flint (carinated). Almost as numerous as the endscrapers are the triangular, bifacially retouched knives with concave butts — the most distinctive form of the Streletskaya Culture. Other artifacts — burins, chisel-type tools, borers — are few (Grigor'yev 1970:48).

The lower stratum of Kostenki XVII (Spitsyn Culture), which dates from about 21,000 B.P. (see Appendix 1–58f), is believed to be broadly contemporaneous with the Streletskaya Culture. But it is profoundly different in its characteristics, being based upon the working of large prismatic blades.

Many other nonconformities have been proposed by Grigor'yev for the Kostenki sites. Some, however, may be due to errors of dating; typologically and geologically based correlations fail to coincide with radiocarbon datings by thousands of years, in several instances.[12]

In the Urals the cave site of Smelovskaya II, which is characterized by an Upper Paleolithic fauna (*Equus caballus, Coelodonta antiquitatis,*

---

[12] For example, Grigor'yev (1970:48) dates Kostenki XII (Volkhovskaya) as contemporaneous with Kostenki VIII (Tel'manskaya) and much younger than Kostenki I or XVII, although GIN–89 (Cherdyntsev *et al.* 1968:431) gives a date of 23,600 ± 300.

Bison priscus, and others), has a typologically archaic stone inventory. It includes fifty-three flint artifacts, thirty-one talc pendants, and ten talc pieces and plates. The artifacts include only twenty-three flakes, six blade-like flakes and blades, two cores, and other unfinished objects. The characteristics of the artifacts are generally Mousterian, compatible with central Asiatic sites. At the same time, the presence of drilled talc pendants, as well as the fauna, indicate an Upper Paleolithic age for Smelovskaya II. The site remains enigmatic (Bader 1971b:200–208).

In Siberia most of the typologically archaic sites, such as Tuekta (Krylova and Pavlyuchenko 1962), apparently remain undatable. Grigor'yev ascribes only Sagly in the Sayan Range and Ust'-Kanskaya in the Altay to the Mousterian epoch. Detailed descriptions for the former are unavailable. The stone inventory of the latter, which has been described at length by Rudenko (1961), has been analyzed comparatively by Anisyutkin and Astakhov (1970). These authors regard part of the artifacts, that is, the Châtelperron knife (Rudenko 1961: Figure 16–1) and the thin prismatic blades (Rudenko 1961: Figure 15–1–8), as later admixtures. The rest of the inventory falls completely within the Levallois Mousterian complex, as defined by Bordes. In fact, the inventory appears to be essentially included within the types represented at Starosel'ye, a terminal Mousterian site in the Crimea, albeit with different frequencies, as is evident from Table 4, compiled from Anisyutkin and Astakhov (1970:3) and Klein (1969b:260).[13]

Anisyutkin and Astakhov see distinct similarities between the inventory at Ust'-Kanskaya and the nearby late Upper Paleolithic site at Strostki, which the excavators related to the Kokorevo Culture on the Yenisey, especially Kokorevo I (Sosnovskiy 1941:123).

In general, Grigor'yev identifies two large lithic traditions in Siberia (see also Abramova 1966). One, characterized by flake tools, especially sidescrapers and points, is centered on the Yenisey. It includes the Afontova Gora and the Kokorevo sites, which can be differentiated as subcultures; Strostki in the Altay; Oshurkovo in the Transbaykal; and a number of later sites on the upper Lena. Of key importance in this group is the Lower Stratum of Afontova Gora II, which Abramova characterizes as follows:

The bulk of the stone tools comprise sidescrapers of various types and primarily flake scrapers. There are also borers, drills, chisel-type tools bifacially worked at the tip, cobble chopping tools, and retouched blades, with knife-like blades of regular outline notable among the last. Points and burins are rare and ill-defined. Both cobble and wedge (blade) cores occur (1966:11).

[13] A Levallois component has also been identified within the late and terminal Mousterian cultures of Central Asia, especially at Khodzhikent in the Uzbek SSR (Ranov 1971:230).

The other tradition is found at Mal'ta, Buret', and the later Krasnyy Yar, all in the Angara region, and also at Sannyy Mys, on the lower Uda River, across Lake Baykal and 300 kilometers east of Mal'ta (see also Okladnikov 1961). The anomalous European characteristics of the Mal'ta tradition were identified by P. P. Yefimenko (1953); recent data, especially I. G. Shovkoplyas' monograph on Mezin (1965), serve only to corroborate this remarkable nonconformity. To quote Yefimenko:

One of the most common groups of stone tools at Mal'ta, as at Mezin, consists of scrapers and every variety of small boring tool, which in part are true punches, and were used, evidently, for the sewing of fur clothing, which is indicated by the discovery of numerous bone needles. But most of them [i.e., the boring tools] served, rather, as cutting tools for the tailoring of furs and the cutting of bone and antler. Such also were the functions of knives with more massive points; some have a working edge made by the removal of a burin spall. Here are, as Gerasimov has shown, more or less typical burins — of central and lateral types — as well; they appear wherever bone is widely used. However, they are not so frequent here [at Mal'ta], often being replaced, evidently, by other tools, e.g., larger and stronger blades with varied cutting tips.
One of these instruments [a Châtelperron knife][14] has been preserved in its reindeer antler handle. . . .
In the collections of M. M. Gerasimov are ordinary end scrapers on a blade; small, round scrapers; and 476 massive instruments of the type of round core-like scrapers and flensers — certain analogues with which are found at Mezin. We may also indicate concave instruments, e.g., flint blades with concavities at the tip, which are peculiarities of the stone inventory of Mezin and certain Solutrean settlements of western Europe. A very curious category of tools is the "ax-like" instrument [Gerasimov] or "disk-like" artifact. In fact, this is fully comparable with the small flint disks encountered in Aurignacian-Solutrean sites . . . which, when attached to a handle, substituted for an ax (1953:474–475).

These broad generalizations on the stone industries of north-central Eurasia can be augmented by a number of specific site and type relationships.

On the Russian plains, both Sungir' and Byzovaya appear to be related to the Streletskaya Culture already associated with the Lower Stratum of Kostenki I. Bader (1961) has characterized some 5,000 worked pieces of flint found at Sungir'. All but 6 percent were debris. Eighty-five percent of the worked flint consisted of flakes and the remainder, blades. The composition of the artifacts, numbering about 300, was as follows:

1. Retouched blades: 35.8 percent;
2. Retouched flakes: 10.5 percent;
3. Endscrapers: 13.3 percent;
4. Sidescraper-like forms: 12.5 percent;
5. Burins: 6.2 percent;

---

[14] See Yefimenko 1953:475. Figures 229–234. The analogue at Mezin is twice as large and may have been used without a handle (Shovkoplyas 1965:162, Table XXV, No. 21).

6. Pièces écaillées: about 5 percent;
7. Other: about 17 percent.

Bader ascribed Sungir' to the Streletskaya Culture because of the following common features:

1. Cobble flint as the basic raw material, with a total absence of high-quality Cretaceous flint.
2. The primitive techniques of splitting the rocks and preparing most of the tools.
3. The high predominance of flakes over blades and the relatively low quality of the latter.
4. The absence of insert tools.
5. The appreciable role of sidescraper-type tools.
6. The similarity in form of endscrapers, especially carinated ones.
7. The presence of triangular flint points with slightly concave bases (Bader 1961:126).

Kanivets (1969) found sixty-three worked flint objects, including only thirty-seven cores, flakes, and chips, at Byzovaya. There was clearly no local manufacture, the nearest veins of flint being at least thirty kilometers distant. The tools, with the exception of one regular, large blade, were from flakes. However, the retouching technique of the working ends of the endscrapers — long, almost parallel, facets — indicated an advanced technology. The tools discovered in 1963–1964 included two hammer stones, ten endscrapers, a combination endscraper-borer, a knife-borer retouched on both edges, corner burins, some unfinished objects, and a leaf-shaped, bifacial knife or point. The last especially links with Sungir' and the Streletskaya Culture (see also Yefimenko 1958:247–248).

Thus far, the predominance of probable western influences in the stone inventories of north-central Eurasia has been emphasized. There is, however, important evidence of influences from the Yenisey northwestward to the Kama River (Talitskiy site) and the Pechora River (Bear Cave).

Bader (1960, 1965b) has identified Talitskiy as a site with predominantly Siberian characteristics, albeit with a number of evidently western features.

Thus, neither regularly-shaped prismatic cores nor regularly-shaped knife blades are found at the site. Knife blades comprise only 17 percent of the total [number] of blades and flakes jointly. Most of the endscrapers are made from flakes; sometimes they are made from short blades of poor quality; little round scrapers, 1.5–3 cm. in diameter, comprise an appreciable proportion of the total. Burins are almost absent. There are inserts — small knifelike blades with blunted and unblunted edges — and even bone tools with inserts, most like the points from Afontova Gora III. Finally, there are also found rather large chopping tools and sidescrapers, mostly of slate but some of flint. Only one was made from a split cobble.... (Bader 1965b:133).

At the same time the Talitskiy stone inventory is characterized by some distinctly European features, as one would except from its geographical location:

Such are several endscrapers at the tips of broken blades; carinated scrapers with canted working ends (usually turned to the right); knives from elongated flakes, and flakes with retouched edges, pièces écaillées, etc. (Bader 1965b:135).

The lithic industry at Bear Cave on the Pechora has, in turn, been correlated with that of the Talitskiy site. The fifty-eight artifacts found at Bear Cave include a hammer stone, seven retouchers, three knives, several blades (especially inserts), twenty-five double sidescrapers, thirteen simple sidescrapers; a burin made on the corner of a broken blade, and, finally, a mammoth tusk artifact used for digging. These tools differ substantially from those found nearby, at Byzovaya. The lamellar flint (*plitchatyy kremen'*) limited the size of artifacts at Bear Cave to an average of three to four centimeters. Nevertheless, 15 percent of the flint objects were made up of blades, elongated flakes (*plastinchatyye otshchepy*), or implements made from them. While the poor quality of the Bear Cave materials gives them a local specificity, the resemblances to Talitskiy arise not only from general features of technique but also from specific peculiarities: small cores with multiple striking surfaces (*ploshchadki*) from which spalls were struck off in various directions; short, often irregular, blades; small blade inserts; endscrapers on short, thick flakes; and concave (*vyyemchatyy*) scrapers (Guslitser and Kanivets 1965:98; Kanivets 1969:141–142).

Summary and Problems for Further Study

To summarize, Zamyatnin's generalizations (1951) for stone typologies can be restated currently as follows:

1. In north-central Eurasia, Upper Paleolithic stone technologies appear, to an appreciable degree, to have Mousterian roots.
2. In the western and central Ukraine, great continuities in localized traditions predominate.
3. The Kostenki sites on the Don River have had a more complex and discontinuous history, both locally and interregionally. In particular, the Streletskaya Culture associated with the Lower Stratum of Kostenki I seems to have some sources in the North Caucasian Mous-

terian (Il'skaya) and, in turn, to have influenced the northern sites of Sungir' and Byzovaya.

4. In the Altay, the Ust'-Kanskaya site has profound similarities to the terminal Mousterian inventory at Starosel'ye in the Crimea as well as some distinctly Upper Paleolithic features, which may be later admixtures.

5. Ust'-Kanskaya, in turn, may have contributed to the development of the predominant cultures of the Siberian Upper Paleolithic (the Afontova Gora, Kokorevo, and allied traditions).

6. The stone inventory of Mal'ta (and of related sites) in the Angara region remains nonconformal within the Siberian milieu. To this day the lithic industry at Mal'ta appears most similar, in many details, to that at Mezin, on the Desna River in the central Ukraine.

7. A northwestward extension of lithic traditions from the Yenisey appears to be represented at Talitskiy and Bear Cave on the Pechora.

In addition to the analysis of the characteristics and interrelationships of the lithic industries of entire sites and regions, Soviet archeologists have devoted attention to the functional, developmental, and comparative analysis of particular categories of tools. These include researches on axes and adzes in both Europe and Siberia, which may represent a historic entity (Astakhov 1967; Shovkoplyas 1965:173–174; Yefimenko 1958:280–283). They also include the comparative examination of slotted bone points, in which the Siberian series appear to be sharply distinct from the European, except at Talitskiy. In the former case, the slots were designed for the insertion of prismatic flint blades; in the latter, for better stability in flight and better bloodletting (Abramova 1967).

Further progress in the study of stone technology will most likely result from three trends. One is the standardization of terminology to facilitate exact and comprehensive comparisons. To date the Bordes classification has been used, with some success, in the study of both Mousterian and Upper Paleolithic inventories (see, for example, Anisyutkin and Astakhov 1970; Chernysh 1967; Klein 1969b; Litovchenko 1969). Clearly, however, much added work is needed in developing more detailed subcategories useful in differentiating local types of artifacts and, above all, in formulating standard descriptions for the classes of artifacts unrepresented in the Bordes (1968) classifications.

Stress on quantitative descriptions of large collections is also needed. Such quantitative descriptions often reveal significant revisions of approximate frequencies obtained from preliminary data; compare, for example, Klein (1969b:101) and the later materials from Litovchenko (1969:112–113), both on Stratum II of Kostenki VIII (Tel'manskaya). Both sources show the predominance of backed bladelets and points; both note a high frequency of burins. However, while Klein noted "some" blades and fragments of blades with continuous retouch, Litov-chenko attributes a fifth of the entire industry to this category.

Finally, the need for many more radiocarbon and other absolute dat-ings of sites — and, by extension, their industries — is clearcut. Without this, historical processes will remain confused. This particularly applies to key sites and strata, such as the Lower Stratum of Kostenki I and Mezin.

Bone Tools and Weapons

In his 1951 characterization of tools in north-central Eurasia, Zamyatnin made the following statement about tools (and other objects) made from bone:

All this mass of heterogeneous stone tools is complemented by numerous and varied bone tools, decorations, and artistic objects.

Among bone tools, along with the common awls, punches, bone dart points, and polishers, are found extremely fine needles from bone or mammoth ivory, with exceedingly artfully drilled eyes; bone points with deep side grooves for the insert of flint bladelets, which form a sharp stone edge; devices for the kneading of straps in the form of sections of reindeer antler with pierced holes [i.e., "batons de commandement"] (1951:137).

Bone working is believed to have had its origins in the efforts of Lower Paleolithic man to extract marrow from bone, and the use of fire and flint to work bone also probably dates to that time (Semenov 1964:145). In the area of the present-day Soviet Union there is evidence from Mous-terian cave sites (Kiik-Koba, Chokurcha, Kosh-Koba) of elementary bone working, including ivory fragments from Chokurcha that had been whittled with flint (Semenov 1964:147). It was Upper Paleolithic advances in stone technology, especially the full development of the burin, which made possible the manufacture of sophisticated bone artifacts such as eyed needles, bone hafts for flint inserts, weapons, and ornaments and chattel art. Bone tools from Soviet sites have not received the attention given to stone typology, although both Gerasimov (1941) and Semenov (1964) have described the techniques of working bone, horn, and ivory.

In the early period of the Upper Paleolithic the material of choice was mammoth ivory for its qualities of hardness, smoothness, and elasticity. Reindeer horn has closely comparable qualities, and during the later period of the Upper Paleolithic it was used widely. Ordinary bone, although not as durable as and more brittle than ivory and reindeer horn, also was employed: large bones (such as a mandible) were employed in a semiworked condition, and small bones were carefully manufactured into awls, needles, and so on. Weapons, such as daggers and dart points, were often made of mammoth ivory; massive spears, from long bones of large animals. Hafts for inserts were variously made from horn, bone, or ivory.

Percussion and splitting techniques were employed for breaking up long and flat bones and ivory; a mammoth scapula from one of the Kostenki sites showed the combined use of percussion and burin techniques. Circular grooving was the method employed for cutting through mammoth tusks; antlers were severed by chopping them with a sharp tool. Long bones of small animals such as hare and arctic fox, intended for manufacture into needles, awls, beads, and so on, were sawn through with a retouched bladelet. For the longitudinal flaking of ivory, a pointed tool would strike off irregular flakes, preliminary grooving with a burin would produce more regular flakes. As previously mentioned, ivory and bone were also whittled with flint tools.

While ivory can be split more easily when dry than in the fresh state, other types of working can be more easily carried out by restoring the ivory's plasticity, either by soaking in water or steaming. The ivory coronet found in the child's burial at Mal'ta was probably treated in this way, and the long ivory spears found at Sungir' were probably straightened by similar methods.

Types of Bone Tools

Partly because of the relative paucity of detailed reports on bone inventories, and partly because various writers often differentiate a tool of a particular type, bone tool types are difficult to categorize. Nevertheless, a broad characterization is attempted below. Weapons, mainly dart points, are treated separately.

LARGE BONES IN A SEMIWORKED STATE.   Large bones used as grinding stones date from the Mousterian (Kiik-Koba), with analogues found at Yeliseyevichi. Likewise, the use of long bones for retouchers continued from the Mousterian into the Upper Paleolithic. The mandible of a carnivore with attached canine was often made into a tool for cracking long bones. Deer and mammoth ribs (some bearing traces of ocher) formed burnishing tools for dressing skins; examples are known from Kostenki I and Avdeyevo. A mammoth rib found at Kostenki I had apparently been used as a palette. Mammoth scapulae embedded in the living surface of a dwelling may have formed some sort of table or workbench; several such scapulae were found at Kostenki I (Semenov 1964:169–171, Figure 89). Ribs and tusks probably formed simple digging sticks.

RIBS AND TUSKS. When ribs and tusks were lashed to wooden handles (see Semenov 1964:Figure 94), as is believed to have been the case, they then became mattocks and picks; if this assumption is correct, they could then be classified as compound tools. Implements of this type have been found at Pushkari I, Yeliseyevichi, Avdeyevo in European Russia, Bear Cave in the Urals, and at Pavlov in Czechoslovakia.

KNIVES. Knives were most often made from long-bone splinters, with edges sharpened, presumably by whittling. Those found in small numbers at Mal'ta averaged eighty-seven to ninety millimeters in length and were probably used for skinning game (Gerasimov 1941:74). Bone tools and weapons that incorporated their own handles usually have a chipped or roughened surface on the haft for improved grasp.

HAMMER-LIKE IMPLEMENTS. Hammer-like implements of deer horn are widely distributed. Sometimes a naturally shed horn was used, as in the "hammer" at Mezin made from the shed horn of a giant deer. If the aperture in the working end was intended for a flint insert, the implement would then have to be characterized as the haft portion of a compound tool. Horn hammers with similar apertures have been found at Chulatovo I (as well as Willendorf). Since none has been found to date with the flint insert actually in place, their classification remains uncertain. Analogues, though usually not in the number found at Mezin, are known from Chulatovo I and II, Yeliseyevichi, Udinovo, Gontsy, Dobranichivka, and Suponevo.

CHISELS AND WEDGES. Straight pieces of bone, or horn with a sharpened, somewhat squared-off edge, either bifacially or unifacially worked, which could have served as wedges for severing animal skulls, for preparing simple wooden tools, or for work requiring a chisel-like tool, are variously called wedges (*Klin'ya*) or chisels (*dolota*). Of the three found at Mal'ta, two were of reindeer horn and the third of long bone. One of the reindeer horn chisels was unifacially worked, and the other smaller one was bifacially worked. Analogues to the Mal'ta chisels were found at Afontova Gora. Two sections of reindeer antler (15.5 by 3.0 to 3.5 centimeters and 16.5 by 2.5 to 3.0 centimeters, respectively) found in Horizon 3 at Borshevo II had beveled edges, and although listed as mattocks, perhaps could be more accurately described as chisels (Klein 1969a:206, Table 36).

IMPLEMENTS PRIMARILY USED FOR WORKING SKINS AND PELTS. These include many types of tools, some very obviously connected with these tasks and some which have only been so interpreted. Ribs and sometimes ivory flakes used for hide burnishing have already been mentioned. Decorated rods with rounded, flat ends, made of mammoth ivory found at Kostenki I, have been interpreted also as being hide burnishers, but they may actually have served some other function.

Strap stretchers, which are straight instruments with a large round aperture at one end, usually made of reindeer horn but sometimes of ivory, have variously been interpreted as dart straighteners or implements for stretching thongs. The Russian term is *vypryamitel'*, literally "a rectifier"; this implement is also sometimes called *zhezl nachal'nika*, a translation of the French term "baton de commandement." One found at Mezin, as described by Shovkoplyas (1965:205), was made of mammoth tusk, with a somewhat oval opening around three centimeters in diameter in the wider end; the narrower end was somewhat pointed. The length was 20.5 centimeters and the maximum width, 5.6 centimeters. Whatever its function or functions, this implement is widely distributed in Soviet Upper Paleolithic sites — Kostenki I, Molodova V, Afontova Gora II, Buret' — as well as at sites in central and western Europe.

Points, punches, and awls (depending on nomenclature) are small pointed implements made of bone, antler, or ivory, round or oval in cross-section, probably used for making and widening holes in pelts and hides. Of the numerous punches found at Mezin, the majority were made of thin ivory flakes or long bones of small animals, mostly arctic fox and hare. The length was usually six to ten centimeters; simply prepared, they were easily broken (Shovkoplyas 1965:199, Figures XLII and XLIII). The small ivory points at Mal'ta were not more than ten centimeters long, round in cross-section and tapering to a point; a larger one, made from the long bone of a large animal, was sixteen centimeters long and five millimeters thick and was probably intended for widening the openings in pelts (Gerasimov 1941:77). As with the thong stretcher, these bone points are widely distributed.

Likewise, *eyed needles*[15] are widely found in both European Russian and Siberian sites — Mezin, Gontsy, Yeliseyevichi, the Kostenki sites, Sungir' (in the child burial), Afontova Gora II, and Mal'ta. Analogues are also known for central and western European sites. Long bones of small animals and ivory fragments were the materials most commonly used. In describing the bone inventory at Mal'ta, Gerasimov (1941:77–78) characterizes the various types of needles found there. One type is large and round, up to 150 millimeters long and about 4 millimeters in diameter, with a slightly curved upper end and a narrow aperture; needles of this type were usually made from deer long bone. Small needles of mammoth ivory were 40 to 60 millimeters long and about the thickness of modern steel darning needles; the round eyes were intended for very thin "thread." Other ivory artifacts, found only in fragments, may possibly have been either needles or portions of small ornaments. They were large

[15] Note that in Russian usage, eyed needles are called "needles with ears" (*igolki s ushkami*).

and flat, curved, with wide eyes up to 3 millimeters in diameter, and sometimes ornamented with a series of shallow pits.

The manufacturing process for eyed needles was, briefly, as follows. After preparing the blank, first by percussion against an anvil stone, and then scraping and smoothing with fine retouched flint tools, the eye was drilled by means of a flint punch (see Gerasimov 1941:78, Figure 10). Drilling the eye was evidently a difficult process, judging by the number of needles found with a second eye drilled after breakage of the original one. Stone slabs were used for sharpening the point. All the flint tools needed for making eyed needles, as well as sharpening slabs, were found in significant quantities at Mezin (Shovkoplyas 1965:202).

Uneyed needles, on the other hand, are regarded by Shovkoplyas (1965:202) to be indicators of sites dating to earlier periods of the Upper Paleolithic ("Aurignacian-Solutrean" as opposed to "Magdalenian"). Examples found at Kostenki I (horizon unspecified), Kostenki VIII (upper horizon) (Tel'manskaya), Gagarino, and Avdeyevo are larger than the eyed needles; the thread was held in place by transverse or slanting cuts in the needle. Another implement found at Lipa VI, with an analogue from Molodova V Horizon 5, Savich (1969:137) characterizes as a "weaving" tool for lacing sinew through hides and pelts. It was made from a mammoth ivory flake, oval in cross-section (diameter five to seven millimeters), and it had a hooked working end.

HAFTS.   Handles made of bone, ivory, horn, or wood with apertures for the insertion of flint blades, thus forming a compound tool, represent an important development, since, as Semenov states:

The technical role of a handle is very significant: it multiplies several times the mechanical strength and efficiency of a tool . . . in cutting tools (knife, burin) it amplifies the mechanical force of the pressure by bringing more powerful muscles of the hand and arm to bear (1964:173).

The simplest surviving form is illustrated by the Châtelperron knife embedded in a portion of reindeer horn from Mal'ta. Analogues, also made from reindeer horn, are known from Lipa VI Stratum 2a and Molodova V (Savich 1969:39), as well as Mezin, Timonovka, and Afontova Gora II (Shovkoplyas 1965:204–205). At Lipa VI, the typical antler haft was about 185 millimeters long, 30 millimeters diameter, nearly round in cross-section, with an oval aperture cut into the spongy interior. Two smaller reindeer horn hafts at Mezin measured 8 to 9 centimeters long. It is possible that glue made from tree resin mixed with other substances was used to fasten the insert, by analogy with the practice of the modern-day Evenki, as cited by Gerasimov (1941:75–76).

Another type of haft, usually made from long bones of small animals, carried a slit in one end, making it possible to replace the flint insert. "Such a changeable handle is known from Eliseevich [Yeliseyevichi] made of a deer long-bone and probably used for burins. The clip consisted of the diaphysis for ejection of the stump" (Semenov 1964:173). Handles for small flint inserts, made from arctic fox, wolverine, and other small animal bones, are cited by Shovkoplyas (1965:204) as analogues to one another from Chulatovo I and Mezin. It is not clear whether they provided for interchangeable inserts, but it is felt that they were probably of this type.

A third variant is a haft, usually of bone as opposed to horn, with a slot cut into the length of the bone instead of the end. Hafts of this type from stratum IIa at Lipa VI consisted of rib bones. One from mammoth rib was 215 millimeters long, with an elongated incised slot 95 millimeters long, 5 millimeters wide and 8 millimeters deep. A second, made from reindeer rib, was even larger (350 millimeters long, diameter 35 millimeters, slot 180 millimeters long and 15 millimeters wide). This type of haft apparently has direct analogues only with Molodova V Horizons 2–4, 6, and 7 and Pavlov, Czechoslovakia (Savich 1969:140–141). However, tools with longitudinal slots for the insertion of blades are reported for Afontova Gora II and Kokorevo I on the Yenisey (Abramova 1967:14–15). These Abramova interpreted as knife handles. Insert tools are also reported for Talitskiy site in the Urals, suggesting its affinities with Siberian sites (see also section on stone typologies, pages 254–261).

MISCELLANEA AND OBJECTS OF INDETERMINATE FUNCTION.   These include a variety of artifacts, some possibly of ornamental or ritual purpose. One find at Mezin may possibly be a fragment of a fish hook, made from a small ivory flake, 5.6 centimeters long, curved, and tapering to a point (see Shovkoplyas 1965: Figure XLIV, Number 12, for a drawing of the reconstructed artifact). Also at Mezin, a mammoth ivory object (10 centimeters long, 1 centimeter wide and around 3 millimeters thick) was found. It has an aperture at one end, and it is shaped like a needle, but it is obviously too large for sewing fur clothing. Shovkoplyas (1965:202–204, Figure XLIV, Number 9) suggests that it might have been used for weaving coarse fabric, presumably of vegetable fiber. Pairs of slanting incised lines on the Mezin object also occur on analogous items at Yudinovo and in Czechoslovakia and France. The incised ivory rods from Kostenki I Horizon 1 have already been mentioned (see Klein 1969a:Figure 41, Numbers 15–19). Likewise, the two ivory "egg-shaped" objects, resembling spindle whorls, from Kostenki I Horizon 1 are of undetermined function (Klein 1969a:122, 125, Figure 39, Number 6). The paddle-shaped shovels at Kostenki XV (Gorodtsovskaya), made of mammoth long bone, are reported to have analogues only at Kostenki XII Horizon 1 and Předmost, Czechoslovakia (Klein 1969a:97–98,

Figure 27). At Sungir', however, a mammoth ivory tool found during the 1969 excavations, may, although it is evidently smaller than the objects found at Kostenki XV, be generally analogous (see section on dwellings pages 201–227).

Weapons among bone inventories consist mainly of dart points. During the early Upper Paleolithic flint dart points were predominant, but they were largely replaced during the later period ("proto-Magdalenian" or "Magdalenian") by a preponderence of points made from ivory, horn, or bone. It is commonly assumed that dart handles were of wood, and the bases of many bone points carry slots, cuts, or other evidence of working for hafting. Very large "boar" spears, their points fire-hardened, also were probably made of wood (Shovkoplyas 1965:207).

Bone points found at Upper Paleolithic sites in the Soviet Union are few and usually fragmentary. Only one dart point in the rich bone inventory at Mezin was found in perfect condition; the remaining dart points were fragmentary and few in number to the many bone artifacts at the site. Likewise, at the Amvrosiyevka killing ground twenty-two dart heads were found; only two fragments were found at the site itself. The fragmentary flint points at Kostenki I Horizon 1 illustrate the same phenomenon. The explanation obviously stems from the fact that dart points were lost in the bodies of hunted animals and never retrieved.

There appears to be a basic distinction in dart points: the presence or absence of flutings or grooves along one or both sides. Some of these flutings are too wide and shallow for the insertion of flints. Hence, they probably were intended to improve the flight qualities of the dart and increase bloodletting. Many of the darts found at Mezin have such flutings, and analogues are known from various European Russian sites. Dart points with narrow slits for small flint inserts apparently are known on the Russian plain and in the Crimea only from sites dating to later periods — the Epipaleolithic and Neolithic.

On the Yenisey, however, at the Afontova Gora and Kokoreva sites, Abramova (1967) has established the existence of points with narrow slots intended for flint inserts. Fluting appears also on some of the points (see Abramova 1967:14, Figure 5, for points from Kokorevo I and II). Radiocarbon dates for the Kokorevo sites range from approximately 14,500 to 12,500 b.p. Dates for Afontova Gora II are 20,900 ± 300 and 11,335 ± 270 b.p.; the latter is questionable because of the lack of preliminary chemical treatment. Bone points from Oshurkovo are similar to those from Kokorevo III; Oshurkovo is attributed by Abramova (1967:17) to the very end of the Upper Paleolithic. Harpoons found at Oshurkovo (as well as Verkholenskaya Gora) were technically analogous and also point to the late age of the sites. The only Upper Paleolithic European analogue to these dart points from the Yenisey was found at Talitskiy site, again confirming its Siberian affinities.

At Mal'ta, Gerasimov found a dagger-like point, oval in cross-section, made from mammoth long bone; long, thin mammoth ivory weapons, sharpened on both sides, were of undetermined function (Gerasimov 1941:78–79). Ivory weapons occur in burials: an ivory dagger in the child burial at Mal'ta and sixteen spears, darts, and daggers in the double burial at Sungir' (see section on burials pages 227–235). A dagger from Yeliseyevichi, made from young mammoth tusk, was twenty-six centimeters long and four and a half centimeters wide across the handle. The point had been sharpened by whittling, and cuts had been made on both sides of the handle for a grip (Semenov 1964:151,152, Figure 75, 3–5).

Summary and Problems for Further Study

Although conditions of preservation have inevitably created an uneven picture of bone tool and weapon inventories, recovered materials indi-

Table 4.   Frequency and percent distribution of stone tools: Ust'-Kanskaya and Starosel'ye

Bordes classification No(s) and type designation	Ust'-Kanskaya[b]		Starosel'ye	
	frequency	percent	frequency	percent
1–2. Typical and atypical Levallois flakes	59	53.6	5	0.6
3. Levallois points	5	4.5	1	0.1
4. Retouched Levallois points	1	0.9	0	—
6–7. Mousterian and elongated Mousterian points	3	2.7	13	1.5
9. Simple, straight sidescraper	4	3.6	98	11.1
10. Simple, convex sidescraper	9	8.2	248	28.0
11. Simple, concave sidescraper	1	0.9	51	5.8
23. Straight, transverse sidescraper	1	0.9	47	5.3
25. Sidescraper on the ventral surface	2	1.8	9	1.0
29. Sidescraper with alternate retouch	1	0.9	8	0.9
30–31. Typical and atypical endscrapers	3	2.7	16	1.8
32–33. Typical and atypical burins	4	3.6	14	1.6
34. Typical borer	1	0.9	3	0.3
39. Raclette	1	0.9	6	0.7
42. Notched tool	2	1.8	37	4.2
43. Denticulate tool	3	2.7	60	6.8
48–49. Piece with fine, abrupt, or alternate retouch	4	3.6	258	29.1
54. End-notched tools	1	0.9	2	0.2
62. Miscellaneous tools	4	3.6	10	1.1
63. Foliate piece	1	0.9	0	—
Total	110	99.6	886	100.1

[a] This excludes types not found at Ust'-Kanskaya.
[b] After Anisyutkin and Astakhov (1970).
[c] After Klein (1969b).

cate the presence of a widespread, diversified, and sophisticated complex of bone, ivory, and antler artifacts throughout the Upper Paleolithic of north-central Eurasia. Although these artifacts have not yet been subjected to comprehensive quantitative study founded on a general taxonomy, some general categories basic to more refined analysis are suggested above. Delineation of regional or temporal variations is not yet possible beyond the widespread types and local specializations already noted.

In addition to the establishment of a general taxonomy, apparent regional ties require further study. Specifically, affinities between Lipa VI and the Molodova sites and central European sites, and those between the Yenisey sites and Talitskiy in the Urals. Finally, the appearance of the dart point with flint insert, in both European Russia and Siberia, would repay continued investigation.

ART AND POSSIBLE RELIGIOUS AND COGNITIVE INTERPRETATIONS

Perhaps one of the most striking achievements of the Upper Paleolithic people was their art. It has been claimed that the very regular geometric forms of some finely worked handaxes are evidence of an aesthetic sensibility already in the later stages of the Lower Paleolithic, and there is little doubt that these objects were finished with more care and refinement than was necessary for purely functional purposes. However, it is only in the Upper Paleolithic cultures of Europe that the arts of carving, engraving and painting are known to have developed (Ucko and Rosenfeld 1967:11).

And in north-central Eurasia the presence of mobile (and rarely parietal) art and definite styles of ornamentation appears also to be an indicator of Upper Paleolithic culture. In the territory of the present-day Soviet Union art objects, beads, and similar artifacts are not reported in the site inventories ascribed to the Lower and Middle Paleolithic (Beregovaya 1960:1–56). Likewise, in commenting upon the differences between the Mousterian of European Russia and the succeeding Upper Paleolithic cultures, Klein states: ". . . art objects and ornaments are entirely lacking in the Mousterian" (Klein 1969b:264).

The first find of Upper Paleolithic art in Russia is reported to have occurred at the Irkutsk military hospital site in 1871. During the last years of the nineteenth century and the early ones of the twentieth, Khyoyko found ornamented mammoth ivory objects, attributed by Volkhov to the "Magdalenian," at Kiyevo-Kirillovskoye site in Kiev. Excavations at Mezin, beginning in 1909, revealed ivory objects with geometric ornamentation. Most of the study of Upper Paleolithic art found within the territory of the Soviet Union, however, has been carried on since the Revolution.

While the representational art from Upper Paleolithic sites in the Soviet Union shares with that of western Europe a general identity of *subject matter* — women and animals — its *form* differs in that it is primarily mobile art, as opposed to the many cave paintings found in France and Spain. In the Soviet Union only one example of cave painting, located at Kapova Cave (Shulgan Tash) in the Southern Urals, is known, and there are pictographs of Upper Paleolithic age at only two sites: Mgvimevi grotto in the Transcaucasus and Shishkino, a very late site on the Lena, in Irkutsk Oblast'. On the other hand, there are quite evident ties between the mobile art styles of central Europe and those of the Russian plain.

Z. A. Abramova (1970a), the recognized authority on Upper Paleolithic art in the territory of the Soviet Union, divides this art into three provinces. The first, from the Black Sea area (Caucasus and Crimea), belongs in the Mediterranean tradition and is outside the purview of this paper. The second province encompasses the art found in European Russia, mostly in the basins of the Don and Desna, with affinities to central Europe, as mentioned earlier. The art of eastern Siberia, especially from Mal'ta and Buret', comprises the third province. The following discussion is selective, emphasizing forms and styles at particular European Russian sites as compared with material from Siberia and describing the Kapova Cave paintings. Finally, some possible religious and cognitive interpretations suggested by these materials are briefly considered.

Techniques and Materials

As with bone tools and weapons, advances in flint-working techniques made possible the production of Upper Paleolithic chattel art and ornaments: the whittling and carving of bone or ivory; engraving; the drilling of shells, animal teeth, ivory, bone, stone beads and pendants.

Ivory and bone, immediately available by-products of the hunt, were the most commonly used materials. Pendants of mammoth ivory were found at Mezin; if one judges from the burial inventories at Sungir', mammoth ivory beads were especially numerous and valued at that site. Marl, locally available in the Don region, is distinctive for the Kostenki sites. Pierced animal teeth, especially of arctic fox, are practically ubiquitous; at Yeliseyevichi, beads made from the tubular bones of small animals or perhaps birds were found. Pierced shells are known from several European Russian sites, especially at Mezin, Timonovka, Yudinovo, and Kostenki. At Borshevo I objects described as "flat, circular mother-of-pearl 'beads' " are the only ornaments from this material known for the Kostenki sites (Klein 1969a:202–203). The presence of

Black Sea shells (and perhaps the mother-of-pearl) at sites so distant from the Black Sea confirms the existence of some form of trade or exchange, either direct or by secondary stages. The amber beads and unworked amber found at Dobranichivka and Mezhirich could either have been gathered on the banks of the Dnepr or obtained in local trade.

In Siberia pendants of calcite crystal were found in the fifth dwelling at Mal'ta (see Table, Number 22, page 211); other pendants and beads from Mal'ta were made of nephrite and fish vertebrae as well as ivory. At Buret' beads, as well as rectangular pendants, had been carved from bluish-green serpentine; blanks for the rectangular ornaments were found in a "workshop" in the ruins of Dwelling 3. At Afontova Gora II the inventory included pendants and beads of soapstone.

Since it is perishable, there is no way of telling whether wood was used for decorative or cult objects, or whether wooden artifacts were carved or painted.

Ocher, usually red but sometimes yellow, as well as other coloring matter, was important in the culture of Upper Paleolithic peoples, in both European Russia and Siberia. Large amounts of ocher have been found in many sites; for example, about ten kilograms was found in the dwelling at Mezin (Pidoplichko 1969:98). It was also used in quantity in some burials, as at Sungir'. Paint made from mixing ocher with other materials was widely employed. The mammoth bones from Mezin (see Figure 3 on page 275) were painted with ocher paint, and red ocher paint was the material applied for the contours of the animal representations at Kapova Cave. Particularly interesting is the wide variety of mineral colorings found by Gerasimov (1941:74) at Mal'ta: verdigris (green), various iron compounds (cherry, lilac, light red), and chalk and limestone (white). Traces of paint were found on limestone slabs in one dwelling, as well as deeply embedded bits of mineral coloring on a reindeer horn artifact. Coloring materials, usually ocher, were probably also used in dressing skins, judging from the traces of ocher found on bone burnishers. Gerasimov, Polikarpovich, and others have also suggested that coloring matter mixed with animal fat may have been used for body paint, for decorative or magical purposes, or, perhaps, for protection against cold or insects.

Ornaments

A wide variety of materials, as indicated earlier in this section, was used for decorative objects and "amulets." Pierced ivory and bone beads, animal teeth, and shells were presumably strung on sinew or some other material for making necklaces; the same would have been true for pendants. The unique and magnificent bracelets with geometric ornamentation found at Mezin were made of engraved ivory strips. Those from the Sungir' burials were made of ivory beads, and strings of ivory beads and shells evidently decorated the clothing and shroud. An ivory coronet was found in the Mal'ta burial. Other decorated ivory fragments found at various sites may have been portions of head ornaments.

Ornamentation Styles

Ornamentation constitutes a special division of Paleolithic art. It can be observed not only on female statuettes, but also on objects of varied type: adzes, trowels, rods, needle cases, bracelets, head and breast ornaments, as well as on plates and fragments of ivory and bone. . . . Ornamentation in Paleolithic art from the territory of the USSR still has not been specially studied. The summary table of the elements of ornamentation presented is a first effort in this area. The elements of ornamentation and their combinations can be divided into groups, beginning with the simplest (Abramova 1970a:85).

Abramova lists ten groups of ornamentation styles (see Figure 1), beginning with the small paired parallel lines observed on the edges of flat bone artifacts, progressing through simple geometric combinations of straight or slanting lines to more complicated designs forming crosses, zigzags, chevrons, honeycomb designs (distinctive for Yeliseyevichi), ladders, and so on; notable also is punctate ornamentation on the heads of statuettes from Kostenki and Mal'ta. The two final categories are the complex geometric, chevron, and meander engravings from Mezin and the wavy-line punctate decoration from Mal'ta.

Mobile Art

It is the mobile art of sites in European Russia and Siberia that has received the most detailed study and in which the differences of style and, to a degree, subject matter between the two areas are most notable. Included within the category of mobile art are objects that are not easily identifiable but that, perhaps, had cult or cognitive significance, especially the "phallic" and "bird" statuettes from Mezin. The painted mammoth bones from Mezin, as well as the engraved object from Mezhirich (see Figures 2 and 3), are treated in the discussion of objects that might have had cognitive significance.

Human Representations

ANTHROPOMORPHIC AND STYLIZED REPRESENTATIONS.   The inventories of a number of European Russian sites — Mezin, Kostenki I – 1, Kostenki II,

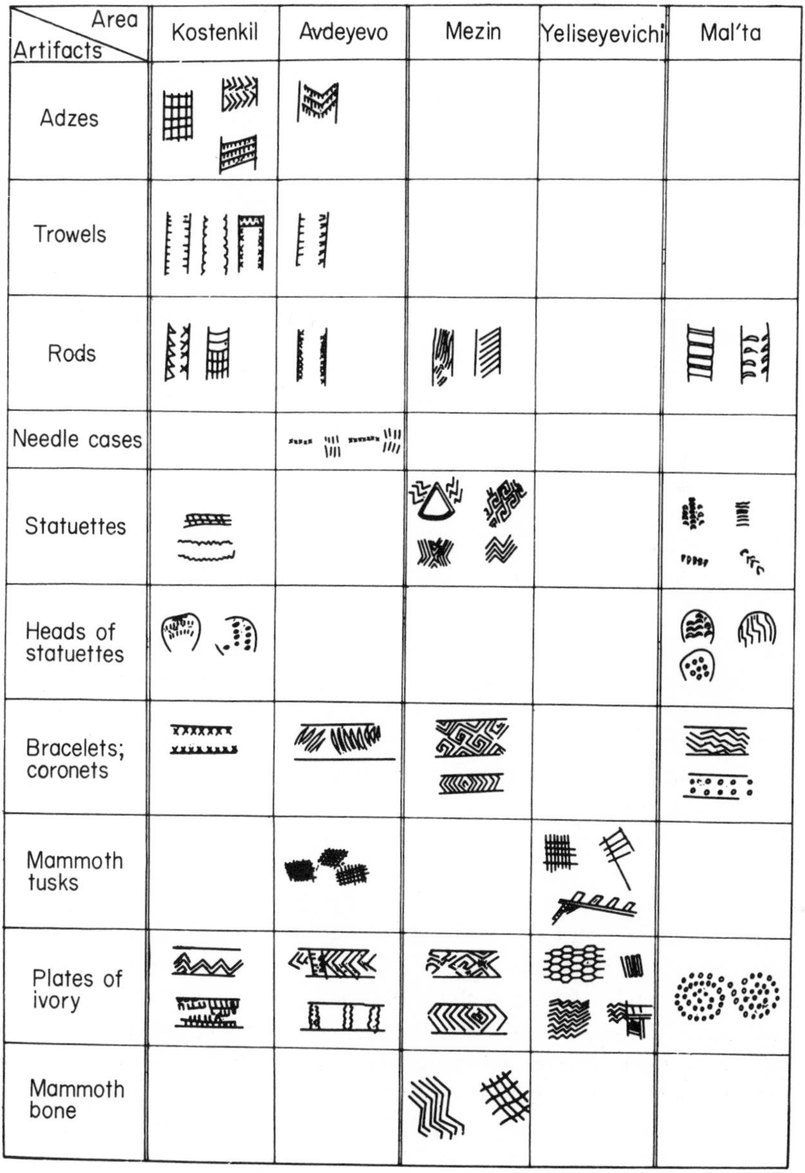

Figure 1.   Ornamentation styles: selected European Russian sites and Mal'ta.
Source: Abramova 1970a: Figure 6

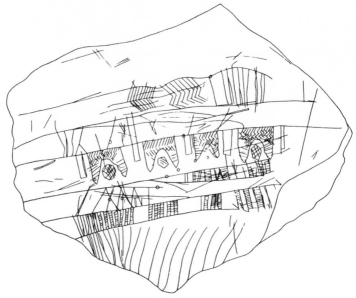

Figure 2.   Possible line drawings of dwellings on a mammoth-tusk fragment from the Mezhirich dwelling (Square 7). *Note*: The four dome-shaped figures along the mid-line are supposedly dwellings. *Source*: Pidoplichko 1969: Figure 58

and Kostenki IV – 1, particularly — include crude ivory objects vaguely indicating female bodies, with or without heads, which are usually classified as anthropomorphic figurines. In addition, the stylized statuettes of ivory with their distinctive geometric ornamentation found at Mezin have been the subject of much discussion. They are headless and legless with the buttocks, which are stylized, the distinctive feature. Their similarity in profile to engravings and paintings at French sites (La Roche, Les Combarelles, and Pech-Merle) and, especially, the figurines from Petersfels, Germany, should be noted. (For illustrations, see Ucko and Rosenfeld 1967:212–213; Coles and Higgs 1969:Figure 123, Numbers 5 and 6.) Some of the stylized Mezin figurines have also been interpreted as phallic objects and stylized bird sculptures (see Shovkoplyas 1965:220). At Kostenki I –1 small marl objects, measuring some two to five centimeters wide, have been interpreted from their markings: "as schematic representations of the lower half of the female torso — " (Klein 1969a:139).

At Mal'ta and Buret' tiny rod-like female figurines were found; one at Mal'ta was found in a case made from a dorsal vertebra of a reindeer which had been placed on the bull shoulder-blade shelf. (See the section on dwellings on pages 201–227.)

STATUETTES.   Clearly identifiable as representative of human beings, statuettes are known from both European Russian and Siberian sites.

Figure 3.   Painted mammoth scapulae, mandibles and femur from the Late Paleolithic dwelling at Mezin. *Note*: Painted with red ocher. *Source*: Pidoplichko 1969: Figure 31

Those from the Russian plain are obviously female, as are the ones from Mal'ta, but there is some question as to the sex of the figurines from Buret'. The Buret' figurines and two from Mal'ta, besides their stylistic distinctiveness, are the only known representations of clothed individuals.

The human figurines from European Russian sites are all female and naked, sharing certain physical characteristics and poses. Carved in the round, they are standing figures, though usually lacking lower legs and feet; the heads, usually bent downward, are unfinished or have been knocked off. The body type is that of a pregnant woman with pendulous breasts, protruding belly, immense buttocks, fat thighs, and knock knees. The arms, which are very thin and are incompletely finished, are crossed under the breasts or held along the side of the body. Most of these figurines are of ivory, although some from Kostenki are made of marl. Many are shown with a band across the chest; other markings appear to be necklaces; markings across the back above the buttocks may be decorations or tattooing.

There are some individual differences among statuettes from European Russian sites. One statuette from Gagarino (with complete legs and feet) appears to be walking; the figure is pigeon-toed. An ivory statuette from Yeliseyevichi (with the head broken off) has a slender torso, and while the buttocks and upper legs are fat, the body type is nearer that of an actual person.

Analogues to the figurines in European Russia occur in both western and central Europe. The "Venus" of Lespugue has the same unfinished, downward-bent head, exaggerated breasts and buttocks, legs ending in a rounded oval knob; some sort of skirt or apron is indicated below the buttocks. A stone bas-relief from Laussel shows a woman with the same general body configuration and proportions as the figurines in the round. The head and face were either unfinished or deliberately defaced. The treatment of the arms, however, is very different: the left arm, finished even to the fingers, is laid across the upper abdomen, while the right holds up what appears to be an animal horn. The knock-kneed legs, which are finished only to mid-calf, give the same suggestion of a pigeon-toed stance as the figure from Gagarino. Other bas-reliefs from Laussel (including one male figure) have outstretched arms. Two female figures carved in bas-relief from La Magdelaine are reclining, but they have the same general physical characteristics.

Figurines from central Europe bear the most obvious resemblance to those from European Russia. The Willendorf "Venus" is the same body type, with exaggerated breasts, abdomen, and buttocks and thin arms, which are represented as bent at the elbows and laid above the breasts. The perfectly round head is featureless, but the hair is represented and could be interpreted as coiled braids. On the other hand, a female torso from Ostrava-Petrkovice, carved from hematite, five centimeters high, is totally different: it is that of a young woman or girl, with small breasts, a defined waist, and naturalistic pelvic girdle and upper legs, As Clark notes: ". . . [it] compares with much larger sculptures of modern European art" (1969:59).

The figurines from Mal'ta and Buret' present some interesting similarities and contrasts to the conventional Venus figurines. One female figurine from Mal'ta has the same general body configurations (arms clasped below the breasts and unfinished lower portions) as those from European Russia. However, it has a very large head. Although the face had been left featureless, the head had been worked to indicate either hair or a cap, with what appears to be a braid hanging across the right shoulder. A second figurine, again without lower legs and with the arms in the usual position, not only has carving showing either hair or a cap, but individualized features of somewhat Mongoloid type. A third miniature figurine is highly stylized, with a rod-like torso.

Two other ivory figurines are covered with horizontally carved ridges and have representations of long tails down the backs of the legs. Gromov (as reported by Yefimenko 1953:480) believed these to be representations of women wearing pelts of "cave lion" with tiger-like markings.

Another distinctive clothed figurine was found at Buret'. This figurine, Number 1 in Okladnikov's description (1960:281), was found in 1936 in a ruined dwelling in what was evidently a special hollow, in association with bones. The body type is slender and flat, with an oval head and short legs and the arms stretched alongside the body. The face is individualized, with a short nose and somewhat squinting eyes. The garment is one piece, covering the entire body, with attached hood. The ivory of the garment is covered with parallel rows of thumb-nail or half-moon shaped incised cuts, believed to represent fur texture.

Statuette Number 2 was found lying face down near a small hearth in the ruins of another dwelling (Okladnikov 1960:281–282). The back and lower portions have been partially destroyed by erosion, however, there was no evidence of intentional destruction. This statuette has a dis-proportionately large head with the features only suggested, sloping shoulders, pendulous breasts with the arms apparently crossed under-neath them, and the female triangle indicated. The head treatment sug-gests a fur cap or perhaps, a headdress of beads. The length of the figurine is 5.1 centimeters, and the width of the shoulders, 1.8 centimeters.

The remaining three statuettes, numbered 3, 4, and 5, were found during the 1940 excavations (Okladnikov 1960:282–286). All three were in association with Dwelling Number 2 (see Table 1, page 210). Numbers 3 and 4 were of ivory, and Number 5 is made of the bluish-green serpentine. Figurine Number 3 is relatively small (height, 5.5 centi-meters; width of shoulders, 1.6 centimeters) with a large head. The arms are apparently crossed under the bulge of the abdomen. From the front the legs are very short, but from the back the groove separating the legs reaches far up the back, making them look very long. Whether these effects were intentional or stemmed from the ineptitude of the artist is impossible to judge. The face of the statuette is barely indicated, and the carved wavy lines on the head suggest hair.

Figurine Number 4 is the largest of those found at Buret'. It measures 8.5 centimeters long and 2 centimeters wide and is unfinished, with the head and limbs only roughly indicated. From the side, it appears bent forward at the hips; possibly this pose was dictated by the shape of the ivory blank.

Figurine Number 5 is miniaturized and rod-like, 4.3 centimeters long and 0.3 centimeters wide, with a narrow body and an oval head of elongated proportions. The torso is not detailed, although the arms appear to be crossed under the abdomen, as with Figurine Number 3.

In addition, an ivory blank for a figurine was found at Buret'. A stylized ivory figurine was also reportedly found at Krasnyy Yar in the Angara region, indicating ties with both Mal'ta and Buret'.

THE SIGNIFICANCE OF FEMALE REPRESENTATIONS. As Abramova (1970a:82) points out, female statuettes almost everywhere have been found in dwelling remains, alongside hearths, and/or in special pits and corners. At Kostenki I mammoth ivory statuettes were found in pits where they had been intentionally placed at the edge of the dwelling area. At Gagarino statuettes were found at the walls of the dwelling; others lay in a pit alongside the hearth. At Buret' one statuette was found near the entrance tunnel in dwelling Number 2, and two more at dwelling walls.

It appears that the heads of many of the statuettes have been intentionally knocked off. Also at Kostenki I–1: ". . . sixteen small sphere-like marl objects were isolated which resemble figurine heads, but which were evidently manufactured separately. By and large they lack a fracture which could establish previous attachment to a larger piece" (Klein 1969a:139). Likewise at Mal'ta, Gerasimov noted that two of the dwellings that he excavated had "male" (right-hand) and "female" (left-hand) inventories. In both cases, the "female" inventories included female statuettes. The implication that the female figurines, both stylized and modeled, had some significance connected with woman's role in Upper Paleolithic society, both in European Russia and Siberia (as well as in central and western Europe), seems obvious, but the exact nature of that significance is open to question. The conventionalization of most of the figurines, as well as the unfinished heads and faces, lends credence to such an interpretation, as do the knocking off of the heads in many cases and the blanks for separate heads found at Kostenki I – 1. Some of the figurines from Mal'ta had been pierced as though they were to be hung about the neck. Nevertheless, the fact that some Upper Paleolithic female representations were individualized, appearing to be portraits of actual people, makes questionable sweeping generalizations about "fertility," "Mother-Goddess" cults or simple erotic symbolism. The famous ivory head from Brassempouy, France, gives the impression of being a portrait, although the mouth and chin appear unfinished. An even more striking exception comes from Dolni Vestoniče. An ivory plaque and the head of a woman with a distortion of the facial muscles from paralysis were found here; the associated body, not only unusual in that it was of a woman, showed, upon examination of the skull, the existence of facial paralysis on the left side as shown in the two portraits. The finished faces on two of the statuettes from Mal'ta and Buret' may be portraits of actual individuals, differentiating them from the faceless, conventionalized statuettes from European Russian sites.

Animal Representations

Small figurines of varying styles, state of finish, and several species of animals have been found at many European Russian sites. These, it should be noted, were associated with habitation sites, unlike the paintings at Kapova Cave.

Representations of mammoth are predominant; over thirty are known from Kostenki I, Anosovka II, and Kostenki IV. Many of the animal statuettes are of bone or ivory, with marl the material used to a great extent at the Kostenki sites. The animals, insofar as they are identifiable as a particular species, are shown in profile. There are small animal heads, however, which are modeled in the round. Representations of rhinoceros are few, corresponding to this animal's rarity. Some figurines from Kostenki IV may represent bison. Two ivory animals from Sungir' (see the section on burials, pages 227–235 with punctate decoration and traces of ocher are most likely of horses. Nowhere in the literature are sculptures of reindeer reported.

Some of the sculptured heads of predators such as wolf and lion from Kostenki I – 1 appear to be the most completely modeled and recognizable. Particularly notable is the head of a lioness, a tiny (3 centimeters long) masterpiece of representational animal art. This head, judging from photographs and drawings, closely resembles the head of a young present-day lioness, except perhaps for the extremely small ears. Abramova (1970a:83) points out that cave lion bones — fragments of a skull, separate teeth, tail vertebrae, and especially paw bones, both broken and in anatomical order — were found in relatively large numbers at Kostenki I. The paw bones in anatomical order had been intentionally secreted in pits within the dwelling floor. This fact, taken in conjunction with the carved heads, may indicate that this predator had some special magical or religious significance for the inhabitants of the site.

The bird statuettes at Mezin resemble "phallic" figurines, though whether they were actually intended to portray birds is questionable. They bear the overall geometric ornamentation distinctive for this site. One stylized representation of a bird has angled meanders covering the body and long straight lines down the center of the "tail" which is edged on both sides with slanting strokes thought to represent tail feathers.

Abramova also mentions that: "certain ornamental motifs at

Timonovka and Suponevo on the Desna could be regarded as stylized representations of fish" (1970a:84).

In contrast to the bird figurines at Mezin, the bird sculptures at Mal'ta are quite clearly intended to represent actual birds. One is a partridge and another is a standing swan (or perhaps a large goose); two birds, shown with outstretched wings and necks as though in flight, represent a swan and a duck or loon. One ivory piece, perhaps a breast ornament, carries engraved representations of snakes with rounded, exaggerated heads. The obverse of this plaque bears the circular punctate design shown in Figure 1 (see page 273). On an ivory plaque there is an entirely recognizable profile engraving of a mammoth.

The Shishkino Pictographs

At Shishkino on the Lena pictographs of horses and a wild bull (or bison) were discovered by Okladnikov in the 1949's (Okladnikov 1955:49–56). The animals are shown in profile, the outlines executed in red paint. One of the horse pictographs is very large, measuring 2.8 meters long; the other horse is 1.8 meters long, the wild bull is 1.12 meters long. These paintings are on a cliff some forty to sixty meters above the level of the river. The location, therefore, while open-air and associated with remains of a nearby very late Upper Paleolithic site, is inaccessible. Beregovaya (1960:91) mentions the cliff was considered sacred by the Buryat tribes and that it bears pictographs from later periods. Okladnikov dated the horse and bull pictographs to the Upper Paleolithic on the basis of the style of execution, the resemblance of one of the horse paintings to the Przewalski horse, and environmental grounds — the fact that the Post-Pleistocene taiga of the Lena valley could not have supported herd animals such as horses. The site at Shishkino is probably related to Makarovo archeologically (see Map 1, Number 55 on page 196).

The Kapova Cave Paintings

Kapova Cave, one of the largest in the southern Urals, is in the Bashkirian ASSR, on the Belaya River. (See Map 1, Number 25, on page 196, for the approximate location; Ucko and Rosenfeld 1967:37 incorrectly place the cave in "southern Russia".)

The entrance to the lower-level galleries is 7.5 meters above the river. These lower-level galleries reach some 300 meters into the mountainside; their floors gradually rise to some 26 meters above water level. This portion of the cave is very damp, especially during seasonal rains and winter snow-melt. Certain charcoal drawings on this lower level were determined to be very recent; likewise, what had been earlier taken to represent relief carvings are natural formations (Bader 1963:126–128).

The route to the second level opens on the left some 140 meters from the cave entrance and is very difficult to reach. The upper level gallery is drier than the lower one; the floors are usually covered with boulders overlain with clay. The floor of the basic portion of the upper gallery is about 50 meters above the river level, and the room containing the wall paintings of Pleistocene animals (Groups I and II) is some 300 meters from the cave entrance.

The species represented include two paintings of horses, seven of mammoth (three each in Groups I and II and an additional painting discovered in 1971), and two of what are apparently intended as rhinoceros. The paintings were done with red paint; the silhouettes of the animals are in dark red, and the inner contours of some of them are in lighter tones. Upon analysis, two samples of paint from Group I were found to consist of red ocher mixed with animal glue. Presumably, all the paint used for Groups I and II, Group III (the abstract designs on the lower level), and the single mammoth discovered in 1971 was of this same composition.

There are seven animals in Group I — horses, mammoth, and rhinoceros — all, represented in profile, walking with all four legs shown. All seven figures are on a different scale and do not appear to have been intended as components of a unified composition. One mammoth lacks tusks, and the head of the rhinoceros is difficult to distinguish, although the general contours of the body are entirely recognizable. The central horse, facing left, clearly resembles the Przewalski horse.

In the same room of the second level Group II consists of four animals, walking one after another, placed at differing levels at an even distance above the sloping cave floor. According to Bader's description, the first animal appears to be a rhinoceros, the other three, mammoth. The third mammoth may be intended to represent a young one following its mother. The fourth mammoth is fully silhouetted in the style of the Group I paintings (Bader 1963:132).

The animal paintings of Groups I and II inevitably invite comparison with the cave paintings of France and Spain. Their location within the cave, their inaccessibility, and the fact that they are not associated with a habitation site provide a basic similarity of context with the deep cave paintings of western Europe. Bader (1963:132) states, however, that the Kapova paintings are not directly analogous in manner of execution, since the Kapova figures are painted with only traces of engraving, whereas in France animal figures are either entirely engraved (Les Combarelles) or painted after preliminary contour engravings (Font de Gaume). In Spain red-painted elephants at El Castillo and El Pindal had also been contoured. Black frescoes are known for Niaux; the black painted horse from the "Salon Noir" at Niaux is an example (Ucko and Rosenfeld 1967:81, Figure 49). Compared among themselves, the Kapova paintings differ somewhat in style and artistic quality, but they are probably contemporaneous with one another. Further judgments about the relationship of these paintings to the art of Upper Paleolithic sites in European Russia or Siberia or to western Upper Paleolithic art in general, and their dating are matters for the expert in Paleolithic art.

In reporting on further study of Kapova Cave and the investigation of neighboring caves in 1971, Bader writes that in the process of cleaning the upper and lower levels of soot, mud, and the defacements of tourists further drawings were discovered, including that of the eighth mammoth, as well as more schematic drawings (Group III). Construction of a projected reservoir on the Belaya River may affect this cave, but it is to be hoped that this unique monument of the Upper Paleolithic will be preserved intact.

Examples of Mobile and Parietal Art with Possible Cognitive Significance

In essence, Marshack's theory is that resource management and, perhaps, social regulation in Upper Paleolithic societies rested upon a large body of detailed systematic knowledge, the acquisition and maintenance of which was helped by symbolic records (that is markings and representations in both mobile and parietal art) (Marshack 1970, 1972a, 1972b). Marshack's data are predominantly from the Magdalenian period in France; his most decisive case has been the discovery of records of lunar counts (Marshack 1972b).

For the Upper Paleolithic of north-central Eurasia a few examples can be cited that perhaps, also are symbolic records in line with Marshack's theory. Here, no attempt will be made to interpret their meaning: the examples singled out are only cited as possibly fruitful objects for future study.

The Group III schematic drawings in the lower level of Kapova Cave, although poorly preserved, are believed, from internal evidence (style, technique of application, and composition of the paint), to be contemporaneous with the representational animal paintings of the upper gallery (Bader 1972:197). The main group of schematic drawings were on the sloping ceiling of a rear chamber of the lower gallery at a distance of 275 to 280 meters from the cave entrance. The geometric figures consisted of a "hut," "ladders," and slanting strokes covered to a considerable extent with mineral deposition. Through these depositions further red patches reportedly could be discerned above the visible drawings (Bader 1963:133–134). Bader (1963:133–134) believes, by analogy with similar drawings in French and Spanish caves, that the Kapova Cave drawings are pre-Neolithic, but of relatively late age (that is, contemporary with the Magdalenian of France and Spain). In particular, similar designs are known for Niaux, and at Font de Gaume there is a similar combination of realistic paintings and abstract representations of "huts" and "ladders."

Some movable objects from the Ukraine also suggest cognitive interpretations. At Mezhirich a line drawing on a fragment of mammoth tusk contains straight, angled, and zigzag lines, triangles, and dots (see Figure 2 on page 274). The fourth band from the (supposed) base contains figures that Pidoplichko (1969:135, 137) has interpreted as representations of dwellings, ornamented with slanting and zigzag lines.

The ocher-painted mammoth bones found at Mezhirich and Mezin are also very intriguing. At Mezhirich a mammoth skull, found at the dwelling entrance, appears to have originally been in an upright position with the maxillary portion dug into the ground. The skull had been painted in red slanting lines and dots. There was also a branching central linear figure. This composition could be interpreted as a schematic representation of fire with "tongues of flame and sparks" (Pidoplichko 1969:134). Likewise, a portion of another ornamented skull was found at the old entrance (Quadrant 11).

At Mezin mammoth bones (scapulae, lower jaws, pelvic and thigh bones) painted with red slanting lines and zigzags (see Figure 3 on page 275) were found in the western half of the dwelling (Quadrant 24 and part of 25) in what was believed to be the "cult corner." Also a portion of a frontal bone in the foundation of the eastern half of the dwelling (Quadrant 33) had been partially painted. It was found that the ocher that had been used for these paintings could be easily washed off. The question then arises as to whether the paintings on the bones were intended as permanent decorations or symbols. Perhaps, the ease of removal means that some sort of modifiable recordkeeping system was intended.

Summary and Conclusions

Within the provinces assigned to European Russian and Siberian mobile art by Abramova (1970a), differences between the two are in style and ornamentation rather than subject matter. Within this context of subject matter — representations of women and animals — the association is in all cases with habitation sites.

The study of ornamentation styles is only in its initial stages; a preliminary analysis by Abramova includes ten different ornamentation styles (see Figure 1 on page 273). Further work may lead to a modification of this classification, especially in what are currently the apparent relationships between the art of different sites.

The paintings within Kapova Cave in the southern Urals appear to be a unique example of parietal art within the confines of the present-day Soviet Union. These paintings share certain common elements with the cave art of western Europe: (1) the subject matter shows a combination of realistic animal paintings and schematic drawings, and (2) the paintings are also somewhat inaccessible and show an apparent lack of relationship to a habitation site. Further exploration of the Urals is continuing and may in time bring to light other cave paintings and possibly habitation sites that will provide clues to the place of Kapova Cave in the Upper Paleolithic of north-central Eurasia, as well as its overall relationship to the larger province of Old World Upper Paleolithic art.

Finally, both the schematic drawings in Kapova Cave and the ocher-painted bones, line drawings, and other subjects of mobile art (as well as, perhaps, some bone artifacts) suggest possible cognitive significance and might repay study in line with Marshack's current research on the western European Magdalenian.

GENERAL CONCLUSIONS

Summary of Evidence

The Upper Paleolithic in north-central Eurasia — from the Russian plain to central Siberia — existed at the end of the interglacial preceding the ultimate glaciation and during that last glaciation itself. The time profile for the Siberian sites, coterminous with the onset of the Sartan and continuing through its later stages, is, however, generally younger than that for sites on the Russian plain. Absolute datings are not available for the Urals sites, while a recent dating for Volch'ya Griva in western Siberia is in the 14,000 B.P. range (see Appendix I–133).

Cultural features and geological information, however, also provide important clues for tentative site datings, both singly and in relation to one another. For instance, at Bear Cave in the Urals the faunal composition, from which inferences on climate and landscape can be drawn, the possible indications of structures within the cave, and a mixed, but Upper Paleolithic, tool inventory, definitely indicate an Upper Paleolithic age. On the other hand at Byzovaya, apparently the northernmost European Russian site, while the tools show Upper Paleolithic traits and there are mammoth remains, with bone dated to 18,000 B.P. (see Appendix I–26), the presence of polar bear bones (if accurately identified and not intrusive) would probably place the site later in the time horizon. Again, the absence of mammoth and rhinoceros in the lowest horizon at Chernoozer'ye II on the Irtysh would definitely indicate a late Paleolithic age.

While the southern Siberian cave site of Ust'-Kanskaya has not been dated and does not contain hearths, Tseytlin's opinion as to its relatively great geological age (Tseytlin 1972:119, 124), the faunal remains, and the stone typology with its indications of terminal Mousterian traits point to an early age for Siberia. The single radiocarbon date for the lower horizon of Afontova Gora II (ca. 21,000 B.P.) (see Appendix 1–2a) is in good concordance with its tundra-dry steppe-mountain fauna and its geological age (early Sartan) (Tseytlin 1972:120, 124). In the case of the Angara region site at Mal'ta the estimated geological age (post-Karginsk — early Sartan) (Tseytlin 1972:120, 124) and the use of rhinoceros bone in dwelling construction do not conform with the single date of 14,750 ± 120 (see Appendix I–66a). This is true even allowing for the fact that many bone datings are too young, since Tseytlin (1972:121) states that in southern Siberia remains of rhinoceros occur nowhere, "either in geological deposits or cultural horizons," later than 15,000 B.P. In addition, there are questions as to the origins and dating of Mal'ta's unique tool inventory.

As one turns from indications of age provided by cultural and faunal data, the evidence available, even though incomplete in many details, confirms that the Upper Paleolithic culture of north-central Eurasia was both complex and sufficiently viable to maintain its populations and penetrate into unsettled areas. Attesting to its complexity are the sophisticated stone and bone tools and weapons; elaborately constructed dwellings and interior hearths (see Table 1); indications of trade in flints, amber, and shells; elaborate burials such as those found at Sungir'; and the presence of "art" objects with magical or religious meaning or cognitive significance (see Figures 2 and 3). Some form of recordkeeping and, perhaps, mapping were probably in use, following Marshack's proposals (Marshack 1970, 1972a, 1972b).

The maintenance of viability required first of all the procurement of large game, supplemented seasonally, no doubt, by small game, birds and eggs, fish, and roots and berries. Since game numbers fluctuate seasonally and from other causes, food storage for times of scarcity is necessary. The storage pits found at many sites would have permitted meat to be frozen and kept over the winter months. Possibly methods of drying or smoking meat were also in use, but there is no direct evidence to this effect. The hearths found inside many dwellings, constructed in some cases with stone slabs, and those with channels found at Kostenki I–1, suggest that cooking was practiced.

Adequate protection against the cold, especially during the severest stages of the last glaciation, was another necessity. The dwellings, many partially dug into the ground (described in the relevant section and Table 1), gave protection against the weather as well as unfriendly intrusions. Bone fragments, especially in sparsely wooded areas, provided good fuel. For outdoor activities, the manufacture of fur or hide garments similar to those in use today in subarctic and arctic environments is confirmed by three types of evidence: eyed bone needles and other sewing implements, the clothed statuettes from Buret' and Mal'ta, and the configuration of the ocher covering the remains of Sungir' man.

Although direct evidence on population numbers is lacking, the very density of sites and site groups on the Russian plain indicates a sizable population. Some sites are estimated to have been occupied for periods ranging from a few months to, perhaps, five to ten years, or even longer. Viable group size would probably have been between thirty-five and fifty persons. Population numbers probably decreased to the north and east into the Urals and western Siberia, but central Siberia had fairly dense settlement. There also are sites, some recently discovered, far to the north and east. There were no doubt short-term migrations following game herds, and the Urals particularly seem to have been an area of hunting camps, but so far hard information on permanent movement into Siberia or from east to west or (earlier) from the south is still lacking.

There are many individual variations between features at sites and site groups, which, taken together, sometimes present a highly contradictory picture. For instance, the round dwellings discovered at Mal'ta closely resemble some on the Russian plain, but the two rectangular dwellings are unique for the Upper Paleolithic dwellings of the area under consideration. This is true unless the remains of rectangular dwellings at Timonovka are regarded as analogous; these structures may have represented an entirely different tradition, possibly to the south. Likewise, the child burial at Mal'ta and that at Sungir' have affinities, but, perhaps, both simply belong within the overall Old World tradition of child burials beginning evidently in the Mousterian. The art at Mal'ta shows an apparent mixture of western and Siberian traditions. Most intriguing, however, is the similarity between stone inventories at Mal'ta and related Angara sites to that at Mezin in the Ukraine.

At the Kostenki sites there are great dissimilarities in tool types; on the other hand, there are similarities between the round and oval dwellings and, to a degree, in "art" objects.

Problems for Further Study

In suggesting this list of problems that require further study, there is an awareness, as previously noted, of the continuing extensive exploration and research being carried out by Soviet scientists on many of these questions. It is possible that work in progress has already gone far toward solving some of them. The following problems are the ones that appear currently most relevant, and they are presented as a basis for discussion.

1. With the continuing exploration of the Urals and north Russia now underway, the location and study of sites with remains of dwellings and hearths would give clues as to the permanence of settlement of these regions. Cultural inventories — tool types, art, and ornaments — as well as faunal remains, pollen analyses, and radiocarbon datings would further help to clarify the position of this area in relation both to the Russian plain and central and western Siberia.

2. With a better definition of the paleogeography of western Siberia during the final interglacial and glacial periods of the Upper Pleistocene, perhaps corridors favorable for human movement both from west to east and east to west could be defined. Further study of the regions lying south and west of the Minusinsk basin and Altay systems and also south of Lake Baykal would help to clarify the ages and cultural relationships of the sites at Ust'-Kanskaya on the upper Yenisey and in the Angara region.

3. Additional Upper Paleolithic burials, wherever found, would be valuable for comparison with those at Sungir' and Mal'ta from the standpoints of orientation of the grave, position of the remains, and cultural inventories or lack of them. Human remains sufficiently well preserved for study, especially any found in Siberia, would provide information on the physical characteristics of the Upper Paleolithic population.

4. As indicated in the summary on stone typologies (see page 260), the formulation of standardized terminologies for classes of artifacts unrepresented in the Bordes classification is needed. Accomplishment of this task would help (1) in a definition of the relationships involved between inventories found in widely separated areas, such as Ust'-Kanskaya and Starosel'ye in the Crimea and, in turn, the Upper Paleolithic cultures of the Yenisey sites; (2) an explanation of the resemblance of Mal'ta's lithic inventory to that of Mezin on the Desna; and (3) the definition of the apparent northwestward extension of the tool traditions of the Yenisey region to the Urals. For bone tools, attempts at establishing a general taxonomy should help to define the relationship in these classes of artifacts between central European sites and those in western European Russia and between the Yenisey and the Urals.

5. In art, three aspects of further study appear most intriguing. The classification of ornamentation styles is now being worked out. The cultural context of the unique cave paintings at Kapova Cave and the search for other caves with paintings of Upper Paleolithic age would help to clarify their position within both north-central Eurasian Upper Paleolithic culture and the larger question of the general relationship to the Upper Paleolithic art of the Old World. The analysis of "art" objects, bone and ivory artifacts with markings, line drawings and paintings, and the schematic paintings found at Kapova Cave may give clues as to recordkeeping connected with the maintenance of a complex, viable Upper Paleolithic culture.

APPENDIX 1: LIST OF SITES AND SITE GROUPS[a]

Site or site group	Location Region	Location Coordinates	Map Number	¹⁴C Dates Lab. No(s). and Reference	¹⁴C Dates Age B.P.	Stratum(S); cultural stratum (C.S.); depth(D.)	Reference(s) Beregovaya number[b]	Reference(s) Other
1. Achinsk	W. Siberia: Chulym R.; Ob' Basin	56°20'N, 90°20'E	42	—	—	—	323	—
2. Afontova Gora Group	C. Siberia: Upper Yenisey R.	56°00'N, 92°50'E	49	—	—	—	334-337	Astakhov 1966:9-14 (Afontova Gora I)
a. Afontova Gora II	—	—		GIN-117; Cherdyntsev et al. 1968:435	20,900 ± 30	Lower C.S.	—	—
				MO-343; Vinogradov et al. 1966:319	11,335 ± 270	Lower/Middle S.		
3. Akhshtyr Cave group a. Navalishino	Caucasus: Mzymta R.	43°32'N, 39°59'E	1	GIN-926; Cherdyntsev et al. 1968:432	15,500 ± 500	Base of U. Paleo-lithic Strata; D., ca. 7.0 m.	254	Panichkina and Vekilova 1962:37-43
				LE-646; Sementsov et al. 1970:253	20,600 ± 650	S: 4; D., not given	—	—
4. Aleksandrovskaya (Kostenki IV): see Kostenki-Borshevo group	—	—		—	—	—	—	—
5. Amvrosiyevka group (Kamennaya Balka)	Azov Sea: Krynka R.	47°45'N, 38°30'E	6	—	—	—	828-831	—

	Region							
7. Anikeyev rov I (Pushkari II): see Pushkari settlement group	—	—	—	—	—	—	—	—
8. Anosovka I (Kostenki X); Anosovka II (Kostenki XI/ Streletskaya I): see Kostenki-Borshevo settlement group	—	—	—	—	—	—	—	—
9. At-Daban	Yakut Assr: Lena R.	60°18'N, 120°15'E	58	—	—	—	423	—
10. Avdeyevo settlement	Russian Plain: Ragozna R., Desna Basin	51°25'N, 35°35'E	14	—	—	—	256	—
11. Baday I, II, III: see Mal'ta settlement group	—	—	—	—	—	—	—	—
12. Bateni (Tashtyk) camp group	C. Siberia: Upper Yenisey	54°37'N, 90°55'E	45	LE-771: Dolukhanov, et al. 1972:356	12,180 ± 120	Uppermost	—	Abramova 1968:161–162
13. Bear Cave (Medvezh'ya Peshchera)	N. Urals: Upper Pechora R.	ca. 62°00'N, 58°00'E	28	—	—	—	—	Guslitser and Kanivets 1965:86–103
14. Bear Rock Cave (Medved' Kamen' Grot)	S. Urals (E. Slope): Taliga R.	57°58'N, 59°53'E	30	—	—	—	305	—
15. Beloyarovka (Shirokaya Balka): see Amvrosiyevka group	—	—	—	—	—	—	—	—

APPENDIX 1: (*continued*)

Site or site group	Region	Coordinates	Map Number	Lab. No(s). and Reference	Age B.P.	Stratum(S.); cultural stratum (C.S.); depth(D.)	Beregovaya number[b]	Other
		Location			¹⁴C Dates		Reference(s)	
16. Biryuchiy Log (Kostenki IX): see Kostenki-Borshevo settlement group	—	—	—	—	—	—	—	—
17. Biryusa camp group	C. Siberia: Upper Yenisey	55°53'N, 92°15'E	48	—	—	—	344-345	—
18. Biyisk	N. Altay; Biya R.	52°25'N, 85°05'E	38	—	—	—	316	—
19. Bliznetsova Cave	C. Urals: Chan'va R.	59°40'N, 57°45'E	27	—	—	—	—	Bader 1968:115-116; 1969:145-146
20. Bugach (Kacha I) see Afontova Gora settlement group	—	—	—	—	—	—	—	—
21. Bugorok: see Pushkari settlement group	—	—	—	—	—	—	—	—
22. Bukhtarma Cave (Malyy Grot)	N. Altay: Upper Irtysh R.	49°30'N, 83°40'E	35	—	—	—	915	—
23. Buranovskaya: see Yuryuzan Cave group	—	—	—	—	—	—	—	—
24. Buret' settlement	C. Siberia: Angara R.	52°55'N, 103°40'E	53	—	—	—	389	—

Site	Location	Coordinates		Date (method; reference)	Date	Depth		Reference
26. Byzovaya settlement group	Upper Yenisey R. N. Russia	65°08'N, 57°30'E	29	TA–121; Punning et al. 1968:379	18,320 ± 280	D., 1.5–2.0m.	—	1971:240–281
27. Chastinskaya	E. Siberia: Lena R.	58°40'N, 110°50'E	56	—	—	—	413	Guslitser and Kanivets 1965:86–103
28. Cheremushnik: see Mal'ta settlement group	—	—	—	—	—	—	—	—
29. Chernoozer'ye	W. Siberia: Irtysh R.	55°30'N, 73°30'E	33	—	—	—	—	Aksenov 1966:23–37
30. Chokurcha	Crimea (nr. Simferopol')	44°57'N, 34°10'E	—	—	—	—	120	Gening 1969:198–200; Petrin 1972:255–256
31. Chulatovo I: see Pushkari settlement group		—	—	—	—	—	—	Vekilova 1971:117–161
32. Deukovskaya	C. Urals: Kama R. Region	55°40'N, 53°05'E	24	—	—	—	284	—
33. Dobranichevka	Dnepr Basin Ukraine: Supoy R.	50°10'N, 32°40'E	—	—	—	—	745	Pidoplichko 1969:62–76
34. Dneprovo-kamenka	Ukraine: Dnepr R.	48°45'N, 34°05'E	—	—	—	—	749	—
35. Dureny	Buryat-Mongol ASSR	50°20'N, 106°50'E	62	—	—	—	467	—
36. Gagarino settlement	Voronezh Obl.: Don R.	52°40'N, 38°55'E	19	—	—	—	237	Tarasov 1969:39–41
37. Glinishche (Kostenki III): see Kostenki-Borshevo settlement group		—	—	—	—	—	—	—
38. Gontsy settlement	Ukraine: Uday R., Desna Basin	50°00'N, 32°55'E	8	—	—	—	811	Pidoplichko 1969:45–61

APPENDIX 1: (continued)

Site or site group	Location Region	Location Coordinates	Map Number	¹⁴C Dates Lab. No(s). and Reference	¹⁴C Dates Age B.P.	Stratum(S.); cultural stratum (C.S.); depth(D.)	Beregovaya number[b]	Reference(s) Other
39. Gorodtsovkaya (Kostenki XV): see Kostenki-Borshevo settlement group	—	—	—	—	—	—	—	—
40. Grensk Group (incl. Berdyzh)	Belorussian SSR: Sozh R.	52°55'N, 30°50'E	9	LE-450; Sementsov et al.1969:253	20,570 ± 430	Lower C.S.	487, 488	—
41. Il'skaya Camp	N. Caucasus: Il' R.	44°45'N, 38°20'E	3	—	—	—	131	Gorodtsov 1941:7–25
42. Irkutsk Camp group	C. Siberia: Angara region	52°10'N, 104°20'E	54	—	—	—	396–400	—
a. Verkholenskaya Gora				MO-441; Vinogradov et al.1969:1176–1177	12,500 ± 180	C.S.; D., 2.2–2.4m.	397	—
43. Kacha I (Bugach); Kacha II: see Afontova Gora settlement group	—	—	—	—	—	—	—	—
44. Kamennyy log (Kokorevo III): see Kokorevo camp group	—	—	—	—	—	—	—	—
45. Kapova Cave	Urals: Belaya R.	ca. 53°00'N, 56°00'E	25	—	—	—	—	Bader 1963, 1965c, 1972
46. Karacharovo	Russian plain: Oka R.	55°20'N, 72°00'E	21	—	—	—	268	—

Site	Location	Coordinates		¹⁴C info	Date	C.S.	Count	Reference
47. Ravenno. see Podsosenka Verkhnyaya	—	—	—	—	—	—	—	—
48. Kayskaya Gora:— see Irkutsk camp group	—	—	—	—	—	—	—	—
49. Kel'siyevskaya (Kostenki XIII): see Kostenki-Borshevo settlement group	—	—	—	—	—	—	—	—
50. Khvoykovskaya: see Kostenki XVIII	—	—	—	—	—	—	—	—
51. Kipernyy Log (Kokorevo IV): see Kokorevo camp group	—	—	—	—	—	—	—	—
52. Kiyevo-Kirillovskoye	Ukraine: Kiev City	50°15'N, 30°35'E	—	—	—	—	742	Pidoplichko 1969:20–44
53. Kiik-Koba	Crimea	45°05'N, 34°05'E	—	—	—	—	115	Vekilova 1971:117–161
54. Klyuchevskaya Cave: see Yuryuzan Cave group	—	—	—	—	—	—	—	—
55. Kokorevo camp group a. Kokorevo I	C. Siberia: Upper Yenisey	55°05'N, 91°10'E	46	See ¹⁴C Dates Below: LE-628; Dolukhanov et al.1970:146	14,450 ± 150	C.S. 3	348	Abramova 1971:240–281
				GIN-91; Cherdyntsev et al.1968:435	13,300 ± 50	C.S. 3(?)		
				LE-526; Dolukhanov et al. 1970:146	12,940 ± 270	C.S. 2		

APPENDIX 1: (continued)

Site or site group	Location Region	Location Coordinates	Map Number	¹⁴C Dates Lab. No(s). and Reference	¹⁴C Dates Age B.P.	¹⁴C Dates Stratum(S.); cultural stratum (C.S.); depth(D.)	Beregovaya number[b]	Reference(s) Other
55 b. Kokorevo II	—	—	—	GIN-90; Cherdyntsev et al. 1968:435	13,300 ± 100	C.S.	349	—
c. Kokorevo III	—	—	—	LE-629; Dolukhanov et al. 1970:146	12,690 ± 140	C.S.	350	—
d. Kokorevo IV	—	—	—	LE-540:1970:146	15,460 ± 320	C., 5.2m.	351	—
				LE-469:1970:146	14,320 ± 330	C.S. 3–5; D., 4.0–4.5m.	352	—
e. Kokorevo V	—	—	—	—	—		—	—
56. Koroviy Log I–III: see Afontova Gora settlement group	—	—	—	—	—		—	—
57. Kosh-Koba	Crimea	45°05'N, 34°25'E	—	—			116	Vekilova 1971:117–161
58. Kostenki-Borshevo settlement group	Russian Plain: Don R.	—	18	See ¹⁴C dates below[c]	—	—	215–236	Velichko and Rogachev 1969:75–87; Klein 1969a
a. Kostenki I (Stoyanka Polyakova)	—	51°25'N, 39°01'E	—	GIN-86; Cherdyntsev et al.1968:430–431	14,020 ±60	Upper C.S. (2nd Terrace)	—	—
b. Kostenki II (Zamyaininskaya)	—	51°24'N, 39°01'E	—	GIN-93; Cherdyntsev et al.:431	11,000 ± 200	C.S.; (2nd Terrace)	—	—
c. Kostenki XI (Anosovka II)	—	ca. 51°24'N, 39°01'E	—	GIN-85; Cherdyntsev et al.:431	9,610 ± 190	Upper C.S.; (2nd Terrace)	—	—
				TA-2?, Rogachev	15,200 ± 600	C.S. 2;		

Site	Location	Coordinates	No.	Lab no.; reference	Date	Description	Reference
e. Kostenki XIV — (Markina Gora)		51°24'N, 39°00'E	—	GIN-79; Cherdyntsev et al. 1968:431	14,300 ± 460	C.S. 3; (2nd Terrace)	—
f. Kostenki XVII — (Spitsynskaya)		51°24'N, 39°01'E	—	GIN-77,[e] Cherdyntsev et al.1968:431	20,000 ± 350	S.4a; D., 3.6–3.7m.	—
				GIN-78; Cherdyntsev et al. 1968:431	20,100 ± 200	S.6; D., 6.3–6.4m. (2nd Terrace)	
				MO-465,[f] Vinogradov et al.1970:173	21,300 ± 400	C.S.; D., 6.15–6.4m.	
				MO-435; Vinogradov et al.	23,900 ± 600	C.S.; D., 2.4m.	
g. Kostenki XIX —		51°25'N, 39°00'E	—	GIN-107; Cherdyntsev et al.1968:432	11,800 ± 500	C.S.; D., 1.0–2.5m. (1st Terrace)	—
h. Borshevo II —		51°20'N, 39°06'E	—	MO-636; Vinogradov et al.1970:174	11,760 ± 240	D., ca.3m.	—
				GIN-107; Cherdyntsev et al.1968:432	12,300 ± 100	Underlying lower C.S.; D., 3.35m. (1st Terrace)	
59. Krasnny Yar	C. Siberia: Angara R.	53°40'N, 103°30'E	51		—		Abramova 1962a; 147–156; 1970b
60. Kravtsov Rov (Pushkari VIII) see Pushkari settlement group		—			—		—
61. Krutaya Gora see Byzovaya settlement group		—			—		—
62. Kursk I	Russian plain: Seym R.	51°40'N, 36°10'E	15	GIN-40; Cherdyntsev et al.1968:430	11,600 ± 200	C.S.; D., 1.2m.	—

APPENDIX 1: (continued)

Site or site group	Location Region	Coordinates	Map Number	Lab. No(s). and Reference	Age B.P.	Stratum(S.); cultural stratum (C.S.); depth(D.)	Beregovaya number[b]	Other
63. Kuznetsov Log: (Borshevo I) see Kostenki-Borshevo settlement group	—	—	—	—	—	—	—	—
64. Lipa camp group	W. Russia: Pripyet basin	50°25'N, 25°50'E	—	—	—	—	716–718	Savich 1969:136–141
65. Makarovo camp group (incl. Shishkino)	E. Siberia: Lena R.	54°00'N, 105°45'E	55	—	—	—	406–407	Aksenov 1970:43–52
66. Mal'ta settlement group	C. Siberia: Angara region	(see below)	52	14C Dates: see below	—	—	383–384	Gerasimov, M.M. 1964
a. Mal'ta		52°52'N, 103°25'E	—	GIN-97; Cherdyntsev et al.1968:436	14,750 ± 120	Lower C.S.; D., 1.0m.	—	—
b. Ust'-Belaya	—	52°55'N, 103°35'E	—	GIN-96; Cherdyntsev et al.1968:435–436	8,960 ± 60	C.S. 3–4	—	Medvedev 1966:38–50
67. Malyy Grot: see Bukhtarma	—	—	—	—	—	—	—	—
68. Markina Gora: (Kostenki XIV): see Kostenki-Borshevo settlement group	—	—	—	—	—	—	—	—
69. Mar'yeva Gora Azov Sea	—	47°32'N, 38°52'E	5	—	—	—	249	—
70. Medved'	—	—	—	—	—	—	—	—

Site	Location	Coordinates	No.	Sample / description	¹⁴C Date	Lab no.; source	No.	Reference
72. Mezhirich	Ukraine: Ros'/Rosava R.	49°45'N, 31°25'E	—			—	—	Pidoplichko 1969:111–144
73. Mezin settlement	Ukraine: Desna R.	51°45'N, 33°05'E	10			—	806	Pidoplichko 1969:77–110; Shovkoplyas 1965
74. Military hospital see Irkutsk camp(?) group	—	—	—			—	—	—
75. Min'yevskaya group	Ukraine: N. Donets R.	48°45'N, 37°30'E	17			—	820–821	—
76. Molodova Sites	W. Russia: Dnestr R.	48°30'N, 27°10'E	—	¹⁴C Dates: see below		—	—	Ivanova 1969:111–119
a. Molodova I	—	—	—	Late Mousterian Hearth; D., ca. 10m.	>44,000	GrN-3659; Vogel and Waterbolk 1967:119	60,558	—
				D., 6.5–7.0m.	22,850 ± 120	GIN-72; Cherdyntsev et al.1968:427		
b. Molodova Vᵍ	—			C.S. 11; D., ca. 10m.	>45,600	LG-17; Arslanov et al.1972:189	561	Ivanova 1966:32–66
				"Sooty Streak"; D., ca. 8.0m.	>35,500	LG-16; Arslanov et al.1972:189		
				C.S. 9, Horizon "A"; D., ca. 5m. (Upper paleo)	29,650 ± 1320	LG-15[a]; Arslanov et al.1972:189		
				Insoluble fraction of charcoal, LG-15[a]	28,100 ± 1000	LG-15[b]; Arslanov et al.1972:189		
				C.S. 8; D., ca. 4.5m.	>24,600	LG-14; Arslanov et al.1972:189		
				C.S. 7; D., 3.1–3.25m.	23,700 ± 320	GIN-10; Cherdyntsev et al.1968:421		

APPENDIX 1: *(continued)*

Site or site group	Location		Map Number	¹⁴C Dates		Reference(s)		
	Region	Coordinates		Lab. No(s). and Reference	Age B.P.	Stratum(S.); cultural stratum (C.S.); depth(D.)	Beregovaya number[b]	Other
b. Molodova V[g] *(contd)*				MO-11; Vinogradov et al.1968:319	23,000 ± 800	C.S. 7; D., ca. 3.5m.		
				GIN-106; Cherdyntsev et al.1968:427	23,100 ± 400	C.S. 10; D., 4.4–4.9m.		
				GIN-147;[h] Cherdyntsev et al.1968:426	17,100 ± 1400	C.S. 4; D., 1.9–2.0m.		
				GIN-52; Cherdyntsev et al.1968:427	17,100 ± 180	C.S. 5; D., 2.2–2.4m.		
				GIN-105; Cherdyntsev et al.1968:427	16,750 ± 250	C.S. 6; D., 2.6–2.8m.		
				GIN-9; Cherdyntsev et al.1968:421	13,370 ± 540	C.S. 3; D., 1.6–1.8m.		
				GIN-56; Cherdyntsev et al.1968:426	12,300 ± 140	C.S. 2; D., 1.2–1.4m.		
				GIN-8; Cherdyntsev et al.1968:420	11,900 ± 230	C.S. 2 (Fossil bones); D., 1.2–1.4m.		
				GIN-54; Cherdyntsev et al.1968:426	10,940 ± 150	E. Mesolithic; D., 0.5–0.8m.		
				GIN-7; Cherdyntsev et al.1968:420	10,590 ± 230	S. la (E. Mesolithic); D., 1.0–1.1m.		
					250 ± 160			

Site	Location	Coordinates	Elev.	Lab no. / Reference	Date B.P.	Type		No.	Reference
78. Navalishino Cave: see Akhshtyr Group	—	—	—	—	—	—	—	—	—
79. Novgorod Severskiy: see Pushkari settlement group	—	—	—	—	—	—	—	—	—
80. Novoklinovka II: see Amvrosiyevka group	—	—	—	—	—	—	—	—	—
81. Nyangi camp group (*incl.* Zarubino)	Buryat-Mongol ASSR: Selenga R.	50°35′N, 106°15′E	61	—	—	—	—	443, 444, 439	Abramova 1970b:9–16
82. Nyuya	Yakut ASSR: Lena R.	60°35′N, 116°15′E	57	—	—	—	—	421	—
83. Ogurdinovo (Mesolithic)	C. Urals: Upper Kama R.	59°30′N, 56°30′E	—	—	—	—	—	286	—
84. Oshurkovo	Buryat-Mongol ASSR: Selenga R.	57°53′N, 107°27′E	60	—	—	—	—	459	Okladnikov 1961:486–497
85. Paseka: see Pushkari settlement group	—	—	—	—	—	—	—	—	—
86. Pavlov (Pollau) Czechoslovakia	C. Europe: Dyje R.	48°50′N, 16°25′E	—	GRO-1272;[i] de Vries 1958:14	26,400 ± 230	C.S.; D., not given	—	—	Coles and Higgs 1969:298; Ivanova 1966:32–66
				GIN-104; Cherdyntsev et al.1968:426	26,000 ± 350	C.S. (?); D., not given			
				GRO-1325; de Vries 1958:14	24,800 ± 150	C.S.; D., not given			

APPENDIX 1: (*continued*)

Site or site group	Location		¹⁴C Dates				Reference(s)	
	Region	Coordinates	Map Number	Lab. No(s). and Reference	Age B.P.	Stratum(S.); cultural stratum (C.S.); depth(D.)	Beregovaya number[b]	Other
87. Pereselencheskiy Punkt settlement	C. Siberia: Upper Yenisey	56°05'N, 93°05'E	50	—	—	—	338	—
88. Podsosenka Verkilnyaya (Kaverino)	Russian plain: Tsna R.	54°10'N, 41°47'E	22	—	—	—	272	—
89. Pogon: see Pushkari settlement group	—	—	—	—	—	—	—	—
90. Pokrovskiy Log (Khvoykovskaya/ Kostenki XVIII): see Kostenki-Borshevo settlement group	—	—	—	—	—	—	—	—
91. Predmost, Czechoslovakia	C. Europe: Morava R.	49°25'N, 17°20'E	—	—	—	—	—	Coles and Higgs 1969:298; Ivanova 1966: 32–66
92. Prishibskaya: see Min'yevskaya	—	—	—	—	—	—	—	—
93. Pristenskaya see Sharukanskaya group	—	—	—	—	—	—	—	—
94. Pushkari settlement group	Russian plain: Desna R.	52°00'N, 33°15'E	11	—	—	—	781–783, 788–790, 799	—

	Laiiiu-Ola (mm.)						
96. Sannyy Mys	Transbaykal: Uda R.	52°00'N, 107°30'E	59	—	—	—	1970:59 Okladnikov 1961:486–497
97. Shan Koba	Crimea	44°30'N, 33°50'E	—	—	—	847	—
98. Sharukanskaya group (*incl.* Pristenskaya)	Ukraine: N. Donets R.	49°05'N, 37°20'E	16	—	—	818, 819	—
99. Shirokaya Balka (Beloyarovka): see Amvrosiyevka group	—	—	—	—	—	—	—
100. Shishkino: see Makarovo camp group	—	—	—	—	—	—	—
101. Smelovskaya Cave group	S. Urals: Ural R.	53°35'N, 58°50'E	32	—	—	302	Bader 1971b:200–208
102. Sosonnitskiy Rov: (Pushkari III) see Pushkari settlement group	—	—	—	—	—	—	—
103. Spitsynskaya (Kostenki XVII): see Kostenki-Borshevo settlement group	—	—	—	—	—	—	—
104. Srostki camp	N. Altay: Katun R.	52°25'N, 85°50'E	39	—	—	317	Sosnovskiy 1941:109–125
105. Starosel'ye	Crimea	45°42'N, 33°52'E	—	—	—	127	Vekilova 1971:117–161
106. Stoyanka Polyakova (Kostenki I): see Kostenki-Borshevo settlement group	—	—	—	—	—	—	—

APPENDIX 1: (*continued*)

Site or site group	Location		¹⁴C Dates				Reference(s)	
	Region	Coordinates	Map Number	Lab. No(s). and Reference	Age B.P.	Stratum(S.); cultural stratum (C.S.); depth(D.)	Berego-vaya number[b]	Other
107. Stoyanka Spitsynskaya (Kostenki XVII): see Kostenki-Borshevo settlement group	—	—	—	—	—	—	—	—
108. Stoyanka Valukinskaya (Kostenki XIX): see Kostenki-Borshevo settlement group	—	—	—	—	—	—	—	—
109. Stoyanka Zamyatninskaya (Kostenki II): see Kostenki-Borshevo settlement group	—	—	—	—	—	—	—	—
110. Streletskaya I; Streletskaya II (Kostenki VI): see Kostenki-Borshevo settlement group	—	—	—	—	—	—	—	—
111. Sungir'	Russian plain: Sungir' Brook, Klyaz 'Ma R.	56°10'N, 40°35'E	20	GIN-326b;[j] Cherdyntsev et al.1969:184	22,500 ± 600	C.S.; D., not given	—	Bader, 1959:144–155; 1961:122–145; 1965:57 ff;

Site	Location	Coordinates		Cherdyntsev et al. 1969:184 GIN-15: Cherdyntsev et al.1968:422 GIN-14: Cherdyntsev et al. 1968:422	16,200 ± 400	14,600 ± 600	Soil below C.S. (see date description) C.S.; D., not given (bone)		References
112. Suponevo: see Timonovka settlement group	—	—	—	—	—	—	—	—	—
113. Svyatoy Log (Kostenki V): see Kostenki-Borshevo settlement group	—	—	—	—	—	—	—	—	—
114. Syuren'	Crimea: Bel'bek R.	44°35'N, 53°55'E	—	—	—	—	—	842–843	Vekilova 1971:117–161
115. Talitskiy	Urals: Chusovaya R.	58°10'N, 56°30'E	26	—	—	—	—	289	Bader 1965b:129–141
116. Tashtyk: see Bateni camp group	—	—	—	—	—	—	—	—	—
117. Telezhnyy Log (Kokorevo II): see Kokorevo camp group	—	—	—	—	—	—	—	—	—
118. Tel'Manskaya (Kostenki VIII): see Kostenki-Borshevo settlement group	—	—	—	—	—	—	—	—	—
119. Tetyushi: see Undory site	—	—	—	—	—	—	—	—	—
120. Timonovka settlement group	Russian plain: Desna R.	53°13'N, 34°25'E	13	—	—	—	—	259, 260	Grekhova 1969:88–97; Velichko 1969:97–102

APPENDIX 1: (*continued*)

| Site or site group | Location | | Map Number | ¹⁴C Dates | | Stratum(S.); cultural stratum (C.S.); depth(D.) | Reference(s) | |
	Region	Coordinates		Lab. No(s). and Reference	Age B.P.		Beregovaya number[b]	Other
121. Tomsk camp	W. Siberia: Tom' R.	56°30'N, 85°12'E	41	—	—	—	322	—
122. Tuekta	N. Altay: Ob' Basin	50°50'N, 85°55'E	36	—	—	—	313	Krylova and Pavlyuchenko 1962:61–64
123. Uglyanka (Kostenki XVI): see Kostenki-Borshevo settlement group	—	—	—	—	—	—	—	—
124. Ulazy	C. Siberia: Upper Yenisey R.	54°55'N, 91°20'E	47	—	—	—	347	Abramova 1971:240–281
125. Undory site (Tetyushi)	S. Urals: Volga R.	54°40'N, 48°30'E	23	—	—	—	276	—
126. Ushkanka: see Irkutsk camp group	—	—	—	—	—	—	—	—
127. Uspenka (Belaya Gora): see Amvrosiyevka group	—	—	—	—	—	—	—	—
128. Ust'-Belaya: see Mal'ta settlement group	—	—	—	—	—	—	—	—
129. Ust'-Kanskaya Cave	N. Altay: Charysh R.	50°45'N, 86°10'E	37	—	—	—	312	Rudenko 1961:203–215; Anisyutkin and

Site	Location	Coordinates	No.	Lab/Source	Date	Context	No.	Reference
130. Ust'-Kuyum	N. Altay, Katun' R.	51 30 N, 88 00 E	40	—	—	—	314	—
131. Verkholen-skaya Gora: see Irkutsk camp group	—	—	—	—	—	—	—	—
132. Vishunov Log (Borshevo II): see Kostenki-Borshevo settlement group	—	—	—	—	—	—	—	—
133. Volch'ya Griva	W. Siberia: Kargat R.	55°10'N, 80°15'E	34	Soan-78; Firsov et al.1972:196	14,200 ± 150	C.S.; D. not given	—	Firsov et al. 1972:196
134. Volkovskaya (Kostenki XII): see Kostenki-Borshevo settlement group	—	—	—	—	—	—	—	—
135. Vorontsov Cave	Caucasus	43°37'N, 39°52'E	2	Le-700; Sementsov et al.1969:253	14,100 ± 140	C.S. 1; D. not given	136	Lyubin and Solov'yev 1971:5–40
136. Voyennyy Gospital' (Military Hospital): see Irkutsk Camp group	—	—	—	—	—	—	—	—
137. Yeliseyevichi settlement group	Russian plain: Sudost' R., Desna Basin	53°10'N, 33°35'E	12	GIN-80; Cherdyntsev et al.1968:430	33,000 ± 400	Base of Hearth; S. of Loessal Loam; D., 2.3m	262	Yefimenko 1953:543–545; Polikarpovich 1968:37–139
138. Yudinovo: see Yeliseyevichi settlement group	—	—	—	—	—	—	—	—

APPENDIX 1: (*continued*)

| Site or site group | Location | | Map Number | ¹⁴C Dates | | | | | Reference(s) | |
	Region	Coordinates		Lab. No(s). and Reference	Age B.P.	Stratum(S.); cultural stratum (C.S.); depth(D.)			Berego-vaya number[b]	Other
139. Yuryuzan cave group (Buranovskaya; Klyuchevskaya)	S. Urals: Yuryuzan R., Ufa Basin	54°55'N, 58°10'E	31	—	—	—			293, 294 295	—
140. Zabochka (Kokorevo I): see Kokorevo camp group	—	—	—	—	—	—			—	—
141. Zarubino: see Nyangi camp (?) group	—	—	—	—	—	—			—	—

[a] Compiled by Demitri B. Shimkin and Edith M. Shimkin, University of Illinois, Urbana.

[b] Beregovaya, N. A. *Paleoliticheskiye Mestonakhozhdeniya SSSR.* (Translated as *Paleolithic sites in the USSR.*) Moscow-Leningrad: Izd. Akad. Nauk SSSR, 1960.

[c] See also Klein 1969a:45–57 and Table 3 with dates tabulated by terrace. Dates of Institute of Archeology, Leningrad Branch (A. A. Sementsov *et al.* 1969 for charred bone, Kostenki I (LE-451) and Anosovka II/Kostenki XI (LE-409 and LE-403) also for charred bone, omitted because too young for technical reasons.

[d] Listed as Kostenki XVIII in Cherdyntsev *et al.* 1966:1414, Grichuk *et al.* 1966:272, and Cherdyntsev *et al.* 1968:431, but tabulated here under Kostenki XI since location is given as Anosovskiy Log (Anosov Ravine) in date description.

[e] Incorrectly listed under Kostenki XVIII in Grichuk *et al.*1966:272 and Cherdyntsev *et al.*1968:431.

[f] Discrepancy in ages for MO–465 and MO–435 probably result of redeposition.

[g] See also Ivanova 1966:Figure 20 and section on faunal remains.

[h] GIN-147, 52, 105, are listed from older to younger for consistency, but note younger dates (105 and 52) are from lower cultural strata (5th and 6th) than GIN-147 (4th).

[i] Incorrectly listed as GRO–1242 in Cherdyntsev *et al.*1968:426 and Grichuk *et al.*1966:270; samples for all three dates from charcoal.

[j] GIN-326a and b both from campfire charcoal; GIN-14, 15, probably too young.

REFERENCE ABBREVIATIONS

AN SSSR —   Akademiya nauk SSSR
                 (Academy of Sciences, USSR)
AN USSR —   Akademiya nauk Ukraynskoy SSR
                 (Academy of Sciences, Ukranian SSR)
AO 19 - - g —   *Arkheologicheskiye otkrytiya 19 - - goda*
                 (Archeological Discoveries of 19 - -).
                 (Note that the year of publication is always one year later than
                 that of the title.)
BKIChP —   *Byulleten' Komissiyi po izucheniyu chetvertichnogo perioda*
                 (Bulletin of the Commission for the Study of the Quaternary
                 Period).
Izd. —   Izdatel'stvo
                 (Publishing House).
KSIA —   *Kratkiye soobshcheniya Instituta arkheologiyi Akademiyi*
                 nauk SSSR
                 (Brief Reports of the Institute of Archeology of the Academy of
                 Sciences, USSR).
MIA —   *Materialy i issledovaniya po arkheologiyi SSSR*
                 (Materials and Research on the Archeology of the USSR).
SA —   *Sovetskaya arkheologiya*
                 (Soviet Archeology).
SOAN —   Sibir'skoye otdeleniye Akademiyi nauk SSSR
                 (Siberian Division, Academy of Sciences, USSR)
                 (Novosibirsk).
TIA —   *Trudy Instituta arkheologiyi Akademiyi nauk SSSR*
                 (Memoirs of the Institute of Archeology of the Academy of
                 Sciences, USSR).
TKIChP —   *Trudy Komissiyi po izucheniyu chetvertichnogo perioda*
                 (Memoirs of the Commission for the Study of the Quaternary
                 Period).
T VII MKAEN —   *Trudy k VII Mezhdunarodnomu kongressu antropologiches-*
                 kikh i etnograficheskikh nauk
                 (Memoirs of the VII International Congress of Anthropological
                 and Ethnographic Sciences).

REFERENCES

ABRAMOVA, Z. A.
  1962a Krasnyy Yar. A new Paleolithic site on the Angara. *SA* No. 3:147–156.
  1962b *Paleoliticheskoye iskusstvo na territoriyi SSSR (Paleolithic art in the*
        territory of the USSR). Arkheologiya SSSR. Svod arkheologicheskikh
        istochnikov, vypusk A4—3. (Translated as *Archeology of the USSR.*
        Collection of archeological sources, No. A4—3). Moscow-Leningrad:
        Izd. AN SSSR.
  1966 Local differences in the Paleolithic cultures of the Angara and Yenisey.
        SA No. 3:9–16.
  1967 On insert tools in the Yenisey Paleolithic. *KSIA* 11:12–18.
  1968 "Research on the Paleolithic of the Yenisey," in *AO 1967 g.* Edited by
        B. A. Rybakov, 161–162. Moscow: Izd. "Nauka."

308   EDITH M. SHIMKIN

1970a   "Paleolithic art," in *Kamennyy vek na territoriyi SSSR*. (Translated as *The Stone Age in the territory of the USSR*.) Edited by B. A. Rybakov, 78–89. Moscow: Izd. "Nauka."
1970b   "The Paleolithic of southern Siberia," in *Drevnyaya Sibir', vypusk 3: Sibir' i yeyo sosedi v drevnosti* (Translated as *Ancient Siberia, No. 3: Siberia and its neighbors in antiquity*). 1–16. Novosibirsk: Izd. "Nauka," SOAN.
1971   New data on the Paleolithic of the Yenisey, *MIA* 173:240–281.

AKSENOV, M. P.
1966   "Cheremushnik campsite," in *Sibirskiy arkheologicheskiy sbornik (Siberian archeological collection)*. Edited by A. P. Okladnikov, 23–37. Novosibirsk: Izd. "Nauka," SOAN.
1970   "The complex of the lower cultural horizon of Makarovo campsite on the Lena," in *Drevnyaya Sibir', vypusk 3: Sibir' i yeyo sosedi v drevnosti*. Translated as *Ancient Siberia, No. 3: Siberia and its neighbors in antiquity*. 43–52. Novosibirsk: Izd. "Nauka," SOAN.
1972   "Research in the valley of the Lena," in *AO 1971 g*. Edited by B. A. Rybakov, 245–255. Moscow: Izd. "Nauka."

ANISYUTKIN, N. K., S. N. ASTAKHOV
1970   "On the question of the most ancient sites of the Altay," in *Drevnyaya Sibir', vypusk 3: Sibir' i yeyo sosedi v drevnosti*. (Translated as *Ancient Siberia, No. 3: Siberia and its neighbors in antiquity*). 27–33. Novosibirsk: Izd. "Nauka," SOAN.

ARSLANOV, KH. A.
1968   Khlopin Institute radiocarbon dates I. *Radiocarbon* 10(2):446–447.

ARSLANOV, KH. A., L. I. GROMOVA, YU. A. RUDNEYEV
1968   All-Union Geological Institute Radiocarbon dates I. *Radiocarbon* 10(2):448–450.

ARSLANOV, KH. A., L. I. GROMOVA, N. I. POLEVAYA, YU. P. RUDNEYEV
1972   Dates from the radiocarbon laboratory of the All-Union Geological Research Institute. *BKIChP* 38:186–189.

ASTAKHOV, S. N.
1966   "The collection of I. T. Savenkov from Afontova Gora I campsite," in *Drevnyaya Sibir': Sibirskiy arkheologicheskiy sbornik (Ancient Siberia: Siberian archeological collection)*, 9–14. Novosibirsk: Izd. "Nauka," SOAN.
1967   Adzes in the Late Paleolithic of the Yenisey. *KSIA* 111:19–23.

BADER, O. N.
1959   The Paleolithic campsite of Sungir' on the Klyaz'ma River. *SA* No. 1:144–155.
1960   Basic stages of the ethno-cultural history and paleogeography of the Urals. *MIA* 79:88–103.
1961   Sungir' campsite: its age and position in the Paleolithic of eastern Europe. *TKIChP* 17:122–145.
1963   The Paleolithic paintings at Kapova Cave (Shulgan-Tash) in the Urals. *SA* No. 1:125–134. Moscow: Izd. AN SSSR.
1965a   "Sungir' campsite and its archeological aspect," in *Stratigrafiya i periodizatsiya Paleolita vostochnoy i tsentral'noy Yevropy k VII Kongressu INQUA (S Sh A, 1965). (The stratigraphy and periodization of the Paleolithic of eastern and central Europe, VII Congress INQUA [USA, 1965])*. 86–103. Moscow: Izd. "Nauka," *BKIChP*, AN SSSR.

1965b "The Paleolithic of the Urals and its position in the most ancient history of Europe," in *Chetvertichnyy period i ego istoriya k VII Kongressu INQUA (The Quaternary period and its history. VII Congress, INQUA)*. Edited by V. I. Gromov et al., 129–141. Moscow: Izd. "Nauka."

1965c *La Caverne Kapovaïa*. Moscow: Izd. "Nauka."

1967 An Upper Paleolithic burial and grave at Sungir' campsite. *SA*, No. 3:142–159.

1968 "The northern Paleolithic expedition" [Bliznetsova Cave], in *AO 1967 g*. Edited by B. A. Rybakov, 115–116. Moscow: Izd. "Nauka."

1969 "Northern Paleolithic expedition," [Bliznetsova Cave], in *AO 1968 g*. Edited by B. A. Rybakov, 145–146. Moscow: Izd. "Nauka."

1970 "A second Paleolithic grave at Sungir'," in *AO 1969 g*. Edited by B. A. Rybakov, 41–42. Moscow: Izd. "Nauka."

1971a "Northern Paleolithic expedition, in *AO 1970 g*. Edited by B. A. Rybakov, 33–34. Moscow: Izd. "Nauka."

1971b Smelovskaya II Paleolithic site in the steppes of the southern Urals. *MIA* 173:200–208.

1972 "Northern Paleolithic expedition" [Kapova Cave], in *AO 1971 g*. Edited by B. A. Rybakov, 197–198. Moscow: Izd. "Nauka."

BEREGOVAYA, N. A.
1960 *Paleoliticheskiye mestonakhozhdeniya SSSR*. (Translated as *Paleolithic sites in the USSR*). *MIA* 81:45–215.

BERG, L. S.
1950 *Natural regions of the USSR*. (Translated by O. A. Titelbaum) New York: Macmillan.

1941 "Kirillovskoye Paleolithic site." *MIA* 2:86–103.

1971 "The Paleolithic site of Anosovka I [Kostenki X] in the Kostenki group." *MIA* 173:182–199.

BINFORD, S.
1968 A structural comparison of disposal of the dead in the Mousterian and the Upper Paleolithic. *Southwestern Journal of Anthropology* 24:139–154.

BORDES, FRANÇOIS
1968 *The old Stone Age*. Translated by J. E. Anderson. New York: McGraw Hill.

BORISKOVSKIY, P. I.
1958 The study of Paleolithic dwellings in the Soviet Union. *SA* No. 1:3–19.

BUTZER, KARL W.
1964 *Environment and archeology: An introduction to Pleistocene geography*. Chicago: Aldine.

CHERDYNTSEV, V. V., V. A. ALEKSEYEV, N. V. KIND, et al.
1965 Radiocarbon dates of the Laboratory of the Geological Institute (GIN), AN SSSR. *Geokhimiya* 12:1410–1422.

1968 Geological Institute radiocarbon dates I–III. *Radiocarbon* 10(2):419–445.

CHERDYNTSEV, V. V., F. S. ZAVEL'SKIY, N. V. KIND, et al.
1969 Radiocarbon dates of the Geological Institute, AN SSSR (Report No. 4). *BKIChP* 36:172–193.

CHERNYSH, A. P.
1967 The nomenclature of Upper Paleolithic tools. *KSIA* 111:3–13.

CLARK, J. G. D.
1969 *The Stone Age hunters*. New York: McGraw-Hill.

COLES, J. M., E. S. HIGGS
1969   *The archaeology of early man.* New York: Praeger.

DEBETS, C. F.
1946   Fragment of a human frontal bone from the cultural horizon of Afon-tova Gora II campsite near Krasnoyarsk. *BKIChP* 8:73–77.
1967   A skeleton of late Paleolithic man from the burial at Sungir' campsite. *SA* No. 3:160–164.

DE VRIES, H.
1958   Radiocarbon dates for Upper Eem and Würm-interstadial samples. *Eiszeitalter und Gegenwart* 9:10–17.

DOLGIKH, B. O.
1952   "The origins of the Nganasany," in *Sibirskiy etnograficheskiy sbornik (Siberian ethnographic collection).* Edited by L. P. Potapov and M. G. Levin, 5–87. *TIA,* n.s. volume 18. Moscow-Leningrad: Izd. AN SSSR.

DOLUKHANOV, P. M., YE. N. ROMANOVA, A. A. SEMYONTSOV
1970   Radiocarbon dates of the Institute of Archaeology II. *Radiocarbon* 12(1):130–155.

FIRSOV, L. V., V. A. PANYCHEV, L. A. ORLOVA
1972   Radiocarbon dates of the Laboratory of Geochronology of the Institute of Geology and Geophysics, Siberian Branch, AN SSSR, Novosibirsk. *BKIChP* 38:190–197.

GENING, V. F.
1969   "Studies of a complex of sites at the village of Chernoozer'ye on the Irtysh," in *AO 1968 g.* Edited by B. A. Rybakov, 198–200. Moscow: Izd. "Nauka."

GENING, V. F., N. K. YESHCHENKO, O. M. KONDRAT'YEV, et al.
1970   "Studies in the middle Irtysh region," in *AO 1969 g.* Edited by B. A. Rybakov, 187–189. Moscow: Izd. "Nauka."

GEPTNER, V. G., A. A. NASIMOVICH, A. G. VANNIKOV
1961   *Mlekopitayushchiye Sovetskogo Soyuza.* (Translated as *Mammals of the Soviet Union.*) Volume 1. Moscow: Gos. Izd. "Vysshaya shkola."

GERASIMOV, M. M.
1941   The working of bone at the Paleolithic campsite at Mal'ta. *MIA* 2:65–85.
1964   "The Paleolithic site Mal'ta: Excavations of 1956–1957," in *The archaeology and geomorphology of northern Asia: selected works.* Edited by Henry N. Michael, 3–32. Toronto: University of Toronto Press.

GORODTSOV, V. A.
1941   Results of the investigation of Il'skaya Paleolithic campsite (Prelimi-nary report), *MIA* 2:7–25.

GREKHOVA, L. V.
1969   "The Upper Paleolithic in the Basin of the Middle Desna," in *Priroda i razvitiye pervobytnogo obshchestva na territoriyi yevropeyskoy chasti SSSR.* (Translated as *Nature and the development of primitive society in the territory of the European part of the USSR*). 88–97. Moscow: Izd. "Nauka." (VIII Congress INQUA, Paris).
1971   "Work of the Desna expedition of the State Historical Museum," in *AO 1970 g.* Edited by B. A. Rybakov, 46–47. Moscow: Izd. "Nauka."

GRICHUK, V. P.
1969   "The vegetation of the Russian plain during the Upper Paleolithic," in *Priroda i razvitiye pervobytnogo obshchestva.* (Translated as *Nature and*

the development of primitive society.) Edited by I. P. Gerasimov, 58–69. Moscow: Izd. "Nauka."

GRICHUK, V. P., I. K. IVANOVA, N. V. KIND, E. I. RAVSKIY, editors
1966 *Verkhniy pleystotsen. Stratigrafiya i absolyutnaya geokhronologiya.* Moscow: Izd. "Nauka."

GRIGOR'YEV, G. P.
1967 A new reconstruction of the above-ground dwelling of Kostenki I. *Current Anthropology* 8:344–349.
1970 "Upper Paleolithic," in *Kamennyy vek na territoriyi SSSR* (Translated as *The Stone Age in the territory of the USSR*.) Edited by B. A. Rybakov, 43–63. Moscow: Izd. "Nauka."

GUSLITSER, B. I., V. I. KANIVETS
1965 "Paleolithic sites on the Pechora," in *Stratigrafiya i periodizatsiya Paleolita vostochnoy i tsentral'noy Yevropy k VII Kongressu INQUA* (SShA, 1965), (Translated as *The stratigraphy and periodization of the Paleolithic of eastern and central Europe, VII Congress INQUA [USA, 1965.]*) *BKIChP*, AN SSSR 86–103. Moscow: Izd. "Nauka."

GUSLITSER, B. I., V. I. KANIVETS, E. I. LOSEVA
1970 Field seminar on the stratigraphy of the Anthropogene and Paleolithic of the Polar Pechora region. *BKIChP* 37:160–170.

IVANOVA, I. K.
1966 "The stratigraphy of the Upper Pleistocene of Central and Eastern Europe from the data of loessal studies," in *Verkhniy pleystotsen. Stratigrafiya i absolyutnaya geokhronologiya.* (Translated as *The Upper Pleistocene. Stratigraphy and absolute geo-chronology*.) Edited by V. P. Grichuk et al. 32–66. Moscow: Izd. "Nauka."

KANIVETS, V. I.
1969 "Paleolithic man on the Pechora," in *Priroda i razvitiye pervobytnogo obshchestva na territoriyi yevropeyskoy chasti SSSR.* (Translated as *Nature and the development of primitive society in the territory of the European part of the USSR*.) 136–142. Moscow: Izd. "Nauka." (VIII Congress INQUA, Paris, 1969).

KLEIN, R. G.
1969a *Man and culture in the Late Pleistocene: a case study* [Kostenki-Borshevo]. San Francisco: Chandler.
1969b Mousterian cultures in European Russia, *Science* 165:257–265.

KOWALSKI, KAZIMIERZ
1967 "The Pleistocene extinction of mammals in Europe," in *Pleistocene extinctions: the search for a cause.* Edited by P. S. Martin and H. E. Wright, Jr., 349–364. New Haven: Yale University Press.

KRANTZ, GROVER S.
1970 Human activities and megafaunal extinction. *American Scientist* 58(2):164–170.

KROEBER, A. L.
1939 *Cultural and natural areas of native North America.* Berkeley: University of California Press.

KRYLOVA, A. A., I. M. PAVLYUCHENKO
1962 Stone Age tools in the mountain Altay. *KSIA* 92:61–64.

KVASOV, D. D.
1966 "The paleohydrology of the Caspian in the Khvalinsk period," in *Verkhniy pleystotsen. Stratigrafiya i absolyutnaya geokhronologiya.* (Translated as *The Upper Pleistocene, stratigraphy and absolute geochronology*.) Edited by V. P. Grichuk et al., 175–181. Moscow: Izd. "Nauka."

LITOVCHENKO, L. M.
  1969   Tel'manskaya Paleolithic campsite. *SA* 3:110–123.
LYUBIN, V. P.
  1970   "The Lower Paleolithic," in *Kamennyy vek na territoriyi SSSR.* Edited by B. A. Rybakov, 19–42. Moscow: Izd. "Nauka."
LYUBIN, V. P., L. N. SOLOV'YEV
  1971   The study of Little Vorontsov Cave on the Black Sea coast of the Caucasus (Excavations in 1950, 1951, 1964). *MIA* 173:5–40.
MARSHACK, A.
  1970   The baton of Montgaudier. *Natural History* 79:56–63.
  1972a Upper Paleolithic engravings. *Current Anthropology* 13:445–477.
  1972b Upper Paleolithic notation and symbol. *Science* 178:817–828.
MEDVEDEV, C. I.
  1966   "New data on the lower strata of Ust'-Belaya," in *Sibirskiy arkheologicheskiy sbornik (Siberian archeological collection).* Edited by A. P. Okladnikov, 38–50. Novosibirsk: Izd. "Nauka," SOAN.
  1971   "New Paleolithic sites in the valley of the Angara," in *AO 1970 g.* Edited by B. A. Rybakov, 183–184. Moscow: Izd. "Nauka."
MOCHANOV, YU. A.
  1972   "Research on the Paleolithic on the Indigirka, Kolyma and western shore of the Sea of Okhotsk," in *AO 1971 g.* Edited by B. A. Rybakov, 251. Moscow: Izd. "Nauka."
MOSKVITIN, A. I.
  1970   The history and climate of the interglacials and interstadials in Europe. *BKIChP* 37:14–32.
MOVIUS, H. L., JR.
  1953   The Mousterian Cave of Teshik Tash, south-eastern Uzbekistan, Central Asia. *American School of Prehistoric Research.* Bulletin 17:11–71.
NYDAL, R
  1961   Trondheim natural radiocarbon measurements. *Radiocarbon* 3:178–180.
OKLADNIKOV, A. P.
  1955   *Yakutiya do prisoyedineniya k russkomu gosudarstvu.* (Translated as *Yakutiya up to the time of its annexation to the Russian state.*) Moscow-Leningrad: Izd. AN SSSR.
  1960   Paleolithic female statuettes from Buret'. *MIA* 79:281–288.
  1961   The Paleolithic of Trans-Baikal. *American Antiquity* 26(4):486–497.
PANICHKINA, M. Z., YE. A. VEKILOVA
  1962   The study of Akhshtyr Cave in 1961. *KSIA* 92:37–43.
PETRIN, V. T.
  1972   "Chernozer'ye II campsite," in *AO 1971 g.* Edited by B. A. Rybakov, 255–256. Moscow: Izd. "Nauka."
PIDOPLICHKO, I. G.
  1969   *Pozdnepaleoliticheskiye zhilishcha iz kostey mamonta na Ukraine.* (Translated as *Upper Paleolithic dwellings of mammoth bone in the Ukraine*). Kiev: Izd. "Naukova Dumka."
POLIKARPOVICH, K. M.
  1968   *Paleolit verkhnego Podneprov'ya.* (Translated as *The Paleolithic of the upper Dnepr region.*) Minsk: Izd. "Nauka i Tekhnika."
POPOV, A. A.
  1948   *Nganasany.* (Translated as *The Nganasany.*) Moscow-Leningrad: Izd. AN SSSR *TIA*, n.s. 3(1).

PRASLOV, N. D., A. K. FILIPPOV
1967   The first find of Paleolithic art in the south Russian steppes. *KSIA*
       111:24–30.

PROTSCH, R., R. BERGER
1973   Earliest radiocarbon dates for domesticated animals. *Science*
       179:235–239.

PUNNING, J. M., A. LIIVA, E. ILVES
1968   Tartu radiocarbon dates III. *Radiocarbon* 10(2):379–382.

RANOV, V. A.
1971   On the study of Mousterian cultures in Central Asia. *MIA*
       173:209–232.

ROGACHEV, A. N.
1966   "Excavations of the Paleolithic [period] in the Kostenki sites," in *AO*
       1965 g. Edited by B. A. Rybakov, 40–42. Moscow: Izd. "Nauka."
1970a "Paleolithic dwellings and settlements," in *Kamenny vek na territoriyi*
       SSSR. (Translated as *The Stone Age in the territory of the USSR*).
       Edited by B. A. Rybakov, 64–77. Moscow: Izd. "Nauka."

RUDENKO, S. I.
1961   The Ust'-Kanskaia Paleolithic cave site, Siberia. *American Antiquity*
       27(2):203–215. Edited by C. S. Chard and translated by H. M.
       Wormington.

SAVICH, V. P.
1969   Bone artifacts at Lipa VI campsite. *BKIChP* 36:136–141.

SEMENOV, S. A.
1964   *Prehistoric technology*. Translated by M. W. Thompson. Boston:
       Barnes and Noble.

SEMENTSOV, A. A., YE. A. ROMANOVA, P. M. DOLUKHANOV
1969   Radiocarbon dates of the laboratory of the Leningrad Branch, Institute
       of Archeology. *SA* No. 1:251–261.

SEMYONTSOV [SEMENTSOV], A. A., P. M. DOLUKHANOV, YE. N. ROMANOVA, *et al.*
1972   Radiocarbon dates of the Institute of Archaeology III. *Radiocarbon*
       14(2):336–367.

SHER, A. V.
1971   *Mlekopitayushchiye i stratigrafiya pleystotsena kraynego Severo-*
       vostoka SSSR i Severnoy Ameriki. (Translated as *Mammalian fauna*
       and the stratigraphy of the Pleistocene of the extreme northeastern USSR
       and North America.) Moscow: Izd. "Nauka."

SHOVKOPLYAS, I. G.
1965   *Mezinskaya stoyanka k istoriyi srednedneprovskogo basseyna v pozd-*
       nepaleoliticheskuyu epokhu. (Translated as *Mezin campsite in relation*
       to the history of middle Dnepr basin in the late Paleolithic epoch.) Kiev:
       Izd. "Naukova Dumka."

SIDEROV, V. V.
1969   A stone age campsite in central Tuva. *SA* 4:126–140.

SOSNOVSKIY, G. P.
1941   The Paleolithic campsite at Srostki village on the Katun. *MIA*
       2:109–125.

STUIVER, M., S. E. DEEVEY, L. J. GRALENSKI
1960   Yale natural radiocarbon measurements V. *Radiocarbon* 2:49–61.

TARASOV, L. M.
1969   "Research on the Gagarino dwelling," in *AO 1968*. Edited by B. A.
       Rybakov, 39–41. Moscow: Izd. "Nauka."

TOLMACHOFF, I. P.
1933   The carcasses of the mammoth and rhinoceros found in the frozen ground of Siberia. *Transactions of the American Philosophical Society*, n.s. 23:1–74.

TSEYTLIN, S. M.
1972   Some questions of the geology and geological periodization of Paleolithic sites of Siberia. *BKIChP* 38:116–125.

UCKO, P. J., A. ROSENFELD
1967   *Paleolithic cave art.* New York: McGraw-Hill.

VEKILOVA, YE. A.
1971   The Stone Age in the Crimea. Some notes and problems. *MIA* 173:117–161.

VELICHKO, V. V.
1969   "The paleogeography of Upper Paleolithic campsites in the basin of the middle Desna," in *Priroda i razvitiye pervobytnogo obshchestva na territoriyi yevropeyskoy chasti SSSR.* (Translated as *Nature and the development of primitive society in the territory of the USSR.*) Edited by I. P. Gerasimov, 97–103. Moscow: Izd. "Nauka" (VIII Congress INQUA, Paris, 1969).

VELICHKO, A. A., A. N. ROGACHEV
1969   "Paleolithic settlements on the middle Don," in *Priroda i razvitiye pervobytnogo obshchestva na territoriyi yevropeyskoy chasti SSSR.* (Translated as *Nature and the development of primitive society in the territory of the USSR.*) Edited by I. P. Gerasimov, 75–87. Moscow: Izd. "Nauka" (VIII Congress, INQUA, Paris, 1969).
1970   New datings of late Quaternary deposits by the radiocarbon method. *BKIChP* 37:171–177.

VELICHKO, A. A., I. K. IVANOVA, V. M. MURAMOV
1969   "The geological history of the Russian plain, the Crimea and Caucasus in the Pleistocene, and the age of Paleolithic cultures," in *Priroda i razvitiye pervobytnogo obshchestva.* (Translated as *Nature and the development of primitive society.*) Edited by I. P. Gerasimov, 8–41. Moscow: Izd. "Nauka" (VIII Congress INQUA, Paris, 1969).

VERESHCHAGIN, N. K.
1967   "Primitive hunters and Pleistocene extinction in the Soviet Union," in *Pleistocene extinctions: the search for a cause.* Edited by P. S. Martin and H. E. Wright, Jr., 365–398.

VIKTOROV, V. P., V. F. GENING, N. K. YESHCHENKO, *et al.*
1971   "Studies in western Siberia," in *AO 1970 g.* Edited by B. A. Rybakov, 197–198. Moscow: Izd. "Nauka."

VINOGRADOV, A. P., A. L. DEVIRTS, E. I. DOBKINA, N. G. MARKOVA
1966   Radiocarbon dating in the Vernadsky Institute I–IV. *Radiocarbon* 8:292–323.
1968   Radiocarbon dating in the Vernadsky Institute IV–V. *Radiocarbon* 10(2):451–464.

VOGEL, J. C., H. T. WATERBOLK
1967   Groningen radiocarbon dates VII. *Radiocarbon* 9:107–155.

YEFIMENKO, P. P.
1953   *Pervobytnoye obshchestvo (Primitive society).* Kiev: Izd. AN USSR.
1958   *Kostenki I.* Moscow-Leningrad: Izd. AN SSSR.

ZAMYATNIN, S. N.
1951   "On the development of local differences in the cultures of the Paleolithic period," in *TIA*, n.s. 16:89–152.

Map References

BELOGLAZOVA, O. A. *editor*
  1955 *Atlas SSSR.* (second edition). Moscow: Glavnoye upravleniye geodeziyi i kartografiyi MVD SSSR.
GRICHUK, V. P., I. K. IVANOVA, N. V. KIND, E. I. RAVSKIY, *editors*
  1966 *Verkhniy pleystotsen. Stratigrafiya i absolyutnaya geokhronologiya.* Moscow: Izd. "Nauka."
MARKOV, K. K., A. I. POPOV, *editors*
  1959 *Lednikovyy period na territoriyi yevropeyskoy chasti SSSR i Sibiri.* (Translated as *The ice age in the European portion of the USSR and Siberia.*) Moscow: Izd. Moskovskogo Universiteta.
MARKOV, K. K., G. I. LAZUKOV, V. A. NIKOLYEV
  1965 *Chetvertichnyy Period (The Quaternary Period).* t. I. *Territoriya SSSR* (volume I. *The territory of the USSR*). Moscow: Izd. Moskovskogo Universiteta (VII Congress, INQUA).
NALIVKIN, D. V., *editor*
  1955 Geologicheskaya karta 1:5,000,000 (Geological Map, 1:5,000,000). Moscow: Ministerstvo geologiyi i okhrana nedr.
SINITSYN, V. I.
  1959 *Tsentral'naya Aziya (Central Asia).* Moscow: Gosudarstvennoye izdatel'stvo geograficheskoy literatury.
VAS'KOVSKIY, A. P.
  1959 "A short sketch of the vegetation, climate and chronology of the Quaternary period on the headwaters of the Kolyma and Indigirka rivers and on the northern shore of the Okhotsk Sea," in *Lednikovyy period na territoriyi yevropeyskoy chasti SSSR i Sibiri,* t. I. Edited by K. K. Markov and A. I. Popov, 510–556. Moscow: Izd. Moskovskogo Universiteta.

Man in the Italian Alps: A Study of the Pleistocene and Post-Glacial evidence

F. G. FEDELE

Fresh fieldwork by different scholars is giving a new start to prehistoric research in Northern Italy and is providing relevant data on the presence and life style of Paleolithic and more recent communities in some parts of the Alps. These data, however, have not yet been interpreted in the light of a "man–mountain" problem. On the other hand, multidisciplinary research on some samples of populations living within the Italian Alpine territory has been recently undertaken, in an attempt to clarify aspects of the interrelations between man and the mountain habitat (Chiarelli and Fedele 1969; Fedele 1971a; Masali, Rabino Massa and Fedele 1972; Lasker *et al*. 1972).

Problems concerning man–mountain relationships arise for contemporary as well as for Pleistocene times. Variations in these relationships during the Pleistocene have to be studied particularly against the background of the oscillatory conditions of that period, both local and general, i.e., in a "diachronic" perspective. The Alps are one of the major high mountain systems in the world, so we may assume they form a relief area suitable for penetrating research into this subject.

Only the southern side of the chain is dealt with here. This arbitrary break is merely contingent, for while a fundamental unity of the Alps as regards human ecology is acknowledged, any attempt at a more comprehensive synopsis is felt to be rather premature.

This paper is simply a tentative and problem phrasing introduction to the subject under study. More space is given here to the discussion of the Paleolithic record, since it is in this field that the most innovative data have been gained. This may result in an unbalanced presentation, but

This research is partly supported by National Research Council of Italy (C.N.R.) grants to the author. This paper is contribution No. 3 of the "History of the human settlement in the Western Alps" project; see Fedele 1973c and in press b, 1973b, for previous contributions.

"mountain" Paleolithic has been so rarely made the object of more than passing and vacant consideration that a formal reappraisal is thought stimulating. The following heuristic assumptions are central to the research of which the present writing is a contribution: (1) man–mountain relationships should be singled out as a topic of its own forming a *distinct* problem; (2) these relationships should be viewed according to the concept of an environmental *system* with its inherent interactions (D. L. Clarke 1971; Fedele in press b).

These topics are discussed in three sections. Attention will first be given to what "mountain" means in the present context, both ecological and geographical. Then the relevant archeological evidence will be critically reviewed. In the last section, some anthropological and paleoecological considerations developed in this survey and by current research will be presented.

MOUNTAIN BIOTA: THEIR ESSENTIAL CHARACTERISTICS

Mountainous environments have no clear-cut lower boundaries. Nevertheless, the specific physiognomy they display immediately after a "transitional" zone justifies putting forward an overall definition of them. The valuable description of the high-altitude environment by Clegg, Harrison and Baker (1970) may be appropriately used to supplement our brief account.

This definition encompasses at least three major, distinct classes of environmental abiotic attributes: (1) *geomorphology* — or the values and the combination of small/large scale landform attributes; (2) *altitude* — a merely metric feature relative to the atmospheric layers; and (3) *climatology*, with particular consideration for its diachronic dynamics in the past. Morphological and metric attributes are the most immediate markers of mountain; the others rather show a relative shading of values, and the variables involved become effective at different points. For example, the hypoxy gradient — one of the few environmental stresses man cannot mitigate by cultural means — becomes truly relevant only above 2,000 meters.

Altitude is generally associated with rugged terrain, but this is not always the case. Other factors affecting high altitude areas are combinations of low temperature, high precipitation rates, and high weather variability. In general, a mountain can be defined as any distinctly elevated, relatively uneven area, with significant climatic differences from any area below.

Mountain environments coincide with a distinct set of biota. Mountains provide a hard environment for every kind of living being, humans included. This holds true for high mountains, but also for rugged lands of lesser height, where other sets of restrictions for habitation prevail. In general, animal populations are most affected by the adversity of mountain environments. As absolute and relative altitudes increase, the number of species drops and that of individuals per species rises; but on the whole, animal population densities tend to decrease and high mountains are virtually devoid of animal life above a certain elevation. This fact conditions the carrying capacity of (especially pre-agricultural) human ecosystems. One may use the term "bio-repulsive factors" for the constraints assumed to be responsible for this inhospitality.

Photosynthetic CO_2 fixation is enhanced by hypoxy, but the vegetation growing season is very reduced and snow cover severely limits the availability of food and of nearly every important raw material. Highly seasonal life cycles become the rule. The lack of wood for fuel may be in some instances a notable limiting factor, unless other cultural devices are applied. One of the more common characteristics of this type of environment is not so much the extreme nature of particular physical or biotic traits, but rather the amplitude of the seasonal variations in energy flow. Immaturity, and thus a continued instability, of the total ecosystem results.

Under such circumstances, some prehistoric populations found in pastoralism an advantageous way to inhabit and exploit mountain environments. In a sense, they used animals as energy exchange intermediaries, biologically suited to subsist on the more or less meagre resources of the ecosystem.

NORTHERN ITALY AND THE ITALIAN ALPS: PHYSIOGRAPHIC BACKGROUND

This paper is concerned with the relief area on the inner side of the Alpine range, from Liguria in the west to its Giulian tract in the east (Blanchard 1952, 1954; Sestini 1957; Dainelli 1959; Walker 1967; Veyret and Veyret 1967; Nangeroni 1967). The essential geographical feature of the chain is a nearly 200° arched, dead-end enclosure, relatively open toward the east with potential barrage conditions toward the west. The highest peaks in Europe are here: Gran Paradiso, 4,061 meters; Mt. Rosa, 4,633 meters; Mt. Blanc, 4,810 meters.

The Alps are considered to begin west of the low altitude Cadibona Pass, which connects the Po Plain with the Ligurian Riviera; to the east the Apennine range begins. It is lower and narrower than the Alps and has quite different geological characteristics. The Italian Alps are conventionally divided into many segments whose names still reflect to some extent the former presence of mountaineers who settled there in protohistoric times (the first millennium B.C.). As an overall subdivision closer to the actual physiographic characteristics, the following major divisions can be considered: (1) the *Western Alps*, from the Ligurian tract to the Ticino–Simplon furrow; (2) the *Central Alps* to the Adige–Resia Pass furrow; and (3) the *Eastern Alps*, which dwindle into the Slovenian highlands.

The western segment of the chain is very high and narrow, with huge offshoots opposing each other on either side of the ridge. It is distinguished by a remarkable dissymmetry between its sides. The Piedmontese side is definitely shorter and steeper than the French one, as a result of the peculiar thrusts that acted here in Alpine orogenesis. The mean distance between the watershed and the plain's border averages only 45 kilometers, and the relief/plain fillet is commonly sharp.

The Western Alps coincide with the Upper Po river basin and are very evenly segmented by the fan-shaped headwaters of the Po itself and of its drainage system, the largest in Italy. The Po alluvial plain is remarkably level throughout; the surrounding relief generally emerges from it in a very clear-cut shape. The Po Plain surface is only interrupted by the low, undulating or fragmented, Monferrato-Langhe Plateau in the central and southern Piedmont region, which is linked with the Apennines; and by the isolated Berici and Euganei hills in the Veneto. Pleistocene conoids and end moraines edge the contour of the plain and in several areas encircle the local foothills, making the transition to the relief less sharp.

A great number of streams descend from the Central Alps and join the central axis of the Po, but they do not follow the regular rayed pattern observed in the western part of the basin. Such irregularity has its roots in the regional morphology; the Central Alps form a large region of quite tangled design, with multi-oriented valleys and differently dissected plateaus. The Adige River is second in size to the Po and cuts through the alluvial plain parallel to it. Beyond the Adige furrow to the east, the rivers descending from the Eastern Alps flow out individually into the Adriatic Sea.

The bulk of the Alps along its main axis is essentially built up of crystalline rocks, with the exception of the Ligurian and Maritime segment where sedimentary lithology is dominant. In front of the inner edge of the Central and Eastern Alps, and throughout their extension, a fringe of lower relief stretches out in which Mesozoic and Tertiary carbonate formations are the common component; this is the Pre-Alps. Morphology and elevation of the Pre-Alpine belt are much varied; as a rule an overall uniformity may nevertheless be recognized, with respect to both the alluvial plain and the higher mountains behind. Where dolomites and certain types of hard limestones are exposed, cliff morphology predominates (cf. Sparks 1971; 226 and 241–242). It is pertinent here to remark that this condition is quite frequently associated with the existence of caves and shelters with archeological potential.

Alpine compactness is broken by many local discontinuities. These are created by valleys and lakes, which ultimately join corresponding watershed sinkings and passes. The gouging done by the Pleistocene glaciers is easy to see. Major valleys represent an effective digitation of the plain environments into the mountain territory right to the feet of the highest relief, where peaks ascend abruptly. Despite some obvious influences from the surrounding mountains on intermontane valley microclimates, the ecology of these eccentric strips of elevated plain matches more or less closely that of the Po Plain itself.

Moving eastward, the major valleys and the altitudes of the main valley-head towns and their shortest distance from the Alpine drainage divide are: (1) the Susa Valley (Susa, 500 meters, 10 kilometers); (2) the Aosta Valley, run through by the Dora Baltea River (Aosta, 580 meters, 15 kilometers); (3) the Ossola and the Upper Ticino Valleys, continuing respectively the western branch and the northern end of Lake Maggiore (Domodossola, 270 meters, 20 kilometers; Bellinzona, in the Swiss Canton Ticino, 230 meters); (4) Valtellina, a longitudinal valley run through by the upper Adda River, continuing Lake Como (Sondrio, 300 meters, 20 kilometers); and (5) the long and straight Adige Valley (Trento, 190 meters; Bolzano/Bozen, 265 meters; Merano/Meran, 310 meters, 15 kilometers).

The main passes (Carandini 1961) are, west to east: Tenda, 1,908 meters; Maddalena or Argentière, 1,996 meters; Monginevro/Montgenèvre, 1,854 meters, and Moncenisio/Mont Cénis, 2,084 meters, to the Susa Valley; Little St. Bernard, 2,188 meters; Great St. Bernard, 2,473 meters; Sempione/Simplon, 2,005 meters; San Bernardino, 2,065 meters, to the Ticino Valley; Resia/Reschen Scheideck, 1,507 meters, and Brennero/Brenner, 1,375 meters, to the Adige Valley; and Predil, 1,156 meters. Many others which are unimportant now were probably crossed by prehistoric mountaineers (Laviosa Zambotti 1950; Bocquet 1968; Agavit 1969; Barfield 1971), as historical records show for the Western Alps in later times (Gribaudi 1928; Sestini 1957; De Lavis-Trafford 1960; Barocelli 1968; Prieur 1968; Agavit 1970).

The main factors in the climate of the Alpine area (Sestini 1957; Mennella 1967) are its elevation and exposure, which are highly varied from place to place. The climatic features of particular interest are: low summer temperatures; a lessening of thermal amplitudes as altitude increases; a stronger solar radiation; higher air dryness; abundant rains (summer maxima); abundant snow precipitation from autumn to spring and snow cover persistence for a half to three-quarters of the year. But these characteristics are more or less common to all mountainous regions of the temperate belt. The snow line in the Italian Alps commonly ranges between 2,500 and 3,000 meters.

A peculiar phenomenon is brought about by *föhn* winds, i.e. a rapid and durable temperature rise which is produced either by northward or southward currents on the lee side of a chain (Perrill 1970).

The Pre-Alpine climate is more humid and rainy and has higher and more constant temperatures; this is partly the result of the presence of large lakes. Over the years, these lacustrine environments also exerted considerable attraction and influence upon man's dispersal into this area.

A REVIEW OF THE CULTURAL EVIDENCE

At present, research is still at the stage of assembling the basic factual evidence. Analyses and evaluations to supply firm data for "human paleoecological" reconstructions are severely limited and related "model" building is in its absolute infancy. The evidence available for the earlier times is archeological and paleoenvironmental, and generally is very meagre as far as the Alps are concerned. Historical sources may add valuable information from classical times onward, but a gap persists in the evidence between the end of the documented Roman period and the conditions which we are still witnessing today.

North Italian prehistory has been recently and competently summarized by L. H. Barfield (1971). For reviews, particular periods, areas or problems, the following surveys may be consulted: Leonardi 1957, 1963; Leonardi and Broglio 1965; Barocelli 1960; Pittioni 1962; Radmilli 1962, 1963; Broglio 1967, 1971, 1972a; Barfield and Broglio 1971; Fedele 1966b. A detailed review of Barfield's book is also available (Fedele 1973d).

Relevant though preliminary information is graphically conveyed by Figure 1 and Maps 1 to 3. These distribution maps must be used with caution, since in the present state of knowledge the overall pattern intensities and regional diversities may be affected considerably by sampling error.

Lower and Middle Paleolithic

PALEOECOLOGICAL BACKGROUND.   Sites assignable to Lower and Middle Paleolithic stages are very rare in Northern Italy in general and absent from the core of the Alps in particular. But the view once held that their lack was caused by actual inhospitality due to the severe adversity of climate during much of the Pleistocene period is no longer tenable. A number of discoveries can be expected in the forthcoming years as proper scientific research focuses upon the problem (Fedele 1966b; Blanchard 1952:294); recent developments, to be discussed later, lend strong support to such expectations.

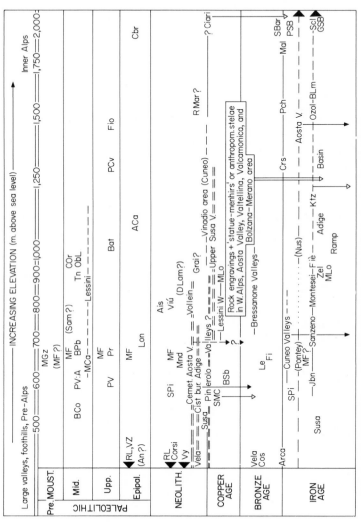

Figure 1. Distribution of main archeological sites according to their altitude above sea level. (From the sources quoted in the text)

General Legend for the sites Recorded in Figure 1 and in Maps 1 to 3

ACa   Cariadeghe plateau, W. of Lake Garda, Lombardy

Ais   Aisone Cave, Stura Valley, SW. Piedmont

An   Angera Cave, E. shore of Lake Maggiore, Lombardy

Arca   Dos dell'Arca hill-site, Valcamonica, Lombardy

Bat   R. Battaglia Shelter, Asiago plateau. 1050 m

BCo   Buco del Corno Cave, Cavallina Valley, Central Lombardy

Blm   Bellamonte hill-fort, Val Travignolo, Trentino. 1548 m

BPb   Buco del Piombo Cave, W. Lombardy. 695 m

BSb   Buco della Sabbia Cave, near Civate, NW. Lombardy

Cbr   Colbricòn open-air sites, near Rolle Pass. 1900–1950 m

Ciari   Gias del Ciari Shelter, Mt. Bego, SW. Piedmont/France. 2100 m

COr   Cava degli Orsi (or del Bisele) Fissure, Asiago plateau. 950 m

Corsi   Ai Corsi di Isera open-air site (hill), S. Trentino

Cos   La Cosina Cave, Cavedine Valley, W. Trentino

Crs   Crissolo, Turin province, Piedmont

DLam   San Donà di Lamon, Central Veneto. 885 m

Fio   I Fiorentini open-air site, Tonezza-Folgarìa plateau. 1482 m

Fi   Fiavè peat-bog site, SW. Trentino

Grai   Arma del Grai Cave, Cuneo province, S. Piedmont

GSB   Great St. Bernard Pass. 2473 m

Jbn   Colle Joben (Jobenbühel), Bolzano area. 609 m

Ktz   Colle Katzenlocher, Bolzano area. 1164 m

Le   Ledro Lake sites, SW. Trentino, W. of Garda Lake. 650 m

Lon   Covoli di Lonedo cave sites, Asiago plateau

Mal   Malciaussià Lake, Upper Viù Valley, Piedmont. 1850 m

MCa   Monte Calvarina, E. Lessini Mountains

MF   Monfenera site system, N. Piedmont — MF1 Ciutarùn Cave; MF2 Ciota Ciara Cave; MF4 Belvedere Shelter. 650–700 m

MGz   Monte Gazzo, Lessini Mountains

MLo   Monte Loffa open-air site, Lessini Mountains

Mnd   Grotta del Mondo cave site, Lessini Mountains

ObL   Obar de Leute Cave, Asiago plateau. 950 m

Ozol   Caslìr di Monte Ozol, Val di Non, Trentino. 1513 m

Pch   Pontechianale-Castello, Varaita Valley. c. 1550 m

PCv   Piancavallo open-air site, Central Veneto. 1300 m

Pr   Pradis Cave, NE. Veneto

PSB   Little St. Bernard Pass. 2188 m

PV   Ponte di Veia cave system, W. Lessini. 602 m

Ram   Ciaslè di Ramponio, Val d'Intelvi, Lombardy. 1045 m

RL   Loc di Romagnano cliff-foot sites, I–III, Trento area

RMar   Balma di Rio Martino Cave, W. Piedmont. 1525 m

Sam   Grotticelle di Sambughetto Valstrona cave site, N. Piedmont. 760 m

SBar   St. Barthélemy, Aosta Valley, c. 2000 m

Scl   Mt. Sciliar/Schlern, Trentino. 2520 m

SMC   St. Martin-de-Corléans, Aosta. 585 m

SPi   St. Pierre, Aosta area

Susa   Susa area, Susa Valley. 500–520 m

Tn   Tanùn Cave, W. Lombardy. 900 m

Vela   La Vela di Trento, Trento area: 1. open site; 2. shelter

Viù   Versino di Viù open-air site. Viù Valley, W Piedmont. 820 m?

Vy   Vayes "Shelter," Susa Valley, Piedmont

VZ   Vatte di Zambana Shelter, Trento area

Zel   Dos Zelor, Fiemme Valley, Trentino. 950 m

General Legend for Maps 1 to 3

Physiographic base map of Northern Italy:

  a. Alpine-Apennine drainage divide; culminations simulated; passes: *a1* pass
     notably crossed in prehistory (adapted from Barfield 1971); *a2* other important
     passes.
  b. Diagrammatic drainage network; the main component is the Po River system, its basin
     covering more than 70,000 square kilometres.

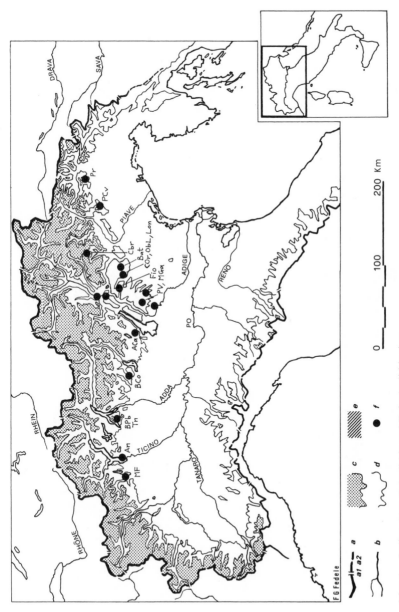

Map 1. Italian Alps, Paleolithic and Epipaleolithic sites.

    c. Elevation above 1,500 metres (at northern latitudes) or 1,700 metres (at southern latitudes).
    d. Elevation above 500 metres (at northern latitudes) or 700 metres (at southern latitudes).
Distribution of archeological phenomena:
    e. Distribution areas; surface scatters; or traces.
    f. Major site.
On the index map the Italian administrative boundary, not the geographical, is shown.

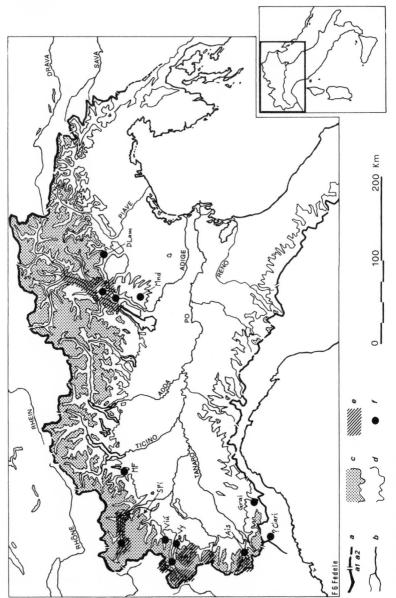

Map 2.   Italian Alps, Neolithic sites.

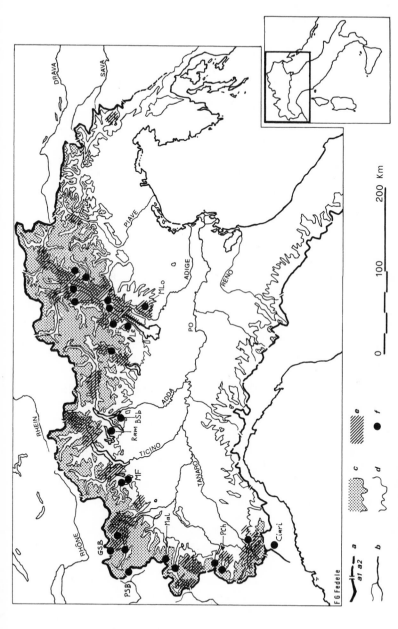

Map 3.   Italian Alps, Copper to Iron Age sites.

This statement does not mean to minimize the size and the far-reaching consequences of the Pleistocene events in this area, however. The Alps fostered impressive glaciations on their southern side, beginning shortly after the Adriatic Sea had started to contract. At the end of the Pliocene period, the sea still extended westward into what is now the Po Plain and reached as a deep gulf the paleo-valleys of the Western Alps.

Pleistocene glacial geology has been well understood in Northern Italy since the times of Penck and Brückner's pioneering inspection and interpretation, early in the century (1909). Glaciers repeatedly increased in relation to the fall of the snow line and the drop of spring–summer temperatures and expanded toward the valley mouths, building high moraines there. For reasons of morphology and feeding, only a few of the glaciers in the Western Alps reached the plains and left signal deposits on their retreat, even if backed by the highest massifs in the chain. The Susa Valley and the Dora Baltea glaciers are the only remarkable instances in this respect (Carraro and Petrucci 1972; Carraro, Medioli and Petrucci, in press). In the Sesia Valley — to be seen later in connection with a Paleolithic locality — the glacier fed by Mt. Rosa's huge snow fields never attained the valley mouth (Sacco 1930). This is not, however, to say that glaciations in the West did not affect the general climate and the regional conditions of microclimate and practicability to a pronounced degree.

The glaciers in the Central Alps were especially large. Nearly every valley is bordered at its entrance by morainic systems protruding into the plain. The succession of valleys now occupied by the sub-Alpine lakes and the spacious Adige Valley (cf. Venzo 1965) is noteworthy. Lesser glacial effects are known farther east.

The consequences of fluctuations of Pleistocene glaciers on the landscapes are easily recognizable everywhere. Glacier-dependent stream regimens projected these effects far down valley to create rhythmical phases of aggradation and erosion which terraced the alluvial plain. As a further result, fluctuations of the watertables both in level and flow were reflected in the regimens of the springs which abound near the relief/plain contact, and were and are so important a factor of man's biotope choices. These facts should be evaluated, too, in the context of the feasibility of human movement in the terrain.

Coastline movements, in accordance with the eustatic oscillations of the sea level, were also strong; but this kind of process is not strictly relevant to the present study.

It is now generally agreed that the Mindel (Elster) and Riss glaciations on the southern side of the Alps were far more extensive than both the previous and the later ones. The earlier glacial events are still little known, while the Würm Glaciation is profusely documented nearly everywhere. It is quite apparent that its glacial termini did not surpass the Riss moraines (Venzo 1965). What is still badly needed — partly as a result of the immaturity of Paleolithic archeology in the area — is a coherent framework of correlations between valley and plain fluvio-glacial sequences and the sedimento-climatic phases derived from the archeological deposits in caves (Fedele 1972a).

The Würm period south of the Alps seems to comprehend roughly two "glacial" sub-periods parted by a milder interval (Pasa 1969; Fedele 1971b, 1972a); they will be referred to here as Lower and Upper Würm. Lower Würm starts strongly oceanic in character and remains to some extent that way for its whole time-span. Faunal associations comprise temperate species such as red deer, fallow-deer, alpine ibex, chamois, cave bear, locally supplemented by marmot or even glutton. Vegetation cover is made up mainly of mixed pine and temperate deciduous tree species. The latter part of this subperiod is marked nevertheless by an increase in continentality and dryness and is characterized by a relative spread of grasslands and associations in which horse and hamster are numerically dominant. This subperiod can be correlated with the Würm I of central European periodizations (cf. Woldstedt in Rankama 1967; W.1^E in the present writer's notation) and E. Schmid's *Frühwürm* of the Swiss Alps (1958, and subsequent works). On the other hand it is to be correlated with the Würm I+II of F. Bordes and other recent French scholars (Bordes 1954; Valoch and Bordes 1957; Bonifay 1964; Leonardi and Broglio 1965; Lequatre 1966; Alimen in Rankama 1967; De Lumley-Woodyear 1969) and my W.1–2^F.

On the whole the Upper Würm shows a predominance of distinctly rigorous, continental climates. Cyclical events, such as wind deposits, congelifraction of flint artifacts or cryoclastic rubble layers are a recurrent feature of this subperiod. Coniferous woodlands, then willow–birch formations and open land tracts, became widespread. *Sicista*–hamster associations are typical in faunal assemblages. During the decreasing phase of this glaciation a shift towards the establishment of an impoverished mountain fauna (ibex, brown bear, snow vole) may be seen, eventually leading to the remnant faunas of today. Such a fauna is locally supplemented by elk and red deer. Cave bear bones increasingly reveal pathological degeneracies. This is quite probably the Würm $2 + 3^E$ as defined north of the Alps, Schmid's *Hauptwürm*, and Bordes's W.$3 + 4^F$ (Leonardi and Broglio 1965; Fedele 1966a, 1968, 1972b).

The main Würm Interstadial (now renamed Hengelo-Quinson in Western Europe) seems to be marked by sedimentation pauses and soil-formation, but it still raises many problems of definition and detail. In Northern Italy as well as elsewhere it generally separates Middle from Upper Paleolithic cultures (cf. Leonardi and Broglio 1966).

The Pleistocene climatology of this territory has been summarized haphazardly in relatively recent works (Mancini 1963; Follieri 1965; Marchesoni and Paganelli 1966; Bertolani Marchetti 1967; Pasa 1969; Charrier 1967, 1970), mainly discussing palynological contributions.

CULTURAL EVIDENCE.   The Lower Paleolithic is sparsely represented in
the Veneto region of northeastern Italy. Examples of the Abbevillian-
like hand ax from Quinzano near Verona in the Plain, supposedly from a
Riss interstadial. A few supposedly post-Riss, "Acheulian" hand axes
and flake artifacts come from upper levels at Quinzano and from surface
sites (Lughezzano di Valpantena) in the nearby Lessini Mountains, a
harshly dissected but unelevated plateau (Zorzi 1959). Even the Mount
Gazzo hand ax and other surface finds, despite some claims (Barfield
1971:20), has only marginal relevance to our theme. All over the Old
World, Acheulian and Clactonian hunters frequented the low and mid-
altitude plateaus (cf. G. Clark 1967; Collins 1969). The same pattern
occurred in peninsular Italy (Radmilli 1963, 1964). But in fact all these
old finds need to be re-examined in depth (Leonardi and Broglio 1965).

Elsewhere in Northern Italy, Lower and more generally pre-Würm
Paleolithic sites are generally unknown (Leonardi 1957; Broglio 1967;
Fedele 1966b). The only exception north of the Po, though remarkable, is
a Late Acheulian campsite which is being investigated in central Piedmont at the time of writing (discovered in 1974; Fedele and coll., unpublished). The true status of three unretouched flakes found at Ciutarùn
Cave on Monfenera in Piedmont cannot be assessed (Fedele 1974a,
1974b).

In summing up, the evidence for a pre-Mousterian human presence in
the Italian Alps is all rather inconspicuous so far as man's first venturing
into the true mountainous territory is concerned. The phenomenon is
substantially the same all around the outer edge of the chain.

Demonstrable Middle Paleolithic sites are clearly more frequent than
the earlier ones. They compose a well-known group in the Veneto region.
West of the Lake Garda–Mincio line on the contrary, in an area of 55,000
square kilometers, this stage is now reported from no more than a
few scattered points (Fedele 1966b, a general survey; 1972b, 1973b,
1973c). Relevant sites are listed in Figure 1. All of them may be referred
to variants of the Mousterian complex (in the current, Bordes' sense)
and are roughly datable to the Lower Würm. Unfortunately, the information at hand for many of these sites is hardly adequate for the requirements of modern research.

The karst fissure site at Cava degli Orsi (Bears' quarry) and the Obar
de Leute Cave, on the escarped Asiago Plateau in the Veneto region,
yielded small collections of worn flint artifacts, which were claimed to be
"Alpine" denticulate Mousterian. "Technical" Levallois indexes are
rather high. Reliable stratigraphy could not be observed in either case;
the faunal remains comprise cave and brown bear, wolf, red deer, marmot, and hamster (Leonardi and Broglio 1965; Broglio 1969b). Surface
traces of probable Mousterian artifacts were collected extensively on Mt.
Calvarina and elsewhere on the Lessini Mountains as high as 1,200

meters (Zorzi 1959, 1960; Radmilli 1962). But in many instances these finds are barely distinguishable from other surface flint débris more clearly pertaining to the Neolithic and post-Neolithic exploitation of the rich flint-bearing plateau. This fact should perhaps justify a little skepticism or prompt a reappraisal of the available evidence. There are other traces which come from Cave A, layers 5-6, at the Ponte di Veia, a remarkable complex of sites under a natural limestone bridge which is situated more inside in the Lessini area.

The Tanùn site demands different considerations. A handful of stone artifacts were found in Buco del Piombo and Tanùn Caves between the lower branches of Lake Como in the Pre-Alps of Lombardy (Leonardi 1957, 1963; Fusco 1958) as a result of unsystematic collections begun in 1935. Many flint and limestone flakes were thought to have definite "Paleolithic" features; this is likely to be true, but neither deposit deserves consideration as more than a mere "presence sign" (Fedele 1966b). The only clue to their chronological assessment was provided by a rather loose association with cave bear bones.

In 1971, it was announced that a denticulate Mousterian assemblage in a rich faunal context, including a human vertebra and two humeral fragments, had been found at Buco del Corno Cave, in the lower Cavallina Valley in Lombardy (Fusco 1971, and personal communications; cf. Fedele 1972b, 1973b).

The Monfenera site cluster in Piedmont is the westernmost Paleolithic locality so far discovered in Northern Italy. Moreover, it seems to be the only one which can substantiate more intimate inferences about man's early activity close to mountainous glaciated areas. On this cliffed mountain, dolomite walls between 650 and 700 meters above sea level, overhanging the Sesia *thalweg* by 350 meters, are carved into a belt of caves and rock-shelters filled with impressive deposits. In Pleistocene times this point was exposed several times to the nearby Sesia Glacier when it descended from the huge snow fields in the Mt. Rosa massif. Scientific investigations there did not begin before 1964, after decades of pillaging and sparse reporting. Currently it is proving very rewarding (Fedele 1966a, 1972b, 1973b, 1974b).

Regular excavations on Monfenera since 1966 have provided strong evidence for the existence of a "system" of close Stone Age sites. Stratified cultural sequences are now known which extend from the Middle Paleolithic to the Neolithic, the Iron Age, and up to the Late Roman and Early Medieval periods.

Definite Mousterian assemblages were discovered in Ciota Ciara Cave and at the Belvedere Rock-Shelter, and more recently in the surviving section at Ciutarun Cave. The number of Mousterian artifacts recovered from Monfenera sites may total 250 up to the present. At least two slightly different industries seem to occur. The first is well documented at the entrance to the Ciota Ciara; it seems to be a non-Levallois, typical Mousterian industry, rich in sidescrapers and denticulate types. Nearly 95 percent of the artifacts are made of milky vein quartz, a quite remarkable choice; some cores were found (Fedele 1966a, 1973c).

The other industry is definitely represented in the richer levels of the Belvedere, 1967 test pit, layers 7–9, and probably in several levels of the Ciutarun "inner" deposit. It may be tentatively described as a *faciès denticulé* Mousterian (*sensu* De Lumley-Woodyear 1969) perhaps to be linked to a typical Mousterian industry (Fedele 1972b, 1973c). Among its most interesting recurring peculiarities are the great variety of good and inferior stones used for manufacture (vein quartz, many crypto-crystalline siliceous stones, porphyry), the scarcity of waste byproducts, the high frequency of microlithic or near-microlithic size, the non-incidence of Levallois flaking technology, and the abundance of use-chipped edges as well as of *pièces écaillées*. Excellent exotic flints have been exceptionally employed. Only a few cores have hitherto been recognized. Two bone *retouchoirs* and bone splinters with thin slicemarks due to flesh removal were found.

The artifact assemblages are commonly associated with selected mammalian faunas among which cave bear remains are prominent. At the Belvedere, megafaunal remains can be generally considered as cultural food refuse; they point to the game specialization of the Mousterian inhabitants (cave bear was supplemented to some extent by ibex, bison and cervids), while the findings from the inner "chamber" of Ciota Ciara Cave better display the broader spectrum of the natural faunal environment (Fedele 1966a, 1968, 1973b). So, Monfenera as a whole affords a signal opportunity to study the internal patterning of a "close site system" and the much-debated problems of activity differentiation and "inter-group" vs. "inter-locational" functional variability (Mellars 1970; Bordes and Bordes 1970; Marks 1971).

Pollen analytical data from the Monfenera sites are still under laboratory processing.

A group of small caves cut by a quarry at Sambughetto Valstrona, in a valley 22 kilometers north of Monfenera, must be dismissed as Paleolithic sites on the basis of the present evidence (Fedele 1966b, 1973c). Nevertheless, many circumstantial signs suggest that a resumption of qualified field research there could eventually bring to light additional proofs of Mousterian penetration into the Western Alps (Maviglia 1952; Venzo 1954; Radmilli 1963; Fedele 1974b, Appendix).

In summing up, one is struck at first by the overall patterning of the geographical distribution of these sites, which show a remarkable alignment in the Pre-Alpine upland and foothill fringe. In Piedmont and Lombardy the sites being discussed are the only ones yet known, while in Veneto many others apparently exist closer to the plain. One may legitimately suspect that west of the Veneto region this patterning is mainly due to inadequate investigation and differential "findability" which strongly favors the Pre-Alpine caves. (On the other hand, the numerous caves existing in southwestern Piedmont at altitudes averaging 1,000 meters, have never yielded any Paleolithic material, so far as can be ascertained.)

If this distribution pattern reflects reality to any extent, the presumptive location of sites along transitional ecological zones or "ecotones" (cf. Harris 1969:8-9) with easy access to the resources of several different major eco-systems — rocky plateaus, middle mountain woodlands, floodplains — is worth taking into account.

Upper Mousterian assemblages from the Broion Cave, in the Berici Hills (Veneto), are radiocarbon dated on charcoal samples as follows: 44,450±1,500 B.C. (GrN–4637), 38,650±1,270 B.C. (GrN–4638) (Leonardi and Broglio 1966).

Upper Paleolithic and Epipaleolithic

Knowledge about the Upper Paleolithic and Epipaleolithic stages has rapidly increased in recent years as a result of lucky discoveries and thorough research in the Veneto and Trentino regions. During the same time, a major new focus was found on Monfenera in the northwest. Finally in 1971–1974 a few minor sites were reported in the intermediate territory and on the Emilian Apennines. Such an increase in knowledge ranks among the outstanding achievements in prehistoric investigation in Italy over the last decade. All the evidence now at hand is thoroughly summarized in the papers by A. Broglio (1967, 1969a, 1971, 1972a, 1972b).

Following Laplace–Broglio's nomenclature (Laplace 1966; Broglio 1969a), the Upper Paleolithic is almost exclusively represented in Northern Italy by the Epigravettian "complexes." This long-lived, backed micro-point tradition seems to continue the Gravettian culture with relatively unimportant changes far after its decline in France and elsewhere, and well into early Post-Glacial times. The Epigravettian tradition seems thus to be synchronous with the French Solutrean, Magdelenian, and Azilian cultures, linking Italy to Eastern more than Western European culture areas. Evidence of preceding Upper Paleolithic cultures (Aurignacian, Gravettian) is extremely rare and controversial in Northern Italy and not documented in the mountain area so far. An assemblage from Ponte di Veia Cave A was ascribed to a Châtelperronian-like industry (pending re-examination), while a few similar finds come from the nearby Grotta del Mondo.

The Epigravettian tradition is superseded at about the seventh millennium B.C. by cultures that almost exactly match the Sauveterrian and the Tardenoisian cultures which are well represented in Western Europe. In the fifth millennium B.C. — or a millennium earlier if the tree-ring calibration chart for radiocarbon measurements is accepted — a local "neolithization" now seems to have occurred in the eastern Po Plain, grafting pottery manufacture and early cereal agriculture into a late Epipaleolithic/Mesolithic (Tardenoisian) lithic industry (Broglio 1972a).

Valid evidence of man's presence on the inside of the Alpine mountains first emerges at the Upper Paleolithic stage of culture. This evidence consists in the first place of Epigravettian assemblages which were found at Ponti di Veia, Caves C and E, and irregularly at Pradis Cave in the Friùli province. But the most striking information is provided by the series of open-air and rock-shelter sites located well above 1,000 meters in the Central Veneto uplands, from the northwestern end of the Asiago plateau to the Cansiglio near Pordenone. The R. Battaglia Shelter (1,050 meters) and the sites at Fiorentini (1,482 meters) and on the Piancavallo Flats (1,300 meters) fall within geological contexts which suggest that the local Würm 3^E ice sheets had begun to retreat just a short time before. When Late Paleolithic hunters pushed as high as Fiorentini, for instance, wood cover had not yet re-ascended so far. The distribution patterning of flint tools and trimming waste at the R.Battaglia site has been taken to show that an encampment of huts or tents was aligned along the limestone cliff foot on the surface of Late Würm aeolian deposits. Faunal and other direct environmental data are unfortunately lacking for all the sites. But the tool-kits themselves certainly point to intensive, perhaps specialized and seasonal, hunting activities (Bartolomei and Broglio 1967; Broglio 1969b; Bartolomei, Broglio and Gaspardo 1971).

All the mentioned assemblages are assignable to the Evolved Italic Epigravettian (Broglio 1969a, 1972a). The artifacts comprise burins, short endscrapers, backed and hump-backed points, simple-backed bladelets and truncatures. A comparison with the radiocarbon-dated series of the Veneto (Tagliente Shelter near Verona) may put this phase in the eleventh to tenth millennia B.C.

In all northwestern Italy the only locality which has hitherto supplied a comparable clue is still the Belvedere Shelter on Monfenera (Fidele 1971b, 1972b, 1973c; Broglio 1972a). So far the Belvedere only yields evidence of repeated but rather erratic visits by small Upper Paleolithic groups. There undoubtedly are signs of human presence well into an early phase of Upper Würm, but a cultural specification is not yet possible. Three deposits have given evidence of such undefined Upper Paleolithic industries on Monfenera so far. Later on in the series, two more definite assemblages occur which are seen best assignable to an Epigravettian very like that of the Veneto plateaus. Bilateral-backed bladelets, arched-backed points, and rough endscrapers, commonly made of choice exotic flints, are reported. Affinities with the Veneto region especially point to the Evolved-Terminal Epigravettian assemblages such as Piancavallo, where for instance protogeometric microliths appear. One may therefore predict that a notably complete, though numerically poor, Upper Paleolithic sequence is documented at the Belvedere Shelter.

One must also foresee, in our opinion, that other Epigravettian and Epipaleolithic resting places and camps will be found on the mountains which surround Monfenera. This assumption leads us to the Epipaleolithic evidence. In fact, few flint microliths from Angera Cave and the Cariadeghe karst plateau, at the opposite ends of Lombardy and in similar situations to Monfenera, are now reported and referred to this culture period on Broglio's authority (Broglio 1972a; Biagi 1972; cf. Fedele 1972b). In the northeast, the Epipaleolithic is mainly known from the important deposits of the Adige Valley, Vatte di Zambana and Loc di Romagnano III, near Trento. The latter is a true "key-site," containing a series which extends with remarkable continuity from a Sauveterrian-like to a Tardenoisian-like layer, up to "Pottery Epi-Tardenoid," Neolithic (different horizons) and the Bronze Age (Perini 1971b; Broglio 1971, 1972b). More recently, Epipaleolithic sites have been discovered high on the Emilian Apennine ridge (Cremaschi and Castelletti 1973).

In 1971, Sauveterrian-like assemblages were recovered between the two small Colbricòn lakes in the vicinity of the Rolle Pass at about 2,000 meters elevation (Bagolini 1971), in close association with hearths (Bagolini 1972b; Dal Ri 1973). Findings such as Colbricòn have brought the southern side of the Alps into the wider picture already emerging from foreign circum-alpine discoveries: Isère (Bocquet 1969), Savoye, Switzerland (Bandi 1963; Egloff 1965), and Slovenia. The latest hunter-gatherers in this territory did not turn to the sorts of mixed subsistence economies apparently documented in the coastal regions to the south, but relied more and more on evolved hunting/gathering practices of a late Paleolithic type, in which high mountain resources evidently gained a substantive role. (The term Mesolithic is therefore avoided, as far as the Alps and the Po Plain are concerned.) This process seems to be almost exactly replicated in the Pyrenees and in the Central Massif area of France, and should be investigated in further detail.

Neolithic

The case of a transition from indigenous Tardenoid substrata to the Neolithic in a technological sense, mentioned above (Loc di Romagnano III, layers AA1-2), is still rather isolated. Ongoing excavations of Gabàn Rock-Shelter, in a suspended valley near Trento (Bergamo Decarli *et al.*

1972), will certainly supply important new information on the Tardenoid and Early "Neolithic" cultures in the northeastern Alpine region.

The well-known Neolithic culture whose lithic component has a clear Epipaleolithic ascendancy (Fiorano culture) was settled in the Emilia region far from the mountains; only scattered imports reached Romagnano and probably other sites in the Adige Valley (Bagolini 1972a; Broglio 1972b). (So far, radiocarbon dating puts the Fiorano culture between 3,900 and 4,400 B.C., tree-ring calibrated to 4,800-5,400 B.C.) The early cultivated cereals were probably unsuited to upland conditions, and economy in the valley communities continued to be mainly based on modified hunting and gathering strategies.

A certain human presence near the core of the Alps develops with the onset and the spread of the Square-Mouthed Pottery (SMP) culture, which was probably parallel to Fiorano at least in its initial stage. An oval hut of the early phase of this culture, 7 x 4 meters in diameter, is reported from Garniga near the summit of Mt. Bondone, which overlooks the town of Trento (Bagolini and Perini 1973). But the push into the mountains appears to have really developed only in the second of Barfield's three phases of the SMP culture, as they were first distinguished in the Veneto and Emilia settlements (Barfield and Broglio 1971, Broglio 1972a). L. H. Barfield (1971:45–6) says,

The choice of naturally fortified hill-tops, strategically dominating river routes, ... marks a divergence from the types of settlement location listed for the Finale-Quinzano phase, and it may reflect the increasing importance of trade routes or an unstable political climate.

(A shift in population pressure and a search for new breeding procedures may perhaps provide an alternative explanation, for example, an assay of transhumance methods.)

In the Adige valley, some shoe-last adzes found at La Vela and in other Late Neolithic contexts are akin to the Hinkelstein and Flomborn types of the *Bandkeramik* and Aichbühl Cultures of Central Europe. They are thus considered the earliest sure evidence for direct communication through the Brenner or the Resia Pass (Barfield 1970). There is indeed a growing body of evidence showing that in a period between the Late Neolithic and the Bronze Age the Upper Adige Basin was closely linked to developments in the *Nordalpiner Kreis, sensu* Driehaus (Pfyn, Altheim, Baalberg, Ievišovice B; see Perini 1973). About this time, stone cist burials appear as a regular funerary style throughout the Trento area and far afield in some of the Adige Basin branches up to Bolzano (Barfield 1970; Broglio 1970). This funerary manifestation seems to have lasted till the Early Bronze Age (Fasani 1965; Barfield 1970). Despite some statements to the contrary, one may still raise the question as to whether or not these cist burials are related to the "Neolithic" cist cemeteries long known in the Aosta Valley (Piedmont), another major valleys of the Alps.

The cemeteries in the Upper Aosta Valley are characterized by crouched, often multiple inhumations in cists of stone slabs. Their usual locations are on escarped spurs hanging high above the *thalweg* (e.g., Montjovet, Vollein). They are very poorly furnished, or at any rate material useful for dating has not yet been reported. But undoubtedly a rather close correspondence exists there with the parallel series of cemeteries carefully explored in the upper Rhône Valley, Canton Wallis (Dellenbach 1935; Sauter 1950, 1955a, 1955b, 1963, 1969; Barocelli 1951, 1956, 1962b; Sauter and Gallay 1969). These Swiss sites are admittedly connected to Cortaillod-influenced, Chassey local groups, usually thought of as Swiss "Middle" (actually "Early," as far as Wallis is concerned) Neolithic. Accordingly, Aosta Valley graves are referred to as the Italian counterpart of that culture complex, the "Upper Neolithic" Lagozza Culture (Radmilli 1963).

On the basis of recent chronometric datings (Thomas 1965; Broglio 1972a) and of revisions in interpretation, I wonder whether the chronological overlap among Swiss Chassey-Cortaillod, Italian Logozza, and the SMP culture middle phase may not be much wider than supposed (Fedele 1973c, and in press b). One square-mouthed vessel sherd was found right in the type settlement of the Swiss group referred to (St. Léonard I) (Sauter 1969, 1970).

Generally speaking, the Neolithic cist grave subcultures in the Alps are more likely to form part of a large complex whose distribution is significantly concordant with the broad boundaries of Pyrenean–Alpine relief (Sauter 1955b; Ripoll and Llongueras 1963; Guilaine and Muñoz 1964). They might be looked at as a mountain-specific, or a mountain-born, phenomenon (Fedele, in press b).

The appearance of the SMP culture in the mountain area may be well observed in the Piedmont Alps. Some old and poorly studied sites are of little interpretive utility: Vayes "Shelter" in the lower Susa Valley (Piolti 1902; Taramelli 1903; cf. Fedele 1971b, 1973c; Brown 1965) or Viù-Versino (Barocelli 1962a). But Aisone Cave, St. Pierre near Aosta, and Monfenera, provide substantive indications of the event.

A child burial in the Aisone Cave, in Cuneo province (Rittatore 1951, 1952a, 1952b, and personal communication 1971; Radmilli 1962), has been radiocarbon dated 3,875±75 B.C. (R-95; tree-ring calibrated date after Renfrew's 1971 chart: *c.* 4,800 B.C.); but the relevance of this occupation site to the early phase of the culture (Barfield and Broglio 1971; Broglio 1972a) cannot be definitely ascertained. St. Pierre is a hill a few kilometers upstream from Aosta; it conceals a multi-component settlement which preliminary recoveries of scattered materials suggest is important (Mollo 1972; Mollo and Mezzena, personal communication

1972). A sherd from a square-mouthed vase and a square polished ax may show the first evidence of the actual presence of this culture on the Italian side of the Great St. Bernard Pass. On the Swiss side again, "Middle" Neolithic remains have been recognized at Sembrancher (Dellenbach 1938; Sauter 1971: 262, and 1972).

The latest excavations on Monfenera have produced evidence that a dwelling structure was built by SMP members right inside the Belvedere Shelter, partitioning the receding cave where the rock roof ends with a sort of post wall. Several post-holes of light inner substructures and two hearths have been found. Neolithic remains from this site are quite consistent with the peculiar association of the Chiozza–Rivoli Spiazzo phase in the East (Fedele 1973a, 1973c). Here, too, an extraordinarily dominating location is linked to this phase of the culture. Some traces of a rock-crystal industry may allow a comparison with the Vollein cemetery in the Aosta area (Daudry 1969:222–5; R. Mollo, personal communication) and St. Léonard in Wallis (Sauter 1959). Though disturbed and fragmentary, the Belvedere evidence justifies the inference that this site has a bearing on the problem of the diffusion and adaptations of the SMP culture to mountain biotopes (Fedele, in press b). Further field research there should add new data.

According to reliable radiocarbon datings, the chronology of the three main phases of the SMP culture is, respectively: Finale-Quinzano, c. 4,100–3,400 B.C.; Chiozza–Rivoli Spiazzo, 3,500-3,100 B.C.; Rivoli Rocca–Castelnuovo, undated. The tree-ring calibrated chronology (Renfrew 1970, 1971) would be: c. 5,000–4,300 B.C. and 4,400–?4,200/?3,900 B.C.

From a middle–late phase of the Neolithic onward, the presence and activity of human communities appear to have been quite intensive in the Western Alps. A number of surface finds — mainly greenstone polished axes — come from high valleys and slopes still crossed by cattle-tracks — Cuneo, Turin, and Aosta Valleys (Barocelli 1933, 1962b, 1968; Blanchard 1952). A test excavation intentionally looking for a prehistoric occupation in a cave at 1,525 meters elevation near the sources of the Po, failed to substantiate this assumption (Richard 1932; Barocelli 1933:12-3), as did our own recent exploration of a cave 2,110 meters high in the Varaita Valley (Fedele, unpublished). Another interesting attempt was made in the area of the famous Mt. Bego rock engravings at Gias del Ciari Shelter, 2,150 meters above sea level. The lower cultural horizon yielded a few materials ascribed to Lagozza (Louis and Segui 1951; Louis and Isetti 1964).

All these cultural ascriptions must be considered quite controversial, as they commonly disregard any explanation in Alps-oriented, rather than plain-oriented, terms. At best they probably prove an autonomous activity in a general time-span from the Neolithic to the permeation of Alpine routes by bronze-bearing groups. Gias del Ciari, and perhaps the poorly-excavated Grai Cave in the southern part of Piedmont (Novelli 1968), should also be viewed as reflecting a well established transhumance economy.

The Metal Stage

Radiocarbon-dated Lagozza sites span the first half of the third millennium, tree-ring calibrated to the first half of the fourth (Renfrew 1970). The Copper Age thus appears to have been introduced as early as the mid-third, or the fourth, millennium B.C.

Many authorities now agree that the first important outburst of so-called rock art in the entire Alpine territory goes back to the early Copper Age of the surrounding lowlands (Anati 1964, 1966, 1972; Barfield 1971; Fedele, in press b). In recent years, outstanding discoveries have occurred at Sion in Switzerland and at St. Martin-de-Corléans, an Aosta suburb. They have revealed monumental centers composed of cist burials, dolmen tombs on podia, decorated "statue-menhirs," and engraved anthropomorphic stelae. Standing "statue-menhirs," that appear to belong to a little-known Late Neolithic/Copper Age culture, were later pulled down and subsequently re-used as walling slabs in Bell Beaker graves at Sion (Bocksberger 1966, 1968a, 1968b; Sauter 1972; A. Gallay, unpublished), or in Early Bronze cist graves at St. Martin, according to a Polada-like elbow-handled cup found in one of them (Mollo 1972).

These discoveries can ultimately relate to each other all the different rock art manifestations previously known within and around the Alps, showing that they are aspects of a single cultural whole. (Santacroce 1969 provides a bibliography on the Alpine rock art.) Moreover, the new finds throw light on cultural events and chronological relationships within the troubled period of the circum-Alpine Copper Age.

Leaving out details, the resulting picture seems that of a relatively long-lasting Copper Age (*c.* 2,500–1,800 B.C., Barfield 1971; around the third millennium, Renfrew 1970), during which the Alpine chain was situated at a crucial crossroads of several European interests, influences, and routes of migration or raiding (Bocksberger 1964, 1968b, 1969; Brown 1965; Barfield 1971:63; Fedele 1973d). In this context one might examine the problem of the persistence of self-contained mountain communities in these times and their interactions with foreign elements.

Copper Age cultural groups of the Po Plain only occasionally attained the Pre-Alps, as for example the Collective Cave Burial group at Buco della Sabbia (Lombardy).

In subsequent periods the amount and quality of evidence about man in the mountains speedily increases. Information is especially rich for the Eastern Alps and the Adige surroundings. Ledro Lake and Fiavè Peat-bog have large settlements, and many upland localities in the Bressanone valleys may be mentioned in this context.

A major shift in frequency is apparent when one considers the Final Bronze and the Early Iron ages. This change may be related to the general break in cultural continuities between the Late and Final Bronze Age that is perceivable in the archeological record south of the Alps. Beyond the watershed, a corresponding maximum population recorded, for example, in Savoy, is specifically dated to the Final Bronze Age (Combier 1962).

Evidence of visits, transits and stays even at considerable altitudes become numerous (Gias del Ciari; Little and Great St. Bernard passes; Mt. Sciliar/Schlern; Malciaussià Lake at the head of the Viù Valley; St. Barthélemy in the Aosta Valley, etc.) and scattered finds of bronze tools, weapons or hoards of this period are almost commonplace. Prolonged occupation is proved by mountain villages and "hill-forts" (commonly called *castellieri* or *castellari*) and by cemeteries with different burial types: cremation and urn; extended with metal grave-goods; or cairns, as in the Cuneo valleys. The French counterpart of this evidence is notewor-thily abundant (cf. Courtois 1957, 1961, 1968; Bellet 1965; Bodard 1967; Bocquet 1969; Fedele, in press b).

Some sites might be interpreted as summer camps related to trans-humance, but specific research to test this hypothesis is still to be done. One-hundred hill-top centers have been recorded in the Cuneo valleys, in the Aosta Valley up to 2,400 meters (Mollo 1972), in the Lombard and Venetian Pre-Alps, and throughout the Adige Basin. A small "eagle's-aerie" cave on Monfenera seems to have been occupied in this period (Fedele 1972b). Where thorough excavations have been undertaken, many regularities in house construction and associated evidence appear to link the Iron Age communities to the cultural inheritance surviving in the Alpine territory today.

A possible Atestine outpost established by 800 B.C. at Rivoli Veronese to secure the border against the Raeti mountaineers, pre-figured in the Iron Age what would later be common under the Romans. It points to the existence of distinct, strong sociocultural systems in the inner Alps. As a rule, Celtic movements and harsh Roman intervention did not very much alter the basic protohistoric culture complex established in the Alpine range (cf. Rittatore 1972). Classical sources reflect a respectful attitude toward the national identity of the mountaineers and their expertise of control over the high routes (see Allais 1890 and Gribaudi 1928, as well as Finocchi 1960, Prieur 1968, Agavit 1970). Quite probably at the same time the reduction of the Alpine region into a conservative enclave also set in.

MAN–MOUNTAIN RELATIONSHIPS IN ANTHROPOLOGICAL PERSPECTIVE: SOME CONCLUSIONS

1. Despite specific bio-repulsive factors, man has been present in mountain regions widely and persistently. No other hominoid, and almost no other primate species, displays this capacity to such an extent.

The present theme may be viewed as only a chapter in a more comprehensive problem — that of the conquest by man of "difficult" environments. Such environments are represented for instance by higher latitudes in both hemispheres and by mountainous territories (some deserts and the tropical rain forest might of course be added). By difficult environment is meant any combination of states of environmental subsystems under which individual survival and/or the homeostasis of the human ecosystem is put in danger.

Even if a partial mastery of difficult habitats was reached much later in human evolution, the evidence secured in the Alps concur to show that success was initiated by groups at the Middle (or Lower?) Paleolithic technological socio-cultural level. High altitude sites, or sites very near to Pleistocene glaciated areas, are useful in providing information on this topic (e.g., Méroc 1953; Wendorf and Miller 1959; Lyubin and Kolbutov 1961; Lyubin 1971; MacDonald 1968; Ravskii and Tseitlin 1968; Bader 1968, 1971a, 1971b; Kanivec 1969; Bryan 1969; Jelínek 1969: 477). This argument has been recently raised with some original approaches (Watanabe 1969; Collins 1969; G. Clark 1970:72ff.; Butzer 1972).

Current ecological research on living human ecosystems which function while coping with more or less extreme environments (e.g., Burton and Edholm 1955; Dunbar 1968; Roberts 1970; Clegg, Harrison and Baker 1970; Freeman 1971) has a potential bearing on the explanation of the record from the past. As a result of continued environmental stresses and severe demands, plasticity and adaptive responses are elicited and high, selective pressures are generally established. The nature and specificity of human responses, as well as the inherent processes of selection and evolution, both somatic (Billy 1966; Ferembach 1967; Vallois 1968; Etingen, Nikityuk and Belkin 1969) and cultural, are the object of the above investigations.

Unfortunately, we are still unable to detect the same phenomena in the archeological record (see Watanabe 1969 for an insightful discussion; cf. Fedele 1966b, 1973b, and in press b). The actual source of man's interest in mountainous lands is not always understood in depth.

2. The evidence of "mountain" Paleolithic from the Italian Alps may be evaluated in the light of the wider comparisons mentioned. It seems likely that the Sesia Valley was extensively occupied by its glacier when the outstanding rampart of Monfenera was being visited by some Mous-

terian and many Upper Paleolithic hunters. Periglacial frost phenomena, such as cryoturbation or cryoclastic collapses of the vault, mark the climaxes of this period at the Belvedere Shelter, which faces towards the Sesian corridor. These archeological data reveal an incipient Paleolithic intrusion into, if not an occasional living in, the northwestern Alps by Mousterians; the same seems to be true for the rest of the chain.

Perplexing manifestations have often been observed in the Alpine and circum-Alpine area in connection with Mousterian assemblages. The name, "Alpine Mousterian," was proposed to single out this geographical complex of doubtful finds as a culture, according to Emil Bächler in Switzerland and Raffaello Battaglia in Italy (cf. Combier 1956; Müller-Karpe 1966). But now this theory is being disproved. The assemblages found at many sites along the Alps show structural divergences that prevent us from envisioning a homogeneous, separate whole. "Alpine" Mousterian sites appear commonly associated with cave bear deposits, but now the problems peculiar to the behavior of cave bears in caves have been cleared up enough to warn against old misunderstandings (Spahni 1954; Leroi-Gourhan 1964; Andrist, Flükiger and Andrist 1964; Lequatre 1966; Fedele 1966b, 1974b; Egloff 1971). Artifactual processes such as microlithic trends or expanding denticulation may well reflect adaptations to the mountain environment of the Würm Glaciation — a raw material economy, for instance. Alpine Mousterian is probably not a distinct culture (Bordes 1968), but the result of an "adaptive" convergence depending upon common demands of the contemporary Alpine environment (Fedele 1973b, 1973c).

3. If we turn now to Upper Paleolithic groups, it is important to emphasize the probable evidence of artificial sheltering at a site on the Asiago Plateau. One might wonder whether this is an indication of actual overwintering, but the question cannot be answered as far as that site is concerned.

As is well known, the building of huts or tents by Oriental Gravettian and other Upper Paleolithic groups has a long tradition in Eastern European plains. These cultures mastered fairly well the adverse environments of their territory, whether it was the mountains above 1,500 meters, as is testified by the Mladeč point industries of Poland (cf. Broglio 1968), or the *Inlandsis* borders up to about 66° North on the middle Pečora River, at Byzovaia (Bader 1971a).

A great increase in human presence and activity appears peculiar to the last phases of retreat of the Würm Glaciation and to the Anathermal. Extreme Epigravettians and — after a gap in the present record — active Epipaleolithic hunter–gatherers, seem to have attained notable population densities in certain privileged, moderate altitude zones, from there raiding far upward.

Human skeletal remains have occasionally been found in association with the Paleolithic and Epipaleolithic assemblages mentioned above, but they are too meagre to allow reliable ascriptions. Mousterian-associated remains studied so far would have Neanderthal characters (Mezzena Shelter near Verona: Corrain 1968). The Buco del Corno finds and the remarkable Vatte di Zambana Sauveterrian burial are unpublished.

4. Although the idea of an "Alpine" Paleolithic has been dismissed, an "Alpine" Neolithic might still perhaps be conjectured. The traces of the SMP culture now coming from the Piedmont region and from Switzerland could be hastily viewed as the first evidence of the use of a western pass (Great St. Bernard). But simple transit is not a satisfactory explanation. There may be early evidence of a permanent settlement in the major intermontane valleys. The basic problems affecting the first encounters by agriculturists and breeders with the Alps were resolved. A combination of valley-floor cultivation and incipient mountain stock-rearing might be presumed to be in existence at this time or shortly later (cf. Higham 1967; Phillips 1971, 1972). Environmental changes which accompanied the gradual shift from an Atlantic to a sub-Boreal climate (Frenzel 1966) must also be considered.

From a general standpoint, explanations in terms of *permanent settlements* in the Alps can be opposed to the traditional concepts in which stress was laid on use of passes for transit alone. Transit across passes may eventually prove to be subordinate, at least when viewed in our modern sense. In the Piedmontese–Swiss tract and in the Adige Valley–Tyrolese region as well, a unique complex of socio-cultural systems spanning either side of the ridge, connected by internal networks pivoting upon the passes, may provide an alternative model based on the Late Neolithic record. As research on living Alpine communities shows, watersheds unite, while often rivers and valleys divide (Fedele, in press b; Lasker *et al.* 1972).

Mountain groups had relations with the lowland cultural groups mainly in the larger valleys. The clearly exotic elements (traders, warriors, Childe's "prospectors"?) who criss-crossed the Alps in the eventful Copper Age, touched the mountain communities but probably involved them only slightly. A substantial part of the populations of the mountains may have pursued the traditional, "Neolithic" way of life well into the second millennium, in an increasing integration within their own ecosystems. These mountaineers may even have played central, not peripheral roles, in the economic context of the time (for example in connection with the mining of metal ores, in the Central and perhaps in the Piedmontese Alps). But this is still difficult to verify (cf. Peroni 1971a).

As previously stated, the next important phase of occupation in the

Alps seems to coincide with the Final Bronze and Iron Ages. An effectual control over the environment, within the limits of the carrying capacities of the exploited biotopes, was attained. No conclusive break with tradition is really perceivable in the subsequent history of many of these mountain settlers — until yesterday. Monfenera among other sites makes this emerging picture of strong continuities from protohistory to the Mediaeval and modern periods particularly impressive (Fedele, in press a).

Populations in the Western Alps, and perhaps elsewhere in the chain and in the Pyrenees, thus appear to have a 3,000-year history of relative biological segregation and cultural independence (Arbos 1922; Burns 1963; Matley 1968; Morton and Hussels 1970). Approximately 150 generations lived without interruption in this environment, this continuity leading them to achieve a high degree of integration with their mountain setting. Today a definitive disintegration has perhaps begun.

REFERENCES

AGAVIT, EMILIA
    1969   I valichi della Valle d'Aosta in epoca preromana. *Bulletin d'Etudes Préhistorique Alpines* 1:5–45.
    1970   I valichi della Valle d'Aosta in epoca galloromana e romana. *Bulletin d'Etudes Préhistoriques Alpines* 2:5–65.
ALLAIS, G.
    1890   *Le Alpi Occidentali nell'antichità.* Torino: Vincenzo Bona.
ANATI, EMMANUEL
    1964   *Civiltà preistorica della Val Camonica.* Milano: Il Saggiatore.
    1966   *La datazione dell'arte preistorica camuna.* Studi camuni 2. Capo di Ponte: Centro Camuno di Studi Preistorici.
    1972   La stele di Ossimo. *Bollettino del Centro Camuno di Studi Preistorici* 8:81–119.
ANDRIST, D., W. FLÜKIGER, A. ANDRIST
    1964   *Das Simmental zur Steinzeit.* Acta Bernensia 3. Bern: Verlag Stämpfli.
ARBOS, P.
    1922   *La vie pastorale dans les Alpes françaises. Etude de géographie humaine.* Grenoble: F. Allier.
BADER, O. N.
    1968   New data on the original inhabitation of North-East Europe. *Quartär* 19.
    1971a The most ancient human settlement of Northern Europe in the light of recent research. (In Russian.) *Kratkie soobščeniya Instituta Arkheologii (Akademii nauk SSSR)* 126:3–13.
    1971b Abitati dell'estremo Nord dell'Europa nel Paleolitico. *Rivista di Scienze Preistoriche* 26:325–345.
BAGOLINI, BERNARDINO
    1971   Colbricon (Passo Rolle–Rolle Pass). *Preistoria Alpina* 7:342–344.

1972a Risultati dello scavo 1969 a Chiozza di Scandiano e considerazioni sull'insediamento della Cultura di Fiorano documentato a Chiozza. *Preistoria Alpina* 8:31–71.
1972b Primi risultati delle ricerche sugli insediamenti epipaleolitici del Colbricon (Dolomiti). *Preistoria Alpina* 8:107–149.

BAGOLINI, B., R. PERINI
1973 Garniga (Monte Bondone–Trento). *Preistoria Alpina* 9:236–237.

BANDI, H.-G., *editor*
1963 *Birsmatten-Basisgrotte.* Acta Bernensia 1. Bern: Verlag Stämpfli.

BARFIELD, LAWRENCE H.
1970 La stazione neolitica de "la Vela" presso Trento. Considerazioni sulle tombe a cista nel Trentino — Alto Adige. *Rendiconti, Società di Cultura Preistorica Tridentina* 5:154–174.
1971 *Northern Italy before Rome.* Ancient peoples and places 76. London: Thames and Hudson.

BARFIELD, LAWRENCE H., ALBERTO BROGLIO
1971 Osservazioni sulle culture neolitiche del Veneto e del Trentino nel quadro del Neolitico padano. *Origini 5.*

BAROCELLI, PIERO
1933 *Edizione archeologica della Carta d'Italia al 100 000. Foglio 66, Cesana. Foglio 67, Pinerolo.* Firenze: R. Istituto Geografico Militare.
1951 La préhistoire en vallée d'Aoste. *Augusta Praetoria* 4:143–155, 199–211.
1956 "Parallelismi culturali tra la Valle d'Aosta ed il Vallese nella preistoria," in *Relazioni e comunicazional XXXI Congresso storico subalpino, Aosta 1956,* 7–28. Torino.
1960 Raffaello Battaglia e la paletnologia veneto-padana. *Sibrium* 5:9–58.
1962a *La stazione preistorica di Viù.* Società Storica delle Valli di Lanzo, Pubblicazioni 6. Torino: O. Falciola.
1962b *Edizione archeologica della Carta d'Italia al 100 000. Foglio 27, M. Bianco. Foglia 28, Aosta* (second edition). Firenze: Istituto Geografico Militare.
1968 *La via romana transalpina degli alti valichi dell'Autaret e di Arnàs. Note di escursioni archeologiche nelle valli di Lanzo Torinese.* Società Storica delle Valli di Lanzo, Publicazioni 16. Torino: O. Falciola.

BARTOLOMEI, G., A. BROGLIO
1967 Il giacimento dei Fiorentini sull'altipiano di Tonezza-Folgaria. *Origini* 1:11–36.

BARTOLOMEI, G., A. BROGLIO, D. GASPARDO
1971 Un insediamento epigravettiano sul Pian del Cavallo (Pordenone). *Rivista di Scienze Preistoriche* 26:393–401.

BELLET, J.
1965 "Préhistoire et protohistoire de la Vallée de Maurienne et leurs relations avec les vallées voisines," in *Actes du Congrès des Sociétés savantes de Savoie, Moûtiers, 1964,* 12–24. Belley: Imprimerie du Bugey.

BERGAMO DECARLI, G., L. BERTOLDI, G. FIORITO, L. POSTAL
1972 Riparo Gaban (Trento). *Preistoria Alpina* 8:269–274.

BERTOLANI MARCHETTI, DARIA
1967 Vicende climatiche e floristiche dell'ultimo glaciale e del postglaciale in sedimenti della laguna veneta. *Memoirie di Biogeografia Adriatica* 7:193–225.

BIAGI, PAOLO
1972   Il giacimento sopra Fienile Rossino sull'Altipiano di Cariadeghe (Serle
       — Brescia). *Preistoria Alpina* 8:177–197.
BILLY, G.
1966   Formation et évolution sur place de la brachycéphalie alpine. *Homo*
       17:147–159.
BLANCHARD, RAOUL
1952   *Les Alpes occidentales. 6: Le versant piémontais*. 1. Paris and Grenoble:
       B. Arthaud.
1954   *Les Alpes occidentales. 6: Le versant piémontais*. 2. Paris and Grenoble:
       B. Arthaud.
BOCKSBERGER, O.-J.
1964   *Age du Bronze en Valais et dans le Chablais Vaudois*. Lausanne:
       Imprimerie Centrale.
1966   Mise au point sur les découverts préhistoriques du Petit-Chasseur à
       Sion (Valais). *Ur-Schweiz* 30:21–36.
1968a Nouvelles recherches au Petit-Chasseur, à Sion. *Ur-Schweiz* 32:6–14.
1968b Dalles anthropomorphes, tombes en ciste et vases campaniformes
       découverts à Sion, Suisse. *Bollettino del Centro Camuno di Studi Preis-
       torici* 3:69–95.
1969   "Les nouvelles découvertes au Petit-Chasseur à Sion." Lecture deli-
       vered in Turin, March 29, 1969.
BOCQUET, A.
1968   Quelques gisements dauphinois et la voie du col du Lautaret à la fin du
       Ier Age du Fer. *Cahiers Rhodaniens* 13:104–115.
1969   L'Isère préhistorique et protohistorique. *Gallia Préhistoire*
       12:121–258, 273–400.
BODARD, PIERRE
1967   Les Alpes-Maritimes. Répertoire bibliographique, topobibliogra-
       phique et biobibliographique. *Mémoires de l'Institut de Préhistoire et
       d'Archéologie des Alpes-Maritimes* 10:8–73.
BONIFAY, E.
1964   Pliocène et Pléistocène méditerranée. Vue d'ensemble et essai de corré-
       lations avec la chronologie glaciaire. *Annales de Paléontologie — Ver-
       tebrés* 50:1–197.
BORDES, FRANÇOIS
1954   *Les limons quaternaires du Bassin de la Seine. Stratigraphie et
       archéologie paléolithique*. Archives de l'Institut de Paléontologie
       humaine, Mémoire 26. Paris: Masson and Cie.
1968   *L'antica età della pietra*. Milano: Il Saggiatore.
BORDES, FRANÇOIS, DENISE DE SONNEVILLE-BORDES
1970   The significance of variability in Palaeolithic assemblages. *World
       Archaeology* 2:61–89.
BROGLIO, ALBERTO
1967   Il Paleolitico dell'Italia settentrionale. *Arheološki Vestnik* 18:247–254.
1968   "Culture paleolitiche," in *Introduzione allo studio della preistoria*,
       85–160. Pavia: Editrice Succ. Fusi.
1969a "Considerazioni sui complessi epigravettiani del Veneto," in *Scritti sul
       Quaternario in onore di Angelo Pasa*, 137–148. Museo Civico di
       Storia Naturale di Verona, Memorie fuori serie 3. Verona.
1969b Gli insediamenti paleolitici degli altipiani vicentini. *Natura e montagna*
       3:30–38.

1970 Risultati delle recenti ricerche sul Neolitico e sul-l'Eneolitico del Veneto, del Trentino e del Friuli. *Odeo Olimpico* 8:65–79.
1971 Risultati preliminari delle ricerche sui complessi epipaleolitici della Valle dell'Adige. *Preistoria Alpina* 7:135–241.
1972a Cronologia delle culture del Paleolitico superiore, dell'Epipaleolitico e del Neolitico della Valle Padana. *Bollettino del Centro Camuno di Studi Preistorici* 8:47–79.
1972b I più antichi abitatori della Valle dell'Adige. *Preistoria Alpina* 8:157–176.

BROWN, DONALD F.
1965 "The chronology of the Northwestern Mediterranean," in *Chronologies in Old World archaeology*. Edited by Robert W. Ehrich, 321–342. Chicago and London: University of Chicago Press.

BRYAN, ALAN L.
1969 Early man in America and the Late Pleistocene chronology of Western Canada and Alaska. *Current Anthropology* 10:339–365.

BURNS, ROBERT K., JR.
1963 The circum-alpine culture area: a preliminary view. *Anthropological Quarterly* 36:130–155.

BURTON, A. C., E. G. EDHOLM
1955 *Man in a cold environment*. London: Arnold Press.

BUTZER, KARL W.
1972 *Environment and archeology* (second edition). London: Methuen and Co.

CARANDINI, L.
1961 I passi delle Alpi occidentali. *Le Vie d'Italia* 67:1343 ff.

CARRARO, F., F. MEDIOLI, F. PETRUCCI
i.p. "Geomorphological study of the morainic amphitheatre of Ivrea, Northern Italy," in *Quaternary studies, Selected papers from IX INQUA Congress, Christchurch, New Zealand, 1973*. Edited by R. P. Suggate et al.

CARRARO, F., F. PETRUCCI
1972 "Carte géologique de la plaine du Piémont à l'échelle du 1:400 000," in *Etudes sur le Quaternaire dans le monde, VIIIe Congrès INQUA (Paris 1969)*, 569–571. Paris.

CHARRIER, GIOVANNI
1967 La torbiera del Colle di Sestriere (Torino): suo significato per la storia del clima e della vegetazione del versante italiano delle Alpi Cozie nell'Olocene superiore. *Allionia* 13:221–250.
1970 Ricerche sull'evoluzione del clima e dell'ambiente durante il Quaternario nel settore delle Alpi Occidentali italiane. 1: I legni fossili di larice del Colle di Sestriere (Torino) datati con il metodo C14. *Allionia* 16:155–164.

CHIARELLI, B., F. FEDELE
1969 Ricerche antropologiche sul popolamento umano delle Alpi occidentali. *Archivio per l'Antropologia e l'Etnologia* 99:209–210.

CLARKE, DAVID L.
1971 *Analytical archaeology* (second edition). London: Methuen and Co.

CLARKE, GRAHAME
1967 *The Stone Age hunters*. London: Thames and Hudson.
1970 *Aspects of prehistory*. Berkeley, Los Angeles, London: University of California Press.

CLEGG, E. J., G. A. HARRISON, P. T. BAKER
1970   The impact of high altitudes on human populations. *Human Biology* 42:486–518.

COLLINS, DESMOND
1969   Culture traditions and environment of early man. *Current Anthropology* 10:267–316.

COMBIER, JACQUELINE
1962   "Aperçu sur les trouvailles de l'âge du Bronze dans le Département de Savoie," in *Actes du Quatre-vingt-cinquième Congrès National des Sociétés Savantes, Chambéry — Annecy 1960*, 43–58. Chambéry.

COMBIER, JEAN
1956   La grotte des Ours à Chateaubourg (Ardèche) et le problème du "Moustérien Alpin." *Cahiers Rhodaniens* 3:3–14.

CORRAIN, CLETO
1968   Resti scheletrici umani del "Riparo Mezzena." *Memorie del Museo Civico di Storia Naturale di Verona* 16:97–101.

COURTOIS, J.-C.
1957   Objets de l'Age du Bronze trouvés dans le département des Hautes-Alpes. *Gallia 15*: 63–78.
1961   L'âge du Bronze dans les Hautes-Alpes. *Gallia Préhistoire* 3:47–108.
1968   *Découvertes archéologiques de l'Age du Bronze et de l'Age du Fer dans les Hautes-Alpes, 1955–1967*. Gap: Vollaire.

CREMASCHI, MAURO, L. CASTELLETTI
1973   Passo della Comunella (Reggio Emilia). *Preistoria Alpina* 9:267–276.

DAINELLI, GIOTTO
1959   *Le Alpi.* Torino: UTET.

DAL RI, LORENZO
1973   Colbricon (Dolomiti). *Preistoria Alpina* 9:227–229.

DAUDRY, DAMIANO
1969   Atti dell'Associazione. *Bulletin d'Etudes Préhistoriques Alpines* 1:212–226.

DE LAVIS-TRAFFORD, M. A.
1960   Etudes sur les voies transalpines dans la région du Mont-Cenis depuis l'Antiquité classique jusqu'au début du XIIIème siècle. *Bulletin Philologique et Historique* 1.

DELLENBACH, M. E.
1935   La conquête du massif alpin et de ses abords par les populations préhistoriques. *Revue de Géographie alpine* 23:170–191.
1938   Une pointe de lance néolithique trouvée dans une vallée des Alpes valaisannes à Sembrancher. *Annales Valaisannes* 13:476–477.

DE LUMLEY-WOODYEAR, HENRY
1969   *Le Paléolithique inférieur et moyen du Midi méditerranéen dans son cadre géologique*. 1. Supplément à "Gallia Préhistoire" 5. Paris: Editions du Centre National de la Recherche Scientifique.

DUNBAR, M. J.
1968   *Ecological development in polar regions. A study in evolution.* Englewood Cliffs: Prentice-Hall.

EGLOFF, MICHEL
1965   La Baume d'Ogens, gisement épipaléolithique du plateau vaudois. *Jahrbuch des Schweizerischen Gesellschaft für Ur- und Frühgeschichte* 52.

1971   "Deux nouvelles grottes à Ursus spelaeus dans les Préalpes vaudoises,"
        in *Actes du 4e Congrès suisse de Spéléologie, Neuchâtel, septembre
        1970*, 215–225. Neuchâtel.

ETINGEN, L. E., B. A. NIKITYUK, V. Š. BELKIN
1969   Sur les causes de brachycéphalie chez les montagnards. *L'An-
        thropologie* 73:401–407.

FASANI, LEONE
1965   Le tombe a cista di M. Loffa e le attuali conoscenze sulle sepolture
        neolitiche a ciste del territorio collinare e montano del Veronese.
        Memorie del Museo Civico di Storia Naturale di Verona 12:309–322.

FEDELE, F. G.
1966a   La stazione paleolitica del Monfenera in Valsesia. 2: Le ricerche
        dell'Istituto di Antropologia di Torino negli anni 1964–66. *Rivista di
        Studi Liguri* 32:27–76.
1966b   La stazione paleolitica del Monfenera in Valsesia. 3: I giacimenti
        quaternari del Monfenera e il Paleolitico dell'Italia nordoccidentale.
        Rivista di Studi Liguri 32:77–106.
1968   Ricerche sui giacimenti quaternari del Monfenera. Studio sui macro-
        mammiferi della caverna "Ciota Ciara" (scavi 1966). *Rivista di
        Antropologia* 55:247–269.
1971a   editor. "Rapporto N. 1 del Gruppo per lo studio multidisciplinare delle
        popolazioni delle Valli cuneesi." University of Turin, Institute of
        Anthropology. (Mimeographed.)
1971b   Gli scavi nel riparo del Belvedere sul Monfenera, Valsesia. Cam-
        pagne 1969 e 1970. *Archivio per l'Antropologia e l'Etnologia* 101:231–
        244.
1972a   "Prime informazioni sul clima würmiano delle Alpi Occidentali da un
        giacimento di grotta (Monfenera, Valsesia)," in *Atti del VII Convegno
        speleologico dell'Emilia-Romagna, Bologna 1971*, 176–188. Memorie
        di "Rassegna Speleologica Italiana" 10. Como.
1972b   Aperçu des recherches dans les gisements du Monfenera (Valsesia,
        Alpes Pennines). *Bulletin d'Etudes Préhistoriques Alpines* 4:5–68.
1973a   Una stazione Vaso a bocca quadrata sul Monfenera, Valsesia (scavi
        1969–72). Rapporto preliminare. *Preistoria Alpina* 9: 151–222.
1973b   "Stone Age discoveries on Monfenera, Northwestern Alps, and their
        bearing on human paleoecology," in *Actes du VIIIe Congrès interna-
        tional des Sciences préhistoriques et protohistoriques, Beograd 1971*. 2:
        140–146. Edited by G. Novak et al. Beograd.
1973c   Paleolitico e Neolitico nelle Alpi Occidentali. *Bulletin d'Etudes Préhis-
        toriques Alpines* 5: 49–98.
1973d   A proposito del libro di L. H. Barfield sulla preistoria dell'Italia setten-
        trionale. *Bulletin d'Etudes Préhistoriques Alpines* 5: 151–157.
1974a   "La serie stratigrafica della grotta Ciutarun (Monfenera, bassa Val-
        sesia)," in *Atti dell'XI Congresso nazionale di speleologia, Genova
        1972*. Memorie di "Rassegna Speleologica Italiana," 11, 189–194.
        Como.
1974b   Monfenera 1973. Rapporto preliminare. *Bulletin d'Etudes Préhistori-
        ques Alpines* 6:53–83. [Includes Appendix on Ciutarun Cave find No.
        118:1 and the problem of Mousterian bone "buckles," by L. Fozzati,
        77–80.]
i.p. a   Scoperte e ricerche di archeologia medievale sul Monfenera. *Bollettino
        Storico-bibliografico Subalpino* 73 (1).

i.p. b   "Stadi di popolamento nelle Alpi Occidentali dal Neolitico all'Età del Ferro," in *CeSDIR, Atti*, volume 7 [Symposium held in 1974]. Milan: Cisalpino-Goliardica.

FEREMBACH, D.
1967   L'origine de la race alpine. *Scientia* vii 102:225–234.

FINOCCHI, SILVANA.
1960   "Aspetti del popolamento e della poleografia alpina nel Piemonte romano," in *Atti e memorie del terzo Congresso Piemontese di Antichità ed Arte — Congresso di Varallo Sesia — Septembre 1960*, 223–233. Torino.

FOLLIERI, MARIA.
1965   Alcuni tratti caratteristici della vegetazione interglaciale in Italia. *Bollettino della Società Geologica Italiana* 84:63–8.

FREEMAN, MILTON M. R.
1971   Social and ecologic analysis of systematic female infanticide among the Netsilik Eskimo. *American Anthropologist* 73:1011–1018.

FRENZEL, B.
1966   "Climatic change in the Atlantic/sub-Boreal transition on the Northern Hemisphere: botanical evidence," in World climate from 8,000 to 0 B.C. proceedings etc. Edited by J. S. Sawyer, 99–123. London: Royal Meteorological Society.

FUSCO, V.
1958   Reperti litici di facies paleolitica in una grotta dell'Alta Brianza. *Rivista "Archeologica" dell'Antica Provincia e Diocesi di Como* 140:5–9.

1971   Buco del Corno sopra Vigano (Val Cavallina, Prov. di Bergamo). *Rivista di Scienze Preistoriche* 26:450.

GRIBAUDI, D.
1928   *Il Piemonte nell'antichità classica. Saggio di corografia storica. Il paese.* Biblioteca della Società Storica Subalpina 114. Torino: Silvestrelli.

GUILAINE, JEAN, ANA MARIA MUÑOZ.
1964   La civilisation catalane des "sepulcros de fosa" et les sépultures néolithiques du Sud de la France. *Rivista di Studi Liguri* 30:5–30.

HARRIS, DAVID R.
1969   "Agricultural systems, ecosystems and the origins of agriculture," in *The domestication and exploitation of plants and animals.* Edited by P. J. Ucko and G. W. Dimbleby, 3–15. London: Gerald Duckworth.

HIGHAM, C. F. W.
1967   A consideration of the earliest neolithic culture in Switzerland. *Vierteljahrsschrift der Naturforschenden Gesellschaft in Zürich* 112:123–160.

JELÍNEK, JAN
1969   Neanderthal Man and *Homo sapiens* in Central and Eastern Europe. *Current Anthropology* 10:475–503.

KANIVEC, V. I.
1969   "Paleolitičeskii človek na Pečore," in *Priroda i razvitie pervobytnogo obščestva.* Moskva.

LAPLACE, GEORGES
1966   *Recherches sur l'origine et l'évolution des complèxes leptolithiques.* Ecole Française de Rome, Mélanges d'Archéologie et d'Histoire, Supplément 4. Paris: E. De Boccard.

LASKER, G. W., B. CHIARELLI, M. MASALI, F. FEDELE, B. A. KAPLAN
1972   Degree of human genetic isolation measured by isonymy and marital distances in two communities in an Italian Alpine valley. *Human Biology* 44:351–360.

LAVIOSA ZAMBOTTI, PIA
1950 Funzione dei passi centrali alpini durante la preistoria. *Jahrbuch des Schweizerischen Gesellschaft für Urgeschichte* 40:193–201.

LEONARDI, PIERO
1957 "Il Paleolitico dell'Italia padana," in Atti del 1° *Convegno interregionale padano di Paletnologia, Milano 1956*, 13–40. Firenze: Istituto Italiano di Preistoria e Protostoria.
1963 Il Paleolitico nel versante meridionale delle Alpi. *Rendiconti della Società di Cultura Preistorica Tridentina* 1:62–85.

LEONARDI, PIERO, ALBERTO BROGLIO
1965 "Il Paleolitico del Veneto," in *Miscelánea en homenaje al Abate Henri Breuil* volume 2. Edited by E. Ripoll Perelló, 31–73. Barcelona.
1966 Datazione assoluta di un'industria musteriana della Grotta del Broion. *Rivista di Scienze Preistoriche* 21:397–405.

LEQUATRE, P.
1966 La Grotte de Prélétang (commune de Presles, Isère). 1: Le repaire d'Ours des cavernes et son industrie moustérienne. *Gallia Préhistoire* 9:5–83.

LEROI-GOURHAN, ANDRE'
1964 *Les réligions de la préhistoire. (Paléolithique).* Paris: Mazenod.

LOUIS, M., G. ISETTI
1964 *Les gravures préhistoriques du Mont-Bego* (second edition). Bordighera: Institut International d'Etudes Ligures.

LOUIS, M., J. SEGUI
1951 Le Gias del Ciari (Mont Bego) (Commune de Tende, Alpes-Maritimes). *Gallia* 7:141–159.

LYUBIN, V. P.
1971 "Les cavernes paléolithiques de Koudaro (Le Caucase)," in *Les rapports et les communications de la délégation des archéologues de l'URSS* (to the 8th Congress of Prehistoric and Protohistoric Sciences, Beograd, 1971), 12 pp. Moskva. (Mimeographed.)

LYUBIN, V. P., A. D. KOLBUTOV
1961 Drevne jšhee poselenie čeloveka na territorii SSSR i paleogeografiya antropogena. *Byulleten' Komissii po izučeniyu četvertičnogo perioda* 26:74–88.

MACDONALD, GEORGE F.
1968 *Debert. A Palaeo-Indian site in central Nova Scotia* (second edition). Anthropology Papers 16, National Musuems of Canada. Ottawa.

MANCINI, F.
1963 Le variazioni climatiche in Italia dalla fine del Riss all'Olocene. (Tentativo di ordinamento cronologico). *Bollettino della Società Geologica Italiana* 81:181–214.

MARCHESONI, V., A. PAGANELLI
1966 Tavola cronologica del Quaternario. *Studi Trentini di Scienze Naturali* B 43:179–188.

MARKS, ANTHONY E.
1971 Settlement patterns and intrasite variability in the Central Negev, Israel. *American Anthropologist* 73:1237–1244.

MASALI, M., E. RABINO MASSA, F. G. FEDELE, *editors*
1972 "Report 2 of the Multidisciplinary study group of the Cuneo Valleys populations." University of Turin, Institute of Anthropology. (Mimeographed.)

MATLEY, IAN M.
1968   Transhumance in Bosnia and Herzegovina. *Geographical Review* 58:231–261.

MAVIGLIA, CARLO
1952   "Le cosiddette 'fibbie' del musteriano alpino, rinvenute a Sambughetto Valstrona (Novara)," in *Atti del I Congresso Internazionale di Studi Liguri. (Monaco — Bordighera — Genova, 1950)*, 41–7. Bordighera: Istituto Internazionale di Studi Liguri.

MELLARS, PAUL
1970   Some comments on the notion of "functional variability" in stone-tool assemblages. *World Archaeology* 2:74–89.

MENNELLA, C.
1967   *Il clima d'Italia*. 1. Napoli: Editrice EDART.

MÉROC, L.
1953   "La conquête des Pyrénées par l'homme et le rôle de la frontière pyrénéenne au cours des temps préhistoriques," in *I\u{er} Congrès international de Spéléologie*, volume 4, 33–51. Paris.

MOLLO, ROSANNA
1972   "Tre anni di nuove scoperte e ricerche archeologiche in Val d'Aosta (1969–1971)." Lecture delivered in Turin, February 12, 1972.

MORTON, N. E., IRENE HUSSELS
1970   Demography of inbreeding in Switzerland. *Human Biology* 42:65–78.

MÜLLER-KARPE, HERMANN
1966   *Handbuch der Vorgeschichte. 1: Altsteinzeit*. München: C.H. Beck'sche Verlagsbuchhandlung.

NANGERONI, G.
1967   Alpi e Prealpi. *Bollettino del Club Alpino Italiano* 46:125–130.

NOVELLI, G.
1968   Relazione sul rinvenimento di insediamento preistorico all'Arma del Graj, sul confine tra Ormea e Garessio – Cuneo. *Bollettino della Società per gli studi storici, archeologici ed artistici della Provincia di Cuneo* 59:33–40.

PASA, ANGELO
1969   "Appunti sul Quaternario," in *Scritti sul Quaternario in onore di Angelo Pasa*, 15–38. Museo Civico di Storia Naturale di Verona, Memorie fuori serie 3. Verona.

PENCK, A., W. BRÜCKNER
1909   *Die Alpen im Eiszeitalter*. Leipzig: Tauchnitz.

PERINI, R.
1971a I depositi preistorici di Romagnano–Loc (Trento) (notizia preliminare). *Preistoria Alpina* 7:7–106.

1971b *L'età del Bronzo nella penisola italiana. 1: L'antica età del Bronzo*. Firenze: Leo Olschki.

1973   Un deposito taro neolitico al Castelaz di Cagnò (Valle di Non). *Preistoria Alpina* 9:45–52.

PERRILL, DONALD M.
1970   The foehn wind phenomenon: a climatological inquiry into pleistocene habitats. *Anthropology University of California at Los Angeles* 2: 19–28.

PHILLIPS, A. P.
1971   Attribute analysis and social structure of Chassey-Cortaillod-Lagozza populations. *Man* n.s. 6:341–352.

1972   Population, economy and society in the Chassey-Cortaillod-Lagozza cultures. *World Archaelogy* 4:41–56.

PIOLTI, G.
1902   I manufatti litici del "riparo sotto roccia" di Vayes (Val di Sisa). *Atti della Reale Accademia delle Scienze di Torino* 37:476–491.

PITTIONI, RICHARD
1962   "Italien. Urgeschichtliche Kulturen." in *Real-Encyclopädie der Klassischen Altertumswissenschaft*. Edited bt A. Pauli, G. Wissowa and W. Kroll. Stuttgart.

PRIEUR, JEAN, ABBÉ
1968   *La province romaine des Alpes Cottiennes*. Publications du Centre d'Etudes Gallo-Romaines de la Faculté des Lettres et Sciences Humaines de Lyon 1. Villeurbanne: Imprimerie R. Gauthier.

RADMILLI, A. M., *editor*
1962   *Piccola guida della preistoria italiana*. Firenze: Sansoni.
1963   *La preistoria d'Italia alla luce delle ultime scoperte*. Firenze: Istituto Geografico Militare.
1964   *Abruzzo preistorico. Il Paleolitico inferiore-medio*. Origines 7. Firenze: Sansoni.

RANKAMA, K., *editor*
1967   *The Quaternary*, volume 2. New York, London, Sydney: Interscience Publishers.

RAVSKII, E. I., S. M. TSEITLIN
1968   Geological periodization of the sites of the Siberian Paleolithic. *Arctic Anthropology* 5:76–81.

RENFREW, COLIN
1970   New configurations in Old World archaeology. *World Archaeology* 2:199–211.
1971   Carbon 14 and the prehistory of Europe. *Scientific American* 225:63–72.

RICHARD, C.
1932   La Caverna di Rio Martino e la regione di Crissolo in relazione alla preistoria. *Bollettino della Società Piemontese di Archeologia e Belle Arti* 16:74–79.

RIPOLL PERELLÓ. E., M. LLONGUERAS CAMPAÑÁ
1963   *La cultura neolítica de los sepulcros de fosa en Cataluña*. Diputación Provincial de Barcelona, Instituto de Prehistoria y Arqueología, Monografías 21. Barcelona.

RITTATORE, F.
1951   Chiusa Pesio (Cuneo). Bec Berciassa (Roccavione, Cuneo). Aisone (Cuneo). Narzole (Cuneo). *Rivista di Scienze Preistoriche* 6:190–191.
1952a   Ricerche paletnologiche nel territorio di Cuneo. *Bollettino della Società storica, archeologica e artistica della Provincia di Cuneo* 30:96–100.
1952b   Ricerche sull'Età del Ferro nel Cuneese. *Rivista di Studi Liguri* 18:32–45.
1972   "I popoli indigeni della Transpadania dall'età del Bronzo alla romanizzazione." Lecture delivered at Aosta, May 21, 1972.

ROBERTS, D. F.
1970   Genetic problems of hot desert populations of simple technology. *Human Biology* 42:469–485.

SACCO, F.
1930   *Il glacialismo nelle Valli Sesia, Strona, Anza e nell'Ossola.* Ufficio Idrografico del Po, Pubblicazione 10, 4. Roma: Ministero dei Lavori Pubblici.

SANTACROCE, A.
1969   Brevi notizie sulle incisioni rupestri ed alcuni suggerimenti per la loro ricerca. *Bulletin d'Etudes Préhistoriques Alpines* 1:122–167

SAUTER, MARC-R.
1950   Préhistoire du Valais des origines aux temps mérovingiens. *Vallesia* 5:1–165.

1955a Préhistoire du Valais des origines aux temps mérovingiens. Premier supplément à l'inventaire archéologique (1950–1954). *Vallesia* 10:1–38.

1955b Sépultures à cistes de la vallée du Rhône et civilisations palafittiques. *Sibrium* 2:133–139.

1959   Sur une industrie en cristal de roche dans le Valais néolithique. *Archives suisses d'Anthropologie générale* 24:18–44.

1963   Aspects du Valais il y a cinq millénaires. *Actes de la Société helvétique des sciences naturelles* 143:19–30.

1969   Le Néolithique moyen du Valais et ses relations circumalpines. *Bulletin d'Etudes Préhistoriques Alpines* 1:46–54.

1970   "Les relations du Néolithique du type de Saint-Léonard (Valais, Suisse) avec Cortaillod, Chassey et Lagozza," in *Actes du VIIe Congrès international des Sciences préhistoriques et protohistoriques, Prague, 1966*, volume 1, pp. 561–563. Praha.

1971   Fouilles récentes en Suisse occidentale. *Bulletin de la Société Préhistorique Française* CRSM 68:262.

1972   "Les relations transalpines avant les Romains." Lecture delivered at Aosta, May 21, 1972.

SAUTER, MARC-R., A. GALLAY
1969   "Les premières cultures d'origine méditerranéenne," in *Ur- und Frühgeschichtliche Archäologie der Schweiz. 2: Die jüngere Steinzeit.* Basel: Schweizerisches Gesellschaft für Ur- und Frühgeschichte.

SCHMID, ELISABETH
1958   *Höhlenforschung und Sedimentanalyse. Ein Beitrag zur Datierung des alpinen Paläolithikums.* Schriften, Institut für Ur- und Frühgeschichte der Schweiz 13. Basel.

SESTINI, ALDO, *editor*
1957   *L'Italia fisica.* Milano: Touring Club Italiano.

SPAHNI, J. C.
1954   Les gisements à *Ursus spelaeus* de l'Autriche et leurs problèms. *Bulletin de la Société Préhistorique Française* 51:364–367.

SPARKS, B. W.
1971   *Rocks and relief.* London: Longman.

TARAMELLI, A.
1903   La stazione neolitica Rumiano di Vayes in Val di Susa. *Bullettino di Paletnologia Italiana* 29:1–23, 126–136.

THOMAS, HOMER L.
1965   "The archaeological chronology of Northwestern Europe," in *Chronologies in Old World archaeology.* Edited by R. H. Ehrich, 343–372. Chicago and London: University of Chicago Press.

VALLOIS, H. V.
1968   "Les hommes du Néolithique et des premiers âges des Métaux: un essai de synthèse," in *La Préhistoire. Problèmes et tendances*, 453–463. Paris: Editions du Centre National de la Recherche Scientifique.
VALOCH, KAREL, F. BORDES
1957   Loess de Tchécoslovaquie et loess de France du Nord. *L'Anthropologie* 61:279–288.
VENZO, S.
1954   Osservazioni sulla fauna delle Grotticelle di Sambughetto Valstrona e sugli Stadi würmiani del Lago d'Orta (Novara). *Atti della Società Italiana di Scienze Naturali* 93:409–431.
1965   *Rilevamento geologico dell'anfiteatro morenico frontale del Garda dal Chiese all'Adige.* Memorie della Società Italiana di Scienze Naturali, 16 (1). Milan.
VEYRET, P., G. VEYRET
1967   *Au coeur de l'Europe les Alpes.* Paris: Flammarion.
WALKER, D. S.
1967   *A geography of Italy* (second edition). London: Methuen and Co.
WATANABE, HITOSHI
1969   "Neanderthalers *vs.* H. Sapiens. Behavioral adaptability to arctic winter," in *Proceedings of the VIIIth International Congress of Anthropological and Ethnological Sciences. 1968. Tokyo and Kyoto*, volume 1. Edited by Endo et al., 280–283. Tokyo.
WENDORF, FRED, JOHN P. MILLER
1959   Artifacts from high mountain sites in the Sangre de Cristo Range, New Mexico. *El Palacio* 66:37–52.
ZORZI, F.
1959   Un'amigdala acheuleana scoperta a Lughezzano di Valpantena nel quadro del Paleolitico inferiore e medio veronese. *Memorie del Museo Civico di Storia Naturale di Verona* 7:297–334.
1960   Monti Lessini (Verona). *Rivista di Scienze Preistoriche* 15:223–224.

Mesolithic Coastal Economies in the Levant and North Africa

EARL C. SAXON

The eastern and southern Mediterranean coasts offer a wide range of ecological zones within a short distance of the sea itself. It is thus a suitable area for the investigation of the relationships between site location preferences and the selection of species for economic exploitation. The Kebaran culture in Palestine and the Iberomaurusian culture in Algeria may be compared in order to see which economic aspects of the cultures show common behavioral responses to similar environmental circumstances — despite cultural separation and reliance on different animal species. Thus one may test the hypothesis that responses to ecological stress (which are successful in the long term) must reflect natural adaptations of relationships between species.

If the research is oriented towards "origins," evidence of technical capacity for innovation may overshadow the emphasis of the economy under study on stable, adaptive behavior. The Mesolithic economies on which the search for the origins of agriculture has been concentrated may not have found it desirable to exploit the cereal cultivation technology which they possessed. However, Higgs (1972) has shown that the practice of herding is much more ancient than its application to ovicaprines would suggest. The evidence from the Levant and the Maghreb supports the hypothesis that a close man–animal interdependence existed as long ago as the Upper Paleolithic, while a close man–plant interdependence may be no older than the early Chalcolithic.

Herd animals can be successfully exploited by hunter–gatherers only at a very low kill level in an economy relying chiefly on other food sources; and there is no evidence of major exploitation of any resource other than herd animals by the Kebaran and Iberomaurusian people. It is unlikely that they could have survived long without carefully and consciously organizing their culture's impact on the indigenous fauna.

The choice among indigenous species varies from site to site and period to period, and it is likely that the environmental and human behavioral conditions affecting any single species were not the same in all times and places. Human behavior in the past may be viewed in terms of those economic activities which have proved stable. Then such variations are assumed to reflect adaptive advantages. Unfortunately, the introduction of foreign species is a phenomenon difficult to assess, because the economy of the period immediately preceding the introduction of the sheep–wheat economy is unknown (Perrot 1966).

If there were no hunter–gatherers fleeing before the relentless on-slaught of the agriculturalists, what became of the people responsible for the abundant epipaleolithic material? Why did the gazelle–fallow deer economy of the Kebaran and Natufian cultures collapse? What became of the barbary sheet–hartebeest system of the Iberomaurusian in eastern Algeria? Their successors, the Pre-Pottery Neolithic (PPN) and Capsian, intensified the exploitation of goats and land snails respectively, but neither of these became the chief resource base of their economy. In each case, one of the previously exploited species predominates as it never had before (Legge 1972; Balout 1955). Speculation on the explanation of these phenomena may be guided by recently refined research methods.

Site catchment analysis (Vita-Finzi and Higgs 1970) provides a basis for understanding the possible resource exploitation patterns. But it does not readily distinguish which of the possibilities are the most likely to have been used unless population pressure is assumed to necessitate the maximum sustainable productivity. Using faunal analysis, the research may clarify what constituted the economic staples, but not how these were utilized. Since any actual prehistoric economy would have to exploit the indicated staples within the framework indicated by site catchment analysis, the number of possibilities is limited. If the relative chronology of the sites is poorly understood, or if the environment is homogeneous for all sites, it will be difficult to test hypotheses regarding the economic interrelationships between sites. A short list of economic alternatives may be as far as the prehistorian can go.

Stratified sites can provide the basis for a relative chronology, but in an area undergoing ecological changes a level may be most similar to other sites in similar ecological circumstances with which it is not necessarily contemporary.

The Kebaran and Iberomaurusian faunal picture reflects part of the variety of resources available to site occupants. The species include both grassland and woodland ungulates. Marsh dwellers, riverine fauna, and marine species are present only in small numbers. By drawing on the resources of woodland and grassland, the economy could be insulated from minor fluctuations in the productivity of either area.

Specialization would have increased yield and stability in an ecologically homogeneous area, but in an ecologically varied catchment, specialization has a destabilizing effect. If the productivity of the catchment ever declined, specialization would be fatal in the subsequent stress situation. Thus in the varied catchments of the Mediterranean basin, the most stable economies are those exploiting a combination of species from different ecological zones. The increasing specialization on gazelle and deer at the expense of *Bos* in Palestine may have had no immediate adverse repercussions because both woodland and grassland herds were still involved in the economy, but any subsequent limitation on the availability of deer or gazelle would seriously weaken the economic flexibility. Thus the Natufian villages prospered with an economy largely based on gazelle alone, but may have insufficiently developed alternatives like the available grain resources.

The long-term consequence was that the deer–gazelle system eventually failed completely, and there is no archeological evidence of subsequent exploitation of the area before the arrival of sheepherders. Something failed in the economic system, which had become increasingly dependent on fewer and fewer species, but archeological evidence gives no direct indication of what it was. In order to test whether that factor is specific to the Kebaran–Natufian–PPN sequence, we can compare its fate with that of the Iberomaurusian along the east Algerian littoral.

The coast of eastern Algeria consists of mountainous regions separated from one another by marshy plains at the mouth of each major river. Recent dunes overlie much of the shoreline. Some sites are known from these dunes (Brahimi 1970), but most are in the foothills of the mountains which form the southern boundary of the coastal plains. Small sites overlook the ends of each narrow valley leading inland and others are found in the mountains wherever a ravine widens sufficiently for the formation of an upland meadow. Many of the sites include Aterian elements in their assemblages (Morel 1953), confirming that site preferences were consistent from the Upper Paleolithic through the epipaleolithic in Algeria as well as Palestine.

The species exploited from the Iberomaurusian sites is overwhelmingly the barbary sheep (*Ammotragus lervia*). *Alcelaphus*, *Bos primigenius*, *Megaceroides algericus*, *Connochaetes*, and *Hippotragus* complete the faunal assemblage in the Beni Segoual caves (Arambourg 1935). The degree of specialization cannot be quantified accurately until further excavations are conducted in Algeria, but there are definitely more *Ammotragus* remains in the collections from Tamar Hat Cave and Afalou bou Rhummel than all the other species together. As at the Kebaran sites, the fauna reflects the accessibility of both woodland and grassland ungulates, but with a degree of specialization more typical of the Natufian. It is reasonable to expect less specialization in the earliest Iberomaurusian, but it is not as yet possible to get further than noting the presence of gazelle in the lower levels of Tamar Hat and its virtual absence from the upper levels. After a brief phase when mollusca were added to the diet in substantial quantities, the Algerian littoral seems to have been abandoned and the archeological record remains blank virtually until historical times.

The shift towards intensive exploitation of one species might be attributed to cultural preference, economic innovation to increase productivity, and the extinction of alternative species. The success of the shift in evolutionary terms is, of course, independent of whether its cause was a matter of taste, inventiveness, or necessity. The slow, simultaneous intensification of gazelle and ammotragus exploitation at opposite ends of the Mediterranean Sea in similar ecological conditions favors the explanation that such a shift was necessitated by similar changes in the catchments of both areas, reflecting the impact on local geography of the Post-Pleistocene rise in sea levels. The ecological change might have led to overexploitation of the traditional species, reducing their numbers below a level where their exploitation was economically feasible, but not leading to complete extinction. The way was thus prepared for the introduction of new herd animals.

While the emphasis on gazelle may have been a contributory factor to the success of the semipermanent Natufian villages in Palestine and the *Ammotragus* and mollusca specialization a forerunner of the primarily hartebeest economy of the Capsian escargotières, neither of the former cultures was as long lived as their more broadly based predecessors. Within the scope of current research it is thus possible to glimpse why the prepottery Neolithic successors of the Natufians and the Neolithic of the Capsian tradition appear to represent even less successful adaptations, but impossible to be sure until the role of cereal cultivation is better known for these cultures. At any rate, no stable economy well fitted to the available resources seems to have been found before the introduction of the typical Mediterranean diet based on sheep, wheat, olives, and wine.

REFERENCES

ARAMBOURG, C.
1935   Les Grottes Paléolithiques des Beni Segoual (Algérie). *Archives de l'Institut de Paléontologie Humaine*, Paris, Mém. 13.
BALOUT, L.
1955   *Préhistoire de l'Afrique du Nord*. Paris: Arts et Métiers Graphiques.
BRAHIMI, C.
1970   l'Ibéromaurusien littoral de la région d'Alger. *Memoirs du Centre des Recherches Anthropologiques, Préhistoriques et Ethnographiques*, Alger, Mém. 13.

HIGGS, E. S., *editor*
  1972   *Papers in economic prehistory.* Cambridge: Cambridge University
         Press.
LEGGE, A. J.
  1972   "Prehistoric exploitation of the Gazelle in Palestine," in *Papers in
         economic prehistory.* Edited by E. S. Higgs, 119–124. Cambridge:
         Cambridge University Press.
MOREL, J.
  1953   L'Outillage lithique de la station du Kef-Oum-Touiza, dans l'est Con-
         stantinois. *Libyca* 1:157–181.
PERROT, J.
  1966   La troisième campagne de fouilles à Munhatta (1964). *Syria* 43:49–63.
VITA-FINZI, C., E. S. HIGGS
  1970   Prehistoric economy in the Mount Carmel area of Palestine: site catch-
         ment analysis. *Proceedings of the Prehistoric Society* 36:1–37.

Late Cenozoic Climate, Mammalian Evolutionary Patterns and Middle Pleistocene Human Adaptation in Eastern Asia

KUBET LUCHTERHAND

Interpretation of the evolutionary position, phylogenetic affinities, and the adaptive pattern of Middle Pleistocene man in East Asia has been a lively topic of discussion in anthropology since the first East Asian *Homo erectus* specimens were recovered. In the pages that follow a considerable amount of recent information about the climate, fauna, and flora of mainland Asia and the North Pacific Basin is discussed as it relates to our understanding of the environment in which Middle Pleistocene man lived in Asia. In Section 1 the late Cenozoic climate of East Asia and the North Pacific Basin is discussed and summarized, and in Section 2 the major features of mammalian evolution in the late Cenozoic of Asia are analyzed and interpreted. In both of these sections it has been necessary to extend the time focus of the study back into the Tertiary in order to present a meaningful picture of macroevolutionary trends in the vegetation and fauna of the region. In Section 3, however, the focus of study is restricted to the Middle Pleistocene hominid occupation sites.

LATE CENOZOIC CLIMATE IN EAST ASIA AND THE NORTH PACIFIC BASIN

The Pleistocene climate and stratigraphy of the Pacific Basin and the Asian continent are not as well known as many other areas of the world, but there has been a substantial amount of recent work in the area which makes it possible to present a fairly comprehensive set of conclusions. Three main bodies of evidence relate to the reconstruction of late Cenozoic climate and environment in Asia.

1.   Climatic data from deep-sea cores pertaining to ocean surface temp-

eratures, correlation with continental glaciations, and circulation within and between the world's ocean basins during the late Cenozoic.

2. Data derived from the study of terrestrial floral and vegetational patterns during the late Cenozoic relating to general features of the formation of the modern climatic zones and regional floral and vegetational patterns.

3. Geological and geomorphological data which provide direct indications of geomorphological processes and events and, therefore, provide data on specific features of the environments in which they occurred.

Each of these topics is reviewed in the following pages and the relevant conclusions drawn. But considerable selectivity has been exercised in writing this section, and the interested reader is referred to the references cited for entrance to the primary literature on these subjects.

Evidence from Deep-Sea Cores

Deep-sea core studies can tell us two different kinds of things about the Pleistocene climate of the ocean basins. (1) They can provide evidence of whether or not Pleistocene climatic fluctuations are synchronous and parallel in the various ocean basins, and (2) they can provide evidence of the actual nature of both specific climatic regimes and the overall climatic cycle.

Many investigators believe that the climatic history of the Pacific Basin is closely parallel to that of the Atlantic and cite general correspondences between the foraminiferal stratigraphy of deep-sea cores as the main body of evidence in support of their position (see Morin, Theyer, and Vincent 1970; Blackman and Somayajulu 1966). It seems likely that their main conclusions are correct since they have shown that the major items of evidence contradicting the hypothesis of synchroneity are due to studies where an inadequate range of foraminiferal species were considered. Ericson and Wollin (1970) had argued that there is direct opposition between climatic cycles in Pacific and Atlantic cores. They reiterated this argument in another article (Wollin, Ericson, and Ewing 1971), but Morin, Theyer, and Vincent (1970) point out that their conclusions are based on a single planktonic form, the *Globorotalia menardii* complex, and that this faunal group is a very small part of the total planktonic fauna in the areas where their cores were taken. This, plus the fact that the area from which their cores were taken is well outside the typical habitat of the *Globorotalia menardii* complex (which has its main distribution in the tropical Atlantic), makes variations of this group very uncertain evidence upon which to base general conclusions about synchrony between Atlantic and Pacific Pleistocene climates. The point is that the discrepancies reported by Ericson and Wollin (1970) concerning *Globorotalia menardii* frequencies in Pacific and Atlantic cores can more easily be explained in terms of competition with other plankton forms in an area well outside the typical habitat of the group than by the construction of sweeping generalizations about the Pleistocene climate of the area.

However, the problem of climatic synchrony between the Atlantic and Pacific during the Pleistocene cannot be resolved from the sort of "paleotemperature" analysis which Emiliani (1966a) has done for the Caribbean and Atlantic. Instead, it must depend upon stratigraphic correlations which do not have absolute temperature scales built into them; this is so because of the conclusion originally drawn by N. Shackleton (1967) and recently reiterated by Dansgarrd and Tauber (1969) that the paleotemperature curves originally proposed by Emiliani really do not index ocean surface temperature so much as they reflect the amount of ocean water tied up in glaciers. The paleotemperature data from the Atlantic and Pacific are based on oxygen isotope temperature analysis and, according to their arguments, may only reflect the degree to which glacial meltwater with relatively low Oxygen–18 content is mixed into the surface waters of the ocean where the cores are taken and have little or nothing to do with water surface temperature. This also means that the magnitude of ocean surface water temperature variations is in doubt, and that the 6°–8°C flux suggested by Emiliani (1966a) may no longer be acceptable.

A further conclusion from these data ought to be pointed out here: If Shackleton and his supporters are correct, oxygen isotope compositions in planktonic stratigraphic studies might be expected to show synchrony between the world's ocean basins to exactly the extent that world ocean currents resulted in thorough mixing of the surface waters of the world's oceans with meltwater derived from wasting glacial sheets. Since the work cited above seems to show such synchrony, Shackleton's interpretation indicates that surface current flow between the oceans proceeded at a rate rapid enough to produce it.

An interesting result concerning the nature of Pleistocene glaciations in general emerges from the appreciation of the use of the oxygen isotope curves from deep-sea cores as "paleoglaciation" indexes; both Broecker and van Donk (1970) and Emiliani (1972) have emphasized that these curves indicate that periods during which glaciers were expanding must be considered "normal" in the sense that glacial growth apparently took place during about 90 percent of the time since continental glaciers first appeared. While these two papers interpret the specific nature of the climatic patterns indicated by the oxygen isotope data in somewhat different ways, they agree that the warm periods between phases of glacial expansion were relatively brief and strongly marked. Broecker and von Donk (1970) also develop a model of glacial expansion according to which continental glaciers grew for periods of approximately 100,000 years and then wasted quite rapidly during times when seasonal contrasts were at a maximum. Even if one rejects Broecker's and von Donk's posited causal relationships between glacial growth and cycles of solar insolation due to periodicities in the wobble of the earth on its rotational axis and in the gradual deflection of the earth's rotational orbit around the sun, the implications of the oxygen isotope curves for indicating the general pattern of Pleistocene glacial growth cycles remain.

Moreover, there is evidence that intervals of carbonate deposition in the equatorial Pacific show close correspondences to the chronology of continental glacial growth. Hays et al. (1969) used magnetic reversal sequences to establish correlations between rates of carbonate deposition in cores from the equatorial Pacific and the paleotemperature curves of both Emiliani (1966b) and Ericson and Wollin (1968) which can be interpreted as indicating a correlation between glacial growth and total carbonate deposition cycles there. However, Flint (1971:722–723) points out an interesting contrast between carbonate productivity in the Atlantic and Pacific Basins. He believes that the temperature of surface waters is the dominant controlling factor of carbonate production in the Atlantic, with the result that high carbonate production is correlated there with "interglacial" or warm surface water phases. In the Pacific, on the other hand, he points out that the evidence favors the result presented by Hays et cd. (1969) cited earlier: In the Pacific carbonate production seems to correlate with periods of cold surface temperatures and, therefore, with periods of glacial growth. Flint (1971) suggests this is due to the presence of proper nutrients as the controlling factor in carbonate production and is influenced by the influx of nutrient-rich but cool currents from Antarctic waters into the Pacific.

It seems then, that until the conditions affecting carbonate production and deposition are clarified in local sequences, it is not possible to attach any temperature analysis to the stratigraphic columns. Even though surface water temperatures have considerable influence on carbonate production in the upper levels of ocean water, actual production also depends upon local abundance of nutrients and, perhaps, on other as yet unidentified factors affecting foraminiferal populations. Moreover, the deposition of the carbonate material which is produced depends upon other factors including the following: (1) the amount of carbonate already dissolved in the water through which it must pass on its way to the ocean floor; (2) ocean currents which might transport it over considerable distances thus both moving it away from the environment affecting production and increasing the probability that it will go back into solution; and (3) the total depth of the column of water through which it must pass before deposition.

With these reservations in mind, the conclusions which may currently be drawn from the marine sediments of the Pacific Basin are as follows:

1. General synchrony of foraminiferal stratigraphy, though not of overall carbonate production, seems to be established between Pacific cores and those from the Atlantic and Caribbean. This indicates both that whatever the causes of the stratigraphic variations they seem to be parallel in the two areas, and that ocean surface currents apparently operated efficiently enough between the two basins to account for that part of the parallel stratigraphy due to the effects of glacial meltwater being returned to (primarily) the Atlantic Basin.

2. Carbonate deposition cycles in the Pacific correlate, in general, with the glacial-interglacial cycle documented for northern continents, but they are out of phase with those in the Atlantic. This indicates a general causal framework which affected such cycles linked to the mechanisms which produced continental glaciation on both sides of the North Atlantic Basin. However, these mechanisms are not identical with those affecting overall carbonate production in the Atlantic.

3. Periods of glacial expansion are probably normal in the sense that they appear to account for as much as 90 percent of the time during which glacial growth has been a periodic feature of continental areas during the Pleistocene. This result is of considerable interest in analyzing late Cenozoic floral and faunal evolution, as it is in the periods of relatively warm climate, or interglacials, during which many of the dramatic compositional changes take place in continental biosystems of the Pleistocene (Leopold 1967; West 1968).

Evidence from Late Cenozoic Vegetations and Floras

The plant communities which lived on the continents of the Northern Hemisphere during the late Cenozoic have a comparatively well-documented history which allows some insight into the development of the present zonation and phytogeographical associations of East Asia. Leopold (1969a:379–387) has provided a summary of some of the general features of the evolutionary history of late Cenozoic floras which includes the following points:

1. Late Tertiary floras are generally less rich in species and other taxa than earlier assemblages. This tendency is seen in both pollen and megafossil assemblages and is more pronounced in higher latitudes than in tropical and subtropical areas.

2. Late Tertiary floras contain a higher proportion of living forms, especially at the generic level of classification, than do earlier ones. While

extinct genera of angiosperms are common in European early Eocene floras (they comprise more than half the forms recorded there), this percentage drops to about 40 percent in the late Eocene and to about 15 percent by the Oligocene. There are many extinct herbaceous forms from Miocene and Pliocene deposits, but that is to be expected in view of the adaptive radiation which took place in herbaceous families in the Neogene.

3. Some families of herbaceous plants first appear in the fossil record in Miocene times and others which have earlier records are first abundant in Neogene deposits. The earliest occurrence of fossil Compositae is taken as an indicator of late Oligocene or early Miocene time worldwide, and such families as Gramineae and Chenopodiaceae also conform to this pattern.

4. A comparatively large number of plant genera identified from late Tertiary fossil floras now live near the localities where they occur as fossils. This is in marked contrast to earlier Tertiary floras and is a feature of temperate and high latitude floras wherever we have fossil records.

5. Late Tertiary floras tend to be much more provincial in character than do earlier ones; this makes the affinities of Neogene fossil floras with their modern counterparts even more striking.

In view of these general trends, it is especially important to distinguish between the composition of the flora and the nature of the vegetation communities which those floras form. This can be done upon a variety of different geographic scales to produce very different levels of inferences about the climate and other environmental factors involved. The distinction between flora and vegetation is crucial; studies of plant community structure and development allow phylogenies to be fitted into an overview of the environment to which each individual species is adapted, but the tremendous number of different ways that a given vegetational type can be comprised floristically suggests that it is the analysis of vegetational patterns rather than floral histories which will yield the best results in the analysis of past climates.

This situation is analogous to the way we study higher taxonomic groupings of mammals; we focus on a given level of organization in a geological community because it provides implications about the environment and ecological organization of the community at a specific level of generalization. Given the incompleteness of the fossil record with respect both to geographical range of a given species or higher taxonomic group and to the anatomy and physiology of any particular organism, it is clear that we must be primarily concerned with the development and distribution of gross vegetational types. We will focus on other levels of generalization in plant evolution only as the data is available and as they relate to understanding the history of vegetation patterns and the climatic history we hope to infer from them.

Since the floral and vegetational successions available from terrestrial deposits in the Far East are incomplete and geographically disparate, we turn to a very well documented floral sequence from the Cook Inlet region of Alaska for the information it provides on late Cenozoic vegetational change in the northern portions of the North Pacific Basin. Described by Wolfe, Hopkins, and Leopold (1966), this vegetational succession spans a considerable portion of the late Cenozoic. The vegetational history has been summarized by Wolfe and Leopold (1967:205) as follows:

The mixed mesophytic forest of the early and middle Miocene was continuous from Japan through Alaska and into conterminous [*sic*] northwestern United States.
    At high altitudes, mixed conifer-broadleaved-deciduous forests were present.
    In the late Miocene, a severe decline in summer temperatures in Alaska resulted in the disjunction of the Mixed Mesophytic Forest.
    In Alaska and adjacent Siberia, the late Miocene vegetation was a rich Boreal Forest, i.e., conifer-dominated, with a few hardwood tree species.
    The rich Boreal Forest was gradually depauperated in the north during the Pliocene, but survives today in regions such as the Amur River Valley and coastal Oregon and Washington.
    By the early Pleistocene, the forests around the North Pacific basins were similar to the extant forests of the same region. A few exotic plants persisted locally, but mixed forest-tundra was present in Beringia.
    The Boreal Forest was effectively partitioned during the late Miocene — probably by edaphic factors and by the opening of Bering Strait — and during the Pliocene by both edaphic and climatic factors.

The picture provided is consistent with a model of general climatic deterioration during the late Cenozoic, but also suggests that the decline may have been marked by oscillations. This view is developed and supported by Wolfe and Hopkins (1967) from an analysis of the climatic implications of the proportion of smooth-margined leaves in fossil floras and defended by Wolfe (1971) from criticisms raised against it, most notably by Axelrod and Bailey (1969). It seems that Wolfe and Hopkins are largely correct in their analysis and that the Neogene climatic deterioration was somewhat less uniform and unidirectional than is often assumed. However, the single most important result from these analyses is that the flora of the northern margins of the Pacific Basin was essentially modern by the end of the Pliocene or, at the latest, by the beginning of the Pleistocene. The climate of the Pacific Northwest (of North America) is indicated as warm temperate to subtropical during the Miocene and temperate in the Pliocene. Very little modification of either floral inventory or vegetational type has taken place in that area since.
    Late Cenozoic floral changes in Japan have been summarized by Tanai (1961) from macroplant assemblages; several studies of pollen sequences from Japanese Tertiary deposits are also available (Sato 1960, 1963;

Tokunaga 1964) and generally support his conclusions. Tanai (1961:243–244) summarizes the floral transitions in the late Tertiary of Japan as characterized by the following:

1. A generally temperate climate throughout the late Tertiary;
2. A gradual decline of temperature since late Miocene times;
3. A gradual disappearance of warm exotic elements from the flora;
4. A lack of revolutionary changes in generic associations in the flora;
5. An evolutionary increase in broad-leaved temperate tree species in late Miocene times; and
6. A nearly complete modernization of the flora by the end of the Pliocene.

It is of some interest that floras on islands in the South Pacific tended to contain many more genera of Micronesian plants during the Miocene than is now the case. Leopold (1969a:409) stresses that Miocene pollen floras from Fiji, Bikini, Palau, and Guam show this pattern, and she has also analyzed fossil pollen from Eniwetok Atoll in the Marshall Islands and found it consistent with this generalization (Leopold 1969b). From the sparse evidence available it is not certain whether this depauperization of the island floras indicates a general decline of temperature or general climatic deterioration, or whether it might be a result of past climatic fluctuations which resulted in local extermination of various plant forms which have not been able to recolonize the islands.

The late Cenozoic floras of New Zealand provide an interesting body of data related to this issue. Couper (1960) has presented evidence for a Miocene pollen flora somewhat more warm-loving than the present one. In New Zealand, as in mainland floras of the Pacific Basin, the composition of the flora was essentially modern by the end of the Pliocene. Even though Couper apparently subscribes to a pattern of uniform, global-scale, climatic fluctuations during the continental glaciations of the Pleistocene, he stresses that "with few exceptions, floras of this [Pleistocene] age [in New Zealand] contain no definite extinct species" (1960:32). In view of the relatively small geographic area of New Zealand and of its latitudinal position between 35° and 45° South, this suggests that the latitudinal shifts in biozones during the Pleistocene can not have been nearly so marked in the South Pacific as they were in Western Eurasia where even late Pleistocene floral assemblages contain genera of plants not now native to the area.

Similarly, Leopold (1969a:405–409) reports that the Miocene and Pliocene floras of the Rocky Mountains of the North American West show a gradual and progressive compositional change in the direction of the modern plant assemblages. Moreover, the late Pliocene–early Pleistocene floras of this area are essentially modern with the occasional exception of a genus that finally goes out locally at about that time, and usually such plants are still found in more eastern areas of North America.

Late Cenozoic pollen studies and macrobotanical analyses are quite rare in the eastern parts of the United States. Leopold (1969a:405–409) suggests that the general pattern for the region is similar to that for other parts of North America. Several middle and late Miocene deposits in Maryland which Leopold surveyed contain floras in which most of the plants are still growing locally, and those which are not found locally are represented in ranges further south in the United States or in Central America. We might note, however, that Watts (1969, 1970, 1971) has recently provided a series of studies of the vegetational flux between glacial and interglacial conditions in southeastern United States which is consistent with the generalization of little floral modification for the eastern part of North America as a whole but which nonetheless indicates a shift in vegetational patterns by at least 1,100 kilometers in some instances. We will return to this data and its implications in the next section.

It is only in Western Eurasia that substantial modification of late Cenozoic floral assemblages continued actively through the Pleistocene, though, of course, there is ongoing vegetational change in all middle and high latitude continental areas during Pleistocene times. There is a large literature on floral change in the European Pleistocene, and we can cite West (1968:110–134, 292–335), and van der Hammen, Wijmstra, and Zagwijn (1971) as providing the best available summaries of this subject. The general picture is one of progressive depauperization of the European flora proceeding at least until middle Pleistocene times, with occasional examples of local extermination of plant genera known also from even the latest parts of the Pleistocene.

The flora of Western Eurasia was modified during the Pleistocene in a way that virtually no other regional flora was. In view of the contrasts that the European flora shows with respect to that of Eastern Eurasia, it seems that the European Pleistocene sequence is somewhat inappropriate as a model for interpretation of the Far Eastern Pleistocene. Understanding of the Pleistocene climate of the Far East requires that the contrast between the vegetational histories of Eastern and Western Eurasia be examined in some detail, and it is to that problem which we now turn.

The Late Cenozoic Vegetation of Northern and Eastern Eurasia

There is reasonably wide agreement that the Pleistocene was a period of substantial shifts in vegetation zones throughout the Eurasian landmass. Flint (1971:424–441) cites a number of climatic sequences from all parts of the globe which show broad parallels between late Pleistocene climatic changes, and Frenzel (1968) has presented a summary statement of his work on the Pleistocene vegetation of Northern Eurasia which concludes that all across the northern part of the continent Pleistocene climatic shifts were reflected by repeated alternations between open steppe-like vegetation and various sorts of forest.

Speaking of Eastern Siberia, Flint (1971:667) summarizes environments outside glaciated regions as follows:

The vast region outside the rather limited glaciers spans as much as 25° of latitude. The belts of vegetation today, like those in North America, are latitudinal in a general way except where conspicuous highlands interrupt the pattern. At the last glacial maximum the pattern was similar, but was displaced toward the south. . . . Where it was not covered by glacier ice the Arctic Coast was flanked by a broad belt of tundra, which graded with long transition into cold steppe. The major highlands, where not covered with glaciers, were clothed in montane grass and herbs. Toward the southeast the steppe graded into woodland, with small areas of forest in Pacific Coastal areas receiving sufficient rainfall. Although generalized, the pattern, reconstructed from pollen data, presents a consistent and reasonable picture. It differs from the corresponding map of Europe in that it reflects a much drier, more continental climate except along the Pacific Coast. . . .

The Siberian vegetation, thus dominantly treeless, supported mammal faunas in which grazers predominated. On the tundra were mammoth, musk-ox, reindeer, and lemming, while overlapping these and extending far southward through the steppe were woolly rhinoceros, elephants, horse, bison, antelopes, cattle, and various rodents.

Frenzel (1968) has reconstructed the full-glacial vegetation of this region as characterized by substantial shifts of the vegetation pattern southward in both northern and midlatitude sections of Asia. His reconstruction is accepted by Flint (1971) and is consistent in general with that of Gitterman *et al.* (1968) reproduced in Flint (1971:670).

It is clear that the exact locations of vegetational boundaries within East Asia during the Pleistocene cannot be now determined. Frenzel (1968:642–643) labels his reconstruction of this region as "hypothetical evergreen broadleaf trees" and "chiefly hypothetical mixed forest dominated by conifers," and until a great many more detailed pollen and macroplant studies on Pleistocene sites in China are available, the reconstruction will remain that way. However, there is evidence from both Taiwan and Japan that a displacement of the magnitude indicated by Frenzel probably occurred. Tsukada (1966, 1967a, 1967b) has published a series of pollen diagrams and interpretations indicating that vegetation zones shifted in the mountains of both Japan and Taiwan in much the same way that vegetation zones are known to have shifted elsewhere in the world, though the pollen records in Japan so far do not go back beyond 10,000 B.P. and, therefore, do not fully confirm the vegetation shifts posited for full-glacial conditions in the Far East.

Flint (1971:432–433) has presented Tsukada's data from Taiwan in graphic form along with comparable pollen climate reconstructions from all over the world. His conclusion seems justified that East Asia experienced shifts of vegetational zones comparable to those elsewhere in the world, and, that with the exception of showing some unexplained anomalous inverse relations in the climatic curves within the last continental glaciation, it apparently experienced them simultaneously.

This result is especially interesting here in that one of the pollen profiles comes from the Olympic Peninsula of Washington State (Heusser 1964). This area now supports a subtropical rain forest community which was transformed to tundra and park-tundra at the height of the Wisconsin glaciation of North America, but which suffered none of the depauperization of its flora during the Pleistocene typical of European localities. A second area of North America from which similar data is forthcoming is that of the southeastern United States. Watts (1969, 1970, 1971) has produced a number of studies on the glacial vegetation of this region and the nature of the glacial-interglacial vegetational flux. Watts (1970) notes that the full-glacial vegetation of Georgia indicates a displacement of modern vegetation zones by some 1,100 kilometers, if the presence of a pine-spruce dominant forest flora there at the height of the Wisconsin glaciation is to be explained. He also comments that the aquatic plant assemblage of the area in full-Wisconsin time shows marked similarities and affinities with the corresponding group of plants now growing in northern New England.

What is truly remarkable about these two sequences, however, is that both indicate that considerable climatic flux in midlatitude climatic zones need not produce the sort of disruption in the ecological structure of an area that is seen in the Pleistocene record of Europe. This is true so long as the specific factors which apparently produced the major disruptions in Europe are not also present elsewhere. Those factors would appear to be the following: (1) limitations on the total north-south movement of vegetation zones possible in an area; and (2) absence of refuge zones of size sufficient to maintain a large enough area of a given vegetational type to preserve the internal structure of the plant community and enough of the animal forms living there to preserve the overall ecological structure.

The relative compositional stability of the floras of North America and East Asia in the face of the sort of climatic fluctuation and the resultant shifts in vegetation zones during the Pleistocene suggests that whatever the nature of those fluctuations and shifts, they apparently proceeded at rates and in ways that allowed the original structure of the plant communities to be preserved. This inference is a major result in the argument being presented here and will be further developed later.

Evidence from Continental Geology and Geomorphology

The geological and geomorphological evidence for Pleistocene climate in the Far East consists primarily of glacial and periglacial features which help to indicate past climates by their latitudinal and altitudinal positions. Figure 1 indicates the areas known to have been glaciated during the last continental glaciation, and from it we can see that comparatively little of the land area of East Asia was covered by ice sheets during the Pleis-

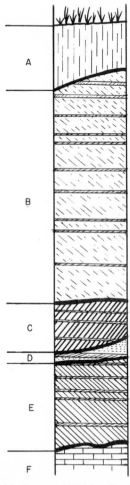

Figure 1.   Schematic section of the loess stratigraphy of northern China (redrawn after Kes 1959). The total height of the column is some 220 meters. A — Yellow (Malan) Loess, Upper Pleistocene; B — Upper Red Loess with buried paleosols, Middle Pleistocene; C — Lower Red Loess with buried paleosols, Middle Pleistocene; D — Pink Clay with buried paleosols, Villafranchian; E — Red Clay with buried paleosols, Villafranchian or Upper Pliocene; F — Mesozoic bedrock

tocene. It might be noted that while there is general agreement between the various plottings of local glaciation in Northern Eurasia (for example, compare Frenzel 1968; Flint 1971:662) there are also numerous areas of difference of opinion concerning exactly how much of the highlands of Eastern Siberia or of the western fringes of the Tibetan Plateau and Himalayan massif or of other areas any particular author will show as glaciated. There are also substantial differences concerning the total extent of glaciated area during the different major glacial stages, as well as variations of interpretation within those differences. There is, however, general agreement that the Far East, in general, and China, Japan, and Southeast Asia, in particular, were not subject to glaciation during the Pleistocene except for a relatively few areas where local conditions produced small valley glaciers. Kozarski (1963) has summarized the available data on Pleistocene glaciations of all ages in China and found evidence only for very local occurrences of valley glaciers. Similarly, Jen (1960) is only able to cite data for small and local occurrences of Pleistocene ice fields in Yunnan: Kobayashi (1965:377–380) also cites only small local occurrences of cirques in the Japanese Alps as evidence of Pleistocene glaciation in Japan.

The existence of such local evidence indicates, however, that there must have been some combination of increased snowfall and decreased wastage in those areas to produce ice sheets where there are none now. This indication is fully consistent with the sort of vegetational shift and inferred climatic cooling discussed earlier.

Kobayashi (1965) discusses a number of river terrace formations in Japan, but he concludes that they do not correspond to a climatic cycle in any direct way. His suggestion is that tectonic activity in the Japanese islands during the Pleistocene effected drainage and downcutting patterns so frequently and strongly that whatever climatic cycle might be reflected there is effectively masked. Elsewhere in Asia, for example, in the Irrawaddy River Valley of Burma and in various river valleys of Malaysia there are terrace systems which may relate to cycles of sea-level movement. However, the climatic factors affecting terrace formation are very difficult to interpret because of the intricate set of local factors which determine the way in which large-scale climatic or meteorological patterns will be expressed in any particular erosional situation (see Butzer 1971:178–185). At the present state of our knowledge of the nature of the sediments and associated landforms of terrace systems in Asia, interpretation of the climatic regimes associated with them is impossible.

There is, however, one major type of landform and sediment in northern China which is indicative of a particular climatic regime and which is used to draw inferences about the Pleistocene climate of East Asia; all across the northern margin of what is now China there are tremendously thick deposits of loess over the pre-Pleistocene land surface. These deposits were the subject of an intensive investigation carried out by Russian and Chinese scientists in the late 1950's, and the results of that investigation are reported in the volume edited by Popov (1959).

The stratigraphy of loess deposits in northern China is long and complex; Kes (1959) reports a typical stratigraphic column of some 200 meters which apparently spans late Pliocene to late Pleistocene deposits. The general stratigraphy includes an upper loess member called the Malan Loess unconformably over a long series of buried soils in loess thought to be of Middle and Upper Pleistocene age overlying a red loess formation (the Sanmen Formation) of the Lower Pleistocene. This general stratigraphic column is repeated monotonously over every area of the Chinese loess so far reported.

Climatic interpretation of the loess deposits is somewhat difficult, however, and even the precise origin of the deposits is in many cases unknown. Flint (1971:264–265) comments:

In northern Asia the extent of loess is still poorly known. Although . . . no close relation between former ice sheets and loess is apparent, this may result in part from inadequate information. In central Asia the mapped areas of loess coincide with tectonic basins in arid and semiarid terrain. There is little doubt that in such environments the source of loess consists of sediment washed down by streams from adjacent mountains. To what extent such sediment was pro-glacial is not known; some of it definitely was, but a substantial part of it may have been nonglacial alluvium. Still another likely source consists of relict sediments of pluvial lakes. The great area of loess in eastern China is thought to be mainly nonglacial, and indeed the aggregate area of glacier ice in the region was very small.

Therefore, the major conclusion one can draw about the presence of loess over much of northern China is that it reflects the presence of the sort of climatic fluctuation suggested by other lines of evidence. Kes (1959:89) shows a total of ten different buried soil formations in the middle level of the stratigraphic column; we may infer that both (1) the deposits involved could represent a timespan of the magnitude assigned them, and (2) the climatic fluctuations seem to have been cyclical and broadly similar to one another over that range of time. Thus, the loess deposits do not add a great deal of detail to our knowledge of the Pleistocene climate of East Asia, but they confirm the general picture already developed.

Summary and Conclusions

The material summarized above gives a reasonably comprehensive picture of the general features of the climate of East Asia during the Pleistocene. A number of specific points emerge.

1. The deep-sea core data indicate that the marine environment in oceans adjacent to East Asia was subject to fluctuations which correspond broadly in time with the fluctuations of the continental ice sheets on continental areas adjacent to the North Atlantic Basin, but which do not necessarily reflect identical and parallel changes in the world's ocean basins. Generally, climate and environmental factors in the North Pacific fluctuated during the Pleistocene more or less in synchrony with those elsewhere in the world. But the nature of the climatic changes involved seems to have been both locally variable and somewhat different from those elsewhere, especially those in the North Atlantic.

2. The flora of East Asia changed during the Tertiary in ways closely parallel to other Northern Hemisphere floras of the period, and, like the majority of Northern Hemisphere floras of the world, achieved its modern floristic composition by the end of the Pliocene or the very beginning of the Pleistocene. In this latter trait, the floras of East Asia and of most other regions in the Northern Hemisphere differ from the flora of Europe which continued to show marked compositional changes (mostly as progressive depauperization of the flora) during middle and even late Pleistocene times.

3. The nature and distribution of vegetation communities in East Asia, however, was much modified during Pleistocene times, as were the vegetation patterns of all the middle and high latitude areas of the earth. This pattern is more marked in higher latitude zones than in subtropical or tropical zones. Thus, the zonation of vegetation communities changed considerably in East Asia during late Cenozoic times, but it did so without great modification of the structure and composition of subtropical and tropical forest communities. This suggests that the nature of climatic fluctuations in East Asia was such that they proceeded with less disruption of ecological systems than was the case on the western side of Eurasia. This tendency toward ecological stability was probably greatest in tropical and subtropical regions and decreased with higher latitudes.

4. East Asia was never the scene of continental-scale glaciation during the Pleistocene, but the geomorphological evidence available for the region suggests a model of climatic change fully compatible with that indicated by the marine and floral data.

The picture that emerges, then, is one of a sub-continental area subject to a series of climatic fluctuations which may have been of considerable magnitude, but which were able to proceed without great structural modification of the botanical communities of the region, especially at lower latitudes. While the vegetation zones were shifted southward during periods of continental glaciation, the full-glacial pattern of climate in the area was such that none of the communities was either completely eliminated or forced into small relict areas. It seems that the north–south zonation of the region remained much as it had been before except for being somewhat compressed in the north–south direction. With this model of Pleistocene climatic change and environmental structure, we can now turn to the study of Pleistocene mammalian evolution in East Asia.

LATE CENOZOIC MAMMALIAN EVOLUTION IN EAST ASIA

Throughout this section the major emphasis is on the structure and organization of the mammalian communities rather than upon the evolutionary history of individual phylogenetic lines. As with the distinction made earlier between floral and vegetational patterns, the reason for focusing on community structure rather than on lower taxonomic units is that we are interested in the relation of middle Pleistocene hominids to the Pleistocene environment of East Asia, and analysis of community structure through time provides the most useful generalizations relevant to that interest. We will proceed (1) to describe the major zoogeographical divisions in the modern fauna of East Asia, (2) to outline the late Cenozoic chronology of the region with respect to the fossil faunas, (3) to consider the faunas of the major zoogeographic divisions in terms of the evolutionary patterns seen within the various orders of mammals found in them, and (4) to characterize the zoogeographic divisions of the region in terms of the structure and stability of the mammalian communities found within them.

The Modern Zoogeographic Divisions of East Asia

The major zoogeographical dichotomy in East Asia is that between the Oriental and Palearctic faunal regions. This division was originally described by Wallace (1876:181–250, 314–386) and is an accepted part of virtually all modern zoogeographical schemes (cf. Darlington 1957; Lattin 1967). The Oriental region is essentially the tropical part of Asia and extends from the Indus Valley through Indochina and into southern China. It also includes Sumatra, Java, Borneo (but not Celebes), and the adjacent smaller islands of the Sunda Shelf. The Palearctic includes all of Eurasia except that belonging to the Oriental region and a small area in the southwestern corner of the Arabian Peninsula (which is classified with sub-Saharan Africa), but also includes the area of extreme northwestern Africa called the Maghreb. In East Asia, then, the Oriental region comprises the southern portion while the northern is within the Palearctic. The discussion that follows is derived from Darlington (1957), and the reader is referred there for greater detail than can be given here.

In their nonmammalian vertebrate faunas, the Oriental and Ethiopian

(African) regions show very strong affinities, though there are some differences related to Oriental affinities with the Palearctic in which Africa is most similar to the New World tropics. One interesting contrast is that the Orient generally has a much greater diversity of snakes than of lizards, while the Ethiopian region has more different kinds of lizards than snakes. Oriental birds are strongly related to Ethiopian forms, though they also have many Palearctic and Australian affinities.

The nonmammalian vertebrate fauna of the Palearctic is much less diverse than that of either the Orient or Ethiopian regions. Darlington (1957:441) sees it as transitional between the Old World tropics and the Nearctic (North America) and points out that Palearctic reptiles tend to be northward extensions of either Ethiopian or Oriental forms and that Palearctic birds are related forms from either Old or New World tropics.

Oriental mammals include a large number of forms of very wide distribution (for example, felid, canid, and mustelid carnivores; sciurid rodents; and so on), many forms with strong Ethiopian affinities (for example, lorosid, cercopithecid, and pongid primates; scaly anteaters; proboscideans; hyaenid carnivores; and so on), a few forms with pan-Old World distributions (for example, viverrid carnivores and many bovid artiodactyls), and a few forms with Holarctic and Neotropical relationships (for example, ursid carnivores and flying squirrels). In addition, there are several important mammalian groups endemic to the Oriental region; they include tarsiiform primates, tupaiiform insectivores, echinocorine insectivores (hairy hedgehogs) and platycanthomyid rodents (spiny dormice). Paleoarctic mammals are partly related to North American forms (for example, moles, pikas, a beaver, and jumping mice), partly related to both North America and the Oriental region (for example, ursid carnivores and cervid artiodactyls), partly related to the Old World tropics (for example, hedgehogs, suid and bovid artiodactyls, and cercopithecid primates), partly endemic (for example, one subfamily of shrews and a few rodent groups), and partly forms with very wide distributions (for example, canid, felid, and mustelid carnivores; various bats; and many lagomorphs and rodents). The affinities to North America are especially strongly marked in the north where a truly Holarctic community prevails.

In his study of the mammals of China and Mongolia, Allen (1938–1940:9–19) distinguished seven areas which now have their own distinctive faunal assemblages: (1) the northern transcontinental forest area, (2) the Gobi grassland and desert area, (3) the northern China forest and grassland area, (4) the southern China forest area, (5) the western China highlands area, (6) the subtropical forest area in southern China, and (7) the Tibetan Plateau area. The first three of these areas fall within the Palearctic region, and the last four are in the Oriental region.

It is noteworthy that the division between the Oriental and Palearctic

regions also closely coincides with the line in East Asia between vegetation zones with open grassland communities as a substantial part of the
total area and regions without such communities. As we will see in the
following section, this vegetation difference is strongly reflected in the
relative emphasis on grazing versus browsing herbivore forms throughout
the late Cenozoic history of the East Asian mammalian faunas. The
modern vegetation zones of East Asia are shown in Map 1.

Late Cenozoic Stratigraphy and Chronology of East Asia

Late Cenozoic stratigraphic sequences in East Asia ordinarily do not span
more than the Pliocene–Pleistocene range of time. The Miocene is not
ordinarily present at the bottom of Pliocene sedimentary sequences, but

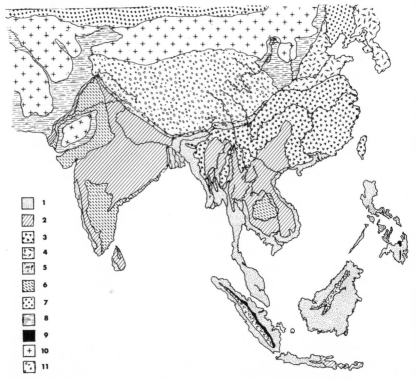

Map 1.   Partially schematic map of modern vegetation communities in East Asia. 1 —
tropical rain forest; 2 — monsoon tropophilous woodland and open jungle; 3 — sub tropical
and temperate rain forest; 4 — broad-leaved deciduous forest and meadow; 5 — montane-
boreal coniferous forest; 6 — open jungle and xerophilous scrub; 7 — temperate grassland;
8 — steppe; 9 — tropical savannah; 10 — Gobi and Central Asiatic deserts; 11 — high
plateau steppe. Distribution and vegetation names modified after Ginsberg *et al.*
(1969:141) and Wang (1961)

it tends to occur in remnants at the top of older peneplain surfaces on uplands flanking the Pliocene–Pleistocene sedimentation basins. There was apparently a combination of factors at about the time of the Miocene–Pliocene boundary that resulted in renewed erosion and the formation of a series of new lacustrine basins in which mammalian and other vertebrate fossils are preserved (de Chardin 1941:1–4). Figure 2 shows two diagramatic sections through fairly complete Late Cenozoic depositional sequences in the Nihowan and Yushe Basins of North China; from them the general stratigraphic relationships of the units discussed in the following pages can be seen.

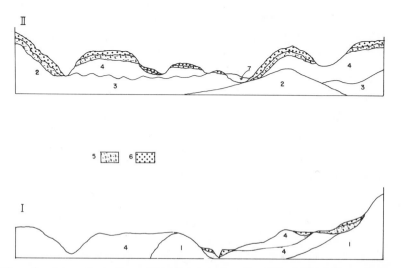

Figure 2. Schematic sections of late Cenozoic deposits of North China: I — Nihowan Basin, northwestern Hopei (12 km. long); II — Yushe Basin, southeastern Shansi (8 km. long). Redrawn after de Chardin (1941:3). 1 — quartzite and sandstone bedrock; 2 — Triassic sandstone; 3 — Early Pliocene; 4 — Villafranchian; 5 — Middle Pleistocene; 6 — Late Pleistocene (Loess); 7 — Holocene sand

In his summary discussion of the late Cenozoic stratigraphy of northern China, de Chardin (1941:1–54) distinguished the following units: (1) Early Pliocene (Pontian), (2) Villafranchian, (3) Early Pleistocene, (4) Late Pleistocene, and (5) Holocene. This sequence is discussed in the following pages, and the terminology used in this paper is related to it. It should be noted that most authors writing before the Second World War treated both the Pontian and the Villafranchian as parts of the Pliocene. Since the Villafranchian is now included within the Pleistocene, and in view of the recent tendency to return the Pontian to the Miocene, the terms "Pontian" and "Villafranchian" are used here rather than "early," "middle," and "late" divisions of the Pliocene. This has been done to avoid confusion.

The most recent assessment of the temporal correlations between the units discussed in the following pages and those of the late Cenozoic of Europe is that of Aigner (1972). The reader is referred there for the best available current summary on the subject and for a discussion of the East Asian fauna and flora as it is often used to establish relative chronology.

THE PLIOCENE.   This stratigraphical unit is identical to what de Chardin and other Asian workers have called "Early Pliocene" or "Pontian," and it represents a single prolonged period of sedimentation that gave rise to the lowest members of many sequences in northern China. In some basins, however, the sediments are divided into two or more subunits with the lower unit(s) typically comprised of gravels and "red clays" and the upper, of lacustrine sediments; this is the case, for example, in both the Paote and Yushe Basins (de Chardin 1941:2–4).

The fauna of the East Asian Pliocene is usually referred to as the *"Hipparion"* fauna and is characterized, according to de Chardin (1941:9) by a number of unique features including an impoverished assemblage of giraffes, the presence of several relatively specialized rhinocerotids (for example, *Sinotherium*), an abundant group of antelopes, a pig-like Aceratherid (*Chilotherium*), and a number of indigenous mustelid carnivores (for example, *Plesiogulo*, and so on). De Chardin believed that the north China fauna of the Pliocene was already a relatively distinct faunal province, and when compared to the *"Hipparion"* faunas of more southern areas, important compositional differences are seen. The faunas from the Siwaliks in West Pakistan and from the Lower Irrawaddy deposits of Burma are the only available assemblages from the Oriental region at this range of time, for Pliocene deposits from South China are so far unknown. As we will see later, one of the major differences between the two areas is in the development of a strong grazing component in the north which failed to appear in the southern faunas.

THE VILLAFRANCHIAN.   This unit is identical to that referred to by the same name in the work of de Chardin and other Asian scholars, except that it is here considered part of the Pleistocene. In the sedimentation basins of North China, the Villafranchian is marked by a unit of very coarse conglomerates lying (sometimes unconformably) above the Pliocene sediments and by a general rearrangement of the sedimentation basins; these features both indicate a period of relatively rapid uplift or tilting of the areas involved. Generally speaking, the period is represented by lacustrine or riverine facies, the best known of which are the Nihowan and Yushe lacustrine basin series and the Sanmen riverine deposits. There is strong evidence for at least two cycles of downcutting by the Huang Ho River in this range of time; de Chardin (1941:12) provides a schematic section of terraces in the Huang Ho gorges between Shensi and Shansi that is reproduced here as Figure 3.

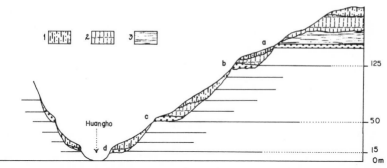

Figure 3. Schematic diagram of the Huang Ho terraces in the gorges between Shansi and Shensi, near Paote. Redrawn afer de Chardin (1941:12). 1 — Loess; 2 — Red Clays, undifferentiated Villafranchian and Middle Pleistocene; 3 — *Hipparion* Red Clays, Pliocene (Pontian); a — Early Pliocene surface; b — Villafranchian surface; c — Middle Pleistocene terrace; d — Late Pleistocene terrace, with rolled paleolithic implements

The Villafranchian fauna of East Asia is marked by the appearance of a number of definitely modern mammalian forms: *Bison, Equus,* and *Paracamelus* appear for the first time along with a variety of modern cervids, and modern forms of *Canis, Ursus, Lutra, Lynx,* several different rhinoceros forms, and several elephants occur for the first time. The best known sites from this range of time in East Asia are those of the Nihowan and Yushe Basins and Locality 18 at Choukoutien; only the Hoshantung Cave in Yunnan has fossils of this age in South China, and that site is probably quite late Villafranchian. Elsewhere in East Asia, the Tatrot and Pinjor levels of the Siwaliks, the Upper Irrawaddy fauna from Burma, and the Djetis levels of Sangiran in Java provide a record of the southern fauna for this time range. The only general difference between the northern and southern Villafranchian faunas is the continued absence of grazing forms in the south. There is also a greater tendency for faunal replacement or dramatic evolutionary change in the north than in the south. All, in all, the southern faunas tend to be quite conservative and to show very little alteration in the basic compositional pattern of the fauna, while the northern faunas are more variable.

MIDDLE PLEISTOCENE. This unit refers to the section of the Pleistocene stratigraphic column usually called "early Pleistocene" by authors writing before the Second World War; the change in terminology is caused by our assignment here of the preceding Villafranchian to the bottom of the Pleistocene. The Middle Pleistocene is apparently marked over much of East Central Asia by a general uplift of the continental shelf or by some modification of the climatic regime which resulted in the rejuvenation of many rivers of the area. It is also the time at which a large number of karstic fissures appeared, especially in South China (de Chardin 1937, 1941:18).

This block of time is sometimes called the "Age of Conglomerates," referring to many extensive gravel conglomerate formations of this age in the Gobi Desert and elsewhere in both Inner and Outer Mongolia, as well as to the "Boulder Conglomerate" formation of the Siwaliks (de Terra and Patterson 1939). The downcutting of many of the drainage systems of Asia at this time may be responsible for the exposure of the many karstic fissures at the ground surface as well as for the lowering of the water table to below their level. These solution cavities are often discovered filled with fossiliferous deposits of Middle Pleistocene age, and an abundant series of mammalian remains has been recovered from them. This is also the time during which the "red loess" deposits of the North Chinese loess sequence are thought to have been deposited. As we mentioned in the first section, the red loess deposits in question show a long series of successively buried paleosols indicating some sort of cyclic climatic change; the suggestion is that the climatic cycle reflected in the loess paleosol formations is coincident with and causally related to the climatic fluctuations that produced Middle Pleistocene glaciers elsewhere in the world.

The fauna of North China is even more strongly marked by outside forms, mostly of Palearctic affinities, during the Middle Pleistocene than was the case during the Villafranchian: *Hipparion*, *Postschizotherium*, and *Hypolagus* are no longer present and various modern carnivores, perissodactyls, and artiodactyls appear and develop. There is also a remarkable evolutionary radiation of rodents at this time in North China, and several lines produce "giant" forms. In South China, on the other hand, the fauna shows the development of a series of indigenous forms, but very little dramatic compositional change. The presence of a few distinctive forms in both faunas (for example, *Bubalus brevicornis*) provides faunal evidence for the temporal correlation of the two assemblages (de Chardin 1941:21–27). The sites referred to this period include most of the localities at Choukoutien and a considerable number of new sites and localities discovered and worked since 1949 in the greater Huang Ho drainage, as well as an equally large number of cave and fissure deposits from South China. Perhaps the most famous of the fissure deposits of South China is that of Wanhsien, Szechwan, the type-site for the *Stegodon–Ailuropoda* faunal complex typical of the Middle Pleistocene of South China and Southeast Asia.

LATE PLEISTOCENE.   This unit is defined stratigraphically in North China as the period during which the "yellow loess" deposits were deposited above the Middle Pleistocene red loess beds and is taken to end at the end of the last continental glacial period, approximately 10,000 B.P. The yellow loess is frequently a redeposited eolian sediment, though there is no question that at least part of it is of primary eolian origin. The deposit lies in a mantle over even the highest parts of the terrain in North China, and in such deposits the yellow loess often has considerable depth and remarkable homogeneity. These deposits sometimes lie conformably over the Middle Pleistocene red loess levels, but, especially in terrace and alluvial fan formations in Shensi and Kansu, they may also occur unconformably above them (de Chardin 1941:33).

Unfortunately, the yellow earth deposits of North China have no clear stratigraphic counterpart in South China, and stratigraphic distinctions between Middle and Late Pleistocene deposits in South China are difficult to determine. It is quite likely that some of the karstic fissure deposits of the South China *Stegodon–Ailuropoda* faunal complex are actually of this age, but the only way to date them is in terms of the relative stages of evolution of the mammals found within them.

Though the loess areas of North China are almost barren of vertebrate remains in Late Pleistocene times except for a few small lacustrine basin areas in Mongolia, the fossil record that is available indicates a somewhat impoverished but quite modern mammalian fauna: *Hyaena sinensis*, *Rhinoceros mercki*, *Equus sanmeniensis*, *Ochotonoides*, *Trogonotherium*, *Siphneus tingi*, and *Siphneus arvicolinus* have disappeared, and *Crocuta*, *Rhinoceros tichorhinus*, *Euryceros ordosianus*, *Spirocerus*, *Elephas namadicus*, and *Bubalus* persist in nearly modern form (de Chardin 1941:34). Moreover, this is the time when the wild ass (*Equus hemionus*), *Bison occidentalis*, *Alces*, and *Elephas primigenius* appear for the first time in this fauna. South of the Tsinling Shan, the *Stegodon–Ailuropoda* fauna may have been somewhat restricted in its range, but this can not be demonstrated conclusively. We can say, however, that the southern fauna shows little structural or compositional change from the Middle Pleistocene.

HOLOCENE. The Holocene, taken here to be the last 10,000 years of the geological record, is remarkable in China for its lack of stratigraphic definition. Partly because erosional processes are dominant over sedimentation in most of East Asia today, and partly because there was apparently no dramatic climatic boundary that showed up in the geomorphological record (other than variable local cessation of loess deposition), it is very difficult to establish a stratigraphic marker for the period. De Chardin (1941:38–39) cites a series of "black earth" deposits atop some Late Pleistocene loess profiles as Holocene deposits, but he also notes that there is no appreciable physiographic or faunal break between the yellow loess times and the beginning of the historic period in the sedimentation basins. As was the case with the Late Pleistocene, there is no marker horizon or faunal break to define the Holocene in South China either.

Late Cenozoic Mammalian Assemblages of East Asia

The sites which have yielded mammalian fossils from the late Cenozoic of East Asia are discussed briefly in the following pages according to their stratigraphic position and whether they belong to the northern or southern faunal groups. There is not enough space here to give complete faunal lists from each of these sites, but the references listed for each site contain such lists. The northern versus southern distinction is made here according to whether the site is now located in the Palearctic or Oriental faunal regions.

NORTHERN PLIOCENE SITES.   There are two major localities which have provided Pliocene mammal records in North China. One is the Yushe Basin in southeastern Shansi and the other is Locality 12 of Choukoutien near Peking, in Hopei. The Yushe Basin contains a rich series of faunas that span most of the Pliocene and overlap with the Villafranchian series of the Nihowan Basin (see page 383). First surveyed in 1932, a number of localities were excavated in 1934 and subsequent years by Licent and Trassaert. The fossils recovered in these excavations were to have been published in a series of seven fascicles of *Paleontologia Sinica*, but the project was disrupted by the political situation in China in the 1930's and 1940's and the fauna is even now not completely published. The most important publications on the sites are de Chardin and Young (1932), Licent and Trassaert (1935), de Chardin and Trassaert (1937a, 1937b, 1938), and de Chardin (1942). The basin and fauna are also discussed in general terms in de Chardin (1941). The fauna is divided into two distinct assemblages: Zone I is of Pontian age and Zone II is considered to be of later Pliocene age. The earlier fauna is typical of the *Hipparion* faunal formation of the Pontian and includes a large assortment of large proboscideans, ungulates, and carnivores, as well as a few rodents. The later fauna contains many more rodents, fewer proboscideans and carnivores, a very rich artiodactyl fauna, but no perissodactyl ungulates.

Locality 12 at Choukoutien (CKT) was described by de Chardin (1938) and yielded a fauna rich in small mammals of later Pliocene age. It is remarkable in containing remains of baboon or macaque-like primates and is dated stratigraphically within the series of CKT localities as later than the Locality 14 Pontian fish fauna, but earlier than the majority of the CKT localities.

SOUTHERN PLIOCENE SITES. There are no Pliocene sites known from China proper, but two localities, the Siwalik Beds in West Pakistan and the Lower Irrawady deposits in Burma, furnish a picture of the southern fauna at this time range.

The Dhok Pathan fauna from the Siwaliks is usually correlated with the Middle or Late Pliocene and contains a very rich mammalian *Hipparion*-type fauna. There is a very large literature on Siwalik mammals; Colbert (1935) has written a major monograph on the faunas, and the bibliography of that publication provides entrance to the literature on the site. The Dhok Pathan fauna is very interesting for our purposes in that it contains many early forms of mammals later to be typical representatives of the *Stegodon–Ailuropoda* fauna including *Hystrix, Rhizomys*, and *Stegodon*.

The Lower Irrawaddy fauna of Burma is much smaller and was also described by Colbert (1938). It is assigned to the Pliocene on faunal grounds and is comprised entirely of ungulate forms.

NORTHERN VILLAFRANCHIAN SITES. There are three faunas of Villafranchian age known from North China. As already mentioned, the Yushe Basin (Zone III) has mammalian fossils from this time, and the others are the Nihowan Basin in Shansi and Locality 18 at CKT. The Yushe Basin has already been discussed above, and the references given also apply to the Villafranchian fossils. The Nihowan Basin contains a long series of Villafranchian sediments containing a large series of mammalian forms; de Chardin and Piveteau (1930) have described this fauna, often taken as the type occurrence of the earliest Pleistocene faunas of Northeast Asia under the faunal-stratigraphic term Sanmenian. Locality 18 of CKT is a small solution cavity with a total sediment depth of some 7 meters that contained a large number of mammalian fossils. The locality is dated to the Villafranchian on faunal grounds, and the fossils were described by de Chardin (1940). The brief discussion of the Villafranchian fauna of North China given in the section on Pleistocene chronology (see page 383) is based on these three sites.

SOUTHERN VILLAFRANCHIAN SITES. While there is only one site in South China of Villafranchian age (and that may actually be earliest Middle Pleistocene), there are four other faunal assemblages from elsewhere in the southern area that probably belong to this time block. The site in South China is Hoshantung Cave in Yunnan and was originally described by Young (1932a); it was subsequently the subject of an article by Bien and Chia (1938) and is also included in Kahlke's summary (1961) on the *Stegodon-Ailuropoda* fauna. While not a large fauna, it contains a series of carnivore genera now typical of the southern fauna, the most frequent and typical fossil elements of the southern Pleistocene faunas,

Hystrix, *Stegodon*, and *Ailuropoda*, as well as the primates, *Pongo* and *Macaca*.

The other four southern Villafranchian sites include (1) the Tatrot and (2) Pinjor faunas from the Siwaliks, (3) the Djetis levels of Sangiran in Java, and (4) the Upper Irrawaddy fauna from Burma. The Siwalik faunas (Colbert 1935) contains both typically Asian forms and a strong admixture of mammals of Ethiopian affinities, especially among the artiodactyl ungulates. The Djetis fauna (see von Koenigswald 1939; but also de Terra 1943:443) has been tentatively dated at $1.9 \pm 0.4 \times 10^6$ years (Stross 1971:836), and it contains many typical southern mammals of the Asian Villafranchian as well as a relatively large inventory of fossil primate forms and a large array of artiodactyls. The Upper Irrawaddy fauna (Colbert 1938) includes only large herbivorous mammals and is marked by the presence of a few archaic forms including *Hipparion*.

NORTHERN MIDDLE PLEISTOCENE SITES.   There are twelve separate sites or localities in North China which are referred to the Middle Pleistocene; nine of them are localities at Choukoutien near Peking, and the other three are separate sites in Shensi. These twelve localities are listed in Table 1 along with the most important references for each. As we mentioned above, this fauna is strongly marked by the presence of outside forms and by the disappearance of earlier and archaic Villa-

Table 1.   Middle Pleistocene sites of the northern faunal region of East Asia

Sites and localities	References
1. Choukoutien, Hopei, Locality 1	Pei (1934); Young (1932a, 1934); Chia (1959); Kahlke and Chow (1961); Weidenreich (1937, 1941, 1943); Breuil (1939); Movius (1944, 1949)
2. Choukoutien, Hopei, Locality 2	Young (1932a); de Chardin and Leroy (1942)
3. Choukoutien, Hopei, Locality 3	Pei (1936)
4. Choukoutien, Hopei, Locality 5	de Chardin and Young (1931)
5. Choukoutien, Hopei, Locality 6 (Chi Ku Shan Hill)	Young (1930)
6. Choukoutien, Hopei, Locality 7	Young (1932a); de Chardin and Leroy (1942)
7. Choukoutien, Hopei, Locality 9	de Chardin (1936)
8. Choukoutien, Hopei, Locality 13	de Chardin and Pei (1941); de Chardin and Leroy (1942)
9. Choukoutien, Hopei, Locality 15	Pei (1939); de Chardin and Leroy (1942); De Terra (1941:33 ff.)
10. Chen-Chia-Ou, Lantian, Shensi	Chow and Li (1965); Dai and Chi (1964); Woo (1964, 1966a 1966b)
11. Yulin Basin, Localities 14 and 15, Shensi	de Chardin and Young (1931:59–60)
12. Hui-Tui-Po, Tungchuan, Shensi	Hsieh (1964)

franchian, and Pliocene mammals. It is also the period during which the so-called "giant" forms appeared in China; the details of these evolutionary developments will be treated in more detail in the next section.

SOUTHERN MIDDLE PLEISTOCENE SITES.   There are a total of twenty-two sites in South China which are referred to the Middle Pleistocene, plus four more from Southeast Asia and the islands of the Sunda Shelf; they are listed along with the most important references pertaining to each in Table 2. Of these, the one which is best-known and often designated as the typical occurrence of the *Stegodon—Ailuropoda* fauna of the Middle Pleistocene of South China is the site of Yenchingkou in Szechwan. It contains a range of mammalian forms which is, with the exception of a few extinct forms, still typical of South China and which fully justifies the generalization that the fauna shows little compositional or structural change from the Pliocene and Villafranchian communities in Southeast Asia. This southern fauna will also be treated in more detail in the following pages.

NORTHERN LATE PLEISTOCENE SITES.   There are three Late Pleistocene mammalian sites in the northern faunal area. They are Sjara-Osso-Gol in Inner Mongolia, Locality 13 of the Yulin Basin in Shensi, and the site of Tingtsun in Shansi. The fauna from Sjara-Osso-Gol was originally described by Boule *et al.* (1928) and is considered the type-site for the fauna of North China during the Late Pleistocene. It was also discussed by Andersson (1943). It includes a variety of forms with affinities to the Palearctic (and especially the arid zones). The fossils from Locality 13 of the Yulin Basin were described by de Chardin and Young (1931:58–59) and include only rodents and lagomorphs. Tingtsun, on the other hand, contained a full range of mammalian forms with Palearctic (and especially arid zone) affinities (Pei *et al.* 1958).

SOUTHERN LATE PLEISTOCENE SITES.   There are three sites which can be referred here: (1) from Java, is the Solo River Terrace fauna described by von Koenigswald (1939) and discussed by de Terra (1943:453); (2) the site of Mapa in Kwangtung, China; and (3) younger fauna from Tzeyang in Szechwan, China. The Mapa fauna was published in a preliminary note from the Kwangtung Museum (1959) and the hominid skull material from the site was described by Woo and Peng (1959); the fauna is typical of the *Stegodon–Ailuropoda* complex of South China and differs from those of the Middle Pleistocene in that it contains fewer extinct species. The Tzeyang site was described by Pei and Woo (1957) and is also typical of the southern faunal complex, though it contains fewer species than the Mapa assemblage.

Table 2.   Middle Pleistocene sites of the southern faunal region of Eastern Asia

Sites and localities	References
1. Yenchingkou, Szechwan	Matthew and Granger (1923); Osborn (1929); Granger (1932, 1938); Young (1935, 1936, 1939); Colbert (1934); Hooijer (1946, 1951a, 1951b); Hooijer and Colbert (1951); Kurtén (1956); Young and Chow (1955); and a major monograph by Colbert and Hooijer (1953)
2. Tzeyang, Szechwan (Old Fauna)	Pei and Woo (1957)
3. Koloshan, Szechwan	Young and Liu (1950)
4. Hoshangpo, Chungking, Szechwan	Young and Mi (1941)
5. Aikang River, Tungnan, Szechwan	Chow (1957)
6. Yang-Chia-Chung, Taanchai, Szechwan	Mi (1943); Kahlke (1961)
7. Chiapei, Yunnan	Bien and Chia (1938); Kahlke (1961)
8. Chaotung, Yunnan	Chow and Zhai (1962)
9. Ma-Kai Valley, Yunnan	Colbert (1940); Kahlke (1961)
10. Tatsaike, Funming, Yunnan	Young and Mi (1941); Kahlke (1961)
11. Hsingan, near Kweilin, Kwangsi	Chang (1934); Pei (1935); Kahlke (1961)
12. Tahsin, Kwangsi	Pei and Woo (1957); Pei (1957d); Young and Chow (1956); Kahlke (1961)
13. Wuchow, Kwangsi	Young (1929)
14. Hsin-Hsueh-Chung-Tsun, Liucheng, Kwangsi	Pei (1957a, 1957b, 1957d); Young and Chow (1956)
15. Liuhsia, Chekiang	Pei and Chiu (1957); Kahlke (1961)
16. Kiangshan, Chekiang	Wang (1931); Kahlke (1961)
17. Tanyang, Kiangsu	Pei (1940a); Kahlke (1961)
18. Hsia-Chao-Hwan, Sihong, Kiangsu	Chow (1959); Young and Chow (1955); Kahlke (1961)
19. Lungtung Cave, Changyang, Hupei	Chia (1957); Kahlke (1961)
20. Chi-Li-Shan, Lungyen, Fukien	Mi (1943); Kahlke (1961)
21. Chihchin, Kweichow	Hsu, Lee and Hsieh (1957); Kahlke (1961)
22. Shaochin, Kwangtung	Chang (1959); Kahlke (1961)
23. Trinil Fauna, Java	Von Koenigswald (1939); De Terra (1943:448–449)
24. Mogok Cave, Burma	Colbert (1942); Colbert and Hooijer (1953:15–21)
25. Lang Son, Vietnam	Mansuy (1916); Patte (1928); Colbert and Hooijer (1953:16)
26. Tam Lang, Vietnam	Arambourg and Fromaget (1938); Colbert and Hooijer (1953:16)

HOLOCENE SITES.   The Holocene fauna of East Asia is known only from two sites in North China and from studies of the living fauna. The Choukoutien Upper Cave fauna was described by Pei (1940b), and that from the historical site of Anyang in Honan was published by de Chardin and Young (1936). Both have their primary affinities to the living fauna of North China and Mongolia, though the Anyang site also contained a number of forms typical of South China. The suggestion has been that they were introduced to Anyang as zoo animals or as game for the hunt (de Chardin and Young 1936). As we have mentioned earlier, Allen

(1938–1940) has written a large work on the mammals of East Asia, and it is to his work that we turn for the most definitive work on the Holocene faunas of the area.

Late Cenozoic Evolutionary Trends in East Asian Mammals

Change in the mammalian faunas of the late Cenozoic in East Asia parallels the ongoing differentiation of zonal communities which took place in middle and high latitude communities of Northern Hemisphere continental areas all over the world at that time. When the faunas of the Yushe Basin and of the Siwaliks are compared, it is apparent that a considerable difference was already in evidence between the two areas by the Pliocene. The Yushe Basin Pliocene faunas include both a substantial number of primitive deer genera of forest-browsing affinities and a substantial number of open-country grazing forms, notably the larger *Hipparion* species and a variety of primitive bovids. The Siwalik faunas, on the other hand, show fewer open-country forms and a far greater diversity of forest-browser types including a large array of giraffids, browsing perissodactyls, and proboscideans.

As we pass forward in time, the contrasting features between northern and southern areas becomes even more pronounced. The Villafranchian sites of the two areas show, if anything, a reduced role for forest-dwelling species in the northern fauna and a continuation of the diversity and development of forest-browsers in the southern areas. Since the Nihowan fauna contains both open-country and forest-dwelling types, it may be a mistake to see a decline in the browsing forms, but by late Villafranchian times at Hoshantung Cave in Yunnan there is no sign of a grazing component in the fauna at all, contrasting sharply with the balanced condition in the more northern areas. This result seems to be more than local environmental effect, since the more than twenty Middle Pleistocene sites from South China show exactly the same pattern from a large series of different localities.

In fact, by Middle Pleistocene times the distinction between the structure of mammalian communities in northern versus southern Asia is even more strongly marked than it is earlier, and the sorts of distinctions drawn by Allen (1938–1940) between the northern and southern areas of the modern fauna are already present in the fossil record. In Late Pleistocene times the appearance of typical representatives of the last-glacial Palearctic fauna such as woolly rhinoceros (*Coelodonta antiquitatis*) and both Przewalski's horse and the wild kulan (*Equus przjewalskyi* and *Equus hemionus*) at Sjara-Osso-Gol and Tingtsun confirm the Palearctic affinities of the northern area, while the distinctive *Stegodon–Ailuropoda* complex of the southern region continues little modified.

In order to examine the development of these evolutionary trends in more detail and also in order to consider the overall structure of the faunal communities of Asia in terms of the diversity of forms and degrees of specialization of different animal forms, we turn now to a discussion of the evolutionary trends and patterns within some individual orders of mammals.

ORDER PERISSODACTYLA.   There are four families of perissodactyls which are represented in late Cenozoic faunas of East Asia: the Equidae, the Rhinocerotidae, the Chalicotheridae, and the Tapiridae. Of these, the Equidae are the most familiar, but all four show distinctive evolutionary patterns which help to understand mammalian evolution in Asia.

The Chalicotheridae were strange, hoofed animals with large claws on their feet; they first appeared during the Eocene and persisted in Asia and Africa until late Pleistocene times (Romer 1966:269). The classification of the chalicotheres is reviewed by Colbert (1935:162–167) and by Romer (1966), and the interested reader is referred there for further discussion of the family. For our purposes, we may simply note that the chalicotheres diverge into two groups in late Cenozoic times. One group, represented by *Postschizotherium* in China (for example, at CKT Locality 12), is characterized by relatively elongate skulls, hypsodont molar teeth, forelimbs of length nearly equal to their hindlimbs, and elongate metapodials; the other division, represented by *Nestoritherium* and *Macrotherium* in the late Cenozoic of eastern and southern Asia, shows a pattern of relatively short skulls, brachydont molar teeth, forelimbs much longer than hindlimbs, and feet with short metapodials and flattened phalanges (Colbert 1935:165). Interestingly enough, the *Postschizotherium*-type of chalicothere is known only from the northern faunas (CKT Locality 12 and Yushe) and the *Nestoritherium*-type is native to more southerly areas (Yenchingkou, Djetis, Pinjor).

It is tempting to parallel the dichotomy in the chalicotheres with some analog in artiodactyl evolution. The forelimb-longer-than-hindlimb pattern of *Nestoritherium* is also seen in the Giraffidae, and the brachydonty fits well with a hypothetical browsing pattern, but the other parts of the pattern are not at all similar to that seen in giraffids such as *Okapia* which might be compared here. We may conclude that *Nestoritherium* may represent some sort of perissodactyl approximation to a giraffe-like browsing pattern, but the similarity is not close enough to allow any detailed analogies. *Postschizotherium* seems to represent a more open-country-oriented form in its limb modifications for running and the indications of a grazing pattern from its hypsodont molar teeth.

The Tapiridae are interesting here in that they are widely distributed during the late Cenozoic in the study area, and in that they represent in a general way the sort of adaptation from which the rhinocerotids sprang in early Tertiary times. *Tapirus* and a closely related "giant" form, *Megatapirus*, are regularly represented in Villafranchian and Middle Pleistocene faunas of South China and of Java, but only in Pliocene times (and then in only one instance in the Yushe Basin) does *Tapirus* occur as part of the northern fauna of East Asia. The evolution of the Tapiridae is discussed by Radinsky (1969) and entrance to the literature on this family as well as on problems of perissodactyl evolution generally is provided by his bibliography.

Given the general conservativeness of the tapir evolutionary pattern, it seems likely that the tapirs have always occupied approximately the same niche that they exploit today, though their formerly more extensive range may also indicate that their niche became more restricted and narrowly defined as their total range decreased. In any event, there is every suggestion that they have always been present in low densities to forage in swamps and streams for the leaves and grasses they prefer.

The Rhinocerotidae were a very diverse family during the middle Cenozoic, but by the Pliocene most of the early extreme forms have already disappeared or are on the wane. We see the primitive *Aceratherium* represented in the Siwalik faunas and also in the Lower Irrawaddy fauna in Pliocene times, but by the Villafranchian the rhinoceros are of more modern type. *Elasmotherium* and *Rhinoceros tichorhinus* are represented in the northern area (for example, Nihowan), and *Coelodonta* and *Rhinoceros* spp. are present in the southern area. During the Pleistocene the southern fauna does not show any great radiation of rhinoceros forms, and faunal lists consistently show "*Rhinoceros* sp." or "*Rhinoceros sinensis* Owen" representing the family. In the northern area, however, the rhinoceros evolutionary pattern closely parallels that known for the European side of the Palearctic fauna; Merck's rhinoceros (*Dicerorhinus kirchbergensis* or *Rhinoceros mercki*) is present along with the woolly rhinoceros (*Coelodonta antiquitatis*) as part of the northern faunal assemblage. The close correspondences between the stages of evolutionary development in the eastern and western sections of the Palearctic in mid-Pleistocene times suggests that, even though there may have been some time lag between the first appearance of a species in one area and its first appearance in another, the Palearctic was a single continuous faunal zone across which many mammalian forms eventually made their way. This is a point worth remembering when we consider the distribution of mid-Pleistocene man in the Far East and try to construct an adaptational model to explain his presence there.

According to Romer (1966:272), the living Sumatran rhinoceros is probably descended from the woolly rhinoceros line; if that is so, it is probable that some of the records of rhinocerotids in South China during Middle Pleistocene times represent *Coelodonta* as well. Given the generally confused state of rhinoceros taxonomy, it will not be possible to draw any detailed conclusions about the rhinoceros of East Asia during the Pleistocene until the phylogeny is clarified for the family as a whole and the Asian material is restudied in the light of whatever conclusions are forthcoming.

The Equidae are the last of the perissodactyl families to be considered here, and they show one of the most interesting patterns of evolution of any of the mammalian forms present in the fauna. The family is represented in the Pliocene fauna by various species and varieties of the genus *Hipparion*, a form so common in the Pliocene faunas of Eurasia that it gives its name to the very widespread and relatively homogeneous fauna of the Old World at that time. *Hipparion* showed considerable adaptation for the running and grazing adaptation with which we are familiar in modern horses, but it retained a three-toed pattern in its feet. The genus was successful enough in Pliocene environments that the late Pliocene saw a substantial radiation of species which differed from one another in overall size, details of molar cusp arrangement, and, most important, in relative body and limb proportions. This radiation presumably reflects a series of dietary and locomotor specializations in local populations related to efficient exploitation of a variety of locally defined niches. Between Pliocene and Villafranchian times, however, *Hipparion* is replaced almost completely and relatively quickly by *Equus*. In all of Asia in Villafranchian time, the two genera occur together in the same site and level only at Nihowan, and *Hipparion* is absent in this area by Middle Pleistocene times.

The dramatic replacement of *Hipparion* by *Equus* probably took place as a result of the *Equus* stock entering Eurasia from North America, but regardless of the point of origin of the *Equus* stock, the replacement is interesting in the light of Shotwell's study (1961) of a similar replacement in the Great Basin of North America. Shotwell was able to correlate the replacement of *Hipparion* by *Equus* with a vegetational change from forest-savannah to open grassland conditions. He suggests that this may indicate that the lateral toes in *Hipparion* provided enough advantage over *Equus* in terrain with obstacles to dodge around while running as to neutralize whatever other advantages the *Equus* pattern may have provided. If Shotwell's idea is correct, it could lead us to surmise that the *Hipparion* niche in Asia was largely an open-country adaptation since *Equus* replaced it very readily, and also to suggest that the Nihowan Basin may have supported a forest-savannah environment during Villafranchian times which was able to support both forms for a time.

In any event, *Hipparion* has never been recorded in a Pleistocene fauna in the southern area, though *Equus* is occasionally present at such sites (for example, Tatsaike, Chaotung, and Ma-Kai in Yunnan) and therefore is probably represented by both browsing and grazing forms. In the Middle and Late Pleistocene, *Equus* is an important part of the total composition of the mammalian fauna of the northern area, and in the Late Pleistocene both Przewalski's horse and the wild ass (*Equus przjewalskyi* and *Equus hemionus*) are present.

ARTIODACTYLA. The artiodactyla are the dominant hoofed mammals in the modern mammalian faunas of the world and have comprised at least five major subgroups. Colbert (1969:420) lists these subgroups as Paleodonta, Suina, Ancodonta, Tylopoda, and Ruminantia. Of these, only the Paleodonta is extinct and never had a place in the late Cenozoid faunas of East Asia, while all the rest are represented there.

The suid artiodactyls have left a substantial fossil record in the Siwalik faunas, and Colbert (1935:263–266) has reviewed their classification and phylogeny, but the suids are not very important elements in the East Asian fauna. Only in the Siwaliks and in the Irrawaddy faunas of Burma do we find pigs other than *Sus*, and frequently the identification is only at the generic level. The pigs of South Asia developed a variety of dental and cranial patterns apparently related to different dietary patterns, but it is to the typical modern wild *Sus* that the suids of Pleistocene Asia are related, though in the modern fauna of Celebes the babirusa provides an example of an aberrant Asian form. Wart hogs (*Phacochoerus*) and the bush pig (*Potamochoerus*) now found only in Africa were once native to the Indian region as well.

The anthracotheres and hippopotamuses comprise a second group of very primitive artiodactyls, and both Colbert (1969:425) and Romer (1966:279) suggest that the hippopotamus is a direct descendant of the anthracothere *Merycopotamus*. *Merycopotamus* is known from the late Pliocene and Villafranchian of the Siwaliks and Burma, but elsewhere in Asia — especially in the southern area — hippopotamus is the form recorded. Kurtén (1968:156–157) concurs in the suggestion of anthracothere ancestry for the hippopotamuses and notes that they were present in Europe as early as the Villafranchian and reappeared there regularly during interglacial times as part of both the forest- and cool-steppe faunas. Hooijer (1950) has reviewed the fossil hippopotamuses of Asia, and Colbert (1935:288–294) presented an early discussion of their phylogeny and evolutionary adaptations. Both *Merycopotamus* and *Hippopotamus* are thought to have been highly aquatic forms feeding on water plants and so are taken as indicating the presence of such environments.

The tylopod artiodactyls, the camels and their allies, have also played a part in the mammalian faunas of Asia. There is a camel (*Camelus sivalensis*) from the Pinjor fauna of the Siwaliks, and *Camelus* (? = *Paracamelus*) is a common feature of the Villafranchian faunas of the northern area, appearing, for example, at both Nihowan and Yushe. Since the camelids experienced the major part of their evolutionary history in North

America (Colbert 1969:428; Romer 1966:282–283), the camel in East Asia in Villafranchian time would seem to indicate the presence there of an arid grassland zone. It is interesting that *Camelus* is now also known from the Omo Basin in East Africa at approximately this same time range (Howell, Fichter, and Wolff, 1969), and fossil camelids are also known from the Pleistocene of Kenya and Tanzania (Gentry and Gentry 1969). This distribution of camelids in the northern area of East Asia as well as in the Siwaliks and far to the west in East Africa — all apparently derived from a single North American radiation — suggests the existence of a continuous arid biome between Northeast Africa and Northeast Asia during the early Pleistocene that is apparent from some modern inverte-brate zoogeographical distributions but which is not often seen in the orders of large mammals (R. Wenzel, personal communication).

The Ruminantia are the most varied and numerous of the living artiodactyls and are divided into four families which figured in the late Cenozoic faunas of East Asia. The families are the Tragulidae, the Giraffidae, the Cervidae, and the Bovidae, and they are considered here in turn.

The Tragulidae are represented by the single genus *Tragulus* in the forests of southern Asia today, though the fossil record of southern Asia includes both *Tragulus* and *Dorcatherium*; the latter is known from the Siwaliks only, while the former occurs there and in both Trinil faunas in Java. Apparently the chevrotains have always been confined to deep tropical forest, and they represent the best living model of the earliest ruminants both in their habitat and their anatomical pattern (Colbert 1969:430–431; Romer 1966:283–285). *Dorcatherium* seems to have developed in parallel to the living African chevrotain, *Hyaemoschus* (Colbert 1935:313).

Giraffes and their allies are also part of the Siwaliks fauna where they occur in a variety of forms including not only the genus *Giraffa*, familiar from the contemporary African fauna, but also a number of less extremely specialized forms such as *Vishnutherium* and *Hydaspitherium*, quite similar to the living *Okapia*, and the extremely modified *Sivatherium* with its great "horns" and relatively gigantic size. Giraffids also occur in the Yushe Basin Zone I deposits (Pliocene) — they are represented there by the genera *Paleotragus* and *Honanotherium* — and in the Lower Irrawaddy fauna (*Vishnutherium*), but by the late Pliocene, the Giraffidae seem to have left the northern area, and they are presently confined to Africa. It is interesting in this respect that Colbert (1969:438) reports a Sumerian statue of an animal which may indicate the presence of giraffids in the Near East in historical time.

There is little evidence to suggest that the Giraffidae were ever a part of the South China fauna and their disappearance from the late Cenozoic faunas of the more northerly parts of the Old World coincides with and may have been caused by the dramatic radiation of the closely related and directly competitive Cervidae in those faunas at that time. In fact, the Giraffidae are a tropical parallel to the more northerly Cervidae, though they never attained the evolutionary success seen among forest-browser forms in the more dynamic temperate latitudes during the late Cenozoic times (Colbert 1969:436; Romer 1966:288).

In contrast to the giraffid pattern of evolutionary decline in the faunas of East Asia, the Cervidae experienced there a very dramatic and wide-spread evolutionary radiation which left the Oriental fauna to this day the repository of the most varied cervid faunal assemblage in the world. The tremendous variety of cervid forms which have evolved in the late Cenozoic has left the taxonomy of the family in great confusion and makes it very difficult to assign levels of taxonomic affinity, especially in fossil forms. It is, therefore, all the more interesting that the Siwalik fauna is remarkably poor in cervid forms; only two genera, *Cervus* and *Dicroceros*, are represented, and the latter only in the Chinji fauna (Colbert 1935:35). The complementarity between cervids and giraffids is clearly seen here as it is in the other faunas of East Asia where giraffids are completely absent and cervids are present in great abundance.

Cervids have remained browsers throughout their evolutionary career, and, as a result, their teeth have remained low-crowned. The most striking and diagnostic differences between cervids are to be found in their overall body size and in the variety of antler formations which they have developed (Colbert 1969:434; Romer 1966:287–288).

There are a number of genera of cervids recorded from the earlier levels of the Yushe Basin fauna which have no close living counterparts, but by Villafranchian times most of the deer in the fossil record are quite similar to forms still living in Asia. In the absence of a recent review of the taxonomy of the fossil Cervidae, Whitehead's classification (1972:151–169) of the living cervids is summarized in Table 3, and this taxonomic scheme will be used in discussing the fossil forms.

From the list of living cervids in Table 3, it can be seen that every living genus of the subfamilies Moschinae, Hydropotinae, Muntiacinae, and Cervinae is represented in East Asia, along with the genera *Capreolus*, *Alces*, and *Rangifer* of the primarily New World subfamily Odocoileinae (though *Alces* and *Rangifer* occur in East Siberia, outside our study area). Only the typical deer of North America (*Odocoileus*) and the various exclusively South American genera are not represented there. The only fauna in the world which rivals that of East Asia in the diversity of its cervid fauna is that of South America. This is especially interesting in view of the generally conservative and primitive nature of many of the mammalian forms in South America and the absence there of competition from the dominant artiodactyl browsers of the Old World tropics, the Giraffidae.

Table 3.   Taxonomy of the living cervidae[a]

Subfamily	Genus	Subgenus	Common name and distribution
Moschinae	*Moschus*		Musk deer: East Asia
Hydropotinae	*Hydropotes*		Water deer: China, Korea
Muntiacinae	*Muntiacus*		Muntjac: East Asia
	Elaphodus		Tufted deer: East and Central China
Cervinae	*Dama*		Fallow deer: Europe, Southwest Asia
	Axis	(*Axis*)	Chital: India, Ceylon
		(*Hyelaphus*)	Hog deer: Southeast Asia
	Cervus	(*Przewalskium*)	Thorald's deer: Tibet
		(*Rucervus*)	Swamp deer: North India
		(*Cervus*)	Red deer, "elk" or Wapiti: Holarctic
		(*Panolia*)	Thamin: Southeast Asia
		(*Sika*)	Sika deer: Southeast Asia, Japan
		(*Thaocervus*)	Schomburgk's deer[b]: Thailand
		(*Rusa*)	Sambar, Rusa deer: Southeast Asia
	Elaphurus		Pere David's deer: captivity, formerly North China
Odocoileinae	*Odocoileus*		Mule and White-tail deer: North and South America
	Capreolus		Roe deer: Eurasia
	Alces		Moose, Elk: East Asia and North America
	Rangifer		Reindeer: Holarctic
	Blastoceros		Marsh deer: South America
	Ozotoceros		Pampas deer: South America
	Hippocamelus		Huemul: South America
	Mazama		Brocket: South America
	Pudu		Pudu: South America

[a]   After Whitehead (1972).
[b]   Extinct?

In the Middle Pleistocene faunas of East Asia we see a pattern of *Muntiacus* and *Cervus* (*Rusa*) appearing in the southern faunal area with only an occasional *Moschus* or *Axis* record to upset their complete dominance of the cervid presence there while in the northern faunal areas *Hydropotes*, *Pseudaxis*, *Euryceros*, and *Megaceros* are the most common forms. We should notice that *Muntiacus* is not known in any northern fossil site, regardless of age, while the *Cervus* (*Rusa*) group is represented in the northern area during Villafranchian time at both Nihowan and the Yushe Basin, though by the Middle Pleistocene it, too, is confined to the southern area. *Hydropotes* and *Pseudaxis* are likewise confined to the northern faunal area in the Middle Pleistocene, and *Hydropotes* is not known in the fossil record before that time. *Pseudaxis* does not occur in the southern faunal sites studied here, but *Axis* occurs in the southern area in the Middle and Late Pleistocene, as well as in the northern area during the Pliocene and Villafranchian. Given the uncertainties of cervid taxonomy, not much can be made of the *Axis-Pseudaxis* distribution, but in the *Dama-Euryceros* and *Sinomegaceros* group a more definite pattern emerges. The *Dama* lineage is apparently ancestral to the famous "pachyosteous" deer of North China in the Middle Pleistocene (see also Kalhke 1961 and his bibliography). The genera *Megaceros*, *Euryceros*, and *Sinomegaceros* have all been erected at one time or another to refer to that Middle Pleistocene form; it is probable that there is only one valid genus — *Megaceros* — to which all the forms ought to be referred and which lived in both Eastern and Western Eurasia during the Middle Pleistocene. Regardless of the taxonomic details, this lineage of cervids has been confined to the northern faunal area throughout the late Cenozoic, though it is known in arid highland regions of Southwest Asia and was also present in Europe during the Pleistocene. The possibility exists that this lineage is present in the northern fauna of East Asia during the Pleistocene by virtue of faunal connection across the arid Central Asian desert areas which may also have included camelids and various rodents.

In any event, the cervid evolutionary pattern in East Asia during the Pleistocene shows a clear pattern of conservatism in the *Muntiacus–Cervus* (*Rusa*) association in the southern fauna and a more dynamic radiation pattern in the north where several new genera appear and develop. In view of this conservatism in the southern area, the absence of giraffids there is less surprising than it might otherwise be.

The Bovidae, taken here to include the sheep, goats, muskoxen, antelopes, and cattle, experienced a surprisingly minor success in East Asia during the late Cenozoic. This is especially so when their development in the East Asian fauna is contrasted with that in other faunas of the Old World. Especially in the southern faunal area, the Bovidae are represented commonly by only *Bubalus* (buffalo) and *Bibos* (wild cow) though in some sites *Damaliscus*, *Capricornis*, *Naemorhedus*, and *Ovis* may also be present. In the northern area, on the other hand, there is often a variety of sizes of antelopes of various genera present, as well as less plentiful *Bison*, *Bubalus*, *Ovis*, and occasionally *Boopsis* (an extinct ovibovine form).

While it is quite likely that the antelope forms in North China and Mongolia comprised a substantial total ungulate biomass, the area over which this was the case must have been quite small compared to that in which the Cervidae were the dominant ungulate forms. This parallel development of cervid and bovid forms in the northern area is a very interesting contrast to the Pleistocene evolution of bovid forms in Africa. In Africa, with the Cervidae completely absent and the more extreme browsing niches occupied by Giraffidae, the Bovidae had a much more diverse radiation that produced a number of bovid tribes which are now endemic to that continent. These forms were formerly present in Europe and South and Southwest Asia, but they either never reached the Oriental fauna or reached it only early in the latter half of the Cenozoic (see also Darlington 1957:355–357).

Among the Bovidae, however, there is a very interesting tribe of the subfamily Caprinae which also fits with the hypothesis of faunal connections across the arid Central Asian deserts. The tribe in question is the Saigini, of which the saiga "antelope" (*Saiga*) is the only living representative, which has a (now discontinuous) distribution from Southwest Russia to Mongolia (Kurtén 1968:173; Matthews 1971: volume 1, p. 397). The saiga antelopes, along with other alpine and subalpine caprine forms, have probably had more or less continuous ranges across this area for much of the Pleistocene.

ORDER RODENTIA.   The rodents are the single most successful order of mammals and comprise about half the total living mammalian population of the world (Matthews 1971: volume 2, p. 142), and as a consequence of their tremendous variety and long evolutionary history their taxonomy is quite unsettled. For the purposes of the discussion which follows, the rodents have been somewhat arbitrarily divided into groups with family designations; this elevates some distinctions and may obscure others, but it will serve for this discussion. The taxonomic divisions used here are meant primarily as an aid in associating unfamiliar generic names into higher taxonomic groupings with which the reader may be more familiar; the breakdown is presented in Table 4.

Of the thirty-seven genera in the taxonomic list, thirty-five are found in one or more fossil assemblage in the northern faunal area, while only ten of the genera (*Hystrix* and *Rhizomys*) occur in more than two different late Cenozoic sites. It is also interesting to note that more than twenty of the known fossil genera of rodents from the late Cenozoic of East Asia occur only in the northern fauna while only two genera (*Sylvaemus* and *Nesokia*) are confined to the southern fossil record. (*Rhizomys* is considered here as endemic to the southern fauna despite its appearance in the Holocene assemblage from Anyang; its presence there is almost certainly a result of human interference.)

Among the living Sciuridae, only *Petaurista* and *Citellus* occur in the southern area, while all the known fossil genera of this family occur in the north; the family does not seem to have undergone any substantial radiation in the known fossil record and this is consistent with its position as one of the older lineages within the order. Similarly, in the Microtidae, only *Ellobius* occurs in the southern area in the fossil record while all recorded fossil genera of the family are represented in the northern fauna; this distribution pattern is quite consistent with its distribution in East Asia today. In fact, the only anomaly in the distribution of these two families is that of *Petaurista*; it is recorded in both the Middle Pleistocene

Table 4. Simplified taxonomy of the rodents

Family	Genus	Common name
Sciuridae	*Sciurus*	Squirrel
	Tamias	Chipmunk
	Sciurotamias	Rock squirrel
	Petaurista	Giant Asian flying squirrel
	Marmota (=*Arctomys*)	Marmot, woodchuck
	Citellus (=*Spermophilus*)	Ground squirrel
Microtidae	*Microtus*	Field vole, meadow vole
	Micromys	Harvest mouse
	Pitymys	Vole
	Phaiomys	Field vole
	Alticola	Vole
	Arvicola	Water vole
	Ellobius	Ground vole, "mole" vole
	Eothenomys	Vole
	Clethrionomys	Bank vole, red-backed mouse
Muridae	*Mus*	Mouse
	Rattus	Rat
	Apodemus	Long-tailed mouse
	Epimys	Rat
	Stephanomys	— (fossil only)
	Sylvaemus	Forest mouse
	Nesokia	Bandicoot rat
Cricetidae	*Cricetinus*	Small hamsters
	Cricetulus	Small hamsters
Gerbillidae	*Gerbillus*	Gerbil
	Bahomys	— (fossil only)
Myospalacidae	*Myospalax* (=*Siphneus*)	Mole rat
	Prosiphneus	— (fossil only)
Rhizomyidae	*Rhizomys*	Bamboo rat
	Brachyrhizomys	— (fossil only)
Dipodidae	*Dipus*	Three-toed jerboas
	Alactaga	Five-toed jerboas
Castoridae	*Castor*	Beaver
	Eucastor	— (fossil only)
	Sinocastor	— (fossil only)
	Trogontherium	Giant beaver
	Dipoides	— (fossil only)
Hystricidae	*Hystrix*	Porcupine (Old World)

and Holocene in the north, but is today confined to the southern provinces (Allen 1938–1940:730 ff.).

Among the fossil Muridae, *Nesokia* (probably equivalent to the modern *Bandicota*) has the most definite southern affinity in the modern fauna (Allen 1938–1940:1046 ff.). It is found only in the southern area fossil fauna, but the family has a broad distribution, and, as with the generally distributed sciurid and microtid genera, their absence in the fossil faunas of the south is probably more due to accidents of preservation than to former distribution patterns.

The Cricetidae are known as fossils only in northern faunas, and these hamsters are also associated with more northern latitudes in the living fauna (Allen 1938–1940:756 ff.). The Myospalacidae constitute another family of rodents with fossil and modern distributions very similar to the cricetids; the mole-rats are also especially interesting in that they experienced a dramatic, well-documented radiation during the late Cenozoic in the northern faunal area. De Chardin (1942:33 ff.) discusses this group and illustrates some of the diverse forms which evolved in that radiation.

Both the Gerbillidae and the Dipodidae also have northern distributions throughout the late Cenozoic; the gerbills and jerboas of these two families inhabited the arid grasslands and desert zones of the Gobi and the surrounding areas and constitute two groups of rodents with close affinities with North African and Central Asian forms. They constitute part of the same arid-zone faunal complex to which the camels, saiga antelopes, and, perhaps, some of the alpine-oriented caprine and ovine artiodactyls belong that has its distribution from the Gobi in the east to the Sahara in the west. Clearly it is unlikely that any one species would extend over the entire distance, but the presence of a distinctive faunal complex in that zone is an important feature of late Cenozoic Asian zoogeography.

The Rhizomyidae, by way of contrast, are primarily associated with the southern faunal area; except for a single occurrence of *Rhizomys* at Anyang in historical times, this genus is known in fossil form only in the south, though its modern distribution also extends up into North China. As its name suggests, this rodent is closely associated with bamboo groves, and its distribution can be expected to closely parallel the distribution of that plant. *Rhizomys* derives a good deal of its food from bamboo, but also eats a variety of other grasses and plants (Allen 1938–1940:902 ff.). *Rhizomys* is one of the most common elements of the *Stegodon–Ailuropoda* faunal complex and with *Hystrix* is the only rodent commonly occurring in the fossil assemblages of that fauna. The late Cenozoic evolution of the Rhizomyidae is summarized by de Chardin (1942:27–32).

The Hystricidae in Asia are represented by the genus *Hystrix* with a variety of subgeneric designations. As just mentioned, *Hystrix* is commonly present in the fossil occurrences of the *Stegodon–Ailuropoda* fauna, often occurring there with *Rhizomys*. The porcupine is, however, a commonplace element in all parts of the Asian fauna.

The last rodent family to be considered here, the Castoridae, or beaver family, is one which is today represented in Asia only by members of the genus *Castor* in extreme North Mongolia (Allen 1938–1940:753–754) as part of a general Holarctic north temperate zone distribution. The family has a substantial evolutionary history in East Asia, however, which has been discussed by de Chardin (1942:1–26) and which included the unusual giant beaver *Trogontherium*. Except for a single occurrence of this giant form in the southern area at Hsia-Chao-Hwan in Kiangsu, the family is confined to the northern area throughout its Asian History.

ORDER LAGOMORPHA. This order is comprised of two groups: (1) the Leporidae, including hares (*Lepus*) and rabbits (*Oryctolagus*); and (2) the Ochotonidae, comprised of the single genus *Ochotona*, the pika. Hares and rabbits occurred in both the northern and southern faunas during the late Cenozoic, but the pikas are confined to the northern fauna and are even fairly common there in the Middle Pleistocene. Since pikas are predominantly alpine forms today and are confined to the Himalayan zone in their Eurasian distribution, their modern distribution coincides nicely with their occurrence in the fossil record, except that they seem to have been somewhat more widespread in the past than is now the case. They are, however, an example of an animal species which shows a continuous distribution between Northeast Asia and Southwest Asia across the northern fringes of the Himalayan highlands.

Hares differ from rabbits in being more specialized for life in completely open-vegetational communities, but neither form is at all restricted in the type of communities it occupies today. Hares occur from tropical latitudes to the high arctic, and rabbits are distributed over the same area except that they do not extend into the tundra in the north. Thus, there is no ecological interpretation of the East Asian fossil record of this group possible beyond what has already been said of the Ochotonidae.

ORDER PROBOSCIDEA. The taxonomy of this order has recently been reviewed, and the classification of the family Elephantidae within it thoroughly revised (Maglio 1973). Maglio has argued (1) that there are only two major evolutionary groups within the order and (2) that they should be classified as two superfamily groups: the Mammutoidea, including the various mastodons, the stegodons, and the stegolophodons; and the Gomphotherioidea, including the two living elephants, their ancestral lines, and the now-extinct mammoths and their ancestors. He suggests that our present understanding of the order Proboscidea indicates that a group of very primitive mammals (including genera *Moeritherium* and the closely related *Deinotherium*) that has usually been placed there are probably not proboscideans at all. However,

Deinotherium occurs in the late Cenozoic East Asian fauna and is mentioned here until its taxonomic status is finally clarified.

Since Maglio's revision of proboscidean taxonomy is concerned only with groupings above the family level outside the Elephantidae, the discussion that follows retains all the various generic names used in the literature except within the Elephantidae. Maglio's classification is summarized in Table 5, with generic names listed only within the Elephantidae.

Table 5.   Taxonomy of the proboscidea[a]

Superfamily	Family	Subfamily	Genus
Mammutoidea	Mammutidae Stegodontidae		
Gomphotheroidea	Gomphotheriidae Elephantidae	Stegotetrabelodontinae Elephantinae	*Stegotetrabelodon* *Primelephas* *Loxodonta* *Elephas* *Mammuthus*

[a]After Maglio (1973:15).

The genus *Deinotherium* is known from East Asia from only one of the sites in our sample; it occurs in the Dhok Pathan fauna of the Siwaliks and is unknown in both Europe and Asia after that time, though it lasts into the mid-Pleistocene of Africa (Romer 1966:386). As just mentioned, the taxonomy of this form is in question and since not much is known about its adaptations and it does not figure in the late Cenozoic faunas of Asia, we will not discuss it further here.

Among the Mammutoidea, the family Mammutidae is well represented in the Pliocene faunas of both northern and southern East Asia, though these forms are gone from the northern region by Villafranchian time and remain in the southern fauna only into the Middle Pleistocene. *Trilophodon* and *Tetralophodon* are known in the Yushe Basin and Siwalik Pliocene faunas; *Pentalophodon* is known from the Siwaliks and from Java in the Villafranchian and from the Yushe Basin Pliocene; *Anancus*, *Rynchoterium*, and *Synchonolophus* are known from the Siwalik Pliocene; *Mastodon* occurs at Yushe in the Pliocene and at the *Gigantopithecus* cave and from Java in the Middle Pleistocene; while *Zygolophodon* is listed from the Middle Pleistocene site of Chaotung, Yunnan.

The other mammutoid family, the Stegodontidae, has a somewhat different evolutionary history; *Stegodon* is present at both levels of the Yushe Basin Pliocene, and it is a dominant element of the southern fauna all during the late Cenozoic and is known from more than half the sites in the southern area sample. The related genus *Stegolophodon* is also present in the southern fauna from the Pliocene through the Middle Pleistocene, but it is much less common than *Stegodon*. The persistence of this mammutoid genus into the Middle and Late Pleistocene is a strong indication of the generally conservative evolutionary pattern among larger herbivores in southern East Asia during the Pleistocene, an indication so strong that *Stegodon* lends its name to the distinctive *Ailuropoda–Stegodon* fauna of the region at that time.

In studying the evolution of the proboscidea, it is interesting to notice that the only major faunal area on earth which saw total replacement of the mastodons by elephantids before the Late Pleistocene was Europe; in North America, as in Africa and South Asia, mastodons persist much longer than they do in the Palearctic fauna. In view of the discussion presented earlier in this paper concerning the gross patterns of vegetational evolution in the late Cenozoic faunal areas, this can only be seen as confirming our conclusions about the special nature of the European late Cenozoic sequence.

Within the Elephantidae, according to Maglio's taxonomy, only two genera occur in the late Cenozoic of East Asia — genus *Elephas*, represented by the species *Elephas hysudricus*, *Elephas platycephalus*, and *Elephas namadicus*; and the genus *Mammuthus* (= *Archidiskodon*). Of these, the most common form is *Elephas namadicus* which is known from eleven sites in the Villafranchian and Middle and Late Pleistocene of the southern area and from seven sites scattered through the Pleistocene of the north. *Mammuthus* is recorded from only two sites in the sample — the uppermost levels of the Yushe Basin and the Pinjor fauna of the Siwaliks. *Elephas hysudricus* is confined to the southern fauna. *Elephas platycephalus* is reported from the Pinjor Siwalik fauna, but it does not occur elsewhere in our sample. In the original site reports *Palaeoloxodon* Matsumoto, *Hypselephas*, *Platelephas*, and *Archidiskodon* are all listed as valid elephantid genera, but Maglio (1973) has sunk *Palaeoloxodon* Matsumoto into *Elephas namadicus*, *Platelephas* into *Elephas platycephalus*, *Hypselephas* into *Elephas hysudricus*, and *Archidiskodon* into *Mammuthus*.

It should be emphasized here that none of the proboscidean forms present in the late Cenozoic of East Asia are other than relatively brachydont browser forms; even the forms identified as *Archidiskodon* and referred to here as *Mammuthus* represent quite early and unspecialized forms of the lineage that was later to give rise to the woolly mammoths of the Late Pleistocene tundra communities. Thus, the overall pattern of proboscidean evolution in East Asia during the late Cenozoic is consistent with the picture developed in our discussion of other herbivorous mammalian orders. The southern fauna remained much less modified in structure and composition (witness the dominance of *Stegodon*-type mammutoids) than did the more northerly faunas, but throughout East Asia the browsing fauna remained to coexist with the newer grazing forms.

ORDER CARNIVORA.   The carnivores of the late Cenozoic of East Asia are a very interesting group. Since they represent the next higher level of the mammalian food chains from those occupied by the herbivorous forms described earlier, the evolutionary patterns seen in this group are very interesting as a way of confirming the general conclusions drawn about the nature of those herbivore faunas. Since they do represent a higher position on the mammalian food chain, however, they are generally much less common in the fossil record than is the case with herbivorous forms. For that reason little detailed analysis is possible from the carnivore fossil record, and they are not treated in detail here. Several general observations concerning carnivore families are possible, however, including the following:

1. Among the ursid carnivores, the most primitive forms (for example, *Agriotherium*) are gone by the end of the Pliocene and are replaced by various species of the genus *Ursus*. Ursids are much more commonly present in the southern fauna than in northern ones and occur in many of the known southern Middle Pleistocene sites. An especially notable genus in this respect is *Ailuropoda*, the giant panda, one of the most distinctive and common elements of the southern *Ailuropoda–Stegodon* fossil fauna that is still native to the area today.

2. Viverrid carnivores are occasionally represented in the fossil faunas and are much more common in the southern area than in the northern. This corresponds well with the fact that they are today found only in the southern faunal region.

3. Hyenid carnivores were frequently present in both northern and southern faunas and are represented by both *Hyena* and *Crocuta* in those areas. Since hyenids are no longer native to East Asia, it is difficult to speculate on their exact ecological position there; they must have been part of both the browsing and grazing types of faunas since they occur very widely, but they can be observed today only as part of savannah-type communities in Africa. It is probably that there is no living analog in modern Africa of their role in Asian forest-dwelling faunas.

4. Canids are widely present in Asian fossil faunas and are also an important element in the modern faunas of the areas. The distinctive *Nyctereutes* is known from ten sites scattered throughout the late Cenozoic of the northern fauna and has no fossil record in the south. A similar fossil history is seen for genus *Vulpes* which may indicate that these two canids evolved to fill some particular small mammal-eating niche in the northern zone (perhaps associated with arid zones), but since

both genera are known in the southern fauna today, any such conclusions remain somewhat uncertain.

5. The procyonid genus *Ailurus* is known from one site from the Villafranchian of the southern faunal region (Hoshantung, Yunnan) and is today confined to the southern faunal area; such a limited fossil record, however, hardly justifies any general conclusion regarding its late Cenozoic range.

6. Mustelid carnivores are often present in the sites in our sample; *Meles* and *Gulo* are the only genera which approximate an exclusively northern distribution, while *Arctonyx* and *Charronia* are the only ones primarily associated with the southern area. The similarities between the mustelid (and canid) faunas of the northern and southern regions indicates that smaller carnivores did not change much during the late Cenozoic of Asia, but this result is neither dramatic nor surprising in view of the rodent evolution sketched earlier.

7. Felid evolution is also undramatic during the late Cenozoic of Asia except for the disappearance of the Asian machairodonts. Aside from the elimination of this archaic group, the felids show little evolutionary or distributional change during the late Cenozoic.

Other orders of mammals have fossil records from the late Cenozoic of East Asia, but the evolutionary patterns to be seen in them are not particularly instructive as concerning the structural history of East Asian ecological communities. Thus, they are not discussed here.

Summary and Conclusions

From the fossil record of the late Cenozoic mammalian communities of East Asia it is possible to extend our observations on the basically conservative nature of the southern communities relative to those in the north into the past. The conclusions that are apparent from the fossil record are (1) that the structural differences which exist between the modern faunas of the northern and southern regions are of considerable antiquity, with the origins of the differences extending well back into Tertiary time, and (2) that the southern fauna has a long history of relative isolation from other faunal regions, while the northern faunas of East Asia show strong influence from other parts of the Palearctic.

In view of the fundamentally different structures of the northern and southern faunas, it is apparent that there was no possibility of diffusion of Palearctic forms through or across the Oriental faunal region and that the presence of similar mammalian forms in the northern East Asian and European Middle Pleistocene faunas must, therefore, represent continuity across Asia north of the Himalayan massif and Tibetan Plateau. As has been pointed out above in the discussions of perissodactyl, artiodactyl, and proboscidean forms, strong pan-Palearctic affinities are present in the Northeast Asian faunas all during the Pleistocene, but especially during the Middle and Late Pleistocene. Thus, the indications are that for at least part of the Middle and Late Pleistocene there must have been a considerable degree of faunal continuity across northern Eurasia.

It has already been mentioned that an alpine and arid-zone fauna may well have been continuous across the northern fringes of the Himalayan–Tibetan Plateau highlands and the associated desert zones of northern, central, and southwestern Asia. The animal forms that may have been involved in such a community included the following: camelid artiodactyls, gerbillid and dipodid rodents; perhaps, hare-type lago-morphs in the arid-zone communities, saigine, caprine, and ovine bovid artiodactyls; some alpine rodents; and cony-type lagomorphs in the more alpine communities. In addition to this relatively dispersed and low-biomass zone, there must also have been a continuous connection involving the large herbivorous forms that lived on the developing tundra communities of northern and midlatitude Eurasia during the Pleistocene. This latter community may not have been continuous through the Middle and Late Pleistocene, but it seems certain that there must have been blocks of time involving thousands of years at a time when the connection was present. Moreover, our ideas of continuity between Eastern and Western Palearctic communities reflect the present climatic and zonal structure of the northern half of Eurasia. There is now considerable evidence (Frenzel 1968) to suggest that the present situation is not a particularly good model of the Pleistocene climate and zonal structure of Eurasia. In fact, the suggestion that continuity was present for blocks of time totaling "thousands" of years is much more likely to be too conservative an estimate of their duration than it is to be an overestimate.

MIDDLE PLEISTOCENE HOMINID DISTRIBUTION AND ADAPTATION IN EAST ASIA

Middle Pleistocene Hominid Sites

The Middle Pleistocene hominid sites of East Asia are distributed in two widely separated areas. One group of sites is found in Southeast Asia and the Indian subcontinent, and the other occurs in the part of North China where the deciduous forest vegetational community is grading off into the arid grasslands of Shensi and Shansi. There is no record of hominid occupation in South China until well into the Late Pleistocene, and it is upon that apparently anomalous fact that much of the interpretation of

Middle Pleistocene hominid adaptation in the latter pages of this paper is built.

There is neither space nor need to go into any detail on the Middle Pleistocene hominid sites of East Asia. The argument here is based not on any detailed analysis of behavior or subsistence patterns in the sites (and such analysis is not possible on most of the sites in question anyway) but upon their temporal and geographical position relative to the late Cenozoic mammalian communities we have been discussing.

In the southern region, there are only three sites that have yielded actual hominid fossil material, and all are in Java: the sites of Trinil Modjokerto, and Sangiran have yielded Middle Pleistocene hominids and fauna. Other sites in the southern region from which human presence is inferred from the recovery of stone-tool assemblages include several localities grouped together under the cultural name Anyathian from the Irrawaddy River Valley in Burma, the locality of Kota Tampan in Malaysia, and a large list of sites scattered over India and West Pakistan. One area of the Indian subcontinent, the Soan River Valley (a tributary of the Indus), has produced stone tools from a context that can be stratigraphically correlated with the top of the Siwaliks faunal sequence, but the rest of the sites from the Indian subcontinent are assigned to the Middle Pleistocene entirely on the basis of the morphology of the stone tools recovered from them.

Sites of the Middle Pleistocene from the northern region include only two localities: Locality 1 at Choukoutien near Peking and the site of Lantian in Shensi. There are a large number of sites in the Fen River Valley (Movius 1956) which have been argued to be of Middle Pleistocene age, but they are probably early Late Pleistocene at earliest. In the Late Pleistocene there is also the hominid-bearing site of Mapa in Kwangtung, China, but it is associated with a fauna with clear Late Pleistocene affinities. References to the Chinese and Javan sites mentioned here have already been given in Tables 1 and 2 (see pages 388 and 390); the other sites mentioned here are treated in Movius (1944, 1949) and in Sankalia (1962).

Theoretical Perspectives on Middle Pleistocene Hominids

It has usually been assumed that the early hominid remains from all areas of East Asia were part of the same geographic population and derived from the same adaptive radiation of Middle Pleistocene hominids out of Africa. This theory has always been incompatible with the claims for australopithecine status for the *Meganthropus* specimens from the Djetis (early) faunal levels at Sangiran, since it posits an African origin for the Hominidae and a Middle Pleistocene date for both the Djetis and Trinil faunas from Java. This theory also either ignores the morphological differences between the *Meganthropus* specimens and the other Javan early hominids or allows australopithecine status for these specimens without following out the implications of such an assignment for Middle Pleistocene human evolution.

Given the reasonable, but as yet uncorroborated, date of $1.9 \pm 0.4 \times 10^6$ years date on the Djetis levels at Sangiran (Stross 1971:836), it would seem that Southeast Asia may have been inhabited by australopithecine populations well before the Middle Pleistocene. If this premise is accepted, it follows that the Middle Pleistocene hominid occupation of Southeast Asia and adjacent areas of the Indian subcontinent can be seen either as a local evolution of australopithecine-grade hominids to the *Homo erectus* grade present in Java or as a secondary radiation of such advanced hominids into southern and southeastern Asia from an origin point elsewhere in the australopithecine range. Regardless of whether one favors a local origin for the Middle Pleistocene hominids of Java, Southeast Asia, and India or not, there is no reason to automatically suppose that they are part of the same hominid population as those of North China other than the weight of traditional assertions to that effect.

The Middle Pleistocene hominid sites of the southern fringes of East Asia are all associated with local occurrences of broken ecological systems. They are found either in areas with open-grassland vegetation, on beaches, or river terraces. The open-grassland communities are azonal features of South Asia and occur in areas where rainfall is insufficient to maintain a climax forest community, and beach and river terrace areas are, by their nature, regularly disrupted by both short-term variations in water level and erosional activity and by the long-term variations in late Cenozoic climates and sea-level. This association of the Middle Pleistocene hominid sites with "broken" ecological systems is a feature of all known sites, and it is my contention that at least local disruption of community structures is a necessary precondition for the presence of Middle Pleistocene hominids in Asia.

The sites of North China also fall within an area of disrupted environmental conditions, but, in this case, environmental disruption is zonal rather than local in nature. The hominid sites of North China that date to the Middle Pleistocene are associated with a pan-Palearctic fauna that apparently evolved in direct response to the climatic fluctuations of North Eurasia during the late Cenozoic. Thus, their chronological and zoogeographical affinities suggest that they are probably more closely related to the Middle Pleistocene hominid sites of Western Eurasia and Northwest Africa (Howell 1960) than they are to their Middle Pleistocene counterparts in South Asia. They are separated from the South Asian sites by the undisrupted Oriental faunal region and are associated with the European occupations via a common affinity with the pan-Palearctic Middle Pleistocene fauna.

A corollary of this argument is (1) that the Middle Pleistocene hominid radiation that resulted in the presence of *Homo erectus* in both North China and in Europe is associated with the radiation of a mammalian fauna including modern ungulate grazing forms into those areas and (2) that both the hominid radiation and the broader mammalian radiation are closely related to vegetational communities that had been seriously disrupted by Pleistocene climatic events. A second corollary of the argument is that the Middle Pleistocene radiation of *Homo erectus* must have involved an adaptation pattern that was only effective in ecological communities in which disruption of one sort or another had opened a reasonably broad spectrum of resources to whatever exploitative techniques the *Homo erectus* populations in question had at their disposal.

These conclusions have important implications for our understanding of hominid adaptations, generally, and for understanding the range of local adaptive patterns, lithic assemblages, and types of sites that were present throughout Europe and Asia during the Middle Pleistocene. Rather than positing a single niche or subsistence pattern as characteristic of *Homo erectus* populations, it seems more reasonable in the light of our arguments here to expect regional variability in all aspects of Middle Pleistocene hominid adaptation. It also seems likely that the relative maturity and degree of disruption of any given local ecological system was the single most important factor in determining the nature and success of Middle Pleistocene human adaptation there. Thus, there is no need to posit that all Middle Pleistocene hominids were big game hunters, fishermen, mollusk gatherers, and so on. Rather, they seem to have been diverse and opportunistic in their subsistence bases, with strong regionalism a frequent and important feature of their overall adaptive pattern.

This viewpoint requires that the once-popular image of early man as a hunter be substantially modified. It is unlikely, on theoretical grounds, that a mammal entering a new and "broken" ecological system would do so as a carnivorous specialist. The resource base for a meat-eating mammal is much smaller and less dependable than that available to a herbivore, and while Middle Pleistocene man may have occasionally or locally hunted animals for food, it is very likely that his primary subsistence pattern was one of broad-spectrum gathering.

There is not enough space here to enter into a detailed discussion of all the ways in which our picture of Middle Pleistocene hominid adaptations is likely to be affected by the conclusions here, but they are likely to be many and far-reaching. Moreover, if Middle Pleistocene hominids are understood in the terms presented here, many of our conclusions concerning later hominid populations must also be reexamined. For example, it is frequently pointed out that Late Pleistocene archeological assemblages show greater internal diversity and variability than do earlier ones, and this observation is often taken to imply some sort of evolutionary advance of Late Pleistocene over Middle Pleistocene hominids. It will now certainly be necessary to consider what part of this increased diversity and variability can be understood in terms of increasing maturity of local ecological systems (of which hominid populations are a part), rather than only in terms of different stages of human physical or cultural development. The maturation process in ecological systems is exactly the process of division and subdivision of the niches they contain as the organisms within them adapt and diversify with respect to one another; increased diversity and variability in archeological assemblages may, therefore, reflect the general maturing process of the ecological systems in which humans found themselves during the Middle and Late Pleistocene as well as progressive "living into" those systems. Only when the relations between local ecological systems and the human populations they contained are understood against the general developmental changes in Middle and Late Pleistocene environments and ecological systems will it be possible to generalize about how much of the change in Middle and Late Pleistocene hominid adaptations is actually due to changes in the hominids. Once done, however, the results ought to lead to much clearer understanding of both Pleistocene hominid adaptation and the environmental setting and evolutionary process by which man moved to his present ecological position.

The issues being raised here cannot be resolved from the analysis of individual local sequences or even from a series of such local sequences. The detail available from individual sites and sequences can only be brought to bear on such questions after they have been integrated into a general model of the structural changes in ecological systems that were taking place on global and continental scales during the time that hominids were evolving. Of course, it is also true that such integration would not be possible without the local sequences and the detailed data they provide, but those data can only be fully understood when placed in the broadest possible context of environmental change, ecological development, and human evolution during the Pleistocene. This paper represents a case study in this sort of approach, and while it does not provide complete answers to the questions it poses, it does illustrate that there are answers at hand to questions which have not yet been asked.

REFERENCES

AIGNER, JEAN S.
    1972   Relative dating of North Chinese faunal and cultural complexes. *Arctic
            Anthropology* 9(2):36–79.

ALLEN, GLOVER M.
1938–1940 *The mammals of China and Mongolia*. Central Asiatic Expedition, Natural History of Central Asia, American Museum of Natural History, volume 11, Parts 1 and 2.

ANDERSSON, J. G.
1943 Researches into the prehistory of the Chinese. *Bulletin of the Museum of Far Eastern Antiquities* 15.

ARAMBOURG, CAMILLE, JACQUES FROMAGET
1938 Le gisement quaternaire de Tam Nang (Chine Annamitique septentionale). La stratigraphie et ses faunes. *Comptes Rendus,* l'Academie des Sciences, Paris 207:793–795.

AXELROD, DANIEL I., HARRY P. BAILEY
1969 Paleotemperature analysis of Tertiary Floras, *Palaeogeography, Palaeoclimatology, Palaeoecology* 6(3):163–195.

BIEN, M. N., LAN-PO CHIA
1938 Cave and rock-shelter deposits in Yunnan. *Geological Society of China Bulletin* 18:325–348.

BLACKMAN, ABNER, B. L. K. SOMAYAJULU
1966 Pacific Pleistocene cores: faunal analysis and geochronology. *Science* 154:886–889.

BOULE, M., H. BREUIL, E. LICENT, P. DE CHARDIN
1928 Le Paléolithique de la Chine. *Archives de l'Institut de Paléontologie Humaine Memoires* 4:1–136.

BREUIL, HENRI
1939 Bone and antler industry of the Choukoutien *Sinanthropus* site. *Palaeontologia Sinica* 6D:1–141.

BROECKER, WALLACE S., JAN VAN DONK
1970 Insolation changes, ice volumes, and the 0–18 record in deep-sea cores. *Reviews of Geophysics and Space Physics* 8(1):169–198.

BUTZER, KARL W.
1971 *Environment and archaeology*. Chicago: Aldine-Atherton.

CHANG, H. C.
1934 "On some fossil mammals from Kwangsi, South China," in *Geological Survey of Kwangtung and Kwangsi*. Special Publications 15:1–14.

CHANG, Y. P.
1959 Pleistocene mammals from Shaochin, Kwangtung. *Paleovertebrata et Paleoanthropologia* 1(3):141–143.

CHIA, LAN-PO
1957 Notes on the human and some other mammalian remains from Changyang, Hopei. *Vertebrata Palasiatica* 1(3):247–257.

CHOW, MIN-CHEN
1957 Note on a small collection of Pleistocene mammals from Tungnan, Szechwan. *Vertebrata Palasiatica* 1(1):57–58.
1959 New species of fossil Proboscidea from South China. *Acta Paleontologia Sinica* 7(4):251–258.

CHOW, MIN-CHEN, CHUAN-KUEI LI
1965 Mammalian fossils in association with the mandible of Lantian Man at Chen-Chia-Ou, in Lantian, Shensi. *Vertebrata Palasiatica* 9(4):387–393.

CHOW, MIN-CHEN, REN-JIE ZHAI
1962 Early Pleistocene mammals of Chaotung, Yunnan, with notes on some Chinese Stegodonts. *Vertebrata Palasiatica* 6(2):144–147.

COLBERT, EDWIN H.
1934   Chalicotheres from Mongolia and China in the American museum. *American Museum of Natural History Bulletin* 67:353–387.
1935   Siwalik mammals in the American Museum of Natural History. *American Philosophical Society Transactions*, n.s. 26:1–401.
1938   Fossil mammals from Burma in the American Museum of Natural History. *American Museum of Natural History Bulletin* 74(6):255–436.
1940   Pleistocene mammals from the Mai Kai Valley of northern Yunnan, China. *American Museum Novitates* 1099:1–10.
1942   Pleistocene vertebrates collected in Burma by the American Southeast Asiatic Expedition. *American Philosophical Society Transactions* 32(3):395–429.
1969   *Evolution of the Vertebrates* (second edition) New York: Wiley-Interscience.

COLBERT, EDWIN H., DIRK A. HOOIJER
1953   Pleistocene mammals from the Limestone Fissures of Szechwan, China. *American Museum of Natural History Bulletin* 102(10):1–134.

COUPER, R. A.
1960   New Zealand Mesozoic and Cainozoic plant microfossils. *New Zealand Geological Survey Paleontological Bulletin* 32:1–87.

DAI, ER-JIAN, HUNG-GIANG CHI
1964   Discovery of Palaeoliths at Lantian, Shensi. *Vertebrata Palasiatica* 8(2):152–162. (Chinese with English abstract.)

DANSGAARD, W., HENRIK TAUBER
1969   Glacier Oxygen-18 content and Pleistocene ocean temperatures. *Science* 166:499–502.

DARLINGTON, P.
1957   *Zoogeography*. New York: Wiley

DE CHARDIN, PIERRE TEILHARD
1936   Fossil mammals from Locality 9 of Choukoutien. *Paleontologia Sinica* 7C(4):1–61.
1937   The post-Villafranchian interval in North China. *Geological Society of China Bulletin* 17(1):169–176.
1938   The fossils from Locality 12 of Choukoutien. *Paleontologia Sinica*, n.s. 5C:1–51.
1940   The fossils from Locality 18 near Peking. *Paleontologia Sinica*, n.s. 9C:1:101.
1941   Early man in China. *Institut de Géo-Biologie, Peking Publications* 7:1–99.
1942   New Rodents of the Pliocene and Lower Pleistocene of North China. *Institut de Géo-Biologie, Peking Publications* 9:1–101.

DE CHARDIN, PIERRE TEILHARD, PIERRE LEROY
1942   Chinese fossil mammals: a complete bibliography, analyzed, tabulated, annotated and indexed. *Institut de Géo-Biologie, Peking Publications* 8:1–142.

DE CHARDIN, PIERRE TEILHARD, WEN-CHUNG PEI
1941   The fossil mammals of Locality 13 in Choukoutien. *Paleontologia Sinica*, n.s. 11C.

DE CHARDIN, PIERRE TEILHARD, JEAN PIVETEAU
1930   Les Mammiferes Fossiles de Nihowan (Chine). *Annales de Paléontologie* 19:1–134.

DE CHARDIN, PIERRE TEILHARD, M. TRASSAERT
1937a Pliocene Camelidae, Giraffidae and Cervidae of South-Eastern Shansi. *Paleontologia Sinica*, n.s. 1C.
1937b The Proboscideans of South-Eastern Shansi. *Paleontologia Sinica* 13C(1):1–85.
1938 Cavicornis of South-Eastern Shansi. *Paleontologia Sinica,* n.s. 6C:1–107.

DE CHARDIN, PIERRE TEILHARD, C. C. YOUNG
1931 Fossil mammals from the late Cenozoic of North China. *Paleontologia Sinica* 9C(1):1–88.
1932 The late Cenozoic formations of S.E. Shansi. *Geological Society of China Bulletin* 12:207–247.
1936 On the mammalian remains from the archaeological site of Anyang. *Paleontologia Sinica* 12C(1):1–79.

DE TERRA, HELMUT
1941 Pleistocene formations and Stone Age man in China. *Institut de Géo-Biologie, Peking Publications* 6:1–54.
1943 Pleistocene geology and early man in Java. *American Philosophical Society Transactions* 32(3):437–464.

DE TERRA, HELMUT, HALLAM L. MOVIUS, JR.
1943 Research on early man in Burma. *American Philosophical Society Transactions* 32(3):264–464.

DE TERRA, H., T. T. PATTERSON
1939 Studies on the Ice Age of India. *Carnegie Institution of Washington Publication* 493:1–354.

EMILIANI, CESARE
1966a Isotopic paleotemperatures. *Science* 154:851–857.
1966b Paleotemperature analysis of the Caribbean cores P6304–8 and P6304–9 and a generalized temperature curve for the last 425,000 years. *Journal of Geology* 74(6):109–126.
1972 Quaternary paleotemperatures and the duration of the high-temperature intervals. *Science* 178:398–401.

ERICSON, DAVID B., GOESTA WOLLIN
1968 Pleistocene climates and chronology in deep-sea sediments. *Science* 162:1227–1234.
1970 Pleistocene climates in the Atlantic and Pacific Oceans: a comparison based on deep-sea sediments. *Science* 167:1483–1485.

FLINT, RICHARD FOSTER
1971 *Glacial and quaternary geology.* New York: Wiley.

FRENZEL, BURKHARD
1968 The Pleistocene vegetation of northern Eurasia. *Science* 161:637–649.

GENTRY, ALLEN W., ANTHEA GENTRY
1969 Fossil camels in Kenya and Tanzania. *Nature* 222:898.

GINSBERG, NORTON, HAROLD FULLARD, H. C. DARBY, *editors*
1969 *Aldine University Atlas.* Chicago: Aldine.

GITTERMAN, R. E. *et al.*
1968 The main development stages of the vegetation of north Asia in Anthropogen. *USSR Academy of Sciences, Geological Institute Transactions* 177:1–270. (In Russian.)

GRANGER, W.
1932 "Palaeontological exploration in eastern Szechwan," in "The new conquest of Central Asia." Edited by R. Andrews, *Natural History of Central Asia (AMNH)* 1:501–528.

1938   Medicine Bones. *Natural History* (New York) 42(4):264–271.

HAYS, JAMES D., T. SAITO, N. D. OPDYKE, L. BURCKLE
1969   Pliocene–Pleistocene sediments of the equatorial Pacific: their paleomagnetic, biostratigraphic, and climatic record. *Geological Society of America Bulletin* 80:1481–1514.

HEUSSER, C. J.
1964   Palynology of four bog sections from the western Olympic Peninsula, Washington. *Ecology* 45(1):23–40.

HOOIJER, DIRK A.
1946   Prehistoric and fossil rhinoceroses from the Malay Archipelago and India. *Zoologische Mededelingen, Museum Leiden* 26:1–138.
1950   The fossil Hippopotamidae of Asia, with notes on the recent species. *Zoologische Verhandlingen Leiden* 8:1–124.
1951a The geological age of *Pithecanthropus, Meganthropus*, and *Gigantopithecus*. *American Journal of Physical Anthropology*, n.s. 9(3):265–282.
1951b Two new deer from the Pleistocene of Wanshien, Szechwan, China. *American Museum of Natural History Novitates* 1495:1–18.

HOOIJER, DIRK A., EDWIN H. COLBERT
1951   A mastodont tooth from Szechuan, China. *Fieldiana: Geology* 10(12):129–134.

HOWELL, F. CLARK
1960   European and Northwest African middle Pleistocene Hominids. *Current Anthropology* 1:195–232.

HOWELL, F. CLARK, LYNN S. FICHTER, R. WOLFF
1969   Fossil camels in the Omo Beds, Southern Ethiopia. *Nature* 222:150–152.

HSIEH, HSIANG-HSU
1964   Mammalian fossils from the Pleistocene of Huituipo, Tungchuan, Shensi. *Vertebrata Palasiatica* 8(4):394.

HSU, Y. H., Y. C. LEE, H. H. HSIEH
1957   Mammalian fossils from the Pleistocene cave-deposits of Chihchin, northwestern Kweichow. *Acta Paleontologia Sinica* 5(2):343–350.

JEN, MEI-GNO
1960   La Glaciation du Yulungshan, Yunnan, Chine. *Annales de Géographie* 69:50–56.

KAHLKE, H. D.
1961   On the complex of the *Stegodon–Ailuropoda* Fauna of southern China and the chronological position of *Gigantopithecus blacki* v. Koenigswald. *Vertebrata Palasiatica* 5(2)83–108. (In Chinese with English summary.)

KAHLKE, H. D., BEN-SHUN CHOW
1961   A Summary of stratigraphical and paleontological observations in the lower layers of Choukoutien, Locality 1, and on the chronological position of the site. *Vertebrata Palasiatica* 5(3):212–240. (In Chinese with English summary.)

KES, A. S.
1959   "The question of the origin of loess in northern China," in *Loess of Northern China.* (Proceedings of the Commission for the Study of the Quaternary Period, Academy of Sciences of the USSR.) Edited by V. V. Popov, 85–105. Moscow: Academy of Sciences of the USSR.

KOBAYASHI, KUNIO
1965   *Problems of late Pleistocene history of central Japan.* Geological Society of America. Special Paper 84:367–391.
KOZARSKI, S.
1963   Problem of Pleistocene glaciations in the mountains of east China. *Zeitschrift für Geomorphologie* 7:48–70.
KURTÉN, BJÖRN
1956   The status and affinities of *Hyaena sinensis* Owen and *Hyaena ultima* Matsumoto. *American Museum of Natural History Novitates* 1764:1–48.
1968. *Pleistocene mammals of Europe.* Chicago: Aldine.
KWANGTUNG MUSEUM
1959   Preliminary report on the excavation of human and mammalian fossils, locality at Mapa, Kwangtung. *Vertebrata Palasiatica* 3(2):104.
LATTIN, GUSTAF DE
1967   *Grundriss der Zoogeographie.* Jena, Germany: Gustav Fischer.
LEOPOLD, ESTELLA B.
1967   "Late Cenozoic patterns of plant extinction." In *Pleistocene extinctions.* Edited by Paul S. Martin and H. E. Wright, Jr., 203–246. New Haven, Conn.: Yale University Press.
1969a "Late Cenozoic palynology," in *Aspects of palynology.* Edited by Robert H. Tschudy and Richard Scott, 377–438. New York: Wiley-Interscience.
1969b *Miocene pollen and spore flora of Eniwetok Atoll, Marshall Islands.* U.S. Geological Survey Professional Paper 260–II:1133–1182.
LICENT, E., M. TRASSAERT
1935   The Pliocene lacustrine series in Central Shansi. *Geological Society of China Bulletin* 14:211–219.
MAGLIO, VINCENT J.
1973   Origin and evolution of the Elephantidae. *Transactions of the American Philosophical Society* 63(3):1–149.
MANSUY, H.
1916   Sur quelques mammiferes fossiles recemment découverts en Indochine (Memoire préliminaire). *Memoire de la Sérvice Géologique d'Indochine* 5(2):1–26.
MATTHEW, W. D., W. GRANGER
1923   "New fossil mammals from the Pliocene of Sze-Chuan," *American Museum of Natural History Bulletin* 48:563–598.
MATTHEWS, L. H.
1971   *The life of mammals,* two volumes. New York: University Books.
MI, T. H.
1943   New finds of late Cenozoic vertebrates. *Geological Society of China Bulletin* 23(3/4):155–167.
MORIN, RONALD W., FRITZ THEYER, EDITH VINCENT
1970   Pleistocene climates in the Atlantic and Pacific Oceans: a reevaluated comparison based on deep-sea sediments. *Science* 169:365–366.
MOVIUS, HALLAM L., JR.
1944   Early man and Pleistocene stratigraphy in southern and eastern Asia. *Peabody Museum of American Archaeology and Ethnology, Harvard University Papers* 19(3):1–125.
1949   The Lower Paleolithic cultures of southern and eastern Asia. *American Philosophical Society Transactions* 38(4):328–420.

1956   New Palaeolithic sites, near Ting-Ts'un on the Fen River, Shansi Province, North China. *Quaternaria* 3:13–26.

OSBORN, H. F.
1929   New Eurasiatic and American Proboscideans. *American Museum of Natural History Novitates* 393:1–23.

PATTE, E.
1928   Comparison des faunes de mammiferes de Lang Son (Tonkin) et du Se Tchouen. *Bulletin Société Géologique de France, Serie 4*, 28:55–63.

PEI, WEN -CHUNG
1934   On the Carnivora from Locality 1 of Choukoutien. *Paleontologia Sinica* 8C(1):1–216.

1935   Fossil mammals from the Kwangsi Caves. *Geological Society of China Bulletin* 14:413–425.

1936   On the mammalian remains from Locality 3 at Choukoutien. *Paleontologia Sinica* 7C(5):1–121.

1939   A preliminary study on a new Palaeolithic station known as Locality 15 within the Choukoutien region. *Geological Society of China Bulletin* 19:147–188.

1940a   Note on a collection of fossil mammals from Tanyang in Kiangsu Province. *Geological Society of China Bulletin* 19:379–392.

1957a   Discovery of lower jaws of giant ape in Kwangsi, South China. *Science Record*, n.s. 1(3):49–52.

1957b   New links between ape and man. *China Reconstructs* 6(6):2–5.

1957c   The zoogeographical divisions of quaternary mammalian faunas in China. *Vertebrata Palasiatica* 1:9–23.

1957d   Discovery of *Gigantopithecus* mandibles and other material in Liucheng district of central Kwangsi in south China. *Vertebrata Palasiatica* 1(2):65–71.

PEI, WEN -CHUNG et al.
1958   *Report on the excavations of Paleolithic man at Tingtsun, Hsiangfenhsien, Shansi Province, China.* Peking: Science Press.

PEI, WEN -CHUNG, C. L. CHIU
1957   On a collection of mammalian fossils from Liuhsia, Hongchow, Chekiang, China. *Vertebrata Palasiatica* 1(1):42–46.

PEI, WEN -CHUNG, JU -KANG WOO
1957   Tzeyang Paleolithic man. *Institute of Vertebrate Paleontology and Paleoanthropology, Academia Sinica Memoirs* 1:1–71.

POPOV, V. V., editor
1959   *Loess of northern China.* Proceedings of the Commission for the Study of the Quaternary Period. Academy of Sciences of the USSR 14 (Translated from the Russian by the Israel Program for Scientific Translations, Jerusalem, 1964.) Moscow: Academy of Sciences of the USSR.

RADINSKY, LEONARD B.
1969   The early evolution of the Perissodactyla. *Evolution* 23:308–328.

ROMER, ALFRED SHERWOOD
1966   *Vertebrate paleontology.* Chicago: University of Chicago Press.

SANKALIA, H. D.
1962   *Prehistory and protohistory in India and Pakistan.* Bombay: University of Bombay Press.

SATO, SEIJI
1960   Palynological study on the Haboro coal seam of the Haboro coal-bearing formation. Palynological Study on Neogene Coal 1. *Journal of*

the Faculty of Science, Hokkaido University, Series IV. Geology and Minerology 10(3):513–536.
1963 Palynological study on Miocene sediments of Hokkaido, Japan. *Journal of the Faculty of Science, Hokkaido University, Series IV. Geology and Minerology* 12(1):1–110.

SHACKLETON, NICHOLAS
1967 Oxygen isotope analyses and Pleistocene temperature re-assessed. *Nature* 215:15–17.

SHOTWELL, J. ARNOLD
1961 Late Tertiary biogeography of horses in the northern Great Basin. *Journal of Paleontology* 35(1):203–217.

STROSS, FRED H.
1971 Application of the physical sciences to archaeology. *Science* 171:831–836.

TANAI, TOSHIMASA
1961 Neogene floral change in Japan. *Journal of the Faculty of Science, Hokkaido University, Series IV. Geology and Minerology* 11(2):119–398.

TOKUNAGA, SHIGEMOTO
1964 "Tertiary plant records from Japan: the microfossils," in *Ancient Pacific floras: the pollen story*, 10th Pacific Science Congress Series. Edited by Cranwell, 13–18. Honolulu: University of Hawaii Press.

TSUKADA, MATSUO
1966 Late Pleistocene vegetation and climate in Taiwan (Formosa). *Proceedings National Academy of Sciences, U.S.* 55:543–548.
1967a Vegetation and climate around 10,000 B.P. in central Japan. *American Journal of Science* 265:562–585.
1967b Vegetation in subtropical Formosa during the Pleistocene glaciations and the Holocene. *Palaeogeography, Palaeoclimatology, Palaeoecology* 3:49–64.

VAN DER HAMMEN, T., T. A. WIJMSTRA, W. H. ZAGWIJN
1971 "The floral record of the late Cenozoic of Europe," in *Late Cenozoic glacial ages*. Edited by K. K. Turekian, 391–424. New Haven, Conn.: Yale University Press.

VON KOENIGSWALD, G. H. R.
1939 Das Pleistocän Javas. *Quartär* 2:28–53.

WALLACE, A. R.
1876 *The geographical distribution of animals*, two volumes. Published in facsimile edition. New York: Hafner, 1962.

WANG, CHI-WU
1961 *The forests of China with a survey of grassland and desert vegetation.* Maria Moors Cabot Foundation Publication (Harvard) 5:1–313.

WANG, K. M.
1931 Die Höhlenablagerungen und Fauna der Drachenmaul-Höhle von Kiangsen, Chekiang. *National Research Institute, Geology, Academia Sinica, Nanking, Contributions* 1(3):41–67.

WATTS, W. A.
1969 A pollen diagram from Mud Lake, Marion County, north-central Florida. *Geological Society of America Bulletin* 80:631–642.
1970 The full-glacial vegetation of northwestern Georgia. *Ecology* 51:17–33.
1971 Postglacial and interglacial vegetation history of southern Georgia and Central Florida. *Ecology* 52:676–690.

WEIDENREICH, FRANZ
1937   The dentition of *Sinanthropus pekinensis*. *Paleontologia Sinica*, n.s. 1D.
1941   The extremity bones of *Sinanthropus pekinensis*. *Paleontologia Sinica* 5D:1–151.
1943   The skull of *Sinanthropus pekinensis*: a comparative study on a primitive skull. *Paleontologia Sinica* 10D:1–485.

WEST, RICHARD G.
1968   *Pleistocene geology and biology.* New York: Wiley.

WHITEHEAD, G. KENNETH
1972   *Deer of the world.* New York: Viking Press.

WOLFE, JACK A.
1971   Tertiary climatic fluctuations and methods of analysis of Tertiary floras. *Palaeogeography, Palaeoclimatology, Palaeoecology* 9(1):27–57.

WOLFE, JACK A., DAVID M. HOPKINS
1967   "Climatic changes recorded by Tertiary land floras in northwestern North America," in *Tertiary correlations and climatic changes in the Pacific — Symposium Volume.* Edited by K. Hatai. Proceedings, 11th Pacific Science Congress, Tokyo, August–September 1966. 25:67–76.

WOLFE, JACK A., D. M. HOPKINS, E. B. LEOPOLD
1966   *Tertiary stratigraphy and paleobotany of the Cook Inlet Region,* Alaska. U.S. Geological Survey Professional Paper 398–A:A1–A29.

WOLFE, JACK A., ESTELLA B. LEOPOLD
1967   "Neogene and Early Quaternary vegetation of northwestern North America and northeastern Asia," in *The Bering land bridge.* Edited by David M. Hopkins, pp. 193–206. Stanford, Calif.: Stanford University Press.

WOLLIN, G., D. B. ERICSON, E. EWING
1971   "Late Pleistocene climates recorded in Atlantic and Pacific deep-sea sediments," in *Late Cenozoic glacial ages.* Edited by K. K. Turekian, 199–214. New Haven, Conn.: Yale University Press.

WOO, JU-KANG
1964   Mandible of the *Sinanthropus*-type discovered at Lantian, Shensi — *Sinanthropus lantianensis*. *Vertebrata Palasiatica* 8(1):1–17. (Chinese with English summary.)
1966a The skull of Lantian man. *Current Anthropology* 7(1):83–86.
1966b The Hominid skull of Lantian, Shensi. *Vertebrata Palasiatica* 10(1):1–22. (Chinese with English summary.)

WOO, JU-KANG, RU-CE PENG
1959   Fossil human skull of early Paleanthropic stage found at Mapa, Shaoquan, Kwangtung Province. *Vertebrata Palasiatica* 3(4):176–182.

YOUNG, C. C.
1929   Notes on the mammalian remains from Kwangsi. *Geological Society of China Bulletin* 8:125–128.
1930   On the mammalian remains from Chi Ku Shan near Choukoutien. *Paleontologia Sinica* 7C(1):1–24.
1932a Fossil vertebrates from Localities 2, 7, and 8 of Choukoutien. *Paleontologia Sinica* C7(3):1–101.
1932b On some fossil mammals from Yunnan. *Geological Society of China Bulletin* 11:383–394.
1932c On the Artiodactyla from the *Sinanthropus* site at Choukoutien. *Paleontologia Sinica* 8C(2):1–158.

1934   On the Insectivora, Chiroptera, Rodentia, and Primates other than *Sinanthropus* from Locality 1 at Choukoutien. *Paleontologia Sinica* 8C(3):1–160.

1935   Note on a mammalian microfauna from Yenchingkuo near Wanhsien, Szechuan. *Geological Society of China Bulletin* 14:247–248.

1936   New finds of fossil *Bubalus* in China. *Geological Society of China Bulletin* 15:505–516.

1939   Some fossils from Wanhsien. *Geological Society of China Bulletin* 19:317–331.

YOUNG, C. C., M. M. CHOW

1955   Pleistocene stratigraphy and new fossil localities of Shihhung and Wuchow, northern Anhwei. *Acta Paleontologia Sinica* 3(1):47–53.

1956   Latest discoveries in vertebrate paleontology in China. *Scientia Sinica* 5(3):603–610.

YOUNG, C. C., P. T. LIU

1950   On the mammalian fauna of Koloshan near Chungking, Szechuan. *Geological Society of China Bulletin* 30:1–4, 43–90.

YOUNG, C. C., T. H. MI

1941   Notes on some newly discovered late Cenozoic mammals from southwestern and northwestern China. *Geological Society of China Bulletin* 21:97–106.

Biographical Notes

PAVEL I. BORISKOVSKIJ (1911–   ) has been Head of the Department of Paleolithic Studies since 1961 at the Institute of Archaeology (Leningrad Branch) of the Academy of Sciences, U.S.S.R. He has been Professor of Archaeology at the University of Leningrad (1952–1960 and 1961–1972) and Professor of Archaeology at the University of Hanoi, Vietnam (1960–1961). His special interests include the Paleolithic and Mesolithic of the U.S.S.R. and the Prehistory of Southeast Asia, especially of Indo-China.

G. A. CLARK (1944–   ) was born in Philadelphia, Pennsylvania, and studied anthropology and prehistoric archaeology at the University of Arizona, where he received B.A. (Hon.) and M.A. degrees in 1966 and 1967. He was awarded the Ph.D. (anthropology) by the University of Chicago in 1971. An Associate Professor in the Department of Anthropology at Arizona State University, he is the author or co-author of a number of articles and two monographs concerned with Late and Post-Pleistocene adaptations in Cantabrian Spain, and with statistical applications to anthropological research in general. He is currently editor of the *Anthropological Research Papers* monograph series at ASU, and co-director (with L. G. Straus) of the National Science Foundation-supported La Riera Paleoecological Project (1976/8).

FRANCESCO G. FEDELE (1942–   ) is Research Director in prehistory and human paleoecology at the Institute of Anthropology of Turin University, Italy. He received his D.Sc. in natural sciences (anthropology) from Turin in 1969. Since 1966 he has carried out pioneering excavations and research projects in northwestern Italy and the Alps, focussing on "Early Man" problems, Alpine adaptations, and the dynamics of human ecosystems. He has worked on the same topics and as a physical anthropologist in other North Italian areas; in 1975 he co-operated as Visiting Scholar with the Northern Yukon Research Programme sponsored by the University of Toronto. He taught human ecology and paleoecology at Columbia University in 1976, and is the author of a hundred publications. In 1978 he was appointed Professor of Anthropology and Director of the Institute of Anthropological Science at Sassari University, Sardinia, Italy.

LESLIE G. FREEMAN (1935–   ) was born in the United States. Educated at the University of Chicago, he is now Associate Professor of Anthropology there. He is the author of numerous articles on paleolithic prehistory. He assisted F. Clark Howell at the excavation of Torralba and Ambrona, two Acheulean sites in north-central Spain and, with J. González Echegaray, jointly directed excavations at Cueva Morin, on the Spanish north coast, which have been the subject of a multi-volume monograph.

J. GONZÁLEZ ECHEGARAY (1930–   ) was born in Santander, Spain. He is Vice-Director of the Museo de Prehistoria y Arqueología of Santander. He received his Ph.D. from Deusto University (Bilbao). His field work includes excavations and studies on paleolithic and mesolithic sites in northern Spain and the Near East. Among his publications are *Excavaciones en la terraza de El Khiam (Jordania)*, 2 vols. (1964–66); *Cueva Morin*, 2 vols. (with L. G. Freeman) (1971–73), and *Pinturas y grabados de la Cueva de las Chimeneas* (1974).

P. E. HARE (1933–   ) did his undergraduate work in chemistry at Pacific Union College. He earned a master's degree at the University of California (Berkeley) and received his Ph.D. degree in geochemistry from the California Institute of Technology. He joined the Geophysical Laboratory of the Carnegie Institution of Washington as a staff member in the field of organic geochemistry. His interests have been in developing analytical techniques in amino acid geochemistry and in the application of amino acid reactions to the age-dating of fossils of archeological and geological significance.

FEKRI A. HASSAN (1943–   ) is Assistant Professor of Anthropology at Wayne State University, Detroit. Born in Cairo and a resident of the United States since 1968, he holds a B.Sc. (1963) and an M.Sc. (1966) in geology from Ain Shams University (Cairo) and an M.A. (1971) and a Ph.D. (1973) in anthropology from Southern Methodist University, Dallas. He participated in archaeological fieldwork in Egypt, Lebanon, Ethiopia, and Algeria, as well as in the United States. His special interests are in the fields of North African and Near Eastern palaeoanthropology, prehistoric demography, geoarchaeology, and the analysis of lithic artifacts with the ultimate aim of providing processual models of culture change in prehistory, especially that of the transition from hunting-gathering to agriculture. Recent publications: *Population growth and cultural evolution* (1974), *Mechanisms of population growth during the Neolithic* (1973).

KUBET LUCHTERHAND (1945–) is Associate Professor of Biological Anthropology at Roosevelt University in Chicago. He received his B.A. in mathematics at Northwestern University, Evanston, and studied anthropology at the University of Chicago where he received his M.A. in 1968 and Ph.D. in 1974. He has studied fossil mammals at many museums in Europe, Africa, North America and South America and wrote a doctoral dissertation on mid-Pleistocene hominid evolution in eastern Asia. His most recent field research is concerned with reconstructing paleoecological systems that included primates and other small mammals in the Middle and Late Cenozoic of South America.

LINDA R. RICHARDS. No biographical data available.

EARL C. SAXON. No biographical data available.

EDITH M. SHIMKIN is an Associate of The Russian and East European Center at the University of Illinois at Champaign-Urbana. She was educated at The College of William and Mary, Williamsburg, Va. and The George Washington University, Washington, D.C., receiving her B.A. in 1934. She has held positions with The National Geographic Society and the War Department General Staff (1941–43). Later she did advanced study at George Washington University (political science) and the University of Illinois (Slavic). Her publications include translations of articles on Soviet archeology (published by the Peabody Museum) and edited translations of Soviet radiocarbon date lists published in *Radiocarbon*. With Demetri B. Shimkin and Dennis A. Frate she is co-editor of *The extended family in black societies* (1978).

RONALD SINGER (1924–) is Professor of Anatomy and Anthropology, and the Robert R. Bensley Professor in Biology and Medical Sciences, as well as Professor in the Committee on Evolutionary Biology, the Committee on Genetics and the Committee on African Affairs, at the University of Chicago (since 1962). He studied at the University of Cape Town, South Africa where he received the M.B., Ch.B. degree in 1947 and D.Sc. in 1962. While on the faculty of the University of Cape Town (1949–1962) he conducted extensive research at fossil sites in southern Africa and was co-discoverer of the Saldanha Skull, and also directed expeditions in South Africa and Namibia to study the biology of living indigenous populations. Since 1970 he has directed excavations at Clacton-on-Sea and Hoxne in Great Britain, and has investigated Pleistocene deposits in Iran. He was a Rotary Foundation Fellow at the Carnegie Institution of Washington Department of Embryology and Foreign Fellow of Johns Hopkins University, 1951–1952, and he served as Visiting Professor of Anatomy at the University of Illinois College of Medicine in Chicago, 1959–1960. He has published more than 120 papers in scientific journals.

LAWRENCE STRAUS (1948–   ) was trained at the University of Chicago (A.B., 1971; A.M., 1972; Ph.D., 1975), and is Assistant Professor of Anthropology at the University of New Mexico. His research interests are in the adaptations of Upper Paleolithic hunter-gatherers in Western Europe. He is currently engaged in investigations at La Riera Cave, a Late Würm-PreBoreal site in Asturias, Spain. He has published numerous articles on the Solutrean and Magdalenian of Cantabria and the Basque Country, and on faunal assemblages from that region.

R. E. TAYLOR (1938–   ) is Associate Professor of Anthropology and Director of the Radiocarbon Laboratory at the University of California, Riverside. He received his Ph.D. in 1960 from the University of California, Los Angeles (UCLA). While at UCLA he was attached to the Isotope (Radiocarbon) Laboratory in the Institute of Geophysics and Planetary Physics. His most recent publications are edited volumes on *Advances in obsidian glass studies: Archaeological and geochemical perspectives* (1976) and *Chronologies in New World archaeology* (1978).

H. F. TURNBULL (1943–   ) is a senior graduate student specializing in biological anthropology at the University of California, Riverside. He transferred to anthropology after receiving his B.Sc. in biochemistry at U.C.R. in 1971. He has conducted studies pertaining to amino acid dating methodology and to Basque genetics and demography. Currently he is completing his doctoral dissertation based on a study of the population structure of Spanish Basque mountain villages.

PHILLIP L. WALKER (1947–   ) is an Assistant Professor of Anthropology at the University of California, Santa Barbara. He received his Ph.D. in Anthropology from the University of Chicago in 1973. His research has been primarily concerned with primate evolution and human paleoecology.

JOHN J. WYMER (1928–   ) Archaeologist at Reading Museum, England, from 1956–65. Specialized in Quaternary archaeology and, since 1965, has been a Research Associate of the Department of Anatomy, University of Chicago, and conducted investigations on Paleolithic sites in Africa and England. He has an honorary degree, M.A., from Durham University, 1970.

Index of Names

Index of Subjects

Acheulean stage: artifacts and hand axes, Italian, 330; bone artifact sites, 32; factor analysis of assemblages, 59; hand axes, 15, 16, 17, 18, 19; hunting areas, Iranian, 24; lithic tool finds, Kazakhstan, 27; migratory hunters, 14, 22, 24; tradition, and Cantabrian Mousterian, 30

Afontova Gora II, central Siberia, 223; lithic artifacts, 256; *zemlyanka* faunal remains, 224

Africa. *See* Algeria, coastal; Sebilian, Nile Valley

Alcelaphus, 359; *buselaphus*, 170

Algeria, coastal: faunal resources, 358, 359; herding hunter-gatherers, Iberomaurusian, 357–358; sites, geographical, 359. *See also* Coastal economies, Mesolithic

Alps, Italian: environmental factors, 318–319; föhn winds and climate, 321–322; geographical areas reviewed, 319-322; geological divisions, 320; Iron Age routes and outposts, 340; valleys and passes, 321, 340

Alps, Italian, archaeological: Acheulean artifacts, 330; Copper Age, 339–340; Bronze Age, 340; Epigravettian complexes, Upper Paleolithic, 333–334; Evolved-Italic, 334; Evolved-Terminal, 335; Finale-Quinzano phase, 336; Fiorano Culture dating, 336; glacial geology, Pleistocene, 321, 328; Iron Age, 340; Paleoecological background, 322; prehistory, North Italian, surveys of, 322; rock art, 339; Sauveterrian assemblages, Colbricon, 335; sites, by period and distribution, 323–327; Square-Mouthed

Pottery (MP) Culture, dating of, 336, 337, 338; rock-crystal industry, 338; studies of Pleistocene man in, 317; Würm climates, fauna and Glaciations, southern, 328–329

Alps, Italian; sites: alignment, geographical, 332–333; Belvedere shelter, Monfenera, 334–335, 338; Bronze Age villages and *castellari*, 340; caves, 330–331, 332, 333, 334, 338; dating, Upper Mousterian, 333; dwellings, Monfenera, 338; Epipaleolithic, Trento, Adige Valley, 335–336; fortified hilltop settlements, 336, 340; Late Paleolithic, hunting, 334; Middle Paleolithic, Veneto group, 330–331, 334; Monfenera Mousterian, 331–332; mountain area complex, 337; Mousterian assemblages, 331; Piedmont, 330, 337; sites charted and mapped, 323–327; summer camps, transhumance, 340; rock-art sites, Copper Age, 339; Tanùn, Lombardy, 331

Amber: beads, 271; worked, Ukrainian, 205, 212, 213

Amerind sites and factor analysis, 59, 60

Amino acid dating research: calibration and environmental temperature, 8; chemical nature of, 2; fossil studies, Californian shell, 7; racemization age, isoleucine, 9, 10; ratios, quantified, 7–8; temporal variations, 7–8

Ammotragus lervia (barbary sheep), 359, 360

Antelope, Saiga, 400

Anthropomorphism, artifact: Kostenki figurines, 217; stelae, Alpine, engraved, 339

stone cist, Italian, 336–337; Sungir', 220; Upper Paleolithic, 227, 232

Burins: angle, Polyhedral, 178; La Riera, 125–126, 127, 135, 136, 137, 140, 144, 149; prismatic, 179, 187; use of, 261

Calluna vulgaris (*Erica* sp.), 118

Camelus, and camelids, distribution of, 395–396

Cancer pagurus, 128, 131

Canis, 383

Canis lupus, 123, 126, 129, 130

Cantabrian Asturian, 117–118; artifacts, lithic, ceramic, 139, 142; plan and elevation La Riera, 120, 121; sketch map of sites, 119

Cantabrian Mousterian: artifact collections, 95, 96; factor analysis of frequencies, 58–59; factor analysis tabulations, 97–111

Capra, ibex *pyrenaica*, 123, 126, 129, 130, 136

Capreolus capreolus, 130

Cardium edulis, 128, 131

Carnegie Institution, Washington; fossil bone analysis, 8

Caspian Sea area: expeditions, 14–15, 19; meltwater floodings, 197

Caucasus, the, 19, 24, 27; hunting drives in, 245

Cave art: engraving, Italian, 338; Kapova, Urals, 280–282; painted horses, Niaux and Kapova, 244

Cave dwellings: Cueva Morin, 60; Cueva La Riera, 117; Guela Cave, Haifa, 32; Iberomaurusian, 359; Italian, Veneto, 330; seasonal, west Siberia, 223; Soviet Mousterian, 201; Torralba, Acheulean, 60; Ural, 221, 222, 240

Celts, European Neolithic, ground, 55

Cenozoic studies. *See* Climate, late Cenozoic; Stratigraphy

Ceramics: statistical analysis of, data-patterning and design motifs, 58–59; Asturian, 139

Cervus elaphus, 123, 125, 126, 129, 130, 133, 136, 138, 141, 145

Chevrotain (*Tragulidae*), 396

Chicago, University of: Abbot Memorial Fund, 13n; archaeological analyses, 58; Computation Center, 63; Department of Anthropology, 117n; Paleoecology Laboratory, 145; Paleology Laboratory, 117n

China: areas of faunal assemblage, 379, 382; Anyang, Honan, 390; bamboo rats, 402; deer, *pachyosteous*, 399; loess stratigraphy, schematic section of, 374,

381; mammals, 379; mammalian records, Choukoutien, 386; Middle Pleistocene fauna, Palearctic, 384, 393; Pliocene, 382; Szechwan, typical fauna of, 389; Yunnan fauna, 387, 391, 394, 404

Choukoutien: Holocene, Upper Cave, 390; Hopei bone artifacts, 31; late Cenozoic, 386; mammalia, Pliocene, 386; sites, Middle Pleistocene, 384, 388

Chronologies: Amudian, 183–184; Cantabrian, Late Pleistocene, 129n; East Asian, 380–386; Sebilian sites, 156–157; Square-Mouthed Pottery periods, 338; tree-ring calibration, 338

Chronometric dating techniques, 2, 337; biochemical and radiocarbon, 7

Clarias anguilaris, 170

Climate, late Cenozoic, 164; carbonate deposition cycles, 366, 367; cycles, Atlantic and Pacific, 364, 365; deep sea core evidence, 364, 365, 366; glacial, Far East, 374–375, 377; loess deposits, Chinese, 375–376; ocean basins, Pleistocene, 364; paleotemperature analysis, 365; river-terrace systems, Asian, 375; stratigraphic studies, 366, 367

Coastal economies, Mesolithic, Mediterranean, 357–360

Coelodonta antiquitatis, 255

Columella columella, 236

Comisión de Investigaciones Arquelogicas, 117

Concheros. *See* Shell-middens, concheros

Connochaetes, 359

Crimean hunting drives, Mousterian, 245

Cueva Morin, Santander: archaeological sequences, 93, 96; artifacts in detail, illustrated, 35–46; bone artifact classification, 33–35; faunal bone identification, 32-33; geology and topography, 93, 94; levels of occupation, 29, 30, 31; lithic artifacts, 30; 'macaroni' figurative art markings, 47, 48, 49n; Mousterian site studies, 29; occupation distributions, 111-112; statistical analysis, 60; worked bone tools, 31, 32. *See also* Factory Analysis

Cultures: 'Alpine Mousterian', 342; 'Alpine' Paleolithic, conjectural, 343; European, various, 333, 334, 335; Fiorano Epipaleolithic, 336; Iberomaurusian, Algerian, 357; Kebaran, Palestinian, 357; Late Neolithic-Copper Age, 339; Natufian, Palestine, 360; Russian, nomenclature of, 194–195; Square-Mouthed Pottery, Italian, 336, 338

Cultures, Upper Paleolithic, Eurasian: classification by tool types, 254;

Palestinian Upper Paleolithic, 177–179; Russian dwellings, 202; Solutrean, La Riera, 123; Torralba tools, 71, 86, 87, 88, 89; Ukraine, Dobranichevka, 212; Ukraine, Mezhirich, 205

Lithic industries: Acheulean quartzite, 124–125; Amudian, 183, 184; Arabian, 19; Armenian, 19; Asturian, tabulated, 133–137, 138, 139; Antelian, 185–187; Atlitian, 187–188; Azilian, La Riera, 126–127; Baluchistan, 15; Cueva Morin tool, 30-31; Emiran, 184–185; flint and quartzite, La Riera, 139, 140; *illustrated*, 140, 141, 142, 143, 144, 145; graphs, cumulative percentage, 31; Iranian stone sources, 20–21; Iran as a land-link, 14; Kebaran, 188; Italian, hunting, 334, 335; La Riera Solutrean, 123; Levantine, 16–18; Lower Paleolithic, Africa-Asia, 14; Palestinian cave, dated sequences, 16; Ukraine, 19; Upper Paleolithic, Palestine, 177–179; Sebilian, Paleolithic, 153, 157, 158, 159–161, 163–164, 168–169

Lithic materials: basalt, 19; chert, 154; diorite, 153–154; quartz, 21, 23; sandstone, 157, 218. *See also* Flint; Quartzite; Stone tools

Lithic terminology, 123n

Littorina: *littorea*, 123, 126, 127, 131; *obtussata*, 123, 126

Lower Paleolithic occupation, Iran, 3

'Macaroni' cave art incisions, French and Spanish, 47, 48, 49n

Mal'ta, central Siberia: artifacts, ivory, 264; bone-working tools, 262; burials, 227, 229, 230, 231; dagger, child burial, 268; dwellings, detailed, 224–226; ivory coronet, 261, 272; mineral colours in art, 271; stone tools and industry, 257, 286

Mammals: of East Asian community, Oriental and Palearctic, 379; faunal forms, distinct, Oriental, Palearctic, 407–408; temporal continuity, faunal community, 408

Mammalian evolutionary patterns: Eastern Asia, 378; China, Mongolia, faunal assemblages, 379, 380, 383, 389; loess area proboscidean fossil records, 385; Middle Pleistocene carnivores, 384, 387; Middle Pleistocene cervids, 398, 399; Mongolian type site, Sjara-Osso-Gol, 389; Oriental region, 378, 379, 382; Palearctic region, 378, 379, 389, 391, 393, 394; north and south, distinctions between, 391; rodents, distribu-

tion of, 400, 401; Stegodon-Ailuropoda southern complex, 384, 385, 387, 388, 391; Villafranchian, 383, 387, 391

Mammalian orders and subgroups: Ailuropoda, 406; Artiodactyla, 395–397; Bovidae, 399–400; Castoridae, 402–403; Carnivora, 406–407; Cervidae, 397, 398, 399; Chalicotheridae, 392; Elephantidae, 405, 406; Equidae, Pliocene *Hipparion*, 394; Giraffidae, 396–397; Gomphotheroidea, 403, 404; Lagomorpha, Leporidae, 403; Mammutoidea, 403, 404; Ochotonidae, 403; Perissodactyla, 392; Proboscidae, 403; Rhinocerotidae, 393; Rodentia, 400–403; Ruminantia, 396–400; Suina, 395; Tapiridae, 392–393; Tylopoda, 395–396; Ursids, 406

Mammoth: Mousterian abundance of, 237; hunting, 245; radiocarbon dating, 242–243; Russian, important, 241–243; varying incidence of, 235, 236, 238, 239, 240

Mammoth bone remains: Afontova Gora, 224; Avdeyevo, 216; Buret', 224; as building material, Ukraine, 204, 205; Gontsy, 213, 214; ivory, in art and ornament, 270, 274, 275; ivory working, 261–262; Kostenki, 217, 218, 219; Mal'ta, 224–226; Mezin, 212, 213; Moldova, 201, 203; painted, artifact, 205; paintings, Kapova Cave, 281; Pushkhari, 214; Siberian, 222–226; Sungir', 220–221; weights of, as food source, 248; Yeliseyevichi, 215

"Mammoth complex", faunal, 239–243

"Mammoth fauna", 141, 403

Man: adaptive to mountain environment, 341, 342, 344; calorific needs of, 248–249; Cro-Magnon stature, 248; evidence of, Eastern Alps, 340; as *Homo erectus*, 411; maximum populations of, Final Bronze Age, Savoy, 340; persistence of as mountain dweller, 342, 343; survival of, Siberian, 252; wintering, and artificial shelter, 342

Mastodon, 404, 405

Mediterranean lithic sites, 16–18

Megaceroides algerica, 359

Meles meles, 126, 130

Mezin tradition, stone tools of, 257

Microliths: Italian Epipaleolithic, 335; Upper Paleolithic, 181n, 187

Migrations, human, intercontinental, 14

Molluskan evidence: Algerian, 360; boreal forms, 236, 239; concheros, Asturian, 123, 126, 129, 130, 131, 132